Margherita Antona · Constantine Stephanidis (Eds.)

Universal Access in Human-Computer Interaction

Theory, Methods and Tools

13th International Conference, UAHCI 2019
Held as Part of the 21st HCI International Conference, HCII 2019
Orlando, FL, USA, July 26–31, 2019
Proceedings, Part I

Springer

Editors
Margherita Antona
Foundation for Research
and Technology – Hellas (FORTH)
Heraklion, Crete, Greece

Constantine Stephanidis
University of Crete
and Foundation for Research
and Technology – Hellas (FORTH)
Heraklion, Crete, Greece

ISSN 0302-9743   ISSN 1611-3349 (electronic)
Lecture Notes in Computer Science
ISBN 978-3-030-23559-8   ISBN 978-3-030-23560-4 (eBook)
https://doi.org/10.1007/978-3-030-23560-4

LNCS Sublibrary: SL3 – Information Systems and Applications, incl. Internet/Web, and HCI

This Springer imprint is published by the registered company Springer Nature Switzerland AG
The registered company address is: Gewerbestrasse 11, 6330 Cham, Switzerland

Foreword

The 21st International Conference on Human-Computer Interaction, HCI International 2019, was held in Orlando, FL, USA, during July 26–31, 2019. The event incorporated the 18 thematic areas and affiliated conferences listed on the following page.

A total of 5,029 individuals from academia, research institutes, industry, and governmental agencies from 73 countries submitted contributions, and 1,274 papers and 209 posters were included in the pre-conference proceedings. These contributions address the latest research and development efforts and highlight the human aspects of design and use of computing systems. The contributions thoroughly cover the entire field of human-computer interaction, addressing major advances in knowledge and effective use of computers in a variety of application areas. The volumes constituting the full set of the pre-conference proceedings are listed in the following pages.

This year the HCI International (HCII) conference introduced the new option of "late-breaking work." This applies both for papers and posters and the corresponding volume(s) of the proceedings will be published just after the conference. Full papers will be included in the *HCII 2019 Late-Breaking Work Papers Proceedings* volume of the proceedings to be published in the Springer LNCS series, while poster extended abstracts will be included as short papers in the HCII 2019 *Late-Breaking Work Poster Extended Abstracts* volume to be published in the Springer CCIS series.

I would like to thank the program board chairs and the members of the program boards of all thematic areas and affiliated conferences for their contribution to the highest scientific quality and the overall success of the HCI International 2019 conference.

This conference would not have been possible without the continuous and unwavering support and advice of the founder, Conference General Chair Emeritus and Conference Scientific Advisor Prof. Gavriel Salvendy. For his outstanding efforts, I would like to express my appreciation to the communications chair and editor of *HCI International News,* Dr. Abbas Moallem.

July 2019   Constantine Stephanidis

HCI International 2019 Thematic Areas
and Affiliated Conferences

Thematic areas:

- HCI 2019: Human-Computer Interaction
- HIMI 2019: Human Interface and the Management of Information

Affiliated conferences:

- EPCE 2019: 16th International Conference on Engineering Psychology and Cognitive Ergonomics
- UAHCI 2019: 13th International Conference on Universal Access in Human-Computer Interaction
- VAMR 2019: 11th International Conference on Virtual, Augmented and Mixed Reality
- CCD 2019: 11th International Conference on Cross-Cultural Design
- SCSM 2019: 11th International Conference on Social Computing and Social Media
- AC 2019: 13th International Conference on Augmented Cognition
- DHM 2019: 10th International Conference on Digital Human Modeling and Applications in Health, Safety, Ergonomics and Risk Management
- DUXU 2019: 8th International Conference on Design, User Experience, and Usability
- DAPI 2019: 7th International Conference on Distributed, Ambient and Pervasive Interactions
- HCIBGO 2019: 6th International Conference on HCI in Business, Government and Organizations
- LCT 2019: 6th International Conference on Learning and Collaboration Technologies
- ITAP 2019: 5th International Conference on Human Aspects of IT for the Aged Population
- HCI-CPT 2019: First International Conference on HCI for Cybersecurity, Privacy and Trust
- HCI-Games 2019: First International Conference on HCI in Games
- MobiTAS 2019: First International Conference on HCI in Mobility, Transport, and Automotive Systems
- AIS 2019: First International Conference on Adaptive Instructional Systems

Pre-conference Proceedings Volumes Full List

1. LNCS 11566, Human-Computer Interaction: Perspectives on Design (Part I), edited by Masaaki Kurosu
2. LNCS 11567, Human-Computer Interaction: Recognition and Interaction Technologies (Part II), edited by Masaaki Kurosu
3. LNCS 11568, Human-Computer Interaction: Design Practice in Contemporary Societies (Part III), edited by Masaaki Kurosu
4. LNCS 11569, Human Interface and the Management of Information: Visual Information and Knowledge Management (Part I), edited by Sakae Yamamoto and Hirohiko Mori
5. LNCS 11570, Human Interface and the Management of Information: Information in Intelligent Systems (Part II), edited by Sakae Yamamoto and Hirohiko Mori
6. LNAI 11571, Engineering Psychology and Cognitive Ergonomics, edited by Don Harris
7. LNCS 11572, Universal Access in Human-Computer Interaction: Theory, Methods and Tools (Part I), edited by Margherita Antona and Constantine Stephanidis
8. LNCS 11573, Universal Access in Human-Computer Interaction: Multimodality and Assistive Environments (Part II), edited by Margherita Antona and Constantine Stephanidis
9. LNCS 11574, Virtual, Augmented and Mixed Reality: Multimodal Interaction (Part I), edited by Jessie Y. C. Chen and Gino Fragomeni
10. LNCS 11575, Virtual, Augmented and Mixed Reality: Applications and Case Studies (Part II), edited by Jessie Y. C. Chen and Gino Fragomeni
11. LNCS 11576, Cross-Cultural Design: Methods, Tools and User Experience (Part I), edited by P. L. Patrick Rau
12. LNCS 11577, Cross-Cultural Design: Culture and Society (Part II), edited by P. L. Patrick Rau
13. LNCS 11578, Social Computing and Social Media: Design, Human Behavior and Analytics (Part I), edited by Gabriele Meiselwitz
14. LNCS 11579, Social Computing and Social Media: Communication and Social Communities (Part II), edited by Gabriele Meiselwitz
15. LNAI 11580, Augmented Cognition, edited by Dylan D. Schmorrow and Cali M. Fidopiastis
16. LNCS 11581, Digital Human Modeling and Applications in Health, Safety, Ergonomics and Risk Management: Human Body and Motion (Part I), edited by Vincent G. Duffy

17. LNCS 11582, Digital Human Modeling and Applications in Health, Safety, Ergonomics and Risk Management: Healthcare Applications (Part II), edited by Vincent G. Duffy

18. LNCS 11583, Design, User Experience, and Usability: Design Philosophy and Theory (Part I), edited by Aaron Marcus and Wentao Wang

19. LNCS 11584, Design, User Experience, and Usability: User Experience in Advanced Technological Environments (Part II), edited by Aaron Marcus and Wentao Wang

20. LNCS 11585, Design, User Experience, and Usability: Application Domains (Part III), edited by Aaron Marcus and Wentao Wang

21. LNCS 11586, Design, User Experience, and Usability: Practice and Case Studies (Part IV), edited by Aaron Marcus and Wentao Wang

22. LNCS 11587, Distributed, Ambient and Pervasive Interactions, edited by Norbert Streitz and Shin'ichi Konomi

23. LNCS 11588, HCI in Business, Government and Organizations: eCommerce and Consumer Behavior (Part I), edited by Fiona Fui-Hoon Nah and Keng Siau

24. LNCS 11589, HCI in Business, Government and Organizations: Information Systems and Analytics (Part II), edited by Fiona Fui-Hoon Nah and Keng Siau

25. LNCS 11590, Learning and Collaboration Technologies: Designing Learning Experiences (Part I), edited by Panayiotis Zaphiris and Andri Ioannou

26. LNCS 11591, Learning and Collaboration Technologies: Ubiquitous and Virtual Environments for Learning and Collaboration (Part II), edited by Panayiotis Zaphiris and Andri Ioannou

27. LNCS 11592, Human Aspects of IT for the Aged Population: Design for the Elderly and Technology Acceptance (Part I), edited by Jia Zhou and Gavriel Salvendy

28. LNCS 11593, Human Aspects of IT for the Aged Population: Social Media, Games and Assistive Environments (Part II), edited by Jia Zhou and Gavriel Salvendy

29. LNCS 11594, HCI for Cybersecurity, Privacy and Trust, edited by Abbas Moallem

30. LNCS 11595, HCI in Games, edited by Xiaowen Fang

31. LNCS 11596, HCI in Mobility, Transport, and Automotive Systems, edited by Heidi Krömker

32. LNCS 11597, Adaptive Instructional Systems, edited by Robert Sottilare and Jessica Schwarz

33. CCIS 1032, HCI International 2019 - Posters (Part I), edited by Constantine Stephanidis

34. CCIS 1033, HCI International 2019 - Posters (Part II), edited by Constantine Stephanidis
35. CCIS 1034, HCI International 2019 - Posters (Part III), edited by Constantine Stephanidis

http://2019.hci.international/proceedings

13th International Conference on Universal Access in Human-Computer Interaction (UAHCI 2019)

Program Board Chair(s): **Margherita Antona and Constantine Stephanidis,** *Greece*

- Gisela Susanne Bahr, USA
- Armando Barreto, USA
- João Barroso, Portugal
- Rodrigo Bonacin, Brazil
- Ingo Bosse, Germany
- Anthony Lewis Brooks, Denmark
- Laura Burzagli, Italy
- Pedro J. S. Cardoso, Portugal
- Stefan Carmien, UK
- Carlos Duarte, Portugal
- Pier Luigi Emiliani, Italy
- Vagner Figueredo de Santana, Brazil
- Andrina Granic, Croatia
- Gian Maria Greco, Spain
- Simeon Keates, UK
- Georgios Kouroupetroglou, Greece
- Patrick M. Langdon, UK
- Barbara Leporini, Italy
- I. Scott MacKenzie, Canada
- John Magee, USA
- Alessandro Marcengo, Italy
- Jorge Martín-Gutiérrez, Spain
- Troy McDaniel, USA
- Silvia Mirri, Italy
- Federica Pallavicini, Italy
- Ana Isabel Bruzzi Bezerra Paraguay, Brazil
- Hugo Paredes, Portugal
- Enrico Pontelli, USA
- João M. F. Rodrigues, Portugal
- Frode Eika Sandnes, Norway
- Jaime Sánchez, Chile
- Volker Sorge, UK
- Hiroki Takada, Japan
- Kevin C. Tseng, Taiwan
- Gerhard Weber, Germany
- Gian Wild, Australia
- Ed Youngblood, USA

The full list with the Program Board Chairs and the members of the Program Boards of all thematic areas and affiliated conferences is available online at:

http://www.hci.international/board-members-2019.php

HCI International 2020

The 22nd International Conference on Human-Computer Interaction, HCI International 2020, will be held jointly with the affiliated conferences in Copenhagen, Denmark, at the Bella Center Copenhagen, July 19–24, 2020. It will cover a broad spectrum of themes related to HCI, including theoretical issues, methods, tools, processes, and case studies in HCI design, as well as novel interaction techniques, interfaces, and applications. The proceedings will be published by Springer. More information will be available on the conference website: http://2020.hci.international/.

General Chair
Prof. Constantine Stephanidis
University of Crete and ICS-FORTH
Heraklion, Crete, Greece
E-mail: general_chair@hcii2020.org

http://2020.hci.international/

Contents – Part I

Universal Access Theory, Methods and Tools

Beyond Usability: Methodologies and Bias – Surveying the Surveys 3
  Troy D. Abel

A.I. Ethics in the City 13
  Marc Böhlen

Empowering Instead of Hindering – Challenges in Participatory
Development of Cognitively Accessible Software 28
  Susanne Dirks

Inquiring Evaluation Aspects of Universal Design and Natural Interaction
in Socioenactive Scenarios 39
  Andressa Cristina dos Santos, Vanessa Regina Margareth Lima Maike,
  Yusseli Lizeth Méndez Mendoza, José Valderlei da Silva,
  Rodrigo Bonacin, Julio Cesar Dos Reis,
  and Maria Cecília Calani Baranauskas

Expectations and Concerns Emerging from Experiences with Assistive
Technology for ALS Patients 57
  Cornelia Eicher, Jörn Kiselev, Kirsten Brukamp, Diana Kiemel,
  Susanne Spittel, André Maier, Ursula Oleimeulen, and Marius Greuèl

Teaching Empathy in Underserved Audiences Through Game
Based Learning 69
  John Gialanella and Kimberly Mitchell

From UX to Engagement: Connecting Theory and Practice,
Addressing Ethics and Diversity 91
  Ole Goethe, Kavous Salehzadeh Niksirat, Ilyena Hirskyj-Douglas,
  Huatong Sun, Effie L.-C. Law, and Xiangshi Ren

Universal Access: The Challenges Ahead 100
  Simeon Keates

Achieving Inclusion with Contextualized User-Sensitive Design 113
  Fang Li and Hua Dong

A Disability-Oriented Analysis Procedure for Leisure Rehabilitation
Product Design 133
  Ming-Chyuan Lin, Guo-Peng Qui, Xue Hua Zhou, and Jing Chen

Getting Smarter About Data and Access in Smart Cities   146
  H. Patricia McKenna

Initiation to Reverse Engineering by Using Activities Based on
Photogrammetry as New Teaching Method in University Technical Studies . . .   159
  Dolores Parras-Burgos, Daniel G. Fernández-Pacheco,
  Francisco Cavas-Martínez, José Nieto, and Francisco J. F. Cañavate

Disrupting Higher Education: Engaging Design Students in UX Processes
to Enhance Innovation in Higher Education   177
  Debra Satterfield, Tom Tredway, and Wesley Woelfel

Novel Approaches to Accessibility

Guideline Definition for the Evaluation of Citizen Experience Using
Urban Interfaces   191
  Luis Carlos Aceves Gutiérrez, Jorge Martín-Gutiérrez,
  and Marta Sylvia del Rio Guerra

Preliminary Findings from a Study of an Arabic Accessibility
Tool Checker   201
  Mona Alnahari and Joyram Chakraborty

Information Technology Based Usable Ballot Interface Design
for Persons with Visual Impairment in Sri Lanka   211
  Madhuka De Silva, Thushani Weerasinghe, and Kapila Dias

User Test Logger: An Open Source Browser Plugin for Logging
and Reporting Local User Studies   229
  Vagner Figueredo de Santana and Felipe Eduardo Ferreira Silva

Research on Wearable Shopping Aid Device for Visually Impaired People. . .   244
  Yu-Hsiu Hung, Chia-Hui Feng, Chia-Tzu Lin, and Chung-Jen Chen

Design and Evaluation of a User-Interface for Authoring Sentences
of American Sign Language Animation   258
  Abhishek Kannekanti, Sedeeq Al-khazraji, and Matt Huenerfauth

Accessibility or Usability of the User Interfaces for Visually Impaired
Users? A Comparative Study   268
  Kamran Khowaja, Dena Al-Thani, Aboubakr Aqle, and Bilikis Banire

Reflections on Elements of a Game Design Model Applied to Inclusive
Digital Games.   284
  Patricia da Silva Leite, Ana Paula Retore,
  and Leonelo Dell Anhol Almeida

Teaching Video Game Design Accessibility: Toward Effective
Pedagogic Interventions in Accessible Design.   301
   Laura Levy and Maribeth Gandy

An Investigation on Sharing Economy Mobile Service Adoption:
How Perceived Risk, Value, and Price Interact?   312
   Shu-Ping Lin and Ya-Hui Chan

The Promotion of Empathy for the Experience of Users with Visual
Impairment in the Game Design Education.   326
   Isabel Cristina Siqueira da Silva

Perceivability of Map Information for Disaster Situations for People
with Low Vision.   342
   Siv Tunold, Jaziar Radianti, Terje Gjøsæter, and Weiqin Chen

Multi-faceted Approach to Computer Simplification via Personalization
and Layering   353
   Gregg C. Vanderheiden and J. Bern Jordan

On Online Banking Authentication for All: A Comparison of BankID Login
Efficiency Using Smartphones Versus Code Generators   365
   Ellen Opsahl Vinbæk, Frida Margrethe Borge Pettersen,
   Jonas Ege Carlsen, Karl Fremstad, Nikolai Edvinsen,
   and Frode Eika Sandnes

Universal Access to Learning and Education

Audiovisual Design for Generative Systems: A Customized
Audiovisual Experiment.   377
   Valdecir Becker, Rafael M. Toscano, Helder Bruno A. M. de Souza,
   and Edvaldo de Vasconcelos

How to Design an Intervention to Raise Digital Competences:
ALL DIGITAL Week – Dortmund 2018   389
   Manuela Becker, Alexandra Benner, Katrin Borg, Jan Hüls,
   Marina Koch, Annika Kost, Annabelle Korn, Marie-Christin Lueg,
   Dominique Osthoff, Bastian Pelka, Carina Rosenberger,
   and Helene Sattler

3D Interaction for Computer Science Educational VR Game   408
   Santiago Bolivar, Daniel Perez, Armando Carrasquillo,
   Adam S. Williams, Naphtali D. Rishe, and Francisco R. Ortega

A Flexible Assessment Platform for Middle School Supported
on Students Goals.   420
    Pedro J. S. Cardoso, Roberto Lam, Rui Penha Pereira, Nuno Rodrigues,
    and Cláudia Herdeiro

A Delphi Study on the Design of Digital Educational Games   433
    Panagiota Chalki, Tassos Anastasios Mikropoulos, and Angeliki Tsiara

Visualizing Student Interactions to Support Instructors in Virtual
Learning Environments   445
    André Luiz de Brandão Damasceno, Dalai dos Santos Ribeiro,
    and Simone Diniz Junqueira Barbosa

A Place to Discover, Imagine, and Change: Smart Learning
with Local Places   465
    Dalit Levy, Yuval Shafriri, and Yael Alef

A Learning Management System Accessible for Visual, Hearing
and Physical Impairments.   481
    Marcos Nascimento, Thiago Oliveira, Nelson Lima, Renato Ramos,
    Lidiane Silva, Francisco Oliveira, and Anarosa Brandão

Expressing the Personality of a Humanoid Robot as a Talking Partner
in an Elementary School Classroom   494
    Reika Omokawa, Makoto Kobayashi, and Shu Matsuura

Evaluation of User-Interface Designs for Educational Feedback
Software for ASL Students.   507
    Utsav Shah, Matthew Seita, and Matt Huenerfauth

HCI Methods and Practices for Audiovisual Systems and Their
Potential Contribution to Universal Design for Learning:
A Systematic Literature Review   526
    Rafael M. Toscano, Helder Bruno A. M. de Souza,
    Sandro G. da Silva Filho, Jaqueline D. Noleto, and Valdecir Becker

Virtual and Augmented Reality in Universal Access

Analysis of Biofeedback Through Heartbeat Obtained by Exposure
to Phobia Through Virtual Reality.   545
    Edvaldo de Vasconcelos, Amaro Neto, Lillian dos Santos,
    and Paula Ribeiro

Using Digital Puppetry to Prepare Physicians to Address Non-suicidal
Self-injury Among Teens.   555
    Kathleen Ingraham, Charles E. Hughes, Lindsay A. Taliaferro,
    Nicholas J. Westers, Lisa Dieker, and Michael Hynes

Using Virtual Reality to Create an Inclusive Virtual
Drumming Environment.   569
   Jacob Jewel and Tony Morelli

Visual Issues on Augmented Reality Using Smart Glasses
with 3D Stereoscopic Images   578
   Masaru Miyao, Masumi Takada, and Hiroki Takada

Automation of Box and Block Test in Virtual Reality
and Augmented Reality   590
   Kouki Nagamune and Yujiro Tsuzuki

Exploration of Physiological Signals Using Different Locomotion
Techniques in a VR Adventure Game   601
   Stanislava Rangelova, Simon Flutura, Tobias Huber, Daniel Motus,
   and Elisabeth André

Editor of O & M Virtual Environments for the Training of People
with Visual Impairment   617
   Agebson Rocha Façanha, Windson Viana, and Jaime Sánchez

AR Contents Superimposition on Walls and Persons   628
   João M. F. Rodrigues, Ricardo J. M. Veiga, Roman Bajireanu,
   Roberto Lam, Pedro J. S. Cardoso, and Paulo Bica

Gaming Background Influence on VR Performance and Comfort:
A Study Using Different Navigation Metaphors   646
   Jose L. Soler-Dominguez, Carla De-Juan-Ripoll, Jorge D. Camba,
   Manuel Contero, and Mariano Alcañiz

Changes in Eye Movements and Body Sway While Viewing
Stereoscopic Movies Under Controlled Consciousness   657
   Akihiro Sugiura, Kunihiko Tanaka, and Hiroki Takada

Effects of Low/High-Definition Stereoscopic Video Clips on the
Equilibrium Function.   669
   Masumi Takada, Syota Yamamoto, Masaru Miyao, and Hiroki Takada

Author Index   683

Contents – Part II

Cognitive and Learning Disabilities

A Collaborative Talking Assistive Technology for People with Autism
Spectrum Disorders   3
  Wajih Abdallah, Frédéric Vella, Nadine Vigouroux,
  Adrien Van den Bossche, and Thierry Val

Usability Enhancement and Functional Extension of a Digital Tool
for Rapid Assessment of Risk for Autism Spectrum Disorders in Toddlers
Based on Pilot Test and Interview Data   13
  Deeksha Adiani, Michael Schmidt, Joshua Wade, Amy R. Swanson,
  Amy Weitlauf, Zachary Warren, and Nilanjan Sarkar

Understanding How ADHD Affects Visual Information Processing   23
  Yahya Alqahtani, Michael McGuire, Joyram Chakraborty,
  and Jinjuan Heidi Feng

Attention Assessment: Evaluation of Facial Expressions of Children
with Autism Spectrum Disorder   32
  Bilikis Banire, Dena Al Thani, Mustapha Makki, Marwa Qaraqe,
  Kruthika Anand, Olcay Connor, Kamran Khowaja, and Bilal Mansoor

Improving Usability of a Mobile Application for Children with Autism
Spectrum Disorder Using Heuristic Evaluation   49
  Murilo C. Camargo, Tathia C. P. Carvalho, Rodolfo M. Barros,
  Vanessa T. O. Barros, and Matheus Santana

Learning About Autism Using VR   64
  Vanessa Camilleri, Alexiei Dingli, and Foaad Haddod

Breaking Down the "Wall of Text" - Software Tool to Address Complex
Assignments for Students with Attention Disorders   77
  Breanna Desrochers, Ella Tuson, Syed Asad R. Rizvi, and John Magee

Feel Autism VR – Adding Tactile Feedback to a VR Experience   87
  Foaad Haddod, Alexiei Dingli, and Luca Bondin

Caregivers' Influence on Smartphone Usage of People with Cognitive
Disabilities: An Explorative Case Study in Germany   98
  Vanessa N. Heitplatz, Christian Bühler, and Matthias R. Hastall

The PTC and Boston Children's Hospital Collaborative AR Experience
for Children with Autism Spectrum Disorder   116
 David Juhlin, Chris Morris, Peter Schmaltz, Howard Shane,
 Ralf Schlosser, Amanda O'Brien, Christina Yu, Drew Mancini,
 Anna Allen, and Jennifer Abramson

Design of an Intelligent and Immersive System to Facilitate the Social
Interaction Between Caregivers and Young Children with Autism   123
 Guangtao Nie, Akshith Ullal, Amy R. Swanson, Amy S. Weitauf,
 Zachary E. Warren, and Nilanjan Sarkar

Taking Neuropsychological Test to the Next Level: Commercial Virtual
Reality Video Games for the Assessment of Executive Functions   133
 Federica Pallavicini, Alessandro Pepe, and Maria Eleonora Minissi

Evaluation of Handwriting Skills in Children with Learning Difficulties.   150
 Wanjoo Park, Georgios Korres, Samra Tahir, and Mohamad Eid

"Express Your Feelings": An Interactive Application for Autistic Patients . . .   160
 Prabin Sharma, Mala Deep Upadhaya, Amrit Twanabasu,
 Joao Barroso, Salik Ram Khanal, and Hugo Paredes

The Design of an Intelligent LEGO Tutoring System for Improving Social
Communication Skills Among Children with Autism Spectrum Disorder   172
 Qiming Sun and Pinata Winoto

An Augmented Reality-Based Word-Learning Mobile Application
for Children with Autism to Support Learning Anywhere and Anytime:
Object Recognition Based on Deep Learning   182
 Tiffany Y. Tang, Jiasheng Xu, and Pinata Winoto

Design and Evaluation of Mobile Applications for Augmentative
and Alternative Communication in Minimally-verbal Learners
with Severe Autism.   193
 Oliver Wendt, Grayson Bishop, and Ashka Thakar

Multimodal Interaction

Principles for Evaluating Usability in Multimodal Games for People
Who Are Blind.   209
 Ticianne Darin, Rossana Andrade, and Jaime Sánchez

A Low Resolution Haptic Interface for Interactive Applications   224
 Bijan Fakhri, Shashank Sharma, Bhavica Soni, Abhik Chowdhury,
 Troy McDaniel, and Sethuraman Panchanathan

A Fitts' Law Evaluation of Hands-Free and Hands-On Input
on a Laptop Computer. . . . .　234
　Mehedi Hassan, John Magee, and I. Scott MacKenzie

A Time-Discrete Haptic Feedback System for Use by Persons
with Lower-Limb Prostheses During Gait. . . . .　250
　*Gabe Kaplan, Troy McDaniel, James Abbas, Ramin Tadayon,
　and Sethuraman Panchanathan*

Quali-Quantitative Review of the Use of Multimodal Interfaces
for Cognitive Enhancement in People Who Are Blind. . . . .　262
　Lana Mesquita and Jaime Sánchez

Statistical Analysis of Novel and Traditional Orientation Estimates
from an IMU-Instrumented Glove. . . . .　282
　*Nonnarit O-larnnithipong, Neeranut Ratchatanantakit,
　Sudarat Tangnimitchok, Francisco R. Ortega, Armando Barreto,
　and Malek Adjouadi*

Modeling Human Eye Movement Using Adaptive Neuro-Fuzzy
Inference Systems. . . . .　300
　Pedro Ponce, Troy McDaniel, Arturo Molina, and Omar Mata

Creating Weather Narratives. . . . .　312
　*Arsénio Reis, Margarida Liberato, Hugo Paredes, Paulo Martins,
　and João Barroso*

RingBoard 2.0   A Dynamic Virtual Keyboard Using Smart Vision. . . . . . .　323
　Taylor Ripke, Eric O'Sullivan, and Tony Morelli

Introducing Pneumatic Actuators in Haptic Training Simulators
and Medical Tools. . . . .　334
　*Thibault Sénac, Arnaud Lelevé, Richard Moreau, Minh Tu Pham,
　Cyril Novales, Laurence Nouaille, and Pierre Vieyres*

ANA: A Natural Language System with Multimodal Interaction
for People Who Have Tetraplegia. . . . .　353
　*Maikon Soares, Lana Mesquita, Francisco Oliveira,
　and Liliana Rodrigues*

An Investigation of Figure Recognition with Electrostatic Tactile Display. . .　363
　*Hirobumi Tomita, Shotaro Agatsuma, Ruiyun Wang, Shin Takahashi,
　Satoshi Saga, and Hiroyuki Kajimoto*

A Survey of the Constraints Encountered in Dynamic Vision-Based
Sign Language Hand Gesture Recognition. . . . .　373
　Ruth Wario and Casam Nyaga

Assistive Environments

Quantifying Differences Between Child and Adult Motion Based
on Gait Features 385
    Aishat Aloba, Annie Luc, Julia Woodward, Yuzhu Dong, Rong Zhang,
    Eakta Jain, and Lisa Anthony

Learning User Preferences via Reinforcement Learning with Spatial
Interface Valuing 403
    Miguel Alonso Jr.

Adaptive Status Arrivals Policy (ASAP) Delivering Fresh Information
(Minimise Peak Age) in Real World Scenarios 419
    Basel Barakat, Simeon Keates, Ian Wassell, and Kamran Arshad

A Feasibility Study of Designing a Family-Caregiver-Centred Dementia
Care Handbook. 431
    Ting-Ya Chang and Kevin C. Tseng

Occupational and Nonwork Stressors Among Female Physicians in Taiwan:
A Single Case Study 445
    Kuang-Ting Cheng and Kevin C. Tseng

Classification of Physical Exercise Intensity Based on Facial Expression
Using Deep Neural Network. 455
    Salik Ram Khanal, Jaime Sampaio, Joao Barroso, and Vitor Filipe

Effect of Differences in the Meal Ingestion Amount
on the Electrogastrogram Using Non-linear Analysis 468
    Fumiya Kinoshita, Kazuya Miyanaga, Kosuke Fujita,
    and Hideaki Touyama

MilkyWay: A Toolbox for Prototyping Collaborative Mobile-Based
Interaction Techniques 477
    Mandy Korzetz, Romina Kühn, Karl Kegel, Leon Georgi,
    Franz-Wilhelm Schumann, and Thomas Schlegel

@HOME: Exploring the Role of Ambient Computing for Older Adults 491
    Daria Loi

Designing and Evaluating Technology for the Dependent Elderly
in Their Homes. 506
    Maria João Monteiro, Isabel Barroso, Vitor Rodrigues, Salviano Soares,
    João Barroso, and Arsénio Reis

Applying Universal Design Principles in Emergency Situations:
An Exploratory Analysis on the Need for Change
in Emergency Management   511
    Cristina Paupini and George A. Giannoumis

Digital Volunteers in Disaster Response: Accessibility Challenges.   523
    Jaziar Radianti and Terje Gjøsæter

The Contribution of Social Networks to the Technological Experience
of Elderly Users   538
    Célia M. Q. Ramos and João M. F. Rodrigues

Automatic Exercise Assistance for the Elderly Using Real-Time
Adaptation to Performance and Affect   556
    Ramin Tadayon, Antonio Vega Ramirez, Swagata Das,
    Yusuke Kishishita, Masataka Yamamoto, and Yuichi Kurita

EEG Systems for Educational Neuroscience   575
    Angeliki Tsiara, Tassos Anastasios Mikropoulos, and Panagiota Chalki

A Soft Exoskeleton Jacket with Pneumatic Gel Muscles
for Human Motion Interaction   587
    Antonio Vega Ramirez and Yuichi Kurita

Author Index   605

Universal Access Theory, Methods and Tools

Beyond Usability: Methodologies and Bias – Surveying the Surveys

Troy D. Abel[⊠]

University of North Texas, Denton, TX 76203, USA
troy.abel@unt.edu

Abstract. Surveys are a tool used in everyday usability testing to gather data and confirm findings amongst target populations; however, usability researchers must be aware of biases which can be introduced through certain types of survey questions. Survey instruments are a popular way to quickly gather qualitative and quantitative data from target populations for use in usability studies. These instruments may, at times, introduce unforeseen bias, and information participants may be unaware of when questions are triangulated and results combined during the analysis phase.

Certain populations may be hesitant to answer certain questions which may divulge immigrations status, sexual orientation, marriage status, age, and socioeconomic status to name a few. Of even greater concern occurs when answers to these, and other, questions are triangulated and combined to form inferences with regard to the population. For example, imagine the survey instrument contained questions regarding sexual orientation, marital status, and income levels – when triangulated and analyzed, the target population could be deemed marginalized and their results deemed unnecessary to the study, when in reality this population could potentially affect the outcome of the survey had their results been included.

Keywords: Usability · Bias · Marginalized populations · Idiosyncratic populations · Data triangulation · Usability testing bias · IRB

1 Introduction to Usability Testing Surveys and Tools

1.1 Usability Testing

According to Usability.gov, "Usability testing refers to evaluating a product or service by testing it with representative users. Typically, during a test, participants will try to complete typical tasks while observers watch, listen and takes notes. The goal is to identify any usability problems, collect qualitative and quantitative data and determine the participant's satisfaction with the product" [1]. In addition to executing 'task-based testing,' quite often survey instruments are utilized to gather information about representative users. These surveys can take place prior to, or in tandem with, a task-based test. The results of these surveys are often analyzed in conjunction with the usability testing to uncover innate problems with a system.

M. Antona and C. Stephanidis (Eds.): HCII 2019, LNCS 11572, pp. 3–12, 2019.
https://doi.org/10.1007/978-3-030-23560-4_1

1.2   The Survey

According to Merriam-Webster, a survey is "[meant] to query (someone) in order to collect data for the analysis of some aspect of a group or area" [2]. "A survey is a tool used to collect data on a large group of people to answer one or more research questions. It is one of the most common research tools used by social science research (sociology, political science, education, and psychology), health fields, and market research" [3]. Surveys are utilized to quickly gather data about target markets, delineate differences amongst populations, and specifically in usability testing, to understand unique differences with regard to usage and ultimate desires of a system.

Surveys are used for several reasons and a broad array of purposes. For example, surveys are utilized by the US Government for evaluating policies. "The Study of Income and Program Participation is a government-funded survey study designed to examine how well federal income support programs are operating. Survey questions from this study include information on housing subsidies, food subsidies, and income supports" [3]. Corporations use surveys to measure customer satisfaction. Social scientists use surveys for basic and applied research. Usability experts rely heavily on quantitative and qualitative data streams, particularly surveys to help define design requirements, drive product innovation, and test the usage of a given system. Usability surveys are mostly delivered via the internet (web and mobile), and several tools exist to help administer such surveys.

Usability studies often employ the use of surveys because they are versatile, cost effective, and generalizable. Surveys can be released and data obtained quickly, and cost-effectively, through the internet. Additionally, surveys are generalizable, "which means that the information found in the survey is representative or reflective of the entire population being studied—not just the sample collected," [3]. if the proper sampling techniques are followed. Usability surveys often contain demographic information as well as socio-economic status information. In additional, several layers of additional self-identified data are collected. With all this data comes extreme ethical considerations to the researcher, the next topic of discussion.

1.3   Research Ethics in Corporate America

Ethics exist to protect the integrity of research, participants, and data obtained. Additionally, "… many of the ethical norms help to ensure that researchers can be held accountable to the public. For instance, federal policies on research misconduct, conflicts of interest, the human subjects' protections, and animal care and use are necessary in order to make sure that researchers who are funded by public money can be held accountable to the public" [4]. Several different policy makers have their own set of Ethics standards for research, such as the National Science Foundation, National Institute of Health, and the Food and Drug Administration. All the entities have varying policies with regard to research and ethics. For purposes of this paper, "Research ethics are primarily concerned with three aspects of research: (1) the research participants themselves, (2) the data collected from the participants, and (3) how we present our findings" [3].

The research participants themselves should be given informed consent and not be harmed in any way, minimizing all possible risks to participants and maximizing benefits of participation. The data collected from the participants should be clearly documented, transparent, replicable, and stored securely. The findings should be responsibly interpreted and stick extremely close to the actual data.

Surveys collect large amounts of data, and often times, usability researchers are not trained in the skillful art of crafting survey questions, and therefore potentially bias their research. "Oftentimes, we think we know the answer to the research question, but we want to confirm it with evidence. Believe it or not, our personal beliefs and assumptions can influence the research design in such a way that the results will reflect our expectations. That is, we can accidentally bias our own research. In fact, even the research questions we ask can expose our biases" [3].

"In 1974, the National Research Act established the Institutional Review Board (IRB) system for regulating research with human beings, which exists today" [3]. The Institutional Review Boards (IRB) are in place to protect human subjects in applied research; however, quite often, usability researchers at private corporations don't have an IRB to protect human subjects and approve their studies; therefore, these studies take place without regard for the participants. However, the IRB mandate only applied to federally funded research, and not private corporation research. Therefore, very few to no corporations, have IRB to review and approve human test subject research- this constitutes a major ethical flaw in Usability Experience (UX) research.

Often times, surveys ask sensitive questions without the necessary support from the sponsoring organization or pressure populations to participate unintentionally. For example, "Asking women questions about sexual abuse or rape might lead to serious emotional harm" [3]. Moreover, protected populations such as children, prisoners, LGBTQ+ participants may feel pressured to participate in surveys if asked.

Without IRB reviews and approvals of human test research, corporations are potentially biasing their data in more ways than one can imagine.

2   The Usability Survey

According to Perlman (2009), "Questionnaires have long been used to evaluate user interfaces (Root & Draper, 1983). Questionnaires have also long been used in elec-tronic form (Perlman, 1985)" [5, 6]. These questionnaires have been used in usability to assist in uncovering problems innate to a designed system. According to Usability.gov, "When conducting an online survey, you have an opportunity to learn: (A) who your users are, (B) what your users want to accomplish, (C) what information your users are looking for" [7]. The structure of a usability survey is quite similar to that of a standard corporate survey: (1) demographics and market segmentation questions, (2) system satisfaction and investigation questions, and finally (3) follow-up questions which probe for deep data. Moreover, survey data, "... is often a main source of input for segmentation, personas, market feasibility, and decisions on prioritizing product functionality" [8].

3 Survey the Survey's: Higher Education Surveys in Action

Currently, two (2) of the most popular surveys being utilized in Higher Education today are the National Survey of Student Engagement (NSSE) and The Freshman Survey (CIRP). These surveys are utilized to help administrators in higher education make changes to their campus in order to facilitate change based on survey responses. Both of these surveys demonstrate usage of potentially biasing questions. Two questions from each survey will be discussed below as examples of potentially biasing participants by reinforcing stereotypes (See Sect. 4.7).

3.1 The National Survey of Student Engagement (NSSE)

According to their website, "The NSSE survey, launched in 2000 and updated in 2013, assesses the extent to which students engage in educational practices associated with high levels of learning and development. The questionnaire collects information in five categories: (1) participation in dozens of educationally purposeful activities, (2) institutional requirements and the challenging nature of coursework, (3) perceptions of the college environment, (4) estimates of educational and personal growth since starting college, and (5) background and demographic information" [9]. This survey is unique in that it is extremely long and tedious for participants to fill out, and potentially suffers from significant participant drop-off.

The NSSE does not ask demographic information until the end of their long survey. After pages and pages of questions, participants are asked personally identifying information such as, "What is your gender identity?" The NSSE only provides 4 choices (See Fig. 1). One of these choices is "Another gender identity, please specify." This is a potentially biasing question, and doesn't explore all potential gender identities, possibly excluding some participants as even with an 'other' option some may feel 'left-out.'

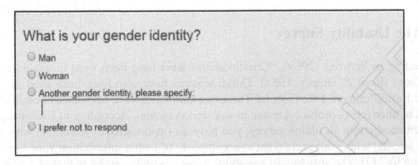

Fig. 1. Demographic question on the NSSE

A few questions below gender identity, the NSSE asks a participant to self-identify mental diagnoses such as sensory impairment, learning disabilities, or even mental health disorders (See Fig. 2). While the importance of this information can be debated, a UX researcher must ask themselves if it is important enough to potentially bias survey results.

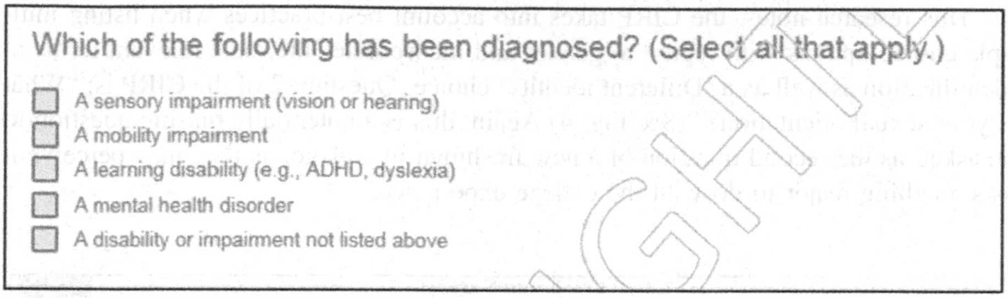

Fig. 2. Demographic question on the NSSE

3.2 The Freshman Survey (TFS: CIRP)

The CIRP survey, according to their website, "… is designed for administration to incoming first-year students before they start classes at your institution. The instrument collects extensive information that allows for a snapshot of what your incoming students are like before they experience college" [10]. When exploring the questions, format, and flow of the CIRP, some participants may be immediately biased towards answering questions.

Take for example, question 1 and 2 of the CIRP. These questions ask participants to self-identify their gender and sexual orientation. Question 1 is: "What is your current gender identity?" (See Fig. 3) Beginning a survey about the new college experience with querying gender identity, may potentially bias some participants. Depending on how the survey is framed, where it is administered, and other factors, some participants may be 'put-off' by this as an initial question and think the entire survey will be about how they personally identify in the world. While this may be a question used to determine market segmentations and demographics, this research would argue placing this question later in the survey, or possibly at the end.

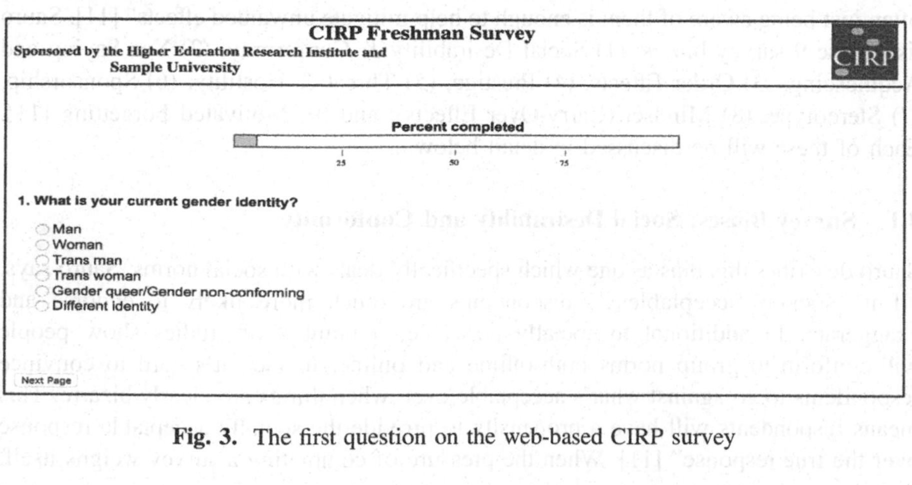

Fig. 3. The first question on the web-based CIRP survey

This research notes, the CIRP takes into account best practices when listing multiple choice options with regard to gender and incorporates the most relevant terms in identification as well as a 'Different identity' choice. Question 2 of the CIRP is: "What is your sexual orientation?" (See Fig. 4) Again, this is a potentially biasing question to be asked as the second question of a new freshman in college, as they may perceive it as something major to do with the college experience.

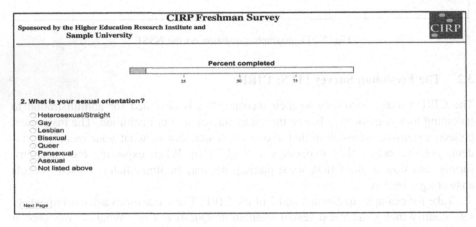

Fig. 4. The second question on the web-based CIRP survey

4   Analyzing Survey Data and Negotiating Bias

Jeff Sauro, an often-cited usability expert in usability statistics, has published what he calls the 9 biases that affect survey responses. These biases, "… can be particularly pernicious because they're harder to spot than more glaring problems …. In fact, there are not always clear remedies to the many biases that can affect your results. However, often just being aware of them is enough to help mitigate unwanted effects" [11]. Sauro lists these 9 survey biases: (1) Social Desirability & Conformity, (2) Yea Saying and Acquiescing, (3) Order Effects, (4) Prestige, (5) Threat & Hostility, (6) Sponsorship, (7) Stereotype, (8) Mindset (Carry-Over Effects), and (9) Motivated Forgetting [11]. Each of these will be discussed in detail below.

4.1   Survey Biases: Social Desirability and Conformity

Sauro describes this bias as one which specifically deals with social norms. Sauro says, "If it's socially acceptable … respondents are much more likely to endorse and exaggerate. In additional to socially desirable, a number of studies show people will conform to group norms both offline and online. In fact, it's hard to convince respondents to go against what's acceptable even when things are clearly bizarre. This means respondents will have a propensity to provide the socially acceptable response over the true response" [11]. When the pressure of completing a survey weighs itself, respondents find themselves subconsciously adhering to the social norms currently in existence.

When analyzing this type of bias, it's important to remember what social norms could influence a response for a particular question, and factor that information into the analysis of responses.

4.2 Survey Biases: Yea Saying and Acquiescing

This type of bias is characterized by those respondents who appear to over-answer 'yes' to a series of questions, even when the questions are negatively phrased and should normally elicit a 'no' response. Sauro says, "Respondents can tend to be agreeable (acquiesce) and respond usually positively to just about any question you ask them in a survey. One of the best way(s) to minimize this "yea" saying is to minimize simple yes-no answers and instead have respondents select from alternatives or use some type of force choice or ranking" [11]. Respondents tend to be amicable, and acquiesce, to satisfy what they believe others want to this.

When analyzing and uncovering this type of bias, it's often difficult to ascertain if a response is truly genuine or not.

4.3 Survey Biases: Order Effects

This bias specifically deals with the linear progression through a survey. Sauro states, "The order you ask questions matters. Mentioning products, brands, or events can affect how people rate their familiarity and attitudes on subsequent questions. This can be especially harmful in branding and awareness surveys as the mere exposure of a brand name first can influence later questions and findings. Response options also matter. A respondent might remember a choice that appeared in an earlier question and be more likely to select the response on later questions. You can often manage many order effects through properly sequenced questions and randomization" [11]. This level of bias is easily mitigated, by carefully scrutinizing the order and wording of usability survey questions.

4.4 Survey Biases: Prestige

Certain questions soliciting information with regard to socio-economic status (SES), income levels, and other 'prestigious' situations, should be carefully scrutinized. Sauro says, "Respondents will likely round up on income (especially men), education, and their reported power and prestige when making decisions. This is different than outright lying or cheating on a survey. If a question asks about prestige, assume the responses are inflated to present the respondent in a more favorable light. Exactly how much they are inflated will depend on the question, context and respondents" [11].

This type of bias, while at times easy to spot, is difficult to judge due to varying levels of respondent inflation and truthfulness.

4.5   Survey Biases: Threat and Hostility

Asking certain questions may trigger respondents and place them in a negative mindset for the rest of the survey. This bias is described by Sauro best, "Getting people to think about unpleasant things and events can get them in the wrong state of mind, which can cast a negative shadow on subsequent questions... Even rather benign questions (like asking people their marital status) may prime respondents with negative thoughts as participants recall bad past experiences (like a divorce or death in the family). Moving more sensitive demographic questions and anything that could potentially elicit negative thoughts to the end of a survey when possible may help" [11]. As Sauro suggests, placing these questions at the end of the survey may mitigate their effect on other answers.

4.6   Survey Biases: Sponsorship

If the survey's sponsor is revealed before or during a survey, be prepared for automatic bias. Sauro says, "When respondents know where the survey is coming from (the sponsor), it will likely influence responses. [For example] if you know the questions about your online social media experience are coming from Facebook, your thoughts and feelings about Facebook will likely impact responses. This can be especially the case for more ethereal measures like brand attitude and awareness that can be affected from the mere reminder of a brand in the email invitation or name and logo on the welcome page. One of the best ways to minimize sponsorship bias is to obfuscate the sponsor as much as possible and/or use a third-party research firm..." [11]. The best way to negotiate this bias is to never reveal who the survey/research sponsor is to the participants.

4.7   Survey Biases: Stereotype

"Asking about gender, race, technical ability, education, or other socio-economic topics may reinforce stereotypes in the mind of the respondents and may even lead them to act in more stereotypical ways. For example, reminding people that stereotypes exist around those who are more technically averse (age), math ability (gender), or intelligence (education level) may affect later responses as the stereotype primes respondents through the questions" [11]. These types of questions potentially 'put-off' participants, and bias their responses throughout the survey. Questions which remind participants stereotypes exist should be avoided if possible, as these will likely bias survey responses for questions to follow.

4.8   Survey Biases: Mindset (Carry-Over Effects)

At times participants remember, or carry-over, remnants from previous questions or biases about a brand or situation they were asked about previously. This type of bias is knows as Mindset according to Sauro [11]. To mitigate carry-over effects when designing survey instruments, consider spacing out questions or inserting 'filler' questions.

4.9   Survey Biases: Motivated Forgetting

"Memories are malleable and in general, we're not terribly good at remembering events accurately. People tend to distort their memories to match current beliefs, also called telescoping. Respondents may recall an event but report that it happened earlier than it actually did (backward telescoping) or report that it happened more recently (forward telescoping). Many research questions rely on participants to recall specific events or behavior. There can be a tendency to recall events that didn't happen or forget the specifics of an event" [11]. When asking participants to recall particular behaviors, be prepared for this type of bias: motivated forgetting. Participants will attempt to provide the 'best answer' to what they hope will be the response the survey is soliciting. Researchers should be aware of this type of bias when analyzing results.

4.10   Survey Inferences

Sauro says, "Just because a survey has bias doesn't mean the results are meaningless". Just because surveys have bias, doesn't necessarily mean a researcher cannot use the resulting data. Sauro says, "Just because a survey has bias doesn't mean the results are meaningless'. It does mean you should be able to understand how each may impact your results. This is especially important when you're attempting to identify the percentage of a population (e.g. the actual percent that agree to statements, have certain demographics like higher income, or their actual influence on purchase decisions). While there's not a magic cure for finding and removing all biases, being aware of them helps limit their negative impact. A future article will discuss some ideas for how to identify and reduce the effects of biases and other common pitfalls in survey design" [11]. Researchers should be aware of inferences and biases as to attempt to mitigate these types of biases.

5   Conclusion and Future Research

This research has demonstrated a need for corporate, academic, and private UX research teams to establish best practices with regard to Human Subject research. In addition, this research provides several classifications of bias, or inferences, in survey research and means to mitigate these biases. Future research includes creating a tool-kit for UX Researchers across all business types which will provide best-practices in UX survey creation, administration, and analysis, including human test subject's ethics.

References

1. usability.gov Usability Testing. https://www.usability.gov/how-to-and-tools/methods/usability-testing.html. Accessed 20 Feb 2019
2. Merriam-Webster No Title. https://www.merriam-webster.com/dictionary/survey. Accessed 5 Feb 2019
3. Ruel, E.: 100 Questions (and Answers) About Survey Research. SAGE Publications, Inc., Thousand Oaks (2019)

4. NIH National Institute of Environmental Health Sciences. https://www.niehs.nih.gov/research/resources/bioethics/whatis/index.cfm. Accessed 15 Feb 2019
5. Perlman, G.: Electronic surveys. Behav. Res. Methods Instrum. Comput. **17**, 203–205 (1985). https://doi.org/10.3758/BF03214383
6. Root, R.W., Draper, S.: Questionnaires as a software evaluation tool. In: Proceedings of the SIGCHI Conference on Human Factors in Computing Systems—CHI 1983. ACM Press, New York, pp. 83–87 (1983)
7. Usability.gov Surveys. http://usability.gov. Accessed 16 Feb 2019
8. Sauro J Surveys. https://measuringu.com/survey-biases/. Accessed 18 Feb 2019
9. Indiana.edu NSSE. http://nsse.indiana.edu/html/survey_instruments.cfm. Accessed 1 Feb 2019
10. UCLA Higher Education Surveys: CIRP. https://heri.ucla.edu/cirp-freshman-survey/. Accessed 1 Feb 2019
11. Sauro J Survey Bias. https://measuringu.com/survey-biases/. Accessed 10 Feb 2019

A.I. Ethics in the City

Marc Böhlen[✉]

Emerging Practices in Computational Media, Department of Art,
University at Buffalo, Buffalo, NY 14260, USA
marcbohlen@protonmail.com

Abstract. Artificial Intelligence (A.I) is the science of making machines act in a way human beings might call intelligent. Ethics of A.I. seek to make A.I. behave responsibly. A recent surge in national and international initiatives in support of A.I and A.I ethics speaks to both the significance of as well as anxieties surrounding the project. This short text is only a sketch with more questions than answers. It points out two factors in the A.I. ethics debate that receive less attention than they should: the significance of situatedness and of decision mechanisms in A.I. The big city, I contend, will be the site where complex A.I ethics conflicts will emerge most prominently; in different ways in different parts of the world.

Keywords: Artificial Intelligence · Ethics · Urbanism

1 Cities as Sites of A.I. Experiences

The city has always been a site of density, of unlikely encounters rendered possible, of voluntary and involuntary exchanges. Part of the lure of the big city is precisely the combination of controlled and uncontrolled events. And big cities today are rich in ingredients that A.I. needs; human capital, data flows and problems to solve.

In the not too distant future, A.I. enabled cities will be blanketed with sensors capable of recording all forms of ambient information, from traffic to biological events with high spatial and temporal resolution. The future omniscient A.I. running the networked city will know, for example, how much water flows to each of its public fountains on any given day. And it will be able to choose precisely which of the fountains to turn off in the event of water shortage during a hot summer.

Contagious diseases no longer go undetected in the A.I. controlled city. Public transportation, armed with these new devices and A.I. algorithms controlling them, keep ever anxious big city dwellers abreast of all contagious hotspots in the city in real time. Optimized against under-reporting a threat, the algorithms are programmed to respond to every possible pathogen detected, even the common cold. Riding in a bus with a fellow sneezing commuter is no longer a shared acceptable risk of life in the city. The offending passenger can be detected, and the danger she poses shared with fellow travelers in real time. In the past, social rules and established but unwritten ethics of everyday behavior dictated that we do not outcast a person just because of a sneeze on a bus.

M. Antona and C. Stephanidis (Eds.): HCII 2019, LNCS 11572, pp. 13–27, 2019.
https://doi.org/10.1007/978-3-030-23560-4_2

A.I. will make the city more controllable; issues left to chance in the past will become decidable. How might the citizens of Rome respond to A.I controlled water fountains during a drought, or the citizens of Hyderabad to biosensing enabled and A.I. controlled public buses during a flu epidemic?

2 A.I. Ethics en Vogue

A.I. tries to efficiently make sense of the world. But A.I. efficiency does not translate to morality, and efficient sense making can cut multiple ways. Leaving out details that might not seem important for algorithm design can mean missing nuance that only becomes apparent when the algorithm operates in the field. The opposition between the power of abstraction and loss of nuance has remained a source of tension in A.I. design and ethics from early experiments to current products.

Some applied A.I. domains, including Ambient Intelligence, have tried to include ethics in design parameters of computing systems, but those approaches, laudable as they were, never scaled to mass deployment. More recently, the topic of A.I. ethics has found resonance again, this time however fueled by unease produced both by spectacular successes in language and image processing as well by ever more glaring A.I. snafus such as biased facial identification [1].

Criticism of A.I from consultants [2], business celebrities [3], and activists [4] has become too intense to ignore even by the most ardent supports of A.I. In response, private industry consortia have taken a lead in A.I ethics debates in order to prevent A. I. from becoming a liability; securing a favorable regulatory framework for A.I. development is of paramount importance to the industry. The fact that there are at the time of this writing over 50 distinct efforts underway to support, oversee and regulate A.I. systems is a clear sign of the general perception of the significance of, and the recognition of the scale of the problems A.I. is generating.

Indeed, not all of the 50 efforts are new. The Organization for Economic Co-operation and Development[1] was a pioneer in the formulation of guidelines for trans-border privacy protection almost 40 years ago and is now is in the process of proposing succinct policy and institutional frameworks to guide A.I. design and use across the planet. The inclusion of the global dimension of A.I. is shared by a variety of other initiatives, each with its own specific focus (the European Union's Communication on Artificial Intelligence in Europe, and the UNESCO World Commission on the Ethics of Scientific Knowledge and Technology, amongst others). Some of the private stake-holder initiatives (The Future of Life Institute; OpenAI; Cambridge University's Center for the Study of Existential Risk; the University of Montreal's Declaration for a Responsible Development of Artificial Intelligence as well as the IEEE's Ethically Aligned Design initiative) combine efforts to manage current A.I. products while considering future A.I technologies far more capable than even the best systems currently in operation.

---

[1] See www.oecd.org/going-digital/ai/initiatives-worldwide/ for an updated list of A.I initiatives.

Many countries view the development of A.I. as a way to increase competitiveness and strengthen national security. The term A.I. nationalism [5] has been coined to denote precisely this nation-first approach to A.I., and several existing and emerging A.I. powerhouses have openly declared their nation-specific aspirations, including China (New Generation of Artificial Intelligence Development Plan); Finland (Age of Artificial Intelligence); France (Strategy for a Meaningful Artificial Intelligence; Italy (Artificial Intelligence at the service of the citizen); Japan (Artificial Intelligence Technology Strategy), as well as the USA (National Artificial Intelligence Research and Development Strategic Plan). China, already a leader in voice and visual recognition technologies, has likely crafted the most ambitious plan [6] for an A.I. fortified future, seeking by 2030 global A.I. dominance in all relevant domains including defense, urbanization, industrialization, social governance and – where necessary – public opinion guidance [6, p. 28].

In addition to the nation-specific interests, many of the current A.I. initiatives respond to popular and current themes such as privacy. Given the current culture of data misuse large and small, it is of little surprise that damage control is applied and that the topics of privacy and security find prominent attention. Certainly the recent history of data theft has brought this part of data culture to the forefront of public scrutiny. And the otherwise desirable ability to learn lessons from large datasets is rapidly becoming a liability when datasets are acquired illegally.

It is also not surprising then that harm prevention would be coupled to the issues privacy and security. The proactive attempt to prevent personal data from being compromised in the first place is the better way to address data security; handling after data breaches occur is mostly ineffective. And harm prevention, applicable to a general public, leads in turn to additional shared themes across the initiatives, namely equity and fairness. Even the concept of well-being is included in some of the initiatives. If nothing else, the inclusion of well-being is a clear indicator of the hope many stakeholder hold for A.I. as a potential source for good. The positivist stance also functions as a powerful rhetorical antidote to evil A.I. that periodically dominates popular debates on A.I. futures.

Specifically the industry supported A.I. initiatives emphasize ethics challenges of future A.I. over those of current A.I. systems. While even the most advanced systems in operation today are probably no indicator of what next generation A.I. will be able to achieve, these superhuman A.I. systems will be so powerful that ethics might not be the most important topic to consider. Indeed, careless mingling of current and future A.I. concerns weakens arguments in support of A.I. governance right now.

Engineers have in the past, at least in principle, been bound by professional standards to act ethically[2], and many A.I. relevant questions can be addressed by existing frameworks. Without questioning the need for deep inquiry into ethics of A.I. at large, some of the most urgent problems can be addressed now: The need to be honest with the general public about what a given A.I. system actually does and the limitations the system has; the acknowledgement of slippages that occur when an A.I. system is

---

[2] See Accreditation Board for Engineering and Technology http://sites.bsyse.wsu.edu/pitts/be120/Handouts/codes/abet.htm.

transferred from one domain to another; control or prohibition of reselling data, etc. Granting A.I. special status because it can be a powerful agent for change weakens calls for constraints to follow basic and established rules of conduct.

3 A.I. Ethics Shapeshifts

Technology-centric approaches to A.I. ethics are often inadequate to address the paths along which A.I. systems impact people. An early yet telling example [7] describes a robotics engineer working on a sophisticated anti-tank mine capable of hopping out of the way of unintended targets such as pedestrians. Certainly one might be tempted to declare this agile robot an example of an ethically designed intelligent machine. Not quite. Because of the mine's clever control system, the device was not classified as a mine, but as a robot and consequently not subject to anti-mine regulation, clearing it for wide distribution as a 'smart' defense device, undermining the procedures designed to curtail the deployment of such weapons in the first place.

Similarly, an A.I. system may become unintentionally harmful with skewed training and questionable design priorities. Imagine service chat bots designed to assist visitors to the US in navigating American customs requirements at ports of entry. With the intent of creating a lifelike experience, the bots are trained on the language habits of American customs officers, who - maybe without malign intent - exhibit threating language use. And in order to make the system efficient, visitor response times are limited to a few seconds. The resultant synthetic rudeness is an unanticipated consequence of poorly selected training sets and pressure to optimize for speedy interaction.

In order to get some understanding of the landscape of unintentional A.I. ethics conflicts, and why cities are likely to become prime sources of generating and experiencing these conflicts, the next section will revisit an early example of a technology-supported intervention into the urban fabric as well as some of the ethical issues that ensued.

4 Road Pricing – Early Technology Ethics

Generally the territory of economists and urban planners, road pricing might seem at first an unlikely candidate for A.I. ethics insights. Yet because road pricing has been applied to many large cities and because scholars have analyzed in depth the forces at work in road pricing projects, a second take is warranted.

A.I. systems, like road transport, impose negative externalities on society [8]. In the case of road transport these externalities include congestion, accidents and pollution. Furthermore, road pricing infrastructures are complex control systems that include data collection and interpretation on an industrial scale. Additionally, road pricing systems are policy dependent, technically enabled responses to urban traffic management and revenue generation needs, as well as responses to calls for fairness in resource use. In A.I. the negative externalities include compromised privacy and constant surveillance, with other factors likely to join the list as the field stabilizes. As such, the dynamics surrounding road pricing interventions parallel several of the issues in A.I ethics.

Road Pricing in Singapore

Singapore was the first country to introduce road pricing with the expressed goal of reducing congestion in the city. Early versions based on manual paper licenses granted access rights to select parts of the city [9]. Additionally, the government discouraged cars from entering downtown with increased parking fees and substantially improved public transportation and park&ride nodes. However, the manual system was labor intensive and unable to charge vehicles per entry and unable to adjust prices rapidly.

In response to these shortcomings an electronic road pricing system (ERP) was introduced in 1998. Vehicles were required to install in-vehicle gizmos with cash cards, and each time a vehicle passes under one of the many overhead gantries installed in rings around the city, the ERP charges are deducted from the cash card via short range radio. The communication is one directional, meaning the gantry tells the in-vehicle unit to charge the cash card rather than the in-vehicle unit signaling the account ID to the gantry. This provision anonymizes the use of the ERP unless a transaction fails, in which case a camera captures the license plate of the vehicle.

Even though the system is designed to operate as an income generator, annual revenue produced by the ERP is about $S150 million [10]. Prior to the actual launch of the ERP, the government of Singapore launched a mass publicity campaign to 'inform and educate' motorists [9]. The campaign included articles in newspapers, on television and radio as well as pamphlets with explanations on how the system works, the location of the gantries and shops to have the in-vehicle control units installed. Singapore's ERP was launched with a three month test period during which no charges were made, allowing a time limited grace period to soften the transition to the subsequent uncompromising oversight.

By traffic control measures, the ERP can be considered a success. It reduced traffic into the downtown core by at least 14% [9]. Yet the Singaporean ERP uncovered otherwise unexpressed anxieties of city dwellers. Complaints filed by users centered on confusion with the pricing structure, the kinetic effects of in-vehicle gizmos in car accidents, radiation exposure from the gantry system, the potential of being tracked, and the fear of being falsely tagged as a violator should some part of the control system fail [9].

Road Pricing in Stockholm

In Stockholm, road pricing followed a quite different trajectory. In Stockholm, the rationale for congestion pricing was based not only on a desire to reduce traffic in a downtown area isolated by waterways but also on a desire to reduce emissions produced by automobiles, a concern not explicitly mentioned in the Singapore case.

The Stockholm congestion tax varies (as others do) based on time and does not depend on direction of traffic in a cordon around the central city [11]. The Stockholm technical model is a fully automatic fee payment system enabled by overhead gantries outfitted with computer vision license plate recognition. No in-vehicle devices nor pre-travel purchases are required. Vehicle owners are sent a monthly bill based on the number and location of license plate recordings.

The history of the project is telling. Congestion charges were introduced in Stockholm first as a trial in 2006, followed by a referendum, and then made permanent from 2007 on. Similar to the Singapore approach, the intervention in Stockholm included an expansion of public bus and train transport, bicycle and pedestrian safety improvements as well as the construction of additional park&ride facilities [10]. The traffic centric debate on the merits of the experiment were paralleled by political maneuvering. A then small interest group, the Green Party, lobbied in favor of the trial in exchange for its support for a national social-democratic government [12, p. 2]. This horse trade in turn negatively impacted public perception of the congestion charge concept. Only after the trial period started did public sentiment turn in favor of the effort as the benefits of the interventions became apparent to individuals and the public at large. Media reports that initially focused on rallying against the costs of road pricing started fantasizing about how the revenues could be put to use [12]. As in Singapore, the benefits generated by the Stockholm system are measurable: 20% decrease in congestion, 14% reduction of CO_2 [12] and about 820 million krona in revenue in 2015 [11].

5   Social-Technical Systems in Context

Road pricing has not been a success story in every urban context in which it has been proposed or introduced. Hong Kong, for example, decided not to adapt electronic road pricing after a large study in the mid-1980s. Not that congestion mitigation was no longer necessary, but traffic reductions occurred through a confluence of other factors, including a new expressway, a stock and property market crash, the opening of a new mass transit railway as well as doubts of the financial viability of the project. The fact that Hong Kong was then slated to return to Chinese rule might have been an additional factor in the city decision not to introduce a large scale surveillance system [13].

Moreover, road pricing is not an urban intervention that produces binary results in every case. In London, for example, traffic has increased after congestion pricing was introduced. But that increase in turn is a function of several factors, including a reduction of road capacity and the introduction of 'exceptions' to the pricing regime [11] for select stakeholders.

The Stockholm case is interesting not because of the novelty of the deployed technology. In fact, license plate recognition was already then a solved problem. What makes the case interesting for the discussion of future urban A.I. ethics is the original oppositional public sentiment, the way it changed over the course of the trial period, and how the political rationality overshadowed the technical debate as the following excerpt demonstrates:

> "Political rationality of congestion pricing may be different from mere public acceptability. While public support certainly affects political actions, it is neither a necessary nor a sufficient criterion for political support for a policy. ... Purely technical rational questions, without a moral dimension or interpretation, may not generate sufficient voter enthusiasm to make them worth any political risk. During the debate, congestion pricing was to a large extent proposed and opposed with moral arguments rather than technical-rational ones in a more limited sense. This line of argumentation may have been necessary to make congestion pricing politically interesting – but may simultaneously have made it a more divisive issue." [12, p. 3]

If oppositional public sentiment almost derailed the Stockholm project, the Singapore ERP never faced such scrutiny. First, because it was created as a successor to an existing and inadequate system, and second, because Singapore's East Asian *electoral authoritarianism* [14] gave the government some leeway to not demonstrate the levels of concern towards public sentiment other democracies might exhibit. Moreover, the implementation of the ERP was by all accounts well organized and produced a smoothly operating system with measurable results.

Road pricing is an example of managing access to a limited, shared urban resource. By and large, the merits of managing limited resources in urban contexts are understood. Problems occur in the distribution of the costs and disadvantages of the intervention. What we can learn from the Singaporean and the Stockholm traffic management examples is that the implementation of a large social-technical system unfolds differently in different cultural and political contexts. The discussion of the merits of the system depend both on its actual performance as well as the way public debate in general occurs. As opposed to road pricing where the costs and merits are comparatively clear, the merits and costs of urban A.I systems are at this moment unstable. Moreover, the paths along which the merits and costs are formed are more complex than in even the newest road pricing systems.

6 Digital Monopolies – A Prelude to A.I. Ethics Conflicts

Road pricing foreshadowed only some of the dynamics of how large scale technical systems in the city are built and perceived by the public. This following section will shift from the automobile to the city dweller and describe how two current urban revitalization initiatives propose to work with large scale urban data flows, and point to some of the debates these efforts are generating.

Sidewalk Labs Toronto

The organizers of Sidewalk Labs [15], part of a large globally operating technology company, want to define, in their terms, what the city of the future might look like. With a local partner, Sidewalk Labs has created a master plan for Toronto's Eastern Waterfront. Promising a people-first design approach, the planners have laid out grand ambitions: sustainability writ large through new construction technologies to create a climate-positive and an inclement weather sensitive neighborhood with mixed income housing; a transit system that combines people, vehicles, freight and garbage disposal; and last but not least data-enabled social services.

Indeed, not only the social services are data-enabled, but every aspect of this new neighborhood is data-driven. Lamp posts, park benches and designer trash bins are optimized for this new urbanity, and they continuously, relentlessly, collect data [16]; data on bench usage, garbage production, dogs marking lamp posts, no event goes to waste. Yet for all its attention to the details of data collection, the original Sidewalk Labs model made no provision for how this new urban resource might be shared with the very people producing it.

Opponents to the plan openly rallied to prevent the new proprietary data infrastructure from becoming effective [17], forcing Sidewalk Labs to agree to declare "privacy as a fundamental human right" [16]. This major shift in approach however has yet to find a path into the details of implementation and oversight. For example, no one outside of Sidewalk Labs understands precisely what the organization will do with the data, which algorithms it will deploy on it and what downstream events it might enable. These are not minor concerns as they can materially impact quality of life along numerous trajectories. For example, will it become harder for a city resident to find an apartment if Sidewalk Labs detects deficiencies in her trash disposal habits? And what would happen if the transgressions were in fact those of a neighbor, and falsely attributed to another person? What kind of recourse could one take? How long would even minor transgressions be stored in databases no citizen has any form of access to?

This ongoing debate makes apparent an increasing discomfort with the cavalier ways digital monopolies collect and process data from people without their consent. The term *surveillance capitalism* has been coined to describe an 'emergent logic of accumulation' [18] that shows itself in the data extraction and control logic of the Sidewalk Labs project where fundamental human rights for data access are included in vague statements only. The opaque data regime envisioned by Sidewalk Labs in Toronto impacts not only the collection of data, but its processing and afterlife. Transparency on the details of data flows are precisely what would make it a meaningful right. Without rigorous transparency, the right simply does not exist.

The End of the Smart City
Sidewalk Labs is an example of a skewed urban concept; a smart city that places a premium on efficiency and in turn reduces the agency of city inhabitants. In response to the disappointment with the smart city concept, some optimistic urban planners and academics coined the term the *responsive city* [19] to describe an alternative notion of software-supported urban existence. In the responsive city, governance is imagined to have all the benefits of information technology enabled efficiencies but without the top-down hierarchy of the smart city. Proponents of the responsive city model hope for administrative efficiencies generated by digital tools that 'sweep away frustrations' and 'free up talent of government workers' [19, p. 6] while enabling new vectors for civic voices [19, p. 52] through open data platforms.

Digital City Barcelona
In Europe, there are several projects that attempt to build from the ground up responsive alternatives to a hierarchical data control model, and Barcelona is currently one of the most prominent examples [20]. Barcelona's effort in finding alternatives to digital monopolies is part of a response to Spain's recent history of austerity politics and the consequences it created for the city. Barcelona en Comù is at the forefront of a new generation of political movements radically opposed to digital innovation without citizen participation. Examples of how en Comù interprets its social mission can be seen in a cooperatively organized internet platform specifically designed to allow citizens of Barcelona voice their preferences and priorities from a list of possible city projects, for example.

One of the main concerns of Barcelona inhabitants has been tourism, in particular the effects of platforms such as Airbnb whose activities have reduced affordable housing options [4]. Furthermore, Digital City Barcelona is invested in building its own software with open source offerings produced by smaller locally operating entities and in adapting the development of these technologies to the changing needs of communities. All government produced datasets reside under sovereignty of the citizens of the city and build the basis of the city's digital commons. One of the stated goals of this approach is the creation of alternatives to the dynamics of the on-demand economic model with a focus on established and new models of sharing.

7   From Fair Data Practices to Ethics of A.I. in the City

The efforts of Digital City Barcelona and other responsive city initiatives cogently address pressing issues of data management in the city. Yet digital literacy, participatory and egalitarian practices and open data access do not speak to the new conditions created by algorithms capable of making decisions without human oversight. It is this class of automated actions that create a paradigm shift, with direct effects on the experience of urban life; algorithmically defined actions are what city dwellers will experience in the A.I. controlled city of the future.

In order to better understand why computer produced decision mechanisms are uniquely problematic and how they impact future A.I. ethics in the city, we take a short detour.

A.I. Makes Decisions

Computers make decisions differently than human beings do. They lack intuition, but can be trained to recognize patterns in large datasets with astonishing results. Supervised learning, learning by instruction – typically from a human being – allows a computer to acquire information without understanding the origin or meaning of the materials at hand. Under supervised learning, a computer builds internal representations of the input and then seeks to detect these patterns in new examples. Today, neural networks are the most expressive models for supervised learning. Neural networks are computational models inspired loosely by biological networks made up of nodes selectively modeled after biological neurons. Each neuron-node receives several inputs, takes a weighted sum over them, passes it through an activation module and responds with an output. And each node is in turn connected to many, many other nodes across multiple layers.

The neural network model has proved to be surprisingly successful in several areas that earlier A.I. methodologies have struggled with: autonomous vehicles, language and image analysis being the most prominent success stories today. Together with faster processors and large data sources, neural networks together with reinforcement learning have come to redefine what computers can achieve, including beating human beings at the game GO [21] even without instruction from humans, by force of trial and (learning from) error.

And A.I. Makes Mistakes

Pedro Domingos does not believe that computers will get too smart and take over the world, rather he believes that they are "too stupid and have already taken over the world" [22, p. 286]. Part of this 'stupidity' in real world situations is due to the specific goals of computer science, namely that of creating general approaches to a problem. A good search algorithm should be able to handle multiple search problems. But in order to achieve this ability to generalize, an algorithm must abstract out details irrelevant to the algorithm yet possibly highly relevant to the real world problem one actually wants to solve. This cleaning up of a real world problem to match the requirements of an algorithm can entail the loss of significant social context and nuance.

Historically, computer science is a child of mathematics and inherits its commitment to abstraction. Even the most basic operation in mathematics, the assignment of number, is an abstraction from reality that sacrifices nuance. But that sacrifice is fully intentional for it allows number to be disassociated from objects. Or, as Alfred Whitehead put it, "the first man who noticed the analogy between a group of seven fishes and a group of seven days made a notable advance in the history of thought" [23]. Without abstraction, the existing foundations of computer science would collapse. Yet when computer science applies itself to real world problems, the blessing of abstraction that give it enormous reach can become a curse.

In the case of reinforcement learning supported neural networks, the contrast between desired and effective operation follow unique patterns. When the output of a learning network produces a result that does not correspond with what the human designer intended, computer scientists speak of an *alignment problem* [24], and it is due to the fact that the optimizing efficiency of an A.I. algorithm cannot guarantee that values aligned with it are maintained. In practice, a machine learning accident occurs when a human had in mind a certain task, but the system designed for that task produced unexpected and possibly harmful results [25, p. 2]. In reinforcement learning, the disjoint between machine action and human expectation typically occurs in the behavior of its ulterior goal, the *objective function*.

Imagine an A.I. enabled drone designed to monitor crowds in public areas. As opposed to drones that use deep learning to attempt to recognize violent individuals [26], this technically more sophisticated and politically more ambitious drone seeks to prevent violence from occurring in the first place. Accordingly, this drone's objective function is formulated to prevent excessive crowd densities that precede the onset of crowd violence. Imagine this drone being deployed in New Delhi during a street protest of farmers, a recurring category of public protest in which farmers call for financial support for their crop production in the face of rising prices, a condition so severe that it results in dozens of suicides per day amongst farmers in rural India [27].

While this drone is not specifically programmed to prevent peacefully protesting farmers from stopping for refreshments at the side of the road, it might be compelled to do so by *reward hacking*. Large groups of people queuing in line could trigger the drone to act against excessive densities of pedestrians. So the drone might attempt to disperse the unassuming crowd wanting nothing more than a drink of water. This class of negative side effect occurs when an objective function over-focuses on one aspect of its environment while not paying attention to other aspects [25, p. 4] such as the presence of a refreshment stand in this case.

Likewise, the tenet of *scalable oversight* could be violated when the drone is unable to make proper decisions in situations that are too expensive to evaluate during training. And what should be the limits to exploration – should the drone be allowed to fly off to a different part of town to inspect a traffic accident and missing the possible onset of a mass panic at the street protest? Or in a case of *lack of robustness to distributional shift* the drone's crowd violence detection algorithm might have been trained on video segments with smaller groups of people at daylight, and then deployed for a particularly large group of farmers carrying candles at night time, rendering the drone unable to make any meaningful assessment.

No doubt there are methods by which many of these conditions can be addressed and the drone's actions aligned with its original goal and the intention of its designers. In this illustrative example, one might train the learning algorithm on many mass gatherings across seasons, during daytime and at night, to expose the algorithm to data of multiple crowd distributions. Or one could attempt to integrate human judgement directly into algorithm training [24]. The point of this simple example is not that any one of these actions can be fixed, but that, taken together, they constitute failure categories that occur within normal operation, not as a consequence of a malfunction or external influences. These are failure modalities other technical systems do not have, and they require a reformulation of what it means to require an algorithm to behave ethically.

One might argue that anxiety is uncalled for. After all, the automobile industry developed safety systems such as the seatbelt, airbag and lane departure warning only after automobiles – unsafe as they were at first - were launched to mass urban markets. Yet the A.I. case is trickier. As autonomous robots become ubiquitous and the A.I. systems controlling them increasingly complex, there is simply a higher chance that A.I. systems produce harmful actions while trying their best to efficiently execute prescribed tasks. And because the problems A.I. systems are asked to solve can be to too difficult, too expensive or too cumbersome for human beings to deal with, these efficient A.I. systems will be deployed. And because there is a race to get powerful (nationalist) A.I. systems into operation before others do, these A.I.s will be deployed even before all the kinks are worked out. As the harm vectors described above are not intentional and likely only detected after they have occurred, the algorithms creating them pose a conundrum to any technology ethics framework seeking to minimize harm.

8   A City Is Not a Laboratory

The outcome of an A.I. system is not just dependent on its design, or how well the technology can perform, but how people respond to its decisions. What works smoothly in a laboratory on synthetic data might not work at all in the wild, and the wildest site for A.I. to be active in is the city.

As a recent case in Boston [28] showed, good A.I. solutions can be defeated by factors completely unrelated to the A.I. itself. In the Boston case, an A.I. system was able to produce a new school busing schedule that changed start times at dozens of schools, rerouted hundreds of buses ferrying students to their respective schools, trimmed the city's transportation costs and shifted the majority of high school student into later start times while offering historically disadvantaged neighborhoods more desirable pickup schedules. Digital transformation of government at its best. So it seemed. But the new schedule proposed shifts in school start times by two hours and more in some cases. Angry parents who were content with the old system and newly disadvantaged by the new 'fair' system made their voices heard and produced a crisis for the city administrators so pressing that the initiative was canceled; the A.I. produced optimal solution suffered political defeat.

As the brief excursion into pre-A.I. electronic road pricing showed, different cities with different cultures respond in unique ways to the opportunities of actively managing individual traffic flow to reduce congestion. Similarly the introduction of A.I. enabled autonomous vehicles (AVs) can be expected have different practical effects and generate varied ethical dilemmas depending on the details of where and how the interventions occur, and the scale at which they occur. Thousands of single occupancy, pricy AVs zipping around a city in designated green traffic lanes with relaxed well-to-do passengers enjoying the view will not solve urban congestion but will foment new experiences of inequality. Without restrictions on AV distribution and occupancy, the convenience of AVs for individual consumers could outweigh the benefits for the public [29], creating a new category of efficiently managed, clean energy enabled unfairness.

In addition to transportation, housing has been a topic of responsive urbanism and A.I. driven innovation attempts. In the US for example, several projects have been launched to alleviate specific aspects of the housing crisis, including streamlining rehabilitation of dilapidated houses through the application of data science to the identification of homes in need of repair [30] and the use of industrial fabrication techniques to lower the cost of housing stock. Critics of technology centric housing crisis approaches point out that housing is a policy problem, one exasperated in the US by stagnating incomes and rising housing costs [31]. Only where zoning laws allow for the placement of low cost units produced by novel fabrication techniques can the social intervention be effective.

The disjoint between A.I fueled hope for a new approach to social equality and the real world constraints opposing change create a new arena for A.I. ethics. This condition is recognized at least by some major technology companies [32] that have recently promised substantial investments in addressing housing needs in their own cities without relying on technical wizardry. Instead, funding has been allocated towards supporting affordable housing developers and new construction initiatives.

9   Megacities as Feeding Grounds for A.I

Over half of the world's population now resides in cities, and some of these cities are growing to immense sizes. The current collection of 33 megacities each with populations of over 10 million is expected to expand to over 40 by 2030 [33]. These megacities will produce massive concentrations of human capital and services, and immense flows of data that urban A.I. systems will not only analyze but use to control the flow of goods and anticipate future events. The combination of intensity of human activities and data creates abundant opportunities for and pressure to develop A.I for urban conditions, and thus the highest concentration of conflicts for A.I ethics to grapple with.

Historians of technology remind us how much effort is required to learn to live with novel technologies. The advent of the telephone, the first electric medium to enter the urban home, created serious confusion in coming to terms with the new dimension of human presence [34], and the emissions of the first automobiles were hardly a cause for concern. There is no reason to assume that our current assessments of A.I. systems will not change. Indeed, they will change simply because A.I. changes, differently and more radically than other technologies, morphing and improving itself as it learns from new data or its own actions.

This is the context in which the recent surge in A.I. initiatives can be understood. There is no lack of lofty goals for A.I. and ethics; from harm prevention to solidarity, fairness and equity to well-being the list is packed, yet the path forward is not clear. The good news is that some technology companies – possibly in response to public pressure - are making efforts to address A.I. ethics violations. In one case an effort was launched to counter bias in facial identification software datasets [35], and in another case the details of an experiment in natural language generation [36] were kept secret because the results were too good. If made public in all its details, the software and training sets might be misused to generate fake news or worse.

Particularly the second case is an example of an effective approach to practical A.I. ethics at this time. *If in doubt, refrain from deployment*; fresh wind in the face of prominent long-winded A.I. ethics initiatives. Yet this can only be a start. More concrete responses to the new A.I. harm vectors should emerge, and any regulation and oversight mechanisms put in place now should remain adaptive to the fluid landscape of A.I. development.

One step towards meaningful oversight could include an honest account of problems industry is encountering as it develops and rolls out the newest A.I. systems to the public. It would be helpful if A.I. creators and providers made available a catalogue of mistakes, complete with project and management history, costs, operation context, failure mechanisms detected and anticipated, analysis and remedies applied. This would allow others to learn from mistakes and would likely enable a powerful new form of collective A.I. improvement over time. And if such a catalogue were publically available, continuously updated and broadcast to public displays in Times Square New York, Shibuya Center Gai Tokyo, and Maracanã Stadium Rio de Janeiro, the global public might even gain some faith in the prospect of a better future for all through A.I.

References

1. Harwell, D.: Amazon facial-identification software used by police falls short on tests for accuracy and bias, new research finds. The Washington Post (2019). https://www.washingtonpost.com/technology/2019/01/25/amazon-facial-identification-software-used-by-police-falls-short-tests-accuracy-bias-new-research-finds/?utm_term=.bae07d3d0eaf. Accessed 31 Jan 2019
2. Townsend, A.: Smart Cities: Big Data, Civic Hackers, and the Quest for a New Utopia. WW Norton & Company, New York (2013)
3. Dowd, M.: Elon Musk's Billion-Dollar Crusade to stop the A.I. Apocalypse. Vanity Fair. (2017). https://www.vanityfair.com/news/2017/03/elon-musk-billion-dollar-crusade-to-stop-ai-space-x. Accessed 3 Mar 2019
4. Morozov, E., Bria, F.: Rethinking the Smart City. Rosa Luxemburg Stiftung (2017). http://www.rosalux-nyc.org/wp-content/files_mf/morozovandbria_eng_final55.pdf
5. Hogarth, I.: A.I. Nationalism (2018). https://www.ianhogarth.com/blog/2018/6/13/ai-nationalism. Accessed 5 Mar 2019

6. State Council.: Notice of the State Council Issuing the New Generation of Artificial Intelligence Development Plan. State Council Document No 35. (2017). https://flia.org/wp-content/uploads/2017/07/A-New-Generation-of-Artificial-Intelligence-Development-Plan-1.pdf. English version, Accessed 7 Mar 2019

7. Nourbakhsh, I.: Lecture: Ethics in Robotics. (2009). https://www.youtube.com/watch?v=giKT8PkCCv4. Accessed 6 Mar 2019

8. Santos, G., Behrendt, H., Maconi, L., Shirvani, T., Teytelboym, A.: Part I: externalities and economic policies in road transport. Res. Transp. Econ. **28**(1), 2–45 (2010)

9. Menon, G., Guttikunda, S.: Electronic Road Pricing: Experience & Lessons from Singapore. SIM-air Working Paper Series: 33 (2010). http://www.environmentportal.in/files/ERP-Singapore-Lessons.pdf

10. Tristate Transportation Campaign.: Road pricing in London, Stockholm and Singapore. A way forward for New York City (2017). http://nyc.streetsblog.org/wp-content/uploads/2018/01/TSTC_A_Way_Forward_CPreport_1.4.18_medium.pdf. Accessed 2 Feb 2019

11. Lehe, L.: A history of downtown road pricing. Medium (2017). https://medium.com/@lewislehe/a-history-of-downtown-road-pricing-c7fca0ce0c03. Accessed 5 Mar 2019

12. Eliasson, J.: The Stockholm congestion pricing syndrome: how congestion charges went from unthinkable to uncontroversial. Centre for Transport Studies, KTH Royal Institute of Technology (2014). http://www.transportportal.se/swopec/CTS2014-1.pdf

13. Hau, T.: Electronic road pricing: developments in Hong Kong 1983–89. J. Transp. Econ. Policy **24**(2), 203–214 (1990)

14. Schedler, A.: Electoral Authoritarianism: The Dynamics of Unfree Competition. Lynne Rienner Publishers, Boulder (2006)

15. Sidewalk Labs Project Vision (2017). http://www.passivehousecanada.com/wp-content/uploads/2017/12/TO-Sidewalk-Labs-Vision-Sections-of-RFP-Submission-sm.pdf. Accessed 1 Feb 2019

16. Barth, B.: The fight against Google's smart city. The Washington Post (2018). https://www.washingtonpost.com/news/theworldpost/wp/2018/08/08/sidewalk-labs/?noredirect=on&utm_term=.29807e353bb9. Accessed 1 Feb 2019

17. Wylie, B.: Deputation to Toronto's Executive Committee on Sidewalk Toronto. Medium (2018). https://medium.com/@biancawylie/my-deputation-to-torontos-executive-committee-on-sidewalk-toronto-jan-24-2018-ee25785bc44e. Accessed 1 Feb 2019

18. Zuboff, S.: Big other: surveillance capitalism and the prospects of an information civilization. J. Inf. Technol. **30**, 75–89 (2015). https://papers.ssrn.com/sol3/papers.cfm?abstract_id=2594754

19. Goldsmith, S., Crawford, S.: The Responsive City: Engaging Communities Through Data-Smart Governance. Wiley, New York (2014)

20. Barcelona Digital City. https://ajuntament.barcelona.cat/digital/en. Accessed 4 Feb 2019

21. Singh, S., Okun, A., Jackson, A.: Learning to play Go from scratch. Nature **550**, 336–337 (2017)

22. Domingos, P.: The Master Algorithm: How the Quest for the Ultimate Learning Machine Will Remake Our World. Basic Books, New York (2015)

23. Whitehead, A.: Mathematics in the History of Thought (1957). http://www-history.mcs.st-andrews.ac.uk/Extras/Whitehead_maths_thought.html. Accessed 7 Feb 2019

24. Irving, G., Christiano, P., Amodei, D.: AI safety via debate (2018). arXiv:1805.00899v2

25. Amodei, D., Olah, C., Steinhardt, J., Christiano, P., Schulman, J., Mané, D.: Concrete Problems in AI Safety (2016). CoRR arXiv:1606.06565.

26. Singh, A., Patil, D., Omkar, S.: Eye in the Sky: Real-Time Drone Surveillance System for Violent Individuals Identification Using ScatterNet Hybrid Deep Learning Network (2018). arXiv:1806.00746v1

27. Agarwal, K.: For the Third Time in Three Months, Farmer to Protest in Delhi. The Wire (2018). https://thewire.in/agriculture/third-time-three-months-farmers-protest-delhi. Accessed 8 Mar 2019
28. Scharfenberg, D.: Computers can solve your problem. You may not like the answer. What happened when Boston Public Schools tried for equity with an algorithm. The Boston Globe (2018). https://apps.bostonglobe.com/ideas/graphics/2018/09/equity-machine/. Accessed 20 Jan 2019
29. Calthorpe, P., Walters, J.: Autonomous Vehicles: Hype and Potential. UrbanLand (2017). https://urbanland.uli.org/industry-sectors/infrastructure-transit/autonomous-vehicles-hype-potential/. Accessed 20 Feb 2019
30. Green, B., Caro, A., Conway, M., Manduca, R., Plagge, T., Miller, A.: Mining administrative data to spur urban revitalization. In: KDD '15: The 21st ACM SIGKDD Conference on Knowledge Discovery and Data Mining (2015). https://scholar.harvard.edu/files/bgreen/files/kdd2015.pdf
31. Badger, E.: Why Technology Hasn't Fixed the Housing Crisis. New York Times (2019). https://www.nytimes.com/2019/01/29/upshot/can-technology-help-fix-the-housing-market.html. Accessed 4 Feb 2019
32. Chan Zuckerberg Initiative (2018). https://chanzuckerberg.com/newsroom/inspiring-young-leaders-to-tackle-housing-affordability/. Accessed 6 Feb 2019
33. United Nations World Urbanization Prospects. The 2018 Revision (2018). https://population.un.org/wup/Publications/Files/WUP2018-KeyFacts.pdf. Accessed 7 Mar 2019
34. Marvin, C.: When Old Technologies Were New. Oxford University Press, Oxford (1990)
35. IBM.: Diversity in Faces Project (2019). https://www.ibm.com/blogs/research/2019/01/diversity-in-faces/. Accessed 5 Mar 2019
36. Radford, A., Wu, J., Child, R., Luan, D., Amodei, D., Sutskever, I.: Language Models are Unsupervised Multitask Learners (2019). https://blog.openai.com/better-language-models/

Empowering Instead of Hindering – Challenges in Participatory Development of Cognitively Accessible Software

Susanne Dirks[✉]

TU Dortmund University, Emil-Figge-Str. 55, 44227 Dortmund, Germany
susanne.dirks@tu-dortmund.de

Abstract. Participative design is a method of involving users in the design and development process through a collaborative approach. This method allows to involve the potential users with their needs and peculiarities from the beginning of the development. In agile software development, the potential user of the software plays a central role as a stakeholder, but the rapid development cycles force users to deal with incomplete and faulty software. With the example of two agile projects for the development of cognitively accessible software, the challenges of participative development with people with cognitive impairments are demonstrated and discussed.

Keywords: Software development · Agile methods ·
Cognitively accessible software · Participatory technology development

1 Introduction

The Internet and other digital resources, such as social media channels, digital magazines, online forums, archives, databases, etc., will increasingly become the most important way for individuals to stay informed about news and services, stay in touch with friends and family, and experience independence. Moreover, with the advent of the Web of Things, everyday physical objects are connected to the Internet and have web interfaces.

Problems with understanding and using these many different and sometimes very complex standard interfaces can be caused by various factors, such as advanced age, congenital or acquired sensory or cognitive impairment, or lack of technical knowledge.

People who are unable to use these interfaces due to disability will experience an increased sense of disability and alienation from society. Their opportunities for participation are severely limited in almost all spheres of life and without improved accessibility of digital resources the digital divide will become more pronounced over time [1].

© Springer Nature Switzerland AG 2019
M. Antona and C. Stephanidis (Eds.): HCII 2019, LNCS 11572, pp. 28–38, 2019.
https://doi.org/10.1007/978-3-030-23560-4_3

1.1 Digital Accessibility

With the ratification of the United Nations Convention on the Rights of Persons with Disabilities [2] and the resulting national measures and laws to implement the affirmations, the overall accessibility of digital resources has improved significantly. In particular, persons with motor and sensory impairments have benefited from progress in the technical development of assistive technologies and the improvement of the accessibility of information and communication technology services. Modern web development technologies such as HTML5, CSS3, and WAI-ARIA help developers to create websites that can be easily accessed by people using assistive technologies [3].

For people with difficulties in understanding content, structures and contexts, whether due to age, cognitive impairments or lack of technical understanding, the situation is clearly different. As a rule, these people do not use assistive technology to access digital information, but rely on the information being structured and prepared in such a way that they are able to capture it.

The most common measures used to enable these people to participate digitally are either a compilation of specific information in a simplified structure and language, or the creation of a dedicated web site offering selected content in an easily understandable form, e.g. the Times in Plain English [4].

While some countries, such as classic immigration countries like the United States of America [5] or countries with very complex writing systems like Japan, have very precise guidelines on how to write documents in an understandable form, there are many countries where, despite the ratification of the CRPD, there is little effort to improve the cognitive accessibility of digital resources.

Despite the good intentions, the problem with the above-mentioned measures is that people with cognitive impairments cannot use the original sources like everyone else, but merely have access to information that has been specially gathered and arranged on their behalf. This clearly violates the CRPD's demand that all persons with disabilities should have equal access to digital information and communication services.

Since the group of people with difficulties in understanding content, structures and contexts is very large and heterogeneous, it is obviously challenging to prepare all digital information in such a way that every potential user can easily handle it.

To be able to deal with the described difficulties in this context, different approaches are being pursued in current research projects.

One of the most promising actual approaches is the development of tools that provide an individual simplification of Internet sites and other digital resources based on current user needs. Although this approach seems very convincing and offers good long-term opportunities for individual adaptation of the cognitive accessibility of digital resources, there are a number of technical and design-related challenges.

1.2 User Participation in Software Development

The idea that potential users play an important role in the development of products and processes has been widely accepted for many years. User Centered Design (UCD) has also gained acceptance in software development projects in recent years. Based on the work of Norman and Draper [6], UCD is an approach in which the needs and perspectives of potential users are integrated in an iterative process of product development. Within the framework of classical approaches to software development, users have often been involved only marginally and at only a few points in the development process. For cost and time reasons, it certainly still happens that users are insufficiently involved in planning and development processes, but the proliferation of agile development methods has made it much easier for potential users to be involved in all development phases Agile development methods like Scrum or eXtreme programming (XP) have many similarities with UCD and offer good possibilities to integrate the potential users with their needs and peculiarities into the development process [7, 8].

Although the main concern of the UCD is the active involvement of the potential user and his interests in the development process, the user is often not part of the team, but is represented by the designers or researchers involved [9]. Due to this 'translation' of user needs, the usability of the developed product may be limited in some areas despite the use of the UCD in the development process.

In order to guarantee users an equal role in the development team, participative approaches for the active involvement of users in software development have been increasingly implemented in recent years. According to the definition of Schuler and Namioka [10], Participative Design can be understood as the active participation of potential users and all other stakeholders in the design and development process. Occasionally, the term Cooperative Design is also used as a synonym.

It is undisputed that the active involvement of potential users in software development usually leads to products that can be better used by the target group and are more readily accepted. Nevertheless, the satisfaction of users, designers and developers with their respective roles in the development process and the product that is created at the end is not always convincing. Both the power relations in the team and the actual consideration of the needs and opinions of the various team members are regarded as sources of dissatisfaction [11, 12]. Other reasons for dissatisfaction include user-related aspects such as user motivation or prior knowledge, communicative aspects such as misunderstandings and conflicts between team members, lack of management support, and project-related aspects such as time constraints and technical problems.

Users with cognitive impairments represent a special target group, both with regard to their requirements for a software system to be developed and with regard to their integration into the development process [13]. People with cognitive impairments have difficulties understanding complex language, reading longer texts, understanding abstractions, generalizing insights and following different perspectives in group discussions [14]. All these skills are relevant for successful work in research teams. Currently, there is no methodologically sound basis for working in research teams with team members with cognitive impairments and many development teams, although generally open-minded, are uncertain of how to deal with these demands.

In the following sections, the challenges associated with participatory software development with people with cognitive impairments are discussed on the basis of two specific research projects.

2 Study

It is indisputable that people with disabilities benefit in many areas of life from the Internet and other digital resources. People with cognitive impairments benefit from these advantages just like other people, but they often have to deal with the fact that their environment does not trust them to be able to handle the Internet independently and safely. The potential risks associated with Internet use in terms of data security, privacy, harassment and unintentional purchase, which all people can encounter, are considered to be more pronounced for people with cognitive impairments [15]. Meanwhile, the potential benefits of the Internet for people with cognitive impairments are also seen as more pronounced. This raises the question of why efforts to enable people with cognitive impairments to access and use the Internet are not being intensified.

The Department of Rehabilitation Technology at TU Dortmund University has been conducting a number of research and development projects to improve the digital participation of people with cognitive impairments over the last few years [16–19]. Two projects focusing on participatory and user centered development of cognitively accessible software will be analyzed in the following.

2.1 Mediata App

The Mediata App is a mobile application that gives people with cognitive disabilities easy access to online platforms and social media [20]. During the development of the app, special attention was paid to communication with friends and family, independent surfing on the Internet and the use of social networks and communication platforms. In addition, a simple and individually configurable single sign-on mechanism was implemented, which enables the user to log in via image selection or pattern input in addition to the text-based login.

To enable people with poor reading and writing skills to access digital resources independently, the app was implemented in a way that an alternative voice input is available in almost all positions (except password input). The search results of the Internet search and the contacts are displayed in a very clear way and the users can initialize a call or send a message directly from the contact overview. For even easier access to certain Internet pages defined in the user profile and for direct contact with the most important contact person, the so-called Easy User Mode was implemented. In the Easy-User Mode, immediately after login, an image-based overview of the specified Internet pages and the most important contact are displayed.

For a better understanding, Fig. 1 shows an example of the image-based login screen and the Easy User Mode of the Mediata app.

The app was developed within an agile approach and the potential users were involved in different phases of the software development. Since the limitations and support needs of the target group are very heterogeneous, a comprehensive user needs analysis was carried out before the start of the actual development. A user needs analysis carried out in advance may be in contrast to a strict interpretation of the principles of agile development in which user requirements are assessed and refined

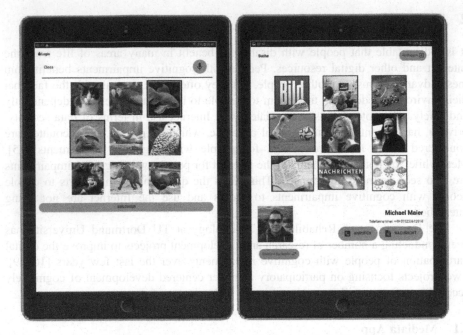

Fig. 1. Mediata-App – image-based login and Easy User Mode

during the iterative development processes. This was considered necessary due to the special characteristics and needs of the target group [21].

During the iterative development of the Mediata app, user tests were carried out at regular intervals. In larger intervals, the current status of the development was thoroughly evaluated and it was jointly decided which changes to the design and functions should be made and which functional enhancements would be useful.

There is no doubt that the results of the participatory development of the Mediata system and the results of the user-centred development accompanying tests have resulted in a product that is beneficial for the target group. Nevertheless, there were a number of difficulties in the development process which affected both the testers and the developers in their work. The testers had difficulties in understanding the test protocols and giving feedback that was comprehensible to the developers. Despite intensive support from the test team, some tests could not be carried out at all or only to a limited extent because functions and design aspects that had not yet been implemented distracted the testers from the functions that should be tested. Another complicating factor was that some of the testers had problems remembering information and test steps already explained or carried out several times. These actions had to be explained or re-executed repeatedly. In addition, some development steps suffered from communication problems between testers and developers, which led to frustration on both sides.

2.2   Easy Reading

A lot of webpages are not accessible for people with cognitive disabilities. But everyone should be able to use the same webpages as everyone else. In the scope of the Easy Reading project a software framework that supports people with cognitive disabilities in understanding web content is developed. The framework provides personalized access to web content and uses tracking technologies to decide if and when the user needs help. The aim of the Easy Reading project is the participative research and development of an open-source based framework for individual adaptation of original websites and other digital content [22].

The inclusive research and development teams in the Easy Reading project have two central research objectives. Firstly, a method is to be developed with which people with cognitive impairments can take an active part into software development projects on the basis of a participative approach. Secondly, an open source framework is to be developed that provides various tools that can be used to adapt any website to the current support needs of the user.

Similar to the previously described project, a comprehensive user needs analysis was conducted in the agile Easy Reading project before the start of the actual implementation. This analysis showed that the 'Read aloud' function was considered to be particularly important. The functions 'adaptability of the layout' and 'additional information on words that are difficult to understand' were also regarded as relevant.

In the Easy Reading project three different inclusive research teams are involved, one German, one Swedish and one Austrian group. Some of the functions requested by the inclusive research teams have already been implemented and integrated into a software environment that can be installed as a browser add-on in Firefox or Safari browsers.

The software environment not only provides various tools and personalization options, such as a screen reader, a synonym indicator or structural simplifications, but also uses technical means to evaluate and analyze the current user behavior. If, for example, the analysis of the user's eye movement patterns reveals that there are problems in understanding certain areas of the website, the system suggests further simplifications and adaptations.

Figure 2 shows the current functional scope and layout of the Easy Reading Framework.

Since the developments in the Easy Reading project have not been completed yet, it is not possible to make an exact statement about the challenges arising in the context of participatory agile software development at this point in time. However, the first user tests accompanying the development have shown similar difficulties as in the previously outlined Mediata project.

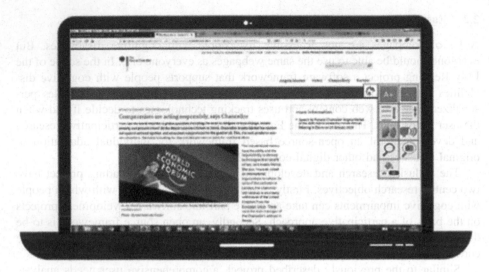

Fig. 2. Easy Reading Framework on an example website

3   Results

Based on the results of theoretical research on user-centered software development and successful practical applications of participatory research methods in general research and development projects, it was expected that participatory development of cognitively accessible software can be carried out in a comparable successful and target-group oriented way.

The two projects presented here, however, showed that the participatory development in agile projects together with people with cognitive impairments leads to a number of challenges.

During the participative development of the Mediata App, various challenges were encountered. In the user needs analysis the main difficulties related to communication and comprehension. During the discussions on user requirements, it became evident that additional support in the form of images and simplified explanations helped to reduce testers' comprehension and memory problems and improve communication and exchange between developers and testers. The use of written material and explanatory images led to a significant improvement of the situation, but resulted in significantly longer meetings than originally planned.

As customary in agile development projects, the first user tests accompanying the development were carried out with prototypes that neither functionally nor in design corresponded to the final state of the Mediata system. Due to the abstraction and concentration difficulties associated with a cognitive impairment, the testers were often distracted by functions that did not yet work or looked 'pretty' and had difficulties in concentrating on the functions to be tested.

In addition, testers had difficulties in focusing on the functions to be tested when other aspects seemed more relevant to them. For example, when testing the contact functions, the layout of the buttons and the poor image quality of the images were considered very relevant for the contacts, and the actual functions to be tested were only partly evaluated. Although the tests accompanying the development definitely led to important results, focused user tests in strict terms could only be carried out in the final test phases, in which the Mediata app was already mature in all functions and only minor deviations in the design existed.

In the Easy Reading project, the analysis of user needs revealed similar problems. In contrast to the Mediata project, however, a larger team with extensive expertise in inclusive research was available, allowing problems to be addressed more quickly and effectively. But again, the special conditions in the inclusive research teams resulted in much more time being needed for the project meetings and workshops than originally planned.

In the development accompanying tests similar problems as in the Mediata project were observed. Features that had not been implemented yet or did not function stable were experienced as very irritating by the inclusive test teams. Design features such as the size or color of the symbols used, which from the developer's point of view were not the focus of the first functional tests, were thoroughly evaluated by the testers, while the existing functional problems were not recognized or only partially evaluated.

Since the Easy Reading Team was significantly larger than the Mediata Team, team communication and the balance of power in the team played a greater role in this project. Here, too, difficulties were observed due to the special characteristics of the target group. The communication difficulties were mainly related to the use of difficult language and abstract terms and concepts. Frequently, it was necessary to translate the discussion content into simple language to allow all team members to follow. In longer and larger project meetings, the long duration of some discussions, the frequent and rapid changes of topics as well as the overall forms of communication not adapted to the target group led to incomprehension and frustration among the testers. Problems and misunderstandings on a personal level also led to problems in the Easy Reading project. In summary, it can be said that developers and researchers had difficulties adapting to the special needs of the target group both on the content level and on the communicative and emotional level. Most of the observed problems could be solved successfully, but resulted in a considerable increase in time and human resources.

Table 1 gives an overview of the challenges in participatory development of cognitively accessible software in the two featured projects.

In addition to the development of the Easy Reading Framework, the Easy Reading project aims to develop adequate solutions and methods for the participative development of cognitively accessible software. As additional important and complex tools will be developed and evaluated in the further course of the project, problems in participative cooperation that have not yet been identified will arise. These problems have to be analyzed and solved continuously.

Table 1. Challenges in participative software development

Project phase	Areas of concern	Description
Requirement analysis	Communication, technical expertise, capacity and strength, time constraints	Difficulties in conveying technical contexts and lack of adequate forms of communication, Inadequate consideration of reduced cognitive and physical resilience, increased expenditure of time due to unscheduled additional explanations and translations
Prototype testing	Communication, abstraction, relevance assessment, technical understanding	Insufficient consideration of difficulties in evaluating prototypes, problems in assessing the relevance of functions and features, and difficulties in performing functions due to lack of technical understanding
Functional testing	Communication, abstraction, relevance assessment, technical understanding	Insufficient consideration of problems in assessing the relevance of functions and features and difficulties in performing functions due to lack of technical understanding
Usability testing	Communication, capacity and strength, time constraints	Insufficient consideration of problems in understanding complex test scenarios, difficulties in describing and documenting test results in a comprehensible way, and the time required for additional explanations and assistance
Project meetings	Communication, capacity and strength, time constraints	Inadequate preparation for difficulties in understanding complex issues and complex communication situations, as well as the emotional distress due to misunderstandings and disagreements

4   Discussion

Empirical evidence from the described projects has shown that the participatory development of cognitively accessible software in agile development projects entails a wide range of challenges. Indisputably, the development of software products for the target group of people with cognitive impairments has to be participative. This is the only way to develop products that are optimally tailored to the needs of the target groups.

But in order to successfully develop a product, the challenges of working together with people with cognitive impairments must be anticipated and understood, and there must be solutions to the emerging problems. For most of the arising issues there are solutions that can be applied if necessary. But this method usually results in a situation in which the tightly calculated projects exceed the available funds and are either terminated prematurely or user participation is reduced to a minimum. The reduction of user participation has particularly serious consequences for users with cognitive impairments, whose needs are often insufficiently taken into account.

A reasonable approach to improve the participative development of cognitively accessible software is the development of a methodological concept, as it is proposed within the Easy Reading project. The special characteristics associated with inclusive research and development teams involving people with cognitive impairments have to be taken into account prior to project planning in order to minimize the problems described in this paper. This allows the entire project team to prepare adequately for the challenges and to adapt the project calculation of development projects appropriately. The reduction of user participation, which is currently a more or less unintended consequence in many projects, causes problems especially for the target group of people with cognitive impairments. In many software development projects, the very heterogeneous needs of this target group are only insufficiently taken into account.

It should be noted critically that the two projects discussed here can only provide an insufficient insight into the complexity of participative software development. Some of the problems may have been caused by the people involved and therefore cannot be generalized. However, since a substantial part of the problems that have been identified within the presented projects were also observed in participatory development projects involving users without impairments, it can be assumed that they are of general relevance for participatory development projects. The development of an adequate methodological approach is therefore certainly beneficial for participative software development in various aspects.

References

1. Dobransky, K., Hargittai, E.: The disability divide in internet access and use. Inform. Commun. Soc. **9**(3), 313–334 (2006)
2. Convention on the Rights of Persons with Disabilities. https://www.un.org/development/desa/disabilities/convention-on-the-rights-of-persons-with-disabilities.html. Accessed 22 Jan 2019
3. Introduction to ARIA and HTML5. https://webaim.org/presentations/2015/CSUN/IntroToARIAandHTML5.pdf. Accessed 22 Jan 2019
4. The Times in Plain English. http://www.thetimesinplainenglish.com. Accessed 22 Feb 2019
5. Plain Writing Act of 2010. https://www.govinfo.gov/app/details/PLAW-111publ274. Accessed 22 Jan 2019
6. Norman, D.A., Draper, S.W.: User Centered System Design. New Perspectives on Human-Computer Interaction. Erlbaum Associates Inc., Hillsdale (1986)
7. Blomkvist, S.: Towards a model for bridging agile development and user-centered design. In: Seffah, A., Gulliksen, J., Desmarais, M.C. (eds.) Human-Centered Software Engineering —Integrating Usability in the Software Development Lifecycle. Human-Computer Interaction Series, vol. 8. Springer, Dordrecht (2005)
8. Chamberlain, S., Sharp, H., Maiden, N.: Towards a Framework for Integrating Agile Development and User-Centred Design. In: Abrahamsson, P., Marchesi, M., Succi, G. (eds.) XP 2006. LNCS, vol. 4044, pp. 143–153. Springer, Heidelberg (2006). https://doi.org/10.1007/11774129_15

9. Sanders, E.N.-B.: From User-centered to Participatory Design Approaches. http://www. maketools.com/articles-papers/FromUsercenteredtoParticipatory_Sanders_%2002.pdf. Accessed 26 Jan 2019
10. Schuler, D., Namioka, A.: Participatory Design: Principles and Practices. Lawrence Erlbaum Associates, Hillsdale, NJ (1993)
11. Zowghi, D., Rimini, F. da, Bano, M.: Problems and challenges of user involvement in software development: an empirical study. In: Proceedings of the 19th International Conference on Evaluation and Assessment in Software Engineering. ACM, New York (2015)
12. Bano, M., Zowghi, D.: A systematic review on the relationship between user involvement and system success. Inf. Softw. Technol. **58**, 148–169 (2015)
13. Nind, M.: Conducting qualitative research with people with learning, communication and other disabilities: methodological challenges. Project Report. National Centre for Research Methods (2008)
14. Cognitive Disabilities – Something to think about. https://webaim.org/articles/cognitive/. Accessed 8 Feb 2019
15. Chadwick, D.D., Quinn, S., Fullwood, C.: Perceptions of the risks and benefits of Internet access and use by people with intellectual disabilities. Br. J. Learn. Disabil. **45**, 21–31 (2017)
16. Brausch, C., Bühler, C., Feldmann, A., Padberg, M.: Supported Employment – Electronic Job-Coach (EJO). In: Miesenberger, K., Bühler, C., Penaz, P. (eds.) ICCHP 2016. LNCS, vol. 9758, pp. 142–149. Springer, Cham (2016). https://doi.org/10.1007/978-3-319-41264-1_20
17. Dirks, S., Bühler, C.: Participation and autonomy for users with ABI through easy social media access. In: Cudd, P., de Witte, L.P. (eds.) Harnessing the Power of Technology to Improve Lives. Proceedings of the 14th European Conference on the Advancements of Assistive Technology. Studies in Health Technology and Informatics 242. IOS Press, Amsterdam (2017)
18. Schaten, M., Lexis, M., Roentgen, U., Bühler, C., de Witte, L.: User centered design in practice – developing software with/for people with cognitive and intellectual disabilities. In: Encarnação, P., Azevedo, L., Gelderblom, G.J. (eds.) Assistive Technology: From Research to Practice: AAATE 2013. IOS Press, Amsterdam (2013)
19. Via4All.: Via4All Project Website (2018). http://www.via4all.de/start. Accessed 22 Oct 2018
20. Bühler, C., Dirks, S., Nietzio, A.: Easy Access to Social Media: Introducing the Mediata-App. In: Miesenberger, K., Bühler, C., Penaz, P. (eds.) ICCHP 2016. LNCS, vol. 9759, pp. 227–233. Springer, Cham (2016). https://doi.org/10.1007/978-3-319-41267-2_31
21. Dirks, S., Bühler, C.: Akzeptanz von assistiven Softwaresystemen für Menschen mit kognitiven Beeinträchtigungen. In: Eibl, M., Gaedke, M. (eds.) Informatik 2017, pp. 345–359. Gesellschaft für Informatik, Bonn (2017)
22. Heumader, P., Edler, C., Miesenberger, K., Wolkerstorfer, S.: Requirements engineering for people with cognitive disabilities - exploring new ways for peer-researchers and developers to cooperate. ICCHP (1), Linz, Austria (2018)

Inquiring Evaluation Aspects of Universal Design and Natural Interaction in Socioenactive Scenarios

Andressa Cristina dos Santos[1]([⊠]),
Vanessa Regina Margareth Lima Maike[1],
Yusseli Lizeth Méndez Mendoza[1], José Valderlei da Silva[1,4],
Rodrigo Bonacin[3], Julio Cesar Dos Reis[1,2],
and Maria Cecília Calani Baranauskas[1]

[1] Institute of Computing,
University of Campinas (UNICAMP), Campinas, SP, Brazil
{andressa.santos,
yusseli.mendoza}@students.ic.unicamp.br,
{vanessa.maike,jreis,cecilia}@ic.unicamp.br
[2] Nucleus of Applied Informatics to Education (NIED), Campinas, SP, Brazil
[3] Center for Information Technology (CTI), Campinas, SP, Brazil
rodrigo.bonacin@cti.gov.br
[4] Paraná State Secretary of Education (SEED-PR), Maringá, PR, Brazil
vander@seed.pr.gov.br

Abstract. New technologies and ubiquitous sysltems present new forms and modalities of interaction. Evaluating such systems, particularly in the novel socioenactive scenario, poses a difficult issue, as existing instruments do not capture all aspects intrinsic to such scenario. One of the key aspects is the wide range of characteristics and needs of both users and technology involved. In this paper, we are concerned with aspects of both Universal Design (UD) and Natural User Interfaces (NUIs). We present a case study where we applied, within a socioenactive scenario, evaluation instruments relying on principles and heuristics from these areas. The scenario involved six children from a hospital that treats craniofacial deformities, playing in a rich interactive environment with displays and plush animals that respond to hugs. Our results based on the analysis of the evaluation conducted in the case study suggest informed recommendations of how to use the evaluation instruments in the context of socioenactive systems and their limitations.

Keywords: Accessibility · Interaction evaluation · Ubiquitous computing · Pervasive · Natural User Interfaces · Universal Design · Universal Access

1 Introduction

The emergence of novel technological devices prompts new forms of interaction involving the body and the environment. This scenario allows people to better express themselves and further exchange information. As ubiquitous and pervasive computing

© Springer Nature Switzerland AG 2019
M. Antona and C. Stephanidis (Eds.): HCII 2019, LNCS 11572, pp. 39–56, 2019.
https://doi.org/10.1007/978-3-030-23560-4_4

becomes a reality in our daily lives, universal access to new technological scenarios and underlying information becomes a necessity and deserves attention [4].

As important as the development of new interactive technologies (*e.g.*, computational devices, their integration and communication in physical contexts), the evaluation of these technologies in diversified scenarios of use by involving users with different characteristics plays a key role for systems acceptance and adequate use. Although there are various classic evaluation instruments and tools for Usability [10], Accessibility [3] and Universal Design [16], they have not been elaborated to address relevant accessibility aspects of this new technological context, which involve ubiquitous and pervasive computing. For example, the heterogeneity of systems and their behaviors, along with the inherent difference between the human side of the interaction, creates an ecosystem where no formal specifications can fully address all accessibility and usability aspects.

Enactive systems, as proposed by Kaipainen *et al.* [6], aim to draw away from goal-oriented and conscious interactions, going towards an interfacing that is "driven by bodily involvement and spatial presence of the human agent without the assumption of conscious control of the system". It is possible to go even further and add a social component to this concept, in a way that collective actions as well as interaction among people affect and are affected in a coupled way by the computer-based system. This concept is the core of what we name "Socioenactive Systems" [2]. These systems require new artifacts and tools, to allow us to evaluate whether such systems provide universal access to information.

In this paper, we investigate evaluation issues regarding the Universal Access provided by socioenactive systems. In particular, we present and discuss the results of applying two evaluation tools within a socioenactive system scenario. The research involved a workshop conducted in the context of a hospital for face deformities correction. Six children, parents and hospital staff participated in the workshop. The system explored in the workshop consisted of plush animals with embedded sensors that measure the intensity of hugs, a display and an interactive Christmas tree. As the children hug the animals, the system offers various feedbacks.

For evaluation purpose, we chose the 7 Universal Design Principles [16], and the 13 Heuristics for Natural User Interfaces (NUIs) [8]. The former was selected because of its relevance and simplicity to look at Universal Design; the latter was chosen because NUIs, or natural interaction, are part of the ubiquitous, pervasive and embodied context of (socio)enactive systems. Our investigation aimed to answer to which extent these instruments are able to analyze key aspects necessary for duly evaluating Universal Access in socioenactive systems.

This investigation provides 2 major contributions. We discuss the instruments limitations and the possibilities of combining and extending them; (1) we provide results and limitations of an exploratory literature review concerning evaluation methods and tools for Accessibility and Universal Design, which are relevant for the context of socioenactive systems. (2) Based on the resulting analysis of the instruments application in the workshop, we provide guidelines on which instruments to apply in the aforementioned technological scenario and recommendations for carrying out the evaluation.

This paper is organized with the following structure: Sect. 2 presents background on NUI Heuristics and Universal Design Principles. Section 3 discusses the findings of our exploratory literature review. Section 4 details the case study, including its context, methodology, results and the lessons learned discussing the findings. Whereas Sect. 5 presents the proposed recommendations on how to use the heuristics and principles as an evaluation instrument, Sect. 6 presents our concluding remarks and points out future research.

2 Theoretical Background

This section describes the theoretical background on (socio)enactive systems (Subsect. 2.1), the 7 Principles of Universal Design (Subsect. 2.2), and the set of 13 NUI Heuristics (Subsect. 2.3).

2.1 (Socio)enactive Systems

The core concept of enaction comes from what Varela *et al.* [18] call the "enactive approach", a two-part circular definition: "In a nutshell, the enactive approach consists of two points: (1) perception consists in perceptually guided action; and (2) cognitive structures emerge from the recurrent sensorimotor patterns that enable action to be perceptually guided". Whereas the first point gives a definition for perception, the second point explains how such perception at the same time builds and is built by the interactions with the world. Kaipainen *et al.* [6] proposed a way to bring this concept into the realm of computer systems, with the concept of "enactive systems". The main idea is to provide a dynamic coupling between the human and the technological parts of the interaction, in a way that there is not necessarily a conscious control of the system, but rather a bodily involvement of the human agent. In this sense, the perceptually guided action consists of feedbacks the system might provide for human actions, and vice-versa; *i.e.*, the human's behavior is affected by the system's responses, and at the same time, the system changes its behavior according to the person's (re)actions.

The concept of *socioenactive systems* [2] adds the social component into the mix, in a way that considers not only the human-technology interactions, but interactions among humans and between different technologies. This creates a complex ecosystem of interactions, where it is purposely difficult to draw the lines separating each agent. Although these ideas are close to the concept of ubiquitous computing proposed by Weiser [19], socioenactive systems represent a novel concept, still under construction. Therefore, there is still no theoretical and methodological basis for their design and evaluation. In particular, a great challenge lies in understanding the needs and characteristics of the environments, technologies and people that are part of the socioenactive systems. Thus, new tools, techniques and processes need to be created. This includes evaluation instruments to assess systems' quality criteria.

2.2   Universal Design (UD) Principles

Universal Design (UD), defined by Story *et al.* [17] consists in the design of products and environments to be usable by all people, to the greatest extent possible, without the need for adaptation or specialized design. It is aligned with the concept of developing accessible interfaces without the discrimination of users. Story [16] has established seven UD Principles, which can serve the following purposes: to guide the design process, to evaluate existing designs, or to teach designers and consumers about the characteristics of more usable products and environments. Each of the seven principles has four or five guidelines describing key elements that should be present in an UD. Table 1 summarizes the short descriptions of each principle.

Table 1. The seven UD Principles

Principle	Definition
P1 - Equitable Use	The design is useful and marketable to people with diverse abilities.
P2 - Flexibility in Use	The design accommodates a wide range of individual's preferences and abilities.
P3 - Simple and Intuitive Use	Use of the design is easy to understand, regardless of the user's experience, knowledge, language skills, or current concentration level.
P4 - Perceptible Information	The design communicates necessary information effectively to the user, regardless of ambient conditions or the user's sensory abilities.
P5 - Tolerance for Error	The design minimizes hazards and the adverse consequences of accidental or unintended actions.
P6 - Low Physical Effort	The design can be used efficiently and comfortably and with a minimum of fatigue.
P7 - Size and Space for Approach and Use	Appropriate size and space is provided for approach, reach, manipulation, and use regardless of user's body size, posture, or mobility.

2.3   Natural User Interface (NUI) Heuristics

Natural User Interfaces (NUIs) refer to an interface paradigm that aims to provide interactions that feel natural to the user, such as gestural, and touch-based interfaces [20]. Norman [11], however, has claimed that, despite harboring great potential, NUIs – and gestures, in particular – are not natural, given they can be hard to learn or to remember. Furthermore, they are also subject to cultural differences, given that a gesture that is friendly in a culture might be offensive in another. This is also true if we think in terms of Accessibility, *i.e.*, how inclusive gestures (or other types of NUIs) can be to people in special conditions, such as those with motor or visual disabilities. Therefore, although NUIs represent a promising paradigm, it is not simple to achieve their promised "naturalness".

Considering these challenges, Maike *et al.* [8] proposed 13 heuristics for the design and evaluation of NUIs in the context of accessibility. These heuristics have been applied and tested in distinct scenarios in which visually impaired users were able to detect and recognize people in the surroundings through Assistive Technology (AT) devices made with NUIs, such as the Microsoft Kinect and a wristband smartwatch. Table 2 presents a summary of the 13 NUI Heuristics.

In this work, we explore these heuristics in an original fashion. Our goal is to understand their potential as part of an evaluation technique for socioenactive systems.

Table 2. The 13 NUI Heuristics

NUI Heuristic	Definition
[NH1] Operation Modes	The system must provide different operation modes. Also, provide an explicit way for the user to switch between the modes, offering a smooth transition.
[NH2] "Interactability"	In the system, the selectable and the "interactable" objects should be explicit and allow both their temporary and permanent selection.
[NH3] Metaphor Adequacy	The sets of interaction metaphors the system provides should make sense as a whole, so that it is possible to understand what the system can and cannot interpret.
[NH4] Learnability	There has to be coherence between learning time and frequency of use. In addition, the design must consider that users learn from each other by copying when they work together, so it is important to allow them to be aware of each other's actions and intentions.
[NH5] Guidance Balance	There has to be a balance between exploration and guidance, to maintain a flow of interaction to both the expert and the novice users. Also, shortcuts should be provided for expert users.
[NH6] Wayfinding	At any time, users should be able to know where they are from a big picture perspective and from a microscopic perception.
[NH7] Comfort	Interacting with the system should not require much effort from the user and should not cause fatigue.
[NH8] Space	The location where the system is expected to be used must be appropriate for the kinds of interactions it requires and for the number of simultaneous users it supports.
[NH9] Engagement	The system should provide immersion during the interaction, at the same time allowing for easy information acquiring and integration.
[NH10] Device-Task Compatibility	The system has to offer kinds of interactions that are compatible with the task for which it is going to be used.
[NH11] Social Acceptance	Using the system should not cause embarrassment to the users.
[NH12] Awareness of Others	If the system supports multiple users working in the same task at the same time, then it should handle and prevent conflicting inputs.
[NH13] Two-way Communication	If multiple users are working on different activities through the same interface, and are not necessarily in the same vicinity, the system must provide ways for both sides to communicate with each other.

3 Related Work

To better understand the subject, we conducted an exploratory literature review looking for papers in the following conferences: HCII (International Conference on Human Computer Interaction), UAHCI (International Conference on Universal Access in Human Computer Interaction), and in the journal UAIS (Universal Access in the Information Society). Two separate searches were conducted. In the first, we searched for papers with all three keywords: "enactive systems", accessibility and usability. Because this search returned a low number of related papers, we did a second search, with the following keywords: "universal design" and evaluation.

This exploratory search found that the overall existing literature emphasizes Web accessibility dealing with specific disabilities instead of a design for all perspective. For instance, Orozco et al. [13] proposed a methodology for heuristic evaluation of Web accessibility, based on the Web Content Accessibility Guidelines (WCAG) 2.0 [5], as defined by the World Wide Web Consortium (W3C). The evaluation process focused on features and specific barriers that people with disabilities needed to overcome to access information on websites, lacking an analysis from a Universal Design standpoint.

On a similar fashion, Mi et al. [9] proposed a heuristic checklist for accessible smartphone interface design. It was developed based on a case study evaluating high-fidelity smartphone prototypes produced by a commercial manufacturer. A comparison was performed between gestures used by people with normal vision condition and those with visual impairments. The authors provided a survey containing the specification and its classification into six general categories as a way to identify the users' requirements. The obtained results provided support for an accessibility checklist, although still limited to design support in the early stages of portable design projects. They relate some Universal Design Principles, by highlighting user's preferences for some of the requirements.

From a device and software standpoint, we found investigations about iTV [12], mobile audio games [1] and a smartphone-based system [14]. Oliveira et al. [12] conceptualized, prototyped and validated an iTV service designed for visually impaired people, which integrates new functionalities based on the Universal Design philosophy. The authors performed a prototype test and evaluation by means of direct observation and semi-structured interview with a group of visually impaired users.

Rahman et al. [14] proposed a smartphone application called *EmoAssist*, which provides access to non-verbal communication for people who have visual impairments. The system analyses person's face to predict their behavioral expressions (*e.g.*, yawn) and the affective dimension (valence, arousal or dominance). Based on these predictions the system provides adequate auditory feedback to the user. The authors applied an usability study, as an evaluation tool, and conducted subjective studies to understand users' satisfaction.

Araújo et al. [1] searched for accessibility guidelines for digital games, then compiled and classified the found ones. The authors focused on specialized games' features for blind people. The authors identified ten recommendations considered to be minimal requirements for the design and development of mobile audiogames. Finally, based on these recommendations, the authors proposed a questionnaire with 32 questions considering the WCAG [5]. These recommendations aid developers in testing their mobile audio games. Although authors mention Universal Design a few times, their work emphasized exclusively visually impaired users.

Aiming to apply UD in the design process, Liu et al. [7] developed specific project criteria, which is based on the seven Universal Design (UD) Principles. To illustrate the scenario, the authors used a voting system, called EZ Ballot, which was designed following Universal Design principles. It has multimodal input and output that eases the voting process and allows electors to simply answer yes/no questions that are presented in different ways. Therefore, people can use the system regardless of their abilities.

Our related work analysis indicates that existing studies focus on specific devices or audiences without considering a systemic view of a scenario. Thus, this review points out a gap in literature, in which the accessibility evaluation is conducted without considering broader contexts or audiences. Our goal, then, is to propose an evaluation method, tool and guidelines suited to promote Universal Design as well as to consider specific characteristics of socioenactive systems, once in these systems human and computational processes interact dynamically and fluidly, providing feedback. They use new technologies, novel interaction modalities and ubiquitous computing, which demand the consideration of new factors such as emotional, physical and cultural that influence the design and evaluation of these systems.

4   Case Study

In this work, we conducted a case study in the context of a socioenactive system, applying evaluation tools to capture: (1) the unique aspects of such context; and (2) Accessibility and Universal Design issues. In the following subsections, we present further details. Subsection 4.1 explains the context in which the case study was developed and the participants. Subsection 4.2 presents the methodology used in conducting the study. The results are presented in Subsect. 4.3, where Subsect. 4.3.1 indicates the Universal Design Principles observed, and Subsect. 4.3.2 contains the details on the analysis of NUI Heuristics. Finally, Subsect. 4.4 discusses the lessons learned.

4.1   Context and Participants

This work is part of a five-year research project named *"Socioenactive systems: investigating new dimensions in the design of the interaction mediated by ICT (Information and Communication Technologies)"*[1] [2]. Its main objective is to formulate the concept of "socioenaction", and build a conceptual framework that supports the design and development of socioenactive systems, taking into account the participants' differences, *i.e.*, their needs, cultural context, abilities and values.

[1] Project funded by the São Paulo Research Foundation (FAPESP) [grant #2015/16528-0].

Our case considered the context of a hospital named Brazilian Society for Research and Assistance for Craniofacial Rehabilitation (SOBRAPAR)[2]. Located inside the campus of the University of Campinas (UNICAMP), this private philanthropic institution offers rehabilitation treatments for people with craniofacial deformities. Their multidisciplinary team is constituted by plastic surgeons, speech therapists, otolaryngologists, psychologists, social workers, orthodontists, neurosurgeons, physiotherapists, nurses, and more. The institution revenue is from donations, government funds and a permanent bazaar where they sell every sort of donated items.

We have established a partnership with SOBRAPAR to conduct experimental research, with the approval of UNICAMP's ethics committee. We invited a small group of children and their parents to participate on "workshops" approximately once a month, usually while they are already on the hospital waiting for treatment. The workshops involved affection aspects, and making the treatment process in the hospital less stressful for the children. In order to do so, the activities were centered around interactive plush animals [15]. Two of these animals, a bear (named Teddy) and a monkey (named Chico), have pressure sensors inside them to detect hugs and their intensity. They also have sound speakers, so they can provide feedback like compliments on the hugs, or asking for more hugs. The intensity of the hugs is represented graphically on a TV screen, by means of a speedometer-like gauge we call "hug-o-meter". From time to time, the TV displays photos of the workshop, taken in real time by another plush animal: an owl with a camera inside it. Figure 1 shows the arrangement of the children in the workshop and the artifacts used.

The workshop reported in this paper happened on December 10th 2018. Six children aged between 7 and 11 years participated in this workshop. At least one of their parents or legal responsible were present, along with a speech therapist from the hospital staff. Before participating, they were all made aware that the activity was part of a research project, and that they had to sign consent forms, but were free to give up at any time. For this specific workshop, we brought an interactive Christmas tree. The idea was to let the children figure out how to light up the tree by hugging the two plush animals, Teddy and Chico. The tree had six horizontal layers of lights, and reaching high levels on the hug-o-meter, made one level of lights blink; repeating that after a certain amount of times made the level stay lit. Our proposal was to make the six levels stay lit, from the bottom to the star on the top. The children did not receive these instructions; they were asked to figure it all out by themselves.

The children were placed in a circle on a carpet on the floor, allowing for more interaction between them, so that they could observe all the action around them. The TV screen that provided the visual effects and the tree were positioned near the circle, at everyone's sight. The owl was placed at a little distance so it could capture good images of the interaction. The stuffed animals were passed around the circle by all children, and as they hugged, the hug-o-meter level was changed.

---

[2] Project approved by the Unicamp Research Ethics Committee [CAAE 72413817.3.0000.5404].

Fig. 1. Artifacts and workshop organization

4.2   Methodology

During the workshop, we had four Human-Computer Interaction (HCI) researchers acting as observers. They focused on the actions, environment and feedback of the proposed solutions. For the evaluation, the seven Principles of Universal Design and the 13 NUI Heuristics were used. The first was selected because of its relevance and simplicity to look at Universal Design; the latter was chosen because NUIs are part of the ubiquitous, diffused and embodied context of (socio)enactive systems.

The research aimed to investigate to which extent these instruments are able to capture the subtleties for the assessment of universal access in socioenactive systems. Both instruments were used as forms to be filled. For each UD principle or NUI Heuristic, there was room for free-text observations, and a compliance scale of −4 (completely not compliant) to 4 (totally compliant), where 0 means "not applicable". Two observers analyzed whether the socioenactive system complied with each UD principle or not, and the other two observers analyzed whether it complied with each NUI heuristic or not.

After the workshop, a debriefing session between the researchers was held for clarification and discussion on the results of the observations. In addition to the initial researchers, 3 others HCI specialists were present. As this session intended to analyze the obtained results in a conceptual way, the participants (children) in the workshop did not attend. The session was conducted in three stages. First, each of the scores attributed to each of the UD Principles were written on a whiteboard for the visibility of all researchers, and a brief discussion was established regarding the observations made by the researchers who took the role of observers during the workshop. The same process was repeated for the NUI Heuristics. Afterwards, we made a general discussion about the results from the UD Principles and the NUI Heuristics, as well as and their application in socioenactive systems scenarios.

4.3 Results

The analysis of the scenario was performed taking into account the NUI Heuristics and the UD Principles. In addition to the scores assigned on the compliance scale, each of the researchers wrote down justifications for their scores. In the following, we present the result analysis concerning the principles, heuristics and the compliance scores.

4.3.1 Assessment of Universal Design Principles

In relation to the seven UD principles, Table 3 shows the scores on the compliance scale and a summary of the justifications given by the observers.

4.3.2 Assessment of NUI Heuristics

Table 4 presents the scores on the compliance scale assigned to each of the NUI Heuristics, and a synthesis of the justifications given by the observers.

4.4 Lessons Learned

The results from the previous subsection were thoroughly discussed in the debriefing session. While discussing the first UD principle *"Equitable Use"*, a question arose regarding how the system would work for a person with no arms. A possible solution that came up was somehow making the plush animal hug the person, instead of the other way around. Another solution would be for the person to press their face against the animal, instead of using the arms. The same question came up in the discussion of the second principle, *"Flexibility in Use"*. In this case, another interesting point was raised, about the (socio)enactive aspect of the system; it was suggested that the threshold of the intensity of the hug to trigger an effect on the tree could vary according to the group. For instance, a group of younger children could have weaker hugs than a group of older children; the system would adapt its threshold accordingly for each group, maintaining consistency. These two questions show how important the debriefing process is, as it brings up features and solutions that are not necessarily considered during the observation of the activity, when there is little time for deeper reflections.

In turn, for the NUI Heuristics, during the debriefing session we noticed that the observations focused on the relationship between the artifacts of the system (*i.e.*, Teddy, Chico, the owl, the TV…). Therefore, while the UD Principles focused more on the microscopic evaluation, looking at individual parts of the interaction, the NUI Heuristics provide a macroscopic view of the system, regarding aspects that are an essential part of the (socio)enactive proposal, such as social, collaboration and engagement. Such aspects were not elicited by the UD Principles, which means that for evaluating socioenactive systems, additional instruments are needed.

Also during the debriefing session, the researchers who observed the UD Principles reported having difficulty in interpreting the principles. This is probably due to the form created as the evaluative instrument; each principle had not only its brief description, but also a set of guidelines that further detailed what had to be observed. However, the compliance scale was relative to the entire principle, so sometimes one single item would drop the score for the entire principle. This suggests that a more refined score strategy is necessary to deal with these aspects.

Table 3. Assessment of the seven UD Principles. For each principle, scores assigned by observers and their observations are described

Principle	Compliance Scores	Observation
"1 - Equitable Use"	2 and 3	The system was not entirely compliant with this principle because some information was presented only in visual form on the TV screen, such as the hug-o-meter. In addition, the sound effects of the animals could have a tactile equivalent, like vibration.
"2 - Flexibility in Use"	3 and 2	The compliance is fairly high because each child can hug the plush animals any way they want, and the dynamics of passing around the animals between them was also self-coordinated, allowing the speed of the handing out to vary during the workshop. It is not entirely compliant for reasons similar to the problems raised in Principle #1, regarding redundancy of information through multiple channels.
"3 - Simple and Intuitive Use"	3 and 4	The association between the turning on of lights on the tree and the hugs was not clear for the children. However, this was purposefully part of the design, *i.e.*, it was meant to be a challenge.
"4 - Perceptible Information"	1 and 3	The compliance is not the highest here because of the same issue raised on Principle #3. Since the children did not perceive the designed correlation between the hugs and the tree lights, they also could not perceive if their actions did not trigger an explicit feedback, or if the system failed. A possible solution would be to improve the feedback.
"5 - Tolerance for Error"	2 and 0	While one evaluator did not find this principle to be applicable to the system, other thought that maybe the intensity of the hug could affect the plush animals, breaking them, which is actually not applicable to this principle since it refers to robustness of the system.
"6 - Low Physical Effort"	1 and 4	One evaluator thought the sensor compatible with the strength of children, while other had doubts if it requires too much strength for some children.
"7 - Size and Space for Approach and Use"	2 and 0	Both evaluators found that the size of the plush animals was suitable for children, and that the space allocated for the workshop was adequate for the activity.

Table 4. Assessment of the NUI Heuristics. For each heuristics, scores assigned by observers and their observations are described

NUI Heuristic	Compliance Scores	Observation
"1 - Operation Modes"	2 and 2	The system provides different forms of feedback and inputs, but you cannot freely change between them.
"2 - "Interactability""	3 and 2	The evaluators questioned whether it is explicit that the plush animals are "interactable", without explaining to the children beforehand. Some children had already participated in the dynamics (so they knew how to interact with the animals), but for the others a brief explanation was made at the beginning of the workshop.
"3 - Metaphor Adequacy"	3 and 4	The meaning and purpose of the hug-o-meter were clear to the children, who seemed enthusiastic and engaged during the workshop. Other elements, like the tree and the owl were more subtle. Some researchers raised questions to the children during the activity, to make them reflect upon the interactions and the effects, but the children's hypotheses raised were not in agreement with the original proposal. There was only some perception and understanding by the children after a comment was made.
"4 - Learnability"	3 and 3	The children who had not participated in the previous workshop learned from the others by observing them interacting with the plush animals. The interaction by hugging was quick to learn, but learning about the effects on the tree would take several iterations, and possibly some intervention by the researchers to lead the children towards the precise answer.
"5 - Guidance Balance"	4 and 4	The environment was free for exploration (through hugs) and the action was encouraged, so it occurred spontaneously and naturally. The interaction between children and the passing around of the plush animals between them reinforces the social factor. With regard to user experience, it did not seem to have distinction between expert users and novices.
"6 - Wayfinding"	4 and 3	From a microscopic perspective, the children understood the effects of hugging the plush animals. In turn, from a macroscopic perspective, the relation with the christmas tree was not entirely understood by the children as expected.
"7 - Comfort"	3 and 4	Hugging requires some strength, and apparently does not seem to cause fatigue. The children could remain seated during the workshop, showinging comfort.

(continued)

Table 4. (*continued*)

NUI Heuristic	Compliance Scores	Observation
"8 - Space"	4 and 4	The space required for the activity and the positioning of the children with the other objects was adequate. The TV and tree were in a visible spot where everyone could have access to the feedback provided. The owl stayed in a strategic location, with a view of all the children, to capture images of the interactions. All this organization generated a pleasant and dynamic environment.
"9 - Engagement"	4 and 4	There was enthusiasm on the part of the children regarding interaction and participation in the workshop. There was no inhibition of participation, even though the children barely knew each other. They were also excited to create a competition between the two plush animals, to see which one would get more hugs.
"10 - Device-Task Compatibility"	3 and 2	Hugs are an appropriate action to the proposal of the system, but the relationship between them and the christmas tree, or the owl, was relatively unclear for the children.
"11 - Social Acceptance"	4 and 4	Even without knowing each other, the interaction between children occurred spontaneously and did not intimidate their participation, leaving them at ease.
"12 - Awareness of Others"	3 and 3	Since there were only two plush animals passing through and six children, there were moments when one of the children did not want to let go and share with the others, thus generating a competition. In the course of the activity, a false hypothesis was raised that the speed of the hugs and of passing around the plush animals had an influence on the christmas tree, thus making some children haste the others to let go faster of the animals.
"13 - Two-way Communication"	0 and 3	One researcher thought that this heuristic is not applicable because although the two interactive plush animals can be hugged simultaneously, the communication between then was unclear due to a technical malfunction. The other observer interpreted that the two plush animals did communicate, regardless of the failure, since the TV display was the interface between them.

5 Heuristics and Principles as an Evaluation Instrument

Comparing the results from the two instruments, we mapped the UD Principles into the NUI Heuristics (*cf.* Table 5). As this table shows, most heuristics have two principles related to them, while some heuristics have one principle. The latter cases could indicate a feature that is not entirely present in the UD Principles. We can also observe that there are heuristics which do not have principles associated with them, which reinforces our hypothesis that the principles were not enough to evaluate the context of socioenactive systems. However, we highlight that the NUI Heuristics are complemented by the principles, with a more specific focus on UD (Table 6).

Table 5. Mapping from of Principles UD into NUI Heuristics.

NUI Heuristics	Principles UD
[NH1] Operation Modes	1 - Equitable Use
	2 - Flexibility in Use
[NH2] "Interactability"	4 - Perceptible Information
	5 - Tolerance for Error
[NH3] Metaphor Adequacy	3 - Simple and Intuitive Use
	5 - Tolerance for Error
[NH4] Learnability	3 - Simple and Intuitive Use
[NH5] Guidance Balance	2 - Flexibility in Use
	3 - Simple and Intuitive Use
[NH6] Wayfinding	Not present in the principles
[NH7] Comfort	6 - Low Physical Effort
	7 - Size and Space for Approach and Use
[NH8] Space	6 - Low Physical Effort
	7 - Size and Space for Approach and Use
[NH9] Engagement	1 - Equitable Use
[NH10] Device-Task Compatibility	2 - Flexibility in Use
	6 - Low Physical Effort
[NH11] Social Acceptance	1 - Equitable Use
[NH12] Awareness of Others	Not present in the principles
[NH13] Two-way Communication	Not present in the principles

The results from using the NUI Heuristics and the UD Principles as evaluation instruments allowed us to propose recommendations on how to use them, particularly in the context of socioenactive systems or similar (*e.g.*, pervasive or ubiquitous). In Table 5, we find which principles share similarities with which heuristics. Based on this information, we propose a checklist to be used by observers while performing an evaluation (*cf.* Table 6). The format of a checklist seems appropriate, especially because it mitigates the issue of one item dropping the score of an entire principle. In addition, the checklist makes it simpler to merge the two instruments together.

Table 6. Checklist for NUI Heuristics and UD Principles

NUI Heuristics	Description
[NH1] Operation Modes	The system must provide different operation modes, with an explicit way to switch between them, offering a smooth transition. Provide the same means for all users: identical whenever possible; equivalent when not. Provide choice in methods of use. Accommodate right- or left-handed access and use.
[NH2] "Interactability"	The selectable and the "interactable" objects should be explicit and allow both their temporary and permanent selection. Use different modes (pictorial, verbal, tactile) for redundant presentation of essential information. Provide adequate contrast between essential information and its surroundings. Provide compatibility with a variety of techniques or devices used by people with sensory limitations. Arrange elements to minimize hazards and errors: most used elements, most accessible; hazardous elements eliminated, isolated, or shielded.
[NH3] Metaphor Adequacy	The sets of interaction metaphors the system provides should make sense as a whole, so that it is possible to understand what the system can and cannot interpret. Be consistent with user expectations and intuition. Accommodate a wide range of literacy and language skills. Discourage unconscious action in tasks that require vigilance.
[NH4] Learnability	Coherence between learning time and frequency of use. Allow users to be aware of each other's actions and intentions, so they can learn from each other by copying when they work together. Eliminate unnecessary complexity. Provide effective prompting and feedback during and after task completion.
[NH5] Guidance Balance	Balance between exploration and guidance, to maintain a flow of interaction to both the expert and the novice users, providing shortcuts for expert users. Facilitate the user's accuracy and precision. Arrange information consistent with its importance.
[NH6] Wayfinding	At any time, users should be able to know where they are from a big picture perspective and from a microscopic perception.
[NH7] Comfort	Interacting with the system should not require much effort from the user and should not cause fatigue. Minimize repetitive actions. Minimize sustained physical effort. Make reach to all components comfortable for any seated or standing user. Accommodate variations in hand and grip size.

(continued)

Table 6. (*continued*)

NUI Heuristics	Description
[NH8] Space	The location where the system is expected to be used must be appropriate for the kinds of interactions it requires and for the number of simultaneous users it supports. Allow user to maintain a neutral body position. Provide a clear line of sight to important elements for any seated or standing user. Provide adequate space for the use of assistive devices or personal assistance.
[NH9] Engagement	The system should provide immersion during the interaction, at the same time allowing for easy information acquiring and integration. Make the design appealing to all users.
[NH10] Device-Task Compatibility	The system has to offer kinds of interactions that are compatible with the task for which it is going to be used. Ensure adaptability to the user's pace. Use reasonable operating forces.
[NH11] Social Acceptance	Using the system should not cause embarrassment to the users. Avoid segregating or stigmatizing any users. Provisions for privacy, security, and safety should be equally available to all users.
[NH12] Awareness of Others	If the system supports multiple users working in the same task at the same time, then it should handle and prevent conflicting inputs.
[NH13] Two-way Communication	If multiple users are working on different activities through the same interface, and are not necessarily in the same vicinity, the system must provide ways for both sides to communicate with each other.

As a result, we present our proposed checklist, which contains a total of 40 items. We suggest using this as a form, where each item has a scale of conformity where a value of correspondence to what is being observed can be marked. Also, for each there will be a box to write notes about it. We disencourage the use of a binary scale (*e.g.*, "compliant" and "non-compliant", or "check" and "unchecked"), since the compliance scale with a wider range stimulates reflexion and discussion, as we have learned from our case study. We point out that four guidelines from the UD Principles were not included in our checklist, two from Principle 4, and two from Principle 5. Mostly, we found that they were redundant with other guidelines from their same principle, so we chose not including them to make the checklist more concise.

6 Conclusion

In the current ubiquitous and pervasive scenario, the emergence of new technological devices brings new forms of interaction. In fact, as we move towards Weiser's [19] vision of an invisible technology, the idea of a "dynamic mind-technology embodiment" [6] from enactive systems becomes increasingly plausible and relevant. Furthermore, the novel concept of socioenactive systems demands new tools and techniques for the design and evaluation of such systems. In particular, there is a need to consider diversified scenarios, environments, and different user characteristics.

Considering such challenging scenario, this paper investigated how much two existing evaluation instruments are applicable to evaluate universal access in socioenative systems. We presented the results of applying existing instruments to evaluate a socioenactive system, seeking to consider the issues that are not typically present in other types of systems.

The results of our case study indicated the principles alone were not able to provide insights into key aspects of socioenactive systems, such as engagement, wayfinding and social factors, like acceptance or awareness of others. However, we found that the principles contribute with a microscopic view, particularly regarding Universal Design, that the heuristics do not have. Therefore, the two complement each other well, which allowed us to merge the two and propose a checklist for the design and evaluation of systems in socioenactive scenarios, or those similar to them. Such results allowed us to propose a new instrument, which intends to supply the demand for design and evaluation tools for socioenactive systems.

Our findings pointed out to recommendations of use for evaluation instruments, such as the proposed checklist. For instance, a debriefing session after the initial collection is great for evaluators to reflect upon their observations, because there is not enough time for that during the data gathering. This way, the discussion among researchers (in this case, in the role of evaluators) is great for raising questions and proposing solutions to problems found either during the observation period, or in the debriefing. We also encourage that the checklist has room for writing notes, and a compliance scale for each item, as these two can feed the later discussion.

Future work involves testing the new instrument with socioenactive systems, possibly along with other existing guidelines, like WCAG. Introducing new tools would allow us to further improve our instrument, and contribute to a framework for designing and evaluating socioenactive systems.

Acknowledgements. This work is financially supported by the São Paulo Research Foundation (FAPESP)[3] (grant #2015/16528-0), by *Coordenação de Aperfeiçoamento de Pessoal de Nível Superior* (CAPES) (grants #01-P-04554/2013 and #173989/2017). We also thank the National Council for Scientific and Technological Development (CNPq) (grants #160911/2015-0 and #306272/2017-2) and the Pro Rectory of Research at the UNICAMP (grant #2018/2132).

References

1. Araújo, M.C.C. et al.: Mobile Audio Games Accessibility Evaluation for Users Who Are Blind. In: Antona, Margherita, Stephanidis, Constantine (eds.) UAHCI 2017. LNCS, vol. 10278, pp. 242–259. Springer, Cham (2017). https://doi.org/10.1007/978-3-319-58703-5_18

---

[3] The opinions expressed in this work do not necessarily reflect those of the funding agencies.

2. Baranauskas, M.: Sistemas sócio-enativos: investigando novas dimensões no design da interação mediada por tecnologias de informação e comunicação. FAPESP Thematic Project (2015/165280) (2015)
3. Consortium, W.W.W., et al.: Web content accessibility guidelines (WCAG) 2.0 (2008)
4. Emiliani, P.L., Stephanidis, C.: Universal access to ambient intelligence environments: opportunities and challenges for people with disabilities. IBM Syst. J. **44**(3), 605–619 (2005)
5. Cooper, M., Reid, L.G.: Web Content Accessibility Guidelines (WCAG) 2.0, pp. 1–24 (2013)
6. Kaipainen, M., et al.: Enactive systems and enactive media: embodied human-machine coupling beyond interfaces. Leonardo **44**(5), 433–438 (2011)
7. Liu, Y.E., Lee, S.T., Kascak, L.R., Sanford, J.A.: The Bridge Connecting Theory to Practice - A Case Study of Universal Design Process. In: Antona, M., Stephanidis, C. (eds.) UAHCI 2015. LNCS, vol. 9175, pp. 64–73. Springer, Cham (2015). https://doi.org/10.1007/978-3-319-20678-3_7
8. Maike, V.R.M.L., de Sousa Britto Neto, L., Goldenstein, S.K., Baranauskas, M.C.C.: Heuristics for NUI Revisited and Put into Practice. In: Kurosu, Masaaki (ed.) HCI 2015. LNCS, vol. 9170, pp. 317–328. Springer, Cham (2015). https://doi.org/10.1007/978-3-319-20916-6_30
9. Mi, N., Cavuoto, L.A., Benson, K., Smith-Jackson, T., Nussbaum, M.A.: A heuristic checklist for an accessible smartphone interface design. Univ. Access Inf. Soc. **13**(4), 351–365 (2014)
10. Nielsen, J.: 10 usability heuristics for user interface design. Nielsen Norman Group 1(1) (1995)
11. Norman, D.A.: Natural user interfaces are not natural. Interactions **17**(3), 6–10 (2010)
12. Oliveira, R., de Abreu, J.F., Almeida, A.M.: Promoting interactive television (iTV) accessibility: an adapted service for users with visual impairments. Univ. Access Inf. Soc. **16**(3), 533–544 (2017)
13. Orozco, A., Tabares, V., Duque, N.: Methodology for Heuristic Evaluation of Web Accessibility Oriented to Types of Disabilities. In: Antona, M., Stephanidis, C. (eds.) UAHCI 2016. LNCS, vol. 9737, pp. 91–97. Springer, Cham (2016). https://doi.org/10.1007/978-3-319-40250-5_9
14. Rahman, A., Anam, A.I., Yeasin, M.: EmoAssist: emotion enabled assistive tool to enhance dyadic conversation for the blind. Multimed. Tools Appl. **76**(6), 7699–7730 (2017)
15. Silva, J.V., et al.: Explorando afeto e sócio-enação em um cenário hospitalar (02 2019) (to be published)
16. Story, M.F.: Maximizing usability: the principles of universal design. Assist. Technol. **10**(1), 4–12 (1998)
17. Story, M.F., Mueller, J.L., Mace, R.L.: The universal design file: designing for people of all ages and abilities. Center for Universal Design, North Carolina State University, Raleigh (1998)
18. Varela, F.J., Thompson, E., Rosch, E.: The embodied mind: cognitive science and human experience. MIT Press, Cambridge (1991)
19. Weiser, M.: The computer for the 21st century. Sci. Am. **265**(3), 94–105 (1991)
20. Wigdor, D., Wixon, D.: Brave NUI World: Designing Natural User Interfaces for Touch and Gesture. Elsevier, Amsterdam (2011)

Expectations and Concerns Emerging from Experiences with Assistive Technology for ALS Patients

Cornelia Eicher[1]([✉]), Jörn Kiselev[1], Kirsten Brukamp[2],
Diana Kiemel[2], Susanne Spittel[1], André Maier[1],
Ursula Oleimeulen[3], and Marius Greuèl[3]

[1] Corporate Member of Freie Universität Berlin, Humboldt-Universität zu
Berlin, and Berlin Institute of Health, Charité – Universitätsmedizin Berlin,
Reinickendorferstr. 61, 13347 Berlin, Germany
cornelia.eicher@charite.de
[2] Evangelische Hochschule Ludwigsburg, Paulusweg 6,
71638 Ludwigsburg, Germany
[3] Pflegewerk Berlin GmbH, Wisbyer Str. 16/17, 10439 Berlin, Germany

Abstract. Amyotrophic lateral sclerosis (ALS) is a neurologic disease effecting
a gradual loss of physical body functionalities with usually unaltered cognitive
functionality. Due to the lack of autonomy, affected persons become dependent
on the support of third parties, such as relatives, friends and informal and formal
caregivers. Autonomy and self-determination play a crucial role in the lives of
ALS patients and can partly be maintained by the implementation of assistive
technologies and devices (ATD). In addition to life-supporting measures, ATD
can support ALS patients in their mobility, communication and help them
control their domestic environment, and thus foster social participation and
autonomy. However, little is known about expectations and concerns of patients
and their informal and formal caregivers regarding ATD. We therefore conducted semi-structured interviews as part of a mixed-methods requirements
analysis to evaluate how ATD influences the lives and living spaces of patients
with ALS as well as their family members and caregivers, and additionally their
expectations and concerns raised by ATD. The presented study research was
conducted as part of the research and development project "ROBINA - robot-
assisted services for patients with ALS".

Keywords: Assistive technology and devices · ATD ·
Amyotrophic lateral sclerosis · Expectations and strengths ·
Concerns and weaknesses

1 Introduction

1.1 Amyotrophic Lateral Sclerosis – ALS

Amyotrophic lateral sclerosis (ALS) is a neurologic disease effecting a gradual loss of
physical body functionalities with usually unaltered cognitive functionality. With the
progression of the disease, affected persons have no longer control over their muscular

© Springer Nature Switzerland AG 2019
M. Antona and C. Stephanidis (Eds.): HCII 2019, LNCS 11572, pp. 57–68, 2019.
https://doi.org/10.1007/978-3-030-23560-4_5

movements up to the point that even respiratory muscles fail to work. Therefore, without assistive technologies and devices (ATD) such as feeding tubes and artificial ventilation systems, the disease ultimately leads to the death of the patients. Around 50% of all ALS patients die between two and four years after onset [1] and only 10% survive longer than 10 years [2]. With a prevalence between 1.44 and 6.25/100.000 inhabitants ALS is defined as a rare disease [3] but characterized by a high level of suffering for both patients and caregivers.

Decreasing body functionality in upper and lower extremities as well as impairments regarding speaking and swallowing adversely effects the performance of activities of daily living (ADL) and has negative effects on the quality of life of patients [4–6]. Persons with ALS experience a continuous decrease and ultimately loss of mobility, communicational skills, and nutrition intake, which is often followed by a restricted social participation, a feeling of worthlessness and frustration [7, 8]. Due to the lack of autonomy, affected persons become dependent on the support of third parties, such as relatives, friends and informal and formal caregivers. In turn, ALS not only affects the quality of life of patients, but also has a huge impact on their social environment.

These issues can partly be compensated by the implementation of a wide array of ATD. In addition to life-supporting measures, ATD can support ALS patients in their mobility, communication and help them control their domestic environment and thus foster social participation and autonomy.

1.2   ATD and ALS – Status Quo

Definition Assistive Technology
Assistive technologies comprise any devices with the purpose to support people with disabilities and help them compensate their impairments. The WHO defines assistive devices and technologies as "those whose primary purpose is to maintain or improve an individual's functioning and independence to facilitate participation and to enhance overall well-being" [9]. The American Assistive Technology Act of 2004 offers a more comprehensive definition and refers to the term assistive technology device as "any item, piece of equipment, or product system, whether acquired commercially, modified, or customized, that is used to increase, maintain, or improve functional capabilities of individuals with disabilities" [10]. ATD includes, but is not limited to, hearing aids, visual aids, walkers and wheelchairs, devices for communication such as software with voice output or computers with gaze control and prostheses.

Types of ATD for ALS
As the ALS disease proceeds, patients experience the loss of mobility and speech and therefore lack of social engagement and communication. Apart from life-supporting measures, communication aids represent a crucial instrument to maintain the personal exchange of patients and their environment, not only for social purposes but also in order to inform about needs and issues.

Therefore, a broad variety of communication devices has been developed and is available on the market. With the progressive character of the disease, which is linked to a decrease of body functionalities, patients acquire a diverse variety of communication systems to meet their requirements. They range from electronic devices such as eye-gaze control systems, which use eye-tracking software to select letters, words or pictures on a screen, to speech apps for smartphones or tablets, simpler writing tableaus and even brain computer interfaces that use a brain's electrical activities to control devices such as computers or prostheses.

ATD that is used to overcome mobility impairments comprise simple crutches or walkers, wheelchairs and power wheelchairs that can be controlled by joysticks, voice input or eye gaze and, related to that, wheelchair ramps to overcome height differences such as staircases. Restraints in mobility also affect transfer tasks such as changing the position for example from bed to chair or from wheelchair to toilet seat. There are several lifter systems available, each adapted to its purpose, with regard to installation position, control unit and extent of reach.

An important issue for persons with ALS is the control of their domestic environment, i.e. control of entertainment devices such as TV or radio, light control, telephone, and computer. Therefore, voice-control systems such as ALEXA or ECHO are from a certain value for people suffering from ALS who are still able to speak clearly. However, there are also alternatives available, that come integrated into one remote control and can for instance be attached on a wheelchair or next to the bed, helping to maintain the patient's independency and autonomy.

Facing breathing muscles affected by the disease, ALS patients must eventually consider respiratory aids. Non-invasive and invasive technologies are available to help patients breathe as well as to cough and to clear their respiratory passages.

There is much more life-supporting and assistive technology available and thoroughly studied. Please refer to [11–13] for more information.

Supply Situation with ATD in Germany

The considerations above show that the need for ATD among ALS patients is very high. However, the supply situation among persons affected by ALS varies widely. To understand the presented study results, it is necessary to look at the German health care system and to understand its strengths and weaknesses regarding ATD supply.

The German health care system consists of two types of health insurances – the statutory health insurance and the private health insurance, with 89.27% and 10.73% insured persons, respectively [14]. The statutory health insurances are financed by their members and employers as well as pension insurance institutes, contributions are income-related and benefit all members who are in need [15]. They conclude contracts with specific care providers such as health care supply stores. Private insurances are financed the same way, but contributions are dependent from age of entry, gender, scope of chosen health care services, and more. Another significant difference between the two insurance types is that private insured persons must pay health services directly to the service provider, the expenses are reimbursed afterwards, and medical doctors can charge up to three times the amount compared to statutory insured persons [15].

The provision of ATD is an essential service of the statutory health insurance. Statutory insurances fund ATD with an additional payment by the insured persons of 10% of the original price (between € 5 and € 10) or the difference between the original price and the price as contracted by the insurance [16]. There are some exceptions, depending on whether the ATD is intended for consumption or not. The insured person must fund additional services beyond the necessary supply as defined by the insurance.

Private insurances fund ATD according to the terms and conditions of the contracts with the insured persons. The contracts are individual for each insurance holder. Most of them are based on a deductible, which must first be exceeded by health services before the private health insurance takes over health care costs [16].

The German health insurance companies are obliged to verify the indicated need for the requested ATD. Thus, health insurances can either accept or reject applications to cover ATD costs, leaving the patients with the choice of objecting or applying again at a later a later stage, private funding or refusing to acquire the requested ATD at all.

A study from 2018 shows that there were failed ATD provisions in different domains such as walking aids, exercise devices and wheelchairs in Germany [17]. 26.3% of the requested ATD was rejected by the health insurance company, showing differences both between the various companies and ATD categories. The amount of rejected powered wheelchairs for example was double compared to orthoses. 9.8% of the requested ATD was rejected by the ALS patients themselves. Reasons for this were not documented but discussed to be a consequence of perceived stigmatization, missing infrastructure for the use of ATD or possibly of supply latency. Especially the delivery of motor-operated or electronic devices such as augmented and alternative communication (AAC) systems and electric wheelchairs lasted very long (96.11 ± 60.6 and 129.7 ± 84.6 days, respectively). This study showed the crucial weakness in the ATD rejection rates and the supply latency in patients with ALS in Germany.

2 Methodology

In order to obtain a detailed overview about experiences with, expectations and requirements of ALS patients to ATD, we conducted a mixed-methods requirements analysis within the research and development project "ROBINA – robot-supported services for an individual and resource-oriented care of patients with ALS".

The semi-structured interviews were conducted with five ALS patients, five informal caregiving relatives of ALS patients and a focus group of five professional ALS caregivers (Fig. 1). All interviews were performed according to a semi-structured guideline, developed by the researchers with experience in qualitative data collection and a medical doctor specialized in the treatment and healthcare provision, including ATD, of patients with ALS.

The semi-structured guideline contained questions related to the living and caregiver/support situation, expectations to and experience with technology, related problems and barriers, and requirements to assistive technology. All interviews were held at an ambulance clinic for ALS treatment. Two researchers were present during all interviews, one led the interviews, and the other researcher filled the relevant information in a standardized protocol form. Additionally, all interviews were recorded with an audio device. The interview guideline was pretested with one representative of each target group. All patients, relatives and professional caregivers received information material about the aim of the study, study process, data protection and gave their written consent prior to the study. The Ethics Committee of the Charité - Universitätsmedizin Berlin approved of the study (no. of approval: EA1/121/17).

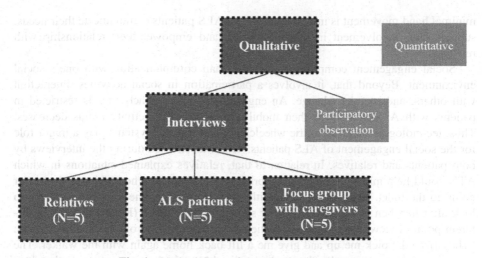

Fig. 1. Methodology of the mixed-methods study

The aim of the interviews was to identify strengths, weaknesses and barriers of assistive technology currently in use by the patients and their (formal and informal) caregivers and to evaluate the technology commitment of the patients and caregivers. Furthermore, to analyze the impact of assistive technology on the different user groups and to identify the requirements of a newly developed robotic system with regard to functionality, safety, operation modalities, positioning, hygiene and appearance. All interviews were transcribed and analyzed in accordance with Mayring [18].

3 Results

In the following paragraph, we present the results of the interviews. The five participating ALS patients were between 50 and 79 years old, four of them were male. The five participating relatives were between 50 and 83 years old, two of them were male, all of them were their partners and had experience in caregiving. The five professional caregivers of the focus group interview were between 50 and 65 years old, all of them were female and had experience with ALS patients.

3.1 Opportunities and Hopes Related to ATD

Due to the circumstances that ALS patients are dependent from ATD for life-supporting measures and for social participation and communication, ATD is expected to fulfill expectations for those purposes. The identified opportunities and hopes could be assigned to the categories of communication, social engagement, and autonomy.

As one of the main issues for ALS patients evident from the interviews is the loss of the ability to communicate with their social environment, depending on the progress of the disease via vocal, body language or both, ATD is anticipated to compensate these restrictions. Consequently, electronic communication operable via eye control or minimal hand movement is important to enable ALS patients communicate their needs, support their involvement in social activities, and empower their relationship with relatives.

Social engagement comprises a lot more than communication with one's social environment. Beyond that, it involves a participation in social activities, interaction with others, and social exchange. An engagement in social activities is restricted in patients with ALS, mainly as their mobility and therefore activity radius decreases. Thus, technologies such as electric wheelchairs and transfer systems play a major role for the social engagement of ALS patients. This was stressed during the interviews by both patients and relatives. In relation to that, relatives explained situations in which ATD could help maintain the patient's privacy, for example when taking a shower or going to the toilet. "This is the same with taking a shower. She does not want me to look after her then or take over tasks or something like that." (Relative, A12). A different point of view was offered by a patient who was afraid to overburden his friends: "They [friends] pick me up and give me a lift back home again with the walker. The walker must be transported and not everyone is able to do that or wants to do that. [...] Maybe at some point it becomes troublesome for them." (Patient, P02).

In this context, a central expectation of all groups was to maintain and retrieve autonomy specifically with regard to ADL. Hence, little activities such as scratching itchy skin or handing over something to drink, can empower patients, and at the same time relieve caregivers and lead to an improved patient-caregiver relationship. "It would be great if could also disburden somebody. Not to need somebody for every little thing, especially feeding." (Patient, P02). Especially iterative processes or activities were perceived as a burden for caregivers, but also for patients who wish not to become a burden to others. To mention an example, one of the interviewed relatives described the scenario that the patient requested a specific sweet several times per hour to support salivation. The relative explained it is very important for the patient but burdensome and tiring for both of them. Any ATD that could overtake this task would relieve not only the relative from iterative walks but also the patient from the requests and highly probable empower the patient's autonomy.

3.2 Concerns Related to ATD

ATD is usually rated positively, empowering patients and supporting their autonomy whilst disburdening formal and informal caregivers. Nevertheless, apart from benefits and strengths, ATD can also raise concerns and fears in affected persons. In our interviews, both patients and caregivers pointed out several situations that constituted or led to fearful or presumably dangerous circumstances. Compared to opportunities and hopes, concerns were mentioned a lot more in our interviews. Identified content could be assigned to the categories of safety, social engagement, handling, information, financing, living situation, stigmatization, and system adaptability.

A central concern ALS patients and relatives mentioned was regarding safety, frequently resulting from negative experiences with ATD. Concrete examples were a transfer system, which was used to transfer the patient from one room to another. The patient was afraid that if the system was installed above his head, it might fall off the ceiling and hit him due to is incapability to move away. Therefore, it was installed further away from his bed, which effected a restriction in usage. Another example from the interviews was a professional caregiver who reported problems with an invasive ventilation system. She perceived this experience as very drastic, up to the point that she was afraid of experiencing similar problems with different ATD. Similar concerns related to technical failure were mentioned by patients and relatives, e.g. a low battery life of an electric wheelchairs and, therefore, getting stuck during transport. Even a little shift of the operating elements, e.g. due to an uneven ground, can become a major issue as this may result in the loss of control over ATD.

Furthermore, assistive technology can entail relevant worries if patients express or are believed to have suicidal thoughts. In one specific example, an electric wheelchair was used to commit suicide. This implied major consequences for the provider, the professional caregivers and the relatives, including interrogations and investigations for a legal reconditioning, causing insecurities and stress in addition to reputation risks. Even though the maintenance and regain of autonomy in patients with ALS is of a high priority, when it comes to self-harm or suicidal thoughts an ethical debate is inevitable.

In the worst case, concerns about safety might have an impact on the use and acquisition of ATD, including non-use, misuse or incorrect installation of the ATD in question, which might result in a reduced effectivity or usability.

Professional caregivers often experienced the handling of ATD as very time-intensive and pointed out worries in relation to correct handling. Since there is a huge variety of ATD available, even for the same purpose, a standardized operation is often impossible. Additionally, some ATD is according to the caregivers not necessarily intuitive in its operation. "Because new assistive technology arrives frequently. Additionally, the [program] language has been altered [...]. I can switch on the light or operate a computer, four or five years that was impossible. We always learn something new." (Professional caregiver, Pf04). Supplier companies offer introduction workshops, but in many cases professional caregivers or relatives cannot take part or would require more than one workshop, i.e. refresher courses on a regular basis. Thus, informal and formal caregivers face fear of incorrect handling and, on the other hand, often need to invest more time than estimated due to lack of training.

At the same time, professional caregivers also criticized the lack of informative catalogs listing assistive technologies specifically for ALS patients, which was reinforced by relatives of ALS patients. Often, a knowledge transfer about available ATD happens via word-of-mouth within self-aid groups or in internet platforms, and sometimes even ATD suppliers can apparently not provide the required information.

Another major concern was the financing of ATD. In many cases, health insurances would not take over the costs for prescribed ATD for several often incomprehensible reasons. I.e. patients had to either object to the rejection with legal support, which causes a lot of stress and is time- and cost-intensive, organize private funding, look for cheaper alternatives or they waived it. "I did it myself. I contacted the mayor, the senator, a representative for people with disabilities, I bugged everyone." (Patient, P08). If the costs for expensive ATD are not covered by the health insurance and with rejections experienced, patients and relatives encounter a huge barrier for the acquisition of appropriate ATD. "We did not hand in the application for the ATD. We knew we would not get it funded anyway." (Relative, A05).

In addition, ATD has lasting effects on the living situation of ALS patients and their family members. Some interviewees pointed out that a spatial separation of patient and the rest of the family can help to maintain a 'normal' life besides nursing aspects. The partners of two ALS patients lived on different floors, and another partner lived in a different flat. They still spent most of the time together but stressed their need for privacy especially in relation to the presence of professional caregivers and the installation of several ATD which makes the living environment look like a hospital environment. They explained that with a spatial separation they could relax from the nursing responsibilities and recuperate easier.

Another issue raised was the topic of stigmatization. Evidence of stigmatization due to a person's appearance or look can be found throughout the literature, throughout history and worldwide. Especially people with visible physical disabilities often suffer from stigma and the feeling to be different compared to most of the people surrounding them. Even though assistive technology can improve a person's quality of life and enhance their autonomy, some of the interviewed ALS patients stated that 'looking disabled' is not an option for them. One patient rejected the implementation of an emergency button because she did not want to look sick. Even after she had experienced a situation in which she could not get up after a fall anymore and had to make her assistant dog to fetch her phone and call help, she would still reject the emergency button. Other statements related to the appearance of ATD. Surprisingly, one patient criticized the lack of color within ATD and required a better quality of her wheelchair. According to this study participant the electric wheelchair was neither comfortable to sit in, nor was its fabric of good quality. The fabric was apparently black and linting everywhere, leaving the user frustrated.

Finally, the lack of adaptability of many systems was described as a huge usage barrier. Due to the progredient character of ALS, the resources and physical abilities of affected persons can decrease quickly. It became clear from the interviews that this fact makes the patients reliant on diverse operating options, ranging from very sensitive joysticks to voice control, eye gaze control or brain interfaces and many more. Since not all ATD are compatible with this range of control options, many devices become difficult to use up to the point of being totally useless for the patient.

One circumstance that additionally affects this issue is that the supply with assistive systems often takes long but is initiated not until the actual need is identified. Therefore, ALS patients do not only repeatedly experience long intervals of limited social participation or communicability, apart from a decline in performing ADL, frequently their body state worsens and thus cannot use the ATD anymore when it is finally being delivered. "And then I received an orthosis for my feet. I cannot use that anymore as I am not able to walk anymore now. Unfortunately, you often wait very long for these things and then when they are finally here, it is too late. This is really bad." (Patient, P08).

4 Discussion

The interviewed persons gave an important insight in their lives with ATD, related hopes and opportunities but also concerns and criticism. Some of the results have been discussed elsewhere with different or additional aspects.

According to the literature, safety concerns are not only related to physical pain or stress, but also to data misuse. It must be a priority to protect personal data and make sure it remains confidential. Computer technology, which often remains the last interaction possibility for ALS patients, constitutes a major issue. Especially privacy concerns take effect in monitoring ATD, such as feedback about movements or heart rates. The misuse of data could also be imaginable in the context of externally controlling ATD. Recent news about theft and purchase of data makes the concern even more concrete. Related to that, other studies argue that caregivers become more and more reliant on monitoring technology rather than focusing on the patient [23]. This constitutes an issue especially among patients whose communication skills are impaired, as technology failure may occur at any time. However, physical pain or stress have a very direct impact on the patients and therefore remain the main worries within safety concerns.

Suicidal thoughts and the use of ATD have not been studied extensively. From an ethical point of view, it is a very sensitive and controversial topic, often crossing social boundaries. Often, affected persons are left alone. Whether they are patients who wish to let got or relatives who miss support from third parties. Different stakeholders are usually involved, such as ATD supplier companies, professional caregivers, institutions such as caregiving facilities, legal representatives and many more. Each of them has their own needs, responsibilities and rights; therefore, a case-sensitive approach is necessary, especially for people in intensive and palliative care.

In the interviews, ATD was associated with an increase of quality of life, e.g. by social engagement. The literature confirms these results. According to several studies, communication technology for example can significantly improve the quality of life of persons with ALS, when implemented in time [19–22]. However, ATD was also linked to a possible loss of contact with other humans, as it is perceived to substitute the support from professional or informal caregivers. It is important to decide the best solution on an individual basis. Each person has different needs and requires different levels of support and autonomy. One must consider that it is not a matter of right or wrong but a matter of quality of life for the patients and their social environment.

The fact, that social engagement might be impeded by ATD as presented has to be considered from two sides. In the mentioned example, the affected ALS patient was afraid his friends would be overburdened with the transfer of patient and walker at some point. Even though that cannot be ruled out, it should be underlined that in this concrete example the walker enables the patient to take part in social activities in the first place. Therefore, such statements should be interpreted with caution und the reasons behind and a possible association with stigmatization should be examined.

The identified issues with the supply and financing of ATD in our study sample have been discussed and verified in several studies (compare also paragraph 1.2) [17, 24]. Nevertheless, results are not generalizable in an international context due to the different characters of health care systems worldwide. However, it raises the question whether the costs of ATD should be the determining factor for the care and supply of patients. Many public places have been adapted or re-built in order to enable a barrier-free access by people with disabilities; however, it is also the responsibility of a state and society to give them access to the means they need to benefit from the inclusion policies.

Appropriately, affected persons should be involved in the establishment of such policies, but also into the development of the means mentioned. The example of ALS shows very clearly, that technology which is not fully adaptable to the changing needs and preferences of its user group will become useless and miss its purpose. Even though the general understanding is that technology should, wherever possible, adapt to consumers [25], this is not always the fact [26, 27]. Reasons can be found both in the companies and in the customers. Personalized items or technology requires investment in innovative and flexible production and logistics, additionally to development time and expertise. This often happens at the cost of reasonable pricing. Apart from that, customer needs are very diverse and potentially not communicated clearly enough, which often constitutes a construction problem.

Related to that are the handling difficulties of formal and informal caregivers who struggle with a variety of non-standardized systems. This might also increase insecurities amongst both patients and caregivers to damage the system. Additionally, and correlating with safety concerns, the collection and processing of data for individual needs is questionable. Especially tracking technology data may reveal sensible information such as absence from home. Nevertheless, it remains a right for patients to receive individualized treatment and therefore module-based technology could represent a key approach for ALS patients.

However, even if assistive technology is perfectly adapted to the user's requirements, one issue may remain unsolved – the feeling of stigmatization. Stigmatization can be found in many groups, among children, older people, people born disabled and persons with acquired disabilities. Especially persons with acquired disabilities often abandon ATD, not wanting to show perceived weaknesses or to avoid social exclusion [28]. There is also the concern that other people might focus on a person's incapability instead of their resources. Even though this may have adverse effects, e.g. social exclusion due to immobility, for many people with ALS it is difficult to accept ATD. ATD is always present and notable for others, and shows a dependency in people who used to be independent and do not want to give up their independency.

Even though the sample size was small with five representatives of each of the three groups, the interviews gave new insights about hopes and concerns related to ATD in patients with ALS. The fact that due to the nature of the R&D project only persons affected by ALS where interviewed makes a generalization for other patient groups using ATD difficult. However, relevant information concerning ATD supply and financing could be derived from this study and will be investigated further using quantitative methods in a bigger sample size including different patient groups suffering from severe physical impairments.

5   Conclusion

The interviews gave an important insight into the lives of ALS patients and formal and informal caregivers using assistive technologies. Assistive technologies and devices offer relevant benefits for patients with ALS and can support their autonomy and social engagement. Nevertheless, the study revealed negative experiences of patients and formal and informal caregivers with ATD. Interview participants expressed several concerns, doubts and fears, especially regarding safety and handling. Therefore, in order to ensure the empowerment of patients through technology, developers, suppliers and caregivers must involve patient needs into all steps of technology development and patient care. Additional attention should be devoted to the requirements from the groups involved in patient care in order to support a good care quality.

References

1. Couratier, P., et al.: Epidemiology of amyotrophic lateral sclerosis: a review of literature. Rev. Neurol. (Paris) **172**, 37–45 (2016). https://doi.org/10.1016/j.neurol.2015.11.002
2. del Aguila, M.A., Longstreth, W.T., McGuire, V., Koepsell, T.D., van Belle, G.: Prognosis in amyotrophic lateral sclerosis: a population-based study. Neurology **60**, 813–819 (2003)
3. Chiò, A., et al.: Global epidemiology of amyotrophic lateral sclerosis: a systematic review of the published literature. Neuroepidemiology **41**, 118–130 (2013). https://doi.org/10.1159/000351153
4. Tramonti, F., Bongioanni, P., Di Bernardo, C., Davitti, S., Rossi, B.: Quality of life of patients with amyotrophic lateral sclerosis. Psychol. Health Med. **17**, 621–628 (2012). https://doi.org/10.1080/13548506.2011.651149
5. Martínez-Campo, Y., et al.: Observational study of patients in Spain with amyotrophic lateral sclerosis: correlations between clinical status, quality of life, and dignity. BMC Palliat. Care **16**, 75 (2017). https://doi.org/10.1186/s12904-017-0260-6
6. Siqueira, S.C., de Vitorino, P.V.O., Prudente, C.O.M., de Santana, T.S., de Melo, G.F.: Quality of life of patients with amyotrophic lateral sclerosis. Revista da Rede de Enfermagem do Nordeste **18**, 139 (2017). https://doi.org/10.15253/2175-6783.2017000100019
7. Oster, C., Pagnini, F.: Resentment, hate, and hope in amyotrophic lateral sclerosis. Front. Psychol. **3**, 530 (2012). https://doi.org/10.3389/fpsyg.2012.00530
8. Pagnini, F.: Psychological wellbeing and quality of life in amyotrophic lateral sclerosis: a review. Int. J. Psychol. **48**, 194–205 (2013). https://doi.org/10.1080/00207594.2012.691977
9. WHO | Assistive devices and technologies. http://www.who.int/disabilities/technology/en/
10. Bausch, M.E., Mittler, J.E., Hasselbring, T.S., Cross, D.P.: The assistive technology act of 2004: what does it say and what does it mean? Phys. Disabil. Educ. Relat. Serv. **23**, 59–67 (2005)
11. Mackenzie, L., Bhuta, P., Rusten, K., Devine, J., Love, A., Waterson, P.: Communications technology and motor neuron disease: an Australian survey of people with motor neuron disease. JMIR Rehabil. Assist. Technol. **3**, e2 (2016). https://doi.org/10.2196/rehab.4017
12. Ball, L.J., et al.: Eye-gaze access to AAC technology for people with amyotrophic lateral sclerosis. J. Med. Speech Lang. Pathol. **18**, 11–23 (2010)
13. Association for the Advancement of Assistive Technology in Europe. In: Assistive Technology from Adapted Equipment to Inclusive Environments: AAATE 2009. IOS Press (2009)
14. GKV und PKV - Mitglieder- und Versichertenzahl im Vergleich bis 2018 | Statistik. https://de.statista.com/statistik/daten/studie/155823/umfrage/gkv-pkv-mitglieder-und-versichertenzahl-im-vergleich/
15. Land, B.: Das deutsche Gesundheitssystem - Struktur und Finanzierung: Wissen für Pflege- und Therapieberufe. Verlag W. Kohlhammer, Stuttgart (2018)
16. Wichert, B., Haufe-Lexware GmbH & Co. KG: Krankenversicherung 2018 Zahlen, Daten, Fakten. (2018)

17. Funke, A., et al.: Hilfsmittelversorgung bei der amyotrophen Lateralsklerose: Analyse aus 3 Jahren Fallmanagement in einem internetunterstützten Versorgungsnetzwerk. Der Nervenarzt **86**, 1007–1017 (2015). https://doi.org/10.1007/s00115-015-4398-2
18. Mayring, P.: Qualitative Inhaltsanalyse: Grundlagen und Techniken. Beltz (2010)
19. Caligari, M., Godi, M., Guglielmetti, S., Franchignoni, F., Nardone, A.: Eye tracking communication devices in amyotrophic lateral sclerosis: impact on disability and quality of life. Amyotroph. Lateral Scler. Frontotemporal Degener. **14**, 546–552 (2013). https://doi.org/10.3109/21678421.2013.803576
20. Linse, K., Aust, E., Joos, M., Hermann, A.: Communication matters—pitfalls and promise of hightech communication devices in palliative care of severely physically disabled patients with amyotrophic lateral sclerosis. Front. Neurol. **9**, 603 (2018). https://doi.org/10.3389/fneur.2018.00603
21. Beukelman, D., Fager, S., Nordness, A.: Communication support for people with ALS. Neurol. Res. Int. **2011**, 1–6 (2011). https://doi.org/10.1155/2011/714693
22. Körner, S., et al.: Speech therapy and communication device: impact on quality of life and mood in patients with amyotrophic lateral sclerosis. Amyotroph. Lateral Scler. Frontotemporal Degener. **14**, 20–25 (2013). https://doi.org/10.3109/17482968.2012.692382
23. Hughes, R.G. (ed.): Patient Safety and Quality: An Evidence-Based Handbook for Nurses. Agency for Healthcare Research and Quality, Rockville (2008)
24. Henschke, C.: Provision and financing of assistive technology devices in Germany: a bureaucratic odyssey? The case of amyotrophic lateral sclerosis and Duchenne muscular dystrophy. Health Policy **105**, 176–184 (2012). https://doi.org/10.1016/j.healthpol.2012.01.013
25. Hagglund, K.J. (Ed.): Handbook of applied disability and rehabilitation research. Springer, New York (2006)
26. Zipkin, P.H.: The limits of mass customization. MIT Sloan Manag. Rev. **42**, 81–87 (2001)
27. Toch, E., Wang, Y., Cranor, L.F.: Personalization and privacy: a survey of privacy risks and remedies in personalization-based systems. User Model. User Adapt. Interact. **22**, 203–220 (2012). https://doi.org/10.1007/s11257-011-9110-z
28. Resources, M.A.: Information: Special and Gifted Education: Concepts, Methodologies, Tools, and Applications. IGI Global, Hershey (2016)

Teaching Empathy in Underserved Audiences Through Game Based Learning

John Gialanella[1](✉) and Kimberly Mitchell[2](✉)

[1] Western Washington University, Bellingham, WA, USA
jgialanella@gmail.com
[2] Bradley University, Peoria, IL, USA
kimberlymelhus@gmail.com

Abstract. To facilitate conversation about design as a profession to an area underserved by the arts, a team of designers worked collaboratively to create a teaching opportunity to reach high school students. Through research we found that in order for someone to learn, they first must be motivated. Introducing a new unfamiliar topic to a group of high schoolers had to be done right if we wanted them to walk away with the learning outcomes we had developed. The primary learning outcome of the project was to create an enjoyable, engaging experience, one in which the students were learning about design thinking, along with developing empathy and problem solving in team-building experiences.

Our card game, "*Parallel – A Game of Creative Spark*," capitalizes on the concept of multiple intelligences by offering a game where these students can exercise their problem solving and critical thinking skills in a group setting, while fostering their culturally diverse background and creativity. Students are not only introduced to design, but they work on their creativity, relationship-building and teamwork skills. Parallel helps facilitate the sharing of rich cultural histories in an alternate dimension. The game allows students to develop skills and perspectives that result in an increased knowledge of design thinking and a sense of pride in their own cultural identity. The students become self-empowered that they can have a voice in creating positive change in their alternate universe, and hopefully they'll see that this also works in their own lives and communities.

In our paper, we illustrate how play can be used to motivate learning and teach empathy.

The team members who collaborated on the creation and design of *Parallel–A Game of Creative Spark* are: Robert Franklin, John Gialanella, Kimberly Mitchell, Jen Pace, Eric Torres.

Keywords: Design thinking · Empathy · Game design

1 Design Thinking in the Form of a Game

The lack of representation from minorities in the design field is problematic in such a diverse world. In a report generated by AIGA, it was found that, "among graphic designers in the field, 2 percent are black, 4 percent Hispanic/Latino, 6 percent Asian/Pacific Islander, and 2 percent other. That leaves 86 percent Caucasian American [1]."

© Springer Nature Switzerland AG 2019
M. Antona and C. Stephanidis (Eds.): HCII 2019, LNCS 11572, pp. 69–90, 2019.
https://doi.org/10.1007/978-3-030-23560-4_6

When our country has one of the most diverse populations in the world, how is it that the graphic design industry is lacking with diversity? It is simple: funds for the arts in middle and high school education is diminishing. This lack in funding disproportionately affects students in low income areas—in addition, these students have limited, if any, access to the technology required to be a designer, and very little exposure to role models in the design industry.

A team of designers worked together for two years brainstorming and developing a tool to expose *design thinking* to underserved high school students in the form of a game. The goal was to empower underserved high school students to become a voice and a leader in social change.

While researching, the team found several existing young student designer kits that were activity based, but did not come across a true game, something that truly engages the target group we were eager to help. Many of the design related tools that existed already were tools that utilize activities and exercises to empower students to explore problem solving through design. What the team found lacking though, was the use of play in introducing underserved students to the world of design.

The iterative planning process brought the team to the solution of utilizing a card game to engage these students. Without the pressures of being challenged to solve design issues beyond their comprehension, students are introduced to concepts of design and design thinking, through some basic principles; teamwork, creativity, communication, and empathy.

By couching these design ideas in the framework of a card game, set in a fictional world based loosely on reality, the students can learn by advancing through the game as a team, meeting challenges as they arise, and striving to earn the highest level of "Design Cred" by the final round. With an enjoyable experience, and ability to always raise their "Cred", the game can be played again and again.

1.1 Methods and Study Procedures

To begin the project, the team first needed to understand the background of the students they were designing for. Questionnaires involving inquires related to the curricular (art and design thinking) and cultural backgrounds of students were created and distributed to high school faculty all throughout the United States, who work directly with underserved students. The surveys were confidential. The results from the surveys helped produce information that was needed to begin designing the game.

In order to be fully immersed with the audience for which they were designing, the team brought on an additional designer who was not only a current undergraduate student, but also from an underserved audience. Additionally, the design team consulted with local faculty who worked directly with underserved students in their community. The faculty also helped serve as cultural consultants for the game play. The goal of forming these relationships was to learn from these consultants as much as possible to inform the game play and underlying educational experience.

After a few a few meetings with each faculty member, the design team worked closely together creating the foundation for the game play. During the user testing stage, the design team distributed pre-questionnaires for the teachers via email. The faculty member or after-school program coordinator who helped facilitate the game play gave each student the pre-questionnaire prior to playing the game. The information collected in the pre-questionnaire asked questions about the student's cultural background, their curricular background with working in groups, and in particular – what their background in art and design was and if that area of study is interesting to them.

The post-questionnaire was distributed by the facilitator following the game play, and it listed similar questions as the pre-questionnaire, but also what they enjoyed and didn't enjoy about the game so that improvements could be made, and if by playing the game, design or art was a more desirable field. All questionnaires were completely confidential.

1.2 Play and Learning

Play: Verb 1. Engage in activity for enjoyment and recreation rather than a serious or practical purpose.

Noun 1. Activity engaged in for enjoyment and recreation, especially by children [2].

Evidence resounds that fun and games are not frivolous pursuits—instead, they come naturally to us as essential parts of being alive [3]. Behavior expert Dr. Stuart Brown considers play to be an evolved behavior that is important to the survival of humans and even highly intelligent animals. His research has linked play with enhanced creative ability, both on and off the job [4]. Developmental Psychologist and Professor Brian Sutton-Smith, says play makes us more adaptable, able to face a wider variety of situations, as well as more optimistic and confident. Playtime is an important part of childhood development: there is often no limits, play allows for experimentation, innovation, and role playing, and often, children who are playing are not afraid of failure, because in play failure doesn't typically exist.

For thousands of years games have reflected profound elements of culture and the struggles inherent in the human condition [5]. Games have the ability to make a lasting impact on society through their play – both positive and negative. Games have been found to "promote and instill prosocial attitudes, behaviors, and emotional responses. For instance, cooperative game play has been shown to reduce intergroup hostility and prejudice [6]". Other research suggests that games can "help facilitate emotional regulation and foster self-actualization and that games can encourage positive shifts in the hearts and minds of players [7]".

We know that play is an integral part of our being and the integration of play in the classroom is not something new. Is it truly possible to teach empathy and design thinking methods to underserved high school students? When the design team was charged with introducing and teaching design thinking amongst high school students with little to no background in the arts, several questions arose. How can you make it exciting and engaging? How has this been done in the past? As stated previously, we know that play is an integral part of our core, so can we use play and gaming to teach empathy and creative thinking?

1.3   Multiple Intelligence Theory and Motivation

Design Researcher and Professor Richard Buchanan, noted that, "design is the bridge between theory and the way we actually live our lives. We need to spend more time teaching non-designers design knowledge [8]." "Design education, as a subject, seems to offer something unique—a tool for creating connections between ideas, information, people and objects" and, according to Buchanan, "it integrates and connects knowledge in new and useful ways [8]." We can use design to address the world's challenges. One of those challenges, in this case, is art and design diversity within minority populations.

In his book, *Frames of Mind*, psychologist Howard Gardner explains the eight dimensions of intelligence: "Visual/Spatial Intelligence, Musical Intelligence, Verbal/Linguistic Intelligence, Logical/Mathematical Intelligence, Interpersonal Intelligence, Intra Personal Intelligence, Bodily/Kinesthetic Intelligence, and the latest Naturalistic [9]." Gardner explains that the "theory of multiple intelligences" (MI Theory, as it has come to be called) makes two strong claims [10]. The first claim is that all humans possess all of these intelligences. The second is that, "just as we all look different and have different personalities and temperaments, we also exhibit different profiles of intelligence [11]." He claims that no two individuals have the same intelligence, even identical twins with the same genetic makeup, because individuals undergo different experiences.

"The MI Theory not only comports with their intuitions that children are smart in different kinds of ways; the theory also holds out hope that students can be reached more effectively, if their favored ways of knowing are taken into account in curriculum, instruction and assessment [11]" Following Gardner, certain tests like the IQ tests have been criticized for emphasizing the logical and linguistic over other cognitive capacities, failing to explain creativity or originality, and disregarding socio-cultural issues and factors such as motivation and perception in the role of understanding [12].

Nearly a decade earlier, American philosopher, psychologist, and educational reformer, John Dewey, was working with the theory of knowledge. Dewey believed that it is the transmission of ideas and practices from the elderly to the newly born that help enhance education. He claimed that there was a necessity of teaching and learning for the continued existence of a society. To him, school was a superficial means of education [13]. He believed that education shouldn't be strictly taught from textbooks but from past experiences. The main concept of John Dewey's view of education was that "greater emphasis should be placed on broadening of intellect and development of problem solving and critical thinking skills, rather than simply the memorization of lessons [14]." John Dewey theorized that learning should not only prepare one for life, but should also be an integral part of life itself [15].

Both Dewey and Gardner believe that the classroom needs multiple ways to educate children to help balance out the different intelligences that children possess. But, how do designers play a role in all of this? Though designers do much more than create games, they innately use the theory of multiple intelligences. Both psychologists, Howard Gardner and John Dewey, believe that in order to move ahead as a society, we need to be accepting of these multiple intelligences and different means of education.

1.4   Engaging Education

IDEO is one of several organizations that has a Design Kit, called *The Field Guide to Human-Centered Design*, which is similar in its idea in that it offers a series of activities that encourage participation from the user, with given steps to solve a certain problem, but its approach is completely different—it is geared towards new and practicing designers, and the end goal for the activities is for these designers to "understand the people they're designing for, to have more effective brainstorms, to prototype ideas, and to ultimately arrive at more creative solutions [16]." The game, "Parallel – A Game of Creative Spark," capitalizes on the concept of multiple intelligences by offering a format where these students can exercise their problem solving and critical thinking skills in a group-like setting, while fostering their culturally diverse background and creativity. They are not only be introduced to design, but they also be work on their relationship-building and teamwork. The game is more than just an activity. It was created to excite the "screenagers" with something that will elicit a response – "winning". Developers and creators found that the play students engaged in through games created energy and were aspirational. In the end, the more fun and engaging the experience, the more plausible that it will be successful.

The end result of Parallel is to encourage participation in the field of art and design and to engage students who probably haven't had any type of prior knowledge with the field, or very limited access to information regarding the design industry. The game helps facilitate the sharing of rich cultural histories in an alternate dimension. All cultures bring their own symbols, designs, and mythologies, and we are the better for it when they are shared. The game will help students develop skills and perspectives that result in an increased knowledge of design thinking and a sense of pride in their own cultural identity. The students become self-empowered that they can have a voice in creating positive change in their alternate universe, and hopefully, through facilitator led discussion following the game-play, they'll see that this also works in their own lives and communities.

2   Parallel – A Game of Creative Spark

The primary mission of the game, "Parallel – A Game of Creative Spark," is to create an enjoyable, engaging experience, one in which the students are learning about design thinking, along with developing empathy and problem solving. By being excited about playing and learning, we are setting them up for a better learning experience in the future.

Without the pressures of being challenged to solve design issues beyond their abilities, students are introduced to concepts of design and design thinking, through some basic principles: teamwork, creativity, communication, and empathy.

Design Thinking is a problem-solving concept that has been used in the creative industry for some time, but increasingly, it is being incorporated into the workplace of many non-design-oriented professions and businesses. The idea that a group of individuals can identify a problem, brainstorm ideas, prototype and test solutions, learn, and adjust, is a process that is beneficial to all students, not just the creative ones.

There are tremendous benefits from Design Thinking to all walks of students, not just the creatively inclined, but for those who excel in traditional core subjects of math and science. Design Thinking introduces, teaches, and encourages students to delve into problems to find the root causes, to view problems from many points of view, and to ultimately discover unique and original solutions that benefit all.

These processes of problem solving and ideating encourage students to think 'outside of the box' and to appreciate the learning processes of their fellow classmates. Students also learn the impact and importance of the unique personal perspectives and experiences they bring to any problem-solving brainstorm.

IDEO defines human centered design as: "embracing human-centered design means believing that all problems even the seemingly intractable ones like poverty, gender equality, and clean water, are solvable" [16]. It means believing that "the people who face those problems every day are the ones who hold the key to their answer. Human-centered design offers problem solvers a chance to design with communities, to deeply understand the people they're looking to serve, to dream up scores of ideas, and to create innovative new solutions rooted in people's actual needs" [16]. Human Centered Design is when a designer fully immerses himself into the lives of others so that he or she finds patterns and themes to help the user solve a problem.

Designers often use design thinking as a creative approach to solving these human-centered problems. By doing this, the designer brings the "who, what, where" into helping find the solution. In Computer Scientist and Nobel Prize laureate, Herbert A. Simon's book, *Sciences of the Artificial*, design thinking was recognized as a way of thinking, comparing it to a scientific method. The tools of design thinking are borrowed from a variety of disciplines and have been used by many great innovators. The problems are solved using human-centric ways where designers are able to fully understand the audience they're designing for. Design Thinking is a problem-solving concept that has been used in the creative industry for some time, but increasingly, it is being incorporated into the workplace of many non-design-oriented professions and businesses.

Parallel is a game about teamwork, creative problem solving, empathy, and strategy within creative professions.

Graphic design is about saying things visually. Illustration, layout, and typography are just a few methods used. Because designers work with many different people, they often get the opportunity to learn a variety of skills. The game, Parallel, was created with this in mind, allowing students to explore characteristics of creative professionals and allow them to work in many different roles alongside classmates/teammates to solve a variety of [fictional] problems.

The card game asks players to work in teams to solve fictional problems (that parallel real-world problems). There are many challenges in the near and distant future that young students face. Some of these challenges are already having an impact on their lives, their family's lives, their community's lives. There are many places in the country where students don't have access to quality education, technology, or the arts. Places where access to healthy meals are non-existent, where healthcare is distant and expensive, where students with disabilities can't attain an equal opportunity. Environmental issues are already having a major impact on these communities, the youth recognize this better than most, but feel voiceless. Many of these places lack safe community spaces, free of violence and negative influences. Poor communities have a shortage of business opportunities, a stifling of an entrepreneurial spirit. Ultimately, students feel their concerns for the future surrounding these issues aren't reflected in their political representation. Parallel sets no expectations that a game could fix these problems. These are deeply embedded social, economic, environmental, and political problems stitched into the fabric of communities across America. Parallel does however, set the lofty hopes, that it can open students in these affected communities to a new way of thinking, an empowering paradigm that they—regardless of their status, can have a positive impact on their communities...and maybe the world.

Parallel requires players to learn how to empathize and work together to solve those problems. Unlike most games in which players are in a challenge against one another, Parallel is cooperative game where players work together against a common antagonist, The Hollow. Players need to learn to communicate clearly and openly with each other, develop strategies for defeating both The Hollow and scoring the most points before the clock runs out. Sometimes, a player can be a leader, building and completing the most projects and scoring the most points for the team. Other times, a player might need to take a supportive role, trading cards that would be beneficial to a teammate, or sacrificing cards or projects for the good of the team.

The ultimate goal of the game is to complete as many projects as a team as possible, and score the highest Cred point total as possible. To enhance the experience and connect with players across the country, teams may upload their scores to the Parallel game website, which will also house game bonus content and resources for players and teachers.

Without the pressures of being challenged to solve design issues beyond their comprehension, we instead introduce students to concepts of design and design thinking, through some basic principles: teamwork, creativity, communication, and empathy.

2.1   The Lore of Parallel

The simplistic design of the cards themselves will encourage player interaction, allowing conversation amongst players by building rapport, evoking stories and exploring emotions, all while designing a solution to a community-wide problem.

Many of the students playing this game will be coming from difficult situations; lack of technological resources, no access to electricity or running water in their home, living in neighborhoods without a grocery store in sight, or severe gun violence problems. Our initial idea was to empower students to face these challenges head-on, by coming up with unique and creative solutions. The more we developed this idea though, the more concerned we were with the possibility of placing these already vulnerable students, into a position of failure—adults, leaders of cities and states, have yet to solve these problems, the last thing we want is for these students to fail early, and be turned off from the possibility of entering the creative world in the future.

Instead of creating specific scenarios, such as; "Less than 10% of homes on the Navajo Reservation have access to Internet service. Students have difficulty doing homework without this access. Your group has been charged with finding a creative solution to this problem," or "The city of Detroit has no grocery stores within the city limits. This lack of food options has led to poor health by the people living in these cities. Your challenge is to develop a creative solution to help these citizens," we instead created a fictional universe, which is based and influenced by the real world. Student players would still face the challenge of trying to win the game and gain "Design Cred", but they wouldn't overtly be reminded of the difficult challenges they face day to day in their own lives.

On Parallel, there are four shape families – Circles, Squares, Triangles, and Hybrids. Each family has their own characteristics and nature. All shapes draw creative spark from The Geode – a majestic structure which powers Parallel. Together, the inhabitants of Parallel use their energy to make useful and beautiful things which advance their civilization.

Yet, their way of life is in constant peril.

Long ago, a collective of shapes called Fractals schemed to steal the Geode's power for themselves. They reasoned that in order to create a perfect world, only an elite few should have the power to create. For a time, their greed made them strong. Just when it seemed the Fractals would possess the power of the Geode, they were shattered by it instead.

But something terrible was brought into existence when the Fractals were defeated. From their broken forms emerged the Hollow, an all-consuming force which devours creative spark. Now, the Hollow roams throughout Parallel enslaving its peoples, threatening its landscapes, and spreading its influence. In spite of this threat, students must help defend Parallel and ensure that it thrives. The Hollow can never be vanquished entirely, but we are the resistance.

2.2 How Does Parallel Work

The game play will last approximately one hour and will ideally be played in the classroom and/or an afterschool program with the facilitation of a faculty member. Following game play, the teacher will be able to facilitate discussions with the class based on prompts given to them in the teacher handbook. Each discussion can be unique to the overall issues or concerns of that particular audience or class, and it is the game's goal that the students can see the connection between how they solved the fictional game problems creatively as a team and how that can be done with existing problems outlined in the discussion.

Parallel is a timed and collaborative game in which students, in groups of four, take turns drawing and playing cards, taking on challenges, building projects, and ultimately scoring as much 'Cred' to battle The Hollow. This process goes on for ten rounds, after which the game comes to an end.

The game features characters that mimic real-life creative professionals, with similar abilities and challenges. The idea is to introduce creatives as 'heroes' to the world of Parallel. The characters, with their varying abilities, work together to pick each other up, compensate for weaknesses, and accomplish as many challenges and projects as possible.

Along the way, an antagonist works behind the scenes of Parallel to try and defeat all that is good. The Hollow represents all things negative, both intentional and by chance. Teaching creative problem-solving using Teamwork – and teaching relationship building and empathy are all end goals of the game play.

Teamwork. Teamwork is a crucial skill for any person wanting to be successful in any field, especially so in a creative industry. Teamwork is about forming connections, sharing ideas, discussing differences, and utilizing the individual skills of a group to find a solution to a problem. Working as a team also allows students to learn how to discuss, disagree, and communicate with people from differing backgrounds. Graphic Designers work with Coders, Copywriters, Photographers, Market Researchers, other Designers and many more specialists. World-class Chefs work with Sous Chefs, Line Cooks, Servers, and Food Suppliers.

Parallel tie-in. In Parallel, the name of the game is teamwork, making it a unique experience to many other games. Students aren't facing off against each other, they aren't trying to defeat or outscore their classmates, they are working together by communicating and strategizing to defeat The Hollow and score Cred before the game comes to an end (Fig. 1).

Fig. 1. Each student will pull one character card (or Hero) that will remain with them for the duration of gameplay. Characters work together to solve problems by using their strengths.

Problem Solving. Problem Solving is the cornerstone for almost all professions. As the world grows, resources dwindle, globalization spreads, and technology advances, humans face new and diverse problems. Being able to identify those problems is an important skill for students to have as they enter the world, and being able to work with others, communicate thoughts, and develop solutions will help them to make a successful and lasting impact on the world around them.

Parallel tie-in. The Hollow represents the dark energy of the Parallel world, when it strikes in the form of a Hollow Storm, it unleashes a dark influence that can impact the motivation of creatives, a creeping doubt, and decay of confidence. These represent unforeseen problems that have an effect on us all. Along with dealing with the unexpected, there are the expected problems that arise; housing shortage, healthy food options, access to clean water. These challenges represent the problems that students can and do encounter in Parallel, and by working together, they can strategize to share cards, defend each other, and work to accomplish goals in providing these needs to the citizens of Parallel (Fig. 2).

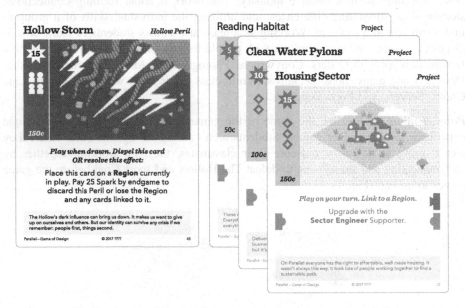

Fig. 2. An example of a Hollow card, besides three Project cards.

Empathy. Being understanding of others, of those who are different, is a vital ability for any person operating in this world. How can someone communicate with, design for, or work with a person of a different background, if they can't envision being in their shoes. Empathy is about understanding the wide range of human experiences, understanding the various cultures, disabilities, families, struggles, and challenges around the world.

Parallel tie-in. Not everyone has the exposure to the same difficulties. Access to clean water in Flint is different than access to clean water in the Navajo Nation. Food deserts that exist in San Francisco, may not be comparable to those in Seattle. The idea though, is that if we can better understand these problems outside of our own communities, we can be better in thinking of solutions. This concept exists in the game as well. One student's Hero may be tasked with building the Reading Habitat, while another is focused on building the Clean Water Pylons. By communicating, sharing resources and ideas, they can help to empathize with each other's mission, and help to work towards a successful resolution (Fig. 3).

Strategy and Planning. After all is considered; Teamwork, Problem Solving, Empathy—creatives need the know-how to get started in tackling their objective. This will not come easy and will not be learned in a class period, a semester, or even a school year. Planning to solve a problem, to build a strategy, takes a long time to

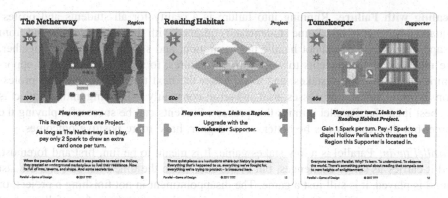

Fig. 3. An example how the cards link with one another.

perfect, with successes and failures. We can encourage students to lean on the strengths of their teammates to supplement their own weaknesses, to share the load, and to appreciate the process.

Parallel tie-in. Parallel is a large, robust world, with many Heroes, Supporting Characters, Regions, Projects, and Enemies, each session of a game played is always a little different. This expansive list of variables causes students to constantly be considering their strategies in the game, adjusting on-the-fly, and learning to be adaptive. Each game will teach them a new successful strategy, as well as failed strategies to avoid the next time.

Exposure to Creative Professions. One of the primary objectives of Parallel is the exposure of Creative Professions to students. Many students are gifted in mathematics, in science and technology, and in business, but just as many who find difficulties in these subjects, have skills and talents that lend well to creative professions. With the growing emphasis on standardized testing and focus on STEM, students who struggle in traditional courses can feel discouraged, hopeless, and left behind. Schools that still have the ability to offer creative courses, are often still limited and seen as non-essential. Some schools have seen these classes eliminated altogether. Our goal with Parallel is to expose students who may struggle with traditional subjects, to the potential of educational and career paths that are tailor made to their skill sets, and to teach those who aren't creatively inclined, to learn how to think and see in different ways.

Parallel tie-in. Parallel has its Heroes who are entrepreneurs, savvy in the sciences, and gifted with the computer, but it also has Heroes who are excel at writing, paint incredible murals, prepare amazing meals. We often focus on design and studio are as being the only arena for creatives, but there is so much more. We want the student who dabbles in mixing her own music, or reads his poetry to friends, to feel they have the same access to a successful career path as anyone else—or even the fact that these career paths exist at all! By making our Heroes diverse in backgrounds, abilities, and professions, we are expanding the idea of what a hero can be. What they can be.

Dealing with Failure. Running into failure is a reality for all students and professionals, it is a part of life. Some students are equipped with the resolve to rebound from disappointment, some cannot handle the frustration, and some lose hope all together. We must encourage students to work through failures, to see shortcomings as opportunities to learn from mistakes, and to do better the next time. Many creative professions work in iterative processes, trial and error, constantly fine tuning until a project is the best it can be. Parallel mimics this process. Students can be successful playing the game, but they can always be better, score higher, have more positive outcomes.

Parallel tie-in. Parallel is a low-stakes game. It is meant to be fun, first and foremost, and it carries its set of challenges, but in the end, when the time runs out, and the last round is played, it is still just a game. The disappointment in not finishing a project, or outscoring their previous Cred total can serve as motivation to learn from falling short and achieving a greater outcome next time.

2.3   Game Characters and How They Relate to Real World

At the beginning of the game, students will draw a random character card. Each card represents a fictional character who has different abilities and traits. The traits of each character can be used and combined with other character cards, and together they can work through solving problems. The character cards, outlined below, demonstrate the abilities:

Hawk. Ability: Farsight. Getting out there comes easy to Hawk. He travels for adventure and adventures lead to great photo ops. Being able to see what's coming next is more than protection, it helps those around you.

Hawk is similar to the student who seems to have good intuition. They have the ability to see in unique ways that offer a different perspective, and have a strong sense of empathy for their peers.

Red. Ability: Transference. Red's all about connecting others with what they need to get things done. For her, creative problem solving starts with getting the right people together. That's when the magic happens.

Red is like the student who always has a positive outlook, always with rose-colored glasses, always glass-half-full. They want to help and find a solution to problems.

Helix. Ability: Etherspeak. Everyone who travels the Etherspace knows about Helix. She's a legend. Hacking, coding, sleuthing, it's all in a day's work. She uses her talents to aid others and knows how to get things done.

Helix is like the student who has an uncanny grasp of technology, who picks up the language of html with ease, and can envision translating that coded language into a visual one.

Cleo. Ability: Asymmetry. Fashion, style, perspective, Cleo has it all. She's a little obsessed with handmade objects, things that require a sense of craft and commitment to make. If that's you too, Cleo's already your friend.

Cleo is like the crafty art student. They are sensitive to style and aesthetics, care about patterns and colors, and are often perfectionists.

Kiryn. Ability: Signature Dish. Kiryn's love of cooking informs her perspective. She doesn't just follow recipes, she invents. From tracking down unique ingredients to taste-testing everything, Kiryn knows what hard work is.

Not all students are ace mathematicians, or poetic writers, or even creative illustrators, some have a passion for food, for experimenting with recipes, making the perfect dish—these students have a lot in common with Kiryn.

Jasper. Ability: Wildcard. Keep everyone guessing, that's Jasper's motto. Jasper embraces risks and chance happenings. He makes the most of dire situations. Oh, and he's been known to laugh in the face of danger.

Students like Jasper have a happy-go-lucky spirit to them, they look for positives in poor situations and shine when they are in the spotlight.

Friday. Ability: Dark Spark. Friday's learned to face the Hollow by embracing a little darkness of her own. Some of Friday's rainy-day hobbies include preserving dead flowers, reading gloomy poetry books, and drawing spiders.

Some students seem sad or withdrawn, sometimes they are, but sometimes they are just the shy type, the types who are deep and quiet thinkers, who work out problems and ideas in their own ways.

2.4   Game Play

Ages ago, an all-consuming force of nothingness known as **The Hollow** invaded the world of Parallel. As it spread, so did fear, anger, and mistrust. Something had to be done.

A girl named Ehm was the first to stand against this threat. With her creative energy and desire to help others, she proved the Hollow could be resisted.

While the people of Parallel haven't found a way to destroy the Hollow, they know it can be repelled using the one thing they all possess – **Creative Spark**.

Objective. Use Spark to complete Projects which help the people of Parallel. Build your network with supporters who can assist your efforts.

Watch out for the Hollow and its minions. Work as a team to stop it from spreading and destroying your creations.

Goal. Score **Credibility Points (Cred)** as a team. The game lasts for 10 rounds. Survive the Hollow and achieve the highest score possible. After 10 rounds tally your Cred score.

2.5   The Cards

While each card is different in terms of its use, all cards have some common areas to make note of, as seen in Fig. 4.

During the game, players will link cards in order to complete Projects and gain benefits. There are four types of link icons to watch for, as seen in Figs. 5, 6, 7 and 8.

There are three main ways to work together during the game to survive the Hollow and gain the highest score.

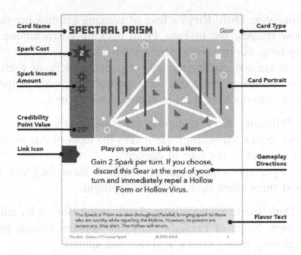

Fig. 4. Card diagram. While each card is different in terms of its use, all cards have some common areas to make note of.

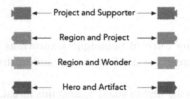

Fig. 5. During the game, players will link cards in order to complete Projects and gain benefits. There are four types of link icons to watch for.

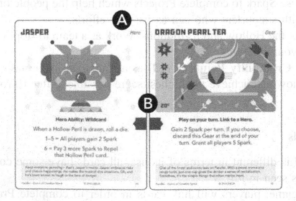

Fig. 6. Example 1: **A.** A Hero is linked to a piece of Gear. The Gear card is played on the table directly next to the Hero so that the two link icons connect. **B.** As long as this Gear is linked to the Hero, the player benefits from the bonuses provided by the Gear.

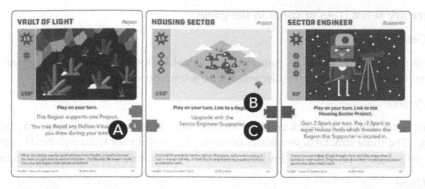

Fig. 7. Example 2: **A**. Regions link to Projects and Wonders. In this case, *Vault of Light* can only link to one Project. No other Projects can be added. **B**. Projects link to Supporters. The *Sector Engineer* is adding benefits to the player as long as it's linked. **C**. This project link icon cannot be used because only one Project can be connected to the *Vault of Light*.

Fig. 8. Example 3: **A**. Wonder cards can be linked to Regions to boost their value. Wonders are placed between the Project cards. **B**. Watch for the number of Projects each Region supports (In this case, one). **C**. IF more Projects can be linked to a Region, they are added here. Supporters are placed between the Project cards.

1. Giving cards

Increasing your Spark income *as a team* is a key way to succeed at repelling Hollow cards. Giving cards to other players that you cannot use OR that they could make better use of, is very important.

2. Sharing Spark

Each player has a Spark Meter of their own. But sometimes, one of your team members may need your help. Share your Spark to give others a boost. This could make a big difference when Hollow cards are drawn.

3. Use Hero abilities

Remember to use your Hero's abilities! These can be easy to overlook as cards are drawn and played, and as Spark Meters are adjusted. Each Hero's ability is geared towards helping the team. When these are used, the team will not only survive, but do great things!

There are seven types of cards in the game

1. *Gear*

These cards can be linked to your Hero for valuable benefits that last throughout the game. Gear cards can also be discarded for onetime benefits.

2. *Project*

Projects are built using Spark and they're the main way to score points at the end of the game. The more structures you build, the more successful your team will be. However, you will need to protect your Projects from the Hollow too. Use your Spark carefully.

3. *Quest*

You may attempt to complete these optional objectives, which will greatly increase your score if you succeed. But be careful not to stray from your main objective – completing Projects.

4. *Region*

Regions provide places to build Projects. In fact, Projects cannot be completed without them.

5. *Supporter*

These characters will help you in your efforts to build Projects. They will also assist you in repelling the Hollow and its minions.

6. *Wonder*

Wonders expand the value of Regions and provide you with added bonuses during the game.

7. *Hollow*

Hollow cards present challenges for individual players or the team as a whole.

3 Teaching Empathy to the Users

Introducing creative problem solving to an underserved audience was one big goal for Parallel. The other goal was that students could tie in their real-life problems with the fictional game play, and use what was learned during game play into solving some of those issues. To help facilitate conversation following game play, the team created a teachers' guide to help direct the teacher or facilitator into leading discussions relevant to what was happening in and around their community.

The topics the team addressed were social, environmental, economic, health, and political. Ideally, students and teachers together would use design thinking and creative problem solving to actively solve community-wide problems. It would be the goal of the facilitator to select one or two topics and discuss how some of these problems could be solved using teamwork, empathy, and creative problem solving, as learned in Parallel.

Education. As high schoolers, students may face some issues with the education they are getting. *This is by no means an attack on education professionals*, but an understanding of the harsh reality that is facing our schools; the cutting of the arts, the lack of updated teaching materials, and a never-ending barrage of standardized tests. Our high school students may not have had adequate access to reading & literacy in their schools at a younger age – or at home. As schools are fighting budget problems, our technology often goes to the wayside, too.

Teachers are then prompted:
When introducing this topic to your students, some starting discussion topics are recommended:

a. Encouraging reading & literacy
b. Expanding access to technology
c. Raising awareness around the benefits of the arts for children/parents

A discussion prompt, specific to this game, may be linked to:
Character: Helix or Red.
Region: Etherspace
Project: Reading Habitat
Supporter: Tome Keeper
Theme: Better Community Spaces

Project: Etherspace Academy
Supporter: Tech Wizard
Theme: Disrupting notion of schools as the only place to gain skills

Project: Tech Access Station
Supporter: Station Controller
Theme: Expanding access to the net

Community. High school students likely have a complicated sense of community, and they may not have any idea that they can, or how to, make a difference in that community. Their community may be embarrassing to them. They may have had to move from community to community. They may not even feel a sense of community.

Teachers are then prompted:
When introducing this topic to your students, some starting discussion topics are recommended:

a. Making vacant and rundown properties useful again
b. Helping underserved communities with financial well-being
c. Providing housing for different family structures
d. Assisting with recovery after natural disasters
e. Encouraging community involvement
f. Improving neighborhood safety
g. Bridging racial issues and conflicts
h. Inclusion/exclusion

A discussion prompt, specific to this game, may be linked to:
Character: Digit (ID-8) - Street poet, writer, and reader of tags.
Region: Axiom
Project: Reading Habitat
Supporter: Tome Keeper
Theme: Better Community Spaces

Project: Housing Sector
Supporter: Sector Engineer
Theme: Sustainable Housing

Project: Animal Shelter
Supporter: Mender
Theme: Providing care to wildlife and pets in need

Environment. This is a topic that some high schoolers may have some background on, but it's probably not a lot, and may even seem so "big picture", that they don't see how they can make an impact. Our future revolves around this generation caring about the environment. They need to understand the importance of becoming good stewards of the planet.

Teachers are then prompted:
When introducing this topic to your students, some starting discussion topics are recommended:

a. Promoting sustainable energy
b. Reducing dependence on fossil fuels

A discussion prompt, specific to this game, may be linked to:
Character: Hawk - Eye spy, wanderer, and explorer of out-of-the-way places.
Region: Vault of Lights
Project: Renewable Energy Nodes
Supporter: Node Controller
Theme: More efficient energy consumption

Project: Clean Water Pylons
Supporter: Pylon Controller
Theme: Clean water for everyone

Project: Housing Sector
Supporter: Sector Engineer
Theme: Sustainable housing

Politics. Politics play a crucial role in all citizens' lives, whether they be old or young, religious or non, rich or poor, black, white, Hispanic or any number of ethnicities. It's well known that the youth of America don't participate in the electoral process like other demographics, but this doesn't mean they don't care or lack interest. Students are very attuned to the issues facing the world, the country, and their own lives, but they feel disenfranchised. We, as their teachers and mentors, can help focus their frustration into action.

Teachers are then prompted:
When introducing this topic to your students, some starting discussion topics are recommended:

a. Informing the public of their rights
b. Participating in the electoral and policy process
c. Investigating politics on the local level

A discussion prompt, specific to this game, may be linked to:
Character: Red - Artifactor, design hero, and part-time writer of fictions.
Region: Forest of Ehm
Project: All projects within Parallel affect all the citizens of Parallel, any of the projects can be taken with a political tinge.
Theme: Government representation for those from all walks of life

Health. Access to healthcare and nutritional food options are issues that face all communities, but are magnified in poor communities, due to the lack of grocery stores, medical centers, and affordable treatment. This is a very broad topic, and the aspect of access to healthcare may be a challenging entry point for young and healthy students, but approaching the subject as a way to discuss and tackle issues surrounding food, water, exercise, addictions, and personal well-being can provide more accessible discussion.

Teachers are then prompted:
When introducing this topic to your students, some starting discussion topics are recommended:

a. Increasing access to healthy foods
b. Providing clean water to all
c. Providing knowledge & resources to victims of domestic violence
d. Encouraging exercising and personal well-being
e. Addictions (drugs, alcohol, gambling, addictive personalities, technology)

A discussion prompt, specific to this game, may be linked to:
Character: Kiryn - Gourmet, food adventurer, and master of tasting things.
Region: The Alt Sea
Project: Sky Garden
Supporter: Arborist
Theme: Promoting healthy foods

Project: Clean Water Pylons
Supporter: Pylon Controller
Theme: Clean water for everyone

Business. Students are incredibly creative and resourceful. Many of the topics discussed prior to this point will spark ideas for solutions in the students' minds, some, if not many of those ideas could become business concepts that could do good for their community. Often, successful business is attributed to those with an "entrepreneurial spirit", and a lack of business knowledge is seen as an insurmountable hurdle. We can encourage all students that their ideas have value, and that with the right direction and knowledge, they can be successful in bringing their business ideas to the public.

Teachers are then prompted:
When introducing this topic to your students, some starting discussion topics are recommended:

a. Promoting "local first"
b. Increasing knowledge sharing for small businesses and start-ups
c. Promoting diversity in the workplace

A discussion prompt, specific to this game, may be linked to:
Character: Cleo - Thread maven, fashion maker, and stylist of the individual
Region: The Netherway
Project: Apprenticeship Circle
Supporter: Polymath
Theme: Helping the youth of Parallel gain skills and business knowledge

Project: Enterpriser's District
Supporter: Visionary
Theme: Resources for small businesses

Project: Etherspace Academy
Supporter: Tech Wizard
Theme: Disrupting notion of schools as the only place to gain skills

Project: Tech Access Station
Supporter: Station Controller
Theme: Expanding access to the net

3.1   User Testing and Recommendations for Changes

Overall Parallel has been well received. The team has presented the game in beta form at several educational conferences and the game has been user tested by a variety of people of all ages and backgrounds. The game is currently being finalized for distribution to underserved high schools all across the United States. Comments received during the user testing were, "The game was fun and I enjoyed the teamwork aspect," "I felt success was tied to how well we worked together." Card sizing, the number of cards distributed at the very beginning of game play, vocabulary adjustments, and the balance of the types of cards were changes made after several rounds of user testing. For Parallel, the audience is students and educators. In testing, we were particularly listening for *how the game makes people feel as they play*. This is important because those impressions may or may not contribute to good conversations with teachers, and that is something we need to facilitate.

Ideally this game is one that people will keep coming back to play over and over. Parallel can be developed further and extension packs with new, updated characters and new projects can be created as necessary.

4 Conclusion

Our findings from the multiple rounds of user testing show that Parallel–The Game of Creative Spark does exactly what was intended: it teaches design thinking in the form of team building. Users communicated to us after the game play that they felt connected to their characters and that they enjoyed the experience of working with one another.

Our research has shown that games are a wonderful outlet for learning. Allowing students to use team building and design thinking to help solve problems in a universe parallel to that of their own will hopefully open their eyes to how they can work together to solve existing problems in their everyday lives. If students do not see the initial connection, it is the goal that the educator's prompted discussion questions help address those concerns.

After the final prototype of the game is complete, the game will be sent off to all AIGA Chapters in the United States (The Professional Association for Design). Each AIGA Chapter is then responsible for seeking their own geographic and socioeconomic areas where this game could be played. We will provide recommended outlets for each state in the teachers' guide, which will be sent along with the game.

The people of Parallel will never be free of the Hollow. It's a force of nothingness and negativity. It'll never be destroyed, only resisted. Just like real-life, students will face negativity in many forms. Parallel–The Game of Creative Spark tries to encourage creative problem solving and energy – in a way that students see that they have the ability to work together to make change.

References

1. Ross, R.: Diversity in Graphic Design. https://pulsevcu.wordpress.com/2012/10/22/diversity-in-graphic-design-rodney-ross/. Accessed 17 Feb 2019
2. Oxford Dictionaries. https://en.oxforddictionaries.com/definition/play. Accessed 17 Feb 2019
3. Kumar, J., Herger, M., Dam, R.: A Brief History of Games. Interaction Design Foundation. https://www.interaction-design.org/literature/article/a-brief-history-of-games. Accessed 17 Feb 2019
4. Englebright Fox, J.: Back-to-basics: play in early childhood, early childhood news. In: The Professional Resource for Teachers and Parents. Excellence Learning Corporation (2007)
5. Kaufman, G., Flanagan, M.: A psychologically "embedded" approach to designing games for prosocial causes. Cyberpsychol. J. Psychosoc. Res. Cyberspace. http://dx.doi.org/10.5817/CP2015-3-5. Accessed 17 Feb 2019

6. Granic, I., Lobel, A., Engels, R.: The benefits of playing video games. Am. Psychol. **69**(1), 66–78 (2014)
7. Granic, I.: Video Games Play May Provide Learning, Health, Social Benefit Review Finds. American Psychological Association. https://www.apa.org/news/press/releases/2013/11/video-games. Accessed 17 Feb 2019
8. Niederhelman, M.: Design Issues, vol. 17, no. 3 (Summer, 2001), 83
9. Gardner, H.: A Multiplicity of Intelligences: In Tribute to Professor Luigi Vignolo. Scientific American, p. 4
10. Gardner, H.: A Multiplicity of Intelligences: In Tribute to Professor Luigi Vignolo. Scientific American, p. 5
11. Gardner, H.: A Multiplicity of Intelligences: In Tribute to Professor Luigi Vignolo. Scientific American, p. 6
12. Dewey, J.: Education as a necessity of life. In: Democracy and Education. http://www.ilt.columbia.edu/Publications/Projects/digitexts/dewey/d_e/chapter01.html. Accessed 17 Feb 2019
13. Project Based Learning. Using Multiple Intelligences. http://pblchecklist.4teachers.org/intell.shtml. Accessed 17 Feb 2019
14. Snyder, L.G., Snyder, M.J.: Teaching critical thinking and problem-solving skills. Delta Pi Epsilon J. **50**(2), 30 (2008)
15. Dewey, J.: Experience and Education, vol. 10. The Macmillan Company, New York (1938)
16. IDEO Design Kit. Resources. http://www.designkit.org/resources/1. Accessed 17 Feb 2019

From UX to Engagement: Connecting Theory and Practice, Addressing Ethics and Diversity

Ole Goethe[1]([⊠]), Kavous Salehzadeh Niksirat[2,3],
Ilyena Hirskyj-Douglas[4], Huatong Sun[5],
Effie L.-C. Law[6], and Xiangshi Ren[2]([⊠])

[1] Kristiania University, Oslo, Norway
ole.goethe@kristiania.no
[2] Kochi University of Technology, Kochi, Japan
xsren@acm.org
[3] École Polytechnique Fédérale de Lausanne, Lausanne, Switzerland
kavous.salehzadehniksirat@epfl.ch
[4] Aalto University, Helsinki, Finland
ilyena.hirskyj-douglas@aalto.fi
[5] University of Washington Tacoma, Tacoma, WA, USA
htsun@uw.edu
[6] University of Leicester, Leicester, UK
lcl9@leicester.ac.uk

Abstract. In the field of Human-Computer Interaction (HCI), engagement bears critical significance, not just for informing a design and implementation of the interface, but also for creating improved and advanced interfaces that can adapt to users. While the idea of user engagement is passively being researched in a range of domains, it has been used to various related but diverse concepts. For instance, engagement is the vital element of an effective HCI design. The primary goal of this paper is to introduce relevant research questions related to the engagement domain. The paper studies engagement from four different perspectives: (i) Theory: identifying key issues that aid in building a pluralism of engagement frameworks, (ii) Practice: developing novel methodologies for user engagement and reliable assessment tools, (iii) Ethics: discussing the ethical aspects of engagement especially for designers and developers of humane technologies, (iv) Diversity: investigating individual differences to develop personalized engaging designs and understanding user diversities to provide equal opportunities for user engagement. The discussion will lead to opportunities for the potential researchers to acquire relevant knowledge, assess the mechanisms of engagement and evaluate the current design frameworks.

Keywords: Engagement · Frameworks · User experience · User interface · Ethics · User diversity · Human-Engaged Computing

1 Introduction

Understanding engagement is a multidisciplinary and interdisciplinary challenge for many technology researchers and designers, a kind of profound knowledge they all seek for. The term engagement itself has been applied in diverse settings, from

© Springer Nature Switzerland AG 2019
M. Antona and C. Stephanidis (Eds.): HCII 2019, LNCS 11572, pp. 91–99, 2019.
https://doi.org/10.1007/978-3-030-23560-4_7

games [1] to social networks [2] to the academic arena [3]. Engagement happens in the utmost complexity of the virtual worlds, but also in a simplicity of the text-based communication.

As stated by Ren [4], "engagement is the state of consciousness where a user is completely immersed in and involved in the activity at hand". At present, HCI researchers and developers have been designing and inventing technologies that engage users for diverse purposes. Engaging users is significant for designers of different products and services of every kind, where a lack of engagement can diminish the efficiency and meaningfulness of interaction between users and technologies. This need to understand users' experiences has motivated a focus on user engagement across computer science. However, to date, there has been limited reviews of how HCI and computer science research interprets and employs the engagement concept. Questions persist concerning its conception, abstraction, and measurement [5].

Engagement is necessary to maintain the meaningfulness and efficiency of the interaction occurring between computers and users. However, engaging/disengaging users with/from technologies is an arduous and potentially a counterproductive endeavor. It can be challenging when a lot of users stop being 'in' the interaction after a few trails out of frustration due to its poor design or absence of motivation. Stopping the interaction means the user seeks for alternative ways to serve their purposes becoming engaged elsewhere. In addition, the ability to be engaged can be hindered upon a user's diverse cognitive and physical differences where they are unable to use a system or technology properly such is the case with very young children. In contrast, other users cannot stop using technology, finding themselves addicted to it impacting their day-to-day life (e.g. gaming and internet addiction [6]). This disequilibrium in the engagement between the computers and users may result from a need of understanding engagement and it could have critical consequences on general well-being of societies. This is even more so the case in diverse use cases, where further reflection is needed to extrapolate the term and involvement with engagement. For instance, the UK government has been pondering upon bringing in new legislations around technologies for children following the French policy to ban smartphones in schools.

This article addresses the challenges of this concept by determining key factors that help development of engagement frameworks (theories), novel approaches to user engagement and effective assessment techniques (practice), ethical considerations (ethics) and individual differences to meet user diversity and provide equal opportunities to all users, including those belonging to minority backgrounds (diversity).

2 Related Work

Engagement is a multifaceted concept that includes both engaged interactions on a micro level and engaged human-technology relations on the macro level. Here micro level is related to the interaction design while macro level has broader perspective about general relationship between human and computer. Research on the micro level often follows "an interaction paradigm" whilst exploration on the macro level tends to adopt "a practice paradigm" [7]. With tech and computing products evolution for many objectives, engagement incorporated "user" next to it. For example, in video games, the user engagement is taken as a preceding stage to presence and immersion [8]. Van Vugt et al. [9] has later assessed engagement with the virtual reality by gauging it as a concept between the distance and involvement. In various other fields such as the development and use of information systems, the user engagement also consists of a sense of involvement, both physically and cognitively [10]. To provide a more nuanced answer to Shneiderman's call that "much work [needs] to be done" to connect macro-HCI and micro-HCI practices [11], Sun approaches engagement from the junction of macro-HCI and micro-HCI with global social media design cases [12]. Here the macro-HCI practice refers to critical design considerations such as agency, identity, values, ideology, structure, power, dominance, and hegemony on a macrosocial level to achieve *engagement* and *empowerment*. The micro-HCI practice refers to design implementations to achieve *efficiency, effectiveness*, and some aspects of *engagement*, with a focus on concrete tasks and different modes of interactions. From the communication and media perspective, macro vs. micro also is associated with the structuration process [13].

Engagement has been considered as an emotional [14], behavioral [15] and cognitive [16] association between computer and the end-user. On the other hand, O'Brien and Toms [17] associated engagement with resilience, challenge, and perceived control by the user. Additionally, engagement has also been related to gratification [18] and visual appeal [19]. Besides, there are also studies that considered engagement beyond User Experience (UX) qualities. For instance, beside the hedonic aspect of engagement (i.e., related to pleasure), Lukoff et al. [20] emphasize the eudemonic aspect of engagement (i.e. related to self-actualization and fulfillment) to study the meaningfulness of engagement.

Lastly, Ren [4] proposed the Human-Engaged Computing (HEC) framework. HEC is a study of the synergized interaction between humans and computers, as well as phenomena around the interaction. It encompasses all aspects of interactions between and within humans and technologies [21]. HEC targets the enhancement of the synergy between humans and technologies through leveraging engagement. HEC demonstrated a holistic view to understand engagement to apply it into interaction design for enhancing human inner capabilities including human softer skills such as mindfulness, focus, creativity, empathy, and self-regulation [22].

As the above conversation denotes, engagement is a multifaceted identity, involving aspects of user experience, physical and cognitive functions, user perceptions and synergism. However, there are many facets of engagement that remain unclear, and yet, there are open questions that need to be addressed.

3 Open Questions on Engagement

The primary goal of this paper is to introduce relevant research questions and future research directions related to the engagement domain. To this end, we review engagement from different angles such as by connecting theory and practice and to address design issues of ethics and diversity concerning technology engagement. These elements chosen to overlap the above mention topics being applicable to all facets (see Fig. 1).

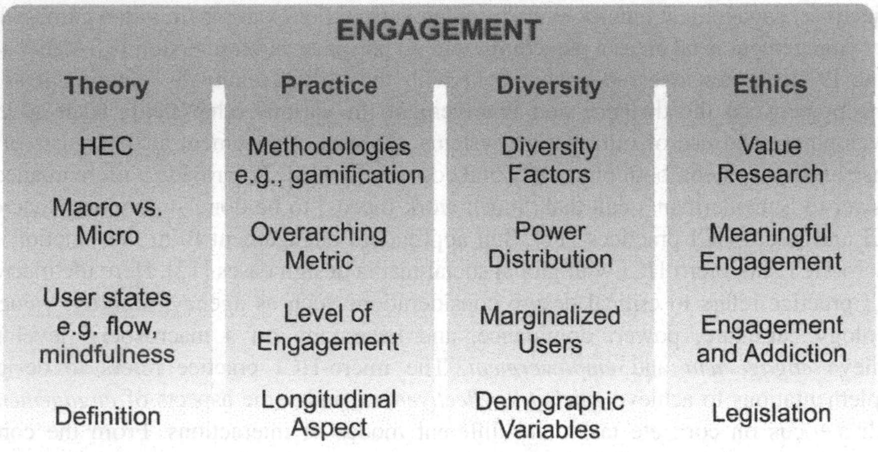

ENGAGEMENT

Theory	Practice	Diversity	Ethics
HEC	Methodologies e.g., gamification	Diversity Factors	Value Research
Macro vs. Micro	Overarching Metric	Power Distribution	Meaningful Engagement
User states e.g. flow, mindfulness	Level of Engagement	Marginalized Users	Engagement and Addiction
Definition	Longitudinal Aspect	Demographic Variables	Legislation

Fig. 1. Open questions on engagement.

3.1 Theory

Traditional HCI considers engagement as the number of clicks, the amount of time a user spent with a product, or even as an affective user state. Despite the traditional perspective, here we see engagement as a holistic consideration of interacting with technology, where it emphasizes the meaningfulness of the interaction, values that technology can add to users, and the longer-term benefits that users can get from technology. However, it is not always clear what terms like 'meaningful' mean to the various users; especially within the diverse user space [23]. Therefore, we need to think about identifying key issues that aid in building a pluralism of engagement frameworks [4]. Thus, we pose these following queries:

- How existing theories or philosophies can be integrated to deepen the understanding of human engagement?
- How the relationships between different aspects of human experiences such as emotion, cognition, behavior, and consciousness should be reframed into frameworks for engagement?
- How should we reconcile different understandings of engagement across the macro and micro levels?
- How should we understand the state of "engaged human" through well-known user states such as flow state (i.e., absorption in the task) or mindful state (i.e., being aware of the present moment)?

3.2 Practice

Developing novel practical techniques and methodologies for engaged users and providing reliable metrics for assessing engagement are highly required. Accordingly, we are interested in following questions:

- How can the existing methodologies in HCI (e.g. Gamification, Persuasive Design) be reframed to develop novel engaging methodologies?
- How to evaluate engagement by proposing an overarching metric that included various facets of engagement (behavior, emotion, cognition, consciousness)? And, how different measurement methodologies such as usage and performance metrics (e.g. experience sampling method, gaze tracking), psychophysiological measurements (e.g. EEG, skin conductivity), and qualitative metrics (e.g. questionnaire, interview) can support the mentioned engagement dimensions?
- How to develop a new metric that can assess engagement from the observable level (i.e., usage metric) to more experiential level (i.e., absorption, immersion), and to the extreme level (i.e., addiction)?
- What is the longitudinal aspect of engagement? How can we evaluate engagement from the perspective of further effects of engagement on a person's life (e.g., decision making) rather than UX level?

3.3 Ethics

Public attention to ethical technology design is on the rise. As technologies hijack the human mind [24] and displease users [25], social initiatives such as Time Well Spent [26] have emerged, and different studies [19, 20, 27] have been conducted to mitigate the perceived detrimental effects of technologies. This detrimental effect has been coined 'dark patterns' in UX/Interaction Design. However, there is still limited work to explore ethical design issues from the aspect of engagement, and it is still critical to raising awareness among researchers, designers, and end users. Here, we see a conflict of interest between overall social good and revenue-driven businesses. Therefore, we would emphasize "ethics for designers and developers", where the people involved within the end-product need to take more responsibility regarding the technologies during design and even after shipping the product.

- How previous theories and studies in Value Research and Value Sensitive Design can be linked to engagement proposing ethics guidelines for designers in this area?
- Is treating engagement as either a meaningful or meaningless approach appropriate? What are the criteria for these categorizations and how are these measured, especially with diverse users? And indeed, is this something that needs to be measured?
- How can engagement lead to addiction? And, what are the solutions that can promote mindful, voluntary engagement? (e.g., design frictions [19])
- Should the tech industry, similar to the pharmaceutical industry, require obtaining an approval before releasing a product in the market? What are the opportunities and threats of such legislation?
- What are the ethical dimensions of engagement that should be the focused upon, beyond responsibility?

3.4 Diversity

Whilst Niksirat et al. [28] have already demonstrated that individuals' experiences such as flow state highly differ based on various factors like gender or culture, there is still much more variables that have not been investigated. Designing for the diverse users and domains focuses design for specific classes of specialized users and these all classes include sub-classes of children, adults, elderly and individuals having cognitive, visual, physical and hearing impairments [29]. The user diversity is further extended to industries like games, healthcare and aerospace. The solutions are being designed in view of addressing user diversity since it has become a core factor to ensure effective engagement. To recognize diversity, the designer considers the kind of user frequenting the system, ranging from different skill levels, to users from diverse backgrounds and different skill sets and abilities. Every kind of user expects the interaction with the technology to accommodate their wants and desires; novice and physically/mentally impaired users possibly needing more structured guidance and specialized technologies, while experts need speed and more advanced options. Accommodating both these styles on the same page is challenging but important to address diversity within this space.

However, by looking at what engagement means for diverse users this force typical assumptions that we hold, such as meaning behind engagement and their typical measurements, to be questioned [30]. This questioning includes both what a user values, and how we know what a user values, and the best way to quantify and scope engagement. By looking at the interchange between these methods, ethics and the interchangeability between diverse users this can bring new understanding into HCI and wider associations [31]. As such, engagement here is not about labeling the user with the formed appellation but instead growing the terminology upon what engagement is through these different perspectives, and how we design for this towards diversity being inherently a preposition.

Thus, engagement for diversity can be considered from two points of view. First, studying the effect of individual characteristics such as age, gender, expertise, and personality on engagement can help researchers for developing personalized engaging technologies [32]. Second, addressing issues regarding the accessibility and meaning of engagement for users from different cultures, ethnicities, socio-economic status can help designers to reach their product to the wider audience, while it can also offer more power to users from relatively deprived communities.

- What individual differences could affect people's engagement with computing technologies? How can we tailor the design to users considering their unique characteristics?
- How can we create technologies that both provide access to marginalized users and allow opportunities for them to engage? What are the current hindrances? And what have we been doing?
- What are the different considerations between engagement and empowerment in this case?
- How do demographic variables such as language and income level can affect the engagement? And how can we tackle those barriers to move beyond this?
- When including and engaging diverse users, what are the safeguards in place to both regulate and allow for engagement?

4 Raising Awareness

Technology is a double-edged sword. While increasingly pervasive technologies create unlimited opportunities for a better quality of life, their domination can cause a disruptive effect on societies. This could be in form of depression after excessive use of social media (i.e., hyper connectivity) [33] or lack of focus after getting too many smartphone distractions [34]. In addition, recent tech scandals have raised serious concerns about the abuse of technology (e.g., a couple was raising a virtual child in an online game that they neglected their baby leaving her to starve to death) [35]. This article aims to raise awareness about challenges that researchers should attack for the future design to develop healthy, meaningful, and safe engagement.

5 Conclusion

This article provides a grounding for the interpretation and measurement of engagement across HCI in terms of theory, practice, ethics, and human diversity, which may allow us to fret less about what engagement 'is' and to instead focus on the value it provides to diverse users. We have examined the theoretical grounding of definitions of engagement and located these interpretations within an HCI, and interaction. The conception of engagement is very often tied to measurement, and so we suggest instead to examine the choice of subjective and objective measures and motivations for their adoption. By individuating strategies for the design of engaging user experiences, we aim towards identifying opportunities for employing the concept within modern design projects. Finally, we annotate the areas for future work, as well as current trends across the engagement literature based on previous works related to user diversity in HCI settings.

References

1. Cheung, G.K., Zimmermann, T., Nagappan, N.: The first hour experience: how the initial play can engage (or lose) new players. In: Proceedings of the First ACM SIGCHI Annual Symposium on Computer-Human Interaction in Play, pp. 57–66 (2014)
2. Freyne, J., Jacovi, M., Guy, I., Geyer, W.: Increasing engagement through early recommender intervention. In: Proceedings of the 3rd ACM Conference on Recommender Systems, pp. 85–92 (2009)
3. Jacques, R.: Engagement as a design concept for multimedia. Can. J. Educ. Commun. 24, 49–59 (1995)
4. Ren, X.: Rethinking the relationship between humans and computers. IEEE Comput. 49(8), 104–108 (2016)
5. Doherty, K., Doherty, G.: Engagement in HCI: conception, theory and measurement. ACM Comput. Surv. 51, 1–39 (2018)
6. Ng, B.D., Wiemer-Hastings, P.: Addiction to the internet and online gaming. Cyberpsychol. Behav. 8(2), 110–113 (2005)

7. Kuutti, K., Bannon, L.J.: The turn to practice in HCI: towards a research agenda. In: Proceedings of the 32nd Annual ACM Conference on Human Factors in Computing Systems, pp. 3543–3552. ACM (2014)
8. Brown, E., Cairns, P.A.: A grounded investigation of game immersion. In: CHI Extended Abstracts, pp. 1297–1300 (2004)
9. Van Vugt, H.C., Konijn, E.A., Hoorn, J.F., Keur, I., Eliëns, A.: Realism is not all! User engagement with task related interface characters. Interact. Comput. 19(2), 267–280 (2007)
10. Kappelman, L., McLean, E.R.: User engagement in the development, implementation, and use of information technologies. In: Proceedings of the Twenty-Seventh Hawaii International Conference on System Sciences, 1994, vol. 4, pp. 512–521. IEEE (1994)
11. Shneiderman, B.: Claiming success, charting the future: micro-HCI and macro-HCI. Interactions 18(5), 10–11 (2011)
12. Sun, H.: Global Social Media Design: Bridging Differences Across Cultures. Oxford University Press, New York, 11 (in print)
13. Giddens, A.: The Constitution of Society. University of California Press, Berkeley (1984)
14. Laurel, B.: Computers as Theatre. Addison-Wesley, Boston (2013)
15. Attfield, et al.: Towards a science of user engagement (position paper). In: WSDM Workshop on User Modelling for Web Applications, pp. 9–12 (2011)
16. Chapman, P.M.: Models of engagement: intrinsically motivated interaction with multimedia learning software. Ph.D. Dissertation. University of Waterloo (1997)
17. O'Brien, H.L., Toms, E.G.: What is user engagement? A conceptual framework for defining user engagement with technology. J. Am. Soc. Inf. Sci. Technol. 59(6), 938–955 (2008)
18. O'Brien, H.L.: The influence of hedonic and utilitarian motivations on user engagement: the case of online shopping experiences. Interact. Comput. 22(5), 344–352 (2010)
19. Cox, A.L., et al.: Design frictions for mindful interactions: the case for micro boundaries. In: Proceedings of the CHI Conference, pp. 1389–1397. ACM (2016)
20. Lukoff, K., Yu, C., Kientz, J., Hiniker, A.: What makes smartphone use meaningful or meaningless? In: Proceedings of the ACM on Interactive, Mobile, Wearable and Ubiquitous Technologies, vol. 2, no. 1, p. 22 (2018)
21. Law, L.-C.E., Silpasuwanchai, C., Ren, X., Bardzell, J., Clemmensen, T., Liu, Y.: Leveraging and integrating eastern and western insights for human engagement studies in HCI. In: Proceedings of the 33rd Annual ACM Conference Extended Abstracts on Human Factors in Computing Systems, pp. 2433–2436. ACM (2015)
22. Salehzadeh Niksirat, K., Silpasuwanchai, C., Mohamed Hussien Ahmed, M., Cheng, P., Ren, X.: A Framework for interactive mindfulness meditation using attention-regulation process. In: Proceedings of the 2017 CHI Conference on Human Factors in Computing Systems, pp. 2672–2684. ACM (2017)
23. Hirskyj-Douglas, I., Read, J.C.: The ethics of how to work with dogs in animal computer interaction. In: Symposium on Animal-Computer Interaction. Proceedings Measuring Behaviour, vol. 16, pp. 434–439 (2016)
24. Eyal, N.: Hooked: How to Build Habit-Forming Products. Penguin, London (2014)
25. Rainie, L., Smith, A., Duggan, M.: Coming and going on Facebook. Pew Research Center's Internet and American Life Project (2013)
26. Harris, T.: Time Well Spent (2018). Retrieved from http://humanetech.com
27. Mark, G., Czerwinski, M., Iqbal, T.S.: Effects of individual differences in blocking workplace distractions. In: Proceedings of the CHI Conference on Human Factors in Computing Systems, p. 92. ACM (2018)
28. Salehzadeh Niksirat, K., Park, K., Silpasuwanchai, C., Wang, Z., Ren, X.: The relationship between flow proneness in everyday life and variations in the volume of gray matter in the dopaminergic system: a cross-sectional study. Personal. Individ. Differ. 141, 25–30 (2019)

29. Peters, C., Asteriadis, S., Karpouzis, K., de Sevin, E.: Towards a real-time gaze-based shared attention for a virtual agent. In: International Conference on Multimodal Interfaces (ICMI), Workshop on Affective Interaction in Natural Environments (AFFINE), Chania, Crete (2008)
30. Hirskyj-Douglas, I., Lucero, A.: On the internet, nobody knows you're a dog... unless you're another dog. In: CHI Conference on Human Factors in Computing Systems Proceedings at CHI (2019)
31. Hirskyj-Douglas, I., Read, J.C., Juhlin, O., Väätäjä, H., Pons, P., Hvasshovd, S.O.: Where HCI meets ACI. In: Proceedings of the 9th Nordic Conference on Human-Computer Interaction, p. 136. ACM (2016)
32. Kulev, I., Pu, P., Faltings, B.: A Bayesian approach to intervention-based clustering. ACM Trans. Intell. Syst. Technol. (TIST) **9**, 4 (2018)
33. De Choudhury, M., Counts, S., Horvitz, E.: Social media as a measurement tool of depression in populations. In: Proceedings of the 5th Annual ACM Web Science Conference, pp. 47–56. ACM (2013)
34. Westermann, T., Möller, S., Wechsung, I.: Assessing the relationship between technical affinity, stress and notifications on smartphones. In: Proceedings of the 17th International Conference on Human-Computer Interaction with Mobile Devices and Services Adjunct, pp. 652–659. ACM (2015)
35. The Guardian: Girl starved to death while parents raised virtual child in online game (2010). Retrieved from https://theguardian.com/world/2010/mar/05/korean-girl-starved-online-game

Universal Access: The Challenges Ahead

Simeon Keates(✉)

Edinburgh Napier University, 10 Colinton Rd, Edinburgh EH10 5DT, UK
s.keates@napier.ac.uk

Abstract. It is approaching 20 years since the first issue of the International Journal on Universal Access was published and also that the first International Conference on Universal Access in Human-Computer Interaction was held. This paper reflects on how the field of Universal Access has evolved over the intervening period and proposes new areas of research challenges that have either emerged following recent advances in technology or still remain comparatively poorly addressed. The proposed challenges have been derived from a examining Maslow's Hierarchy of Needs along with technological development trends.

Keywords: Universal access · Inclusive design · Artificial intelligence · Robots · Healthcare · Telehealth · Cybersecurity · Networks · Functional impairments · Rehabilitation engineering

1 Introduction

It is approaching 20 years since Springer published the first issue of the International Journal on Universal Access in the Information Society in 2001. That was the same year that the inaugural Universal Access and Human-Computer Interaction conference was held in New Orleans. While a 20th anniversary issue is being prepared, it is interesting to consider how far the field has come in that time and consider where it might be heading over the next 20 years.

1.1 Where Were We in 2001?

It is interesting to take a look at the topics of the first issue of the UAIS journal.

The first paper addressed the use of speech recognition software by both able-bodied users and those with spinal cord injuries [1] and evaluated its usefulness based on user productivity and satisfaction. The authors expressed their dissatisfaction with more traditional analyses of the acceptability of software for users with functional impairments.

The second paper focused on developing a model-based schema for representing roles and goals when considering "Design for All" [2]. The aim of the paper was to explore a method for capturing and representing user behaviours more completely so that more effective solutions for the widest possible range of users could be developed.

© Springer Nature Switzerland AG 2019
M. Antona and C. Stephanidis (Eds.): HCII 2019, LNCS 11572, pp. 100–112, 2019.
https://doi.org/10.1007/978-3-030-23560-4_8

Next was a paper that focused on the use of biometric processing to better identify users and their needs [3]. The aim was to identify and respond to users more efficiently and securely.

The penultimate paper proposed that accessibility and high quality of interaction with products, applications, and services by anyone, anywhere, and at any time are fundamental requirements for universal access [4]. The paper discussed how these concepts could be utilised in the development of user interfaces that adapt automatically to the needs of the users.

Finally, the first issue concluded with a paper that looked at the development of user models and a framework to enable user interface developers to be able to respond better to the wider range of users [5].

These topics have been visited and re-visited a number of times further over the 18 years since that first issue. Jumping ahead to the present day, it is clear to see that if the next issue of the UAIS journal came out with an identical table of contents, many readers would not be surprised. That original table of contents would still be as valid today as it was back in 2001, albeit that much of the underlying technology platforms would be more advanced. So what does this tell us about progress in universal access for the past 20 years or so?

1.2   What Has Changed Since 2001?

As discussed above, technology has clearly advanced since 2001. The Internet, already popular back then, is now ubiquitous. This has now expanded to include the Internet of Things, i.e. collections of smart devices and sensors that are able to communicate with each other in both formal and ad hoc networks.

Mobile telephone networks are now capable of supporting much greater bit rates. Coupled with the increase in raw processing power of modern microchips and better battery life with the latest generation of battery cells, the modern smartphone is now at least as capable as many desktop computers from 2001. Tablet computers, such as the iPad, offer new methods of interacting with technology on the move, including multipoint touch. The very nature of we interact with each other is changing, too. We are in the age of the always-on and always-connected citizen. Social media may be evolving from one preferred platform to another every few years, but its overall popularity is still very strong.

Augmented reality displays are now commonplace in cars and aeroplanes. Voice activated systems can be used to control your house or play your choice of music. Even the humble doorbell can be upgraded to offer a form of virtual presence allowing a homeowner to talk to someone on their doorstep via their mobile phone.

Cars are on the cusp of becoming self-driving. Many aeroplanes are capable of flying themselves to their destinations. Companies are exploring the use of drones for delivering parcels to private addresses. Warehouses and factories are continuing to become almost fully automated. Table 1 gives a number of other interesting technological milestones from the intervening period.

Table 1. A summary of a few notable milestones since 2001.

Date	Technology milestone
June 2007	Launch of the iPhone
July 2008	Launch of the App Store
January 2010	Launch of the Parrot Ar. Drone
April 2010	Launch of the iPad
February 2011	IBM Watson competes in Jeopardy!
October 2011	Launch of Siri
February 2012	Launch of Raspberry Pi
April 2012	Launch of Google Glass
April 2015	Launch of Apple Watch

All of these technological advances offer significant opportunities for everyone, regardless of any personal functional impairment(s). There have also been many societal changes. Back in 2001, very few countries had legislation guaranteeing equal rights of access for people with disabilities. The USA had its 1990 Americans with Disabilities Act [6] and the UK had the 1996 Disability Discrimination Act [7], but there were very few other countries that had comparable laws. As we approach 2020, though, the rights of people with disabilities are upheld much more widely, for example with the UN Convention on the Rights of Persons with Disabilities (CRPD) adopted in 2006 [8].

Issues around accessibility and universal access have also become increasingly incorporated into academic conference calls for papers and there is now a wider number of publication outlets for papers in this area than there has ever been.

These are very welcome developments, but it is not yet time for us to be resting on our laurels. The reality is that without a continued and explicit focus on the needs of the widest possible range of users, it is all too easy for those who most need assistance to be left behind. There have also been a number of backwards steps as well. Computer crime continues to grow as criminals develop ever-more sophisticated methods of scamming people. Remote access technologies are also proving vulnerable to criminal attack, such as the use of signal range extenders in a growing number of vehicle thefts.

1.3   What Does the Future Hold?

While there continues to be a debate over how long Moore's Law can continue to hold [9], it is reasonable to expect that computing power will continue to increase for the foreseeable future even if the actual rate of growth is uncertain. It is also expected that form factors will continue to shrink. While Google Glass disappeared somewhat ignominiously, the prospect of truly wearable computing is clearly on the horizon. Furthermore, computers will become increasingly "intelligent" and "smart," however one may wish to define those terms. Machine learning and artificial intelligence are more commonplace than just a few years ago.

The structure of future computer systems will also be far more ad hoc and flexible than in the past. The Internet of Things offers great potential for assembling a collection of sensors and actuators for almost any task imaginable, from refrigerators that tell you when you need to buy fresh milk to burglar alarms that message you to let you know there is a potential intruder [10].

What will not change, though, are the reasons for users to continue to access these new technologies. Although the environment is changing, the fundamental human needs evolve more slowly. Maslow's hierarchy of needs still applies [11], i.e.:

- Physiological needs (heat, food, warmth, etc.)
- Safety needs (safety, security)
- Belongingness and love needs (intimate relationships, friends)
- Esteem needs (prestige and feeling of accomplishment)
- Self-actualisation (achieving ones full potential including creative activities)

These needs have been re-formulated over the years to include activities of daily living (ADLs), instrumental activities of daily living (IADLs) [12] and even areas of life endeavor [13].

Taking all of the above together, it is worth engaging in a bit of blue-sky thinking to consider what the principal challenges for the next 20 years may look like.

2 The Principal Challenges for the Future

Taking Maslow's Hierarchy of Needs as a starting point, along with technological developments that we can reasonably foresee, a possible list of candidate areas of interest might look like the following:

- Applications of advanced machine learning/artificial intelligence
- Access to healthcare services/telehealth and extending independent living
- Personal mobility
- Robotic assistants and control of the environment
- Cybersecurity, physical security and privacy
- Access to work and education
- Access to full citizenship
- Communicating and socializing with friend and family
- Access to the latest technology
- Developing and using rapidly customizable and/or adaptable designs
- Personal recognition and self-worth

The rest of this paper will explore each of these areas. It is worth noting that the list above is not intended to be comprehensive, but instead seeks to inspire new avenues of research or to encourage readers to consider returning to some older paths that may be ready for a fresh perspective by taking advantage of the possibilities of new techno-logical developments.

2.1 Applications of Advanced Machine Learning/Artificial Intelligence

The advent of artificial intelligence (AI) has opened the door to many new applications for computer-based applications. Advanced machine learning techniques allow computers to be trained swiftly on a broad range of data types. Combined together, it is no longer necessary for software developers to have to develop rigorous and fixed models and hierarchies of the world around us to allow computers to be programmed. This transition from a fixed algorithmic view of the world to a more flexible and nuanced understanding offers significant potential for developing computer systems that meet the needs of a wider range of users.

Take, for example, the development of the IBM Watson system [14]. Watson represents the cutting edge in natural language processing and deep question and answer (Q&A) technology. The design intent was to develop a computer system that was inspired by the architecture and structure of the human brain and that could also provide sensible answers to flexibly structured questions asked using natural language. The system was put to the test in February 2011 when it competed against two Jeopardy! grand champions and triumphed. The newspaper coverage of this historic achievement was somewhat ambivalent, though, with a number of articles openly referencing the Terminator movies and the suggestion that the development of Watson was another step along the path towards a Skynet-type supercomputer capable of inflicting untold misery on the human race. The reality is that the applications of the Watson technology have been somewhat more mundane than global domination and enslavement of humankind. Artificial intelligence is one of those areas where public preconceptions and the reality of the technology are really quite out of step.

However, this should not be allowed to dissuade researchers from exploring the possibilities that AI offers for Universal Access. For example, rapid machine learning approaches can help train voice recognition software to recognize an individual person's speech patterns very quickly [15]. Combined with AI techniques to better eliminate background noise and interference, speech recognition systems offer the Star Trek view of computer interaction where members of the crew of the Enterprise can talk directly to the ship's computer. The rise of systems such as Siri, Cortana and Alexa show that such systems are on the verge of becoming commonplace. While such systems can still sometimes struggle with voices they have not been trained for, they are getting better with each new generation of the technology. The potential benefits for users with motor impairments, for example, to be able to speak to a computer rather than have to use their fingers and hands to do so are obvious.

Looking beyond the matter of physical access to computers, though, there are wider questions about what such technology could be used for. For example, while the Watson system is currently limited to the quality and size of the database on which it has been trained, it is easy to envisage a situation where such a system has been trained on a very large and quality-controlled dataset. Now imagine the situation where students are sitting in a classroom and their telephones have now become a gateway to the perfect question-and-answer system. Any question that they ask their telephone will be answered correctly and immediately. What are the implications of such a system being available to them? How will it change how they learn? How will it change how they are taught? It is known that the advent of electronic calculators had an adverse effect on how well people can perform mental arithmetic. A similar effect was seen with GPS systems and the ability to navigate. What will be the implications for learning in general if such a perfect question-and-answer system becomes universally available? [14]

These are all significant questions that need to be considered as new AI and machine-learning approaches are developed.

2.2   Access to Healthcare Services/Telehealth and Extending Independent Living

It is widely accepted that most developed countries have either an ageing or an aged population [16]. As people get older, they generally develop more health conditions that need either monitoring or medical interventions. The cost of providing this healthcare is growing, especially as the traditional family support structures that helped older adults in previous generations are becoming more geographically dispersed as family members move to new areas to find work. The costs of healthcare and social care, especially when an older adult has to be moved into a care home or hospital because their relatives cannot support them at home, are a major source of political debate and discussion as many countries are struggling to meet these demands and costs.

As a consequence, there is a clear role for technology to help ensure better access to healthcare services and also to help older adults maintain their ability to live independently for as long as possible.

In terms of access to healthcare, many GP practices now offer appointment-booking services via the Internet. There is an increasing use of video calls, such as via Skype, for routine appointments or for regular check-ups. Internet-based pharmacies can deliver repeat prescriptions direct to a person's home. All of these services reduce pressures on GP practices. However, more can be done to automate as much of healthcare services as possible [17]. For instance, wearable sensors can be used to monitor blood sugar levels remotely that will send alerts automatically to healthcare providers when a dangerous blood sugar level is encountered.

Such technologies also extend a person's ability to continue to live independently for as long as possible as they offer peace of mind that help is on hand automatically should the worst happen. Staying in ones own home is not only better for society, as it is cheaper to support someone in their own home than in a care home or hospital, but also offers significant psychological and wellbeing benefits to the older adult [18].

The development of the Internet of Things technologies can help expand the range and type of sensors that can be used to help with healthcare and telehealth services. For example, one can envisage a scenario where each room in a house is equipped with high definition video cameras that are monitored either remotely or via an artificially intelligent computer system that is capable of identifying when a medical intervention is required. There is significant scope for research and development of new technologies that respect a person's privacy, but also allow them to remain in their own home for as long as possible.

2.3   Personal Mobility

Indivisible from the notion of independent living is the ability to move freely from one location to another without relying on the assistance of others [19]. Perhaps the ultimate epitome of this notion would be a fully autonomously controlled car that is wholly capable of driving itself without needing manual intervention at any point. While so-called "self-driving" cars are being tested, the reality is that they still require a licensed driver who is able to perform manual interventions when necessary. It is clear that the technology is still some distance away from the point where, say, a blind person could get into such a car, tell it a destination and then sit back to enjoy the ride.

However, even if such vehicles were available now, they would not solve all mobility issues. There are some places where private transport is either impractical or legally proscribed, such as many large city centres. Thus it is still necessary to ensure that public transport is also as accessible as possible. In a city such as London, many improvement have been made over recent years over bus timetabling, for example, where "smart" bus stops now show and speak the next few buses expected to arrive at that stop. Mobile phone apps also allow a person to monitor when buses are due. Trains, though, continue to be a major source of difficulty, with the 100+ year old underground station infrastructure still not accessible to a person in a wheelchair at many tube stations.

There also remain challenges of personal mobility once someone has got out of their car or off public transport. It is still necessary to be able to navigate and walk or move oneself to get to many destinations, such as going into a particular shop or office building. The ubiquity of GPS systems offers great potential for helping with the navigation aspect of this, but there are still comparatively few genuinely accessible GPS systems available for, say, someone who is blind. Many smartphone-based navigation systems are pretty good in this regard, but still typically require the user to either look at the screen or hear the directions. For someone who is blind, the former is not a viable option. Hearing the instructions can work well, but may be at the expense of listening to surrounding traffic, etc., so may not be the safest option. Researchers have explored the possibility of vibrotactile navigation cues, but no such system has achieved commercial viability yet.

2.4   Robotic Assistants and Control of the Environment

Controlling ones environment to ensure that it is safe, secure, warm and dry is a fundamental human need according to Maslow [11]. Home automation systems are becoming increasingly available and are much more sophisticated nowadays than the earlier attempts that often required long, difficult command line instructions [10]. Apps are available for everything from controlling the thermostat to monitoring burglar alarms. However, consumers are faced with a choice of either buying all the systems from the same supplier if they want a single unified interface to control everything, or having to download, install and use multiple apps, one for each system they wish to control. There is a clear need for a more unified approach that allows multiple systems to be controlled via a coherent interface design, somewhat akin to the Apple UI design guidelines adhered to by developers of software to run on Apple Macs.

Looking beyond home automation systems, robots to help people with functional impairments have been proposed and explored many times over the years. For example, robot guide (i.e. seeing eye) dogs have been explored by a number of different research groups. However, very few such robots have achieved commercial viability or market acceptance [20]. Those that have done so are either focused on very particular functions, such as the Handy 1 robot that allows a person with motor impairments to feed themselves, or are typically used in a medical situation, such as prostheses or post-stroke rehabilitation exercises.

Given that it is comparatively straightforward to include speech recognition and Internet connectivity into a robot using current technology, and that robots can be made increasingly lifelike such as the RoboThespian, perhaps now is the time to re-visit the possibility of personal robotic assistants. There is a clear role, for example, in helping older adults remain independent for such a robot [21].

2.5 Cybersecurity, Physical Security and Privacy

Again, according to Maslow, security is a key human need, as is privacy. However, these are issues that are very rarely addressed in the field of universal access. Indeed, privacy is often assumed to be a low priority for many universal access solutions that depend upon users being willing to share information about themselves in the hope of gaining a better "experience" as a result. While it is generally considered that someone with a significant health issue is usually more willing to forego privacy to ensure better healthcare, it cannot be assumed to be true for all users with functional impairments or health issues. More work needs to be done on balancing the need to share information for better support with a person's fundamental right to privacy.

One solution is to explore methods of more informed consent. Another would be to employ more "local" intelligence so only significant information is shared beyond a user's area of personal control. So, for example, consider a robotic assistant in an older adult's home. The robot could be equipped with a camera and motion detection sensors to monitor whether the person is active. Its artificial intelligence could then determine whether the person's behaviour and actions fall within pre-determined acceptable parameters. If they do not, and only if they do not, the robot could then send a message to a monitoring station requesting assistance. However, if the behaviour and actions fall within the acceptable parameters, no information need be shared and the person's privacy is protected. In other words, by putting more local intelligence into the system, personal information can be held within a secure, ring-fenced domain (the person's home environment) and only shared with external agencies when medically necessary.

Another area needing further research is cybersecurity. Scammers and on-line criminals are becoming increasingly sophisticated in their tactics and techniques [22]. Initially such attacks were based on seeking financial gain, through approaches such as the infamous 419 scam. However, there are an increasing number of examples where physical thefts and damage are resulting from the activities of hackers and other criminals. The use of signal range extenders for breaking into cars with keyless remotes is one example. Another is the case of hackers gaining remote control of engine control units (ECUs) in cars. These security risks are bad enough for able-bodied users, but for someone with a functional impairment, the potential risks could be catastrophic. Imagine if a hacker took remote control of a powered wheelchair, for instance, or a medication-dispensing machine.

While security is generally considered in the design of most technologies, is sufficient attention being paid to the particular needs of those requiring universal access solutions? Very few papers in either the UAIS journal or the UAHCI conferences address this particular issue.

2.6   Access to Work and Education

Although not explicit in Maslow's hierarchy of needs, access to both education and work are essential parts of everyday life and this is as true for those with functional impairments as for anyone else [23]. This basic principle was recognized by organisations such as the Papworth Trust, which evolved from its early days as a tuberculosis colony to become a residential centre for those with severe motor and sensory impairments. Central to the philosophy of the Trust was that work was an essential part of any rehabilitation programme. The Trust ran a number of companies, from the famous Papworth Leather and Travel Goods, which made the suitcases used by the British royal family, to the Pendragon Press. It even ran its own vehicle repair shop. All of the residents at the Trust were given a job in one of the companies. This gave them all a sense of purpose and a sense of worth. Later the Trust evolved further to providing skills training so the residents could secure jobs in local companies.

A foundation to any attempt to access work is, of course, to be able to access education. While much of the research in universal access focuses on technologies that can facilitate access to education (such as research into computer access and the like), the development of assistive technologies (for conditions such as dyslexia and dyscalculia) and even the development of curricula for teaching designers how to develop more inclusive solutions [e.g. 23], there is comparatively little research into the design of curricula for people who are functionally impaired beyond usually simple guidelines. Research into cognitive and learning difficulties is also not as widespread as that into sensory or motor impairments [24].

2.7   Access to Full Citizenship

In the 2017 general election in the UK, there were five Members of Parliament who were classified as "disabled" out of 650 MPs. Given that it is generally accepted in 1 in 6 of the population has a functional impairment that generally affects their ability to undertake everyday activities [25, 26], 5 out of 650 cannot be considered representative of the population in general. It is symptomatic of level of participation in some aspects of citizenship for people with disabilities, though. How many debating programmes on television feature disabled people in the audience, for example? While there has been research into the accessibility of voting mechanisms, there have been very few papers exploring the level of participation in political debate or policy-making.

Other developments in society may also exclude people with functional impairments inadvertently [27]. For example, a recent newspaper article was examining the impact of the move to the so-called cashless society on older adults as an increasing number of companies move towards not accept cash payments. Such a move penalises those who are not comfortable with the new payment technologies and a disproportionate number of those who fall into this category are older adults. Thus another challenge is how to ensure that new developments of this type are genuinely inclusive and not driven by one segment of the population to the detriment of others [28, 29].

2.8 Communicating and Socializing with Friends and Family

While there is an increasing variety of possible methods for communicating with friends and family, such as Skype, WhatsApp, FaceTime and the like, many charities still report that there is a very high number of people who feel isolated and alone. Just because the software is available, that does not mean that it is necessarily accessible to everyone.

Equally, a number of mental health professionals are concerned about the impact of social media on the wellbeing of vulnerable individuals, especially with the frequency of bullying and intimidating messages in some forums.

Thus while there may be many new mechanisms for communication, the issues of how to ensure fruitful, productive and healthy interaction have clearly not been solved for everyone.

2.9 Access to the Latest Technology

The issues around basic interaction science are still not fully resolved [30]. While there is a growing body of research into computer access there is still an unacceptably high number of people who experience difficulty interacting with a computer [31]. The development of new forms of technology, such as the advent of smartphones and tablets, offer opportunities and challenges to older adults and those with functional impairments. There is clearly still a need for more research into the fundamentals of human-computer interaction.

2.10 Developing and Using Rapidly Customizable and/or Adaptable Designs

Additive manufacturing, commonly referred to as 3D printing, is frequently held up as an example of rapid prototyping and manufacturing technology. The age of truly personalized products is approaching rapidly [e.g. 32]. Such technology offers significant opportunity for those who do not conform to the usual anthropomorphic datasets. Such people include those who are notably taller or shorter than average, weaker or stronger, larger or slimmer. However, there are comparatively few commercial examples of such technology in use. One example is from skiing. Ski boots can be tailored to ones feet through the use of innovative thermoplastics that can be heated and moulded very rapidly – no different in principle to moulding plastic gum shields for contact sports. This is a very particular example though and only scratches the surface of what these new manufacturing technologies can support. Product designers can, in theory, develop modular kettles that can have handles attached that are 3D printed to the exact contours of ones hand. The challenge here is how best to take full advantage of this new technology and the possibilities it offers.

In the field of software design, developers can go one step further and produce software that is capable of adapting itself to the evolving needs of its users [33]. However, while the principles for accomplishing this are understood, very little commercial software supports such an approach. There is an obvious challenge here to get such principles accepted more widely.

2.11   Personal Recognition and Self-worth

It is difficult to envisage the development of a piece of new software or technology that is designed to improve ones recognition or sense of self-worth. However, what is clearly possible is developing a much better understanding of how we as individuals view and measure our sense of self-worth [34]. This is a continually-evolving notion. Where a few years ago, it may have been measured by the size of ones social circle, for example, these days it may include the number of virtual friends as well as those that we meet in real life.

It is important that designers and developers understand the value of self worth. Any successful design has to meet the needs, wants and aspirations of the users and be both practically and socially acceptable. The notion of "social" acceptance here includes the implicit impact on ones self-worth [35].

3   Conclusions

While there have been many significant developments since the inaugural UAHCI conference and first issue of the UAIS journal in 2001, there remain many notable challenges for researchers in the field of universal access to address. This paper has addressed how far technology has developed over the intervening periods and has also highlighted a number of those challenges that are worth exploring further.

References

1. Sears, A., Karat, C.M., Oseitutu, K.: Productivity, satisfaction, and interaction strategies of individuals with spinal cord injuries and traditional users interacting with speech recognition software. Int. J. Univ. Access Inf. Soc. 1(1), 4–15 (2001). https://doi.org/10.1007/s102090100001
2. Stary, C.: User diversity and design representation: towards increased effectiveness in design for All. Int. J. Univ. Access Inf. Soc. 1(1), 16–30 (2001). https://doi.org/10.1007/s102090100002
3. Fairhust, M., Ng, S.: Management of access through biometric control: a case study based on automatic signature verification. Int. J. Univ. Access Inf. Soc. 1(1), 31–39 (2001). https://doi.org/10.1007/s102090100009
4. Stephanidis, C., Savidis, A.: Universal access in the information society: methods, tools, and interaction technologies. Int. J. Univ. Access Inf. Soc. 1(1), 40–55 (2001). https://doi.org/10.1007/s102090100008
5. Jacko, J., Vitense, H.: A review and reappraisal of information technologies within a conceptual framework for individuals with disabilities. Int. J. Univ. Access Inf. Soc. 1(1), 56–76 (2001). https://doi.org/10.1007/s102090100003
6. ADA: Americans with Disabilities Act. US Public Law 101-336 (1990)
7. DDA: Disability Discrimination Act, DfEE, London (1995)
8. UN: Convention on the Rights of Persons with Disabilities. United Nations (2006)
9. Bright, P.: Moore's law really is dead this time. Ars Technica (2016). Available at: https://arstechnica.com/information-technology/2016/02/moores-law-really-is-dead-this-time/. Last Accessed 05 Feb 2019

10. Keates, S., Bradley, D., Sapeluk, A.: The future of universal access? Merging computing, design and engineering. Universal Access in Human-Computer Interaction. Applications and Services for Quality of Life, LNCS, pp. 54–63. Springer, Heidelberg (2013). https://doi.org/10.1007/978-3-642-39194-1_7

11. Maslow, A.H.: A theory of human motivation. Psychol. Rev. **50**(4), 370–396 (1943). https://doi.org/10.1037/h0054346

12. Bookman, A., Harrington, M., Pass, L., Reisner, E.: Family Caregiver Handbook. Massachusetts Institute of Technology, Cambridge (2007)

13. Keates, S., Kozloski, J., Varker, P.: Cognitive impairments, HCI and daily living. In: Proceedings of International Conference on Universal Access in Human-Computer Interaction. LNCS, vol. 5614, pp. 366–374. Springer-Verlag, Heidelberg (2009). https://doi.org/10.1007/978-3-642-02707-9_42

14. Keates, S., Varker, P., Spowart, F.: Human-machine design considerations in advanced machine-learning systems. IEEE/IBM J. Res. Dev. **55**(5), 4:1–4:10 (2011). https://doi.org/10.1147/jrd.2011.2163274

15. Kinch, M.W., Melis, W.J.C., Keates, S.: The benefits of contextual information for speech recognition systems. In: Proceedings of the 10th Computer Science and Electronic Engineering Conference (CEEC), 19–21 September 2018, University of Essex, Colchester, UK (2018)

16. Coleman, R.: Living longer. In: Clarkson, P.J., Coleman, R., Keates, S., Lebbon, C. (eds.) Inclusive Design: Design for the Whole Population, pp. 120–141. Springer, Heidelberg (2003)

17. Ball, L., Szymkowiak, A., Keates, S., Bradley, D., Brownsell, S.: eHealth and the Internet of Things. In: Proceedings of the 3rd International Conference on Pervasive Embedded Computing and Communication Systems, pp. 139–142. SCITEPRESS, Barcelona, Spain (2013). https://doi.org/10.5220/0004336701390142

18. Keates, S.: Design for the value of inclusiveness. In: Van den Hoven, J., Vermaas, P.E., van de Poel, I. (eds.) Handbook of Ethics, Values and Technological Design, pp. 383–402. Springer, Heidelberg (2014)

19. Coda, A., Gadeselli, R.: The FIAT autonomy programme. In: Clarkson, P.J., Coleman, R., Keates, S., Lebbon, C. (eds.) Inclusive Design: Design for the Whole Population, pp. 216–224. Springer, Heidelberg (2003)

20. Mahoney, R.: Robotic products for rehabilitation: status and strategy. In: Proceedings of the 5th International Conference on Rehabilitation Robotics (ICORR '97), Bath, UK, pp. 12–17 (1997)

21. Keates, S., Kyberd, P.J.: Robotic assistants for universal access. In: Antona, M., Stephanidis, C. (eds.) Universal Access in Human–Computer Interaction. Human and Technological Environments. Proceedings of UAHCI 2017, LNCS, vol. 10279, pp. 527–538. Springer, Heidelberg (2017). https://doi.org/10.1007/978-3-319-58700-4_43

22. Hofman, C., Keates, S.: Countering Brandjacking in the Digital Age – and Other Hidden Risks to Your Brand. Springer, London (2013)

23. Keates, S.: A pedagogical example of teaching Universal Access. Int. J. Univ. Access Inf. Soc. (UAIS) **14**(1), 97–110 (2015). https://doi.org/10.1007/s10209-014-0398-4

24. Keates, S., et al.: Cognitive and learning difficulties and how they affect access to IT systems. Int. J. Univ. Access Inf. Soc. **5**(4), 329–339 (2007). https://doi.org/10.1007/s10209-006-0058-4

25. Grundy, E., Ahlburg, D., Ali, M., Breeze, E., Sloggett, A.: Disability in Great Britain. Department of Social Security, Research Report No. 94, Corporate Document Services, London, UK (1999)

26. Keates, S.: Designing for Accessibility: A Business Guide to Countering Design Exclusion. Lawrence Erlbaum Associates/CRC Press, Mahwah (2007)
27. Keates, S., Clarkson, P.J.: Countering Design Exclusion: An Introduction to Inclusive Design. Springer, London (2003)
28. Keates, S., Lebbon, C., Clarkson, P.J.: Investigating industry attitudes to Universal Design. In: Proceedings of RESNA 2000, Orlando, FL, pp. 276–278. RESNAPress (2000)
29. Dong, H., Keates, S., Clarkson, P.J., Cassim, J.: Implementing inclusive design: the discrepancy between theory and practice. In: Proceedings of the 2002 ERCIM Workshop on User Interfaces for All, Lecture Notes in Computer Science, vol. 2615, pp. 106–117. Springer, Berlin (2002). https://doi.org/10.1007/3-540-36572-9_8
30. Keates, S.: When Universal Access is not quite universal enough: case studies and lessons to be learned. Int. J. Univ. Access Inf. Soc. (2018). https://doi.org/10.1007/s10209-018-0636-2. (Springer Online First)
31. Keates, S., Robinson, P.: Gestures and multimodal input. Behav. Inf. Technol. 18(1), 36–44 (1999). https://doi.org/10.1080/014492999119237
32. Gao, J., El Souri, M., Keates, S.: Advances in Manufacturing Technology, vol. 31. IOS Press, Amsterdam (2017)
33. Stephanidis, C.: The Universal Access Handbook. CRC Press, Boca Raton (2009)
34. Yelding, D.: Power to the people. In: Clarkson, P.J., Coleman, R., Keates, S., Lebbon, C. (eds.) Inclusive Design: Design for the Whole Population, pp. 104–117. Springer-Verlag, Heidelberg (2003)
35. Nielsen, J.: Usability Engineering. Morgan Kaufmann, San Francisco (1994)

Achieving Inclusion with Contextualized User-Sensitive Design

Fang Li[1(✉)] and Hua Dong[2(✉)]

[1] Tongji University, 1239 Siping Road, Shanghai 200092
People's Republic of China
1510084@tongji.edu.cn
[2] Loughborough University, Epinal Way,
Loughborough, Leicestershire LE11 3TU, UK
h.dong@lboro.ac.uk

Abstract. Users and contexts in human-computer interaction systems often have great diversity, which limits the inclusion provided by a single design. Existing user-sensitive design and contextual design methodologies have made useful attempts to pay attention to diversities, but they still cannot provide sufficient design basis for adapting to dynamically changing user capabilities, needs and usage contexts. Based on the analysis of the interaction between the behavior model and various elements in the human-computer system, this paper constructs a contextualized user-sensitive design framework, and studies the diversity and changing factors in the human-computer system from the two basic dimensions of the user and the context. In order to reflect the multi-dimensional dynamic characteristics of users, the authors propose a new user research and analysis tool, the generalized user balance sheet, for user-sensitive design, and takes a questionnaire case to reveal the huge differences of users' needs in different contexts. Based on the contextualized user-sensitive design framework, this paper shows the basic methods and essential system elements of user-sensitive design and contextualized design, as well as the possibility of combining the two for inclusive design.

Keywords: Inclusive design · User sensitive design · Contextual design · User centered design

1 Introduction

When using languages to express certain concepts, we are often constrained and influenced by the language itself. For example, when we express the concept of 'same', we usually only recognize that the referred objects are the same when they are nearly 100% identical. However, when we need to judge 'different', the standard seems to be much lower. 10% or even less inconsistency is enough to make us believe that there are significant differences. As a result, in a complex system of the world, the same/different equilibrium point that we think may be distorted greatly. When we think that most individuals in a group are different, in fact there are only small and partial diversities between different individuals. This difference in semantic concepts requires us to be extremely cautious when choosing words to describe concepts. Therefore, this paper

© Springer Nature Switzerland AG 2019
M. Antona and C. Stephanidis (Eds.): HCII 2019, LNCS 11572, pp. 113–132, 2019.
https://doi.org/10.1007/978-3-030-23560-4_9

chooses 'diversity' and 'similarity' to represent the difference of users from two different perspectives in the same dimension.

Diversities and similarities are like head and tail of a coin, and their complementarity forms a unity of opposites. In most user groups with a certain scale, it is almost impossible to have absolute similarities and diversities if they are based on individual users. Therefore, diversities and similarities must exist at the same time. The combination of the two can fully reflect the overall needs and characteristics of users. The similarity of users enables designers to build core features around which products or services can be scaled up. For this reason, it is usually the focus of user research. This is of course understandable, but if we only focus on the common characteristics of users and ignore the understanding and research of diversities, then the resulting design proposal may easily lead to either a lack of inclusiveness or failure to provide inclusive results in a reasonable, effective and sustainable manner.

2 Design for Diversities

The characteristics of things are the sum of diversities and similarities. Since we have made clear the complementarity of diversities and similarities, we may as well regard 'commonness' as a special form of diversities, which is convenient for us to start from diversities and solve the problem of how to maximize design inclusiveness under the resource constraints.

2.1 Behavior Model and Human-Machine System

For design research, user behavior is one of the research focuses that cannot be avoided. Users interact with products through certain activities to achieve a certain purpose or meet a certain demand, which is always completed in a certain context. Gonzalez and Morer summarized the relationship among the user, product, contexts and activity into the system structure as shown in Fig. 1 from the system view of ergonomics [1]. Fogg's behavior model proposes that behavior is the product of motivation, ability and trigger factors. The behavior can only occur if the actor has sufficient motivation and execution ability and is triggered to execute the behavior [2]. Economists attribute human behavior to making choices among many alternative behaviors in order to eliminate discomfort [3]. Although the expressions and theoretical backgrounds of theories are different, the laws and principles expounded by them are basically the same. Eliminating discomfort is actually the fundamental goal and motivation of human beings, specific behaviors and trigger factors are created by the context of making choices, and making choices among many optional behaviors is based on the evaluation and comparison of the execution ability of different behaviors. For an activity, the higher the actor's ability, the simpler it is to complete the activity and the lower the cost. At the same time, the greater the benefits and value of the behavior, the stronger the motivation. Therefore, if the ability dimension in Fogg's behavior model is transformed into cost through reciprocal, and the motivation dimension corresponds to the interest demand, we can easily reduce Fogg's behavior model to the basic assumption of economics for individuals to pursue self-interest maximization and typical demand curve.

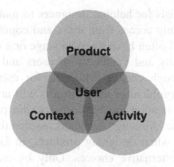

Fig. 1. UCAP map [1].

In the UCAP map of Fig. 1, although the elements constituting the design of human-machine system revolve around users, there is no clear mutual relationship, which reflects that ergonomic research only classifies and roughly locates these elements, and lacks in-depth discussion on the role and logical structure of these elements in the design process. This paper regards products, users, situations and activities as four independent vertices, and connects them with lines with directional arrows to form a tetrahedral structure (Fig. 2). If this tetrahedron is rotated in a three-dimensional space, we can examine its interaction with different elements from the perspective of a certain vertex. At the same time, the diagram also indicates the relationship between this structure and design, external environment and goal, and then we will analyze one by one.

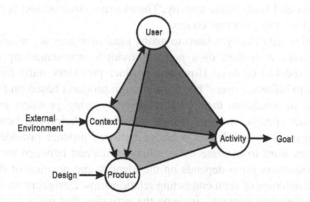

Fig. 2. Human-machine system tetrahedron.

Product. A product is a direct design object. It can be any artifact, service or artificial environment. Designers provide users with choices and means for targeted activities by shaping products, and thus influence and help users achieve goals through activities. As the substantial carrier of supply, the product can be independent or a component in a larger system. Of course, product design will inevitably be constrained by the supply capacity, but this is an inherent constraint outside the human-machine system.

Under this constraint, the basis for helping designers to make design decisions in the human-machine system mainly comes from users and contexts. Once the design of a product is determined, it will often have a certain stage or a certain degree of stability. However, due to the diversity and variability of users and contextual factors, if the product cannot provide enough choices and tools for users to complete the target activities, it means that the problem of inclusiveness will arise.

On the other hand, the relationship between specific products and context-user-activity plane is also unstable. Although designers assume that the product is a part of the human-machine system when designing products, in fact, the design of a single product often faces many alternative choices. Only by maintaining the continuous competitive advantage against alternative solutions can the product keep its position as a member of the human-machine system, which is especially difficult with the change of users and contexts.

Activity. Although we often emphasize taking users as the center in design research and practice, users' needs and goals are always achieved by using products to conduct certain activities in specific contexts. Activities are initiated by users, influenced and restricted by contexts, and are mainly completed through the use of products. Users, products and specific contexts are all indispensable elements of activities, and these three elements have their own motivations.

From the perspective of products, activities can be regarded as an indirect design object. Designers can further support and influence users' activities by product design. From the user's point of view, the main actor of the activity is the user him/herself, that is to say, the user is the final decision-maker and executor of the activity. From the perspective of the context, the context is the inducement that the external environment works on the user and leads to the activity. The external environment here includes all stakeholders of the system in this context.

Since activities are directly related to goals, ideal activities are aimed at the common goals of users with their own needs, providers represented by products and stakeholders in specific context. However, product providers must have their own interests and try to influence users' behavior through products based on these interests. Users also hope to maximize their own interests by using products in games with stakeholders under specific contexts, which makes the relationship between product providers and users very subtle. As a bridge between product providers and users, whether designers want to mediate the conflicts of interest between the two or have obvious tendentiousness often depends on the identity and position of designers, and activities are the outcome of such competing relationships. Designers need to study and understand the users and contexts, imagine the activities that users need to carry out according to the demand goal, and then respond through product design.

User. Users are the group who will choose appropriate product functions to engage in certain activities according to their own situation and the context at that time. The reason why it is called group is that although products and services may be designed for personal use, in most cases, a large number of individual users need to share the same design, so the diversity formed by user diversities puts forward requirements and challenges for the inclusiveness of product design.

Because users and designers have the same sense of autonomy, in human-machine system, the user is actually the core leading factor in system operation. Under certain limited conditions, when the context forces the user to decide to complete the highly challenging activity goal, even if the product fails to provide sufficient and strong support, the user will still try his best to overcome the difficulty of the activity and strive to achieve the goal by creatively using the product or investing more user resources. Similarly, when the system has limited constraints on users, if the products are not usable, users are completely likely to give up solutions based on existing products and adopt more competitive systems to meet their own needs and goals.

Context. Some researchers believe that contexts can also be designed, while we tend to regard contexts as an objective existence independent of the product (design objects) and user. If we can accurately understand that the context is the result of interaction between the user and the external environment, it is not difficult to find that the context itself is not controlled by design. From the perspective of designers, contexts can be found, observed, predicted and evaluated, thus providing a basis for product design.

Contextual factors often change from time to time, from place to place, from person to person, and we can classify these changes into two categories. One is the so-called force majeure, that is, the contextual factors that the user can only passively accept. The contextual factors act on the user unilaterally, forcing the user to respond. Force majeure mentioned here, of course, is also relative. It means that the influence of users on the external environmental factor is very small and negligible. For example, when passengers are waiting for the train at the platform, the arrival time of the train is force majeure for the users, who have to accept it passively. Another kind of context change is the result of interaction between users and the external environment, i.e. both users and the external environment have considerable influence on the context. Changes in either side may cause context changes, such as driving on urban roads, and the context difference at this time will be shown as a function of changes in the external environment and users themselves.

The lack of support for users to engage in certain activities and contexts in product design certainly weakens users' ability to meet their needs. However, due to the existence of user factors, users' needs are not necessarily rigid and irreplaceable. Other activities in other contexts are likely to make up for dissatisfaction with demand and insufficient design support in some contexts. Therefore, it is necessary to look at the role and function of contexts from a systematic perspective in addition to microscopic immersion experience.

2.2   Design Framework and Principles

The research into design has increasingly shifted from industrial design for traditional hardware products to interaction design for smart devices, software and Internet services. A fundamental change in this trend is that the design object itself has gained the possibility and potential to meet and adapt to differentiated needs. Unlike printed labels, mechanical structures, physical switches, clearly defined functional specifications and interactive logic on traditional devices, in an emerging interaction design interface, the typeface, font size, spacing and layout of the page can be adjusted at any time according to user needs; the brightness and color of the screen can be automatically adjusted according to environmental conditions with ambient light sensors; and customized content and commodity information can be pushed to different registered users based on algorithms and big data, or even the iteration of the product can be performed through over-the-air (OTA) upgrade. It means that the diversity of users and contexts has become a design opportunity rather than a design challenge.

Design tools, methods and theories, such as the persona [4] and user profile [5] for analyzing user behavior patterns and preference characteristics, responsive design [6] and adaptive design [7] for different screen sizes and resolutions, as well as contextual design for user-centered system [8], have been created around how to make the full use of this potential to design a more inclusive experience for interaction. These tools, methods and theories propose solutions to a certain kind of factors that cause demand diversities and changes, but they are still not enough to systematically and comprehensively solve the problems caused by complex contexts and user diversity in the design practice.

In order to make the design meet the needs from different users in various contexts as much as possible, the authors argue that the priority goal in interaction design should not be to seek the best design for specific needs, instead, it should focus on how to provide individual users in different contexts with sufficient choices to accommodate their diverse needs under the established constraints, because the duplication and delivery cost of digital products is often as low as zero. Therefore, it is necessary to establish a contextualized user-sensitive design framework (Fig. 3). This framework should contain two core principles: one is to ensure that the individual user has a consistent experience in different contexts, and the other is to ensure that the differentiated needs and preferences of users who have different capabilities could be met equally.

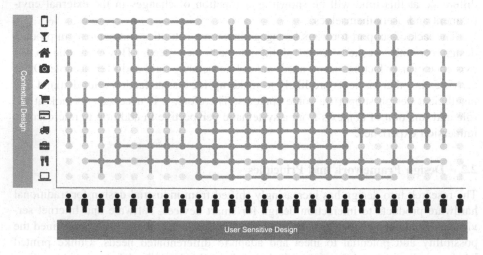

Fig. 3. Contextualized user-sensitive design map

The implementation of the framework is based on some preconditions and necessary system capabilities: for example, the system should be able to identify and record the characteristics of different users respectively, and be able to perceive different usage scenarios. Therefore, the perceptual design of the diversities of users and contexts will be incorporated into the whole design process, and we need to have in-depth understanding of these diversities.

3 User Diversities

The emphasis on perceiving user diversities originates from the user-centered design research methodology. Since Jakob Nielsen put forward the concept of usability design [9] in the early 1990s, user research has been one of the central issues of interaction design. A concept similar to User-centered Design is Human-centered Design, which includes a wider range of stakeholders. The International Organization for Standardization formulated the Human-centered design processes for interactive systems (ISO 13407:1999) [10] in 1999. This standard was revised as Ergonomics of human-system interaction – Part 210: Human-centered design for interactive systems (ISO 9241-210:2010) [11], and has become the basis of many studies. However, as Ekaterina Novoseltseva pointed out in an article on UsabilityGeek.com, although it may be the good wishes of many designers and developers, in fact not all people will become actual users. Therefore, User-centered Design emphasizes more in-depth analysis of users than the Human-centered Design, focusing on the specific habits and preferences of the target users rather than just the general characteristics of people [12]. This is not to say that other stakeholders and environmental and sustainable factors are not important. No design methodology will cover all aspects of the design process. To study the specific habits and preferences of the target users, it is difficult to ignore the diversities of users. Here we focus on the diversities of users, which depend on our main purpose to reduce and eliminate the exclusion caused by diversities.

User diversities can be observed from two different perspectives. One is the individual differences within the user group. The other is the difference of the same user in different contexts. The latter can be regarded as a reflection of the context diversities projected on users, so we will discuss them together when we discuss context diversities in Sect. 4.

3.1 Generalized User Balance Sheet

Ergonomic user research usually starts with physiology, cognition and emotion, and divides physical factors into two aspects: motor and sensory [13]. The research on these factors often does not make a detailed distinction between different functional categories, but generally takes them as the basis for consideration in generating design proposals. However, from the perspective of the relationship between the behavior model and the aspects of human-computer system, different factors play completely different roles in human behavior. As stated in Fredrick Herzberg's hygiene-motivational factors theory [14], some are the motivational or incentive factors of behavior, and some are the hygiene factors of behavior. All designs for human-computer systems are ultimately to assist, support and promote users to complete purposeful behaviors, that is to say, the design activity itself is a purposeful behavior. If users are regarded as the core resources and partners of human-computer systems to complete behavioral activities, then different users will show different execution and cooperation willingness. It is the various user characteristics that determines the cooperation value and ability of users, and it is not static, but constantly changes with the target activities and contexts.

Many ergonomics researches are devoted to improving the execution ability of users in completing activities, which is based on the assumption that users have common understanding of the target activities envisioned by researchers and there is no lack of motivations: as long as users complete activities more easily, the efficiency of the system will be higher, and the user experience will be better. For the productivity equipment and tools with relatively simple usage scenarios, this assumption may not be a big problem. However, once the system is put into operation in a more complex real environment, changes in users and context make the hygiene factors and motivational factors work together on users' behaviors and are affected by more external factors. Not only does the users' behavior intention become at least as important as their behavior ability, but also the uncertainty of behavior ability is greatly increased. In view of this, we need to construct an effective analysis tool to accurately capture and evaluate user diversities.

Since the user's behavior model conforms to the principles of economics and is inspired by finance, investment and accounting, the authors use financial statements as a reference, and introduces a "Generalized User Balance Sheet (GUBS)" to represent and reflect the user's attributes at a certain moment. We set a basic balance formula:

User Abilities (*Assets*) = *User Requirements* (*Liabilities*) + *User Satisfaction* (*Equity*)

Assets represent resources that can be used to accomplish a certain activity. These resources include not only the user's own physical function and cognition, but also emotional intelligence and available economic and social resources. We can simply understand them as the user's comprehensive ability. However, user liabilities include all factors that make users uncomfortable and need to be eliminated, such as unmet demand goals and unsatisfied preferences, all of which require extra efforts from users. User equity is the surplus of user's ability to cope with the demand. The more surplus this part has, the stronger the sense of pleasure and satisfaction, and the better the user experience.

According to a certain kind of classification, we can get a GUBS by properly arranging the specific items of users' abilities, needs/preferences and satisfaction at a certain moment.

The subjects and categories listed in Table 1 are just to show the general usage of this tool. Although there are many potential options, the actual user capabilities and needs involved in a product are usually limited. For specific practical projects, designers and researchers need to select and set appropriate subjects to accurately reflect the user-related capabilities, needs and preferences in their project.

Table 1. An example of generalized user balance sheet

Assets	Liabilities
Current Assets	Current Liabilities
Physical Function	Physical Needs
Motor	Economic Interest
Power	Profit
Agile	Risk
Sensory	Valuation
Visual	Non-Current Liabilities
Hearing	Cognitive Needs and Preferences
Economic Capacity	Convenience
Income	Complexity
Purchasing Power	Emotional Preference
Investment Capacity	Taste
Risk Tolerance	Values/Beliefs
Credit	Character
Non-Current Assets	Habit
Cognitive Ability	Social Preference
Memory	Privacy
Language Ability	**User Equity**
Knowledge	Price Discount
Skills	Save Time

There are two main potential values in using the GUBS. First of all, design researchers can use it as a summary tool for user research results to describe the user's project-related capabilities and requirements, and use it as a basis for product design to determine the product's capability requirements and satisfaction degree for users. Secondly, the GUBS can also be used to identify and evaluate the diversities of different users in interactive product operation. Based on this, dynamic and parametric user profiles can be established. By comparing actual user data with design calibration values, and combining evaluation indexes and feedback of user experience, the reference standards for product optimization, iteration and dynamic response can be formed.

However, although the GUBS uses the form of accounting statements for reference, the types of user's preferences and abilities are very complex, and there is a lack of currency to convert different subjects in a unified way. Therefore, it cannot be used as an accurate quantitative tool at present. It is only helpful to grasp the user diversities on the whole and in individual classification, and to identify the individual diversities. However, the core significance lies in that, compared with other tools such as Persona, GUBS no longer describe users from a static perspective, but are based on dynamic models related to target tasks. Users' capabilities, needs and related equities are dynamic data that change at any time. Such user models are helpful to fit with a richer variety of usage situations and external environments, thus improving user experience and design inclusiveness.

3.2   Multidimensional Analysis of Individual Diversities

By using the GUBS or other various user research tools and methods, the individual diversities of target user groups can be analyzed and studied. In order to grasp the individual diversities of users more comprehensively, user research needs to explore users' capabilities and needs/preferences from multiple dimensions.

Physical. A large number of existing inclusive design studies focus on this dimension. The lost or weakened abilities of the main research objects - disabled and elderly groups - can mostly be attributed to physical functions. These functions are the original functional abilities of individuals. One type is motor functions, such as body type, (each part) muscle strength, muscle memory, speed, flexibility, agility, etc. It is the ability of individuals to feedback or take active actions to the external environment and other individuals through their own physical activities. The other is sensory ability, which is the individual's ability to obtain the external environment state and information. Usually, it is easy to naturally understand the sensory ability as vision, hearing, taste, touch, smell and so on possessed by the five senses, and at most it includes more detailed senses such as color, night vision, etc. These senses are processed by the brain to form perception. However, a broader sense of perception should include not only the acquisition of information on the state and changes of all external environments such as light, sound, temperature, taste, force, friction, etc. and the direct feelings of pain, itching, comfort, excitement, etc. by any individual not limited to human beings or even organisms, since they may become design objects or partners.

These capabilities are the biological basis of all behavioral capabilities, and are also the basic conditions for individuals to participate in competition and cooperation. Traditionally, the definition of disabled people in human society refers to the people who are lack of ability in these aspects. Low motor function will affect the user's ability to complete target activities. Low or even lack of sensory ability will reduce the input of external information and stimulation, which may affect the users' direct and indirect behavioral motivation. However, in some situations, the impact is not all negative. For example, people with visual impairment are less afraid of dark environment than other people. In this dimension, designers need to understand the relevant physical functions and sizes involved in the use of products, environment or services by target users, so as to make the design solution adapt to the size of as many people as possible, and try not to require users to have a high level of physical functions before normal use, or to provide assistive methods and tools to enhance users' functions in some aspects. Many research data and results of human factor engineering can be used for inclusive design in this dimension. Physical functions are independent and bound to individuals, which means that it is difficult for one individual to directly obtain and use functions possessed by other individuals. For severely disabled people and the disabling context, combining appropriate assistive technologies can effectively compensate for the loss of ability, and relying on other capabilities with compensatory function to complete the task is also a common design idea.

In addition to physical functions, physical dimensions also include many passive needs determined by non-subjective consciousness, such as instinct and conditioned reflex. Instinct is congenital demand and desire, highly related to human biological attributes, and is the most direct and basic source of demand. Reflex is an individual's non-subjective response to external environmental stimuli, including instinctive unconditioned reflex and acquired conditioned reflex. Unconditional reflex is the inherent fixed connection between external stimulus and individual response, while conditioned reflex is the temporary connection established between external stimuli and the individual response under certain conditions. It can be obtained and designed through training. The designer should pay attention to the habituation and degeneration of conditioned reflex. This kind of passive demand has relatively high regularity and predictability, and is suitable for empirical scientific research methods, and there are a large number of related disciplines (biology, physiology, psychology, ergonomics, etc.) research results and conclusions can be directly borrowed. The design for passive requirements is usually the bottom line and red line of inclusiveness, and its demand elasticity is very low. However, from the perspective of user diversities, the diversities in passive requirements are relatively limited, and different users have relatively high generality.

Cognitive. More and more products are becoming more and more complex while providing functions and experiences far beyond the past. From being able to know and use various functions provided by products to obtaining excellent user experience, users rely on mastering corresponding knowledge, information and skills. Respecting the users' existing cognition, experience and habits, and making the best use of the users' existing knowledge can make the products easier to understand and learned. Conversely, it will increase the users' burden, which will most likely lead to the users being forced to give up using the products. Sufficient information helps users to make choices that best meet their real needs. Incomplete information will lead to misjudgment and misoperation by users, resulting in adverse consequences. For example, insufficient information will lead to uncertainty expected by users. Uncertainty of behavior results is the risk cost for users. User will tend to increase the margin of safety, thus occupying too many resources.

The cognitive difference of users varies with age, experience and educational level, including both congenital cognitive ability difference and acquired experience, knowledge and skills difference. This makes the diversity in the ability and efficiency of different users in solving problems independently far greater than their physical differences, and even determines the success or failure of many activities. An experienced and skilled printing shop operator can easily accomplish several times the workload of a novice, while users lacking professional knowledge cannot even complete the basic operation of professional software. Distinguishing the difference between knowledge and skills is of great significance to ease the cognitive difference of users. Much knowledge is information that can be quickly known and used, while skills are the ability to complete a certain task that requires a certain amount of time to practice. In the process of interaction between products and users, necessary and lacking knowledge can be conveyed to users, thus eliminating obstacles of users. But for a particular skill, on the one hand, we should try our best to avoid the dependence of interactive operation on this skill, and at the same time, we should give users with this skill sufficient space to display it.

Emotional. Emotional dimension reflects the emotional value of products, environment and services and the user preferences. The emotional attribute of a product is an important feature that the product gets rid of "commodity attribute" and thus has non-materialized meaning. The core aspects of emotional dimension are aesthetic, cultural and psychological. The differences of users in these aspects are often diversified and changeable, which makes the inclusive design of this dimension full of uncertainty. Moreover, the biggest challenge to designers brought by user diversities in this dimension is that these differences often have obvious mutual exclusion, and the evaluation standard is not a single one. For example, some people's fondness is likely to be dismissed or even hated by others. Even if MUJI adopts neutral and simple design to avoid contradictions and conflicts, it cannot satisfy those consumers who are eager to make public and show off. In more complex multi-user platforms, users need to share more design elements, and emotional diversities between different users are more likely to produce conflicts and contradictions. In many cases, design also needs to respond to the consumer's demand for identity, and stimulate some demands by transmitting the value to satisfy consumer's needs, thus generating the desire to buy and use [15]. These rich and diverse needs are usually difficult to satisfy and are often contained by a single design. Fortunately, in most cases, the market has the same diversified supply capacity. Designers can make trade-offs for their own product positioning, so as to ensure that their design language is consistent with the target users, and can also provide different design for different users. The key is accurate matching between different designs and different users.

Economic. The economic dimension reflects the ability of users to exchange and control external resources. The economic ability of users not only restricts their access to products and services, but also influences their ability through leverage factors. Like a joker card, purchasing power can be easily converted into various other external capabilities by the market, thus greatly changing the actual situation of individuals. It is worth noting that the diversities in economic ability between different individuals is further enlarged compared with physical and cognitive diversities, and can also be doubled through credit leverage. However, economic ability does not necessarily affect consumers' value cognition. Good economic ability only gives consumers more freedom and leeway to make choice. In this sense, economic ability is a direct supporting factor for users' various needs. Diversities in economic ability will also bring about diversification of demand, thus generating more design and business opportunities.

Users' demands in the economic dimension are often at odds with users' capabilities in this dimension. Generally, users with poor economic capabilities are more sensitive to price and demand higher economic returns on products. Economic capability is not simply equivalent to an individual's financial situation. For a specific product, the user's willingness to bear risks and consumption ability on the product are the economic capability indicators related to the product design. Therefore, simple high-income groups and high-consumption "credit card slave" may have economic capability opposite to their comprehensive economic strength at a certain stage in a certain subdivision field.

3.3 User-Sensitive Design

Researchers from the Department of Applied Computing in University of Dundee took the lead in proposing the concept of user-sensitive and inclusive design [16, 17], the starting point of which is to bring the elderly and the disabled into the target user group of mainstream products. They think that some groups, such as the elderly, are different from ordinary users and designers, and have high diversity. The relevant user research often involves moral and ethical issues. It is difficult to copy the standard user-centered design methodology to sum up diverse user characteristics. There are not only substantial differences in user characteristics, but also changes in different time scales. User sensitive and inclusive design needs to respond to this dynamic diversity [18]. Compared with industry, the education field has always attached more importance to the implementation of the principle of teaching students according to their aptitude. With the concept of lifelong learning and a learning society being widely accepted, and information technology playing an increasingly important role in the learning process, individual learners are showing a more and more diversified trend, with different backgrounds, skills, interests, professional knowledge, goals and learning styles. In order to meet such diverse requirements, user-centered design and user-sensitive design have become logical choices [19].

Providing an intelligent user interface is an effective means to make products flexible to personalized needs. The framework to deal with user heterogeneity in the early stage envisages two ways: one is the Adaptable System, i.e. the system allows users to customize. The second is the Adaptive System, that is, the system can adjust the appearance and behavior of the interface according to the characteristics of the user [20]. Although this framework was proposed long before the popularity of graphical user interfaces, it is worthy of respect that the idea of starting from both passive and active aspects still has important guiding significance. We can see that the same thinking is still practiced in the latest interactive design of mobile devices and applications.

How to cooperate with specific users in the best way is the core concern of user sensitivity design. It is an ideal scheme to achieve this goal, which has both adaptability and adaptability. To do this, we first need to be able to identify different users. No matter whether login mechanism or anonymous method is adopted, only by separating unique individuals from a wide range of user groups can targeted responses be made to users. After identifying the user, the system needs to judge the degree of understanding of the user, which depends on the system's archiving of the user's profile. If the user's archived complete information is available, the system can match the ideal preset value for the user through adaptive design. On the contrary, if the system identifies a new unfamiliar user, the system can gradually establish the user's profile through novice guidance or other adaptive design methods in the process of interaction with the user (Fig. 4). From this we can conclude that a user-sensitive design system must include the following features:

- User identification capability;
- Archiving system for user profiles and data;
- Adaptive design of system interface and function;
- The system interface and functions can be customized.

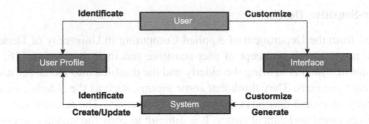

Fig. 4. User-sensitive design framework

4 Contextual Diversities

In addition to individual diversities among users, the diversities that users show due to changes in constraints in different contexts may exceed all others. Even though attention has been paid to the diversities between individual users, if the influence of interaction between users and external environment in different contexts is ignored, contextual exclusion will occur.

4.1 A Cases Study of Contextual Diversities in User Research

Method. In order to analyze and understand the relationship between demand and constraints in user research, the author conducted a survey on MRT (Mass Rapid Transit) payment methods. The survey distributed questionnaires through mobile social networks, and received 519 visits and 201 valid answers. Affected by the media, 200 of them were filled in through mobile phones and only 1 was completed on computers. The purpose of our research is not to understand the user needs reflected in the questionnaire itself and its representation to the real user population, but to study the differences between the individual user needs in the actual environment and the ideal environment, and how to understand the differences and translate them into design insights. Therefore, the data collected by this questionnaire is sufficient for our research.

Result. The first question in the questionnaire is about how often users travel by MRT. The users who choose to travel daily and several times a week account for 22.89% and 31.84% respectively, which together account for more than half of the total. They represent the user group that regards MRT as one of the main modes of travel. The proportion of respondents who choose to take several times a month and occasionally is 16.42% and 26.37% respectively. They can be regarded as low-frequent users with experience of MRT. Only 2.49% of the respondents said that they basically did not take MRT. We will mainly examine their demand characteristics in the ideal environment. Considering that more than half of the respondents come from Shanghai and Beijing, where MRT is well developed (judging by IP addresses, accounting for 47% and 5% of the respondents respectively), this result basically meets our expectations.

The questionnaire asked other users except those who basically do not take MRT what kind of fare collection and payment methods they mainly use when taking MRT. The available answers include "Pay-as-you-go Card", "One-way Ticket", "QR Code", "NFC", "Wearable Device" and a "Other" option that can be filled in by users. The results show that only one interviewee has chosen the "Other" option and filled it in as "AliPay". The answer can actually be classified as "QR Code", which proves that the options provided by the questionnaire basically cover all ticket checking and payment methods currently provided by China's MRT. Specifically, 122 users chose "Pay-as-you-go Card", accounting for 62.2% of the respondents, far ahead of other options and in a dominant position. QR Code was the second choice, with 82 places, accounting for 41.8%. Some mobile phone models with NFC support contactless payment, with 44 users using this relatively "advanced" method accounting for 22.4%; Only 13.3% of the respondents used the most basic and "primitive" one-way ticket. Emerging wearable devices such as bracelets and watches are probably still in the market introduction stage, with the overall user share being the lowest, at 4.1% (Fig. 5).

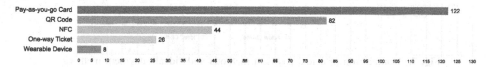

Fig. 5. Number of passengers of various payment methods.

It is worth noting that the answer to this question is actually not the choice made by the interviewee when answering the question, but the expression of their actual choices under real constraints in real life. These actual choices are the optimal solution that the user chooses under the rational guidance after considering all real costs, convenience and potential benefits in a long period of time and putting it into action. Although the reality constraint is not easy for us to perceive and attach importance to because it is pervasive, its influence undoubtedly exists. Users' choices tend to converge at the equilibrium point of supply and demand. In this multi-choice question, the total proportion of all the respondents' choices is 143.9%, which reflects that some respondents - in fact, 31.6% of them - will use more than one method of payment. This may be due to the fact that the same people will encounter different usage contexts and have different preferences for different contexts, but what we see is that more people (68.4%) choose to use the only fare collection and payment method - that is, the best method they choose under the constraints of reality (Fig. 6).

The questionnaire then asked them to choose their ideal payment method. In addition to the original options, we have provided "Identity Card", "Fingerprint Identification", "Face Recognition" and "Voice Recognition" as new options for the four existing payment methods that have not yet been adopted but for which related technology implementation solutions already exist. This question provided more options. However, since this topic is multiple choice, we believe that the new options will not in theory unduly dilute the respondents' positive evaluation of the existing payment methods (Fig. 7).

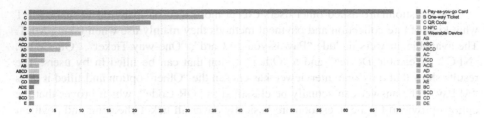

Fig. 6. Number of passengers adopted by various payment combinations.

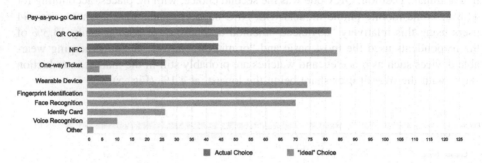

Fig. 7. Comparison of actual payment methods and "ideal" payment methods

Findings. We found an interesting result when we compared the daily payment method previously selected by the user with the "ideal" payment method. We have not made any improvement to the existing payment method, but only asked the respondents to make a new choice by asking questions instead of retelling the actual behavior. However, the results showed that only 20.9% of the respondents thought that the pay-as-you-go card used by the most respondents (62.2%) in daily life was the ideal way, and the number of people who choose QR code and one-way Tickets has dropped significantly. On the contrary, in reality, only 22.4% and 4.1% of the respondents use NFC and wearable devices respectively, 41.8% and 36.8% of the respondents think that they are ideal methods, which have become the two most popular choices among the existing payment methods. Among the four new options, fingerprint recognition and face recognition have achieved relatively high acceptance, which is roughly equivalent to contactless payment of mobile phones and wearable devices, while ID card recognition and voice recognition have not been recognized by most respondents.

The main difference between the two choices is that in the new choice, what we have set is a virtual context. Users do not need to bear any actual costs for their choices, but only need to express their ideal demands. This is similar to the context that researchers will unconsciously construct in most user researches based on questionnaires and interviews. We can see how different users' choices are from the real behaviors in the real context under this virtual context. On the one hand, it shows that the existing research results of users based on virtual contexts need to be evaluated more prudently. On the other hand, it also shows that users' needs and preferences are by no means a stable and static attribute. Any prediction and assumption about users' behaviors and choices depends on clear contextual constraints.

4.2   Contextual Design

Contextual design has been studied and applied in computer hardware [21] and software [22] systems for a long time. In mainstream object-oriented programming languages, functions are triggered by contextual events, which has become a common basic knowledge. However, in the traditional industrial and architectural fields, most products and spaces are not designed for multi-context and complex environment, or the early design research paid little attention to this kind of design. When entering the 21st century, more and more information technologies are integrated into product design, the boundaries between hardware and software systems begin to blur gradually, and multi-functional and multi-mode designs suitable for different contexts gradually increase, thus contextual design has begun to receive more and more attention.

Holtzblatt and Beyer summarized a series of key principles and design processes of contextual design [8], but that process may not substantially differ from other versions of interactive design processes. The focus of their attention is how to understand the user's demands and characteristics from the usage context, so that the design can help users to accomplish the task better. What we want to argue is that the key problem in contextual design is how the product responds to complex and uncertain context changes in real time and accurately. Therefore, through field investigation, user participation and other methods to clarify the needs of users at the design stage can certainly provide valuable insights for design research output, but it is not sufficient to provide sufficient design basis for contextual design. If the product has enough ability to help users accomplish tasks, but cannot coordinate all functions and resources in specific contexts and enter the best mode for specific tasks, then the original intention of contextual design, that is, to ensure users have consistent experience under diverse context, has still not been realized.

Contextual design does not need to reorganize and rebuild a unique design process. Similar to user-sensitivity design, what we need to do is to establish corresponding models for different contexts and usage scenarios, and design corresponding tools and interfaces for system perception of context changes. When the system senses the change of the user's usage context, it needs to be able to respond to the change and adjust the system to adapt to the change of the context. This adjustment mechanism is the focus of contextual design. The specific adjustment mechanism varies according to the relevant subdivisions of the actual project. It is difficult for us to carry out the detailed adjustment mechanism here because of the limited space. However, the authors believe that this topic has a broad space for research and discussion. In addition, even if we have designed an almost perfect adjustment mechanism, we cannot guarantee that it can fully meet the needs of users in that context, so it is always necessary and valuable to give users convenient intervention and adjustment ability to the system.

5   Contextualized User-Sensitive Design

After discussing user-sensitive design and contextual design respectively, it is possible to combine the two and summarize a design framework that can be applied to diverse users in diverse contexts. Through user research in early stage, we can initially understand the distribution of user diversities and context diversities, and establish a preliminary user balance sheet, story board and scenario model for the target users. By cross-examining the diversities between users and contexts, designers and researchers can find the gaps and blind areas of product's inclusion to users in different usage contexts (Fig. 3). These gaps and blind areas can be used as benchmarks for further design improvement (Fig. 8).

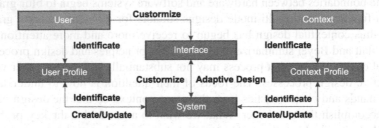

Fig. 8. Contextualized user-sensitive design framework

As mentioned earlier, the implementation of the framework is based on some prerequisites and necessary system capabilities: for example, the system should be able to identify and remember the characteristics of different users and perceive different contexts and scenarios. Consequently, the design of identifying user and context diversities will be integrated into the whole design process. On this basis, the modeling of users and scenarios will go on from design and development till daily operation and maintenance after launch when users are continuously using the product. The target user's persona and scenario storyboards are established, and then the profiles of users and scenarios are created and accurately refined with the data generated by the user's interaction with the system. Thanks to the rapid growth of data calculation and storage capacity, the user profiles and scenario descriptions can be subdivided into a greater extent than ever before. It is even possible to maintain a dynamically updated accurate profile for each user and scenario.

One of the major limitations of the previous product and interaction design is that the granularity of the design is very large, and there are often only a limited number of design schemes to deal with different context, which greatly limits the inclusion of the design to user diversities and context changes. In the framework of contextualized user-sensitive design, in order to match accurate user and context perception ability, the final output of contextualized user-sensitive interaction design will no longer be implemented into a standardized GUI, but rather a parameterized and algorithmic interface and interaction experience. Responsive design is only a partial and preliminary attempt of this kind of design. Through the matching mechanism and algorithm designed in advance by designers, combined with user customization and the application of artificial intelligence technology with broad prospects, the design granularity of digital products will be greatly reduced, thus seamlessly connecting the changing user needs and capabilities. Users will not only obtain completely differentiated and customized content and services, but also include completely differentiated and customized interface and interactions, which keep consistent across different contexts.

6 Conclusion

This paper constructs a contextualized user-sensitive design framework by analyzing the interaction between behavior models and various aspects in human-computer systems. The design framework is based on two basic dimensions of users and contexts, and studies the diversities and changing factors in human-computer systems. In order to reflect the multi-dimensional dynamic characteristics of users, the authors propose a new user research and analysis tool, the generalized user balance sheet, and use a questionnaire case to reveal the huge differences of users' needs in different contexts. Based on the contextualized user-sensitive design framework, this paper shows the basic methods and essential system elements of user-sensitive design and contextual design, as well as the preliminary exploration of combining the two for inclusive design.

The authors believe that when the interaction design of digital products can respond to the differentiated needs and preferences of each user contextually, it is close to achieving the maximum inclusion. Its significance lies in making full use of the possibilities created by technological progress, so that each individual will no longer compromise with the need to share the same interface and design resources with others, thus expanding inclusion.

References

1. Gonzalez, I., Morer, P.: Ergonomics for the inclusion of older workers in the knowledge workforce and a guidance tool for designers. Appl. Ergon. **53**((Part A)), 131–142 (2016)
2. Fogg, B.: A behavior model for persuasive design. In: Proceedings of the 4th International Conference on Persuasive Technology. ACM: Claremont, California, USA (2009), pp. 1–7
3. Mises, L.V.: Human Action: A Treatise on Economics. Shanghai Academy of Social Sciences Press, Shanghai (2015)
4. Miaskiewicz, T., Kozar, K.A.: Personas and user-centered design: how can personas benefit product design processes? Des. Stud. **32**(5), 417–430 (2011)
5. Pfeil, U., Arjan, R., Zaphiris, P.: Age differences in online social networking—a study of user profiles and the social capital divide among teenagers and older users in MySpace. Comput. Hum. Behav. **25**(3), 643–654 (2009)
6. Marcotte, E.: Responsive Web Design (2010)
7. Gustafson, A.: Adaptive Web Design: Crafting Rich Experiences with Progressive Enhancement, 2nd edn. New Riders, San Francisco (2016)
8. Beyer, H., Hultzblatt, K.: Contextual Design: Defining Customer-Centered Systems. Morgan Kaufmann, San Francisco (1998)
9. Nielsen, J.: Usability Engineering, 1st edn. Morgan Kaufmann, San Francisco (1993)

10. ISO 13407:1999: In: Human-Centred Design Processes for Interactive Systems. International Organization for Standardization (1999)
11. ISO 9241-210:2010: In: Ergonomics of human-system interaction—Part 210: Human-centred design for interactive systems. International Organization for Standardization (2010)
12. Novoseltseva, E.: User-Centered Design: An Introduction. https://usabilitygeek.com/user-centered-design-introduction/. Accessed 5 Jan 2019
13. Gonzalez, I., Morer, P.: Developing a workstation design assistance tool for older knowledge workforce inclusion. Univers. Access Inf. Soc. **16**(3), 641–651 (2017)
14. Herzberg, F., Mausner, B., Snyderman, B.B.: The Motivation to Work. Wiley, New Jersey (1959)
15. Sparke, P.: An Introduction to Design and Culture. Yilin Press Ltd, Nanjing (2012)
16. Newell, A.F., Gregor, P.: User sensitive inclusive design—in search of a new paradigm. In: Proceedings on the 2000 Conference on Universal Usability. ACM, pp. 39–44, Arlington (2000)
17. Newell, A.F., et al.: User-sensitive inclusive design. Univers. Access Inf. Soc. **10**(3), 235–243 (2011)
18. Gregor, P., Newell, A.F., Zajicek, M.: Designing for dynamic diversity: interfaces for older people. In: Proceedings of the Fifth International ACM Conference on Assistive Technologies. ACM, pp. 151–156, Edinburgh
19. Glavinić, V., Granić, A.: HCI Research for E-Learning: Adaptability and Adaptivity to Support Better User Interaction. In: Holzinger, Andreas (ed.) USAB 2008. LNCS, vol. 5298, pp. 359–376. Springer, Heidelberg (2008). https://doi.org/10.1007/978-3-540-89350-9_25
20. Matthias, S.-H., Uwe, M., Thomas, K. (eds.): Adaptive User Interfaces: Principles and Practice. Elsevier Science Inc., New York, p. 362
21. Curtis, P., et al.: Customer-focused design data in a large, multi-site organization. In: The SIGCHI Conference on Human Factors in Computing Systems: the CHI Is the Limit. ACM Press, pp. 608–615, Pittsburgh (1999)
22. Rockwell, C.: Customer connection creates a winning product: building success with contextual techniques. Interactions **6**(1), 50–57 (1999)

A Disability-Oriented Analysis Procedure
for Leisure Rehabilitation Product Design

Ming-Chyuan Lin[✉], Guo-Peng Qui, Xue Hua Zhou, and Jing Chen

College of Arts and Design, Sanming University, Sanming City, Fujian, China
mingchyuan1688@gmail.com, 644021962@qq.com,
403393909@qq.com, chenjing_1205@163.com

Abstract. The leisure activities of current disabled people are primary static types rather than dynamic types. However, most marketed leisure exercise products seldom consider the requirements of the disabled people especially their slow reactions on hand grasp and eye perception. This situation always makes the disabled people be unable to do normal lifestyle activities. The preliminary investigation showed that certain cerebral palsy people with minor disorders have strong desires to do leisure rehabilitation activities. As such, the objective of this research is to try to focus on the redesign of certain leisure exercise products for the cerebral palsy people and derive specific combination of functions and design guidelines for designer reference. During the development process, an AIO (A: activity; I: interest; O: opinion) questionnaire regarding user feelings, preferences and requirements is designed and distributed the related subjects to explore more precise user requirements. The analytic results are forwarded to the process of conjoint analysis and quality function deployment to help identify some critical design characteristics for the design of leisure rehabilitation products. Several design alternatives are generated based on the proposed design criteria. The generated design alternatives are represented in 3D rendering images with the assistance of computer-assisted software. It is expected that the proposed design process of the leisure rehabilitation product development and recommended design alternatives can provide designers with disability leisure exercise product design guidelines and requirements.

Keywords: Leisure rehabilitation product design · Disability-oriented design · Conjoint analysis · Quality function deployment

1 Introduction

Rehabilitation apparatuses are considered as part of the body for the disabled persons and have been widely used. In general, rehabilitation apparatuses can be classified as personal assisted apparatuses, skill training apparatuses, rectified implements, personal motion apparatuses, personal medical and protective equipments, living rehabilitation apparatuses, living furniture, communication and information assisted apparatuses, tooling, machining and environmental improvement equipments, leisure assisted apparatuses and multipurpose implements [1, 2]. Due to a gradual increase on the disabled people, a variety of rehabilitation apparatuses techniques and development become important to our society. Previous investigation showed that the existing rehabilitation apparatuses

© Springer Nature Switzerland AG 2019
M. Antona and C. Stephanidis (Eds.): HCII 2019, LNCS 11572, pp. 133–145, 2019.
https://doi.org/10.1007/978-3-030-23560-4_10

can meet daily requirements of the disabled people, but they expect to have the same living quality as normal people, especially on leisure activity requirements [1]. It appears that a good rehabilitation product design should meet the disabled requirements and can help improve their living quality. Therefore, explore living problems and identify requirements for the disabled are an important issue in rehabilitation technique study. Our preliminary research on the requirements of the disabled people has found that some of them such as cerebral palsy people with minor disorder symptoms will expect to have certain types of leisure rehabilitation products for their daily activities. Unfortunately, there are only very limited leisure rehabilitation products in the market and even do not consider the disabled requirements. It is noted that the cerebral palsy people usually have slow reaction on hand control and eye perception and cannot use regular leisure products for rehabilitation. As such this research will focus on the cerebral palsy demands for recreational sports products and explore the best combination of design guidelines and recommendations based on the requirements of cerebral palsy leisure activity lifestyle.

In product design, the designer must collect many types of information including both product-user requirements and design development in related field. Since the designer has his or her own subjected opinion, the integration of knowledge and experience designers of similar products will greatly improve the quality of product design. Current techniques in product design process indicated that conjoint analysis can be used to help identify the optimum combination of user requirements for specific group [3]; while quality function deployment can used to effectively link user requirements with design characteristics and determine design criteria [4–6]. In order to explore suitable designs for the requirements of the cerebral palsy people, the objective for this research effort is to apply the concepts of conjoint analysis and quality function deployment in the leisure rehabilitation product design process to develop suitable leisure rehabilitation products for the cerebral palsy people.

2 Development Procedure

During the development procedure, the research considers not only the requirements of rehabilitation functions and user sensation, but also appropriate product form and multi-purpose. The research has three stages of development. The first stage is identification and analysis of cerebral palsy requirements on recreational sports or rehabilitation products, including: (1) data collection on cerebral palsy characteristics, (2) collection of existing regular leisure products and rehabilitation products, and (3) factor analysis for identifying user requirements. The second stage is employment of conjoint analysis and quality function deployment (QFD) technique that will help determine suitable recreational sports or rehabilitation product design criteria for the cerebral palsy people. In the process of conjoint analysis, the research used an AIO (A: activity; I: interest; O: opinion) questionnaire associated with factor analysis to help identify requirements of the cerebral palsy people. Based on the conjoint analysis, the research will determine specific requirements for groups of the cerebral palsy people. The requirements for the first group of the cerebral palsy people are then chosen and forwarded to the process of QFD analysis. According to the evaluation results from the QFD process, some critical design characteristics are identified. As to the third stage,

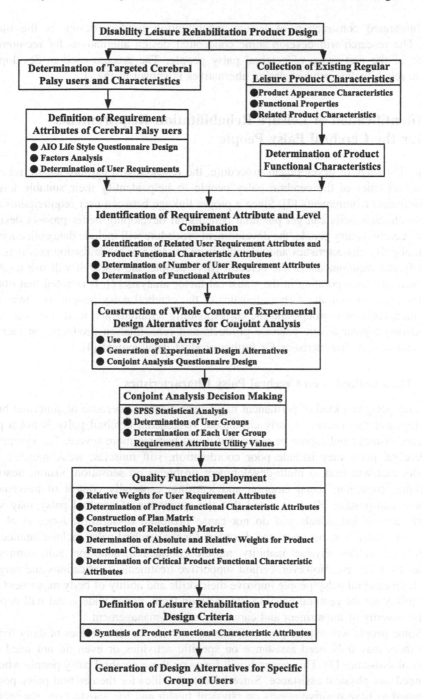

Fig. 1. A conceptual structure showing the procedure for leisure rehabilitation product design

the integrated construction of leisure rehabilitation product design is the major part. The research will develop some conceptual design alternatives for recommendation of the first group of cerebral palsy people. The process used in developing leisure rehabilitation product design alternatives is shown in Fig. 1.

3 Identification of Leisure Rehabilitation Requirements for the Cerebral Palsy People

In the first stage of development procedure, the research will explore leisure rehabilitation activities of the cerebral palsy people to help identify their suitable leisure rehabilitation requirements [7]. Since a proper linkage between user requirements and design characteristics can get potential benefits on developing better product designs for the cerebral palsy people, the development procedure will include data collection on cerebral palsy characteristics and related leisure exercise or rehabilitation products. To identify the requirements of the cerebral palsy people, the research will use an AIO questionnaire incorporating in the statistical factor analysis [7]. It is noted that obtain essential information about characteristics of the cerebral palsy people will help analyze their preference groups and the corresponding requirements; while the collection of existing regular leisure exercise products and rehabilitation products can identify potential design characteristics for further product development [4].

3.1 Data Collection on Cerebral Palsy Characteristics

Cerebral palsy is a kind of permanent movement disorders because of abnormal brain development that occurs in early childhood. In general, cerebral palsy is not a progressive disorder and cannot be cured, but it can become more severe. The symptoms of cerebral palsy may include poor coordination, stiff muscles, weak muscles and tremors that will lead to multi-development problems on sensation, vision, hearing, speaking, cognition, social emotion and learning, especially control of movement, balance and posture [8]. It is noted that the symptoms of cerebral palsy may vary greatly among individuals and do not cause profound disabilities. Jones et al. [2] further indicated that the associated disorders for the cerebral palsy include intellectual disabilities, sudden physical inability, muscle contraction, abnormal gait, communication disorders, etc. However, certain supportive treatments, medications and surgery may help cerebral palsy people improve their skills and ability of body movement [9]. The ability for the cerebral palsy to live independently varies widely and will depend on the severity of impairment and capability of self-management.

Some people will require personal assistant service for all activities of daily living, but others may only need assistance on specific activities or even do not need any physical assistance [2]. This research will focus on those cerebral palsy people who do not need any physical assistance. Since leisure activities for the cerebral palsy people are noted to have positive effects on physical health and life satisfaction, researchers tried to develop some formal or informal activities to help reduce muscle stress, increase coping activities, increase companionship, physical relaxation and enjoyment [1, 10]. This research will focus on those cerebral palsy people who do not need any physical assistance.

3.2   Collection of Existing Regular Leisure or Rehabilitation Products

The study showed that electronic games of leisure rehabilitation products can provide the cerebral palsy people with enjoyable fun and direct operational involvement. These activities also have clear rules and objective that encourage the cerebral palsy people to challenge their capability and help them improve their disability. Current marketed electronic leisure products that are available for the cerebral palsy people seldom consider the cerebral palsy requirements, such as slow movement on eyes and hands, weak ability of grip and operation, and use of a wheelchair. Landreth [11] suggested that specific kinds of toys for the play therapy may include pile up, simulated family living, shooting, hammering, boxing, palm type ragdoll, softball playing and transportation type of simulated driving.

3.3   Factor Analysis for Identifying Cerebral Palsy User Requirements

In designing suitable leisure rehabilitation products for the cerebral palsy people, it is important to take physiological functions of human bodies, comfort, pleasure, aesthetics, maintenance and care, and consumers' lifestyles into consideration [12]. As such the research is developed based on user experiences that apply questionnaires, psychographic analysis and statistical factor analysis to identify requirement attributes and explore their preferences on leisure activity products [13]. The research developed an AIO (A: activity; I: interest; O: opinion) lifestyle questionnaire to help identify candidate user requirements [7]. A total of 36 AIO-type questions were designed, which included 16 types of activities, 12 types of interests and 8 types of opinions. This questionnaire is distributed to the selected test subjects of cerebral palsy people. There were 21 effective questionnaire results obtained from 13 male and 8 female people. The results of questionnaire survey were forwarded to the statistical software SPSS for a factor analysis. According to the result of factor analysis, 36 AIO-type questions were pooled to 12 specific requirement attributes and also formed into five factors, as illustrated in Table 1. Based on the semantic contents of 12 requirement attributes corresponding to each factor, the research defined five factors as (1) appearance, (2) adjustment, (3) operation, (4) safety, and (5) feedback. In Table 1, five factors associated with their attributes were identified: (1) appearance (simple form and big size), (2) adjustment (handle enlargement, button enlargement and speed adjustment), (3) operation (simplified and repetitive operation, easy reading and low speedy display), (4) safety (fixed type, and pressure endurance), and (5) feedback (sound and flash light). The identified five factors and associated requirement attributes are then forwarded to the conjoint analysis to determine the requirements of user groups.

Table 1. Illustration of requirement attributes associated with factors

Factor Matrix after Data Rotation

AIO Life Style Requirement Attribute	Factor				
	1	2	3	4	5
36 Simple Form	.899	.207	-.077	.137	-.023
21 Big Size	.885	.180	.019	.052	-.046
34 Handle Enlargement and Bolder	-.126	.828	.041	.293	.012
32 Push Button Enlargement	.352	.756	.096	.142	-.187
8 Speed Adjustment	.448	.626	-.225	-.208	.420
10 Simplified and Repetitive Operation	.379	.094	.829	.118	.180
13 Readability	.160	.067	.783	-.003	.402
12 Low Display Speed	.168	.232	.730	.388	.093
2 Fastener	.302	.186	-.204	.852	.106
4 Pressurization	-.107	-.054	.413	.830	.161
19 Voice Reminder	-.322	.039	.187	.158	.871
20 Flash Light Reminder	.558	.056	.040	.175	.703

4 Employment of Conjoint Analysis and Quality Function Deployment

Followed by the first stage of development procedure, the second stage of this research conducts the procedures of conjoint analysis and quality function deployment. The conjoint analysis will be used to evaluate the requirement factors and attributes and help identify preference attribute combination of group cerebral palsy people. While the analysis of quality function deployment will link the preference requirements of specific group of cerebral palsy people with design characteristics of leisure rehabilitation products that help determine a combination of critical design characteristics for further product development [4, 14].

4.1 Conjoint Analysis for Identifying Group Requirements of Cerebral Palsy People

When dealing with the process of conjoint analysis, dummy variables and utility values corresponding to the identified requirement attributes are defined. The concept of orthogonal array is applied in the experimental design that helps efficiently conduct the measurement [15]. Note that the statistical computer software SPSS V14 is used throughout the proposed research. Considering a minimum size of the orthogonal array in conjoin analysis, the SPSS V14 software helps generate an orthogonal array with a 16 experimental design and will be called as "Card1", "Card 2", ... and "Card 16", respectively. Each experimental design consists of one requirement attribute assigned from each factor that constitutes design characteristics of a leisure rehabilitation product design alternative. To conduct the experiment, the research designed 16 cards with the size of 10 × 10 cm cardboards and organized each of combined requirement attributes in the cardboard. The original 21 tested subjects were asked to make a pair-wise preference evaluation of combined requirement attributes among the 16 card-boards. It is noted that the concept of multiple linear regression models will be applied in the measurement of component utility values for the combined requirement attributes of a cardboard. In a multiple linear regression model, the value of preference order associated with values of dummy variables will then be considered as dependent and independent variables, respectively. These component utility values of dummy variables for the 21 tested subjects are then forwarded to the SPSS software for a K-means clustering analysis. In this research, the 21 tested subjects were divided into three groups. The results of each component utility value for the corresponding requirement attribute of three groups are illustrated in Table 2.

Table 2. Group component utility values of requirement attributes

Factor	Level	Requirement Attribute	Group Component Utility Value		
			Group 1	Group 2	Group 3
Appearance	1	Simple Form	0	1.188	0
Type	2	Big Size	0.375	0	1.375
Adjustment	1	Handle Enlargement and	1.361	3.000	1.094
Type		Bolder			
	2	Push Button Enlargement	1.944	4.250	0
	3	Speed Adjustment	0	0	3.297
Operation	1	Simplified and Repetitive	1.528	1.813	0
Type		Operation			
	2	Readability	1.856	0.625	1.556
	3	Low Display Speed	0	0	0.859
Safety Type	1	Fastener	0	0.375	0
	2	Pressurization	0.972	0	0.766
Feedback Type	1	Voice Reminder	0	2.563	1.563
	2	Flash Light Reminder	2.333	0	0

4.2   Construction of a House of Quality of QFD

The 9 tested subjects of Group 1 were asked to make a quality function deployment survey to measure the relationships between customer requirement and design characteristic attributes, respectively. To develop a house of quality (HOQ) of quality function deployment, the research made an investigation on identifying suitable leisure rehabilitation design characteristic attributes. The investigation involved the cerebral palsy people, tested subjects, school mentors and supervisors, parents of tested subjects, and current leisure recreational products. The research summarized 12 design characteristic attributes that are thought to be related to the customer requirement attributes. The 12 design characteristic attributes are (1) error reminder, (2) character size, (3) clear indication, (4) control area size, (5) targeted control size, (6) user dominant role, (7) simplified operation process, (8) material selection, (9) sticky fastener, (10) avoid redundant decoration, (11) avoid sharp angles, and (12) simple manual operation. After customer requirement attributes and design characteristic attributes having been defined, the research performed the process of quality function deployment analysis. Since this research will primarily deal with the generation of design alternatives, the development of quality function deployment only considers the core part of the relationship matrix. The general steps for developing a simplified house of quality in quality function deployment are stated as follows [4–6]:

Step 1.   List customer requirement attributes and place them on left side of the house.
Step 2.   List design characteristic attributes and place them on top of the house.
Step 3.   Determine relative weights for customer requirement attributes.
          To evaluate customer requirement attributes, the concept of analytic hierarchy process (AHP) [16] is used. In implementing pairwise comparisons between two customer requirement attributes, a questionnaire survey based on a measurement scale with points 1–9 and their reciprocals is distributed to the tested subjects. The points of 1–9 represent the strength of relative importance of a customer requirement attribute compared with the other customer requirement attribute. The values of 1–9 represent equal, weak, …, and extreme importance between customer requirement attributes. Note that geometric means are calculated to pool evaluation values of all tested subjects. By the summation of the geometric means of all customer requirement attributes, a normalization process is also calculated to obtain relative weights for each customer requirement attribute. The relative weight value of each customer requirement attribute is expressed as a percentage.
Step 4.   Evaluate close relationships between customer requirement attributes and design characteristic attributes to form a relationship matrix.
          The relationship matrix evaluates the strength of the linkages between customer requirement attributes and design characteristic attributes. Each matrix cell indicates a relationship that represents the impact strength of a design characteristic attribute on a corresponding customer requirement attribute. The strength relationship is assessed with a rating scale of 0, 1, 2, 3, 4, and 5 to represent none, very weak, weak, medium, strong, and very strong, respectively. The measured data from all tested subjects are averaged and filled in the corresponding cells of the relationship matrix.
Step 5.   Calculate the absolute weight for each design characteristic attribute.
          To calculate the absolute weight for each design characteristic attribute, simply do the summation of the value by multiplying the relative weight value of each customer requirement attribute with the corresponding relationship matrix cell value of a design characteristic attribute. The summation denotes the contribution of that design characteristic attribute to the overall customer satisfaction.

Step 6.   Normalize the absolute weights of design characteristic attributes to be relative weights.

The relative weight value for each design characteristic attribute is calculated as the absolute weight value of a customer requirement attribute divided by the summation of all absolute weight values of customer requirement attributes. Each relative weight value of the design characteristic attribute is expressed as a percentage.

Step 7.   Determine certain critical design characteristic attributes for further product development.

The relative weights of design characteristic attributes are ranked according to their relative priorities. It means that a higher rank corresponds to a more important design characteristic attribute and needs to pay more attention to product development.

Figure 2 illustrated the construction of a partial house of quality in quality function deployment for the group 1 survey. The result of quality function deployment analysis showed in Fig. 1 revealed that the design characteristic attributes of "targeted control size", "user dominant role", "control area size", and "error reminder" can be considered as critical design characteristics for further improvement in product design.

	User Requirements Relative Weight (100%)	Error reminder	Character size	Clear Indication	Control Area Size	Targeted Control Size	User Dominant Role	Simplified Operation process	Material Selection	Sticky Fastener	Avoid Redundant Decoration	Avoid Sharp Angles	Simple Manual Operation
Simple Form	4.35	2.6	3.0	2.7	3.6	4.6	3.2	3.0	2.4	3.0	3.6	3.0	2.0
Big Size	4.35	3.0	3.8	2.0	3.6	4.6	4.0	3.6	2.0	3.4	3.4	3.3	3.0
Handle Enlargement and Bolder	16.5	3.5	2.2	2.0	4.4	4.5	4.2	2.8	2.4	3.0	2.2	3.0	2.0
Push Button Enlargement	22.1	3.2	2.8	1.7	3.4	4.2	4.2	3.2	3.0	4.4	3.2	3.6	3.5
Speed Adjustment	1.72	3.0	2.8	4.0	2.6	4.2	2.7	2.6	2.2	4.4	3.2	2.6	2.1
Simplified and Repetitive Operation	3.88	3.4	3.2	4.0	2.6	4.0	3.6	1.8	2.2	3.0	3.0	3.6	2.2
Readability	1.87	3.8	3.4	4.2	2.8	4.0	2.7	1.6	2.4	3.4	3.8	2.0	2.1
Low Display Speed	15.8	2.6	2.4	4.2	2.8	4.4	3.4	1.6	2.4	3.4	3.0	2.6	3.0
Fastener	0.92	2.0	3.6	3.0	3.6	4.8	4.2	3.2	2.4	2.4	2.6	2.3	3.0
Pressurization	13.1	4.0	3.4	2.3	4.0	4.8	2.8	3.6	2.6	1.4	2.4	2.6	3.5
Voice Reminder	7.73	2.6	2.0	2.5	2.6	2.2	3.0	2.0	2.6	2.0	2.6	2.0	2.0
Flash Light Reminder	7.73	3.0	2.4	3.4	3.4	3.0	3.6	3.2	3.2	2.0	4.0	2.3	3.2
Design Characteristics Absolute Weight		317	271	266	345	414	363	276	261	305	294	289	284
Design Characteristics Relative Weight (100%)		8.6	7.4	7.2	9.4	11.2	9.9	7.5	7.1	8.3	8.0	7.8	7.7
Design Characteristics Ranking		4	10	11	3	1	2	9	12	5	6	7	8

Fig. 2. Construction of QFD' house of quality for Group 1

5   Generation of Conceptual Design Alternatives

The analysis of quality function deployment for group 1 of the tested subjects shown in Fig. 2 provides designers with clear design criteria for developing design concepts. This research proposed three concepts of design alternatives. These design alternatives will be focused on activities of upper and lower extremity, and eye movement rehabilitation exercise. They are (1) fight rodents game, (2) pedal touch panel, and (3) memory pair-off matching game.

The concept of fight rodent game design is based on the large scale of regular fight rodent game that reduces the size to fit the personal use. When playing the game, the user pushes the central red ON/OFF button. One of the surrounding 12 different colored rodents will rise up randomly in a relatively and reasonably time that allow the cerebral palsy people to use the wooden hammer to press it and get the score. The cumulative score will be displayed on a rectangular panel to encourage the user to make an effort to obtain a good score. Figure 3 illustrates the proposed design alternative of fight rodent game. The pedal touch panel is designed for the lower limb rehabilitation purpose. Basically, the front panel has six or more large circles. When the power is on, the user can apply the foot touching to any circle area and the circle area will emit the light and sound of music. Each time of pedal touch action will emit different color of light and sound of music that will make the user to continue his or her rehabilitation without showing boredom. Figure 4 illustrates the proposed design alternative of pedal touch panel. As to the memory pair-off matching game, it belongs to a kind of card play. The game can be available for single, couple, or multiple persons of play. The figure images of the cards are designed based on the concepts of both 12 Chinese animal signs and 12 constellation signs. Each card is doubled in pairs that make the total box of 48 cards. As to the play rules, it is similar to the game of memory matching in the Internet. However,

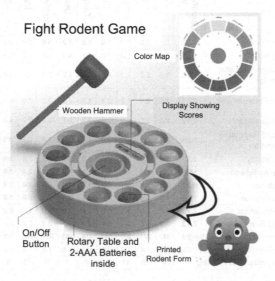

Fig. 3. A fight rodent game design alternative

the memory pair-off matching game is a real entity that help the cerebral palsy people play with friends, train brain memory, increase their play interest and encourage taking a challenge. Figure 5 illustrates the proposed design alternative of memory pair-off matching game. These game activities also have clear rules and objective that encourage the cerebral palsy people to challenge their capability and help them improve their disability.

Fig. 4. A pedal touch panel design alternative

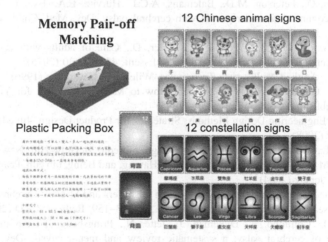

Fig. 5. A memory pair-off matching game design alternative

6 Conclusion

Product design is an activity that the designer must draw upon many types of information including both product-user requirements and design techniques in related fields. Currently, design for the minority has become an important issue that arouses people to pay attention to improving the living quality on the disabled people. Many cerebral palsy people need various types of products to assist their rehabilitation, especially for leisure exercise activities. The investigation also indicated that young people prefer electronic products. The research proposed a design procedure that involving conjoint analysis and quality function deployment to determine requirements of the cerebral palsy people. In the conjoint analysis, factors of user requirements including appearance, adjustment, operation, safety and feedback are identified. Based on the linkage between user requirement attributes and design characteristic attributes in the analysis of quality function deployment, the priority of design characteristic attributes are determined to be the design criteria. Three conceptual design alternatives, "fight rodent game", "pedal touch panel", and "memory pair-off matching game" are presented for further product development. It is expected that this research effort is directed toward the development of the procedures and will enhance the efficiency of design on leisure rehabilitation products to help the disabled persons or even social vulnerable groups in medical rehabilitation and living care.

Acknowledgements. The authors are grateful to the Fujian University Humanities and Social Science Research Base-Product Design Innovation Research Center, China for supporting this research.

References

1. Verschuren, O., Peterson, M.D., Balemans, A.C.J., Hurvitz, E.A.: Exercise and physical activity recommendations for people with cerebral palsy. Dev. Med. Child Neurol. **58**(8), 798–808 (2016)
2. Jones, K.B., Wilson, B., Weedon, D., Bilder, D.: Care of adults with intellectual and developmental disabilities: cerebral palsy. FP Essent. **439**, 26–30 (2015)
3. Sharma, S.: Applied Multivariate Techniques. Wiley Inc, New York (1996)
4. Cohen, L.: Quality Function Deployment How to Make QFD Work for You. Addison-Wesley Publishing Company, Reading (1995)
5. Cross, N.: Engineering Design Methods: Strategies for Product Design, 4th edn. Wiely Ltd, Chichester (2008)
6. Dieter, G.E., Schmidt, L.C.: Engineering Design, 5th edn. McGraw-Hill, New York (2013)
7. Solomon, M.R.: Consumer Behavior: Buying, Having, and Being, 6th edn. Pearson Prentice-Hall, New Jersey (2004)
8. NINDS (the National Institute of Neurological Disorders and Stroke): Cerebral palsy: hope through research. National Institutes of Health, pp. 13–159, Bethesda, MD (2013)
9. Oskoui, M., Coutinho, F., Dykeman, J., Jetté, N., Pringsheim, T.: An update on the prevalence of cerebral palsy: a systematic review and meta-analysis. Dev. Med. Child Neurol. **55**(6), 509–519 (2013)
10. Stone, D., Jarrett, C., Woodroffe, M., Minocha, S.: User Interface Design and Evaluation. Morgan Kaufmann Publishers, San Francisco (2005)
11. Landreth, G.L.: Innovations in Play Therapy: Issues, Process, and Special Populations. Brunner-Routledge, New York (2001)
12. Lehto, M., Landry, S.J.: Introduction to Human Factors and Ergonomics for Engineers, 2nd edn. CRC Press, Taylor & Francis Group, Boca Raton (2013)
13. Preece, J., Rogers, Y.: Interaction Design: Beyond Human-Computer Interaction. Wiley Inc, New York (2002)

14. Chen, M.-S., Lin, C.-C., Tai, Y.-Y., Lin, M.-C.: A grey relation approach to the integrated process of QFD and QE. Concurr. Eng. Res. Appl. **19**(1), 35–53 (2011)
15. Lin, M.-C., Lin, Y.-H., Chen, M.-S., Hung, Y.-C.: An integrated neuro-genetic approach incorporating the Taguchi method for product design. J. Adv. Eng. Inf. **29**, 47–58 (2015)
16. Saaty, T.L., Vargas, L.G.: Decision Making in Economic, Political, Social and Technological Environments: The Analytic Hierarchy Process, vol. VII. RWS Publications, Pittsburg (1994)

Getting Smarter About Data and Access in Smart Cities

H. Patricia McKenna[(✉)]

AmbientEase, Victoria, BC V8V 4Y9, Canada
mckennaph@gmail.com

Abstract. The purpose of this paper is to explore access in relation to new forms of urban data enabled by more aware people and aware technologies in smart cities. Focusing on the constructs of awareness, learning, openness, and engagement, a review of the research literature for data access and universal access in relation to smart cities is provided. As such, a theoretical space for data access is developed as a dimension of the construct of universal access. The research design for this work employs an exploratory case study approach, using multiple methods of data collection including interviews and survey in small to medium to large sized cities, mostly in Canada and extending to cities in other countries. Content analysis is used as an analytic technique for qualitative data to identify insights while descriptive statistics are used in the analysis of quantitative data. This work makes a contribution to: (a) the research literature for smart cities; (b) urban theory by advancing a conceptual framework for ambient access in learning, smart, and future cities; and (c) spaces for debate, inquiry, theorizing, and everyday interactions pertaining to urban data in smart cities, regions, and communities.

Keywords: Ambient access · Ambient data · Awareness · Data accessibility · Data rights · Future cities · Learning cities · Smart cities · Universal access

1 Introduction

At the intersection of rapid urban growth, aware technologies, and more aware people [1] is the emergence of new forms of data in smart cities. Schmitt [2] describes the flow of data "as the new building material of the future dynamic city" while others [3] describe data as a new type of resource requiring access and rights considerations as in, the need for a 31st human right. According to Stephanidis [4], universal access "is intended to inform the evolution of the information society as a human, social, and technological construct," pointing to the "new challenges posed by pursuing proactive accessibility and usability in the context of ambient interaction" [5]. This is important because according to Konomi and Roussos [6], "we are now going beyond the last decade's conception of smart cities" and moving "towards a deeper level of symbiosis among smart citizens, Internet of Things and ambient spaces." As if in anticipation, Stephanidis [4] called for "methods and techniques to be appropriately expanded and enhanced, as well as validated in practice" for "new technological environments and contexts of use." In response, the aim of this work is to explore access in relation to

© Springer Nature Switzerland AG 2019
M. Antona and C. Stephanidis (Eds.): HCII 2019, LNCS 11572, pp. 146–158, 2019.
https://doi.org/10.1007/978-3-030-23560-4_11

new forms of urban data, as a dimension of the universal access construct. Through a review of the research literature for data access and universal access in relation to smart cities, this work formulates a conceptual framework for ambient access in learning, smart, and future cities. This framework is then operationalized using the constructs of awareness, learning, openness, and engagement to explore the potential for getting smarter about data and access in relation to urban life in smart cities. The research design for this work employs an exploratory case study approach, using multiple methods of data collection including interviews and survey, involving a cross-section of people in multiple small to medium to large sized cities in Canada and beyond. Content analysis is used as an analytic technique for qualitative data to identify insights and descriptive statistics are used in the analysis of quantitative data.

Intended to open spaces for emergent thinking about data access in relation to urban life, the key research question posed in this work is – *How and why is there a potential for access to data to form part of smarter human and urban infrastructures?*

2 Theoretical Perspective

A review of the research literature for data access is provided from multiple perspectives in relation to smart cities including associated frameworks. Perspectives from the research literature are then provided on universal access focusing on data for smart cities. With this background, a conceptual framework for ambient data access in learning, smart, and future cities is formulated in Sect. 2.3.

2.1 Data Access and Smart Cities

The rapid growth of cities and urban regions has given rise to the need for smarter, more responsive cities enabled through the increasing development and use of information and communication technologies (ICTs) [7, 8] and other aware technologies [9]. Townsend [10] describes smart cities as "places where information technology is combined with infrastructure, architecture, everyday objects and even our bodies, to address social, economic, and environmental problems." Evolving understandings of the smart city phenomena reveal new opportunities and potentials for people to interact with technologies and with each other in addressing ever more complex urban issues [11]. Gil-Garcia, Nam, and Pardo [12] advance smarter as a new urban agenda while Gil-Garcia, Zhang, and Puron-Cid [13] provide a conceptualization of smartness in government consisting of 14 dimensions, including – creativity, equality, integration, and openness.

Data Access and Value. Gurevich, Hudis, and Wing [14] note that, "due to progress in technology, institutions have become much better than you in recording data" claiming that such "shared data decays into inversely private" and that "more inversely private information is produced when institutions analyze your private data" that "allows institutions to serve you better." However, Gurevich et al. [14] point to the value of access to this information and refer to "the inaccessibility of your inversely private information" as "the inverse privacy problem" whereby "a good solution should not only provide you accessibility but should also make that access convenient."

Data Access and Control. From a law and policy perspective, Scassa [15] focuses on data ownership and control in the context of open government in smart cities, highlighting "rights to re-use the data whether it is for innovation, civic engagement or transparency purposes." From an economics and innovation perspective, Mazzucato [16] argues for the "making of private data into a public good." And the notion of access to "inherent human data" as a fundamental right is being advanced as a 31st human right, "to assure that our data is our property" [3].

Frameworks for Data Access in Intelligent Environments. Frameworks for data in intelligent environments include those identified by Lea [17] in relation to standards while McKenna [18] articulates an ambient data framework for learning cities and smart cities. Liu, Heller, and Nielsen [19] provide a classification of data in smart cities as "sensitive, quasi-sensitive, and open/public" with a flowchart for accessing published data. Liu, Heller, and Nielsen [19] advance a framework for smart city data management encompassing "data collection, cleansing, anonymization and publishing" as a "generic solution." It is worth noting that Lim, Kim, and Maglio [20] provide a word cloud of the "top 100 words representing the smart city literature" based on "a topic modeling method" and the word smart appears in large print with the word data and the word city in slightly smaller print beneath and the word access embedded within a letter of the word smart at a much smaller scale, suggestive perhaps of the notion of smart access to data in cities, with very little literature, as yet, focusing on access. Osman [21] advances a big data analytics framework for smart cities with model management and aggregation functionality and a comparison of "traditional knowledge discovery approaches" is provided. In recognition of "people's concerns about their privacy" van Zoonen [26] advances a privacy framework for smart city technologies and urban big data privacy, attentive to the notion of "legitimate access." Two data dimensions are featured in the framework by van Zoonen [26], the personal and sensitive in relation to the purpose for data collection as service or surveillance related. A framework for adaptive differential privacy is advanced by Winograd-Cort, Haeberlen, Roth, and Pierce [28] where the use of *privacy filters* along with an *adaptive layer* is highlighted, addressing some of the challenges [29].

Data Access and the Toronto Experience with Sidewalk Labs. It is worth noting that Sidewalk Labs, under the parent company of Alphabet, proposed a draft plan for data privacy for the downtown Toronto initiative through articulation of the notion of a *Civic Data Trust* [22] in response to seemingly intractable issues associated with urban data [23, 24]. As an independent organization, the Civic Data Trust "will control the data" for the smart city project and "set the rules around its use" and also "make it open and accessible to people while offering privacy protection." Two types of data collection are identified for the trust as: "that collected without consent" and that "collected with consent" where the former would include "pedestrian counters and streetfacing cameras, though it would be wiped of personal information" and the latter would include data collected "through websites and mobile apps" and "wouldn't be subject to control of the trust." In the interests of "transparency and safety", recommendations from "a panel of millennials" include the need for organizers of the Toronto project to "address meaningful consent" of "data collection in public spaces" and to "maintain an open data portal to encourage innovation for the public good" as well as the creation of "an independent data trust to manage all data collected" [25]. McDonald [27] describes Sidewalk Labs' proposal for the Quayside Project in Toronto as "the world's largest Civic Data Trust proposal."

Data Access Alternatives. Lea [30] introduces a framework for people to "begin to share and control access to their personal data" by advancing the case for the smart city data brokerage idea as a solution to the limitations of open data that is said to be "infrastructure centric"; "anonymized" with the intent "to ensure privacy" and this may in turn "reduce usefulness"; while being described as "often 'low value' data, that is easy for "cities and others to 'give away'." By contrast, the data brokerage notion "focuses on making data available" in a way described as "a controlled manner" enabling "organizations to manage who uses this data and what they do" with the data and in some instances even "monetize their data" where "control is managed through specific licensing" providing "an ability to control how data is being used." As such, Lea describes a "spectrum from a freely available open source data set" to one afforded by the data brokerage model that "could be licensed, for a fee, with a specific license that allows a single use." Pointing to examples such as Google or Facebook where "data is gathered in exchange for free services" where "citizens have no control over the data, its usage" as well as often "not even aware that their personal data is being used by third parties," Lea seeks to reverse this situation, advancing the data brokerage for "empowering citizens" as "a powerful tool to unlock valuable data" while enabling people to have "more control over personal data" [30].

Data Access and Literacies. Edelenbos et al. [31] explore a research agenda for "data sensitive governance" noting that the "accessibility" of big data "is in fact limited and selective" giving rise to the need for a focus on policy; analytics and data literacy; legal and social aspects and associated inequalities; and "the reworking of spatial boundaries" in addressing what is referred to as a paradox of increasing livability on the one hand and the "risk of creating very complex urban governance dynamics" on the other hand. Moore, in an interview with Rocker [32] about the Virtual Singapore Project, focused on digitizing the city, points to a shift in access, highlighting the "benefit" for cities of being able to rethink "the possible business models" and "reassess the value of data" while receiving assistance with how "to integrate the data in a smarter way." In the context of data and information architectures in smart cities, McKenna [33] argues for "smarter access" along with "meaningful access" to "inform evolving urban understandings" focusing on smartness and architectures, governance, and data in smart cities, featuring ambient data for smart delivery; potential to build capacity through infrastructures; data access for constructive uses; and mobile apps for real-time collaboration and decision-making.

2.2   Universal Access and Smart Cities

Smith [34] emphasizes the importance of human infrastructures in smart cities, involving cross-sector dialogue, as does Lea [35] in relation to the sharing, exposing, and using of data. Regarding data infrastructures, Gray, Gerlitz, and Bournegru [36] argue for data infrastructure literacy as a way to "cultivate sensibilities" going beyond data science, and extending to "data sociology, data politics" and even to "wider public engagement with digital data infrastructures" in support of "collective inquiry, experimentation, imagination and intervention around data in educational programmes and beyond." According to Gray et al. [36] such spaces would enable explorations into "how data infrastructures can be challenged, contested, reshaped and repurposed to align with interests and publics other than those originally intended." Pérez-delHoyo, Garcia-Mayor, Mora-Mora, Gilart-Iglesias, and Andújar-Montoya [37] advance "an urban model for improving accessibility" where "the design of intelligent environments, with the automation of processes and functions in urban spaces" is "a safe and effective way to promote inclusion and participation of all citizens." Mollá-Sirvent et al. [38] developed an accessibility index for smart cities involving people in the collection of data in contributing to the visualization of "how accessible a city is" over a period of time. The World Urban Forum (WUF9) advances the importance of accessibility and inclusion in support of "cities for all" [39]. Ang, Seng, Ijemaru, and Zungeru [40] describe applications, architectures, and challenges for the Internet of Vehicles (IoV) articulated as "a convergence of the mobile Internet and the Internet of Things (IoV) while advancing the "novel paradigm" of a "universal Internet of vehicles (UIoV) for smart cities" attentive to various types of access issues. Streitz [41] argues that "a transparent urban ambient intelligence environment" supports "city authorities as well as citizens" in being able to "access and exploit the wealth of all the data collected" in urban spaces.

2.3 Conceptualizing Ambient Data Access in Smart Cities

The theoretical perspective developed in this paper, from a review of the research and practice literature, enables formulation of an ambient data access conceptual framework for learning cities, smart cities, and future cities, as depicted in Fig. 1. The emergence of new forms of data made possible through more aware people and their multisensory capabilities, interacting with more aware technologies enables evolving perspectives on human infrastructures and urban infrastructures. Characteristics of these data infrastructures include adaptive, contextual, connective, interactive, and sensing in support of ambient data and privacy innovations (e.g., ambient, adaptive differential, inverse, etc.) highlighting the potential for accommodating smarter possibilities related to control, creativity, literacies, purpose, rights, and value. As such, this work proposes and develops the construct of ambient data access in support of more dynamic, in-the-moment, and adaptive understandings of accessibility in accommodating the creative, serendipitous, and unpredictable nature of people [42], in keeping with the notion of humans in the loop [41]. This framework builds on work by McKenna [33] where access figured strongly in relation to information infrastructures, governance, and data in smart cities and where creativity and serendipity are highlighted [42].

The framework is operationalized for use in this paper in responding to the research question, reformulated as a proposition under exploration in this study, as follows: in contemporary urban environments:

P: Access to data forms part of smarter infrastructures through *awareness, learning, openness, and engagement* contributing to and influencing urban life for learning, smart, and future cities.

Fig. 1. Ambient data access conceptual framework for learning, smart, and future cities.

3 Methodology

This work employs an exploratory case study approach because it is said to be particularly appropriate for the investigation of contemporary phenomena [43], in this instance, the emergent dimensions of access associated with urban data.

3.1 Process

A website was used to describe the study, enable sign up, and participation in the online survey. During sign up for the urban study, people could self-identify in one or more categories (e.g., student, educator, business, community member, etc.) and demographic data were also collected at this time for age, gender, and geographic location. Interviews were conducted, mostly online, to enable more in-depth discussion of smart city issues and experiences. Notice of the research study was made to online spaces attracting researchers, practitioners, and anyone interested in smart cities and regions. As such, sampling procedures used involved heterogeneity sampling, a form of purposive sampling enabling a broad range of perspectives to emerge [44].

3.2 Data Collection

This study employs multiple methods of qualitative data collection including interviews and survey, involving a cross-section of people in the city. A survey instrument was developed and pre-tested prior to use in the study as well as an interview protocol to guide discussions. As such, quantitative data were gathered through surveys and qualitative data were gathered through interviews and open-ended survey questions in various sized cities in Canada and other areas including northern and southern Europe and beyond.

In parallel with this study, data were also systematically gathered from a wide range of people through group and individual discussions across multiple sectors (e.g., higher education, information technology, business, community members, city councilors, urban educators and innovators, to name a few) in multiple Canadian cities (e.g., Greater Victoria, Vancouver, and Toronto).

3.3   Data Analysis

Content analysis was used as an analytic technique for qualitative data involving pattern matching and explanation building enabling the identification of insights. Descriptive statistics were used in the analysis of quantitative survey data. An iterative approach to all three data sources enabled simultaneous analysis, comparison, and triangulation of data for n = 73 with 41% females and 59% males for people ranging in age from their 20s to their 70s.

4   Results

Findings from this work are presented in relation to the four constructs – awareness, learning, openness, and engagement – used to explore the proposition in this research study.

Awareness. The desire to know more about what is going on in the city on the part of citizens was expressed, as in, "it is hard for the locals to find out what's going on around the city" and by visitors to the city, as in, "what do the locals do", said to be "the most commonly asked question." An individual in St. John's identified the need for information that is "not too dense" enabling people to know "what's happening at a particular point" so that "you can access this type of information and know what's going on in real time almost." When urban interventions are conducted to introduce art in public spaces for example, interest was expressed in the type of data that would assist in understanding how the intervention changed the space in terms of increased usage, quality of use, transformation of urban spaces, and the like. However, in the case of such interventions, it was indicated that funding for identifying, gathering, and making available the data was not yet available. A city councilor pointed to the value of receiving data from people who are interacting with the city through the infrastructures of a bike path on the one hand and a mobile app on the other hand whereby urban users report conditions requiring attention that the city can then act upon in the moment, as in, "through your phone you are able to track accidents" and "create a map with that information" for the city to "create engineering fixes for those intersections."

Learning. A community engagement specialist pointed to the importance and value of pedestrian counts in public spaces to learn more about the vibrancy of the city, referred to by an educator as "human activity in every corner." The importance of the digital and data dimension of information in public spaces was readily acknowledged at the urban level through an expression of interest in learning more about the potential for undertaking small-scale urban data interventions involving the notion possibly of a "smart bench." Similar to urban interventions by Placemaking networks such as a temporary street closure on a Sunday to provide the experience of more pedestrian friendly urban spaces, urban data interventions place an emphasis on learning more about the value, nature, and complexities of data. In such spaces, pedestrian counts would be of value as an indicator of interest and engagement while data interventions more generally provide an opportunity for "rethinking the traditional norms that we have around data." For example, the notion of a smart bench infused with technology elements that provide information related to use on the one hand with the potential for safety on the other hand, depending on the location, give rise to potential implications if people are aware that the bench contains 'smart elements'. Explorations for learning were also articulated by a student for "geofenced location-based content" in relation to "community interactions" with the juxtaposition of "social media" and "closed communities as well as open" enabling "access" for "citizen inquiry" and "educational institutions" featuring informal and "formalized education." City information technology (IT) staff pointed to the need for data literacies along with the need for funding to support such initiatives indicating that "we're very immature in that overall data sense" in that "we're starting to look at tools to help us mine the data that we already have an interest in" while referring to "that hurdle" of "starting to educate" with respect to "what could be done" along with "educating ourselves." When asked what cities need to do to become smarter, 67% of survey respondents selected the option to "Support learning cities by enabling new forms and configurations for education in the city (e.g., school-university-city collaboration, etc.)."

Openness. Speaking of urban data, City IT staff indicated that, "fundamentally there is a desire to be very, very open with the data" and because "it is public data, we manage on behalf of the citizenry" access is important "where there is a purpose to utilize that data" and "maybe it helps improve something." Potential emerges for the expanding of open data beyond "low value" [30] to richer, more valuable data for more meaningful openness. A student pointed to the wicked challenges associated with the "ownership and privacy" of urban data in relation to "how it is housed" and the "infrastructure by which it is shared" suggestive of the range of complexities associated with data access from control to purpose, to rights, to value along with the opportunity potential for creativity and new literacies. When asked whether they associated openness with smart cities, on a 7 point likert scale (e.g., 1 = not at all, 2 = not sure, 3 = maybe, 4 = neutral, 5 = sort of, 6 = sure, and 7 = absolutely), 33% of survey respondents selected 7 at the upper end of the scale, 33% selected 6 near the upper end of the scale, and 33% selected the neutral position of 4 on the scale. City IT indicated that there is "interest in putting physical infrastructure in place" adding that, "how we interpret using it is still open" suggestive possibly of creative and collaborative opportunities influencing data access elements pertaining to control, purpose, rights, and value.

Engagement. An educator and community member observed that, "we're not smart about how we use the technology", suggestive of implications for all aspects of the data and digital dimension. From the perspective of a student, "we will know more what to do with" the data "that is constantly being made, built" in social media and other spaces "as we work out how to sort" what is being generated, giving rise to "notions of smart delivery." City IT described the notion of "documented engagement" giving rise to new types of datasets for sharing and decision-making. Using the example of an eTownHall meeting, City IT indicated that "we furnish some of the elements of engagement" using various technologies to create a meeting space for "questions and sharing answers through Twitter" and other platforms. IT staff in the higher education sector empha-sized the critical element of access in terms of "getting at that data and using it in constructive ways" in order to enable "benefit to the society and the citizens." In the words of one individual, "you can have all the connectivity you like but if there is no access to data in a meaningful manner" as well as "no interpretation of that data leading to good public policy decisions then" smart cities are "all for nothing." When asked what cities need to do to become smarter, survey respondents, without exception, selected the option to "make engagement smarter" as in, "break down the silos and collaborate more." Given a variety of options to choose from, when asked "How does technology help you in the city?" 67% of survey respondents selected "To access city resources."

5 Discussion

Through a review of the research and practice literature for data access and universal access in smart cities followed by an exploration of the experience of smart cities in relation to the constructs of awareness, learning, openness, and engagement in this study, insights emerge about data control, literacies, purposes, and value, aided by the understanding of more adaptive and dynamic forms of access, as in, ambient access, as depicted in Fig. 2.

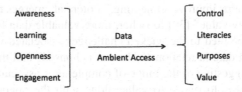

Fig. 2. Ambient access lens for data control, literacies, purposes, and value.

For example, people in this study spoke in terms of the need to be "smart about how we use the technology" while smarter approaches to information delivery were suggested in the form of 'smart delivery'. In discussing the potential for an urban intervention to learn more about data in relation to urban elements such as a bench, a community leader suggested the term 'smart bench' involving data sharing, animating public spaces, and the like. These examples point to a recognition of the potential for ambient access as a more dynamic, adaptive mechanism for rethinking and reconfig-uring current understandings of data control, involving new data literacies, new pur-poses for data, and emerging forms of value for data.

Two dependent variables are identified in this work, as follows: that of *ambient data access and value* and that of *ambient data access and literacies* along with independent variables for each. In the case of *ambient data access and value* the independent variables include: use of mobile apps and urban infrastructures for sharing data in the moment; the generation and sharing of exploratory urban intervention data; and tools and mechanisms for the interpretation of data. In the case of *ambient data access and literacies* the independent variables include: learning about the importance of the digital and data dimension of information in public spaces; learning about the value, nature, and complexities of data; and new forms and configurations of education in support of learning cities.

6 Future Directions

In advancing the construct of ambient access in relation to urban data, to complement and extend evolving understandings of universal access, this work creates openings for future directions for both practice and research.

6.1 Research

Future research opportunities and challenges enabled by this paper relate to the potential for further validation and exploration of the ambient data access conceptual framework advanced and operationalized in this work as well as the variables identified.

Ambient Data Access Conceptual Framework. This work navigates a pathway toward ambient data access as a possibly smarter approach to the seemingly intractable issues, challenges, and opportunities for urban data in smart, learning, and future cities.

Ambient Data Access Variables. Dependent variables (DV) emerge for *ambient data access and value* and *ambient data access and literacies* along with associated independent variables (IV) for each providing opportunities for exploration and validation.

6.2 Practice

This work highlights some of the needs and interests of practitioners at the urban level in that it explores the *ambient data access* construct in the context of involving people more directly with aware technologies in relation to awareness, learning, openness, and engagement. More specifically, areas for practical involvement include:

Exploratory Urban Interventions. Urban interventions of an exploratory nature provide a practical way for involving people more directly with data in relation to awareness, learning, openness, and engagement.

Data-focused Urban Initiatives. Initiatives with a data focus are encouraged that may be city wide or project-based in support of enhancing some aspect of city life while providing opportunities for involving people more directly with data in relation to awareness, learning, openness, and engagement.

Such interventions and initiatives support the potential to provide insight into the concept of *meaningful openness* while raising the value of urban open data beyond that of what is said to be "low value" [30].

Dependent and Independent Variables. Dependent variables (DV) emerge for *ambient data access and value* and *ambient data access and value*. Associated independent variables (IV) for *ambient data access and value* pertain to: mobile data sharing; urban intervention data sharing; and data interpretation tools. Associated independent variables for *ambient data access and literacies* pertain to: digital data in public spaces; the value, nature, and complexities of data; and new forms of education for learning cities.

7 Conclusion

This paper develops the ambient access construct in relation to urban data through a review of the research literature and an exploratory case study conducted in relation to awareness, learning, openness, and engagement at the urban level. As such, this work creates a space for debate, theorizing, and exploration around the construct of ambient access for data in smart cities, learning cities, and future cities. In addition to the contributions this work makes to urban theory, the data dimension of universal access, and the smart cities literature, the dependent variables of *ambient data access and literacies* and *ambient data access and value* are identified, along with several associated independent variables for each.

A key take away from this paper is the importance of urban data literacies with implications for access and in turn, realization of the emerging value potential of urban data along with the complex issues associated with access. This work will be of interest to students, educators, researchers, data managers and analysts, city managers, policymakers, urban planners and designers, and anyone concerned with smarter approaches to urban data and access in contemporary and future cities.

References

1. McKenna, H.P.: Exploring the quantified experience: finding spaces for people and their voices in smarter, more responsive cities. In: Arai, K., Bhatia, R., Kapoor, S. (eds.) FTC 2018. AISC, vol. 880, pp. 269–282. Springer, Cham (2019). https://doi.org/10.1007/978-3-030-02686-8_22
2. Schmitt, G.: Smart cities. Massive Open Online Course (MOOC). edX, ETH Zurich, Zurich, Switzerland (2016)
3. Hu.manity.co: The problem (2018). https://hu-manity.co. Accessed 8 Jan 2019
4. Stephanidis, C.: Universal access and design for all in the evolving information society. In: Stephanidis, C. (ed.) The Universal Access Handbook, pp. 30–40. CRC Press, Taylor & Francis Group, New York (2009)
5. Stephanidis, C.: Emerging challenges. In: Stephanidis, C. (ed.) The Universal Access Handbook, pp. 1032–1040. CRC Press, Taylor & Francis Group, New York (2009)
6. Konomi, S., Roussos, G.: Enriching Urban Spaces with Ambient Computing, The Internet of Things, and Smart City Design. IGI Global, Hershey (2017)
7. Charoubi, H., et al.: Understanding smart cities: an integrative framework. In: Proceedings of the 45th Hawaii International Conference on System Sciences, pp. 2289–2297. IEEE Computer Society Press, Washington, DC (2012)

8. Nam, T., Pardo, T.A.: Conceptualizing smart city with dimensions of technology, people, and institutions. In: Proceedings of the 12th Annual International Conference on Digital Government Research, pp. 282–291 (2011)
9. Streitz, N.A.: Smart cities, ambient intelligence and universal access. In: Stephanidis, C. (ed.) UAHCI 2011. LNCS, vol. 6767, pp. 425–432. Springer, Heidelberg (2011). https://doi.org/10.1007/978-3-642-21666-4_47
10. Townsend, A.M.: Smart Cities: Big Data, Civic Hackers and the Quest for a New Utopia. WW Norton, New York (2013)
11. Ferscha, A.: Implicit interactions. In: Stephanidis, C. (ed.) The Universal Access Handbook, pp. 992–1013. CRC Press, Taylor & Francis Group, New York (2009)
12. Gil-Garcia, J.R., Pardo, T.A., Nam, T.: A comprehensive view of the 21st century city: smartness as technologies and innovation in urban contexts. In: Gil-Garcia, J.R., Pardo, T.A., Nam, T. (eds.) Smarter as the New Urban Agenda: A Comprehensive View of the 21st Century City. PAIT, vol. 11, pp. 1–19. Springer, Cham (2016). https://doi.org/10.1007/978-3-319-17620-8_1
13. Gil-Garcia, J.R., Zhang, J., Puron-Cid, G.: Conceptualizing smartness in government: an integrative and multi-dimensional view. Gov. Inf. Q. **33**, 524–534 (2016)
14. Gurevich, Y., Hudis, E., Wing, J.M.: Inverse privacy. Commun. ACM **59**(7), 38–42 (2016)
15. Scassa, T.: Smart cities: data ownership and privacy issues. Blog (2017). http://www.teresascassa.ca/index.php?option=com_k2&view=item&id=241:smart-cities-data-ownership-and-privacy-issues&Itemid=81#. Accessed 4 Oct 2018
16. Mazzucato, M.: Let's make private data into a public good. MIT Technol. Rev. **121**(4), 74–75 (2018)
17. Lea, R.: Making sense of the smart city standardization landscape. IEEE e-Standards Magazine (2016). https://www.standardsuniversity.org/e-magazine/november-2016-volume-6-issue-4-smart-city-standards/making-sense-smart-city-standardization-landscape/
18. McKenna, H.P.: Civic tech and ambient data in the public realm: challenges and opportunities for learning cities and smart cities. In: Streitz, N., Markopoulos, P. (eds.) DAPI 2017. LNCS, vol. 10291, pp. 312–331. Springer, Cham (2017). https://doi.org/10.1007/978-3-319-58697-7_23
19. Liu, X., Heller, A., Nielsen, P.S.: CITIESData: a smart city data management framework. Knowl. Inf. Syst. **53**(3), 699–722 (2017). https://doi.org/10.1007/s10115-017-1051-3
20. Lim, C., Kim, K.-J., Maglio, P.P.: Smart cities with big data: reference models, challenges, and considerations. Cities **82**, 86–99 (2018). https://doi.org/10.1016/j.cities.2018.04.011
21. Osman, A.M.S.: A novel big data analytics framework for smart cities. Future Gener. Comput. Syst. **91**, 620–633 (2019)
22. CMD Group: Sidewalk Labs unveils draft data, privacy plans for high-tech Toronto project. Daily Commercial News 91(201):1, 18 October (2018)
23. Postmedia Network: Ex-Ontario privacy commissioner resigns from Sidewalk Labs. The Toronto Sun (Online) (2018)
24. Rizza, A.: Critics call for more transparency in decisions. Chronicle Herald (2018)
25. Deschamps, T.: Sidewalk Labs to weigh suggestions from panel for Toronto smart city project. The Canadian Press (2018)
26. VanZoonen, L.: Privacy concerns in smart cities. Gov. Inf. Q. **33**(3), 472–480 (2016)
27. McDonald, S.: Toronto, civic data, and trust. Medium blog (2018). https://medium.com/@McDapper/toronto-civic-data-and-trust-ee7ab928fb68. Accessed 3 Jan 2019
28. Winograd-Cort, D., Haeberlen, A., Roth, A., Pierce, B.C.: A framework for adaptive differential privacy. In: Proceedings of the ACM on Programming Languages, vol. 1, no. 10. ICFP (2017)

29. Mervis, J.: Can a set of equations keep U.S. census data private? Science Magazine (2019). https://www.sciencemag.org/news/2019/01/can-set-equations-keep-us-census-data-private. Accessed 9 Jan 2019

30. Lea, R.: The case for a smart city data brokerage. UrbanOpus: People, Data & the Future of Cities blog (2018). http://urbanopus.net/the-case-for-a-smart-city-data-brokerage/. Accessed 9 Jan 2019

31. Edelenbos, J., et al.: Governing the complexity of smart data cities: setting a research agenda. In: Rodríguez Bolívar, M. (ed.) Smart Technologies for Smart Governments. Public Administration and Information Technology, vol. 24, pp. 35–54. Springer, Cham (2018). https://doi.org/10.1007/978-3-319-58577-2_3

32. Moore, C.: The virtual Singapore project aims to digitize an entire city. Digital Trends (2017). https://www.digitaltrends.com/home/virtual-singapore-project-mapping-out-entire-city-in-3d/. Accessed 20 Feb 2019

33. McKenna, H.P.: Ambient urbanities as the intersection between the IoT and the IoP in smart cities. IGI Global, Hershey (2019)

34. Smith, M.L.: Urban infrastructure as materialized consensus. World Archaeol. (2016). https://doi.org/10.1080/00438243.2015.1124804

35. Lea, R.: Smart cities: technology challenges for the IoT. SenseTecnic Blog (2015). http://sensetecnic.com/technology-challenges-for-the-iot/Blog. Accessed 8 Sept 2016

36. Gray, J., Gerlitz, C., Bounegru, L.: Data infrastructure literacy. Big Data Soc. (2018). https://doi.org/10.1177/2053951718786316

37. Pérez-delHoyo, R., Garcia-Mayor, C., Mora-Mora, H., Gilart-Iglesias, V., Andújar-Montoya, M.D.: Making smart and accessible cities: an urban model based on the design of intelligent environments. In: Proceedings of the 5th International Conference on Smart Cities and Green ICT Systems (SMARTGREENS 2016), pp. 63–70. SCITEPRESS (2016)

38. Mollá-Sirvent, R.A., Mora, H., Gilart-Iglesias, V., Pérez-delHoyo, R., Andújar-Montoya, M.D.: Accessibility index for smart cities. In: Multidisciplinary Digital Publishing Institute Proceedings, vol. 2, p. 1219 (2018)

39. UN: Cities 2030—Cities for All: Implementing the New Urban agenda. Ninth Session of the World Urban Forum (WUF9) (2018). https://www.un.org/development/desa/disabilities/wuf9.html. Accessed 20 Feb 2019

40. Ang, L.-M., Seng, K.P., Ijemaru, G.K., Zungeru, A.M.: Deployment of IoV for smart cities: applications, architecture, and challenges. IEEE Access 7, 6473–6492 (2018). https://doi.org/10.1109/ACCESS.2018.2887076

41. Streitz, N.: Beyond 'smart-only' cities: redefining the 'smart-everything' paradigm. J. Ambient Intell. Humaniz. Comput. 10, 791–812 (2019). https://doi.org/10.1007/s12652-018-0824-1

42. McKenna, H.P.: Creativity and ambient urbanizing at the intersection of the Internet of Things and people in smart cities. In: Antona, M., Stephanidis, C. (eds.) UAHCI 2018. LNCS, vol. 10908, pp. 295–307. Springer, Cham (2018). https://doi.org/10.1007/978-3-319-92052-8_23

43. Yin, R.K.: Case Study Research and Applications: Design and Methods, 6th edn. Sage, Los Angeles (2018)

44. Trochim, W.M.K.: Research Methods Knowledge Base (2006). http://www.socialresearchmethods.net/kb. Accessed 22 Feb 2019

Initiation to Reverse Engineering by Using Activities Based on Photogrammetry as New Teaching Method in University Technical Studies

Dolores Parras-Burgos[✉], Daniel G. Fernández-Pacheco,
Francisco Cavas-Martínez, José Nieto, and Francisco J. F. Cañavate

Graphical Expression Department, Universidad Politécnica de Cartagena,
30202 Cartagena, Murcia, Spain
{dolores.parras, daniel.garcia, francisco.cavas,
jose.nieto, francisco.canavate}@upct.es

Abstract. Nowadays, reverse engineering is used in multiple professional fields that impel to develop different processes for obtaining virtual objects from real objects. Moreover, the importance of providing students with basic knowledge in this type of data collection processes increases, but sometimes the most sophisticated tools are not available because of their high cost and level of knowledge. Among the types of scans that can be found for three-dimensional reconstruction, there is an alternative based on the photogrammetry whose method is denominated Image-based 3D Modeling and Rendering (IB3DMR), which uses a set of photographs in 2D to generate a three-dimensional digital model. With the aim of students learning the basics of scanning and three-dimensional reconstruction of objects, point clouds or mesh of an object, reverse engineering, exportation to other CAD formats and preparation of models for 3D printing, a series of activities with tools of low cost related to photogrammetry are proposed in this communication. This study was performed among students from three different subjects taught at the Technical University of Cartagena during the first term of the 2017/18 course: 'Industrial Design' and 'Graphic Expression' (both from the Degree in Mechanical Engineering), and 'Graphic Expression' (Degree in Industrial Technologies Engineering). The obtained results demonstrate a high level of satisfaction and interest in this type of methodologies during the academic education of the students. Using this type of tools prepares students in new technologies and applications that are increasingly being implemented in all professional fields of society. Universities must be prepared for these new challenges and offer them as a complement to their academic education.

Keywords: Learning · Engineering education · Educational experience · Photogrammetry · Low-cost tools

© Springer Nature Switzerland AG 2019
M. Antona and C. Stephanidis (Eds.): HCII 2019, LNCS 11572, pp. 159–176, 2019.
https://doi.org/10.1007/978-3-030-23560-4_12

1 Introduction

In modern industry, reverse engineering is increasingly becoming more relevant in the design and development process of any product. The use of technologies to obtain information about a product to know how it works, what it is made of or to have an overall view of its shape has become an obligation to be competitive in the market, assuming an advantage that can reduce costs and increase efficiency of any product. To obtain such information requires a device called a 3D scanner that is used to analyze an object or a scene and use the data obtained to build three-dimensional digital models that are used in a wide variety of applications.

In the market, several types of three-dimensional scanners that permit to get a great precision of the acquired data can be found: contact, contactless, active, passive, etc. [1–3]. Some of these technologies are not easy to be obtained due to their high cost and the requirement of qualified personnel for their use. For this reason, other alternatives based on more accessible and economic software are being used more and more. These new alternatives consist of scanning and three-dimensional reconstructing an object by using a set of successive photographs, also called Image-based 3D Modeling and Rendering (IB3DMR). More specifically, this type of methodology is based on the detection, clustering and extraction of characteristics (sides, vertices, etc.) that are present in an image to be later interpreted as common elements of a 3D model.

This method can be divided into two parts. On one hand, there is Image-based rendering (IBR) which uses images instead of polygons. The goal is to get a faster and more realistic rendering, simplifying the process of modelling. This technique consists of either knowing the precise positions of the cameras or carrying out automatic "stereomatching" which, in the absence of data, requires a large number of images close in proximity. On the other hand, there is Image-based modelling (IBM), which refers to the use of images to guide the reconstruction of three-dimensional geometric models.

Despite the fact that 3D scanning is a standard source of data entry, image-based modelling seems to be a complete, economical, practical and flexible alternative to expensive scanners. Rather than render objects or scenes using the traditional approach of polygons, IBMR uses large amounts of images (photographic or synthetic) to achieve a high level of realism. This type of technique has been used for several years and many studies have been conducted on it [4–6].

One of the main objectives of this work is the utilization of low cost tools for its use as a teaching tool. In this sense, several applications based on the described IB3DMR methodology can be found, as for instance Autodesk Recap (the new version of Autodesk Remake and 123D Catch), Microsoft PhotoSynth, Patch-Based Multi-View Stereo (PMVS), PixelStruct, VisualSize, Bundler, BigSFM or OpenPhotoVR, among others. Based on this type of technology, some previous studies have been analyzed to compare the suitability of this type of applications. Cavas et al. [7] studied the behavior of Microsoft PhotoSynth and PMVS for the reconstruction of different types of fruits, offering the PMVS software better results when applying textures. That same year, a later study by the same authors [8] analyzed the software Microsoft PhotoSynth, PMVS and 123D Catch for the reconstruction of mechanical metal parts, demonstrating the high accuracy of the reconstructions using the 123D Catch software compared to the rest. On the contrary, PMVS does not offer good results when textures are applied and Microsoft PhotoSynth only provides a cloud of few points that does not complete the scanned part.

One of the first works that demonstrated the performance of 123D Catch was the study developed by Cervera et al. [9], who used several applications to perform an acoustics analysis by 3D modeling of closed spaces. That same year, Venkatesh et al. [10] studied the 3D models obtained by photogrammetry as a simple and inexpensive source of images for diagnosis and evaluation in the field of dentistry, serving as a complement to other diagnostic images in 2D as X-ray images. A similar study was carried out in the field of architecture by Santagati and Inzerillo [11], in which a study of the metric precision of 123D Catch was performed. In turn, Santamaría y Sanz [12] deepened the use of Autodesk 123D Catch for 3D modeling of terrain, as an alternative to other more complex and expensive topographical methods. Another study to highlight is the one carried out by Lerma et al. [13], where they compared the results of image-based modeling software (Autodesk 123D Catch, Fotoglife and VisualSFM) with the results of time-of-flight laser measurements in two different cave paintings. Even under the sea, this methodology has been used to obtain the reconstruction of aquatic organisms in an easy, fast and non-intrusive way [14].

Taking into account the characteristics and possibilities that 3D scanners provide, this work has looked for an affordable and accessible alternative to recreate a reconstruction process with a really useful purpose for engineering, its application as a didactic tool. After the analysis made to the different mentioned studies, the Autodesk ReCap tool has been selected for this work. The objective of using this type of low cost technologies as didactic tools is to bring students to some knowledge and work methodologies that can later be applied in the labor world through more sophisticated tools. On the other hand, a new process of obtaining photographs is offered to substantially improve the quality of three-dimensional reconstructions with respect to the conventional system recommended by the program. This study was performed among students from three different subjects taught at the Technical University of Cartagena during the first term of the 2017/18 course: 'Industrial Design' and 'Graphic Expression' (both from the Degree in Mechanical Engineering), and 'Graphic Expression' (Degree in Industrial Technologies Engineering). These students conducted a series of activities to acquire basic concepts of scanning and three-dimensional reconstruction of objects, point clouds or mesh of an object, reverse engineering, exportation to other CAD formats and preparation of models for rapid prototyping. At the end of the study, their evaluations and comments are analyzed, highlighting their satisfaction and the usefulness of this type of complementary activities for their education and their future work.

2 Application of ICT Tools in Teaching

There are several examples of how the application of information and communication technologies (ICT) in teaching has a great impact on the teaching-learning process of the student and how he increases his motivation if he becomes an active part of his learning [15, 16]. The universities demand, more and more, complementary formative actions as support to the face-to-face teaching. Camacho et al. [17] showed a didactic resource in the study of mathematics in the Economics and Business degrees, demonstrating an increase in the assimilation of the concepts developed in the classroom and supposing a feedback to the teacher to improve his teaching methodology. In the Engineering field, computer-aided design (CAD) is key in different areas of study where the use of 3D virtual models permits students to acquire different knowledge and skills that complement their academic training [18–20].

More specifically, and relating teaching with 3D scanners, we find examples in the field of Health Sciences, where volumetric representations are increasingly applied in the educational process to allow the student to have a closer visual comprehension to the three-dimensional reality of the object of study. An example is a the teaching innovation project developed by Prados et al. [21] with the aim of obtaining a multimedia material from the most complex areas of the human anatomy that allows an active teaching methodology by the student, using a laser scanner and software for processing and conversion of scanned data. On the other hand, Mateos Quintanilla et al. [22] developed an optical 3D scanner prototype and present how the students learnt to handle the scanner and perform various practices to acquire data, reconstruct elements, compare them, etc.

In relation to reverse engineering, we can find an example where these new technologies of digitalization and reengineering was tried to be brought to students, such as the study by Sinha [23], where a preliminary presentation of different 3D scanning and reverse engineering tools was carried out.

Engineers have to face multiple projects in their working life and, increasingly, this type of scanning and three-dimensional reconstruction tools are used within a reverse engineering process. These technologies are booming and, for this reason, this work proposes a series of activities that permit the students to acquire basic knowledge to face them in the best possible way.

3 Materials and Methods

3.1 Reverse Engineering Process

The purpose of the use of these tools is to show students two ways to obtain virtually mechanical and daily objects, and their subsequent use for possible redesigns or prototypes in a reverse engineering process. The scheme that can be considered traditional for data acquisition of an existing object is the one that requires measurement tools to achieve them (hardware); another alternative is the use of 2D images. Both methods permit to obtain virtual models with which to work and generate 3D-printed prototypes (Fig. 1).

In order for students to know de basic concepts related to reverse engineering, different activities have been performed in every subject of the study. These activities are considered complementary to the subject, and they permit the students to develop all aspects related to the three-dimensional scanning and reconstruction of objects and their transformation for 3D printing of prototypes. Subsequently, the students have completed a series of tests to evaluate every phase and their satisfaction with this type of activities.

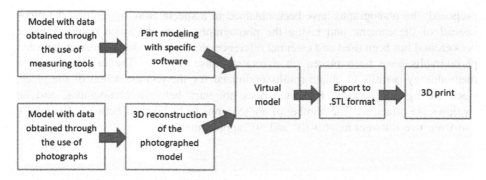

Fig. 1. Scheme for obtaining data from measuring tools and from photographs.

3.2 Objects Used in the Study

For this study, a great variety of pieces with different geometries and textures has been used, enabling the students to work the tasks of scanning and three-dimensional reconstruction. Some of the objects used by the students are shown in Fig. 2.

Fig. 2. Some of the objects used for the study.

3.3 Activities

Scanning Phase

The software used for the three-dimensional reconstruction is Autodesk ReCap, which offers a series of recommendations for obtaining images in this first scanning phase: the photographs must be taken in a dynamic environment, where the pieces remain fixed and the photographs are taken around it. However, in this study a new methodology is proposed: the photographs have been obtained in a special way by rotating the piece instead of the camera, and taking the photographs from the same point. A white background has been used and essential reference elements for the connection between photographs have been placed on a rotating base (Fig. 3). The use of this new methodology permits to obtain results optimized for the reconstruction of the piece, since the lighting remains fixed and does not vary between photographs, and no shadows are produced. The number of photographs to be taken is between 40 and 70, and from two different heights (0° and 30° approximately).

Fig. 3. Scenario used during the scanning phase.

The camera used to take the photographs was a Nikon D80 Digital Reflex Camera, with 10 megapixels of resolution and a sensitivity calibrated from 100 to 1600 ISO. The computer used for all processes of reconstruction, import and export of data is equipped with an Intel® Core™ i7-4790k 4 GHz processor, Windows 7 Professional 64-bit operating system and 32 GB RAM.

The first practice consisted of preparing the scenario for obtaining the photographs of the objects of study, constituting the scanning phase. This process does not require a laboratory or special room, so it facilitates the student's work if a distance modality of teaching is contemplated. This practice, which a priori may seem simple, requires controlling several parameters such as lighting, contrast between the colors of the piece and the environment, reference elements, etc. so that the result is the most optimal in the reconstruction (Fig. 4).

Reconstruction Phase

The application used in this study is ReCap Pro 2018, for Windows 64-bit systems. Autodesk offers the possibility to download a free educational version of the program from its website. Once installed this version, another program called Autodesk ReCap Photo is also installed, which offers new tools for the management of the reconstructed models and that will be later used.

Fig. 4. Students performing the scanning phase.

The reconstruction process begins with acquiring the photographs taken in the previous scanning phase. To perform this, the user must select the "New project" option, which is used to choose the desired photographs for the reconstruction. It should be noticed that Autodesk ReCap Pro performs the reconstruction task on its own servers to later download and view it in the program. This way permits the virtual models to have a good quality at the same time that they are processed quickly and without consuming memory or CPU resources from the user's computer.

Once the reconstruction is finished and visualized on the screen, it can be saved as OBJ or RCM file. For this study, the RCM extension is used. This RCM file is then opened with the Autodesk ReCap Photo application (Fig. 5a). After verifying that the reconstructed object is adequate, those parts of the environment that surround the object must be cleaned (Fig. 5b), and the model can be exported to any of the five formats offered by the application: OBJ, FBX, STL, PLY and PTS. For the present study, the generated models have been exported to STL format.

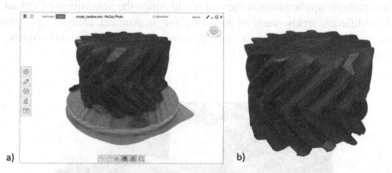

Fig. 5. Piece reconstructed: (a) with environment to be cleaned, (b) without environment.

One of the reasons for obtaining virtual models is their subsequent reproduction through 3D printing. This process consists of manufacturing a three-dimensional solid object from digital models in STL format. The STL format allows defining the geometry of 3D objects, excluding information such as color, textures or physical properties that do include other CAD formats. This format uses a closed triangular mesh to define the shape of an object: the smaller the triangulation size used, the higher the final resolution. Figure 6 shows the meshed surface of the model within Autodesk ReCap with (Fig. 6a) and without texture (Fig. 6b), and the model in STL format in MeshLab (Fig. 6c). This MeshLab tool is used to optimize, if necessary, the mesh of the virtual model, also giving the possibility of exporting to other CAD formats. It is an open source application that offers a number of tools for the editing and processing of surfaces in the form of triangular 3D mesh models, and is based largely on the VCG library, developed by the Visual Computing Laboratory of ISTI-CNR.

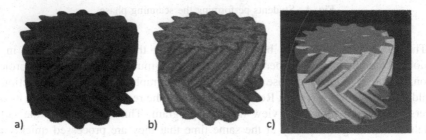

Fig. 6. Meshed surface of the model: (a) with texture (Autodesk ReCap), (b) without texture (Autodesk ReCap), (c) model in STL format (MeshLab).

In this second activity, the students obtain a three-dimensional reconstruction of the objects from the photographs taken in the previous activity (Fig. 7). They should evaluate the degree of similarity in terms of geometry, color and textures between the study piece and the generated three-dimensional model. This phase is very motivating for the students since they are the ones who get results with every given step. This phase has multiple applications in the real world, since the acquisition of virtual models is used in different fields, such as medicine for anatomical analysis and prostheses, archeology for the conservation and dissemination of historical objects, virtual museums, etc.

Fig. 7. Students performing the reconstruction phase.

Prototyping/Exportation Phase

Once the three-dimensional reconstructions of the objects have been obtained, different processes can be performed for their analysis, such as the comparison of pieces. If the objective is to use other software to process and edit the mesh of the virtual object or obtain a prototype by 3D printing, the model can be exported to other file formats from those offered by the program. In this way, students are able to assimilate concepts and processes of reverse engineering and processing of virtual models in a more didactic and motivating way. The activities carried out in this phase include observing the manufacturing process by 3D printing.

The 3D printing technology used during this study was Fused Deposition Modeling (FDM), which provides a great quality-cost relation, and ABS (Acrylonitrile Butadiene Stirene) material (Fig. 8).

Fig. 8. Some prototypes obtained by 3D printing: (a) gear wheel, (b) engine.

Once the final 3D models have been obtained by using reverse engineering software, an STL file must be generated so that the additive manufacturing machine can interpret the geometric information (triangularization) modeled in CAD.

4   Results

4.1   3D Reconstructions

Among all the reconstructions performed by the students of the three subjects analysed during this study, only those that offered the best aspect were selected. Table 1 shows the images of these selected reconstructions and their respective real objects.

4.2   Students Tests

In order to analyze different characteristics of the proposed activities, the students completed a test for every activity: (i) scanning, (ii) reconstruction and (iii) prototyping/exportation. The students also performed a test to assess globally all activities, analyzing the level of knowledge of the most important concepts and their interest in learning more about this type of methodologies.

Table 1. Comparative table for the reconstructions that offered the best results.

Model	Real object	3D Reconstruction
Wooden gear		
Wooden mold		
Gear wheel		
Toy robot		

(*continued*)

Table 1. (*continued*)

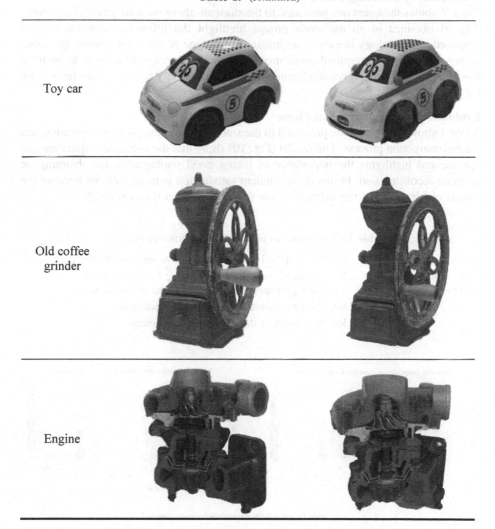

Toy car	
Old coffee grinder	
Engine	

Table 2. Test questions about the scanning phase.

Evaluation questions from 1 to 5 (1 Disagree/5 Agree)	S1. The proposed methodology is easy to understand
	S2. It is necessary a prior knowledge about photography to perform this activity better
	S3. The time to elaborate the activity is sufficient
	S4. The activity carried out is interesting

Evaluation of Scanning Phase

Table 2 shows the questions presented to the students about the scan phase. The results (Fig. 9) obtained in all the study groups highlight the following conclusions: the proposed methodology is easy to assimilate, some type of previous knowledge about taking photographs is required, some more time should be required in order to perform this phase better, and everything learned through this activity has been very interesting for them.

Evaluation of Reconstruction Phase

Table 3 shows the questions presented to the students about the program operation and the reconstruction process. The results (Fig. 10) show that the software is quite easy to operate and highlights the importance of taking good photographs for obtaining an accurate reconstruction. In this phase, student satisfaction is more variable because the results obtained in the reconstructions are not always what they expected.

Table 3. Test questions about the reconstruction phase.

Evaluation questions from 1 to 5 (1 Disagree/5 Agree)	R1. The proposed software is intuitive and easy to use
	R2. Obtaining photographs according to the proposed methodology improves the results in the reconstruction
	R3. The time invested in this phase is adequate
	R4. The results of this phase are satisfactory

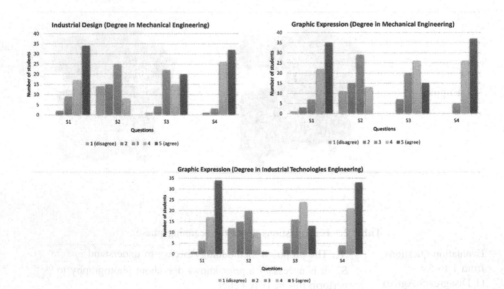

Fig. 9. Results of questions related to scan phase for the three groups of the study.

Evaluation of Prototyping/Exportation Phase

Table 4 shows the questions about the use of CAD formats and 3D printing techniques. The results (Fig. 11) reflect the importance that students give to a good management of the different types of CAD formats and the acquisition of a general knowledge of 3D printing processes and techniques for their professional future. On the other hand, they consider that a little more time should be dedicated to this phase and that the knowledge acquired in this stage could be very useful in other subjects.

Table 4. Test questions about the prototyping/exportation phase.

Evaluation questions from 1 to 5 (1 Disagree/5 Agree)	P1. Handling of different CAD formats is relevant to my academic education
	P2. The knowledge of 3D printing techniques is interesting for my professional future
	P3. The time dedicated to this activity is appropriate
	P4. The knowledge acquired in this phase is useful in other subjects

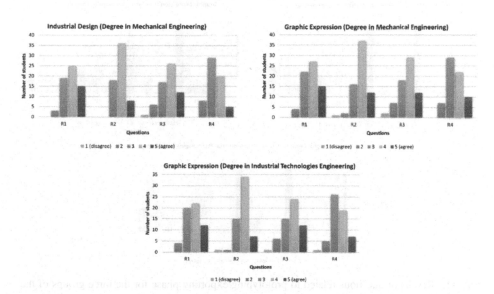

Fig. 10. Results of questions related to reconstruction phase for the three groups of the study.

Global Evaluation of Activities

To analyze different aspects of the activities in a general way, the students assessed the questions shown in Table 5. As can be seen in the different results (Fig. 12), there is no extended knowledge about the concepts of reverse engineering, photogrammetry or the proposed methodologies. On the other hand, there is great interest by most students in continuing to learn more about everything related to this type of methodologies. The general assessment is very satisfactory in all groups and reflects the support and interest that this type of activities has obtained in the considered subjects.

Table 5. Test questions about the global evaluation of the methodology.

Evaluation questions from 1 to 5 (1 Disagree/5 Agree)	G1. Degree of knowledge of the concept of reverse engineering prior to these activities
	G2. Degree of knowledge of the concept of photogrammetry prior to these activities
	G3. Degree of knowledge of the proposed methodologies prior to these activities
	G4. Degree of interest in learning more about this type of reverse engineering methodologies
	G5. The time devoted to the expositions of theoretical content has been sufficient to address these activities
	G6. The practical exercises carried out are sufficient to understand the proposed methodologies
	G7. This type of learning is important for my professional future
	G8. General assessment of activities

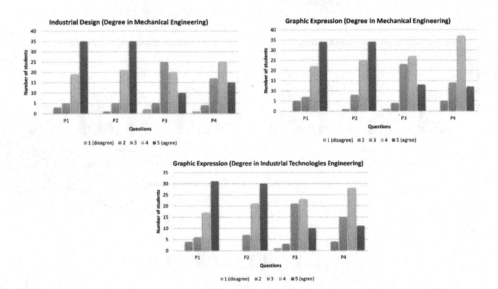

Fig. 11. Results of questions related to prototyping/exporting phase for the three groups of the study.

The students had the possibility of providing personal opinions or suggestions during the tests. Some of them are the following: "More practices of this type should be done", "It has been a good experience, the results have been quite good ", "I think it is a necessary and very interesting activity. Hopefully more time would be devoted to its execution" and "It is a very good initiative; other subjects should do the same". These comments reflect the interest that this type of activity arouses in students.

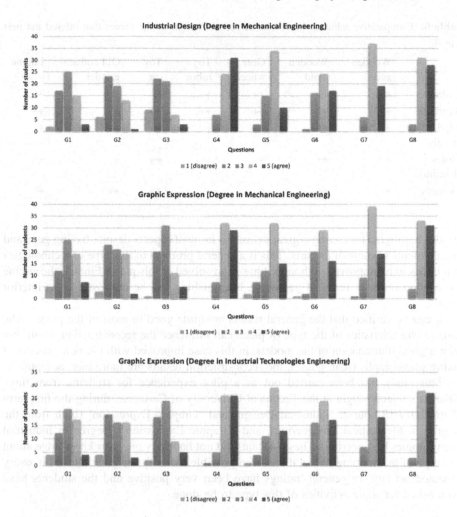

Fig. 12. Results of general questions related to the methodology used during the study.

5 Discussion

A comparative study of the results of reconstruction of the selected pieces that offered the best aspect can be shown in Table 6. In this analysis, different characteristics and shape aspects were taken into account.

If the reconstructions of the wooden gear and the wooden mold are analyzed, a very good quality in all the defined aspects can be observed. This is due to they are compact pieces without hollows or deep holes, so the definition of their shape is very good. The gear wheel also has a pretty good finish, but its definition in the edges and in the holes is deficient, since it is a thin piece. The reconstruction of the toy robot presents good quality in most of the features except in the holes that constitutes the wiring. The toy car also stands out for its good result in both shape and appearance. The old coffee

Table 6. Comparative table of the results of reconstruction of the pieces that offered the best aspect.

	Wooden gear	Wooden mold	Gear wheel	Toy robot	Toy car	Old coffee grinder	Engine
Colours	++	++	++	++	++	++	++
Textures	++	++	++	++	++	++	++
Model details	++	++	++	+	++	++	+
Holes definition	++	++	–	–	++	+	–
Borders	++	++	+	+	++	++	+

grinder highlights for having a great definition in most aspects despite having gaps and thin elements in some of its parts. This is a general problem of this type of technologies that needs to be improved, although it has been solved in this piece. Finally, the engine has a good result in terms of geometry, but finishing can be improved in its interior details.

It can be verified that the general results are quite good in most of the pieces. The surface characteristics of the type of piece can influence the reconstruction result, but with a good illumination of the models, in this case improved with the new process of taking photographs (scan phase), the reconstruction results are more than acceptable.

This study has been carried out as a pilot experience for students from three different subjects taught at the Technical University of Cartagena during the first term of the 2017/18 course: 'Industrial Design' and 'Graphic Expression' (both from the Degree in Mechanical Engineering), and 'Graphic Expression' (Degree in Industrial Technologies Engineering). These students did not have any previous knowledge about this type of methodologies and it has been possible to verify the great interest in every executed activity. In general, ratings have been very positive and the students have even asked for more activities of this type to be done.

6 Conclusions

Nowadays, reverse engineering is used in multiple professional fields that impel to develop different processes for obtaining virtual objects from real objects. This study is a sample of the use of open access applications as didactic tools within a reverse engineering process. This type of practice is only an initiation to this process. The ideal solution would be to use more sophisticated and professional tools, but not always they are reachable.

The present study has shown the process of scanning and 3D reconstruction by images of several pieces. This method, which is denominated Image-based 3D Modeling and Rendering (IB3DMR), uses a set of photographs in 2D to generate a three-dimensional digital model. The tool used during this study is Autodesk Recap, which has been proved to offer a good quality in most reconstructions. In case of requiring a possible mesh editing process, the MeshLab software has been shown. This tool is used to optimize, if necessary, the mesh of the virtual model giving the possibility of exporting to other CAD formats.

Three-dimensional reconstructions obtained from scanning by images can have multiple applications in different fields such as engineering. Acceptable virtual objects can be obtained to perform the required simulations in a design process, analyse characteristics and surface properties of any type of piece, etc. In addition, this type of tools does not highlight by its equipment accuracy, but its ease of use, low cost and flexibility make them very appropriate for the teaching field as didactic tools, and especially for distance learning.

This work has presented a series of activities that allow students to begin in the reverse engineering process, work in the process of scanning and reconstructing objects by images, and exporting them to different formats according to the needs required by the piece. Using this type of tools prepares students in new technologies and applications that are increasingly being implemented in all professional fields of society. Universities must be prepared for these new challenges and offer them as a complement to their academic education.

The analysis of the tests completed by the students highlights that this type of methodologies are unknown and most of the students have a high level of interest in learning them because they consider that it may be important for their professional future.

References

1. Blais, F.: Review of 20 years of range sensor development. J. Electron. Imaging **13**(1), 231–243 (2004)
2. Luhmann, T.: Close range photogrammetry for industrial applications. ISPRS J. Photogramm. Remote Sens. **65**(6), 558–569 (2010)
3. Remondino, F., El-hakim, S.: Image-based 3D modelling: a review. Photogramm. Record **21**(115), 269–291 (2006)
4. Debevec, P.E., Taylor, C.J., Malik, J.: Modeling and rendering architecture from photographs: a hybrid geometry-and image-based approach. In: Proceedings of the 23rd Annual Conference on Computer Graphics and Interactive Techniques. ACM (1996)
5. Nguyen, C.V., et al.: Capturing natural-colour 3D models of insects for species discovery and diagnostics. PLoS ONE **9**(4), e94346 (2014)
6. Sinha, S., et al.: Image-based rendering for scenes with reflections. ACM Trans. Graph. **31**(4), 100:1–100:10 (2012)
7. Cavas Martínez, F., et al.: Reconstrucción tridimensional de frutas a partir de imágenes digitales para su análisis. In: I Symposium Nacional de Ingeniería Hortícola "La Agromótica en la Horticultura". Orihuela (España) (2014)
8. Cavas Martínez, F., et al.: Empleo de imágenes digitales para reconstrucción tridimensional de componentes. In: 18th International Congress on Project Management and Engineering (AEIPRO 2014). Alcañiz (España) (2014)
9. Cervera, O., et al.: Técnicas de modelado tridimensional y su aplicación en la auralización de espacios. In: VIII Congreso Ibero-Americano de Acústica. Évora, Portugal (2012)

10. Venkatesh, S., Ganeshkar, S.V., Ajmera, S.: Image-based 3D modelling: a simple and economical technique to create 3-D models of the face. Int. J. Health Sci. Res. **2**(6), 93–99 (2012)
11. Santagati, C., Inzerillo, L.: 123D catch: efficiency, accuracy, constraints and limitations in architectural heritage field. Int. J. Herit. Dig. Era **2**(2), 263–290 (2013)
12. Santamaría, J., Sanz, F.: 3D land modelling from photos. In: VII Congreso Ibérico de Agroingeniería y Ciencias Hortícolas. Sociedad Española de Ciencias Hortícolas, Madrid (2013)
13. Lerma, J.L., et al.: Range-based versus automated markerless image-based techniques for rock art documentation. Photogramm. Record **29**(145), 30–48 (2014)
14. Lavy, A., et al.: A quick, easy and non-intrusive method for underwater volume and surface area evaluation of benthic organisms by 3D computer modelling. Methods Ecol. Evolut. **6**(5), 521–531 (2015)
15. Li, L.: Interactive and collaborative learning in virtual English classes. J. Cases Inf. Technol. **15**(4), 7–20 (2013)
16. Wu, Y.C., Yang, J.C.: The effects of the social media-based activities and gaming-based learning in construction education. Institute of Electrical and Electronics Engineers Inc. (2016)
17. Camacho Peñalosa, M.E., et al.: Motivar a la autoevaluación y el autoaprendizaje de las Matemáticas a través de las TIC. In: V Jornadas de Innovación Universitaria. Universidad Europea de Madrid, Villaviciosa de Odón (Madrid) (2008)
18. Faath, A., Anderl, R.: Interdisciplinary and consistent use of a 3D CAD model for CAx education in engineering studies. In: ASME 2016 International Mechanical Engineering Congress and Exposition. American Society of Mechanical Engineers (2016)
19. Reisoğlu, I., et al.: 3D virtual learning environments in education: a meta-review. Asia Pac. Educ. Rev. **18**(1), 81–100 (2017)
20. Wong, H.M., et al.: Qualitative and quantitative analysis of the students' perceptions to the use of 3D electronic models in problem-based learning. Knowl. Manag. E-Learn. Int. J. (KM&EL) **9**(2), 128–142 (2017)
21. Prados Salazar, J.C., et al.: Desarrollo de representaciones volumétricas como metodología docente para el autoaprendizaje en el Área de Anatomía. In: V Jornadas de Innovación Universitaria. Universidad Europea de Madrid, Villaviciosa de Odón (Madrid) (2008)
22. Mateos, Q.A., et al.: Aplicación de un escáner 3D a fines didácticos. In: XXII Jornadas de Automática. Universidad Autónoma de Barcelona, Barcelona (2001)
23. Sinha, A.: Preliminary assessment of different 3D scanning and reverse engineering tools for undergraduate projects. In: 2008 ASEE Annual Conference and Exposition, Pittsburg, PA (2008)

Disrupting Higher Education: Engaging Design Students in UX Processes to Enhance Innovation in Higher Education

Debra Satterfield[✉], Tom Tredway, and Wesley Woelfel

California State University, Long Beach, Long Beach, CA, USA
{debra.satterfield, tom.tredway, Wesley.woelfel}@csulb.edu

Abstract. In Fall 2018, California State University, Long Beach initiated an envisioning process for future casting called BEACH 2030. This multi-year event was initiated with a two-day event called "Imagine Beach 2030." Designed to engage a broad audience of stakeholders including students, faculty, staff, alumni, leadership, regional partners, and community members, this event, held on November 14–15, 2018, was an opportunity to host a series of campus activities meant to engage groups of people both in virtual and physical space. This case study discusses an experience design event that was a collaborative strategy to generate innovation strategies to enhance the student experience in higher education. A unique combination of UX research strategies, design course and student engagement events are discussed with regard to how existing courses and resources can be used to create a cohesive process for UX innovation in higher education in design.

Keywords: Collaboration · Connectivity model · Design thinking · Disruptive technologies · Innovation · Sustainability · Team teaching · Triangulated research strategy · UX

1 Introduction

Design students from two courses, DESN 268: History and Theory of Sustainability in Design and DESN 481: Designing for User Experiences, participated in research for an "Imagine Beach 2030" event. Students in DESN 481, an introductory UX design course, conducted a qualitative data collection process to engage a large number of design students in a brainstorming and idea generation process resulting in several "idea generation boards." Students in DESN 268, a design seminar course, formed teams and prepared in-depth research papers and presentations on topics involving future innovation for higher education. These two courses and research strategies were integrated by seeding the idea generation boards with the research topics of the seminar classes.

The culmination of the UX data gathering strategies was a design sprint conducted on November 15, 2018, during the campus-wide "Imagine Beach 2030" event. The sprint included presentations by the DESN 268 seminar students on their deep dive

© Springer Nature Switzerland AG 2019
M. Antona and C. Stephanidis (Eds.): HCII 2019, LNCS 11572, pp. 177–187, 2019.
https://doi.org/10.1007/978-3-030-23560-4_13

research. After the presentations were completed, students at the sprint were given the opportunity to form teams along these topics and were provided with the idea generation boards containing crowd sourced ideas on the same topics. Students used the Connectivity Model, a UX research model based on social, emotional, motivational and physical parameters, to assess and develop final innovation concepts for what the university should be in the year 2030.

The student led brainstorming, classroom engagement, and the use of a design sprint to engage large numbers of student stakeholders in the university envisioning process will be discussed. The specific methods, tools, UX strategies and outcomes of this unique series of events will be presented. In addition, the application of these UX processes as an innovative strategy for self-evaluation and innovation in higher education will be discussed.

2 Triangulated Research Strategy

Our triangulated research strategy reframed several questions of interest in different formats of data gathering and participation. The reframing methods were derived from design thinking techniques made popular by Tim Brown and David Kelly [1]. By applying our methods in different contexts and formats we broadened the spectrum of the data gathered. For the purposes of maximum student engagement and divergent thinking, incorporating in-depth research and critical thinking in problem solving, the following three strategies were combined into a triangulated research methodology:

1. Crowd Sourced Student/Stakeholder Input via Public Crowd Sourced Data Collection;
2. In-Depth Subject Research Papers/Presentations; and
3. Design Sprint Teams.

At the Beach 2030 Design Sprint event held in the California State University, Long Beach's Design Department Gallery, we incorporated in our three strategies several creative problem solving methodologies pioneered by Alex Osborn and Sidney Parnes [2]. One of our goals in data gathering at the design sprint was connecting the "how might we statements" utilized in the other two approaches of our triangulated research strategy. These statements are designed to encourage divergent thinking and are commonly utilized in many design thinking and creative problem solving frameworks. In our sprint, we integrated a series of exercises aimed at promoting the reciprocation of divergent and convergent thinking. Our tools of choice incorporated a combination of white boards, dry-erase pens, writing materials, paper and post-its to emphasize rapid exercises to cultivate the exchange of information in a group setting and synthesize an environment of idea sharing and building.

Fig. 1. Crowd Student and Stakeholder Data was Collected in Public Spaces on our Themes.

3 The Beach 2030 Event

DESN 268: History and Theory of Sustainability in Design explores the intellectual and cultural foundations of sustainability issues across design practices and disciplines in human society including historical, contemporary and future theories. Its BEACH 2030 Sustainable Futures project addressed several student learning outcomes for the course, including: create hypotheses for future scenarios from a base of historical and theoretical understanding; demonstrate effective use of integrative learning skills, including synthesis and interdisciplinary methods of inquiry; and contextualize sustainability topics as influenced by specific and diverse global, local, cultural and historical conditions.

The BEACH 2030 Sustainable Futures project built from the premise that anticipating and shaping future design trends can have a significant influence on sustainability. Students worked together in groups to research and propose future trends in sustainable design and determine potential applications for California State University, Long Beach. Each group selected a certain product category, system, process, or sphere of the physical and/or digital environment and determined what it may look like, from a sustainability perspective, in 2030. They then applied those research insights to determine how sustainability could be improved in that area at CSULB. We discussed methods, models, and practices for determining sustainable design futures in class and our methodological approach began with R. Buckminster Fuller's Comprehensive

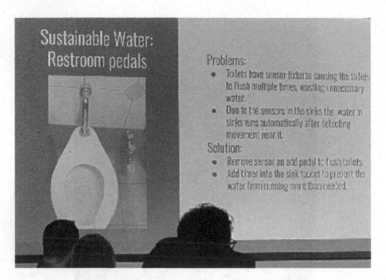

Fig. 2. In-Depth Research Presentations were made during the Sprint prior to the Design Phase.

Anticipatory Design Science as general framework for research-based, iterative futures development [3]. We also looked at contemporary case-studies for design futures research and development projects with a particular focus on issues of ecological, social, and economic sustainability, including design futures approaches to products as explored by Bradley Quinn and sustainable architectural futures projects by Ted Givens, Koen Olthius, and Werner Sobek, among others [4].

Once we explored futures theories, systems, and approaches we built on our previous coursework on sustainable systems and processes for product and service design and building systems. Students were encouraged to combine visionary creativity with rigorous research to anticipate and contextualize sustainability futures. Student groups determined their own research topics, which included academic technology, transportation and parking, energy, water, building technologies, and green roofs, and conducted research into contemporary design and sustainability trends in these areas. Research questions centered around recent changes in the field, developments on the horizon, including problems addressed and anticipated success, and other innovations that may have an impact on sustainability, either in a positive or a negative way, in the near future. Students then determined which trends and developments were likely to continue into the next decade to anticipate the state of sustainable design in each field in 2030 and applied that research to issues or problems faced by CSULB. We utilized design thinking and active learning strategies to approach research, writing, and presentation development as an iterative process best done in diverse, multidisciplinary teams with an emphasis on creative experimentation through prototyping and constructive feedback [5, 6]. Once the teams had selected topics and conducted preliminary research we held a round robin session addressing sustainability developments in each area and brainstorming potential applications for our campus. Based on these sessions students conducted further research and prepared advanced drafts of their presentations for informal review through desk critiques. Feedback from these sessions was incorporated into a final 10-minute public presentation which detailed their research on recent and contemporary sustainability trends in their area and explained their vision for the state of sustainable design in their field at CSULB in 2030.

In anticipation of the presentations, we prepared six "how might we" statements related to the various research areas and used them to seed UX idea generation boards to solicit community engagement and feedback. Each board was titled with one of these statements and armed with an assortment of dry-erase pens then stationed throughout our department in hallways, classrooms and gathering points in the days leading to the final presentations and our design sprint.

4 The Connectivity Model as a Framework

Students participating in the sprint were given research tools to inform them with regard to considerations in the areas of Social, Emotional, Motivational and Behavioral aspects of their designs. The Connectivity Model was used as a framework for the research tools. As a design research methodology, the Connectivity Model uses audience analysis to understand the characteristics of a target audience with regard to their activities, emotions, motivations, and cognition. This model considers the artifact or environment being designed as part of a larger contextualized experience. The social and emotional needs of the user, as well as any physical constraints are integral to the constraints for the final design. Only those solutions that meet these requirements will be considered optimal solutions (Fig. 3).

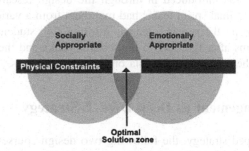

Fig. 3. The Connectivity Model Optimal Solution Zone.

The series of informational research tools included:

1. Disruptive Technologies/Disruptive Economies;
2. Emotional Factors;
3. Social Factors;
4. Behavioral Factors; and
5. Motivational Factors.

The purpose of the informational research tools was to stimulate the thought processes of the sprint participants in each of these areas. They were projected onto the screen during the design sprint as the teams were working. Since the time frame of a sprint is compressed, the purpose of these tools was to insert additional ideas and concepts at critical points in the brainstorming and ideation phase of the project.

5   The T-Shaped Team Concept

The concept of T-shaped people and T-shaped skills have permeated design circles since the early 90 s with David Guest and later IDEO's Tim Brown championing the strategy as the ideal combination of deep knowledge along with breadth of skills and empathy. According to Brown:

> "T-shaped people have two kinds of characteristics, hence the use of the letter "T" to describe them. The vertical stroke of the "T" is a depth of skill that allows them to contribute to the creative process. That can be from any number of different fields: an industrial designer, an architect, a social scientist, a business specialist or a mechanical engineer. The horizontal stroke of the "T" is the disposition for collaboration across disciplines. It is composed of two things. First, empathy. It's important because it allows people to imagine the problem from another perspective- to stand in somebody else's shoes. Second, they tend to get very enthusiastic about other people's disciplines, to the point that they may actually start to practice them. T-shaped people have both depth and breadth in their skills [7]."

The nature of our design innovation strategy for this event used many of the strategies common in T-shaped groups. In our event the breadth was achieved in the crowd sourced data collection and the eclectic composition of the sprint teams. The depth of knowledge was introduced in through the design research and theory presentations. Each of the final sprint teams had members from a variety of backgrounds and representatives from the research teams. Additionally, students were allowed to organically form teams after listening to the research talks and the sprint teams were then provided with the crowd-sourced data on the same subjects.

6   Student Engagement as Deep Dive T-Strategy

Based on the T-Shaped strategy, the following two design courses assigned comprehensive projects to support the Beach 2030 event:

DESN 268 - History and Theory of Sustainability in Design

This course is a seminar class that explores the intellectual and cultural foundations of sustainability issues across design practices and disciplines in human society including historical, contemporary and future theories.

DESN 481 - Designing for User Experiences

This course is an introduction to user experience design. It explores the application of theories, research methods, ethics, and design processes of UX (user experience) design. Students research, develop, and test UX designs. Design strategies are discussed as they apply to physical, virtual, and hybrid solutions.

Six how might we statements were developed from the DESN 268 research topics as a tool to gather feedback and response from outside the course:

- How might we utilize green roofs to increase social and ecological sustainability on campus?
- How might we leverage emerging technologies, including AR/VR, to envision the university education of the future?
- How might we deploy new building techniques and materials to meet the growing demand for student housing and other needs?
- How might we reimagine a transportation network for all stakeholders at CSULB?
- How might we harness new forms of renewable energy to fuel our campus?
- How might we create water systems that address a drought-parched future?

7 Horizontal T-Strategy Using a Design Sprint

The culmination of our triangulated research strategy was expressed in the form of a design sprint immediately following the aforementioned DESN 268 student presentations. We invited students, faculty, staff and community members from throughout the city of Long Beach to participate in the design sprint held within California State University, Long Beach's Design Department Duncan Anderson Gallery. The sprint utilized creative problem solving methods, environmental tone changes, energy, and competition to gather further data.

Our methodology incorporated several creative problem solving exercises formatted in a series of rounds. Each round addressed and slightly reframed a question from the DESN 268 student presentations. One of the key elements of divergent thinking revolves around the problem solving environment. We utilized a format of rounds and prizes aimed at encouraging participation, sharing and fun within the event. Prior to each round we motivated the behavior of the participants to utilize the standards of productive divergent thinking by sharing several guidelines for idea gathering derived from the Creative Problem Solving "CPS" process [8] (defer judgement, seek wild ideas, combine and build, etc.). Each round utilized our "how might we" spark questions and challenged the participants to produce ideas rapidly. Each spark question incorporated our Connectivity Model as a theme:

Social Factors:

1. Knowledge of Social Roles, Rules, and Scripts;
2. Effective Listening Skills;
3. Understanding What Makes Other People Tick;
4. Impression Management Skills; and
5. Verbal Fluency and Conversational Skills.

Motivational Factors:

1. A Need for Achievement-Goals, Standards, Competition;
2. A Need for Affiliation-Liked, Honesty, Reaching out; and
3. A Need for Power-Command and Control.

Behavioral Factors:

1. Aggressive;
2. Assertive; and
3. Passive-Aggressive.

Emotional Factors:

1. Self-Awareness-Emotional Self-Awareness;
2. Self-Management, Self-Control, Adaptability, Outlook;
3. Social Awareness-Empathy, Organizational Awareness; and
4. Relationship Management-Teamwork, Leadership.

Fig. 4. Sprint Teams used the Connectivity Model along with the Information from Presentations and Crowd Sourced Data to design Beach 2030 Innovations for Campus.

Within each round, students were led by faculty members in sharing their ideas onto a movable whiteboard using post-its and colored dry-erase markers.

After several rounds of spark questions and exercises, the participants amassed a healthy library of ideas and approaches to answering each spark question. We then moved into a convergent round in which we changed the perspectives of the participants into ones that promoted thoughtfulness, building, and deliberate decisions based upon guidelines developed by the Creative Education Foundation [8]. Ideas, thoughts, experiences and suggestions on the post-its were collectively categorized and ordered using heuristic creativity ordering techniques within the group setting. We converged the ideas further by labeling and circling each node group of ideas on the whiteboard with our dry-erase markers.

Following this round, and after prizes of course, the cohort of participants battled against each other in a final design charrette in which each group utilized its boards of data to develop a final gestural design that addressed the spark questions from our Connectivity Model methodology. Each team then shared their work and exchanged their thought process (Fig. 4). The sprint offered a forum for the rapid collection and exchange of concerns, thoughts and innovations while leveraging the diversity of our audience (Fig. 5).

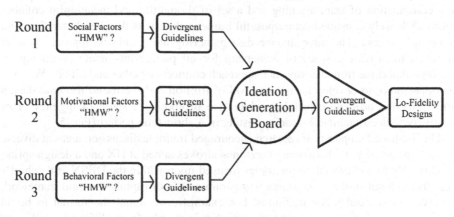

Fig. 5. Design Sprint Team Process.

The Sustainable Instructional Technology Futures presentation focused on how to leverage emerging AR/VR technologies in the classroom to create hybrid environments that help to replicate the social aspects of face-to-face education in order to keep students engaged and promote efficient use of resources. The results from our divergent and convergent design thinking methodology charrette emphasized AI, increasing internationalization of the student body amid globalization, and the need for responsive educational technology. The design phase produced a low fidelity prototype for an AI-enhanced universal language translator that would allow for near real time translation of speech or text in recognition of the fact that language barriers often lead to educational challenges for a variety of CSULB students and that rapid and accurate access to course content can improve learning and academic success (Fig. 6).

Fig. 6. Sprint Teams Created Drawings and Models to Support their Innovation Designs.

8 Analyzing the Event, Experiences and Tools

The triangulated research strategy provided several lenses of data gathering propelled by a combination of team teaching and a set of thoughtful and meaningful collaborations. A loosely construed yet purposeful framework provided a useful, iterative, and thoughtful process. The three diverse data gathering and feedback approaches were leveraged to provide a space of ownership for all participants while producing an unknown that came from the way each approach connects together and differs. We took this opportunity to develop ideas to a level of fruition and we found the final design sprint provided artificial constraints while also promoting a sense of urgency. This effectively yielded tangible lo-fidelity results in a short time period (Fig. 5).

The T-Shaped emphasis of research encouraged multiple discussion areas at diverse levels of granularity. By harnessing horizontal strokes aimed at UX and a design sprint, we were able to add breadth to the topics focused upon within the DESN 268 cohort's deep dive vertical stroke. This format was paramount in disrupting the rigid framework of university schedules and traditions. For example, we found the format to be an effective method of bringing students together not only from different levels and programs within our curriculum, but without the necessity to schedule courses in parallel nor drift from each course's student learning objectives.

Although the team teaching strategy lacked many constraints, this served as an advantage to encouraging diverse participants. It is worth noting that we see our research strategy as a generator of an awareness of diverse and inclusive topics. However, the activities and events held within our triangulated research strategy were not built to be conductive of gathering the utmost diverse and inclusive participation. charrette style is not adherent to accessibility and not everyone can be involved in the traditional settings of brainstorming. Frequently, common thinking comes from brainstorming environments. And while we like to believe in stigma and bias how might we identify the emotional aspects of discomfort and bias? What happens when participant gets an idea but doesn't want others to know they are thinking of it? In retooling this research strategy, how might we design an event that captures and shares the diversity of social sustainability and inclusive design? In future deployments of this research strategy it would be a priority to apply socially sensitive and diverse methods to gather a greater degree of contribution of various participants from a behavioral, emotional, social, and motivational perspective.

This research strategy is flexible and could be easily adapted to be used in many contexts and frameworks. Moving the design approach utilized in our research strategies from stakeholders to professionals appears to require a retooled approach. Sometimes, inclusive discussions that move into a business become ideas that are seized instead of shared and contributed back. There isn't a mechanism in our strategy currently to return the value to those who provide the value.

We hope to utilize our approach as modules and apply them to different events in the future in an effort to validate, evaluate and improve its effectiveness. A set of guidelines or a workbook could be developed to promote deployable and reproducible results which could be documented to expedite improvement. Depending upon the mix of collaborators and coordinators, different lenses can be customized and applied. In redefining each deployment of the triangulated research strategy, we can recruit an expert as a catalyst for the vertical stroke's deep dive of the T-shape collaboration structure or perhaps any subsequent design sprint.

References

1. IDEO.org.: The Field Guide to Human-Centered Design, 1st edn. IDEO.org/Design Kit (2015)
2. Osborn, A.: Applied Imagination: Principles and Procedures of Creative Problem-Solving, 3rd edn. Charles Scribner's Sons, New York (1963)
3. Brown, H., Cook, R., Gabel, M.: Environmental Design Science Primer. Buckminster Fuller Institute. https://www.bfi.org/design-science/primer/environmental-design-science-primer
4. Quinn, B.: Design Futures (London; New York: Merrell, 2011); Building for the Future (New Docs, 2014)
5. Leverenz, C.S.: Design Thinking and the Wicked Problem of Teaching Writing. Comput. Compos. Int. J. Teach. Writ. 33, 1–12 (2014)
6. Bean, J.C.: Engaging Ideas: The Professor's Guide to Integrating Writing, Critical Thinking, and Active Learning in the Classroom, 2nd edn. Jossey-Bass, San Francisco (2011)
7. https://chiefexecutive.net/ideo-ceo-tim-brown-t-shaped-stars-the-backbone-of-ideoaes-collabo rative-culture__trashed/
8. Creative Education Foundation: Creative Problem Solving Resource Guide. Massachusetts, Creative Education Foundation (2015)

Novel Approaches to Accessibility

Guideline Definition for the Evaluation of Citizen Experience Using Urban Interfaces

Luis Carlos Aceves Gutiérrez[1,2], Jorge Martín-Gutiérrez[1(✉)],
and Marta Sylvia del Rio Guerra[1,2]

[1] Universidad de La Laguna, 38202 San Critóbal de La Laguna, Tenerife, Spain
{luis.carlos.aceves,marta.sylvia.delrio}@udem.edu.mx,
jmargu@ull.edu.es
[2] Universidad de Monterrey, 66238 Monterrey, Nuevo León, Mexico

Abstract. This paper presents fourteen useful guidelines to evaluate and determine how much does a digital interface in a public facility provide user experiences for citizens. In addition, it describes the partial outcomes of applying these guidelines to three urban interfaces in the city of Monterrey, Mexico. An ethnographic study was conducted to obtain preliminaries results where the user experience was assessed in these interfaces when applying the proper guidelines. The goal is to validate guidelines with global assessment methods to establish a protocol of design for urban interfaces; in other words, an application that provides the information required to design urban interfaces from point of view of UX. This extended ethnographic study will be implemented in different cities around the world and urban interfaces.

Keywords: Digital interfaces · User experience · Smart cities · Interaction design ·
Citizen-centered design · Design principles and usability test

1 Introduction

We live in an age of constant changes where information technology is reaching a great number of people. In this sense, the context of digital channels and technological devices use has evolved from robust and costly computers and specialized knowledge to a "massive" environment, where a person with scarcely any money or computer skills can use these devices.

Thus, daily activities are being systematized; people are using tools and computer systems aiming to improve their well-being. These automated activities take place while the cities grow, and governments establish technological infrastructure to improve their citizen's well- being. This is how the transition from a "traditional" city to a "smart" city has occurred nowadays [6].

2 Smart Cities and Urban Interfaces

2.1 Smart Cities

A smart city is characterized by offering people different digital channels to interact with each other or with their local government. According to García [9], every time technology

© Springer Nature Switzerland AG 2019
M. Antona and C. Stephanidis (Eds.): HCII 2019, LNCS 11572, pp. 191–200, 2019.
https://doi.org/10.1007/978-3-030-23560-4_14

for residents or tourists is taken into account when the city is carefully designed, an environment of intelligent and sustainable growth is created and promoted.

2.2 Urban Interfaces

Since the 90s, with the commercial boom of the Internet, governments began to offer information and, subsequently, offered services and procedures to users through websites known as government web portals. This was the main and only digital channel of intelligent environment in the cities. Due to the increase of mobile devices, governments realized the importance of having a digital presence, ubiquitous and customized. In the last few years, other technological devices such as kiosks, sensors and ATMs allowed governments to increase their service-offer to people. Digital channels are suited to perform in urban environments such as public roads or special facilities that are part of an urban context design [9]. According to Mazhar [1] and Sakamoto [17], these channels must have a simple and easy digital interface which allows people to offer a faster and more efficient service.

Verhoeff [22] mentions that urban interfaces include an array of technologies, screen forms, formats, facilities, sensorial interfaces and architecture. Those technologies are located in public facilities; they are interactive and connect the user with his closest environment. They are important because they can be shared, are available to everyone, they are also intelligent and are crucial for the city's social welfare.

The most common urban interfaces were not designed with a user-centered approach because it becomes an ordeal for the user to accomplish what he/she desires to do. Authors such as Sandnes [19], Prior [15], mention some aspects they bore in mind when they conducted a research on the train ticket-machines in Taiwan. Their main aspects are: the machine's ergonomics and dimensions, vision angles on the screens and use of deflector materials, the interface's location, data privacy when necessary, use of proper colors, iconography and significant signals, availability in different languages and structured menus.

In spite of these aspects, many existing urban interfaces are neither evaluated nor designed adequately due to a lack of knowledge about the process to validate them.

3 Usability Heuristics

3.1 Brief Review of Existing Heuristics

During the 90s, Nielsen suggested a series of usability heuristics to evaluate user-experience of digital interfaces [12,13]. These heuristics are a qualitative proposal based on the fact that the evaluator must execute an empathy process while using the system to simulate the different scenarios where the final users would be immersed.

As a result of Nielsen's findings, other methods have been developed to evaluate the interface usability; some have had a more quantitative approach such as the Sirius method, published by Suárez, that takes into account a checklist with a set of items [20]. Other proposals such as Weinschenk's psychological heuristics evaluate its usability from a perspective related to the user's senses and reasoning when he/she uses an interface [18, 24].

However, all these proposals aren't very accurate since the evaluator must simulate he/she is the final user. So, the real point of view remains unknown [15].

3.2   Usability Assessment of Urban Interfaces

Since the rise of the first digital channels which were provided by some governments, very little has been done to evaluate citizens who use digital interfaces. If there is some luck, the interfaces of the government's web portals are evaluated by a quantitative heuristic method that only provides a general diagnosis showing how well-positioned is the portal in the user's mind.

Aside from government web portals, there is no other practice to evaluate interfaces in other channels. This lack of assessment is the reason why many of the government's technological initiatives fail, because they are focused on the achievement of a smarter city.

In addition, in the case of urban interfaces, many of these channels have been implemented under a technology-centered perspective or are limited to the government's budget, rather than adopting a citizen-centered perspective [3, 4, 6, 14].

4   User Experience Guidelines to Design Urban Interfaces

4.1   Defining the Guidelines

The collected information from experts in usability, user- experience design and ergonomics was analyzed for heuristics development. The consulted authors and organizations were Nielsen [13], Weinschenk [24], Tognazzini [21], Connell [7], Russo and Boor [2], Rosenfeld [16], Web Accessibility Initiative (WAI) [23] and the Biomechanic Institute of Valencia [11].

The analysis included a heuristic revision of the consulted authors in order to assemble those that share similarities. This information was used to create a comparative table of heuristics [8].

Once the groups were identified, we created the assessment indicators giving a name and a representative description to each group. We ran a verifying process to be sure that all the revised and planned areas of the research were covered.

The final result was fourteen guidelines to be presented in the following paragraphs. The guidelines include aspects of usability, ergonomics, psychology, and accessibility among others. The suggested heuristics are the following: efficiency, assistance and direction, content-structure, environmental resemblance, context relevant information, mistake prevention, feedback, cognitive processes, internationalization, visual design, movement and perception, perception access, complementary and alternative channels [8].

4.2   Guidelines to Assess Urban Interfaces

We offer below, a detailed description of the guidelines required to judge the user-experience in an urban interface. Each guideline has its own description and criteria to enable a proper qualitative assessment.

Guideline 1. Efficiency. This guideline evaluates the extent in which a task is completed without deviations or delays. The goal is to determine whether the interface is flexible when adapted to a person's different requirements. At the same time, we checked if the interface provides various options to perform the tasks depending on the devices where the action takes place.

The method to evaluate this guideline is based on the behavior that is observed in the following situations:

- Does a person have the opportunity to skip a step to complete the task?
- Is he/she able to complete the task without making a mistake?
- Is he/she able to go one step backwards or all the way to the beginning?
- Does a person obtain all the information from only one place?
- Does a person capture the minimum amount of data?

Guideline 2. Assistance and direction. This guideline reviews the way in which the urban interface provides a rapid access to the information that solves all the possible doubts that a person may have.

To assess this guideline we must observe the following situations:

- Does a person have to find information on how to perform a specific step?
- Is there a way to contact someone in case a mistake is made?
- Does he/she know exactly what to do to attain his/her goal?

Guideline 3. Content structure. This guideline measures whether the information is well organized in the interface. It also determines if browsing allows people to find what they are searching for.

The following situations are useful to determine the fulfillment of this guideline:

- Once a person has completed the task, can he/she remember the required steps to complete it?
- Does he/she make mistakes when he/she captures the information?
- Does he/she understand what he/she will find based on the labeling?
- Can a person access the contents in a simple and easy manner?
- Is there a search engine tool?
- Is there any ambiguity in the instructions?
- Is the information grouped in such an order that anybody may comprehend how to complete the format and interpret the results?
- Are there more ways to find the same information?

Guideline 4. Likeness with reality. To assess this guideline, we use metaphors that enable a person to identify familiar situations in a simple and natural way.

The following situation is useful to evaluate this guideline:

- Did a person have previous knowledge of the elements included in the interface before he/she interacted with them?

Guideline 5. Relevant contextual information. It shows the necessary information for interaction. However, it is possible to present more data if required.

This guideline is accomplished by answering the following questions:

- Does the interface show relevant information?
- Does the interface constrain the user to memorize the previous steps?
- Is the information clear and concise?

Guideline 6. Mistake prevention. This guideline determines whether the interface is designed to anticipate a person's needs.

To define the extent in which this guideline is fulfilled, some questions must be analysed:

- Does the interface allow to choose options that are not valid?
- Did a person have to consult the same information more than once?

Guideline 7. Mistake retrieval. This guideline analyses if the interface allows you to correct mistakes and learn from them.

The following conditions must be reviewed:

- Yes, there was a mistake. Was the person able to recognize what caused it?
- Do error messages allow a person to know what went wrong?
- Do error messages allow him/her to discern how to retrieve and correct the error?

Guideline 8. Feedback interface. In this case, it is important to know whether a person identifies what is taking place while the interface performs a specific action.

The following questions must be studied for the evaluation of this guideline:

- Did he/she performed an action more than once or did he/she use an element of the interface that wasn't required?
- Does he/she know his/her progress percentage to complete the task?
- Was it possible to find the desired option without making a mistake?
- Is a person familiarized with the unresolved steps to complete the task?
- Does the interface inform a person whether he/she is performing an action? For example: recording, consulting, information processing

Guideline 9. Cognitive processes. This guideline determines whether the interface was designed for human mental processes. It considers the required work flow and the steps that a person must follow.

The following questions must be revised to evaluate this guideline:

- Does the interface give the impression of being user friendly? This includes not only the screen but also the hardware's appearance.

- Is the information difficult to remember? Does a person need to obtain these data from other sources?
- Does a user find distractors that hinder the process to complete the task?
- Does he/she feel safe when using the interface?
- Does the user feel satisfied after completing the task?

Guideline 10. Internationalization. This guideline determines whether the information in the interface corresponds to the country's cultural background and whether the information is available in different languages.

The following situations must be reviewed to determine the internationalization:

- Is the content available in relevant languages?
- Is the text translated properly?
- Are there available options in the original language to change it to a foreign language?
- Is it possible to choose the desired alphabet?
- Are special characters (accents, ñ, among others) properly used in the text?
- Are the formats adapted to the country? (date, currency, measure units, names, addresses, among others)
- Does the interface use colors that correspond to the country's cultural background and dismisses those that do not correspond?

Guideline 11. Visual design. This guideline revises the first visual appearance of the interface. In other words, it analyses whether the design is appealing, coherent and minimalist, contrasted, and space and hierarchy-designed.

The following information must be analysed to determine whether the interface includes this guideline:

- Do the elements in the whole interface have the same visual design?
- If there are many similar elements, can mental groups be created?
- Is the same grid used in the whole interface and in the interfaces of other devices?
- Can the color palette sustain contrasting colors?
- Is a proper symbology used to distinguish the relation between sizes and objects.

Guideline 12. Movement access. This guideline determines whether the design was developed using a user-centered approach where capabilities, motion and physical limitations were taken into consideration.

The following information must be reviewed to evaluate this guideline:

- Is little effort required to activate the keyboard or tactile screen?
- Do the keyboard keys have the correct form, texture and space between them so fingers neither slip nor press two keys at the same time.

- Is it possible to obtain a nearby wheelchair?
- Does the machine's height correspond to the standards issued by the country?

Guideline 13. Perceptive access. This guideline complements the above-guideline number 12. All possible users, with their abilities and sensorial limitations were considered as references during the design process.

The following questions must be analyzed to review and validate this guideline:

- Is the option for the output-sound via headphones/earphones clearly visual?
- Is the interface applicable to all people and tasks?
- Does the interface show information in layouts that disabled people can identify?
- Is there any way to customize a person's preferences?

Guideline 14. Complementary and alternative channels. This final guideline shows whether there are other digital channels to complement the main channel, for example a mobile phone that accompanies the use of a kiosco, in order that a person may use different communication channels to interact with the interface.

The following questions must be studied to ensure the accomplishment of this guideline:

- Can a person choose one or multiple outgoing information channels? For example, use the e-mail, receive a SMS with the ticket or recharge a card via his mobile device? Can he/she choose one or multiple incoming information channels? (for example, use a bill or printed ticket, use a bar-coded card, scan codes)
- Is it possible to interact by using a mobile digital device?
- In case that it is required, is it possible to pay using other payment procedures besides cash? (debit or credit cards, e-money)

5 Ethnographic Study to Validate the Suggested Guidelines

According to Hernandez Sampieri [10], the qualitative approach must be applied when the goal is to examine the way in which people perceive and experience nearby events and express their viewpoints, interpretations and meanings.

The ethnographic study mustn't be descriptive only; it must make additional inquires by asking people further questions to obtain information about the meaning of things.

A research will be conducted based on a reliable theory. We will observe people's behaviors when they use three similar urban interfaces in the cities of Monterrey and Mexico City, in Mexico.

The final goal is to calculate user-experience in each interface by applying the guidelines previously described.

As it was mentioned, we will analyze three different urban interfaces, which will result in three groups of people. They will be under observation in order to study their user-experience.

Each group will be identified by their common characteristics. To create a model of these groups, we will apply the personas technique to obtain archetypes, which are a fictional but concrete representation of the users- groups that will utilize the product. In other words, these archetypes are based on behavioral patterns recorded during the user-research; their goal is to serve as tools that enable communication during the product-design process [9].

5.1   Number of People to Observe

To determine the number of people that will be part of this research, we must bear in mind that a sample size is never established before collecting the information during the qualitative inquiring. A unit type of analysis has been set up. Thus, we shall obtain an approximate number of cases. But the final sample is only known when we reach the saturation point, where the new data no longer provides new or different information [10].

According to Nielsen [12], at least five users must be considered to get significant results from a usability test. Those five persons, will enable us to identify 85% of the problems in the evaluated system. The purpose of this research is to have eight users in each archetype so we can identify at least 95% of the problems of each interface.

5.2   Suggested Method

The field study includes the comments of each person. The researcher will participate as a full-time observer, taking photos and recording videos [10], followed by the application of an ASQ (After- Scenario Questionnaire). This type of questionnaire was developed by Lewis. The participant must answer questions after completing a scenario or task. The participant will select some sentences by choosing an answer with a grading scale from 1 to 7 (The lowest score would show the highest usability affinity with the system). It also reviews the Likert scale, which employs scales from 5 to 7 options and is mostly used to measure quality in questionnaires.

Open questions will be included in the questionnaire. The goal is to obtain information, showing the opinion, explanations and justifications of the participants [10].

To conclude, the questionnaire's design will take into consideration the problem presented. We will try to determine the fulfillment of each guideline and evaluate the participants' general experience. The questions must be designed in such a manner that they conduct the person through a pondering process which reflects his feelings toward the problem.

Finally, once the participant has finished the questionnaire, we will obtain a score showing the number of questions answered in order to get a "quantification" of the experience in each interface [5].

6   Future Projects

One of the most important goals of this research's effort is to internationalize all the guidelines depicted in this document; it is one of the main challenges. Another test is the creation of an interactive tool that enables people to evaluate urban interfaces.

The urban interfaces will be assessed in Monterrey and Mexico City, in Mexico. Nonetheless, the guidelines are global assessment methods; in other words, they are applicable in different scenarios.

For this reason, in the short term, this ethnographic study can be implemented in other cities and urban interfaces. The purpose of this guide is to be put into operation in important cities of countries such as Canada, UK, Colombia and Spain.

Having obtained this information, we will compare and draw conclusions in other type of scenarios and people. We, then, will be able to create an assessment index of urban interfaces.

Acknowledgments. We would like to thank Andrea Cortés, Alma Velázquez and Edgar Ramírez to their contribution to the heuristics, both in the revision of existing ones and the creation of new one, work done as undergraduates for their final project under the supervision of their thesis advisor, Marta Sylvia del Río at the Universidad de Monterrey.

References

1. Abbas, M.: Challenges in implementation of TVM (ticket vending machine) in developing countries for mass transport system: a study of human behavior while interacting with ticket vending machine-TVM. In: Marcus, A. (ed.) DUXU 2014. LNCS, vol. 8519, pp. 245–254. Springer, Cham (2014). https://doi.org/10.1007/978-3-319-07635-5_24
2. Russo, P., Boor, S.: How fluent is your interface? Designing for international users. In: Proceedings of the INTERCHI '93 on Human Factors in Computing Systems (INTERCHI 1993), Amsterdam, The Netherlands, 24–29 April 1993. IOS Press (1993). http://dl.acm.org/citation.cfm?id=164943. Accessed 12 July 2017
3. Martinez Ballesteros, L.G., Alvarez, O., Markendahl, J.: Quality of experience (QoE) in the smart cities context: an initial analysis. In: 2015 IEEE First International Smart Cities Conference (ISC2), pp. 1–7 (2015). https://doi.org/10.1109/ISC2.2015.7366222
4. Benouaret, K., Valliyur-Ramalingam, R., Charoy, F.: CrowdSC: building smart cities with large-scale citizen participation. IEEE Internet Comput. **17**(6), 57–63 (2013). https://doi.org/10.1109/MIC.2013.88
5. de Castro, F., Silva, S.L., Barbará de Oliveira, S., Augusto, G.A.: Service desk software usability evaluation: the case of Brazilian National Cancer Institute. Proc. Comput. Sci. **100**, 557–564 (2016). https://doi.org/10.1016/j.procs.2016.09.195
6. Concilio, G., Marsh, J., Molinari, F., Rizzo, F.: Human smart cities: a new vision for redesigning urban community and citizen's life. In: Skulimowski, A.M.J., Kacprzyk, J. (eds.) Knowledge, Information and Creativity Support Systems: Recent Trends, Advances and Solutions. AISC, vol. 364, pp. 269–278. Springer, Cham (2016). https://doi.org/10.1007/978-3-319-19090-7_21
7. Connell, I.: Full Principles Set. http://www0.cs.ucl.ac.uk/staff/i.connell/DocsPDF/Principles Set.pdf. Accessed 12 July 2017

8. Flores, A., Velázquez, A., Ramirez, E.: Definicion y aplicacion de un instrumento de evaluacion de experiencia de uso de interfaces digitales urbanas dirigidas a ciudadanos. Universidad de Monterrey, San Pedro Garza García (2017)
9. Garcia, R., Dacko, S.: Design thinking for sustainability. In: Design Thinking. Wiley, Hoboken, pp. 381–400 (2015). https://doi.org/10.1002/9781119154273.ch25
10. Hernández Sampieri, R., Fernández Collado, C., Baptista Lucio, P.: Metodología de la investigación. McGraw-Hill. https://books.google.com.mx/books/about/Metodología_de_la_investigación.html?id=wXMtSgAACAAJ&redir_esc=y. Accessed 12 July 2017
11. Insitituto de Biomecanica de Valencia.: Instituto de Biomecánica-ERGONOMÍA Y MUEBLE. Guía de recomendaciones para el diseño de mobiliario ergonómico (2017). http://www.ibv.org/publicaciones/catalogo-de-publicaciones/ergonomia-y-mueble-guia-de-recomendaciones-para-el-diseno-de-mobiliario-ergonomico. Accessed 12 Oct 2017
12. Nielsen, J.: Finding usability problems through heuristic evaluation. In: Proceedings of the SIGCHI Conference on Human Factors in Computing Systems-CHI '92, pp. 373–380 (1992). https://doi.org/10.1145/142750.142834
13. Nielsen, J., Molich, R.: Heuristic evaluation of user interfaces. In: Proceedings of the SIGCHI Conference on Human Factors in Computing Systems Empowering People-CHI '90, pp. 249–256 (1990). https://doi.org/10.1145/97243.97281
14. Opromolla, A., Ingrosso, A., Volpi, V., Medaglia, C.M., Palatucci, M., Pazzola, M.: Gamification in a smart city context. An analysis and a proposal for its application in co-design processes. In: De Gloria, A. (ed.) GALA 2014. LNCS, vol. 9221, pp. 73–82. Springer, Cham (2015). https://doi.org/10.1007/978-3-319-22960-7_8
15. Prior, P.: Train Ticket Vending Machines: Designing for Usability (2016)
16. Rosenfeld, L.: Bloug: Information Architecture Heuristics (2004). http://louisrosenfeld.com/home/bloug_archive/000286.html. Accessed 12 Oct 2017
17. Sakamoto, M., Yoshii, A., Nakajima, T., Ikeuchi, K., Otsuka, T., Okada, K., Ishizawa, F., Kobayashi, A.: Human interaction issues in a digital-physical hybrid world. In: 2014 IEEE International Conference on Cyber-Physical Systems, Networks, and Applications, pp. 49–54 (2014). https://doi.org/10.1109/CPSNA.2014.17
18. Sanchez, J.: Psychological usability heuristics|UX magazine. In: UX Magazine (2011). http://uxmag.com/articles/psychological-usability-heuristics. Accessed 12 July 2017
19. Sandnes, F.: User interface design for public kiosks: an evaluation of the taiwan high speed rail ticket vending machine (PDF download available). J. Inf. Sci. Eng. pp. 307–321 (2010). https://www.researchgate.net/publication/220587882_User_Interface_Design_for_Public_Kiosks_An_Evaluation_of_the_Taiwan_High_Speed_Rail_Ticket_Vending_Machine. Accessed 12 Oct 2017
20. Suárez Torrente, M.C.: SIRIUS: Sistema de Evaluación de la Usabilidad Web Orientado al Usuario y basado en la Determinación de Tareas Críticas (2010). http://digibuo.uniovi.es/dspace/handle/10651/12866. Accessed 12 Oct 2017
21. Bruce, T.: Bruce Tognazzini's Tog on Interface—Developing User Interfaces for Microsoft Windows. http://flylib.com/books/en/2.847.1.19/1/. Accessed 12 Oct 2017
22. Verhoeff, N.: Urban interfaces: the cartographies of screen-based installations. Telev. N. Media 18(4), 305–319 (2017). https://doi.org/10.1177/1527476416667818
23. Web Accesibility Initiative.: WAI Guidelines and Techniques|Web Accessibility Initiative (WAI)|W3C (2015). https://www.w3.org/WAI/guid-tech. Accessed 12 Oct 2017
24. Weinschenk, S.: The Psychologist's View of UX Design|UX Magazine. In: UX Magazine. https://uxmag.com/articles/the-psychologists-view-of-ux-design. Accessed 12 Oct 2017

Preliminary Findings from a Study of an Arabic Accessibility Tool Checker

Mona Alnahari[✉] and Joyram Chakraborty[✉]

Department of Computer and Information Sciences, Towson University,
Towson, MD 21252, USA
{malnahari,jchakraborty}@towson.edu

Abstract. Research into web accessibility tools in Saudi Arabia is limited. Many Arabic websites have accessibility limitations which prove challenging for people with disabilities. The purpose of this study is to create awareness of web accessibility for Arabic-speaking people and to demonstrate the efficacy of an Arabic accessibility checker prototype. Challenges in the internationalization of the interface design that were overcome using creative solutions to develop this tool are discussed. The first version of the tool solved the limitations of previous Arabic accessibility checkers. The usability of the tool which we called Arabic Accessibility Testing Tool (AATT) was investigated. Specifically, this paper presents work-in-progress research in the area of Arabic web accessibility issues and cross-cultural interface design.

Keywords: Web accessibility tool · Human-computer interaction · Tool checker · Arabic web accessibility

1 Introduction

The necessity of developing websites that provide access to people with different disabilities is widely accepted. Providing people with special needs access to educational, technical, and financial tools through inclusive web accessibility design should not be an afterthought but rather a part of the design process. All nations in the world have citizens with special needs. Saudi Arabia is no exception with about 4% of its population identified with disabilities (Akram and Sulaiman 2017). Arabic Human-computer interaction (HCI) researchers have carried out many studies about the accessibility of websites for people with disabilities (Al-Khalifa 2012a, b; Masood Rana et al. 2011; Shawar 2015). These studies demonstrate the limited accessibility of various Arabic websites. Academic and governmental websites were mostly designed for non-disabled people with little to no consideration for people with disabilities.

Even though the number of universities in Saudi Arabia has increased recently, there are no clear Arabic accessibility guidelines, which promote inclusive design for individuals with disabilities (Akram and Sulaiman 2017; Alayed et al. 2016). Saudi Arabia has shifted manual governmental services to electronic services and has adopted Blackboard and other similar E-learning systems; therefore, it is very important for people with disabilities to have equal access to the web and benefit from government and learning services.

© Springer Nature Switzerland AG 2019
M. Antona and C. Stephanidis (Eds.): HCII 2019, LNCS 11572, pp. 201–210, 2019.
https://doi.org/10.1007/978-3-030-23560-4_15

Although there are several well-developed tools available on the web that check websites for conformance against different accessibility guidelines, such as Web Content Accessibility Guidelines (WCAG) 1.0, Web Content Accessibility Guidelines 2.0, and Section 508 guidelines, none of these tools are designed for Arabic usage, and, thus, prevent Arabic developers from knowing the issues that negatively affect web accessibility. In other words, accessibility issues for Arabic websites may be caused by not having web accessibility checker tools that help Arabic developers understand and solve accessibility issues related to their designs. Having web accessibility checkers eliminate some challenges in educating and engaging web developers and content authors in applying accessibility methods along with raising awareness of usability issues of people with sensory, physical, or cognitive impairments when accessing websites (Sloan 2006).

In our study, we developed an Arabic accessibility checker tool. In order to understand the effectiveness of the tool, a usability study was conducted to understand the challenges faced by the user requirements gathering process to better accommodate inclusive design.

2 Background and Related Work

Several studies have been done that evaluate Arabic web accessibility and all of them show the need to improve the accessibility of Arabic websites. Arabic human-computer interaction (HCI) research has suggested developing Arabic accessibility tool checkers to improve the state of current Arabic websites. Al-Nuaim et al. (2005) developed an Arabic website 1.0 to provide assessments for Arabic websites. Their efforts resulted in a website that meets Bobby accessibility checker requirements. Bobby checker is a tool developed by the Center for Applied Special Technology (CAST). Bobby provided three levels of accessibility compliance which are "A," "AA," and "AAA" (1.0). The Arabic website that was developed allowed users to run Bobby on their website. It also guided users through the Arabic error report and how to correct the errors. The application allowed website designers to evaluate their websites, identify the accessibility issues and fix the errors to improve the accessibility of their websites (2005). However, the website used only WCAG 1.0 guidelines and this version has since been updated to WCAG 2.0. Most of the developers currently use the WCAG 2.0 guidelines, along with Section 508, to test websites for accessibility issues. Also, the Bobby tool is no longer available on the web as it has been closed by the owner in 2008. Another study by Al-Khalifa (2012a, b) resulted in an Arabic web accessibility tool that checks for accessibility issues based on WCAG 2.0 level A success criteria and produces a report in Arabic that includes accessibility issues. The accessibility issues are organized in errors and warnings, and the tool gives a summary and detailed reports. The tool could evaluate some websites based on the implemented modules that handle links, images, forms, and tables accessibility issues. However, the tool does not support the techniques that are mentioned by WCAG 2.0 level one. This tool could not test modern websites that use dynamic URL generation. Both of these tools are no longer available on the web. Our approach aims to develop a tool that is capable of evaluating all kinds of websites based on WCAG 2.0 guideline level one.

3 The Tool Development

In order to develop an accessibility tool checker, existing accessibility tools were studied. Out of the many tools in various languages available on the web, none were in Arabic. After reviewing the existing tools, we noticed that some accessibility checkers had been developed by teams who dedicated their time, effort, and skills for a decade to build robust accessibility evaluating tools. Some tools that are widely used and available on the web for free are Cynthia Says, TAW, WebXACT, HERA, WAVE, AChecker, RAMP, InFocus, and A-Promp. Cynthia Says is an automated testing tool developed from the International Center for Disability Resources on the Internet in cooperation with Hi-Software. This tool evaluates a web page and generates a report based on Section 508 standards and WCAG guidelines. TAW, introduced by the Center for the Development of Information and Communication Technology and has a functionality similar to Cynthia Says, evaluates a web page and generates a report showing whether the checkpoints are satisfied or not. In addition, TAW displays tags on items that should be checked manually. This tool is available in English and Spanish, while Cynthia Says is only available in English (Benavídez et al. 2006). WebXACT was introduced by Watchfire and was a modified version of Bobby. It tests some WCAG checkpoints but recommends that the user should test other checkpoints manually. This tool tests the speed of a website and quality measures (Benavídez et al. 2006). HERA 2.0 is an improvement of the beta version of HERA. The previous version is available in four languages which are Spanish, English, Portuguese and Italian and is being translated into five more languages. The new version of HERA reduces the evaluation time by 40% to 50%. This tool can evaluate a whole website and generate a detailed report of the accessibility issues (Benavídez et al. 2006). WAVE tool was developed and administrated by Web Accessibility in Mind in 2001.

Considering the development of an Arabic tool that provides the same capabilities as the tools mentioned above is not impossible. However, it will be very time-consuming. Since many of these tools provide an application programming interface (API) service, we decided to utilize one of the existing robust tools that provide API services for the current study.

The Arabic accessibility tool checker uses AChecker's web API service. When a developer registers on the AChecker website, a unique "key service" is generated automatically. The "key service" can be used by a developer so that the developer can integrate the features of AChecker in an application. AChecker was chosen over other accessibility checkers because of certain features that were not available in other accessibility checkers. AChecker allows the user to carry out an accessibility review, interact with it, and make a decision on some accessibility issues that no other checker currently allows (Gay and Li 2010). For example, all other accessibility evaluation tools were not able to determine whether the text alternative for a picture on the page was good enough to convey the meaning of the picture. AChecker, on the other hand, guides the user through the process of understanding the error and deciding on the issues that it cannot identify automatically. AChecker provides users with the accessibility issues and associated links for each accessibility issue, which allows the user to access documentation that gives a detailed description of the error and a solution to repair it. AChecker created well-documented guidelines based on WCAG 1.0 (Level 1, 2, and 3), WCAG 2.0 (Level 1, 2, and 3),

Section 508, BITV 1.0 (Level 2), and the Stanca Act. The tool allows users to choose any guidelines available on their system. AChecker was created by a team from Deque Systems and was funded by the Ontario Enabling Change Program (Gay and Li 2010).

AATT has been developed, and the first version of the tool is online. The tool is based on the ASP.Net web-application framework, and the code is written in the C# language. While developing the tool, some challenges have been identified in the internationalization of user interfaces. For example, several words in the markup language do not have linguistic equals in Arabic. To solve the problem, closer meanings have been used and supported by a solution and an example to make the translation understandable as much as possible. The translations were independently tested for contextual verification using Arabic speakers that were not affiliated with the study.

3.1   Evaluating a Website Using AATT

The Integrated Definition Method (IDEF0) diagram (see Fig. 1) explains the processes that the tool uses to generate the results on the interface:

- A user enters a URL of a website in order to get an accessibility review of the site.
- The URL will be evaluated so that if the URL is correct, the system proceeds to the next step; otherwise, the system returns an error message to the user.
- In case the URL is valid, the system sends the URL to AChecker's web service
- AChecker evaluates a website and produces an XML file that contains all the accessibility issues.
- The system imports the XML file.
- The system parses the data on the file and extracts the accessibility review into different categories.
- The system will translate all the information into the equivalent meaning of the accessibility review (see the TranslateError method in Fig. 2).
- Accessibility review will be reported on the interface of AATT in both languages, Arabic and English.

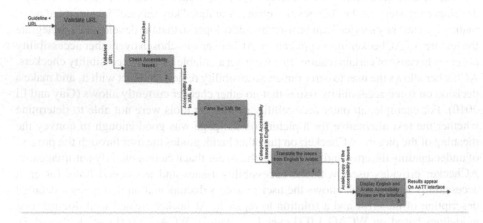

Fig. 1. The automated processes of the proposed Tool

```
XmlNodeList m_nodes = results.SelectNodes("//resultset/results/result");

foreach (XmlNode result in m_nodes)
{
    table1.Rows.Add(result["resultType"].InnerText.ToString(),
    result["lineNum"].InnerText.ToString(),
    result["columnNum"].InnerText.ToString(),
    result["errorMsg"].InnerText.ToString(),
    TranslateError(result["errorMsg"].InnerText.ToString()),
    result["errorSourceCode"].InnerText.ToString());
}
```

Fig. 2. Part of the C# code that explains parsing the XML file and translating the error.

3.2 The Design and Structure of the Interface

Considering usability as an important part of the interface design, we developed a system that was easy to use with clear instructions, which allows the user to navigate through the system easily. The tool currently is available on the web, and it can be accessed and used easily. AATT is expected to provide Arabic web speakers the support with accessibility issues they may have on their websites. This tool also provides users with recommendations and examples to enhance the process of understanding accessibility issues and solving errors. The tool is available in two languages, Arabic and English. Web Content Accessibility Guideline (WCAG 2.0) level one is translated into Arabic, and the users will have the ability to check their websites for conformance with accessibility. Figure 3 shows the interface of the tool before checking a website.

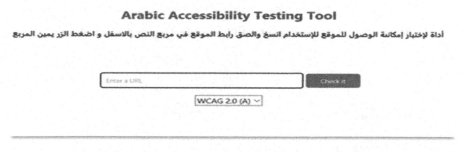

Fig. 3. The interface of AATT. The website link is www.aatt2019.com/

Figure 4 shows the status of the website and number of the known problems, likely problems, and warnings. When the user checks a website, the tool will show error messages in Arabic and English on the site along with column numbers, and source codes. This allows the user to see what is being checked and make the process of locating, understanding, and solving the problem much easier. When scrolling down on the interface, the user can see the first category of the errors, known problems. The list of known problems is the errors that the tool identified with certainty. For instance, if a picture on a webpage does not have alternative text, the AATT can easily determine the problem. Figure 5 shows the second and third type of accessibility errors which are labeled as "Likely Problems" and "Warnings." In this case, no errors are indicated as likely problems while many warnings were noted. Likely problems checked for are the errors that are considered as probable accessibility barriers. For instance, if the tool finds a hyperlink of one word, the tool considers the link text as a probable problem because the link text may not be meaningful. Therefore, a decision from the user is needed to determine whether the text is good enough. It can also identify potential problems that may affect system accessibility. For example, the tool can identify if there is a movie in a web page, but it cannot determine if the movie has closed captions, so human intervention is needed for the errors that are labeled as warnings.

Fig. 4. Part of the interface of AATT after checking an Arabic website

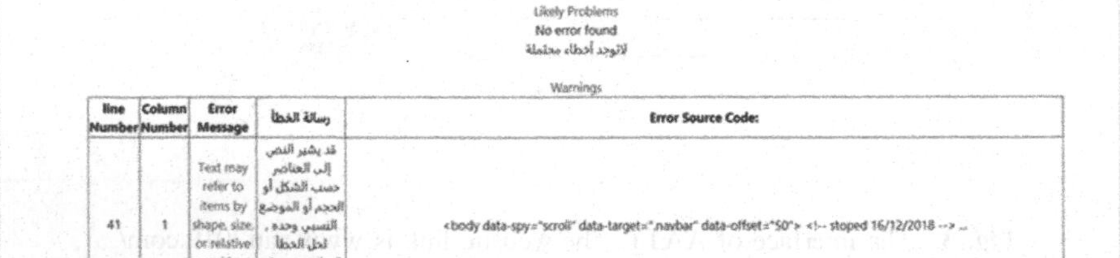

Fig. 5. Part of the interface that shows the second and third type of errors.

4 Usability Testing

The first version of the tool has been developed, and user tested by randomly selected subjects, who speak Arabic and English and live in the US. They were asked to complete a pre-testing questionnaire in order to learn about their background. They were asked to open the link of the AATT, choose any Arabic website they like, and copy and paste the URL of the chosen website in the text box of the tool interface. They were then asked to look at the interface and read through the accessibility errors generated by the tool. Upon completing the interactions with the AATT, a post-questionnaire was given to each subject in order to understand user acceptance, satisfaction, evaluation and needs. The pre- and post-testing questionnaires included a five Likert scale ranging between (strongly agree to strongly disagree), binary questions (yes/no), and open-ended questions. Instructions to the users included directions to fill out the questionnaires and instructions on how to use the tool. The following section highlights and details the usability testing.

4.1 Data Collection and Analysis

Data were collected from 34 undergraduate and graduate students between the ages of 21 and 35. There were 20 male participants and 14 female participants. Seven participants took usability testing at an American university. The rest of the participants took the test remotely through an application called WhatsApp. In the pre-testing questionnaire about 80% of the participants indicated that they would like to learn about web accessibility and about 60% of the participants have never used an accessibility tool checker before.

4.2 Post-test Questionnaire

Every participant was asked to fill out the questionnaire in order to understand their perspectives about the tool. The post-testing questionnaire consisted of the following statements:

1. The instructions given were clear.
2. The tool was easy to use.
3. It took a few minutes to understand how the tool work.
4. The Arabic instructions on the interface were easy to follow and understand.
5. The Arabic instructions helped to complete the tasks.
6. The Arabic accessibility issues were clear and understandable.
7. I think that Arabic accessibility issues were understandable even for people who do not have knowledge about the markup language.
8. I understood the difference between known problems, likely problems, and warnings on the interface of the accessibility tool.
9. I think the tool was useful.
10. I think the tool looks pleasant.
11. I'm satisfied with the interface.
12. I think having Arabic and English instructions on the interface is a good idea.

13. I think it is better to have an English interface of the tool and another Arabic interface of the tool.
14. I recommend the tool to people who are interested in web accessibility.

In the post-testing questionnaire, participants were also asked open-ended questions which were:

Q1: If you think that the Arabic instructions on the interface are not clear, please write some recommendations for improvement.
Q2: If you think that the Arabic Accessibility issues are not clear, please write some recommendations for improvement.
Q3: Do you think the tool will make a difference in Arabic web accessibility, as it is the first tool designed for Arabic speakers?

The results of the post-testing questionnaire revealed that most of the answers were positive, which means that the participants chose either "strongly agree" or "agree" (see Fig. 6). Most participants thought that the instructions of the interface were clear, and the tool was easy to use. Also, regarding the interface of the tool, most of the participants are satisfied with the tool. They also thought that the tool is useful for individuals who are interested in web accessibility. However, other responses indicated that a change must be made to meet the participants' perspectives of an accessibility checker. For example, less than half of the participants thought that the interface is unpleasant, and about 64% of the participants thought that having an interface in Arabic and another interface in English is better than including both Arabic and English instructions on the same interface. Also, most of the participants were not clear about the differences between "Known problems," "Likely Problems," and "Warnings." Not knowing the meaning of different types of errors raises the need to have clear explanations about each type of error in the tool interface. Moreover, about half of the participants did not understand markup languages errors and thought that markup language error generated in the error message section of the interface is only understandable by people who have knowledge about web accessibility. In addition, more than 50% of the participants took a few minutes to understand how to use the tool.

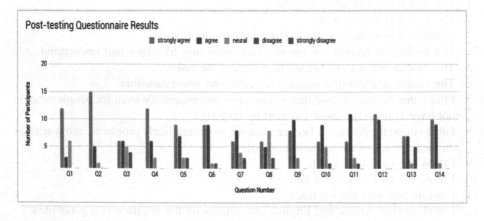

Fig. 6. The results of the first 14 questions in the post-testing questionnaire.

4.3   Discussion

The usability testing aimed to understand the efficacy of our AATT through asking Arabic-speaking participants. The results of the study showed that most of the participants liked the proposed tool. Improvements on the tool must be considered to meet the user's considerations of the final version of the tool. For example, in the open-ended questions, some participants thought that there is a need to explain some accessibility terms, so the purpose of the tool can be understood by people who do not know about accessibility. Other participants thought that the interface needs some improvements. Moreover, some participants thought that the Arabic translation of the accessibility issues need rephrasing and should not be literal. Instead, it should reflect the semantic meaning of the corresponding English accessibility issues. However, all the participants thought that the tool would make a difference in Arabic web accessibility.

5   Conclusion and Future Work

In this paper, we have developed a prototype Arabic accessibility tool, called (AATT), and tested it using Arabic and English speakers. Usability testing was conducted to understand how easy and understandable the tool is for Arabic-speaking users. Most of the usability results are positive. However, there is a need to make changes in the interface to improve the localization translation and explain the meaning of some web accessibility terms. Based on the findings of our usability testing results, the tool will be improved for future research and studies.

In future studies, the tool will be tested by Arabic developers at a University and a hospital in Saudi Arabia to evaluate the university website and solve the accessibility problems. They will be asked to fill out pre-test and post-test surveys to determine whether the tool can be of assistance to users in the field in understanding the accessibility issues and solving the problem. Additionally, some guidelines will be added to the tool such as Section 508.

References

Akram, M., Sulaiman, R.B.: A systematic literature review to determine the web accessibility issues in Saudi Arabian university and government websites for disable people. Methodology 8(6) (2017)

Alayed, A., Wald, M., Draffan, E.A.: A framework for the development of localised web accessibility guidelines for university websites in Saudi Arabia. In: Antona, M., Stephanidis, C. (eds.) UAHCI 2016. LNCS, vol. 9737, pp. 3–13. Springer, Cham (2016). https://doi.org/10.1007/978-3-319-40250-5_1

Al-Khalifa, H.: The accessibility of Saudi Arabia government web sites: an exploratory study. Univ. Access Inf. Soc. 11(2), 201–210 (2012a). https://doi.org/10.1007/s10209-010-0215-7

Al-Khalifa, H.S.: WCAG 2.0 semi-automatic accessibility evaluation system: design and implementation. Comput. Inf. Sci. 5(6), 73–87 (2012b)

Al-Nuaim, H., Alnahdi, N., Alomery, G., Alhebaishi, L., Alhebaishi, L., Khubrany, M., et al.: Design, Development and Assessment of Arabic Accessibility Website 1.0 (2005). Retrieved from https://www.kau.edu.sa/Show_Res.aspx?Site_ID=320&Lng=EN&RN=35856

Benavídez, C., Fuertes, J.L., Gutiérrez, E., Martínez, L.: Semi-automatic evaluation of web accessibility with HERA 2.0. In: Miesenberger, K., Klaus, J., Zagler, W.L., Karshmer, A.I. (eds.) ICCHP 2006. LNCS, vol. 4061, pp. 199–206. Springer, Heidelberg (2006). https://doi.org/10.1007/11788713_30

Gay, G., Li, C.Q.: AChecker: Open, interactive, customizable, web accessibility checking. In: Proceedings of the 2010 International Cross Disciplinary Conference on Web Accessibility (W4A), p. 23. ACM (2010)

Sloan, D.: The effectiveness of the web accessibility audit as a motivational and educational tool in inclusive web design. Doctoral dissertation, School of Computing (2006)

Shawar, B.A.: Evaluating web accessibility of educational websites. Int. J. Emerg. Technol. Learn. 10(4), 4–10 (2015). https://doi.org/10.3991/ijet.v10i4.4518

Masood Rana, M., Fakrudeen, M., Rana, U.: Evaluating web accessibility of university web sites in the Kingdom of Saudi Arabia. Int. J. Technol. Knowl. Soc. 7(3), 1 (2011)

Information Technology Based Usable Ballot Interface Design for Persons with Visual Impairment in Sri Lanka

Madhuka De Silva$^{(\boxtimes)}$, Thushani Weerasinghe, and Kapila Dias

University of Colombo School of Computing, Colombo, Sri Lanka
desilvamadhuka@gmail.com, {taw,gkad}@ucsc.cmb.ac.lk

Abstract. Elections in Sri Lanka are conducted based on a paper-based voting system. Voters with visual impairment requires assistance of another to vote and cannot have an independent vote. In this study, two ballot interfaces were designed and examined that are capable of providing an independent voting experience for voters with visual disabilities: Button Tactile Ballot with button controls, Touch Tactile Ballot based on a touch interface. The design features of the interfaces were based on multi-modality and universal design guidelines. A foam prototype was provided to a group of users and usability metrics were used to measure the results. Feedback received for the test prototype could be interpreted that voters with visual disabilities prefer to use this multi-modal voting solution that provided mean SUS Scores of 88.25 and 84.44 for Button Tactile Ballot and Touch Tactile Ballot respectively. Users preferred the Button Tactile Ballot more than Touch Tactile Ballot while some preferred both. However, in terms of efficiency Touch Tactile Ballot was slightly ahead that of Button Tactile Ballot. Effectiveness wise also Touch Tactile Ballot was slightly higher, which was measured by the number of completed ballots without errors.

Keywords: Electronic voting · Visual impairment · Usability ·
Ballot interfaces · Independent voting

1 Introduction

Around one million people with visual impairment in Sri Lanka have the right to vote, which is 5.1% out of the total population [1]. According to Elections (Special Provisions) Act [2] in Sri Lanka, voter with a disability is allowed to accompany another individual (an eligible individual adhering to the stated requirements by the act) who is capable of marking the vote on the ballot paper upon the preference of the voter with visual impairment [3]. Although paper-based voting systems provide advantages such as ease of understanding for the voter, those do not support individuals with visual impairments voting independently. However, various voting systems that support voters with visual impairment are utilized all over the world. A preliminary study was conducted on those systems and Table 1 shows a summary of the design features available in those existing voting systems relevant to accessibility, privacy and design methodologies [4].

© Springer Nature Switzerland AG 2019
M. Antona and C. Stephanidis (Eds.): HCII 2019, LNCS 11572, pp. 211–228, 2019.
https://doi.org/10.1007/978-3-030-23560-4_16

Table 1. Summary of review of existing voting systems

Category	Findings
Design features relevant to accessibility	Tactile features
	• Buttons
	• Rotation dials
	• Sleeves with punched holes
	Touch features
	• Single/double tap
	• Slide rule
	Multimodal features
	• Combining tactile, touch and/or voice input
Design features relevant to privacy	Security aspect
	• Cryptography-based solutions
	Interface aspect
	• Accessible interfaces
	• Screen off feature
Design methodologies	Design principles and guidelines
	• User centered design (UCD)
	• Universal design (UD)
	Evaluation models
	• Unified theory of acceptance and use of technology (UTAUT)
	• ISO usability standards
	• System Usability Scale (SUS)

In some contexts, voting systems utilize Braille buttons [5]. However, when considering Braille literacy in Sri Lanka context, only 41% of individuals who know Braille are able to use it [6]. Thus, it is important to have other modes of interactions blind voters. Thus, multi-modality concept has been adhered in voting, which is also following the 2nd universal design principle of Flexibility in Use [7]. One such example is 'Prime III' [8], which has accessible modes of buttons and voice-based voting. However, it has only 90% accuracy within a Signal to Noise Ratio (SNR) of 1.44 [9]. Another ballot design, which adheres to multimodal concept is 'Universal Ballot Design' interfaces that provide two ballots, 'Quick ballot' and 'EZ ballot' [10]. In EZ ballot design, interactions based on slide rule [11] are used with a touch interface. Evaluations report that this slide rule is less familiar to blind voters and is less of a natural interaction [12]. However, it also has design issues such as accidental touch on unintended spaces and spending excessive time touching inactive areas due to lack of guidance on the touch interface [12].

Many voting systems consider that ensuring privacy of the vote only as a security aspect. However, some electronic voting machines (e.g. AVC Edge, AutoMARK VAT) have the option of turning off the screen when a blind voter uses the system considering privacy in an interface aspect but voters have reported it less user friendly [5].

Initially, a pre-study was conducted through a design workshop [4]. During the workshop two ballots were designed. Also, the participants of the workshop evaluated the design. The design of the two ballots were aligned with Universal Design [7] guidelines. The remaining sections of the paper are organized as follows. Section 2 summarizes the design features and the findings of the design workshop held in the pre-study (see [4] for more details). Section 3 states the research goal, which drives the present study. Section 4 describes the ballot design and Sect. 5 explains how the research was conducted. Section 6 analyses the data and presents the results. Section 7 discusses the results and finally Sect. 8 concludes this paper.

2 Pre-study: Design Workshop

All the participants had some sort of experience in using mobile phones. However, their experience in using different types of mobile phones varied. The majority had the experience of using smartphones but there were persons who had only the experience of using a basic mobile phone with buttons or keypads. Thus, multimodality concept was adhered for the voting design, which is also accommodating the 2nd Universal Design principle of Flexibility in Use [6]. Since voice-based voting is claimed accurate only within certain environments with respect to sound distortions, voting interactions were directed towards using buttons and touch-based voting. Figure 1 shows the ballot interface designed and evaluated during the design workshop.

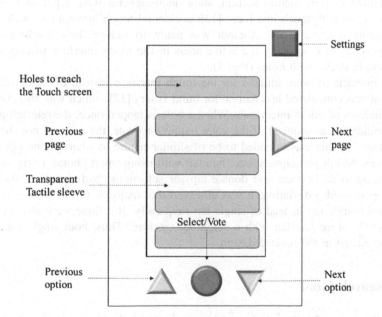

Fig. 1. Voting interface designed and evaluated in the design workshop

2.1 Button Interface

In the button interface, next option, previous option, next page, previous page, and settings buttons are used for navigation and select button (circular green) is used for selections as shown in Fig. 3. Next option button and previous option button are used to navigate the previous and next political party/candidate.

Few participants of the design workshop stated on the difficulties of differentiating colors of buttons, which led to refinement of colors. Also, this indicates that solely depending on color is also not sufficient. Thus, uniqueness of the buttons was also considered by using different shapes.

According to the prototype results, having several navigating buttons as 'next', 'next page', 'previous' and 'previous page' was confusing for many users, which was observed by the participant actions of trial and error to identify the buttons. Thus, instead of going through pages, the suggested approach is to consider a single page, which can be scrolled up and down using simple two buttons. This is more intuitive and natural as it is more similar to the paper-based voting, where only a single long ballot paper is provided for voting in the Sri Lankan context. The aim of placing the buttons in different locations was for easy identification. However, participants had difficulties and several responded it as a bad experience. Thus, the layout of buttons should be refined bringing the buttons to close proximity.

2.2 Touch Interface

As explained in Introduction section, some inefficiencies were reported in existing voting systems with touch interfaces [12]: accidental touch, unfamiliar touch interaction, tapping inactive areas. Attempt was made to reduce these inefficiencies by allowing voters to reach only the active areas in the touch interface placing a transparent tactile sleeve with holes (Fig. 1).

Tap interactions were utilized for the touch interface instead of 'Slide rule' [11] because it was considered less natural for blind voters [12], which was also confirmed by the findings of initial interviews. When a hole is tapped once, the relevant political party/candidate is announced. If the voter requires to vote, the relevant hole had to be double tapped. This was intended to be of similar nature to smart phone tap interactions. Even though participants were familiar with using smart phones using single tap for listening to description and double tap for selections, participants of the design workshop showed a deviation. It was observed that majority of the blind persons are performed double tap instead of single tap frequently. But there were also some participants who were familiar with a single tap gesture. Thus, both single and double were considered in the revised design.

3 Research Goal

During the pre-study, the interfaces were evaluated only for the voting step and no other steps such as language selection, adjusting settings, etc. Thus, a full comprehensive system was not developed.

The aim of this research is to improve the voting design, develop a system for the intended complete voter journey and conduct evaluation. The research goal aimed by this research is, "Designing usable ballot interfaces to provide an independent voting experience for Sri Lankans with visual impairment". These features should enable an accessible vote, which also supports to maintain the secrecy of the vote. The usability is defined and measured according to metrics of International Organization for Standardization (ISO 9241-11, 1998), which lists effectiveness, efficiency and user satisfaction as key factors of usability in a design.

4 Ballot Design

The voter journey begins when the voter wears the headphone (Fig. 2). Subsequently, audio instructions are initiated to play. Initially, the voter has to choose the preferred language. After the language selection, the voter is made aware of the 'settings' button with the available options that can be modified: language preference, audio volume, audio speed, and color contrast. The voting instructions are played next and the voter can wait to listen or skip the instructions. Next, voter is asked whether they are ready to vote. Subsequently, the voting list is displayed mentioning the number of political parties/candidates with the number of pages. The voter can select the preference by pressing the appropriate button or touching the relevant hole as explained in the subsequent sections.

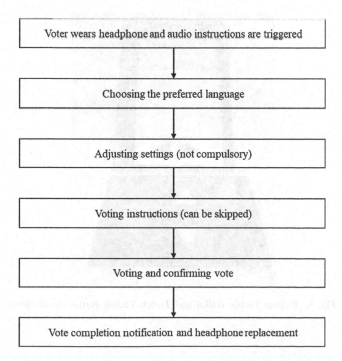

Fig. 2. User flow of the journey of a voter with visual impairment

Then the voter has to confirm the vote in order to complete the voting process. The system acknowledges the voter about the successful completion of the voting and requests the voter to replace the headphone. System replays the list automatically when the voter makes no selection.

In the journey of the voter with visual impairment (Fig. 1), it is required to identify the features that are required for navigation and how the voter interacts with the voting system (Table 2). Thus, voting interfaces with both buttons (Button Tactile Ballot) and touch (Touch Tactile Ballot) were designed as shown in Figs. 3 and 4 based on the results obtained from a preliminary user study and literature review conducted.

Table 2. Navigation and selection actions

Feature type	Actions
Navigation	Navigating through languages
	Navigating through settings
	Navigating through political parties/candidates
Selection	Selecting preferred language
	Adjusting settings
	Selecting the preferred political party/candidate
	Confirming vote

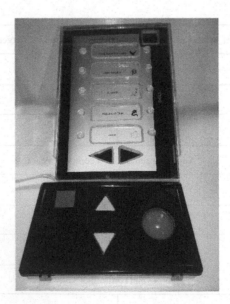

Fig. 3. Button Tactile Ballot and Touch Tactile Ballot (front view)

Fig. 4. Button Tactile Ballot and Touch Tactile Ballot (side view)

Voting systems designed based on touch interfaces have reported in many errors due to accidental touch [12]. The findings of the interviews with users also signified the difficulty of scanning the whole touch screen. Thus, a tactile sleeve (Touch Tactile Ballot) was designed to act as a guidance as shown in Fig. 5. It shows that a tactile transparent sleeve with holes is placed on top of the touch interface.

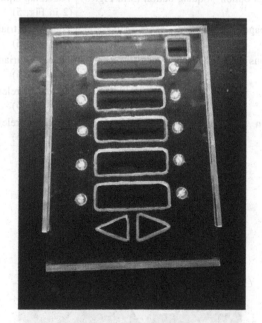

Fig. 5. Transparent sleeve in Touch Tactile Ballot

4.1 Button Tactile Ballot

In the Button Tactile (BT) Ballot (Table 3, Fig. 6), up, down and settings buttons are used for navigation and select (circular red) button is used for selections.

The political parties or the candidates are announced through audio recordings. After each political party/candidate, there is a pause (4 s) allowing the voters to cast their vote. If the voter prefers the particular political party/candidate, then the voter should press the circular red button (Fig. 6). Otherwise the voter can wait until the system announces the next political party/candidate or press the yellow triangular button on the right side (Fig. 6). After a voter presses the circular red button, voter is asked to confirm the vote by pressing the same button again. The list of political parties/candidates in this ballot, has been segmented to number of pages. Thus, navigating through pages is not required (see Table 3).

Table 3. Interactions for navigation and selections using BT Ballot and TT Ballot

	BT Ballot	TT Ballot
Navigating to next option	Down button (1 in Fig. 6)	Touch/tap relevant hole (1 in Fig. 5)
Navigating to previous option	Down button (2 in Fig. 6)	Touch/tap relevant hole (1 in Fig. 5)
Navigating to settings option	Square button (3 in Fig. 6)	Touch/tap square shaped hole (2 in Fig. 5)
Navigating to next page	Null	Touch/Tap triangular shaped hole (3 in Fig. 5)
Navigating to previous page	Null	Touch/tap triangular shaped hole (4 in Fig. 5)
Selecting an option	Round button (4 in Fig. 6)	Touch/tap relevant hole (1 in Fig. 5)
Confirming an option	Round button (4 in Fig. 6)	Touch/tap relevant hole again (1 in Fig. 5)

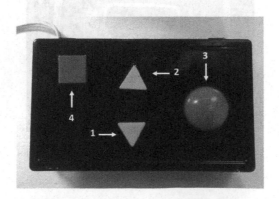

Fig. 6. Layout of Button Tactile Ballot

4.2   Touch Tactile Ballot

The political parties or the candidates are listed as shown in Fig. 7. When a hole is touched/tapped once, the relevant political party/candidate is announced. Then the voter is asked to confirm the vote by tapping again followed by audio instructions (Fig. 7). Here, the transparent sleeve with holes is used as a guidance to reduce the inconvenience of touching unintended areas and screen areas that has no response.

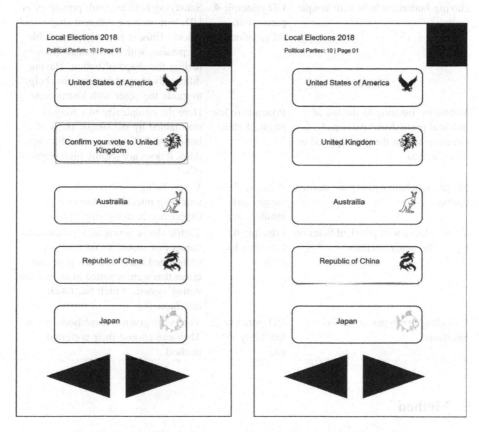

Fig. 7.   Screens illustrating voting list and vote confirmation prompt

4.3   Design Concept

Table 4 summarizes the design features of the ballot interfaces designed to support voters with visual impairment. It explains the justifications for these features and how the Universal Design guideline has been followed.

Table 4. Design and justifications

Design	Universal design (UD) principles	Justification
Providing two types of ballot interfaces	UD principle 2: flexibility in use	Voters are given two methods to vote. They can choose their preferred method
Having button controls with unique features	UD principle 4: perceptible information	Satisfying both two sub principles in UD, buttons have different shapes and colors. Thus, it is easily identifiable by persons with visual disabilities by feeling the shape of button. Having differently shaped buttons also helps to guide the voter with instructions
Voting by listening to the list of political parties/candidates and selecting within the given period of time interval	Principle 6: low physical effort	Here the complexity of voting is maintained by the simple press of a button while listening to audio clips. Also, it does not require high physical effort
Simply touching/tapping the desired option	Principle 3: simple and intuitive use	Voters being familiar with single touch/tap interaction due to their experience in using smart phones
Tactile sleeve with punched holes on top of the touch interface	Principle 6: tolerance for error	Tactile sleeve acting as a guidance for voters that would avoid touching unintended areas and less prone to errors that were reported in an existing voting system, which has touch interfaces [6]
Providing two types of ballot interfaces	UD principle 2: flexibility in use	Voters are given two methods to vote. They can choose their preferred method

5   Method

5.1   Participants

A total of 10 participants with visual disabilities were selected (7 men and 3 women, 20–71 years old, mean age 44.7 ± 5.9 years). Among them, 7 totally blind (5 men and 2 women, 20–71 years old, mean age 50.1 ± 7.2 years) and 3 were partially blind (2 men and 1 woman, 22–46 years old, mean age 32 ± 7.2 years).

Experience in using mobile phones or Automatic Teller Machines (ATM), is considered as a potential to use an electronic voting solution with ease implying that similar interfaces are incorporated [13]. Thus, participants were questioned of whether they have prior experience of using digital devices such as an ATM, computer, mobile phones and for how long they have experienced the usage.

5.2   Procedure

Participant consent was obtained for audio recording. Demographic information was collected from the participants by reading out a questionnaire and answers were noted down. Participants faced the training and performed the voting process in the relevant ballot interfaces and they were randomly assigned for the two ballot interfaces. After using each interface, participants were asked to rate their voting experience by agreeing or disagreeing to the 10 statements provided system usability scale (SUS). After both trials were completed, participants were asked to choose their preferred ballot and feedback was noted. Interactions with the interfaces were video recorded and the feedback was audio recorded. Time spent on conducting all trials with training varied (25–45 min). Evaluation was carried out in three steps: conducting pre-trial interviews, participants performing the tasks and conducting post-trial interviews.

5.3   Tasks

Participants were given an introductory training for both ballot interfaces (BT Ballot and TT Ballot). Participants were randomly assigned to use one of the ballots first and the other second.

Training. The training program of Button Tactile (BT) Ballot described the button placements and its functions. The training for Touch Tactile (TT) Ballot described the positions of the holes and its functions.

Trials. Before using any ballot interface, participants were instructed to listen to voting instructions. If linear navigation was considered instead of page wise navigation, participants were instructed to vote for the 7th political party. Each page displays only five candidates. If page wise navigation is considered, participants were instructed to vote for the 3rd political party in the 2nd page. Here, ballot interfaces used names of countries instead of names of actual political parties.

5.4   Data Collection and Metrics for Analysis

Usability of both Button Tactile (BT) Ballot and Touch Tactile (TT) Ballot were measured using metrics recommended by International Organization for Standardization (ISO 9241-11,1998) and previously conducted studies in a similar research [14] (see chapter 2). Thus, effectiveness, efficiency and user satisfaction were measured. Usability issues observed were noted separately.

Effectiveness. Participant voting choices were captured using logs.

Efficiency. Time stamps were logged when the language selection page was loaded, when the voting list was loaded and when the participant arrives the vote completion page. Ballot completion duration was considered the time between the loading of voting list and loading of vote completion page since initial language selection and instructions were common for all. The durations were marked in seconds.

Satisfaction. The System Usability Scale was adopted and score was calculated by considering the values from 0 to 4. Calculation procedure was followed as explained in literature [15] (see Sect. 3.5.3). For items 1, 3, 5, 7 and 9 the score contribution is the scale position minus 1. For items 2,4,6,8 and 10, the contribution is 5 minus the scale position. Then the sum was multiplied by 2.5 to obtain the overall value which have a range of 0 to 100 [15].

6 Results

Most of the participants (n = 8) completed all the tasks including training and trials of using the ballot interfaces. Two participants (n = 2) were not able to complete the voting task using Button Tactile (BT) Ballot because they did not confirm the vote. One participant (n = 1) avoided and did not want to test Touch Tactile (TT) Ballot due to personal preferences. Thus, the total number of completed ballots was 17 (TB Ballot interface × 1 trial × 8 participants plus TT Ballot interface × 1 trial × 9 participants).

Eight participants have used touch based smart phones (average of nearly 2 years of experience). Remaining participants have used phones with keypads (average of nearly 3 years of experience). All participants had an experience of using screen reader assisted computers. Some participants had an experience of using an Automated Teller Machine (5 participants).

6.1 Effectiveness

Out of the 17 completed ballots, 10 ballots (58.82%) were completed without error: 50% (n = 4 ballots) with BT Ballot and 66% (n = 6 ballots) with TT Ballot (see Table 5).

Table 5. Ballot completion with and without errors

Ballot	Category of impairment	No error	With error	Total
Button Tactile Ballot	Total blind	3	3	6
	Partial blind	1	1	2
	All	4	4	8
Touch Tactile Ballot	Total blind	4	2	6
	Partial blind	2	1	3
	All	6	3	9

Out of the total number of completed ballots (n = 17 ballots), 7 ballots (41.17%) were completed with an error of not marking the intended political party: Overall, 50% (n = 4) of the ballots with BT Ballot contained the stated error. The number of ballots containing this error also varied by group: the total blind group (38%, n = 3) had the highest number of ballots containing the stated voting error, followed by the partially blind (13%, n = 1). Overall, 33% (n = 3) of ballots with TT Ballot contained the stated error. The number of ballots containing this error also varied by group: the total blind (22%, n = 2) had the highest number of ballots containing at least one voting error, followed by partially blind (11%, n = 1).

6.2   Efficiency

It was identified that ballot completion was faster with Touch Tactile Ballot (M = 92.55 s, SD = 24.40) than with Button Tactile Ballot (M = 105.5 s, SD = 49.63). The ballot completion time varied also by the disability of the participants (see Fig. 8). For the total blind participants, ballot completion time was lesser in Touch Tactile Ballot (M = 89.33 s, SD = 28.57) than with Button Tactile Ballot (M = 107.16 s, SD = 58.61). For the partial blind participants, ballot completion time was lesser in Touch Tactile Ballot (M = 99 s, SD = 15.71) than with Button Tactile Ballot (M = 100.5 s, SD = 2.12).

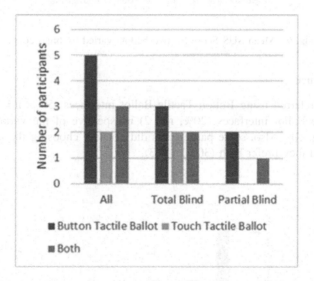

Fig. 8. Mean ballot completion time varied by ballot type and blind context

6.3   Usability with Satisfaction

The mean SUS score of both ballots (Button Tactile Ballot: M = 88.25 and SD = 7.91, Touch Tactile Ballot: M = 84.44 and SD = 6.09) was above the average score (68) [16]. Figure 9 presents how the mean of the SUS score varies for each ballot by the blind disability.

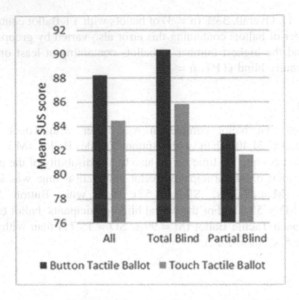

Fig. 9. Mean SUS Score for two ballots varied by blind context

6.4   Preference

Participants preferred using Button Tactile Ballot interfaces (50%, n = 5) than using Touch Tactile Ballot interfaces (20%, n = 2) irrespective of the variation in visual disability (Fig. 10). Also, some participants did not like choosing the most preferred and stated that they prefer both (30%, n = 3).

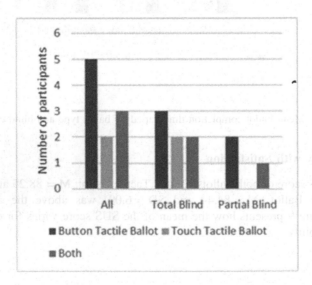

Fig. 10. Preference of the ballot interface type varied by blind context

A majority of total blind participants (30%, n = 3) preferred the Button Tactile Ballot to Touch Tactile Ballot (20%, n = 2). The reasons why they preferred the Button Tactile Ballot to Touch Tactile Ballot included the following: easier to use compared to touch (n = 2), identifying the buttons was easier (n = 2), only few buttons were there to learn (n = 2), pressing of the buttons felt more in touch sensory (n = 1).

The reasons why they preferred Touch Tactile Ballot to Button Tactile included the following: they were familiar with using touch phones so it was easier than using buttons (n = 2), it was quicker (n = 1), no accidental touch when compared to usual touch phones that need whole screen scanning to identify locations (n = 1).

The reasons provided by the participants who preferred both ballots (n = 3) included: both are equally easy (n = 2), 'it was easy to use Touch Tactile, even if the touch concept is given in a different way here' (n = 1), 'buttons were easy to handle but using touch tactile allowed to vote in a different contrast color setting, so I like both' (n = 1).

6.5 Usability Issues

It was observed that, 40% of the participants (n = 4) started touching the holes from the bottom instead of top using Touch Tactile Ballot. Some stated that this issue could have been avoided if audio instructions stated that the hole numbers start from top (n = 2), one suggested that design can be modified to begin hole number from the top and another stated 'this won't be an issue if we are given more time to be familiar with the device physically'. Another issue noted was that two participants accidently used double tap which led to skipping options ahead. Some participants (n = 4) stated that since they are familiar with touch phones, they tend to double tap to do a selection although this design is catered to avoid double tap. One participant stated that the gap is not enough between the holes located in the middle which listed the political parties. Another participant stated that holes sizes are too large and that can lead to accidental touch of holes. Using Button Tactile Ballot, 50% of participants (n = 5) faced a technical issue of hearing response alerts and instructions (dual sound clips playing) together in some situations which was disturbing to them.

In both ballots, two participants reported that language selection and vote ready pages also require response feedback when a selection is made and it should not be limited to the voting list page. Some participants mentioned that waiting period (4 s) was too long (n = 3). However, using Button Tactile Ballot interface, two participants voted mistakenly to the following political party (political party listed after 'Norway') because the waiting period was not enough. One person stated that instead of having separate training interface, it is better to combine training and voting instructions for both ballots.

7 Discussion

The research was aimed at designing usable ballot interfaces having aligned with Principles of Universal Design [7] supporting voters with visual abilities (total blind and partial blind). Results of the study indicate that participants did not perform equally on the two ballots when considering usability metrics of effectiveness, efficiency, and satisfaction.

Effectiveness is achieved when the voters are able to cast their vote for the intended political party/candidate. Only 85% ballots were completed with or without errors because the remaining did not confirm the vote as instructed. However, a majority of 58.82% were able to complete it without error. Participants marked the ballot incorrectly in Button Tactile Ballot slightly than in Touch Tactile Ballot irrespective of the blind category they belonged to. It was observed that few of them were late to press the button when the political party was announced. Errors were reported using Touch Tactile Ballot were mainly due to participants' double tapping rather than single tap because of their prior experience in using smart phones. This can be addressed by adjusting the touch with de-bounce feature [12].

When considering the efficiency measure, participants were slightly faster using Touch Tactile Ballot than using Button Tactile Ballot. This can be due to Touch Tactile Ballot displays candidates all at once and participants can go through it. However, the difference is not high because participants made well use of the 'up' and 'down' buttons of Button Tactile Ballot to go through the voting list quickly.

Although effectiveness was not significant, satisfaction in terms of the SUS score showed beyond average and excellent results (BT = 84.44 and TT = 88.25) according to the grading scales [16]. According to Nielsen Norman Group, 'Users generally prefer designs that are fast and easy to use, but satisfaction isn't 100% correlated with objective usability metrics' [17]. Thus, it is clearly evident that effectiveness and satisfaction can show no correlation as the results gained from the test prototype.

In existing voting systems with touch interfaces [12] the major inefficiencies reported were accidental touch and tapping inactive areas. These inefficiencies can be reduced by allowing voters to reach only the active areas as in Touch Tactile Ballot. Prototype results show that, users are capable and preferred to use the tactile sleeve (Touch Tactile Ballot preference only = 20%, both ballot preference = 30%), which is also evident by the SUS Score gained (84.44). However, it was observed that some participants used trial and error in tracking the holes. Thus, improvements have to be made by including a feature as a guidance to track the holes, so that they do not require to remember the holes or guess. Majority of the participants preferred the Button Ballot Interfaces (Button Tactile Ballot preference only = 50%, both ballot preference = 30%) due to its minimalist design of few unique buttons made with known shapes. It was stated by one the participants that, irrespective of any prior knowledge on touch or other technologies, they can easily use this.

8 Conclusion

Persons with visual disabilities are more accustomed to use mobile phones because inbuilt accessibility features exist. All the participants also had some sort of experience in using mobile phones compared to other IT related devices. However, their experience in using different types of mobile phones varied. Majority (80%) had an experience of using smart phones but there were persons who had only the experience of using a basic mobile phone with buttons or keypads. Also, there can be blind voters without any mobile device experience. Thus, in order to interact with the voting system, voters should be provided with several options such that they will choose the more familiar way, which is bringing in multi-modality concept for voting. Such concept is also aligned to facilitate the universal design principle. Few systems were already designed based on this concept whereas certain challenges remained to be addressed. Aim of this research was to design ballot interfaces that fit into the Sri Lankan context. Results obtained from the test prototype were promising and provided a greater SUS score. However, few usability issues were identified that requires certain modifications to improve the voting experience: Adjusting touch sensitivity to accommodate double tap errors, improving audio instructions, changing how the training is provided. After modifications are made, the ballots have to be tested again by voters with visual disabilities and without visual disabilities both.

References

1. Department of Census and Statistics—Government of Sri Lanka. Census of Population and Housing (2012)
2. Sri Lanka—Elections (Special Provisions) Act, No. 28 of 2011. Sri Lanka (2011)
3. Blind can cast their vote. Sunday Leader (2013). http://www.thesundayleader.lk/2013/08/25/blind-can-cast-their-vote/. Accessed 19 Mar 2018
4. DeSilva, M., Weerasinghe, T., Dias, K.: Designing an IT based voting solution for persons with visual impairment. In: Advanced Computer Human Interactions. IARIA (2019)
5. Burton, D., Uslan, M.: Cast a vote by yourself. Afb.org. (2002)
6. Weerakkody, D.: DAISY implementation in Sri Lanka. Dinf.ne.jp. http://www.dinf.ne.jp/doc/english/resource/srilanka.html. Accessed 10 Jan 2019
7. Connell, B.R., Jones, M., Mace, R., Mueller, J., Mullick, A., Ostroff, E., et al.: The principles of universal design (1997). https://projects.ncsu.edu/design/cud/about_ud/udprinciplestext.htm. Accessed 10 Jan 2019
8. Gilbert, J.E., McMillian, Y., Rouse, K., Williams, P., Rogers, G., McClendon, J., et al.: Universal access in e-voting for the blind. Univ. Access Inf. Soc. **9**(4), 357–365 (2010)
9. Jackson, F., Solomon, A., McMullen, K., Gilbert, J.E.: To start voting, say vote: establishing a threshold for ambient noise for a speech recognition voting system. Procedia Manuf. **3** (AHFE), 5512–5518 (2015)
10. Lee, S., Xiong, X., Yilin, L.E., Sanford, J.: EZ ballot with multimodal inputs and outputs. In: Proceedings of the 14th international ACM SIGACCESS Conference on Computers and Accessibility—ASSETS 2012, vol. 215 (2012)
11. Kane, S.K., Bigham, J.P., Wobbrock, J.O.: Slide rule: making mobile touch screens accessible to blind people using multi-touch interaction techniques. In: Proceedings of the 10th International ACM SIGACCESS Conference on Computers and Accessibility (Assets 2008), pp. 73–80 (2008)
12. Lee, S.: Designing ballot interfaces for voters with vision disabilities. In: CHI 2014 Extended Abstracts on Human Factors in Computing Systems – CHI EA 2014, pp. 933–938 (2014)
13. Tokaji, D.P.: The paperless chase: electronic voting and democratic values. SSRN Electron. J. **73**(4), 1771–1785 (2004). https://doi.org/10.2139/ssrn.594444

14. Lee, S.T., Liu, Y.E., Ruzic, L., Sanford, J.: Universal design ballot interfaces on voting performance and satisfaction of voters with and without vision loss. In: Proceedings of the 2016 CHI Conference on Human Factors in Computing Systems—CHI 2016, pp. 4861–4871 (2016)
15. Brooke, J.: SUS—a quick and dirty usability scale. In: Usability Evaluation in Industry, vol. 189, no. 194, pp. 4–7 (1996). http://hell.meiert.org/core/pdf/sus.pdf
16. Sauro, J.: Measuring usability with system usability scale (2011). https://measuringu.com/sus/. Accessed 6 Dec 2018
17. Nielsen, J.: User satisfaction vs. performance metrics (2012). https://www.nngroup.com/articles/satisfaction-vs-performance-metrics/

User Test Logger: An Open Source Browser Plugin for Logging and Reporting Local User Studies

Vagner Figueredo de Santana[(⊠)] [iD] and Felipe Eduardo Ferreira Silva

IBM Research, São Paulo, SP 04007-900, Brazil
vagsant@br.ibm.com, felipe.ferreiral@ibm.com

Abstract. Tooling user studies tasks is fundamental to reduce the burden of evaluators, practitioners, facilitators, and observers during user interface (UI) evaluations. However, available tools for collecting data beyond clicks are usually paid, count on limited vocabulary of UI events, have complex setup, or do not provide easy download of captured data. In this context, we present a general-purpose data logger for local user studies able to capture up to 40 different types of UI events. It provides detailed data logging, downloading, and reporting features. The evaluation of the tool was performed in a focus group with 4 Human-Computer Interaction (HCI) specialists. The focus group resulted in new features and changes/corrections in existing features. The redesigned tool is open source and freely available to the HCI community. The tool can be used by HCI specialists or data scientists as a core tool for empirical evaluations or an additional data source in mixed methods assessments, offering greater control on types of events captured and counting on multiple types of report.

Keywords: Data logger · Interaction log analysis · User study · User test · Usability · Accessibility · Evaluation

1 Introduction

The study of log files dates back to the first Operating Systems, supporting debugging and auditing processes. Nowadays, interaction logs are used in multiple systems, since interaction patterns represent part of human behavior while interacting with computing systems. Such systems are present in multiple contexts, for instance, e-commerce, education, e-government, business intelligence, analytics, among others. In the context of Human-Computer Interaction (HCI), the possibility of logging detailed interaction data paved the path for multiple approaches based on task grammars/models, e.g., GOMS (Goals, Operators, Methods, and Selection Rules) [11] and Concur Task Trees (CTT) [15], and data-oriented approaches, e.g., as Web Event-logging Tool (WET) [8], MouseTrack [2], and Web Event Logger and Flow Identification Tool (WELFIT) [19], just to name a few.

In this work we present User Test Logger, a general-purpose web browser logging and reporting tool that can be used in a variety of HCI studies. It can be configured to

© Springer Nature Switzerland AG 2019
M. Antona and C. Stephanidis (Eds.): HCII 2019, LNCS 11572, pp. 229–243, 2019.
https://doi.org/10.1007/978-3-030-23560-4_17

record any type of JavaScript or jQuery [19] event and also provides reporting and downloading features to connect with statistical and graph analysis tools.

This work is structured as follows: the next section presents related tools; Sect. 3 presents a description of tool's features; Sect. 4 details the focus group performed to evaluate the tool; Sect. 5 describes the redesign of the tool based on focus group results; Sect. 6 discusses outcomes and possibilities of using the proposed tool.

2 Related Works

The task of comparing tools requires a common ground for attributes, techniques, and data sources considered. In this realm, Santana and Baranauskas proposed a taxonomy for website evaluation tools considering 4 main dimensions [18]:

1. **Participant-evaluator interaction** – refers to the interaction between evaluators and participants during an evaluation. It can be divided into:
   a. *Localization*: Remote or non-remote;
   b. *Time*: Synchronous or asynchronous;
   c. *Use*: Formal or informal;
2. **Effort** – refers to the effort required from the evaluator and from the participant to setup an evaluation scenario. It can be divided into:
   a. *Evaluator (HCI practitioner, facilitator)*: Model/grammar maintenance, environment configuration/setup, or no action;
   b. *Participant*: Actions at the beginning, during the test, or no action;
3. **Automation type** – refers to the automation characteristics of the tool. It can be divided into:
   a. *Capture*: User expressions, physiological signals, ambience, browser events, or customized events;
   b. *Analysis*: Visual reports or statistical reports;
   c. *Critique*: content, structure, or layout;
   d. *Adjustment*. Content, structure, or layout;
4. **Data source** – refers to the data source considered in the evaluation. It can be divided into:
   a. *User Interface*: Structure or content;
   b. *User data*: Interaction data or questionnaire data;

This taxonomy highlights 4 dimensions ranging from data source to automation provided by the tool. Table 1 compares tools based on the presented taxonomy. It is possible to verify that that tools that focus on formal studies are related to local user tests. In addition, critique is offered by few tools. And the types of events captured are usually restricted and evaluators cannot choose which events to capture. When considering studies involving accessibility, most tools are restricted to mouse interaction. From the Universal Design (UD) perspective, the vocabulary of events captured by the tools should cope with the whole diversity of users' interaction strategies and users' devices.

Table 1. Tools for logging and reporting user interaction at the Web.

Tool	Participant–evaluator interaction	Effort	Automation type	Data source
Click heat[a]	Remote, asynchronous, informal	Tool setup	Capture (click), analysis (Heatmap)	Interaction data
Click tale[b]	Remote, asynchronous, informal	Tool setup	Capture (click, mousemove), Analysis (heatmap, mouse path)	Interaction data
Crazy egg[c]	Remote, asynchronous, informal	Tool setup	Capture (click, mousemove), Analysis (heatmap, playback)	Interaction data
Heatmap.com[d]	Remote, (A)synchronous, informal	Tool setup	Capture (click), Analysis (Heatmap)	Interaction data
Morae[e]	Local, synchronous, formal	Tool setup and run the study	Capture (audio, click, keypress, mousemove, screen recording), Analysis (playback)	Interaction data
Mimic [3]	Remote, asynchronous, formal	Tool setup	Capture (blur, click, dblclick, focusin, focusout, keypress, mousemove, resize, keypress, scroll), Analysis (heatmap, timeline, playback)	Interaction data
User test logger[f]	Local, synchronous, (In)formal	Tool setup and run the study	Capture (40 events vocabulary), Analysis (usage graph, heatmap, and mouse path). Critique (accessibility/usability issues)	Interaction data

[a]www.dugwood.com/clickheat/
[b]www.clicktale.com
[c]www.crazyegg.com
[d]www.heatmap.com
[e]www.techsmith.com/morae.html
[f]https://github.com/IBM/user-test-logger/

UD can be defined as the design of products and environments that are usable by everyone, in the widest possible extension, without the need for adaptation or specialized design [6]. In this direction, User Test Logger allows evaluators to select types of events to be captured during the session, beyond mouse interaction.

When considering privacy, laws as General Data Protection Regulation (GDPR) [10] and *Lei Sobre Proteção de Dados Pessoais* [14] highlight the right of privacy, capturing only the needed data, previously stating goals and ways of using the captured data. In this direction, User Test Logger focuses on local studies so that logged data is not transmitted to an external server and participants are properly informed by practitioners/facilitators about types of data being captured in such a way that even users can easily see what was captured if it is the case.

Finally, existing tools lack easy setup and easy access to raw interaction data, key features for Data Scientists aiming at performing further analysis in external software/libraries as R, Python, or SPSS. The proposed tool aims at addressing existing gaps in the connection between HCI and Data Science, supporting field studies, applying interaction log analysis in usability tests, A/B tests, accessibility evaluations, or any type of *in situ* user studies.

3   Proposed Tool

The proposed tool was developed as an add-on for Firefox web browser and is available at Github.com.[1] The rationale of offering it as a browser add-on was to make it a tool easy to setup and use, allowing HCI practitioners to install, configure, and run the tool via web browser UI. The main pillars guiding its development are:

- Inclusive view of data captured;
- Value privacy;
- Prevent disturbing participants during the session;
- Provide easy access to captured data;
- Inclusive way of reporting captured data.

According to the taxonomy for user evaluation tools presented in [18], the User Test Logger is a tool for *capture, analysis and critique for (in)formal local user studies*. This means that the tool counts on features for capturing, analyzing, and pointing out issues related to local user studies considering predefined tasks (i.e., formal) or exploratory studies (i.e., informal). The next subsections present an overview of the initial version of the tool, including its architecture, setup example, capture, and analysis.

3.1   Architecture

The tool was developed inspired by the classic Model-View-Controller (MVC) architectural design pattern [5] applied to the Firefox web extension structure [1].

---

[1] https://github.com/IBM/user-test-logger/.

It considers the Model as being the *background* component, View as *popup* component, and Controller as the *content scripts* (Fig. 1).

- **Model** component (background) is responsible for establishing the communication with the content scripts and storing the data.
- **View** (popup) component is responsible for providing controls, feedback, and reporting features for the user.
- **Controller** (content script) is responsible for capturing and formatting UI events.

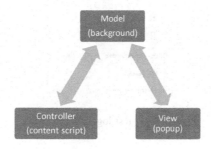

Fig. 1. User test logger architecture overview.

The User Test Logger works as follows: As soon as the plugin is loaded, the background component is loaded in the browser. Once the browser is running, every time the user opens a new web page, a content script is loaded specifically for logging that page, and a connection is established with the background component. All the events logged will be sent by the content scripts to the background, where all logged data is stored. The popup can be displayed by clicking on the "L" button (Fig. 2). This component exposes features to the user and sends the triggered actions to the background. Then, if the settings are changed, the background updates the content scripts.

Regarding components and libraries, the add-on uses jQuery [12] to cope with compatibility issues and to ease the manipulation of events. In order to save the log file on the client-side, the FileSaver [9] is used. Finally, User Test Logger uses D3 [4] drawing library for creating all visualizations.

3.2 Setup

One of the goals of the proposed tool is to ease the setup process of data logging. The easiest way of trying the tool is by loading it as a "Temporary Add-on". The add-on zip file is available at the plugin's github.com page.[2] Once the zip file is downloaded and decompressed at the users' device, the setup can be done by typing *about:debugging* in the Firefox address bar, clicking the button "Load temporary add-on", and selecting the *manifest.json* file downloaded.

---

[2] https://github.com/IBM/user-test-logger/archive/master.zip.

Figure 2 shows the first version of the tool menu, under the "L" button. In this menu, the item "record" starts the data logging, the menu item "report" contains the visualizations and reports for the logged data, the item "dump raw data" allows the evaluator to download logged data and clear the browser's memory, and under the item "events" it is possible to define which events are going to be logged, also called events of interest (Fig. 3).

Fig. 2. User test logger main menu.

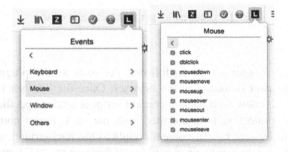

Fig. 3. Selection of events of interest prior to logging.

3.3 Data Capture

The tool supports capturing all standard JavaScript events, jQuery events, touch events, geolocation events, and device orientation events (Fig. 3). The whole set of events captured by the tool (i.e., event vocabulary) includes 40 events. Once the configuration of events of interest is done, the HCI practitioner can click on record to start the capture. After the user test session, the practitioner can pause data capture and explore reporting features or dump the interaction log for analyzing it in an external software. In addition, the tool supports analysis of interaction occurred with UI elements without id attribute and coming from multiple browser tabs. To do so it uses DOM (Document Object Model) tree path for identifying uniquely all UI target elements.

The tool can be used to capture logs from sessions separately or to log a set of participants' sessions, depending only on the evaluation experiment design. Finally, given that the tool supports logging highly detailed data, the tool favors participants' privacy over transmitting logged data to an external server or software component.

3.4   Analysis

The first version of the tool counted on three types of report, namely: usage graph (Fig. 4), mouse fixations heatmap (Fig. 5(a)), and mouse plot (Fig. 5(b)).

Usage Graph. The usage graph is a directed graph used to represent user interaction, event by event, based on the algorithm detailed in [19]. It can be seen as the combination of walks (non-empty alternating sequence of nodes and edges) representing what, where, and when users performed actions. In the usage graph, a node is identified by its label, which is the concatenation of the event name and an identifier of the UI element where the event occurred, e.g., *"mouseover@logo"*, *"click@logo"*, *"focus@/html/document/body"*. Moreover, each node counts on information regarding the total of sessions they occurred, mean distance from the root node (session start), mean timestamp, among others. In addition, all these information supports identifying patterns and usability problems/accessibility barriers candidates.

These candidates are identified via a heuristic that aims at pointing out cyclic actions and deviations, comparing nodes in the usage graph, comparing paths that are far from the starting of the session due to attempts or deviations from the task at hand. For more details, please refer to [19].

The rationale of choosing the usage graph is that it is not restricted to mouse events and allows the identification of repeated sequences of events in one or more sessions. Figure 4 exemplifies how nodes (representing events in UI elements) are distributed and how nodes that are part of cyclic actions are highlighted.

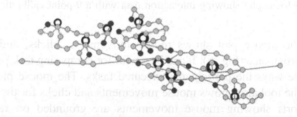

Fig. 4. Usage graph sample report.

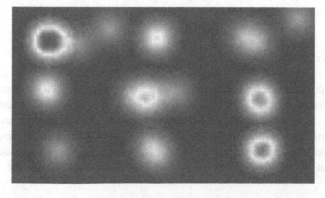

Fig. 5. Heatmap showing interaction data with a 9-points calibration page.

Heatmap. The heatmap provided by the User Test Logger is generated by detecting mouse fixations, as an analogy to eye fixations, by using the dispersion algorithm presented in [17]. In sum, it considers a mouse fixation when mouse movements are close to another and for longer durations in comparison with other mouse movements (i.e., mouse saccades).

In this version the heatmaps count on solid background instead of an overlayer. The rationale for it resides on the fact that reports aim at tracking multiple pages and multiple browser tabs. Hence, the heatmap of the first version of the tool shows mouse fixations for the whole session, which may involve multiple screens and tabs, as a way of summarizing the whole session.

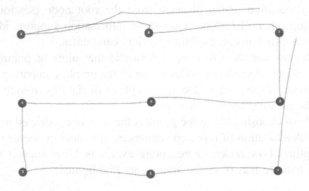

Fig. 6. Mouse plot showing interaction data with a 9-point calibration page.

Mouse Plot. The mouse plot shows mouse movements, clicks, and double clicks performed by participants (Fig. 6). It can be useful for comparing task performance and showing multiple ways the participants executed tasks. The mouse plot report of the first version of the tool also shows mouse movements and clicks for the whole session.

Finally, reports showing mouse movements are grounded on results from [7] showing the high correlation between eye and mouse movements in web browsing tasks. Besides logging and reporting features, the tool provides multiple download formats (e.g., DOT, PNG, and CSV) allowing HCI practitioners and Data Scientists to use the logged data in different analysis tools.

4   Focus Group

A focus group is defined by Krueger [13] as a *"carefully planned discussion designed to obtain perceptions in a defined area of interest in a permissive, non-threatening environment"*. According to Rubin [16], focus group is a valuable technique at early stages of a project to evaluate concepts and get feedback, judgment, feelings, exploring how representative users think and feel towards a product or service. In addition, Rubin discusses that these concepts can be presented in low-fidelity or high-fidelity prototypes. In our case, the first version of the tool was used in the presentation to our representative users.

The goal of the focus group performed in this research was to show the first version of the logger to potential users, HCI specialists with experience on performing user tests, and gather feedback on existing and desired features. The invited specialists act as researchers and possess MSc or PhD titles as highest education degree. The 6 invited participants have background on Design or Computer Science, all of them acting in the realm of HCI. The invitation was performed by email; 5 of them accepted; 4 showed up in the scheduled meeting, performed via video conference. In summary, participants characteristics are:

- **Sex**: 2 men and 2 women;
- **Background**: 2 in Design and 2 in Computer Science;
- **Highest education degree**: 2 MSc title and 2 PhD.

The materials used in the focus group involved the first version of the tool, recording the whole session in video and audio, and the video conference software used for screen sharing. The recording was performed only after specialists agreed in having the meeting recorded.

The focus group took approximately 1 h 30 min. In the first 30 min the facilitator walked through the tool's features then a round of discussion took place. An observer also participated taking notes about specialists' feedback. The round of discussions was driven by the following open-ended questions made to each of the specialists:

1. What do you think about available features?
2. What do you think that is missing?
3. What do you think that must be improved?

4.1 Results

The analysis on the collected was performed according to impact/outcome reported by each of the specialists about available/missing features. For instance, in different occasions specialists exemplified situations based on previous experiences on performing user tests. According to this rationale, the following lists summarize the results obtained in terms of available/missing features and on suggestions on how to improve existing features:

Available Features

- Heatmap and mouse plot should be done for each page, showing all the visualization as an over layer of the actual web page;
- Change the current format for raw data from JSON to CSV, easing the process of analyzing the logs in external software, given that much of existing software have capabilities for importing CSV, not all of them allow importing JSON format;
- Provide multiple ways of downloading/visualizing the available reports;

– Display the number of logged events, showing that the tool is properly capturing and providing feedback to users about the status of the tool;
– Show hints about the impact when capturing certain types of events;
  • This suggestion was made by one of the participants that tried the tool during the focus group. He mentioned that tested it in a current project having a UI with lots of asynchronous components, which results in *DOMInsertedNode* events. Hence, he mentioned that some decisions on what data to record could be informed so that only relevant data would be recorded.
– All the reports should be done for each user separately.

Missing Features

– Upload a setup file for the study, containing the types of event to capture and any additional configuration;
– Upload data captured back to the tool to analyze already downloaded data;
– Display, highlight, or differentiate in any way what are the tabs being logged;
– Provide an easier way to analyze the common patterns performed by the users;
  • Although the usage graph has all the information about the user interaction, they suggested that a simpler and faster way to analyze the common patterns and issues might of interest of specialists performing data analysis.

5   Redesign of the Tool

The redesign resulted in a new version of the tool, combining improvements on available features and implementation of some of the missing features, detailed next. Figure 7 shows the new main menu, now displaying the number of logged events, providing guidance and feedback to the user about the current status of the tool.

Fig. 7. User test logger main menu after redesign.

Fig. 8. User test logger reports menu after redesign.

The raw data format was changed from JSON to CSV as one of the designers suggested, in order to facilitate the specialists' task of importing it in external software in cleaning and analysis stages. Moreover, more control was provided to the specialists, allowing them to see or download individual reports (Fig. 8).

In the report section, improvements were made in the heatmap and mouse plot, considering the suggestion for separating the visualization for each page. After the changes, the visualizations are computed and displayed for each browser tab and web page (Figs. 9 and 10), as an over layer to the Web page. One report page now counts on one section per tab and, inside this section, a report for each URL used in that tab.

Fig. 9. Heatmap report after redesign.

Fig. 10. Mouse plot after redesign.

The new features implemented after the focus group were done considering the need for reports that present relevant information about the user interaction in an easier and more accessible way than the usage graph (Fig. 11). Two reports were developed, namely:

1. **Patterns**: An HTML accessible table that shows the usage graph's nodes whose occurrences are above the 80th percentile, representing nodes representing repeated actions, its source node(s), and its outgoing node(s). This allows specialists to identify UI events repeated during the interaction, their source and they subsequent action;

2. **Incidents**: An HTML accessible table that shows the usage graph's nodes defined as incidents by the usage graph and its SAM-based heuristic (for more details on the SAM-based heuristic, please refer to [19]). The rationale of the incidents report is the same of the patterns report, showing key events in the central column and the corresponding originated and subsequent events in the outer columns.

Finally, regarding features that were not implemented we have the following:

1. Report features for each user – Since the User Test Logger is a web extension, the idea is to keep it as simple as possible. It is not desirable that the proposed tool become too much complex nor demanding extra CPU or RAM usage, which could impact negatively the participants experience the UI in evaluation;

2. Upload setup file for the study – Given that the only setup performed by the specialist is to select the events of interest and that these values persist, the easiest way to select the events to be recorded is by selecting them in the events menu item, as shown in the Fig. 3;

3. Upload data captured back to the tool – Given the goal of the tool of supporting a rich and detailed data capture, allowing specialists to analyze in depth in additional graph or statistical software, the goal was to allow specialists to record and download all reports for further analysis;

4. Indicate what are the tabs being logged – Given that all tabs are logged and that the tool also aims at not disturbing the end user participating in the user test, the "L" button was designed to be as simple and as subtle as possible. In the design phase of the tool, for example, it was considered to have a red circle over the menu to show that it was in use. However, it is known that these indicators end up calling users' attention that, for a logger tool in a local setup, is not desirable.

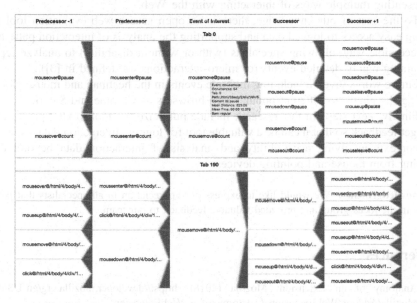

Fig. 11. Patterns/incidents report in the second version of the tool.

5. The tool tip shows additional information for each node contained in the usage graph.

6 Discussion

Although there are multiple tools for interaction logging, the literature still lacks a general-purpose logging tool supporting an easy way for HCI practitioners and Data Scientists to capture detailed interaction data, covering more than clicks and mouse movements. The proposed tool addresses this gap and is available at Github (https://github.com/IBM/user-test-logger). The tool counts on documentation and on videos describing how to install, capture data, and start analyzing highly detailed interaction data.

The participants from the focus group provided valuable feedback and insights to our team. Although the User Test Logger was, by design, developed to fill a gap existing in evaluation tools, the participants needed reports similar to existing ones in similar tools, as the heatmap overlayer that was added after the focus group.

Bearing in mind limitations of the focus group, the number of participants is the main issue, given that it was planned to be run with 6 participants.

The impacts aimed with this tool involve technological aspects, supporting the capture of detailed data, and social aspects, given that it goes beyond of click streams, data usually used in web studies that take from granted sight and use of the mouse. This is one of the key aspects of the tool, considering that one of its pillars is to be inclusive, considering the whole diversity of types of events that can be captured and, hence, representing multiple ways of interacting with the Web.

To the best of our knowledge, there is no open source web evaluation tool providing easy access to logged data and supporting the analysis of interaction patterns in an accessible way, allowing specialists (with or without disability) to analyze reports containing highly detailed events (or micro-interactions, as defined in [3]).

Future works involve including multiple events in the heatmap and mouse plot and porting the plugin to different popular web browsers as Chrome and Safari.

Finally, next steps in this research include publicize the tool to HCI practitioners and get feedback so that it can be a valuable tool for logging interaction data, especially on contexts involving accessibility and analysis of interaction data beyond those coming from mouse and pointing devices.

Acknowledgements. We would like to express our appreciation to all specialists that participated in the focus group and provided valuable feedback to our team.

References

1. Anatomy of an Extension: Mozilla (2018). https://developer.mozilla.org/en-US/docs/Mozilla/Addons/WebExtensions/Anatomy_of_a_WebExtension
2. Arroyo, E., Selker, T., Wei, W.: Usability tool for analysis of web designs using mouse tracks. In: CHI 2006 Extended Abstracts on Human Factors in Computing Systems (CHI EA 2006) (2006)
3. Breslav, S., Khan, A., Hornbæk, K.: Mimic: visual analytics of online micro-interactions. In: Proceedings of the 2014 International Working Conference on Advanced Visual Interfaces (AVI 2014), pp. 245–252. ACM, New York (2014). https://doi.org/10.1145/2598153.2598168
4. Bostock, M.: Data-Driven Documents (D3) (2017). https://d3js.org/
5. Buschmann, F., Henney, K., Schimdt, D.: Pattern-Oriented Software Architecture: On Patterns and Pattern Language. Wiley, New York (2007)
6. Centre for Excellence in Universal Design.: What is Universal Design? (2012). http://universaldesign.ie/What-isUniversal-Design/
7. Chen, M.C., Anderson, J.R., Sohn, M.H.: What can a mouse cursor tell us more? Correlation of eye/mouse movements on web browsing. In: CHI 2001 Extended Abstracts on Human Factors in Computing Systems (CHI EA 2001) (2001)

8. Etgen, M., Cantor, J.: What does getting WET (web event-logging tool) mean for web usability? In: 5th Conference on Human Factors and the Web (1999)
9. FileSaver JavaScript Library.: (2019). https://github.com/eligrey/FileSaver.js
10. General Data Protection Regulation (GDPR) (2016). https://eur-lex.europa.eu/legalcontent/EN/TXT/?uri=CELEX:32016R0679
11. John, B.E., Kieras, D.E.: The GOMS family of user interface analysis techniques: comparison and contrast. In: ACM Transactions on Computer-Human Interaction 3, 4 Dec 1996, pp. 320–351 (1996)
12. jQuery.: (2019). http://jquery.com/
13. Krueger, R.A., Casey, M.A.: Focus Groups: A Practical Guide for Applied Research. Sage Publications, London (2014)
14. Lei de Proteção de Dados Pessoais.: (2018). www.planalto.gov.br/ccivil_03/_ato20152018/2018/lei/L13709.htm
15. Paternò, F.: Model-Based Design and Evaluation of Interactive Applications. Springer, Heidelberg (2012)
16. Rubin, J.: Handbook of Usability Testing: How to Plan, Design, and Conduct Effective Tests. Wiley, Hoboken (1994)
17. Salvucci, D.D., Goldberg, J.H.: Identifying fixations and saccades in eye-tracking protocols. In: Proceedings of the 2000 Symposium on Eye Tracking Research and Applications (ETRA 2000) (2000)
18. de Santana, V.F., Baranauskas, M.C.C.: A taxonomy for website evaluation tools grounded on semiotic framework. In: Antona, M., Stephanidis, C. (eds.) UAHCI 2018. LNCS, vol. 10907, pp. 38–49. Springer, Cham (2018). https://doi.org/10.1007/978-3-319-92049-8_3
19. Santana, V.F., Baranauskas, M.C.C.: WELFIT: a remote evaluation tool for identifying Web usage patterns through client-side logging. Int. J. Hum. Comput. Stud. 76(2015), 40–49 (2015)

Research on Wearable Shopping Aid Device for Visually Impaired People

Yu-Hsiu Hung[1], Chia-Hui Feng[1,2(✉)],
Chia-Tzu Lin[2], and Chung-Jen Chen[3]

[1] Department of Industrial Design, National Cheng Kung University,
No. 1, University Road, Tainan, Taiwan R.O.C.
p38041075@ncku.edu.tw
[2] Department of Creative Product Design,
Southern Taiwan University of Science and Technology,
No. 1, Nan-Tai Street, Yongkang District, Tainan, Taiwan R.O.C.
[3] Department of Visual Communication Design,
Southern Taiwan University of Science and Technology,
No. 1, Nan-Tai Street, Yongkang District, Tainan, Taiwan R.O.C.

Abstract. This study explored the effect of three different shopping modes, namely shopping alone, shopping with a companion, and shopping using a shopping aid device, on the efficiency of in-store shopping and compared the behavioral difference between these three shopping modes using in-depth interviews with visually impaired people, their companions, and sales agents. The goal is to understand the current condition of shopping of visually impaired people and their related needs. Lastly, the researchers of this study designed and developed the prototype of a smart shopping aid wearable device for product recognition for visually impaired people. The study participants were six students, four males and two females, from Huei-Ming School and Home for Blind Children. For all participants, their task performance accuracy rate and task performance time were recorded and then analyzed by one-way repeated measure ANOVA to determine if shopping time was affected by the mode of shopping. System Usability Scale (SUS) was applied to determine the usability score of the wearable device of this study. The study results are as follows: (1) When comparing the average number of correct task performance between the three modes, the difference was statistically significant. From the post-hoc comparison, the correct rate of using a wearable device for shopping (95%) was significantly higher than of shopping alone (75%) and shopping with a companion (75%). Moreover, there was no difference between shopping alone and shopping with a companion. (2) For the task performance time, no significant difference was found between the variables. (3) The average SUS score was 74.2 (grade C) and the percentile rank was 71. This finding indicates that the wearable device developed in this study is easy to understand and easy to use. The participants showed a short learning curve and a high use intention.

Keywords: Assistive technology · Visually impaired people ·
Product recognition · Smart wearable device

M. Antona and C. Stephanidis (Eds.): HCII 2019, LNCS 11572, pp. 244–257, 2019.
https://doi.org/10.1007/978-3-030-23560-4_18

1 Introduction

According to the World Health Organization (WHO), by 2018 worldwide there are about 253 million people with visual impairment, and among them, 3.6 million people suffer from complete blindness; 217 million, medium or serious visual impairment [1]. According to studies based on the 2017 Global Vision Database, the age of populations with complete blindness, medium visual impairment, and severe visual impairment has gone down. In other words, visual impairment is more and more common among young people now [2].

People with visual impairment often need to rely on either their experiences or their family and friends for coping with various dangers and inconveniences in their daily lives. There are welfare organizations providing visually impaired people with vocational training, orientation training, and self-help skill training. Nonetheless, there are still numerous everyday tasks challenging people with visual impairment but no solutions available. Take shopping as an example, some shop owners refuse to have guide dogs enter their stores, making shopping difficult for visually impaired people [3].

Psychologically, studies have shown that because there are many daily matters, such as exploring a foreign environment, that visually impaired people cannot handle independently, and moreover, neither stable nor comprehensive aids are available for visually impaired people in the physical environment, visually impaired people need to look for help. However, seeking help often make visually impaired people anxious because of social and family relationship concerns, time pressure, etc. [4].

Physiologically, studies have shown that the major differences between people with congenital visual impairment and people with acquired visual impairment are the challenges they face and the use of their perception. Congenital visual impairment refers to impairment that happens before the age of five, and people with congenital visual impairment have usually lost their visual memory. In contrast, acquired visual impairment normally happens after the age of five, and people suffering from acquired visual impairment usually have their visual memory partially kept [5]. Visual impairment affects people both mentally and behaviorally depending on how much life experience they have accumulated. The more visual life experience a visually impaired person has accumulated, the more mental characteristics of non-visually impaired people this visually impaired person possesses [6], and the longer time it takes for this visually impaired person to learn to use his/her acute sense of touch and of hearing instead of the vision.

In recent years, shopping for visually impaired people has received great attention. Visually impaired people need to shop for fresh produce and daily necessities, and according to the physical store shopping methods of visually impaired people provided by the American Foundation for the Blind (AFB), common difficulties encountered during shopping by people with visual impairment include navigating among the aisles or reading the price tags or labels to find out the name, production date, list of ingredients, or nutritional facts of grocery products. Depending on their personal backgrounds, for example, people with severe visual impairment often find shopping difficult and are anxious about how to find out the content of products. Currently, people with mild visual impairment can use a shopping cart scanning device or a magnifier to read such information or to ask a shopping assistant to read the information for them. In research, studies have explored problems experienced by visually impaired people when shopping in physical stores and the corresponding solutions, but all these studies are centered on the use of scanning devices to assist visually impaired people in shopping [7–11].

Because of poor eyesight, the most frequently encountered obstacles by visually impaired people in shopping are associated with seeking and reading information. These obstacles include personal obstacles, interpersonal information obstacles, information and media access obstacles, and physical environment obstacles. For personal obstacles, information acquisition is affected primarily by the level of visual impairment and the age, and psychologically and cognitively, some visually impaired people may lack confidence, independence, a sense of security, and motivation for information acquisition [12, 13]. For interpersonal information obstacles, they are mainly caused by the gap between the assistance provided by non-visually impaired people and the actually needs requested by visually impaired people. Moreover, the assistance provided by non-visually impaired people is often affected by the amount of time available and their willingness [14]. In the physical environment, visually impaired people may encounter information obstacles, traffic flow obstacles, fine movement obstacles, and distance obstacles, and the last obstacle is the most problem one [15]. All these obstacles prevent visually impaired people from completing their shopping independently.

According to the above, visually impaired people when exploring new things may encounter physical difficulties, including locating product shelves or reading product labels, and psychological burdens, including social and family relationship concerns and other mental issues, and these issues make people with visual impairment worry about shopping in physical stores. To solve these problems, this study explored the use of a smart wearable device to assist visually impaired people in shopping. More specifically, the objective of this study is to use technology to help visually impaired people to locate product shelves and acquire product information so they can shop independently. Aside from providing useful information for promoting shopping environments and services accessible to visually impaired people, this study also presents insights to researchers investigating the shopping behavior of distinctive user groups.

2   Method

2.1   Subjects

The study participants were six junior high school students, four boys and two girls, aged between 12 and 15 from Huei-Ming School and Home for Blind Children. See Fig. 1. The participating students had to be capable of communicating and expressing their ideas and walking independently. Students with multiple disabilities were excluded from this study. For students participating in this study, the researchers of this study first explained the objectives of this study and the experiment procedure to the school, their parents and themselves and requested them to sign the informed consent for participants in order to protect the rights of these students.

Fig. 1. Interviewing visually impaired students

2.2 Subjects Experimental Design

To compare between the current shopping modes and the shopping mode of using a wearable device of visually impaired people, this study selected 24 products that were available on the market and divided them into four groups: cookies and crackers, beverages, household items, and snack foods. The participating students were asked to perform experimental tasks in three shopping models, and to eliminate the effect of learning, the sequence of the tasks and the location of the products were different between the students. In the following paper, the task of shopping alone is referred to as Task A, the task of shopping with a companion is referred to as Task B, and the task of using the wearable device is referred to as Task C. The sequence of these tasks of the first participating student was A first, B second, and C third (ABC), the sequence of the tasks of the second participating students was B first, C second, and A third (BCA), the sequence of the tasks of the third participating students was C first, A second, and B third (CAB), and the sequence of the rest of the students was arranged in the same fashion. For each task, the participating students had to find four designated products in a simulated shop, and after completing the experimental tasks, the task performance accuracy rate, the task performance time, and data collected from the system usability scale (SUS) regarding the wearable device were analyzed.

2.3 RFID Product Tags

The 24 selected products were divided into four groups, and most of these products were boxed or canned items. A passive RFID tag was attached to the inside of these boxes and cans. Information carried by the tags included the content of the product, the ingredients, the production date, the expiration date, and the price.

2.4   Product Shelves

Product shelves were set up in a simulated shop for displaying the products. These product shelves were arranged based on findings from retail product display studies. The products were arranged on shelves about 60 cm to 150 cm high from the floor for the best visual effect and an easy access [16, 17]. See Fig. 2. Each product shelf was equipped with an active RFID tag, and the sensing range was set to be within one meter for positioning the visually impaired participants and informing them which product shelf it is. Each product shelf displayed three products.

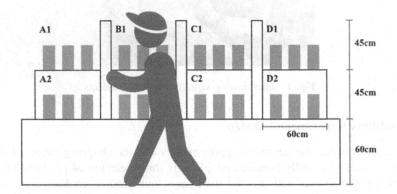

Fig. 2. Product shelf position and recommended optimal access range

2.5   The Wearable RFID Reader Device

This wearable RFID reader was to be worn on the wrist. See Fig. 3. This device was paired with an anti-metal interference high-frequency RFID tag, a Mp3Player module with a memory card, an 5DBI antenna, a RFID read write device, an Arduino RUNO microcontroller board, a read write device, and a speaker.

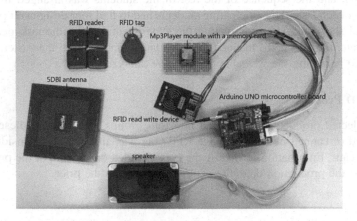

Fig. 3. Wearable device functional components

2.6 IoT Database

This study set up a simulated shop, product shelves, and a product information database. When participants put on the wearable device, information can be transmitted through the cloud network.

2.7 Programming Tools

An Arduino UNO board and Arduino IDE were used for software development and programming. The wearable device used in the experiment here was equipped with a RFID read writ module. On the product shelf, an active RFID tag was installed for transmitting information of the type of the product shelf. A passive RFID tag was attached to each product displayed on the package. A simulated shop information cloud was established to link all equipment used in the experiment to receive information from them.

2.8 System Usability Scale (SUS)

Developed by John Brooker in 1986, the system usability scale (SUS) has been extensively used for a quick test of products, systems, and websites. A major advantage of this scale is that it can be accurately and rapidly implemented for usability evaluation, even if the sample size is small [18]. In 2008, Bangor conducted a study using a large sample and found the reliability of SUS of 0.91. The scores of the scale can be divided into six levels, and each level is paired with a text description [19]. See Fig. 4.

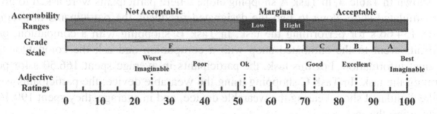

Fig. 4. SUS score cross reference chart

3 Results

This study used IBM SPSS Statistics Version 25 for the quantitative analysis of the acquired data in terms of the task performance time, the task performance accuracy rate, and the SUS score for the wearable device. The objective here is to present the experiment results comprehensively from various aspects.

3.1 Participants' Profile

As shown in Table 1, this study had six participants, and they were all junior high school students from Huei-Ming School and Home for Blind Children. There were four male students (66.7% of the study sample) and two female students (33.3% of the study sample).

Table 1. Descriptive statistics of participants' gender

Item	Sample size	Percentage (%)
Male	4	66.7
Female	2	33.3
Total	6	100

As shown in Table 2, all six participants (100% of the study sample) had retail shopping experience, and no participants (0% of the study sample) had no retail shopping experience.

Table 2. Descriptive statistics of participants' shopping experience

Item	Sample size	Percentage (%)
With retail shopping experience	6	100
Without retail shopping experience	0	0
Total	6	100

3.2   Task Performance Time Analysis Result

As shown in Table 3, in Task A shopping alone where participants were asked to go to the simulated shop alone to find the designated products, the participants in average spent 134.66 s for performing the task. In Task B shopping with a companion, participants went to the simulated shop with a companion and ask the companion for product information. For this task, the participants in average spent 166.50 s for performing the task. In Task C shopping using the wearable device, the participants went to the simulated shop wearing the wearable device, and in average, they spent 190.16 s performing the task.

Table 3. Task performance time analysis

Mode	Item	Mean	SD	Number
A	Time spent when shopping alone	134.66	39.05	6
B	Time spent when shopping with a companion	166.50	75.04	6
C	Time spent when shopping wearing a wearable device	190.16	66.00	6

As shown in Table 4, both the general assumption of variance analysis and the assumption of sphericity were met by the repeated measure ANOVA. Mauchly's W was 0.482, which when used for calculating the chi-square distribution gave a value of 2.922 ($p = 0.232 > 0.05$, nss).

Table 4. Mauchly's Sphericity test: task performance time analysis

| Within subjects effect | Mauchly's W | Approx. chi-square | df | Sig. | Epsilon[b] | | |
					Greenhouse-Geisser	Huynh-Feldt	Lower-bound
Factor	.482	2.922	2	.232	.659	.801	.500

Table 5 shows that the assumption of sphericity was satisfied, and therefore, the data can be the sphericity assumed rows. It was found from between-group effect test that the sum of squares (SS) of the effect of the independent variable was 9307.444, the mean square was 4653.722, the F value was 3.133 (p = 0.088, nss). This finding suggests a lack of significant difference between the three shopping modes in the amount of time spent for completing the tasks.

Table 5. Testing the within-subject effect of task performance time

Source		Type III sum of squares	df	Mean square	F	Sig.
Factor	Sphericity assumed	9307.444	2	4653.722	3.133	.088
	Greenhouse-Geisser	9307.444	1.317	7066.088	3.133	.119
	Huynh-Feldt	9307.444	1.603	5806.596	3.133	.105
	Lower-bound	9307.444	1.000	9307.444	3.133	.137
Error (factor)	Sphericity assumed	14852.566	10	1484.256		
	Greenhouse-Geisser	14852.566	6.586	2255.172		
	Huynh-Feldt	14852.566	8.015	1853.200		
	Lower-bound	14852.566	5.000	2907.511		

Table 6 shows the within-subject test result and it was affected by repeated measures. For the between-subject effect, the repeated measured ANOVA revealed a sum of squares (SS) between-subject of 42717.111, a degree of freedom of 5, and a mean square of 8543.422. Because the between-subject effect was statistically significant (p < .001), the amount of time required for completing the tasks varied among the participants.

Table 6. Testing the within-subject effect of task performance time

Source	Type III sum of squares	df	Mean square	F	Sig.
Intercept	482816.889	1	482816.889	56.513	.001
Error	42717.111	5	8543.422		

See Table 7. The dependent sample sphericity test result indicated that the assumption of sphericity was not violated. Mauchly's W was 0.482 (χ^2 = 2.922, p = 0.232), and therefore no correction was required. The difference between the means of the three tasks was not statistically significant, and for the between-group effect, F (2,10) = 3.133 (P = 0.088 > 0.05), it can be found that the amount of time required for participants to complete the tasks in the three modes (shopping alone, shopping with a companion, and shopping using a wearable device) was not much different. Because the between-group difference for the task performance time was not statistically significant, a post-hoc comparison was not required.

Table 7. ANOVA test result for task performance time of different shopping modes

Source	Between-group variation	df	Mean square	F	Sig.
Between groups	9307.444	2	4653.722	3.133***	0.088
Within group (error)					
Between subjects	42717.111	5	8543.422		
Residuals	14852.566	10	1485.256		
Total	66877.121	17			

3.3 Analysis of Task Performance Accuracy Rate

As shown in Table 8, participants in Task A shopping alone were asked to go to the simulated shop alone to find the designated products, and their average number of correct task performance was 75.00, with a standard deviation of 15.81. For Task B where participants went to the simulated shop with a companion and needed to ask the companion for product information, the participants' average number of correct task performance was 75.00, with a standard deviation of 15.81. For Task C where participants wore the wearable device to the simulated shop, the average number of correct task performance was 95.83, with a standard deviation of 10.20.

Table 8. Analysis of task accuracy rate

Mode	Item	Mean	Std. deviation	N
A	Shopping alone	75.00	15.81	6
B	Shopping with a companion	75.00	15.81	6
C	Shopping using the wearable device	95.83	10.20	6

As shown in Table 9, both the general assumption of variance analysis and the assumption of sphericity were met by the repeated measure ANOVA. Mauchly's W was 0.476, which when used for calculating the chi-square distribution gave a value of 2.966 (p = 0.227 > 0.05, nss).

Table 9. Mauchly's test of Sphericity for task performance accuracy rate

Within subjects effect	Mauchly's W	Approx. chi-square	df	Sig.	Epsilon[b]		
					Greenhouse-Geisser	Huynh-Feldt	Lower-bound
Factor	.476	2.966	2	.227	.656	.797	.500

   Table 10 shows that the assumption of sphericity was met, and therefore, the data can be the sphericity assumed rows. From testing the between-group effect, it was found that the sum of squares (SS) of the effect of the independent variable was 1736.111, the mean square was 868.056, and the F value was 5.435 (p = 0.025, reaching the statistically significance (p < 0.05). This finding suggests that in different shopping modes, participants' task performance accuracy rate was significantly different, and therefore, a post-hoc comparison was required.

Table 10. Test of the within-subject effect for the task performance accuracy rate

Source		Type III sum of squares	df	Lower-bound	F	Sig.
Factor	Sphericity assumed	1736.111	2	868.056	5.435	.025
	Greenhouse–Geisser	1736.111	1.313	1322.595	5.435	.049
	Huynh–Feldt	1736.111	1.593	1089.468	5.435	.037
	Lower-bound	1736.111	1.000	1736.111	5.435	.067
Error (factor)	Sphericity assumed	1597.222	10	159.722		
	Greenhouse–Geisser	1597.222	6.563	243.357		
	Huynh–Feldt	1597.222	7.968	200.462		
	Lower-bound	1597.222	5.000	319.444		

   See Table 11. According to the test result of the between-subject effect, repeated measures had an effect. For the between-subject effect, the repeated measured ANOVA revealed a sum of squares between-subject of 1423.611, a degree of freedom of 5, p < .001, and a mean square of 284.722.

Table 11. Test of the between-subject effect for the task performance accuracy rate

Source	Type III sum of squares	df	Mean square	F	Sig.
Intercept	120868.056	1	120868.056	424.512	.0001
Error	1423.611	5	284.722		

See Table 12. According to the mean difference and the significance from the Bonferroni post-hoc test, the average task performance accuracy rate of shopping using the wearable device was significantly higher than that of shopping with a companion or of shopping alone. As for shopping with a companion and shopping alone, no significant difference was found between their average task performance accuracy rates.

Table 12. Post-hoc comparison of the task performance accuracy rate between different shopping modes

(I) factor	(J) factor	Mean difference (I-J)	Std. error	Sig.[(b)]	95% confidence interval for difference[(b)]	
					Lower bound	upper bound
A	B	.000	9.129	1.000	−23.466	23.466
	C	−20.833*	4.167	.004	−31.544	−10.123
B	A	.000	9.129	1.000	−23.466	23.466
	C	−20.833*	7.683	.042	−40.583	−1.084
C	A	20.833*	4.167	.004	10.123	31.544
	B	20.833*	7.683	.042	1.084	40.583

Note: A for shopping alone, B for shopping with a companion, and C for shopping using the wearable device

As shown in Table 13 that the assumption of sphericity was not violated according to the test result. Mauchly's W was 0.476 ($\chi^2 = 2.966$, p = 0.227), and therefore no correction was required. The mean difference of the three tasks reached statistical significance, and the between-group effect was significant (F (2,10) = 5.435, P = 0.025 < 0.05). In other words, the participants' task performance accuracy rate was significantly different between the three shopping modes (i.e., shopping alone, shopping with a companion, and shopping using a wearable device). It was found from the post-hoc comparison that the average number of correct task performance of Task C (using the wearable device) was 3.38, significantly higher than 3.0 of Task B (shopping with a companion) or 3.0 of Task A (shopping alone). Moreover, the task performance accuracy rate of Task A and Task B did not differ significantly.

Table 13. Analysis of variance of the task performance accuracy rate of different shopping

Source of variation	SS	df	MS	F	Sig.	Post-hoc comparison
Between groups	1736.111	2	868.056	5.435***	0.025	C > B = A
Within group (error)						
Between subjects	1423.611	5	284.722			
Residuals	1597.222	10	159.722			
Total	4756.944	17				

3.4 SUS Result for the Wearable Device

As shown in Table 14, the SUS score of the wearable device of this study was 74.2 of grade C, and because this score exceeded the average SUS score of 68.5, this wearable device passed the usability evaluation test. As for the easy-to-learn score of the device, the device tested in this study was easy to learn and to use. The short learning curve of the participants means that they could easily understand how to use the device, and because the device was easy to use, the participants showed a good use intention and considered that the functions of the device met their daily needs.

Table 14. SUS result of the smart wearable device

No.	1	2	3	4	5	6
Score	82.5	75	77.5	30	87.5	92.5
Rating	B	C	C	F	B	A
Mean	74.2					

According to Fig. 5 of SUS, the wearable device had a grade of C and a score of 74.2 (between 70 and 80). This finding suggests that the participants considered that the device has a good usability, a good acceptability, and no operating problem.

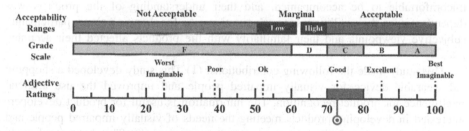

Fig. 5. SUS score cross resulted chart

4   Discussion and Conclusion

According to the participant task performance accuracy rate, task performance time, and the SUS result, the shopping mode of using the wearable device and the functions of the wearable device were accepted by the six participants and received positive feedback from these participants. In other words, this wearable device can meet the daily needs of the participants currently. This study considered that there is still a lot of room for the development of shopping aid devices for visually impaired people. The shopping aid device developed in this study has three major contributions; one is that this shopping aid device can meet visually impaired people's expectation for shopping independently. Another is that this shopping aid device enables visually impaired people to acquire information easily. The other contribution is that this shopping aid device can eliminate the social and family relationship concerns and mental stress experienced by visually impaired people when looking for a companion for shopping.

It can be found from the task performance time analysis that there was no significant difference between the three shopping modes. The reason for spending more time when shopping using the wearable device than the other two shopping modes is that the participants in the experiment had to first touch the products before listening to the information of the products and judging which one is the designated one. The task performance time was increased because the participants might listen to the information more than once.

For shopping with a companion, the amount of time spent performing the task was affected by how extrovert the participants were; those who were more willing to ask for information voluntarily spent relatively more time performing the task than those who were reluctant to ask questions. For shopping alone, the amount of time spent performing the task was affected by participants' subjective product perception; they would touch the products, feel the weight, or smell the products to help identify them. For unfamiliar products, they had to guess and to intuitively and subjectively make decision. In this case, though less time was spent, the error rate was high.

It can be found from the task performance accuracy rate that participants when using the wearable device can identify three to four products correctly. Though this mode was more time consuming than the other two modes, the accuracy rate was better than the other two because the information the participants listened to can help them identify the correct products. For shopping with a companion, some participants felt uncomfortable to be accompanied, and their understanding of the products was dependent upon their willingness to ask questions. As for shopping alone, participants' subjective viewpoints and their familiarity with the products affected their accuracy rate.

This study made the following contributions: (1) This study developed a shopping aid wearable device for visually impaired people and improved the use artificial intelligence for product recognition. The information is useful for product developers interested in developing products meeting the needs of visually impaired people and possessing a good usability and an easy-to-learn feature. (2) This behavioral study investigating the physical retail shopping experience of people with visual impairment offers the pros and cons of shopping alone, shopping with a companion, and shopping using a wearable device. (3) This study found from the experiment that product packages containing metal lead can interfere with the sensitivity of product sensing of the device; (4) The length of time of product voice information should not be too long or visually impaired users may lose their patience and concentration.

References

1. World Health Organization. https://www.who.int/news-room/fact-sheets/detail/blindness-and-visual-impairment. Accessed 31 Dec 2018
2. Bourne, R.R., Flaxman, S.R., Braithwaite, T., Cicinelli, M.V., Das, A., Jonas, J.B., et al.: Magnitude: temporal trends, and projections of the global prevalence of blindness and distance and near vision impairment: a systematic review and meta-analysis. Lancet Glob. Health **5**(9), e888–e897 (2017)
3. Lai, S.L.: The current status and future outlook of adaptive devices for the visually impaired in Taiwan. Spec. Educ. **99**, 31–36 (2006)
4. Wang, Y.Y.: The role of 'personal assistance': the case of visual assistant service. NTU Soc. Work Rev. **12**, 89–138 (2005)
5. Moore, J.E., Graves, W.H., Patterson, J.B.: Foundation of Rehabilitation Counseling with Persons Who Are Blind or Visually Impaired. AFB Press, New York (1997)
6. Sato, T.: Psychology and Education for Children with Visual Impairment. Wu-Nan Book Inc., Taipei (1983)
7. Gharpure, C.P., Kulyukin, V.A.: Robot-assisted shopping for the blind: issues in spatial cognition and product selection. Intell. Serv. Robot. **1**(3), 237–251 (2008)
8. Nicholson, J., Kulyukin, V., Coster, D.: ShopTalk: independent blind shopping through verbal route directions and barcode scans. Open Rehab. J. **9**(2), 11–23 (2009)
9. Kulyukin, V., Kutiyanawala, A.: Accessible shopping systems for blind and visually impaired individuals: design requirements and the state of the art. Open Rehab. J. **2**, 158–168 (2010)
10. Lanigan, P.E., Paulos, A.M., Williams, A.W., Rossi, D., Narasimhan, P.: Trinetra: assistive technologies for grocery shopping for the blind. In: Proceedings of the 10th IEEE International Symposium on Wearable Computers, pp. 147–148 (2007)
11. Yang, C.Y.: Assisting the visually impaired to identity objects using smart phone. Master's thesis (2012). https://hdl.handle.net/11296/8994ev
12. Graeme, D., Christine, C., Sue, P.: The role of the WHO ICF as a framework to interpret barriers and to inclusion. Br. J. Vis. Impair. **25**(1), 32–50 (2007)
13. Saumure, K., Given, L.M.: Digitally enhanced? An examination of the information behaviors of visually impaired post-secondary students. Can. J. Inf. Libr. Sci. **28**(2), 25–42 (2004)
14. Elaine, G.: The benefits of and barriers to computer use for individuals who are visually impaired. J. Vis. Impair. Blind. **97**(9), 536–550 (2003)
15. Gold, D., Simson, H.: Identifying the needs of people in Canada who are blind or visually impaired: preliminary results of a nation-wide study. Int. Congr. Ser. **1282**, 139–142 (2005)
16. Lin, C.H., Huang, Y.C.: Business Strategies for Successful Shopping Center Management. Tiaohe Culture Co., Ltd., Taiwan (1999)
17. Hsieh, C.H.: Retail Store Planning and Management, Highlights. Wu-Nan Book Inc., Taipei (2009)
18. Brooke, J.: SUS: a retrospective. J. Usabil. Stud. **8**(2), 29–40 (2013)
19. Bangor, A., Kortum, P.T., Miller, J.T.: Determining what individual SUS scores mean: adding an adjective rating scale. J. Usabil. Stud. **4**(3), 114–123 (2009)

Design and Evaluation of a User-Interface for Authoring Sentences of American Sign Language Animation

Abhishek Kannekanti[1], Sedeeq Al-khazraji[1,2], and Matt Huenerfauth[1(✉)]

[1] Rochester Institute of Technology, Rochester, NY 14623, USA
{ak9492,sha6709,matt.huenerfauth}@rit.edu
[2] University of Mosul, Mosul, Iraq

Abstract. Many individuals who are Deaf or Hard of Hearing (DHH) in the U.S. have lower English language literacy levels than their hearing peers, which creates a barrier to access web content for these users. In the present study we determine a usable interface experience for authoring sentences (or multi-sentence messages) in ASL (American Sign Language) using the EMBR (Embodied Agents Behavior Realizer) animation platform. Three rounds of iterative designs were produced through participatory design techniques and usability testing, to refine the design, based on feedback from 8 participants familiar with creating ASL animations. Later, a usability testing session was conducted with four participants on the final iteration of the designs. We found that participants expressed a preference for a "timeline" layout for arranging words to create a sentence, with a dual view of the word-level and the sub-word "pose" level. This paper presents the details of the design stages of the new GUI, the results, and directions for future work.

Keywords: Human computer interaction · American Sign Language · Authoring tools · Timeline

1 Introduction

American Sign Language (ASL) is the primary means of communication for over one and a half million people in the United States of America [10], and it is ranked as the third most popular "foreign language" studied in U.S. universities [3]. The grammar of ASL is different than English; it has a unique word-order and vocabulary. Standardized literacy testing has revealed that many deaf secondary-school graduates in the U.S. have lower levels of written and reading English skills [14]. Hence, the use of English text captions on dynamic multimedia content (TV, radio, movies, and computer programs) may also be difficult to understand for such users. Several sign language writing systems have been proposed [12, 13] but have not gained popularity among the deaf community. Therefore, if website or media designers wish to provide information in the form of ASL for these users, they must provide a video or an animation of the ASL information content [6].

© Springer Nature Switzerland AG 2019
M. Antona and C. Stephanidis (Eds.): HCII 2019, LNCS 11572, pp. 258–267, 2019.
https://doi.org/10.1007/978-3-030-23560-4_19

What is required is a practical way for adding sign language to media or websites. While providing video recordings of a human is possible, it is expensive to remake a video of a human producing sign language, for content that is frequently changing. However, with animated characters, the content could be dynamically created from a "script" of the message, which could be more easily updated. Such an approach could provide high-quality ASL output that is easier to update for websites or media. While some researchers have investigated the problem of automatically translating from written English into a script of an ASL message [11], currently a human who is knowledgeable of ASL is needed to produce such a script accurately. Therefore, there is a need for software to help this person produce ASL sentences or longer messages that use ASL signs in proper word-order, with other details of the animation correct [9], such as the timing of words, the facial expression of the animated human, etc.

1.1 Problem Statement

Beyond this broader future use of ASL animation technology to produce content for websites, there is a more immediate need for software tools: Our laboratory uses the EMBR animation platform [8] as a basis for its research on ASL animation technology, and as part of this work, the lab is often producing new animations of sentences (or longer messages) in ASL. For instance, the lab may need to produce sentences that will be shown during an experiment, in order to evaluate some of the technical details of the animation technology. Thus, as an important form of research infrastructure, this tool should enable someone to build sentences as well as to identify and add items from a repository of individual ASL signs (words) that members of the laboratory had pre viously authored and saved for future use. Being able to make use of these pre-built words from the repository reduces the effort needed for creating a new sentence, by allowing someone to use pre-built components (the individual ASL sign animations that have already been created).

This paper reports on our design and evaluation of a software user-interface to enable someone to author sentences (or multi-sentence messages) in ASL. The primary users of this system would be researchers who are investigating ASL animation technologies, but we anticipate that understanding how to produce a useful research system for authoring such sentences may also shed light on how to best design an ASL animation authoring system that could be used in the future outside of a laboratory context. To investigate the design of this software, we utilized participatory design techniques, interviews, and iterative prototyping methodology. The users who participated in this design and evaluation were "expert users" – i.e. researchers at the Linguistic and Assistive Technology (LATLab) at the Rochester Institute of Technology.

While the laboratory had an existing software system for allowing someone to reuse individual signs to build entire sentences (or longer messages), as described in [7], current users of that software reported that it is too complicated to use. For instance, users had reported that, to create a new ASL sentence, it took about 3 h for an experienced user to import pre-built ASL signs from the lab's existing collection, adjust the timing properties of these signs, and to make small modifications to the individual signs to enable them to smoothly flow from one to the next. Hence a more intuitive and efficient user experience was necessary for generating ASL animations.

The laboratory's current animation platform is based on EMBR [9], and the existing user-interface for assembling words into sentences is a Java application called Behavior Builder, which is distributed with the open-source EMBR software. The Behavior Builder software can be used to perform two different functions: (1) creating an individual ASL sign and (2) assembling signs into a sentence or longer message (and customizing aspects of the signs for this purpose, e.g. adding additional details to the animation, such as facial expressions). Therefore, the system allows users to modify different aspects of the virtual human animation (e.g., the hand shapes, facial expressions, torso positions, etc.) to produce an animation of a message.

In work reported in this paper, our focus is on this second functionality (2): enabling the user to assemble signs into a sentence or a longer message. While the existing system had been a Java application, the lab is currently re-implementing the authoring tool as an HTML5 application, based on the proposed final design from the design and usability testing process described in this paper.

2 Prior Work

Some researchers provided an overview of sign language generation and translation [8], technologies that would plan ASL sentences in a fully automatic manner, when given an English input sentence. While there is continuing research on machine translation for sign languages, progress in this field is still limited by the challenging linguistic divergences encountered during text-to-sign translation and the relatively small size of training data (collections of linguistically labeled ASL recordings with parallel English transcription) [7]. Furthermore, members of the Deaf community have expressed concerns about the deployment of such technologies before they are proven to be of high quality [16]. For this reason, as discussed in [1] our laboratory investigates "human in the loop" workflows for generating ASL animation, in which a human who is knowledgeable of ASL produces a script for an intended message (specifying the words in the sentences, their order, and other details), software automatically generates animations of a virtual human performing ASL (more efficiently than if the human author had been required to animate the movements of the virtual character manually). In this context, it is necessary to provide "authoring tools" for users to develop scripts of ASL animations.

Authoring software would allow users to build sentences of sign language by ordering single signs from a database onto a timeline. Later the authoring software produces an animation of a virtual character based on this user-built timeline. There have been several prior commercial and research efforts to create such tools: For instance, Sign Smith Studio [15] was a commercially available software product that allowed users to make ASL animations on a timeline, using a relatively small dictionary of several hundred words. However, at this time, the product is no longer available commercially.

While the Sign Smith Studio system enabled users to build sentences, there was a complimentary product called "Vcom3D Gesture Builder" [15], which could be used to create entirely new signs, to expand the dictionary of words available for use when building sentences in the Sign Smith Studio system. The Gesture Builder software had several intuitive controls for adjusting the orientation and location of the hand through direct manipulation (click and drag) interaction. The software also featured a timeline of the individual "poses" that comprise a sign, to allow the user to flexibly in changing the hand shape and orientation, by adding time segments for both the hands. The software also contained a repository of pre-built hand shapes, categorized based on the number of fingers, which allowed users to select a hand shape to build ASL sign. However, at this time, the product is also no longer available commercially.

Another example of an authoring system for (European) sign languages was the eSIGN project [2], which created a plugin for a web browser that enabled users to see animations of a sentence on a web page. The technology behind the plugin allowed users to build a sign database using a symbolic script notation called "HamNoSys" in which users typed symbols to represent aspects of the handshape, movement, and orientation of the hands. However, that input notation system was designed for use by expert linguists who are annotating the phonetic performance of a sign language word, and it has a relatively steep learning curve for new users [4].

A recent research project [17] has investigated the construction of a prototype sign language authoring system, with design aspects inspired by word-processing software. While building the prototype, the researchers identified two major problems that their users encountered during the authoring task: (1) retrieving the sign language 'words' (from the collection of available words in their system's dictionary) and (2) specifying the transition movements between different words.

Our lab's EMBR-based animation system uses a constraint-based formalism to specify kinematic goals for a virtual human [5, 7, 8]. While this platform enables keyframe-based animation planning for ASL animation, as discussed in Sect. 1.1, the GUI provided with EMBR was not optimized for selecting ASL signs from a pre-existing word-list nor efficiently adjusting timing characteristics specific to ASL. Thus, we investigate a new user-interface for planning ASL sentences.

3 Methodology

3.1 Iterative Prototyping and User Interviews

To design and evaluate a new user-interface for authoring animations using our EMBR web application, we opted to use Lean UX methodologies, which include rapid sketching, prototyping, creating design mockups, and collecting user feedback. Observation of current users of the existing authoring software as they created animations was conducted to understand current limitations of the system. Next, we presented iterative prototypes to users during three rounds of user studies with a total of 8 to 12 participants in each round (1 to 3 female and 7 to 9 males, in each round). The participants consisted of research students working at the Linguistic and Assistive Technologies Laboratory at Rochester Institute of Technology who had some experience in ASL and familiarity with the need for the laboratory to produce animations of ASL periodically in support of ongoing research projects, e.g. to produce animation stimuli for experimental studies.

The designs presented in the study consisted of high-fidelity static prototype images illustrating various steps in the use of the proposed software. In each round, participants provided subjective feedback about the proposed design iteration. At the end of each presentation round, the feedback and suggestions in the form of qualitative data were synthesized (via affinity diagramming), and changes were applied to the designs. User suggestions in each round (e.g. feature request or UI changes) became test hypotheses for the subsequent round.

Participants in each round of feedback were asked to consider how they would create an ASL animation for the English sentence "Yesterday, my sister brought the car." In addition to creating the sentence, participants were asked to add some additional pause time after one word (additional "Hold" time), and they were asked to adjust the overall speed of one of the words in the sentence (the "Time Factor" for the word).

The final design which resulted from this iterative design process is presented in Fig. 1, with detailed images available in subsequent figures. As shown in this figure, there is a "Left Portion" of the GUI that consists of a list (top to bottom) of the sequence of words in the sentence being constructed (beginning to end). Each word that is listed in the Left Portion of the GUI represents an ASL word from our system's available word list. The numbers shown to the right of each word consist of the start-time and end-time for each word on the sentence, in milliseconds. When words are added to a sentence from the dictionary, their duration is initially set to the duration of the word as stored in the dictionary, and an automatic gap of 30 ms is placed between words. The word duration and time between words are both adjustable (as discussed below, when individual elements of the GUI are described in greater detail).

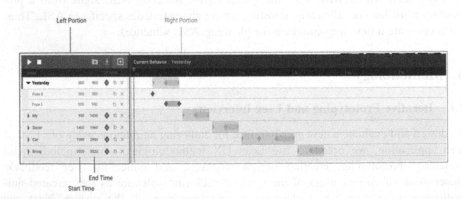

Fig. 1. The final design for authoring ASL sentences, resulting from three rounds of iterative design and testing.

The Right Portion of the GUI contains another view of the information shown in the Left Region. It displays a corresponding representation on the left-to-right timeline for each word of the sentence. As changes are made in one region, the changes are reflected in the other. The rationale for this dual representation of the sentence was that a right-to-left timeline is a more traditional method of displaying a sequence of words in a sentence, yet because an individual ASL sign may consist of multiple "poses" (multiple key frames that occur during time that represent individual landmark positions of the hands in space during time), it is useful to have a method of viewing the detailed numerical information for a sign or a pose in the vertical list-like arrangement in the Left Region of the GUI.

This sentence-authoring user-interface shown in Fig. 1 is only a portion of an overall word-authoring and sentence-authoring tool. In other work at our laboratory, we are investigating methods for controlling the pose of a virtual human character in order to create an individual ASL word (sign), and therefore the upper portion of the screenshot shown in Fig. 2 displays the user-interface elements for that word-authoring task. In this paper, we are specifically focused on our efforts to create a user-interface for assembling signs into a sequence (for a sentence or a longer message), which consists of the lower portion of the screenshot shown in Fig. 2.

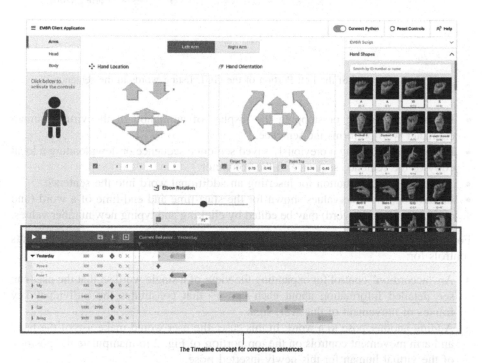

The Timeline concept for composing sentences

Fig. 2. The GUI of our overall user-interface for both word-authoring (moving the arms and hands to create a sign) and sentence-authoring (assembling words into sentences); the highlighted region shows the sentence-authoring timeline, which this the focus of this paper.

3.2 Detailed Discussion of Elements of the GUI's Left and Right Portions

The Left Portion of the GUI (shown in Fig. 3), with its vertical list-like arrangement of information about the words in the sentence contains multiple controls, which include:

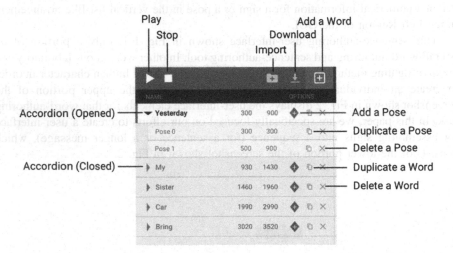

Fig. 3. Detailed of the Left Portion of the GUI, listing words in the sentence.

- Buttons for playing or stopping the display of animation of the virtual human character who performs the sentence.
- Buttons for importing a previously saved sentence sequence or downloading a local copy of the sentence sequence to the computer.
- An "Add a Word" button for inserting an additional word into the sentence.
- In addition, the time values shown for the start-time and end-time of a word (and each sub-pose of a word) may be edited by clicking and typing new number values.

For each individual word in the sentence, the Left Portion of the GUI also presents controls for:

- An "accordion" control for expanding the view of a single word so that the user can see detailed information about each "pose" that constitutes the individual key frames of movement of this ASL sign.
- Adding another pose to a word. In this case, the user would make use of the hand and arm movement controls on the top portion of Fig. 2 to manipulate the position of the virtual human for this newly inserted pose.
- Duplicating a word in the sentence.
- Deleting a word in the sentence.
- In addition, individual words can be dragged and dropped to rearrange their position.

When viewing detailed information about individual poses, there are analogous controls for editing time values, duplicating individual poses, or deleting individual poses.

As discussed above, the Right Portion of the GUI is simply an alternative left-to-right visualization of the sequence of words, which corresponds to the vertical top-to-bottom arrangement of words in the Left Portion of the interface. As shown in Fig. 4, as the animation is played, there is a playhead indicator that moves left-to-right to indicate the current time during the sentence animation. Each word on the timeline is presented as a translucent blue rectangle region, and each individual "pose" of the hands/arms that constitute a word is indicated as a grey diamond. If a "pose" has a non-instantaneous duration in time (i.e. if the virtual human holds its hands and arms motion-less of a brief period of time), then there will be a pair of grey diamond that are linked with a line, to indicate this duration information on the timeline. Notably, if the user uses the "accordion" control on the Left Portion of the interface to expand the view of a word (to see its component poses), then these individual poses are also displayed on the Right Portion timeline – appearing as gray diamonds that are displayed below their parent word.

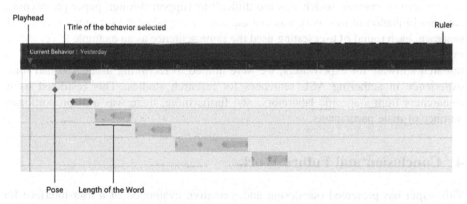

Fig. 4. Detailed view of Right Portion of GUI, showing words and poses.

3.3 Major Recommendations from All Rounds of Testing

While the previous section has described the elements of the final design, this section documents some of the feedback provided by participants during the iterative testing of the preliminary designs. Our first iteration of the interface had a simple design that used the left-to-right timeline metaphor only – without the vertical top-to-bottom list. Overall the left-to-right timeline layout resonated well with the participants, but they also wanted to have a way to control the timing of any selected pose or a word. In the second iteration, we added the Left Portion of the GUI, which revealed numerical values for the "start-time" of each word, as well as a number that represented the "duration" of the word in milliseconds. Participant reacted positively to having this specific numerical information revealed, but some expressed confusion about seeing a "start-time" and a "duration." Several participants mistakenly interpreted the second number as an "end time" for the word, which they believed would be more natural. Thus, our third and field iteration (as shown in Figs. 1, 2, 3 and 4) included both the start-time and the end-time of each word as text input fields (listed to the right of each word in the Left Portion of the interface).

After the final iteration, an additional usability study was conducted via interactive paper-prototyping (utilizing the high-fidelity static images from the final iteration) with four participants who were asked to step through the process of authoring an ASL sentence. No new issues were revealed in this final paper-prototyping session.

3.4 Limitations of This Study

A major limitation of the studies used during the design of this system is that high fidelity static images were displayed to users, rather than an interactive system. Thus, all of the step-by-step screens for the interface were presented as static screens, which limited users' ability to try different ways of arranging the words. While the researcher had several paper prototype images available during these sessions, there were times that participants proposed "playing around with" the sequence of words in a sentence in an exploratory manner, which was too difficult to support through paper prototyping. Another limitation of this work was that the users were asked to consider a single ASL sentence; each round of user testing used the same sentence as an example ("Yesterday, my sister brought the car"). In addition, because we were targeting the design of research software for expert users, we were limited to recruiting users who had some experience in authoring ASL sentences for research studies. This restricted us to researchers from a specific laboratory, and furthermore, there was a disproportionate number of male participants.

4 Conclusion and Future Work

This paper has presented our design and formative evaluation of a user-interface for authoring an animation of an ASL sentence (or multi-sentence messages). Our user studies found that the interface was intuitive for expert users. Three rounds of iterative designs were conducted to understand the factors that influenced the efficiency of composing sentences to create animations. After each round of presentation, the interface design was updated with the feedback given by the participants – and also through validation with subject matter experts and developers, to determine whether the final design was implementable, given our existing software platform.

This work has only presented the design process for prototyping a new user-interface design for this sentence authoring task. The implementation of the GUI is ongoing work at our laboratory. Hence, after the implementation of a working proto-type that is compatible with our animation platform, we anticipate that in future work, we will investigate the usability and efficacy of the resulting system. For instance, we anticipate measuring the time needed to create a sentence on a working prototype – and to conduct an A/B testing with the existing EMBR application to examine the efficiency.

Acknowledgements. This material is based upon work supported by the National Science Foundation under award number 1400802 and 1462280.

References

1. Al-khazraji S., Berke, L., Kafle, S., Yeung P., Huenerfauth, M.: Modeling the speed and timing of American Sign Language to generate realistic animations. In: Proceedings of the 20th International ACM SIGACCESS Conference on Computers and Accessibility (ASSETS 2018), pp. 259–270. ACM, New York (2018)
2. Elliott, R., Glauert, J., Kennaway, J., Marshall, I., Safar, E.: Linguistic modelling and language-processing technologies for Avatar-based sign language presentation. Univ. Access Inf. Soc. **6**(4), 375–391 (2006)
3. Goldberg, D., Looney, D., Lusin, N.: Enrollments in languages other than English in United States Institutions of Higher Education, Fall 2013. In Modern Language Association. Modern Language Association, New York (2015)
4. Hanke, T.: HamNoSys-representing sign language data in language resources and language processing contexts. LREC **4**, 1–6 (2004)
5. Heloir, A., Nguyen, Q., Kipp, M.: Signing avatars: a feasibility study. In: 2nd International Workshop on Sign Language Translation and Avatar Technology (SLTAT) (2011)
6. Huenerfauth, M., Hanson, V.: Sign language in the interface: access for deaf signers. In: Universal Access Handbook. Erlbaum, NJ, p. 38 (2009)
7. Huenerfauth, M., Kacorri, H.: Augmenting EMBR virtual human animation system with MPEG-4 controls for producing ASL facial expressions. In: The Fifth International Workshop on Sign Language Translation and Avatar Technology (SLTAT), Paris, France (2015)
8. Huenerfauth, M., Lu, P., Rosenberg, A.: Evaluating importance of facial expression in American Sign Language and Pidgin Signed English animations. In: The Proceedings of the 13th International ACM SIGACCESS Conference on Computers and Accessibility, pp. 99–106. ACM, New York (2011)
9. Kacorri, H., Lu, P., Huenerfauth, M.: Evaluating facial expressions in American Sign Language animations for accessible online information. In: Stephanidis, C., Antona, M. (eds.) UAHCI 2013. LNCS, vol. 8009, pp. 510–519. Springer, Heidelberg (2013). https://doi.org/10.1007/978-3-642-39188-0_55
10. Mitchell, R.: How Many Deaf People are There in the United States. Gallaudet Research Institute, Graduate School and Professional Programs, Gallaudet University, Washington, DC (2004)
11. Morrissey, S., Way, A.: Manual labour: tackling machine translation for sign languages. Mach. Transl. **27**(1), 25–64 (2013)
12. Newkirk, D.: SignFont Handbook. Emerson and Associates, San Diego (1987)
13. Sutton, V.: The SignWriting Literacy Project. Presented at the Impact of Deafness on Cognition AERA Conference, San Diego, CA (1998)
14. Traxler, C.B.: The Stanford Achievement Test: national norming and performance standards for deaf and hard-of-hearing students. J. Deaf Stud. Deaf Educ. **5**(4), 337–348 (2000)
15. VCom3D. Sign Smith Studio. http://www.vcom3d.com/language/sign-smith-studio/. Accessed 10 July 2018
16. World Federation of the Deaf. WFD and WASLI Issue Statement on Signing Avatars. https://wfdeaf.org/news/wfd-wasli-issue-statement-signing-avatars/. Accessed 15 Jan 2019
17. Yi, B., Wang, X., Harris, F.C., Dascalu, S.M.: sEditor: a prototype for a sign language interfacing system. IEEE Trans. Hum. Mach. Syst. **44**(4), 499–510 (2014)

Accessibility or Usability of the User Interfaces for Visually Impaired Users? A Comparative Study

Kamran Khowaja(✉) ⓘ, Dena Al-Thani ⓘ, Aboubakr Aqle ⓘ,
and Bilikis Banire ⓘ

Division of Information and Computing, Technology,
College of Science and Engineering, Hamad Bin Khalifa University, Doha, Qatar
kamran.khowaja@gmail.com, dalthani@hbku.edu.qa,
{aaqle,bbanire}@mail.hbku.edu.qa

Abstract. The use of the Internet to search and browse information has increased in the recent past from the younger children to adults and older adults with or without any disability. The access to the information is becoming more common through the use of mobile apps as it is ubiquitous. This requires an evaluation to ensure that it can be used by everyone including people with disability. However, there is no generic set of guidelines or heuristics that can be used by anyone to evaluate an interface in terms of usability and accessibility. This paper provides expert evaluation of two apps i.e. Accessible Qatar and LinkedIn using a set of heuristics by Gómez and colleagues, and Web Content Accessibility Guidelines (WCAG) 2.0 in terms of both usability and accessibility evaluation. The data analysis was carried out based on the usability problems and the opinion of experts using the system usability scale (SUS) questionnaire. The usability problems were analysed based on the number of usability problems found and the average severity ratings of the usability problems. The results show that the most frequently violated heuristics from the usability heuristics are *visibility* and *recognition*. The average severity rating of all the problems found using usability heuristics set is a mix of both minor and major. The results also show that the most frequently violated WCAG 2.0 guideline alternatives; the average severity rating of all the problems found using WCAG 2.0 guidelines is major.

Keywords: Visually impaired user · Heuristic evaluation ·
Accessibility guidelines · Web Content Accessibility Guidelines (WCAG) ·
Mobile heuristic · Interface evaluation

1 Introduction

There is a growing trend to make the desktop applications available for the mobile phones/web browsers so that they can be accessed anytime, and anywhere. It is because, the use of the internet for all types of users (children, adults, older adults) with/without disability/impairment has increased in recent years. The use of the website or any application (desktop/mobile phone) to browse user-specific information may

M. Antona and C. Stephanidis (Eds.): HCII 2019, LNCS 11572, pp. 268–283, 2019.
https://doi.org/10.1007/978-3-030-23560-4_20

become difficult for visually impaired users among other users if the website/application has not followed the accessibility guidelines. The Web Accessibility Initiative (WAI) of World Wide Web Consortium (W3C) often referred to as W3C-WAI develop standards for accessibility (W3C Web Accessibility Initiative [W3C WAI] 2019). They also develop supporting materials for an individual to understand and implement accessibility. The web standards produced by W3C are known as "W3C Recommendations". WAI has developed a number of recommendations, and web content accessibility guidelines (WCAG) is one of them. These guidelines are the most popular guidelines since 2000 when the first set of guidelines were made available. WCAG aims to address the accessibility of web pages and make web interaction available for people with disabilities (Web Content Accessibility Guidelines [WCAG] 2019).

Besides accessibility, for the developer working on an application, it is important to identify and fix the usability problems in the application before it is released for the potentials users to use (Yeratziotis and Zaphiris 2017). The potential users are typically involved towards the last stage of the application development, therefore, the domain experts are usually recruited to evaluate the applications on behalf of the potential users. Heuristic evaluation (HE) is one of the many ways in which expert evaluation of an application can be performed (Nielsen and Molich 1990). The HE is quick, cheap and easy to perform over other methods of expert evaluation which include cognitive walkthrough (Polson et al. 1992; Wharton et al. 1994), goals, operators, methods and selection (GOMS) (Card et al. 1983), keystroke-level model (Card et al. 1980), or using results of previous study as a basis to prove or disprove different aspects of the design.

This led to an interesting question that if accessibility or usability at their own is enough? And can they replace each other? From the search, a number of research studies were found in which researcher have emphasised that accessibility and usability cannot substitute each other (Horton and Leventhal 2008; Hudson 2004; Shneiderman 2000); this shows that while following the accessibility guidelines like WCAG 2.0, one can ensure that an application (standalone or web-based) is accessible by everyone including the person with any disability/impairment. On the contrary, following the usability guidelines like Nielsen's heuristics (Nielsen 1995; Nielsen and Molich 1990) or any other user interface guideline like eight golden rules of interface design by Shneiderman et al. (2009), one can ensure that usability problems have been fixed before anyone including the person with any disability/impairment starts using that application.

A study conducted by Correani et al. (2004) has highlighted that there are websites which fulfil the success criteria of accessibility guidelines but lack to meet the usability guidelines due to which users may face difficulty in terms of interaction with the websites.

To the best of our knowledge, there is no specialised set of heuristics or guidelines that can be used to evaluate interfaces for visually impaired users in terms of both the usability as well as accessibility.

In our previous research (Aqle et al. 2018), a search engine (SE) currently being developed as a part of our ongoing research for visually impaired users, was evaluated for both accessibility and usability. The SE has limited functionalities (no images and videos). The SE was evaluated by the experts using WCAG 2.0 and a set of heuristics by Nielsen (1995). Both of these sets have different purposes and cannot replace each other but can complement each other. This was seen in the results as well. Although the results suggested that both sets contributed to the identification of usability issues that had to be fixed before an experimental evaluation with the visually impaired users was carried out. It was realised that one application is not enough to generalise the results on what to do with the evaluation of the systems. Therefore, this research builds on our existing research with an aim to present an expert evaluation of two mobile apps namely Accessible Qatar and LinkedIn. The mobile apps have been carefully chosen in a way that they may be useful for visually impaired users in their daily life. Nielsen's set is generic and not preferred for the evaluation of mobile apps, therefore, a specialised set of heuristic by Gómez et al. (2014) and WCAG 2.0 guidelines are used in this research to evaluate mobile apps in terms of both usability and accessibility.

2 Related Work

2.1 Web Content Accessibility Guidelines (WCAG)

The WCAG 1.0 was released back in 1999 and mainly provided accessibility for the static web pages. The W3C recommendation of WCAG 2.0 was published in December 2008 so that it can be applied on different web technologies and can be tested using a combination of automated tests through an application (web accessibility evaluation tool list[1]) and manual evaluation by a human subject. The WCAG 2.1 is a recent W3C recommendation and was released in June 2018.

The foundation of WCAG 2.0 is based on four principles namely, perceivable, operable, understandable, and robust (Web Content Accessibility Guidelines [WCAG] 2019). Each principle has one or more guideline; there are 12 guidelines altogether. The researchers, developer among others should target each of these guidelines to make content accessible by people with different disabilities (Ellis and Mike 2011). It is to be noted that these guidelines at their own are not testable but each of these guidelines has one or more success criterion from a total of 61 success criterion. Each success criterion is individually testable in terms of the requirements and three levels of conformance: (1) A is the lowest, (2) AA, and (3) AAA is the highest (Caldwell et al. 2008). WCAG 2.1 includes 17 new success criterion which is part of 12 guidelines of WCAG 2.0.

Since WCAG 2.1 has been recently released and it may take time for companies to adopt new success criterion and ensure that their web content complies with the WCAG 2.1 guidelines. Therefore, WCAG 2.0 is used in this research. The conformance of WCAG 2.0 is widely used for web accessibility evaluation (Vigo et al. 2013). The use of the automated tool for the web accessibility evaluation is always subject to criticism as they can produce incorrect or misleading results (Abou-Zahra et al. 2017; Ivory and Chevalier 2002; Vigo et al. 2013). The automated tool can only assist than determining the accessibility. Therefore, human judgment is needed for the evaluation. The human subject referred to as an expert can manually check web content against all the guidelines as a part of the review process.

---

[1] http://www.w3.org/WAI/ER/tools/.

Following is a list of 12 guidelines from WCAG 2.0; these guidelines would be referred to as "accessibility guidelines" throughout the manuscript. One word in the complete name of each guideline is written inside a square bracket which represents the shorter names of the guidelines. These shorter names will be referred to in the subsequent sections.

1. Text [Alternatives]
2. [Time]-based Media
3. [Adaptable]
4. [Distinguishable]
5. [Keyboard] Accessible
6. [Enough] Time
7. Seizures and Physical Reactions [S and PR]
8. [Navigable]
9. [Readable]
10. [Predictable]
11. Input [Assistance]
12. [Compatible]

2.2   Set of Heuristics by Gómez et al. (2014)

Gómez et al. (2014) have compiled a set of heuristic evaluation checklists readapted for the mobile interface. The authors used existing heuristics from the desktop heuristic evaluation as a base, rearranged and expanded with the best practices and recommendations for a mobile interface which were missing in the existing heuristics. Following is a list of 13 heuristics which include 230 subheuristics; these heuristics would be referred to as "usability heuristics" throughout the manuscript. The first 10 heuristics are from desktop heuristics, while, the remaining 3 heuristics are taken from the mobile interfaces. From the subheuristics, 158 are based on the compilation of subheuristics from traditional general heuristic checklists and 72 are based on the compilation of mobile-specific subheuristics. One word in each complete name of the heuristic is written in a square bracket which represent the shorter names of the heuristics. These shorter names will be referred to in the subsequent sections.

1. [Visibility] of system status
2. [Match] between system and the real world
3. User [control] and freedom
4. [Consistency] and standards
5. [Error] prevention
6. [Recognition] rather than recall
7. [Flexibility] and efficiency of us
8. Aesthetic and [minimalist] design
9. Help users recognize, diagnose, and [recover] from errors
10. Help and [documentation]
11. [Skills]
12. Pleasurable and respectful [interaction] with the user
13. [Privacy]

2.3 Screen Readers

There are different screen readers available; some of them are free to use while the other needs to be purchased before it can be used.

Job Access with Speech (JAWS). JAWS is the world's most popular screen reader, developed for visually impaired users (Job Access With Speech [JAWS] 2019). Unfortunately, the trial version can only be installed and used on one personal computer (PC) for a week/month time. For the personal use, a visually impaired user can buy an annually 'home annual license' for $90 or buy a perpetual version for $1000 for personal/non-commercial purpose. Both paid versions of the licenses can be installed and used on three PCs only which means it cannot be used on the smartphones.

NonVisual Desktop Access (NVDA). NVDA allows visually impaired users and blind users to interact with the Windows operating system and many third-party applications for free (NonVisual Desktop Access [NVDA], 2019). As mentioned on their website, "We're free by principle, not by merit! We strive for a world where EVERYONE has equal access to the life-changing benefits of technology—not just the privilege." However, they do provide two options for those who are interested to willingly contribute to the better cause. The first option is 'one-off donation' of a fixed amount in Australian currency which include $30, $50, $100, $250 or other amount based on your preferences. The second option is 'monthly donation' of a fixed amount in Australian currency which include $5, $10, $20, $50 or other amount based on your preferences. Although, NVDA is free for users to use it can only be used on the PCs but not on the smartphones.

TalkBack Accessibility Service. TalkBack is developed by Google and it is being used as a screen reader on the smartphones. TalkBack service provides spoken feedback to the users so it allows them to operate its smartphone without having a look at the screen. The advantages of using TalkBack screen reader are: (1) it is pre-installed with Android operating system (OS), (2) it is free, and (3) it is easy to turn on/off TalkBack screen reader in device settings.

3 Study Design

3.1 Participants and Recruitment

The number of experts to be recruited should be at least three to identify 75% or more problems in the system to be evaluated (Nielsen and Molich 1990). Considering, this requirement and for the consistency in terms of the experts' profile, all experts who participated in our earlier research were invited from which two accepted our invitation. We used an approach of Snowballing to identify more participants and two more experts confirmed their participation. The recruited participants include researchers and faculty members at the university level and have used or use Nielsen's heuristics and WCAG guidelines for the interface design and evaluation (Table 1).

Table 1. Demographic information of the experts

Characteristic	Values
Gender	2 Female, 2 Male
Education	2 PhD, 2 Master's degree
Occupation	2 Employed, 2 PhD Student
HCI Courses	All
HCI experience	2 Expert, 2 Advanced
Screen readers	3 JAWS, 3 NVDA

3.2   Mobile Apps Used

Two Mobile Apps were to be selected for use by the experts to perform an evaluation; the criteria used to select apps is as follow:

1. The app is available on Apple App Store and Google Play Store
2. The app can be downloaded for free and used without any trial period
3. The app is of interest to visually impaired users (Hollier 2012)
4. Visually impaired users can use the app with minimal guidance

Based on the above-mentioned criteria, two apps are selected; the first app is Accessible Qatar. Accessible Qatar is a smartphone app and website where the disabled community is able to view the public and touristic locations and outlets in Qatar and see whether they are accessible and in what way. This research was carried out in Qatar and this app is particularly important in the local context as the number of people with disabilities (Qatari and non-Qatari) is increasing (Gulf Times, 2018).

The second app is LinkedIn mobile app which provides a faster way to tap into your professional world. It allows the user to get the latest news and updates related to their profession, provide a daily brief about users connected with you on the network, and an easy to get in touch with all of them. It may also be useful to establish connections with friends and companies to get updates regarding available jobs and their requirements (Hollier 2012).

3.3   Study Protocol

Following protocol was used as a part of this research:

1. An email was sent to the participants from our existing studies; they were informed that evaluation data submitted as a part of this research will remain anonymous. They were requested to respond to the email and inform about their willingness to be part of the evaluation process.
2. To recruit more participants in the replacement of declined request, an email was sent to new participants using snowball sampling.
3. The experiments were carried out face-to-face on campus. Each participant was given a briefing about the purpose of evaluation, introduction to both apps, and usability heuristics and accessibility guidelines to be used for the evaluation as a part of this research. They were informed about the identification of usability

problems in both the apps and the reporting process of those problems. For each usability problem they identify, they were asked to rate it from 0 to 4 (0 for 'not a problem', 1 for 'cosmetic', 2 for 'minor', 3 for 'major', and 4 for 'usability catastrophe').

4. They were asked to download, install and apps on their smartphones and enable 'TalkBack' accessibility feature on their smartphones to act as screen reader before using any of the mentioned apps. They were given two files; one to report usability problems based on the heuristics by Gomez, and another to report usability problems based on the WCAG guidelines. They were also given a softcopy of the System Usability Scale (SUS) questionnaire and were informed to fill-in once they have gone through both apps in detail and reported all the usability problems in the respective files. They were asked to carry out an evaluation at their own and submitted all three files through an email.

5. The SUS contains 10 statements to gather the opinion of an expert about the app they used. For each statement, expert need to select the best option from the scale of 1 referred to as 'strongly disagree' to 5 referred to as 'strongly agree'.

3.4   Data Analysis

Two data were gathered as a part of evaluation; the first is related to the usability problems in both apps, whereas the second one is related to their opinion using system usability scale (SUS) questionnaire. The data related to usability problems were analysed based on the following two parameters:

Number of Usability Problems Found. It is calculated as a sum of all the usability problems found by all the experts using each heuristic of Gómez and guidelines of WCAG.

Average Severity Ratings of the Usability Problems Found. It is calculated as an average of all the usability problems found by all the experts using each heuristic of Gómez and guidelines of WCAG.

System Usability Scale (SUS). The second analysis is carried out based on the SUS; it includes ten statements which are based on the Likert scale ('strongly disagree' as 1 to 'strongly agree' as 5) and provides an overall subjective assessment of any system. The usability measurements included in SUS cover the effectiveness, efficiency and user satisfaction. Following are the ten statements of SUS:

1. I think that I would like to use the app frequently.
2. I found the app unnecessarily complex.
3. I thought the app was easy to use.
4. I think that I would need the support of a technical person to be able to use the app.
5. I found the various functions in the app were well integrated.
6. I thought there was too much inconsistency in the app.
7. I would imagine that most people would learn to use the app very quickly.
8. I found the app very cumbersome to use.
9. I felt very confident using the app.
10. I needed to learn a lot of things before I could get going with the app.

4   Results

The results of evaluations based on usability heuristics and accessibility guidelines are discussed in the following sub-sections.

4.1   Overall Results

A total of 134 usability problems were found using usability heuristics and accessibility guidelines for Accessible Qatar and LinkedIn apps. The total number of usability problems found using usability heuristics for both apps is (N = 81, 60%), while the total number of usability problems found using accessibility guidelines for both apps is (N = 53, 40%).

Tables 2 and 3 shows the number of usability problems identified, its percentage within severity and percentage within usability heuristics (referred to as "GH" in the table) and accessibility heuristics (referred to as "WCAG") for Accessible Qatar and LinkedIn app respectively.

Table 2. Comparison of usability problems identified in Accessible Qatar app using usability heuristics (GH) and accessibility guidelines (WCAG)

		Accessible Qatar		Total issues
		GH	WCAG	
Severity Rating (SR)	**Count of SR 4**	**5**	**4**	**9**
	% within Severity	55.56	44.44	100.00
	% within Set	9.43	11.43	10.23
	Count of SR 3	**21**	**9**	**30**
	% within Severity	70.00	30.00	100.00
	% within Set	39.62	25.71	34.09
	Count of SR 2	**23**	**22**	**45**
	% within Severity	51.11	48.89	100.00
	% within Set	43.40	62.86	51.14
	Count of SR 1	**4**	**0**	**4**
	% within Severity	100.00	0.00	100.00
	% within Set	7.55	0.00	4.55
Total	**Total count**	**53**	**35**	**88**
	% covered	60.23	39.77	100.00

Table 3. Comparison of usability problems identified in the LinkedIn app using usability heuristics (GH) and accessibility guidelines (WCAG)

		LinkedIn		Total issues
		GH	WCAG	
Severity Rating (SR)	**Count of SR 4**	**4**	**0**	**4**
	% within Severity	100.00	0.00	100.00
	% within Set	14.29	0.00	8.70
	Count of SR 3	**17**	**16**	**33**
	% within Severity	51.52	53.33	100.00
	% within Set	60.71	88.89	71.74
	Count of SR 2	**7**	**2**	**9**
	% within Severity	77.78	4.44	100.00
	% within Set	25.00	11.11	19.57
	Count of SR 1	**0**	**0**	**0**
	% within Severity	0.00	0.00	0.00
	% within Set	0.00	0.00	0.00
Total	**Total count**	**28**	**18**	**46**
	% covered	60.87	39.13	100.00

4.2   Usability Heuristics

Figures 1 and 2 show the usability problems identified and average severity ratings of the identified problems for each heuristic proposed by Gómez et al. (2014). The number of usability problems identified is represented using the vertical axis on the left side, while the average severity ratings of all the usability problems identified are represented using the vertical axis on the right side.

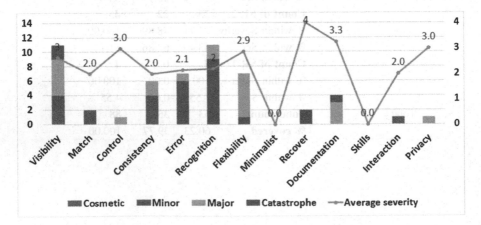

Fig. 1. Number of usability problems and average severity ratings found using usability heuristics in Accessible Qatar app

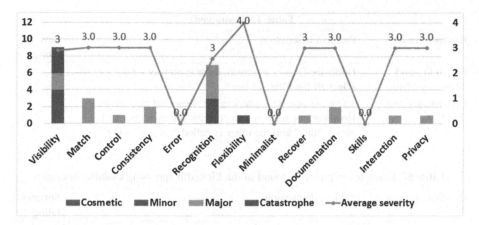

Fig. 2. Number of usability problems and average severity ratings found using usability heuristics in the LinkedIn app

Each heuristic in a usability heuristics is associated with a stacked column which represents the number of usability problems identified for one or more of the four severity ratings using different colours (blue for cosmetic, red for minor, green for major, and purple for catastrophe). The line connecting markers in a circle and running on a horizontal axis represents the average severity ratings of all the usability problems identified.

Number of Usability Problems Found. The most commonly broken heuristics for Accessible Qatar app are *visibility* and *recognition* (each has N = 11) followed by *error* and *flexibility* heuristics (each has N = 7) and *consistency* heuristic (N = 6). Some comments of the most commonly broken heuristics are presented in Table 4. The most commonly broken heuristics for the LinkedIn app are *visibility* heuristics (N = 9) followed by *recognition* heuristic (N = 7). Some comments of the most commonly broken heuristics are presented in Table 5.

Table 4. Examples of problems found in Accessible Qatar app using usability heuristics

Heuristic broken	Problem description	Severity rating
Visibility of system status	When using the search feature, the system doesn't give any feedback once the results are displayed. Hence, the screen reader user will not be able to know that the results are displayed on the screen	4
Recognition rather than recall	Under specific news detail screen, there is an icon to view photos related to the news. When clicks on the icon, it's read as "unlabelled button"	2
Error prevention	Under "Sign up" screen, the textbox of "Email" is read as "Editing, edit box"	2

(*continued*)

Table 4. (*continued*)

Heuristic broken	Problem description	Severity rating
Flexibility and efficiency of use	Under the favourites screen, there is no way for the user to select all the filters at one	3
Consistency and standards	There are two type filters in list view and map view. However, the naming can confuse the users as one is called 'filter' and the other is called 'category filter'	3

Table 5. Examples of problems found in the LinkedIn app using usability heuristics

Heuristic broken	Problem description	Severity rating
Visibility of system status	When clicking a profile photo there is no feedback	4
Visibility of system status	When message alert comes, the voiceover doesn't read it. Thus, the user will not be able to know that an alert message has popped up on the screen	4
Recognition rather than recall	Clicking on "Kudos username" button is read as "Quick comment button". It's confusing	2
Recognition rather than recall	Clicking on an image of those who viewed your profiles in a private, it is read as "group people image" which does not indicate anything about what it is	2

Average Severity Ratings of the Usability Problems Found. The visual analysis of the average severity ratings for Accessible Qatar app shows that the majority are problems are a combination of minor (N = 23, 43%) and major (N = 21, 40%) respectively. The visual analysis of the average severity ratings for the LinkedIn app shows that the majority are problems are major (N = 17, 61%).

4.3   Accessibility Guidelines

Figures 3 and 4 show the usability problems identified and average severity ratings of the identified problems for each accessibility guideline. For the consistency, the format of presenting the usability problems and their severity ratings are the same as of Figs. 1 and 2. Although each expert classified the identified usability problem into 1 of the 51 success criterion, space is limited to show all the information at once. Thus, all the related success criterion were grouped together and instead usability problems are shown using 12 guidelines.

Number of Usability Problems Found. The most commonly broken heuristics for Accessible Qatar app are assistance (N = 11) followed by *predictable* (N = 8) and *alternatives* (N = 7). Some comments of the most commonly broken heuristics are presented in Table 6. The most commonly broken heuristics for the LinkedIn app are *alternatives* (N = 4) followed by *time* and *navigable* (each has N = 3). Some comments of the most commonly broken guidelines are presented in Table 7.

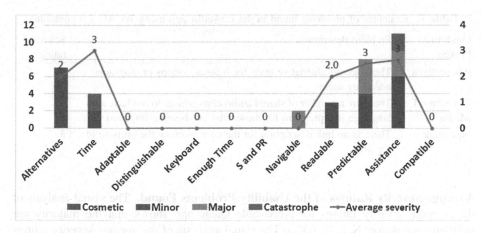

Fig. 3. Number of usability problems and average severity ratings found using WCAG 2.0 in Accessible Qatar app

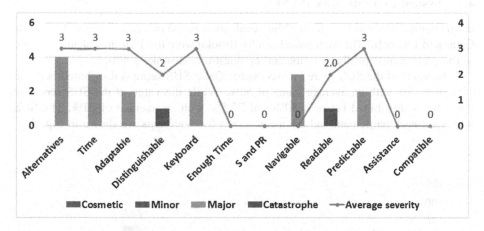

Fig. 4. Number of usability problems and average severity ratings found using WCAG 2.0 in the LinkedIn app

Table 6. Examples of problems found in Accessible Qatar app using WCAG 2.0 guidelines

Guideline broken	Problem description	Severity rating
Predictable	Some navigation buttons are not working when clicked. Such as 'alphabetical and Distance links' and this makes the user to be confused	3
Alternatives	When viewing the photos related to the news, there is no description of each photo which makes it difficult for the user to understand	3

Table 7. Examples of problems found in the LinkedIn app using WCAG 2.0 guidelines

Guideline broken	Problem description	Severity rating
Alternatives	There are no alternative texts for images, videos or diagrams added by users	3
Time-based Media	There are a number of shared audio clips which do not have sign language interpretation for those who are hearing-impaired	3
Navigable	There is no link description for the user to know the purpose of the link	3

Average Severity Ratings of the Usability Problems Found. The visual analysis of the average severity ratings for Accessible Qatar app shows that the majority are problems are minor (N = 22, 63%). The visual analysis of the average severity ratings for the LinkedIn app shows that the majority are problems are major (N = 16, 89%).

4.4 System Usability Scale (SUS)

In this paper, SUS was used for usability evaluation of the two mobile apps: Accessible Qatar and LinkedIn. The SUS guidelines by Brooke were used for the calculation base of the participants' feedback to the survey questions (Brooke 1996).

The value of the SUS score for Accessible Qatar SUS score is distributed between 45% and 55% with an average value of 50%. While the value of the SUS score for LinkedIn is distributed between 50% and 77.5% with an average of 61%. The SUS scores for each participant and the mean scores for both apps are shown in Fig. 5.

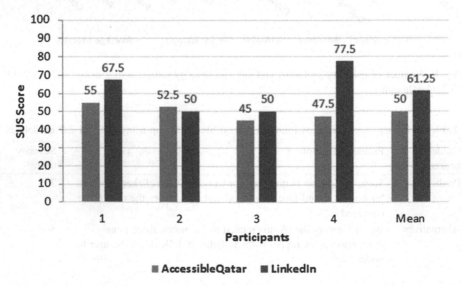

Fig. 5. Accessible Qatar and LinkedIn SUS Scores by participants

The average SUS scores for both mobile apps i.e. Accessible Qatar and LinkedIn are shown in Fig. 6. There are different ways to interpret the SUS scores (Sauro 2018); these include percentiles, grades, adjectives, acceptability, and promoters and detractors. In this research, SUS scores are interpreted using percentiles which also include the grade as well.

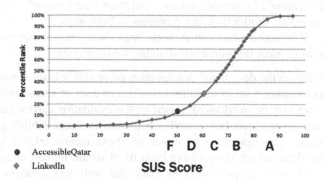

Fig. 6. Mean SUS Scores of Accessible Qatar and LinkedIn

The average SUS score of Accessible Qatar is 50, while the average SUS score of LinkedIn is 61.12. According to the grading scale interpretation of SUS scores by Sauro and Lewis (2016), Accessible Qatar and LinkedIn have "D" and "F" grade respectively. This shows that Accessible Qatar and LinkedIn mobile apps need major improvements and enhancements to meet the minimum usability scale requirements.

5 Conclusion

This research presented an expert evaluation of two apps i.e. Qatar Accessibility and LinkedIn using a set by heuristics by usability heuristics and accessibility guidelines. It was carried out as an extension of our previous study in which a web search interface (currently being developed as a part of our ongoing research) for visually impaired users was evaluated using a set of heuristics by Nielsen and accessibility guidelines. The key findings are as follows:

1. The analysis of results revealed that they were similar to our previous research (Aqle et al. 2018). The usability heuristics and accessibility guidelines both contributed to the identification of usability problems which needs to be fixed in the apps for better interaction experience of the user with both of the apps.
2. In comparison to Nielsen's heuristics, the usability heuristics allowed identification of usability problems especially based on three new heuristics namely, Skills, Pleasurable and respectful interaction with the user, and Privacy. Although, these three heuristics contributed less but supported experts in finding major issues which had otherwise remained undetected.

3. The *visibility* and *recognition* usability heuristics were more commonly broken heuristics in both apps. The ignorance of these and other heuristics means the important usability problem would remain undetected.
4. The *alternatives* guideline was highly broken guideline in both apps.
5. There are a usability heuristics like "error prevention", and "help users recognize, diagnose, and recover from errors" which are similar to accessibility guidelines like "error identification", "error suggestion", and "error prevention". Such heuristics/ guidelines revealed similar usability problems in both apps.
6. The mean SUS score shows that both apps need major improvements and enhancements to meet the minimum usability requirements.

While working on the design and development of an app, it is often possible to give more emphasis on either a set of usability heuristics or a set of accessibility guidelines such that other set may be overlooked. Based on the evaluation carried out as a part of our previous and this research, both usability heuristics and accessibility guidelines are equally important. The ignorance of either of them means critical usability and accessibility problems which should have been fixed would remain undetected.

WCAG is the standard guidelines to make the web accessible to people with disabilities when it comes to the implementation/evaluation of the accessibility of the content. However, the set of usability heuristics varies from the domain to domain; for instance, heuristics for deaf web user experience (Yeratziotis and Zaphiris 2017), heuristics for children with ASD (Khowaja et al. 2015), heuristics for child e-learning (Alsumait and Al-Osaimi 2009) among others. Thus, it is important for researchers to identify an appropriate set of heuristics to identify relevant usability problems in the user interface.

In future, the researchers can evaluate more apps especially in their local context. They can also use WCAG 2.1 guidelines for the evaluation of web content.

References

Job Access With Speech [JAWS] (2019). http://www.freedomscientific.com/products/software/jaws/

Abou-Zahra, S., Steenhout, N., Keen, L.: Selecting web accessibility evaluation tools (2017). https://www.w3.org/WAI/test-evaluate/tools/selecting/

Alsumait, A., Al-Osaimi, A.: Usability heuristics evaluation for child e-learning applications. Paper presented at the Proceedings of the 11th International Conference on Information Integration and Web-Based Applications and Services (2009)

Aqle, A., Khowaja, K., Al-Thani, D.: Accessibility or usability of InteractSE? A heuristic based approach to evaluate proposed search engine for the visually impaired users. Paper presented at the Eighth International Conference on Innovative Computing Technology (INTECH 2018), London, UK (2018)

System Usability Scale (SUS): a quick-and-dirty method of system evaluation user information, 19172650 (1996)

Caldwell, B., Reid, L.G., Vanderheiden, G.: Web Content Accessibility Guidelines (WCAG) 2.0 (2008)

Card, S.K., Moran, T.P., Newell, A.: The keystroke-level model for user performance time with interactive systems. Commun. ACM **23**(7), 396–410 (1980)

Card, S.K., Newell, A., Moran, T.P.: The psychology of human–computer interaction (1983). https://dl.acm.org/citation.cfm?id=578027

Correani, F., Leporini, B., Paternò, F.: Supporting Web Usability for Vision Impaired Users. Springer, Berlin (2004). https://doi.org/10.1007/978-3-540-30111-0_20

Ellis, K., Mike, K.: Disability and New Media. Routledge, New York (2011). https://doi.org/10.1007/978-1-84800-050-6_21

Gómez, R.Y., Caballero, D.C., Sevillano, J.-L.: Heuristic evaluation on mobile interfaces: a new checklist. Sci. World J. **2014**, 434326 (2014). https://doi.org/10.1155/2014/434326

Hollier, S.: SociAbility: Social Media for People with a Disability. Media Access Australia, Ultimo (2012)

Horton, S., Leventhal, L.: Universal usability. In: Harper, S., Yesilada, Y. (eds.) Web Accessibility, pp. 346–355. Springer, London (2008)

Hudson, W.: Inclusive design. Interactions **11**(4), 55–56 (2004). https://doi.org/10.1145/1005261.1005278

Ivory, M.Y., Chevalier, A.: A Study of Automated Web Site Evaluation Tools. Department of Computer Science. University of Washington, Washington, DC (2002)

Khowaja, K., Salim, S.S., Asemi, A.: Heuristics to evaluate interactive systems for children with Autism Spectrum Disorder (ASD). PLoS ONE **10**(7), e0132187 (2015). https://doi.org/10.1371/journal.pone.0132187

Nielsen, J.: Ten usability heuristics (1995). http://www.nngroup.com/articles/ten-usability-heuristics/

Nielsen, J., Molich, R.: Heuristic evaluation of user interfaces. Paper presented at the Proceedings of the SIGCHI Conference on Human Factors in Computing Systems: Empowering People (1990)

NoName (2018). Qatar's efforts to help people with disabilities highlighted. Retrieved from https://www.gulf-times.com/story/591963/Qatar-s-efforts-to-help-people-with-disabilities-h

NonVisual Desktop Access [NVDA], NVDA (2019). https://www.nvaccess.org/about-nvda/

Polson, P.G., Lewis, C., Rieman, J., Wharton, C.: Cognitive walkthroughs: a method for theory-based evaluation of user interfaces. Int. J. Man Mach. Stud. **36**(5), 741–773 (1992)

Sauro, J.: MeasuringU: 5 ways to interpret a SUS Score (2018). https://measuringu.com/interpret-sus-score/

Sauro, J., Lewis, J.R.: Chapter 8: Standardized usability questionnaires. In: Sauro, J., Lewis, J.R. (eds.) Quantifying the User Experience, 2nd edn, pp. 185–248. Morgan Kaufmann, Boston (2016)

Shneiderman, B.: Universal usability. Commun. ACM **43**(5), 84–91 (2000). https://doi.org/10.1145/332833.332843

Shneiderman, B., Plaisant, C., Cohen, M., Jacobs, S.: Designing the User Interface: Strategies for Effective Human-Computer Interaction. Addison-Wesley Publishing Company, Reading (2009)

Vigo, M., Brown, J., Conway, V.: Benchmarking web accessibility evaluation tools. Paper presented at the Proceedings of the 10th International Cross-Disciplinary Conference on Web Accessibility—W4A 2013, Rio de Janeiro, Brazil (2013)

W3C Web Accessibility Initiative [W3C WAI]: W3C-WAI (2019). https://www.w3.org/WAI/

Web Content Accessibility Guidelines [WCAG]: WCAG (2019). https://www.w3.org/WAI/standards-guidelines/wcag/

Wharton, C., Rieman, J., Lewis, C., Polson, P.: The cognitive walkthrough: a practitioner's guide. In: Usability Inspection Methods. Wiley, New York (1994)

Yeratziotis, A., Zaphiris, P.: A heuristic evaluation for deaf web user experience (HE4DWUX). Int. J. Hum. Comput. Interact. **34**(3), 195–217 (2017). https://doi.org/10.1080/10447318.2017.1339940

Reflections on Elements of a Game Design Model Applied to Inclusive Digital Games

Patricia da Silva Leite(✉), Ana Paula Retore, and Leonelo Dell Anhol Almeida

Postgraduate Program in Technology and Society (PPGTE),
Federal University of Technology (UTFPR), Curitiba, Paraná, Brazil
patriciasleite@gmail.com, aretore@alunos.utfpr.edu.br,
leoneloalmeida@utfpr.edu.br

Abstract. Cultural relevance of digital games characterizes them as social objects. In such a way digital games are created based on our culture and society, at the same time they contributed to shaping our world. Thus, digital games need to be accessible to all members of society, including people with disabilities. Based on those points, we discuss how a game development tool, such as game design models, can be articulated with social inclusion principles. This research proposes a series of critical reflections about how digital game elements can be used and thought also regarding people with disabilities. In this way, it is possible to expand game accessibility, and digital game development proceeds towards inclusive digital games.

Keywords: Social inclusion · Inclusive digital games · Accessibility · Game design models · Critical analysis

1 Introduction

Social, cultural, political, economic and historical aspects permeated in digital games by society, make possible to understand these artifacts as social objects which present unfoldings in several areas of human development and knowledge [11,14]. The social relevance of digital games indicates that these artifacts must be accessible to all members of society, including people with disabilities, particularly whereas games be used in other areas beyond entertainment, such as education, health, politics, among others [4,38].

To accomplish the needs and requirements of people with disabilities in games, several researchers and institutions advocate for game accessibility. Their purpose is to contribute to the development of games that have as intended public also people with disabilities, and to contribute to the inclusion of these people in the gamer community as well as in society. Examples of such researches involve Grammenos, Savidis and Stephanidis [12] - which research involves the development of universally accessible games (which are games designed to adapt to player characteristics and abilities without particular adjustments); Yuan, Folmer and Harris Jr. [38] - a survey about 2010's state-of-the-art of digital

© Springer Nature Switzerland AG 2019
M. Antona and C. Stephanidis (Eds.): HCII 2019, LNCS 11572, pp. 284–300, 2019.
https://doi.org/10.1007/978-3-030-23560-4_21

game accessibility; and Westin, Bierre, Gramenos and Hinn [36] - summary of researches between 2005 and 2010 about game accessibility. There are also institutions as International Game Developers Association (IGDA)[1], with Game Accessibility Special Interest Group (GA-SIG)[2] – a group created with the goal of develop digital games playable for everyone and take special considerations for gamers with disabilities; and The AbleGamers Foundation[3] – a nonprofit organization with use digital games to provide social inclusion to people with disabilities.

Considering digital games and their social role, there are several ways to study and develop them, such as by gender, platform, narrative, and so on. There are also some schemes to contribute to accomplishing those tasks, among them are game design models, which are epistemic tools for researching, designing and producing digital games [26].

Taking into account game accessibility researches and movements, digital games as social objects whose access and use is a right of every person, and game development tools; we argue about the possibility to analyze digital game elements, organized in a game design model, regarding people with disabilities context. This analysis involves an articulation of digital game elements and social inclusion principles of Convention on the Rights of Persons with Disabilities (CRPD) [34], henceforth CRPD principles. Our motivation is to reflect on social inclusion principles and to expand game accessibility issues from those carried out by the researchers and institutions cited above; while articulating with a game design model.

It is important to highlight that the game design model used in following sections was selected through comparative analysis between three models: Elemental Tetrad [27], Design, Dynamics, Experience (DDE) [35], and Artifact-Experience Model (AEM) [20]. Our goal were to select a model to support the discussions between game elements and social inclusion principles.

The articulation performed in this research consists on an applied investigation, in accordance with critical analysis method, which is based on the argument that such practice refers to informed judgment on a subject, involving theoretical, practical and reflexive tasks, in order to contribute to analysis and development of artifacts that consider cultural experiences and technical issues [5,7]. By adopting critical analysis method, which is aligned with Human-Computer Interaction (HCI) approaches that involve human sciences and is also concerned with contextual issues [5,13], this paper explores discussions about production and consumption of digital games, regarding with people with disabilities, intending to present other perspectives on the relationship between social inclusion principles and digital games.

This research results in a set of contributions and reflections for the design of inclusive digital games for people with disabilities. This contribution is highlighted by the analysis of 10 examples of elements, in several games, from the

---

[1] https://www.igda.org/.
[2] https://igda-gasig.org/.
[3] https://ablegamers.org/.

perspective of social inclusion principles, intending to present some indications of the feasibility of designing inclusive digital games.

This paper is organized as follows: the second section presents three game design models, their descriptions and our comparative method to select a game design model; the third section presents the social inclusion principles used in this paper, to later establish the relationship between these principles and game elements organized in the selected game design model; the fourth section presents our discussions on how it is possible to articulate elements of the selected game design model with social inclusion principles, articulation performed adopting critical analysis method and examples of that articulation; finally, the last section presents our final remarks and further research appointments.

2 Game Design Models

There are several schemes and models to comprehend, study, structure and produce digital games [26]. Examples of them are game design models – "abstract representations which provide a vocabulary and a set of concepts to support a team to think, analyze and design digital games in a formal process, over the game development process" [8, p. 174].

This research present and discuss three game design models: Elemental Tetrad [27], Design, Dynamics, Experience (DDE) [35], and Artifact-Experience Model (AEM) [20]. Our goal is to select a model to support our main discussion: articulate game elements, organized in a model, with inclusion principles. It's important to highlight that the conducted game design models analysis takes into account the role of persons involved in the game development process, not the players' perspective, sellers or reviewers of concluded games.

To select a game design model, we use a Comparative Analysis Method, which goal is to verify common points or explain divergences between groups or phenomena [22]. In this research, we analyze and compare the models with the following criteria and classification:

1. **How profound is concepts definition?** To this criterion, we consider each definition component: description text, their connection with game elements, and examples. We use these components to analyze: (a) game element detailing; (b) game element relation with other researches (e.g. common points, differences, and divergences); and (c) theoretical foundation, theoretical argumentation, and detected or known limitations on the game element;
2. **Which model better satisfies the digital game's definition used in this research?** In this criterion, we analyze the best set of model's elements to outline digital games as an artifact. To accomplish that, we based on the concept that a game is "a type of play activity, conducted in the context of a pretended reality, in which the participant(s) try to achieve at least one arbitrary, nontrivial goal by acting in accordance with rules." [4, p. 3]. It's important to highlight that these models have different elements compositions, making impracticable to compare them based only on their elements.

Therefore our analysis considers the model's elements group to constitute game as an artifact (our object of interest).

We emphasize that it was not our goal to create a new game design model after these analysis. Instead, we intend to choose a game design model to support our discussions.

2.1   Elemental Tetrad

Elemental Tetrad (Fig. 1) is a model created by Schell [27] to present and organize elements that he considers as game's elements. That model presents four elements: mechanics, story, aesthetics and technology.

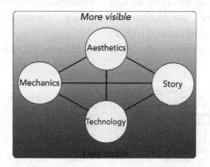

Fig. 1. Elemental Tetrad by Schell [27]

Schell explains that model's elements arrangement doesn't have as goal present an element' relevance between others, thereby all elements have the same relevance level [27]. This model is arranged to illustrate the "visibility gradient", that is, the level in which an element is perceived by the player. Thus, model' elements lower levels indicate they are less "visible" to players than higher levels elements (Fig. 1). Tetrad elements are defined as follows:

- **Mechanics:** Comprehends game procedures and rules. This element describes game goals and how players can achieve that. According to Schell, it is the mechanics that differentiate games from other entertainment artifacts such as books and movies [27];
- **Story:** It is the sequence of events that unfold in the game. According to the author, a story can be linear and predetermined or branching and emerging;
- **Aesthetics:** It is related to the appearance, sounds, smells, tastes, and sensations provided by the game in the gaming experience;
- **Technology:** Any material or interaction that makes the game possible as paper and pencil, plastic chits or computers. The game technology provides or prevent the creation of different types of interaction, applying diverse mechanics, stories, and aesthetics.

2.2 Design, Dynamics, Experience (DDE)

Walk, Görlich and Barrett's [35] work discuss some game design models, such as Mechanics, Dynamics, and Aesthetics (MDA) [15] and Elemental Tetrad [27], for then proposes DDE. To overcome MDA's limitations and to restructure this model, the author's goals are to encompass other game development aspects, which involves the production of a game as an artifact, and also players perceptions [35]. Thereby, the authors' goals with DDE is to provide a game design tool guided to player experience, not to game's functional units [35].

Following DDE sections: "Design" is related to game elements directly controlled by the game development team; "Dynamics" is related to game elements use and, players experience; "Experience" is directly related to players interaction result with the game [35].

Since is not our goal analyze model's elements related to the gaming experience, to analyze DDE, we examine only the "Design" section, which fulfills game's, as an artifact, elements (Fig. 2).

"Design" section has three subcategories: Blueprint, Mechanics and Interface.

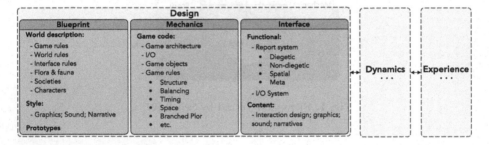

Fig. 2. DDE by Walk, Görlich and Barrett [35]. In the figure is DDE's basic concept, focusing on design section

- **Blueprint:** Related to the concepts and descriptions of the game world (culture, societies, physics, rules of the game, among others), art styles, narrative, characters, and sound;
- **Mechanics:** Related to codes, input and output data components, game rules implementation and game objects interaction;
- **Interface:** Related to the elements that are used to communicate the game world to the player; how it is, how it reacts and interacts with the player.

Based on Elemental Tetrad and DDE comparison, we consider DDE more appropriate to our goals in this research. We make that decision for the reason that DDE presents and incorporate Elemental Tetrad elements on is own structure. Besides that, Walk, Görlich and Barrett presents theoretical articulation with other research to DDE's creation and to support the presented concepts and elements. Although the Elemental Tetrad presents more detailed examples, we did not select this model in our analysis because we consider item 2 as a decisive selection criterion, which analyzes the set of elements in a model. Thus, as previously presented, the Elemental Tetrad's elements are incorporated into DDE's structure.

2.3 Artifact-Experience Model (AEM)

Proposed by Leite and Almeida [20], the Artifact-Experience Model (AEM) was created to connect gameplay with game elements. Based on the literature, the authors also present game elements concepts review. This review and the proposed model has as goal support communication in a game development team, and support game researchers. Considering AEM structure and our goal in this research, we will analyze only model's elements related to the game's structure as an artifact. Thus, we do not consider AEM's section related do gameplay (element presented into the model).

Leite and Almeida [20] discuss works such as Adams [4] and Schell [27] to indicate game elements considered into AEM. Between these elements, are Elemental Tetrad's elements. Based on that literature review, the authors compiled a game elements list, called "essential game elements", which are: technology; visual, aural and haptic elements (V.A.H.Es); narrative; goals; rules and mechanics [20].

Of this game elements list, the authors analyzed the articulation between them (Fig. 3). This articulation is detailed to indicate each element role to structure a game as an artifact. Thus, the AEM's section called "Game as an Artifact", can be comprehended as follows: to create a game as an artifact, it is necessary that the game world, delimited by their rules, be presented to the player by game's narrative and V.A.II.Es, elements that constitute game's simulated reality; to reach game goals, the player manipulates game mechanics and accomplishes actions into that simulated reality; lastly, V.A.H.Es, narrative, goals, rules, and mechanics are presented or limited by the game's technology, which is in charge to implement game elements and to provide players interaction with the game [20].

The AEM elements can be briefly understood as follows:

- **Technology:** Element used to present or express the game;
- **Visual, Aural and Haptic Elements (V.A.H.Es):** They cover the sensory elements of a game, which are related to the senses of sight, hearing and touch;
- **Narrative:** Story events that are narrated (counted or displayed) to the player. They are also non-interactive elements that present part of the story;
- **Goals:** Elements delimitated by game rules and the game world, defined by game's development team, and not trivial;
- **Rules:** A set of definitions and/or instructions accepted by players in the gaming experience;
- **Mechanics:** Refers to the elements with which players can interact to change the game's state. Mechanics also represent rules implementation, to provide resources to players to reach the game world goals.

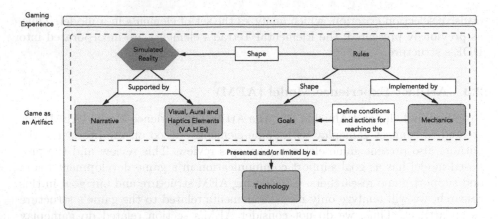

Fig. 3. Artifact-experience model adapted from Leite and Almeida [20]

After DDE - AEM comparison, we consider AEM more appropriate to structure game as an artifact, our goal with this analysis. The primary reasons for this choice are: the precise distinction to each model' elements; the relationships between each element; theoretical argumentation to elements relationships; and adequation to the game's concept used in this research. Based on these arguments, we consider that AEM presents game elements concepts and connections grounded by literature and relating to other works in the game area. Unlike DDE, in AEM, the theoretical argumentation, discussed examples, and concepts are also based on literature review, another analysis criteria. In consequence of foundation in the literature regarding elements' concepts, theoretical foundation, and elements' connections, AEM's elements set presents better articulation when compared to DDE; and more adequate to the game's concept used in this research. These arguments corroborate our choice to AEM as a game design model used in the following sections.

3   Social Inclusion Principles and Inclusive Digital Games

Inclusive digital games are designed considering as intended public also people with disabilities, their elements need to be used as resources to support this development. Thus, it is relevant to consider these elements from the social inclusion principles perspective. The social inclusion principles, applied in this research, are based on principles presented on the Convention on the Rights of Persons with Disabilities (CRPD) [34].

Formally created in 2006, the CRPD had the signature of 158 countries [19]. Nowadays, CRPD is used as a reference to ensure human and fundamental rights of people with disabilities. CRPD is considered central to movements of rights of people with disabilities, as CRPD embraces human rights conceptions and acts as a tool that provides a structure to guide the proposing of national and international policies to build a more inclusive society [1,34].

Based on CRPD relevance to people with disabilities, our research used their general principles so, through them, consider game design elements. CRPD general principles are presented in their third article and organize a group of inseparable values to promote the social inclusion of people with disabilities. Table 1 shows CRPD principles used in this research and the name to reference them later:

Based on CRPD principles, which includes accessibility, we argue that game accessibility is an relevant stage for social inclusion of people with disabilities. Nevertheless, game accessibility is not sufficient. That reinforces this research relevance and the importance of inclusive digital games development.

4 Inclusive Digital Game Elements

Considering game design elements from the perspective of CRPD principles can help in the game development that goes towards to inclusion of people with disabilities. It is important to reiterate that the inclusion process of people with disabilities does not only occurs with the use of games by these people or their representation in games, since inclusion involves issues such as engagement and participation of people with disabilities. It is essential to consider how to design game elements for inclusive game development as part of a larger process, and regard people with disabilities not only as players but also as people with relevant roles in game development.

Following we propose reflections on how some of CRPD principles can be related to each element of the AEM in order to highlight how those principles can be achieved, even though CRPD principles act as a set of inseparable values. It is not our purpose to present prescriptive reflections or to exhaust the discussions about the relation between game design elements and CRPD principles. We intend to present our considerations and examples of how those connections can be achieved or recognized.

4.1 Technology

Inclusive digital game's technology is one that provides the implementation of resources that can increase the number of players who can experience the game, including people with and without disabilities. Thus, technology's features need to be considered in the game design process in order to reach as many players as possible; as well as technologies' different characteristics when compared to another one, such as the difference between arcades and consoles [20].

We understand this perspective about game technology as a contribution to the guidelines presented in digital games accessibility documents, such as the "Includification" [6] and the recommendations of the "Accessible Player Experiences (APX)" [2], an Includification's upgrade. We consider this a contribution because it is not guidelines' goal to present instructions about game design (although the recommendations may interfere in this process), but rather to

Table 1. CRPD principles

Principle code	Principle name	Description
P.AUTON	Respect for inherent dignity, individual autonomy including the freedom to make one's own choices, and independence of persons	This principle is related to people with disabilities interest and desire in their choices and decisions. Decisions based on their independence [28]
P.NDISC	Non-discrimination	Related to guaranteeing the participation of people with disabilities in social life activities, without any discrimination, so as not to, a priori, prevent their participation [28]
P.PARTIC	Full and effective participation and inclusion in society	Regarding the previous item, this principle indicates that people with disabilities should be included in the society and/or in the execution of roles. And in case of doubts of their capacity, they have the right to try to demonstrate their abilities and competencies [28]
P.DIVERS	Respect for difference and acceptance of persons with disabilities as part of human diversity and humanity	When this principle is ensured, it is asserted that there should be no discrimination and that there should be inclusion. That confirms that the principles listed here are interlinked [28]
P.EQUAL	Equality of opportunity	Is related to the issue of differences and elimination of production of inequality mechanisms, so that people with disabilities can use the services and activities of society, as well as people without disabilities [25]
P.ACCESS	Accessibility	Is an instrument for the exercise of other rights and is related to the access, entrance, and permanence to physical means (buildings, streets, squares, among others), media and communication systems, policies, services and programs implemented by society [25, 28]
P.GENDER	Equality between men and women, that in this research, in the light of Louro [21], will be adjusted to "equality between people of different gender identities"	Related to respect for each person's gender identity, as well as their autonomy and independence [28]
P.CHILD	Respect for the evolving capacities of children with disabilities and respect for the right of children with disabilities to preserve their identities	Principle created to highlight the vulnerability of children and to emphasize their potential, not their deficits [25]

solve technical problems identified by the community. In this way, our contribution goes towards considering the choice of technology for which the game will be available, a decision that interferes with the type of audience that will have access to the developed game and the game design process.

Examples of how game technology that can be related to CRPD principles P.AUTON (respect, autonomy, and freedom), P.NDISC (non-discrimination),

P.DIVERS (respect for differences), P.EQUAL (equality of opportunity) and P.ACCESS (accessibility) are games that allow remapping keys, so that people with or without disabilities can adjust the controls to their needs. Remapping keys is an accessibility guideline, and some examples are games such as *Injustice 2*[4], which offers completely remappable controls; and *Overcooked!*[5], which features control mappings options [3].

Another example is the zoom feature implemented in PlayStation 4, which allows, for example, people with low vision to increase the size of parts of the screen such as those that display texts, minimap or other elements [17].

Controller's types used by players are also part of the game's technology selection process. In this case, the use of inclusive technologies may involve considering controls such as the "Xbox Adaptive Controller"[6] and other software and hardware used to achieve accessibility. This game controller was developed in partnership with the community to meet players' needs with reduced mobility so that players can configure the physical control in the way that they need.

In all the previously mentioned examples, people have their differences respected (P.DIVERS); have autonomy and freedom to choose commands configuration or the use of resources (P.AUTON); are not discriminated, since that resources are not designed to assist a specific public but available to all people (P.NDISC); these resources also allow people with and without disabilities to use and enjoy the game (P.EQUAL); and finally, these examples demonstrate the implementation of accessibility guideline recommendations to enable more people to have access to games, such as configuration flexibility (P.ACCESS).

4.2   Visual, Aural and Haptic Elements (V.A.H.Es)

V.A.H.Es from CRPD principles perspective means to promote the articulated use of visual, aural and haptic resources so that players do not rely on only one of these resources to play, players are not harmed if they can not use one of these resources, and players are not favored if they can use all these resources. Game elements and characters are developed considering that they will not represent stereotypes, particularly of people with disabilities, be they, children or adults.

CRPD principles P.NDISC (non-discrimination), P.DIVERS (respect for differences) and P.GENDER (gender equality), can be perceived in the game *Overcooked!*, which includes among its characters people with different races, genres, and disabilities. In this game, characters selection displays only the characters' head, so that only characteristics like gender and race can be noticed. Other characteristics are identified only with level's beginning. In this way, the player will know all the character's characteristics only at playing, which makes it difficult to select a character in a discriminatory way (P.NDISC); and promotes that players realize that the characters with or without disability, man or woman, are all equally skilled to carry out the game activities (P.DIVERS and P.GENDER).

---

[4] https://www.injustice.com/.
[5] http://www.ghosttowngames.com/overcooked/.
[6] https://www.xbox.com/en-us/xbox-one/accessories/controllers/xbox-adaptive-controller.

Approaching V.A.H.Es from CRPD principles perspective may involve accessibility guidelines related to visual and hearing disabilities such as "Changeable Text Colors", "Changeable Font Sizes", "Color Blind Options", "Closed Captioning", among others [6]. However, we consider our proposal a contribution, in relation to accessibility guidelines, since it goes beyond technical aspects such as colors and visual, hearing and tactile feedback. Thus, our proposal also covers issues about representation and game world elements development towards the inclusion of people with disabilities.

4.3   Narrative

A narrative from CRPD principles perspective is the one that presents to the player stories and narrative experiences that can represent the diversity that exists in the world, so that players do not feel excluded or stereotyped, but rather engaged in a series of events that contribute to expressing diversity with respect and dignity.

Frequency Missing is an example of a game with inclusive narrative in relation to P.NDISC (non-discrimination), P.DIVERS (respect for differences), P.EQUAL (equality of opportunity) and P.ACCESS (accessibility). The game was designed to provide similar narrative experiences to people with and without visual disabilities, and its narrative was designed so that the story main elements were displayed with visual and aural elements (P.NDISC and P.DIVERS) [37]. *Frequency Missing* exemplified how a game that goes towards inclusion can contribute to people sharing experiences (P.EQUAL), without these resources harm the game's dynamics or appearance (P.ACCESS).

Inclusive narratives may be related to accessibility guidelines such as "Closed Captioning" and "Alternative Reactionary Inputs" [6], as they discuss ways to present the context of the game in a more accessible way. Thus, inclusive narratives development incorporates the technical issues of the accessibility guidelines.

Our proposal expands the accessibility guidelines in the sense that the construction of an inclusive narrative involves characters development that reflex the world's diversity, such as in the game *Mass Effect*[7], with the character Jeff "Joker" Moreau, and in the game *Grand Theft Auto V*[8], with the character Lester Crest [10]. Both characters are good examples of how the game narrative can meet the principles P.NDISC (non-discrimination) and P.DIVERS (respect for differences), since they are presented by their characteristics on that game world (ship's pilot and strategist), not their disabilities (mobility disabilities).

In addition, involvement and participation of people with disabilities during the process of developing game narrative elements (P.PARTIC), particularly in the story and the characters development, helps to avoid the creation of stereotyped characters or to provide incomplete or incorrect information (P.DIVERS). An example is a character on *Rogue Legacy*[9] with Ehlers-Danlos Syndrome

---

[7] https://www.masseffect.com/.
[8] https://www.rockstargames.com/V/.
[9] http://www.cellardoorgames.com/roguelegacy/.

(EDS) who, because of this deficiency, has a body more flexible than other characters; a game's advantage that hides the real effects of the disability and how it affects the life of persons with EDS [24]. An inclusive narrative, provide a more inclusive game not only in its development process, with people with disabilities engagement in its stages, but also present more inclusive contents and representations that are important for the players, since it indicates what exists and is possible in our society [29].

4.4 Goals

Goals main characteristic is to work as a motivator for the players' actions. Thus, approaching them from CRPD principles perspective means designing challenging goals for the most diverse players, mainly because this element contributes to how challenging or not a game can be for your audience.

Goals from the CRPD principles perspective means creating challenging goals for players with different physical, motor, cognitive, social, economic and cultural characteristics. An alternative to complying with CRPD principles such as P.AUTON (respect, autonomy, and freedom), P.NDISC (non-discrimination) and P.GENDER (gender equality) is to enable the game goals to be achieved by characters and people regardless of their gender or disability, such as in *Overcooked!* and *Dishonored 2*[10] or the *Mass Effect* franchise; that enables players to choose the character's attributes with which they will achieve the game's goals. *Dishonored 2* game can still be related to CRPD principles P.DIVERS (respect for differences) and P.EQUAL (equality of opportunities) as it provides several ways to meet the different game goals, goals that are selected by the players, so that their differences of opinion and abilities are respected (P.DIVERS), and yet several people are nevertheless allowed to have experience with the game (P.EQUAL).

Our approach to game goals can be related to accessibility guidelines that address game difficulty settings or player's assistents [6]. Games like *Mass Effect* and *Horizon Zero Dawn*[11] are examples of games that include several types of game levels difficulty. Although reaching game achievements is not an accessibility guideline, making it possible for people with disabilities is a way of making a more inclusive game, without discriminating players who may or may not perform such actions (P.NDISC and P.EQUAL). This action is possible in the game *Horizon Zero Dawn*, whose achievements can be completed by the players in any difficulty mode (Story, Easy, Normal, Hard and Very Hard).

4.5 Rules

Game rules are directly linked to the items in the game world, to the activities that the player can perform and to the limits of the game goals. So this element has a direct impact on the player's experience. Thus, considering them

---

[10] https://dishonored.bethesda.net.

[11] https://www.guerrilla-games.com/play/horizon.

from CRPD principles perspective involves developing game rules that keep the game world consistent and do not create obstacles for players with or without disabilities.

As presented in the examples of goals section, meeting the principles P.AUTON (respect, autonomy, and freedom), P.NDISC (non-discrimination) and P.GENDER (gender equality) can be related to avoiding rules that explicitly prevent the game's experience from people or characters of different classes, races, genres or disabilities. That said, a way to meet these principles is enabling characters that have different characteristics to realize game actions, such as in *Overcooked!* and *Mass Effect* franchises.

A game in accordance with CRPD principles such as P.DIVERS (respect for differences), P.EQUAL (equality of opportunity) and P.ACCESS (accessibility), avoid rules that require game goals to be achieved in a time limit. This is because that stress created by the time limit may make impossible for people with cognitive or motor disabilities to have fun with the game. *Lara Crof GO*[12] and *Monument Valley*[13] are games whose rules do not require the player to finish the levels in a predetermined time.

As in the goals previous section, accessibility features such as difficulty setting, game speed control, and assists can be related to the development of inclusive game rules. Games like *Spider-man*[14] and *Uncharted 4*[15] are examples of games that implement features that change game events to assist the player, such as disabling quick-time events (QTEs) by holding a button, rather than pressing the button repeatedly [18, 23, 32, 33]. *Celeste*[16] is also one of the most recent game examples with excellent accessibility options like assist and sliders to change game speed [16], which in addition to meeting some accessibility guidelines, can be related CRPD principles P.AUTON (respect, autonomy and freedom), P.NDISC (non-discrimination), P.GENDER (gender equality), P.DIVERS (respect for differences), P.EQUAL (equality of opportunities) and P.ACCESS (accessibility).

4.6 Mechanics

Since mechanics are the game's heart [4, 20], understand this element from CRDP principles perspective can indicate that mechanics is what gives players a variety of ways to perform actions in the game world, without these actions offering benefits or difficulties to people.

CRPD principles P.AUTON (respect, autonomy, and freedom), P.DIVERS (respect for differences), P.EQUAL (equality of opportunities) and P.ACCESS (accessibility), can be considered in the creation of various mechanics that, realizing similar actions or not, allow the players to use different resources to meet the

---

[12] https://laracroftgo.com/.
[13] https://www.monumentvalleygame.com/.
[14] https://insomniac.games/game/spider-man-ps4/.
[15] https://www.unchartedthegame.com/en-us/games/uncharted-4/.
[16] http://www.celestegame.com/.

same goal. Those principles are also considered if all mechanics are available to all players; not just propose a specific mechanic to be used exclusively by a group. Examples of this can be founded in the *Dishonored* franchise, which presents different mechanics for the player's choice and uses according to their abilities or preferences to complete the game's challenges (P.AUTON, P.DIVERS, and P.ACCESS). Thus, the player has several mechanics options to reach the goals, being able, for example, to accomplish game's missions in (1) stealth mode – that provide the speed control and the way that the actions are performed and does not present time-based challenges, and allows the player to have a slower gaming [31]; (2) lethal mode – which demands faster responses from players; or (3) merge the two modes according to players preference to perform actions in the game world that alter the game state and achieve the goals (P.EQUAL and P.ACCESS).

Turn-based game mechanics, such as various games from *Pokemon*[17] franchise, can also meet CRPD principles P.AUTON, P. NDISC, P.DIVERS, P.EQUAL, and P.ACCESS, since they do not present barriers such as time limits, reducing the stress factor of the game (P.DIVERS, P.EQUAL, and P.ACCESS); and make it possible to choose the player's actions by navigating menus with several options (P.AUTON, P.NDISC, P.EQUAL and P.ACCESS). Games like *Lara Croft GO* and *Monument Valley* are also examples of games whose mechanics do not present time limiters for performing actions.

Developing inclusive digital game mechanics can be related to the accessibility guidelines used in the game goals and rules since mechanics are the resources used by players to achieve goals and are limited by rules. Thus, thinking about inclusive digital game mechanics is one of our contributions to the accessibility guidelines, because developing these mechanics is part of the game development process and have people with and without disabilities as the intended audience, as well as participation and involvement of these people in this process. Our contribution is not limited to game accessibility. Instead, game accessibility is as a step to create mechanics of inclusive digital games.

Inclusive game mechanics can also be connected to other games elements, such as game story, as reached by the game *Way of the passive fist*[18]. This game, in addition to implementing accessibility features like sliders to control the game's difficulty (P.AUTON, P.NDISC, P.EQUAL and P.ACCESS), has in its own narrative structure the main mechanics of the game, which is to defend itself before deciding how to immobilize the enemies. In this way, the player does not have to go through frenetic action sequences to defeat the various enemies appearing on the screen, but rather defend himself while recognizing enemies patterns and finding an opening to counterattack. In addition, the game can be considered more inclusive by involving people with disabilities since the beginning of the development process (P.PARTIC) and aiming to meet accessibility requirements from the beginning (P.ACCESS), so that the game could be played by as many players as possible [9, 30].

---

[17] https://www.pokemon.com.
[18] http://wayofthepassivefist.com/.

Our reflections presented in this section highlights the relevance to change the perspective of the concepts of the AEM elements so that they consider CRPD principles since such a change can contribute to the development of more inclusive games, particularly of people with disabilities.

5   Concluding Remarks

Adopting a game design model to support, to understand and to develop a digital game can be a relevant tool to ensure that the game elements are correctly implemented, enabling an entertaining and engaging experience for the players. It is undeniable that utilizing a game design model and its elements do not guarantee the development of a fun game. However, understanding more about the game elements can prevent that game significant details be neglected or forgotten.

Considering a game design model elements for researching or developing an inclusive game can be a relevant resource for inclusion, particularly of people with disabilities in the gamers communities and in other contexts of life in society. To accomplish this task, this research presented reflections on how a game design model elements could be understood when related to the CRPD principles and examples of how CRPD principles can be identified in games. In addition, connecting accessibility guidelines to CRPD principles can be an action towards the development of more inclusive games.

It is important to note that accessibility guidelines should be part of the development of inclusive digital games. The inclusion process discussed in this research does not ignore accessibility, instead, it makes accessibility inherent to the game development process, at the same time it proposes new perspectives and actions for the development of digital games that have as an intended audience, also people with disabilities.

The discussions presented in this research can contribute to the understanding of the relevance of game development that goes towards inclusion, as well as reflections on the actions to accomplish the task of creating inclusive games. However, it is not the objective of this work to determine or prescribe methods and tools to create inclusive elements and possibly inclusive games, but rather to promote the theme discussion of the development of games that have as a intended audience, also people with disabilities, and perceptions about how the development of inclusive games can occur.

Acknowledgments. To Fundação Araucária, CAPES and PPGTE. This study was financed in part by the Coordenação de Aperfeiçoamento de Pessoal de Nível Superior - Brasil (CAPES) - Finance Code 001.

References

1. The UN convention on the rights of persons with disabilities (CRPD) (2018). http://www.internationaldisabilityalliance.org/CRPD

2. AbleGamers Charity: Accessible player experiences (APX) (2019). https://accessible.games/accessible-player-experiences/
3. AbleGamers Charity: Same controls but different (2019). https://accessible.games/accessible-player-experiences/access-patterns/same-controls-but-different/
4. Adams, E.: Fundamentals of Game Design, 2nd edn. Pearson Education, Berkeley (2010)
5. Bardzell, J., Bardzell, S.: Humanistic HCI. Morgan & Claypool Publishers, San Rafael (2015)
6. Barlet, M.C., Spohn, S.D.: Includification: a practical guide to game accessibility. The Ablegamers Foundation, Charles Town (2012). https://accessible.games/wp-content/uploads/2018/11/AbleGamers_Includification.pdf
7. Carroll, N.: On Criticism. Routledge, New York (2009)
8. Cezarotto, M.A., Battaiola, A.L.: Estudo comparativo entre modelos de game design para jogos educacionais. In: SBC - Proceedings of SBGames, pp. 174–181. SBC (2017). https://sbgames.org/sbgames2017/papers/ArtesDesignFull/175240.pdf
9. Couture, J.: Prioritizing accessibility made way of the passive fist much better (2017). https://www.gamasutra.com/view/news/304181/Prioritizing_accessibility_made_Way_of_the_Passive_Fist_much_better.php
10. DisturbedShadow: a look at characters with disabilities in video games (2014). http://tay.kinja.com/a-look-at-characters-with-disabilities-in-video-games-1552513077
11. Feenberg, A.: Transforming Technology: A Critical Theory Revisited. Oxford University Press, Oxford (2002)
12. Grammenos, D., Savidis, A., Stephanidis, C.: Designing universally accessible games. Comput. Entertain. (CIE) **7**(1), 8 (2009)
13. Harrison, S., Tatar, D., Sengers, P.: The three paradigms of HCI. ACM, New York (2007)
14. Huizinga, J.: Homo ludens: o jogo como elemento cultural. Perspectiva, São Paulo (2014)
15. Hunicke, R., LeBlanc, M., Zubek, R.: MDA: a formal approach to game design and game research. In: Proceedings of the AAAI Workshop on Challenges in Game AI, vol. 4, pp. 1–5. AAAI Press, San Jose (2004)
16. Kidwell, E.: Check out celeste's remarkably granular 'assist' options (2018). https://www.gamasutra.com/view/news/313731/Check_out_Celestes_remarkably_granular_Assist_options.php
17. Klepek, P.: Legally blind gamer can finally enjoy more PS4 games (2015). https://kotaku.com/legally-blind-gamer-can-finally-enjoy-more-ps4-games-1695264255
18. Klepek, P.: How one disabled player convinced naughty dog to add more accessibility options to uncharted 4 (2016). https://www.kotaku.com.au/2016/05/how-one-disabled-player-convinced-naughty-dog-to-add-more-accessibility-options-to-uncharted-4/
19. Ladner, R.: The impact of the united nations convention on the rights of persons with disabilities. Commun. ACM **57**(3), 30–32 (2014)
20. Leite, P.S., Almeida, L.D.A.: Modelo artefato-experiência para elementos dos jogos e gameplay. In: SBC - Proceedings of SBGames, pp. 125–134. SBC (2017). https://sbgames.org/sbgames2017/papers/ArtesDesignFull/175100.pdf
21. Louro, G.L.: Gênero e sexualidade: pedagogias contemporâneas. Pro-posições **19**(2), 17–23 (2008)
22. Marconi, M.A., Lakatos, E.M.: Fundamentos de metodologia científica, 5th edn. Atlas, São Paulo (2003)

23. McAloon, A.: In the name of accessibility, spider-man offers toggleable puzzles and QTEs (2018). http://www.gamasutra.com/view/news/326079/In_the_name_of_accessibility_SpiderMan_offers_toggleable_puzzles_and_QTEs.php
24. Parlock, J.: Opinion – disability in gaming: the problem of representation (2014). http://indiehaven.com/opinion-disability-in-gaming-the-problem-of-representation/
25. Resende, A.P.C., de Paiva Vita, F.M.: A Convenção sobre Direitos das Pessoas com Deficiência Comentada. Secretaria Especial dos Direitos Humanos - Coordenadoria Nacional para Integração da Pessoa Portadora de Deficiência (2008). https://www.governodigital.gov.br/documentos-e-arquivos/A%20Convencao%20sobre%20os%20Direitos%20das%20Pessoas%20com%20Deficiencia%20Comentada.pdf
26. Salen, K., Zimmerman, E.: Regras do jogo: fundamentos do design de jogos: principais conceitos: volume 1, vol. 1. Blucher, São Paulo (2012)
27. Schell, J.: The Art of Game Design: A Book of Lenses. AK Peters/CRC Press, Natick/Boca Raton (2014)
28. Secretaria de Direitos Humanos da Presidência da República, Secretaria Nacional de Promoção dos Direitos da Pessoa Com Deficiência: Novos Comentários à Convenção sobre os Direitos das Pessoas com Deficiência. Secretaria de Direitos Humanos da Presidência da República (2014). http://www.pessoacomdeficiencia.gov.br/app/sites/default/files/publicacoes/convencao-sdpcd-novos-comentarios.pdf
29. Shaw, A.: Gaming at the Edge: Sexuality and Gender at the Margins of Gamer Culture. University of Minnesota Press, Minneapolis (2014)
30. Sinclair, B.: Designing for accessibility from day one (2017). http://www.gamesindustry.biz/articles/2017-08-28-designing-for-accessibility-from-day-one
31. Straub, J.: Six mechanics that make any game more accessible (2013). https://dagersystem.com/six-mechanics-that-make-any-game-more-accessible/
32. Straub, J.: Disability game review: uncharted 4 (2016). https://dagersystem.com/disability-review-uncharted-4/
33. Straub, J.: Disability game review: spider-man (2018). https://dagersystem.com/disability-game-review-spider-man/
34. United Nations: Convention on the rights of persons with disabilities (CRPD) (2018). https://www.un.org/development/desa/disabilities/convention-on-the-rights-of-persons-with-disabilities.html
35. Walk, W., Görlich, D., Barrett, M.: Design, dynamics, experience (DDE): an advancement of the MDA framework for game design. In: Korn, O., Lee, N. (eds.) Game Dynamics, pp. 27–45. Springer, Cham (2017). https://doi.org/10.1007/978-3-319-53088-8_3
36. Westin, T., Bierre, K., Gramenos, D., Hinn, M.: Advances in game accessibility from 2005 to 2010. In: Stephanidis, C. (ed.) UAHCI 2011. LNCS, vol. 6766, pp. 400–409. Springer, Heidelberg (2011). https://doi.org/10.1007/978-3-642-21663-3_43
37. Wilhelmsson, U., Engstrom, H., Brusk, J., Ostblad, P.A.: Accessible game culture using inclusive game design: participating in a visual culture that you cannot see. In: 7th International Conference on Games and Virtual Worlds for Serious Applications (VS-Games), pp. 1–8 (2015)
38. Yuan, B., Folmer, E., Harris Jr., F.C.: Game accessibility: a survey. Univ. Access Inform. Soc. 10(1), 81–100 (2011)

Teaching Video Game Design Accessibility: Toward Effective Pedagogic Interventions in Accessible Design

Laura Levy[✉] and Maribeth Gandy

Interactive Media Technology Center,
Georgia Institute of Technology, Atlanta, GA, USA
{laura,maribeth}@imtc.gatech.com

Abstract. Video games are enjoyed as creative, emotional, and social outlets for many. However, for a growing number of people with disabilities and/or those acquiring disabilities due to age-related decline, this kind of media is becoming inaccessible. The future of accessible game design hinges on teaching the next generation of game developer professionals of best practices and providing them experience to create their own accessible games. Still, little is known for effective pedagogic practices that instill domain knowledge and awareness in students on accessibility design. In this early work, researchers explore the impact of one 60-min accessibility lecture on the way student participants sonified a game for those with visual impairments. Results indicate that students receiving the lecture produced a more accessible product for player with visual impairments, while also intimating higher levels of empathy for those with disabilities. Based on these findings, we present recommendations for how instructors can implement a minimum viable pedagogic intervention for accessible game design, if a longer engagement with this material is not possible.

Keywords: Accessibility design · Video games · Human-computer interaction

1 Introduction

Video games provide a number of social [1], physical [2], and cognitive benefits [3, 4] to players. However, games remain or can become out of reach for a growing number of people as the average age of the world increases [5] and age-related decline (e.g. sensory, motor) affects more of the population. Currently in the United States, there are 61 million people [6] with a disability and, of these, there are 33 million gamers with disabilities [7]. This requires increased attention by technology communities towards accessibility design for both hardware (input devices such as smartphones and keyboards) and software (e.g. user interfaces on the web).

Until relatively recently, the part of the gaming industry producing large-scale titles, known as "AAA" games, has largely overlooked early integration of accessibility features into commercial games. Unfortunately, much of the work on accessibility research conducted in academic settings does not find its way into commercial applications because of a balkanization of industry and academic communities, in addition

© Springer Nature Switzerland AG 2019
M. Antona and C. Stephanidis (Eds.): HCII 2019, LNCS 11572, pp. 301–311, 2019.
https://doi.org/10.1007/978-3-030-23560-4_22

to the challenges of appropriately implementing these features in the time pressures these projects face.

Some headway in commercial accessible products has been made, such as the release of the Microsoft Xbox Adaptive Controller [8], which focuses on players with limited mobility. The Adaptive Controller allows players with disabilities to connect their own accessible input devices providing agency over the way the game is played (for example, using a foot pedal for jumping and also a sip-and-puff controller to move the character). However, many accessible devices or software modifications – in gaming or other digital media – remain afterthoughts and add-ons that often work clumsily with the main technology. Additionally, accessible hardware can be prohibitively expensive for a user to purchase on their own (a sip-and-puff controller can cost $450 USD), software documentation for use may be scarce, and/or an accessible software solution simply be non-existent.

Partly, the difficulty of effective implementation of accessibility in technology is due to the substantial challenge in designing for the wide breadth of abilities and disabilities (e.g. sensory, physical, cognitive) that people may experience throughout their lifespans. A first step in promoting the future of accessible design in games, and of technology overall, is through educating the next generation of human-computer interaction (HCI) professionals. We must begin this education practice early in students so that they can employ best practices and principles for the rest of their careers. Professionals must also seek continuing education opportunities to keep abreast of new accessibility requirements, guidelines, and community needs as technology rapidly evolves.

In this early work, we focus on teaching accessible game design to undergraduate students at a university in the United States. As part of a larger project on accessible game design, researchers explored a minimum intervention of an accessible game design lecture given to students and examined how the lecture impacted the ability of students to make a game accessible to visually impaired or blind players, as compared to students that did not receive the lecture. Games are social, creative, and emotional outlets for many, and maintaining the ability to engage in this activity can increase the quality of life for many kinds of people [9–11]. Therefore, new generations of game designers and developers armed with knowledge, awareness, and self-driven interest in accessible game design may serve to support all kinds of gaming communities with the tools needed to successfully play.

2   Related Work

New standards and regulations in the United States, the European Union, Australia, and other large markets continue to be updated with more stringent criteria for accessibility on the web. This growing attention places demands on industry to hire professionals with accessible design skills, and also on higher education institutions to produce these new professionals. Increasingly, universities are implementing accessibility teachings in their program curriculum, particularly in the fields of disability studies and biomedical design. However, encountering this level of instruction in computer science specializations can be more rare [12].

For the field of HCI, several universities (e.g. Universidad Politécnica de Madrid, University of Dundee, University of California Santa Cruz) have successfully implemented stand-alone courses as part of a larger computer science or interactive media program [13–16]. However, many argue [17, 18] that accessibility teachings should be integrated throughout all courses in an undergraduate curriculum, thereby promoting increased experience with this way of thinking, and also to keep students abreast of new developments with rapidly evolving technologies

2.1   Teaching Accessible Design with Authentic Learning Theory

The pedagogic theory of "authentic learning" possesses four main themes of (1) tackling real-world problems reflecting the work of professionals, (2) presenting non-prescriptive problems with open-ended solutions, (3) providing opportunities for discourse and collaboration with other learners, and (4) allowing students agency over directing their learning in the project to develop their own emotional commitments with the subject matter [19]. In a survey of several European Union programs teaching accessibility awareness, researchers found the activities most effective in impacting students reflected themes from authentic learning; particularly in creating meaningful connections between learners and those in disability communities [20].

Videos, including freely available ones from YouTube, have proven successful in instilling deeper connections in learners by raising awareness of accessibility challenges and bringing a human element to those who students are designing for [16, 21, 22]. Additionally, access to design stakeholder members with disabilities also can increase awareness around accessibility domain knowledge, and learner comfort in interacting socially with disabled persons [16, 23]. Laboratory exercises can also be a successful strategy to instill meaningful connections in learners, such as requiring students to use screen readers to interact with the web [24] or using tools to simulate disabilities (e.g. using the Cambridge Capability Loss Simulation gloves or glasses [25]). However, these activities are likely best paired with interactions by those in the disabled community to demonstrate how they can adapt to their abilities, as one study found disability simulator tools can decrease attitudes in the learner about the ability for disabled persons to work and live independently [26].

However, for those educational programs without the luxury of integrating accessibility throughout much of or the entirety of a curriculum, questions remain on the most effective ways of teaching accessibility. What is the minimum viable intervention that can be given to students to instill not only heuristics and procedural domain knowledge, but a sense of awareness of accessibility challenges? Video games are a specific kind of interactive media, and information on dedicated university courses or programs for accessible game design is scarce. Further, less is known for how to teach this kind of accessibility design to new game designers and developers.

3 Study Description

Empirically, we have little understanding of how much and what kind of training is necessary for students to be effective in implementing accessibility design in their work – particularly for accessible games. In this preliminary study, researchers gave a supplementary lecture on sonification accessibility design in video games in a computer audio course to a portion of computer science undergraduate students. The purpose of this study was to examine how a bare minimum intervention (i.e. one lecture of 60 min) impacted the way students made a video game accessible for play by those with vision impairments, as well as how they discussed their justifications behind their design.

A thematic analysis was used to typify the kinds of errors made by participants in each condition to understand how to design the next iteration of pedagogic interventions. Researchers expert in game design and accessibility created a scoring rubric to assess: (1) if critical game elements for accessible play were sonified, and (2) the quality of the sonification (e.g. was the sonification appropriate in communicating its information). Additionally, all student participants submitted a two-page explanation justifying their design and these statements were evaluated using a thematic qualitative analysis for intent, and also evaluated in conjunction with the efficacy of the final product.

4 Methods

In an undergraduate course on computer audio, researchers divided the class into two groups to participate in this study. Both groups of students completed an accessibility design assignment where they were given the same 1-min video of a game called *Bubble Trip* [27–29] to make accessible for visually impaired or blind players. One group of students completed this assignment after receiving a supplementary 60-min lecture on designing for accessibility, while the other group completed the assignment without this lecture. Thirteen students participated in this study, with eight students attending the supplementary accessibility lecture and five not.

4.1 The Lecture

The 60-min lecture on game design accessibility was the first introduction on accessibility for most of the participant students. The lecture introduced topics including the concept of universal design and its intended benefits, multi-modal interaction and feedback design, and how to design sonifications communicating spatial simulation, descriptions of environment, changes in environment, game alerts, player resources, and system controls. Specific instruction on how to map sonifications for loudness, frequency, tempo, and timbre with examples were also provided.

As a technique for students to use in their assignment, Shephard's Tone was described (this creates an auditory illusion of a rising pitch, without exhausting actual rising tones or loudness [30]). Finally, video examples were shown to students exemplifying challenges that visually impaired players experience with games such as Zelda: Ocarina of Time. In this particular example, students watched how a blind player had modified his gaming environment to present himself with stereo sound, and used a Nintendo emulator to frequently and rapidly save game states to return to after failing a level [31]. Other videos shown in the lecture demonstrated games that have been modified for visual impairments using sound, or that were specifically designed for those players with visual deficits.

4.2 The Accessibility Assignment

All students completed the same accessibility assignment, whether they had received the lecture or not. Students were provided a 1-min video clip of the game, *Bubble Trip*, and instructed to use a video editor to add sufficient and appropriate sonifications that would enable a visually impaired or blind player to effectively play the game, while also having an enjoyable experience. *Bubble Trip* was created as a scientifically valid and reliable personality assessment game [27–29], where players read personality questions (from the HEXACO Personality Inventory [32]) and move their fish avatar around the screen to make answer selections. Additionally, players collect bubbles for points and avoid collisions with enemy jellies (see Fig. 1).

Fig. 1. Student participants added sonification to a video of gameplay from *Bubble Trip* for low vision and blind player accessibility

4.3 Scoring Rubric

The suitability and effectiveness of the student's accessibility sonifications were assessed by experts in both game design and accessibility design. Prior to reviewing student videos, these experts independently described elements from the game that they believed required sonification in order for a low vision or blind player to effectively play the game, while also having an enjoyable experience.

To make *Bubble Trip* accessible for those with low vision, the rubric (see Table 1) identifies three categories that must be sonified: (1) verbal support of text, (2) positions of interactive agents, and (3) player status. For example, a very basic accessibility feature should be a voice read-out of the game instructions, as well as every personality survey question presented to the player. Other game elements that should be made accessible through sonification are the Likert scale items pre-selected and then finally confirmed as a submitted answer, location and velocity information on the player's fish avatar, presence of collectable bubbles, and the motion and position of enemy jellies. Finally, periodic (or sustained) updates on player status are important feedback and would include overall score and number of survey questions remaining.

Table 1. Complete list of possible sonifications, as identified by experts in both accessibility and game design, and items used in the scoring rubric for *Bubble Trip*

Accessibility category	Game element	Example
Verbal support of text	Game instructions	"This game uses the arrow keys on your keyboard to..."
	Survey question text	"I would like to go to an art museum"
	Fish position	Communicating the x and y location of avatar
	Fish motion	If avatar is being moved or not
	Survey answer pre-selection	Likert item indicated before final selection
	Survey answer selected	Likert item confirmed as final selection
Positions of interactive agents	Jelly position	Communicating the x and y location of enemy jelly
	Jelly motion	That the jelly is moving across the screen
	Jelly collision	If the avatar collides with an enemy jelly
	Bubble presence	If bubbles were floating up screen
	Point collection	Upon collection of bubbles by avatar
	Screen boundary	If avatar position is on edge of gameplay screen
	Player score	Communicating number of bubbles collected
Player status	Question number	Communicating number of questions remaining

Two researchers independently coded each video and scored against the rubric the following criteria: (1) if these game elements were coded (or to add any new codes if students identified missing sonification element needs), and (2) the quality of the sonification (e.g. if the sound design was effective and appropriate in communicating its information). In addition to the submitted video, each student included a two-page report justifying their chosen sonification elements and explaining their sound design for each. These reports were also examined in terms of procedural knowledge applied to their sound design, explanations indicating a deep understanding behind the chosen design, and empathetic sentiments guiding their process.

5 Observations and Results

The following sections describe observations of students from the accessibility lecture, the produced sonified videos from all students, and the justification reports submitted with the videos by all student participants.

5.1 Students Not Receiving the Lecture

Results indicated that students not receiving the accessibility lecture omitted more sonifications of *critical gameplay elements,* such as audio that read the personality question aloud for the player. No student in this group added verbal read-outs of the *Bubble Trip* instructions, and including text read-outs of the personality questions to be answered was also rare. If a player cannot read the survey questions, it is still possible to technically play the game but neither effectively nor in the way the game was intended to be played.

Students in the no-lecture group also made more *fundamental* mistakes regarding crucial information, such as positions of interactive agents, that would need to be communicated to a visually impaired player. Standard accessibility heuristics would emphasize the need to communicate position of an interactive element, making this a fundamental basis for accessible design – particularly for games. Since the fish avatar can be moved in any direction on the screen but the survey answers are only available at the top, a visually impaired player must have assistance in knowing the position of their avatar in order to answer the questions. Additionally, sonifying the same aspects for the enemy jellies helps players to avoid colliding with them (though enemy collisions have no punitive aspect, they do freeze the player's character for a brief moment).

In the report justifications, these participants indicated that they were more focused on the aesthetic design of the sound rather than accessibility. For example, one student produced a video with a high number of sonifications fitting the underwater nature of the game (e.g. sounds of flowing water, bubbles popping) but the sounds themselves were not able to effectively convey the requisite information for a visually impaired player to play the game. Although the sounds satisfied hedonic elements of the game, they had low bandwidth in communicating useful information such as player position or proximity to enemies.

5.2 Students Receiving the Lecture

Students that did receive the lecture, however, sonified more overall game elements and their audio design communicated more nuanced information to the player.

These participants opined more empathic statements about putting themselves "in someone else's shoes" and thinking of what the game experience would be like if they could not see it clearly. These students more often explicitly mentioned "the player" they were designing for and what they understood the player's needs to be in relation to *Bubble Trip* specifically. For example, "a visually impaired player would have a difficult time knowing where the screen boundaries are, so I am sonifying these to help them orient themselves in the game".

Students receiving the lecture also used more conditional statements in justifying their sonification design. For example, "if I were visually impaired, I know I would get frustrated with menus so those should definitely be sonified to help guide the player" and "because this element [bubbles] is fun to collect in the game, it should be fun for the player to hear but I want to make sure it doesn't hurt their ears either because if I were blind then I think I would be very sensitive to sounds".

Overall, lecture-receiving participant explanations indicated they had thought more deeply about the gameplay experience from an empathic standpoint, and less from a straightforward heuristic approach. Finally, these students wrote more on how their accessible design would benefit players regardless of visual ability – perhaps a consequence of learning about universal design in the lecture.

6 Discussion

An unexpected outcome of the lecture intervention was the sense of empathy it appeared to instill in students receiving it. Although this makes sense in hindsight, elements of the lecture were not included to purposefully create this awareness and yet it appears an effective vehicle in motivating designers to more appropriately design for accessibility. This follows authentic learning theory in several counts. The project had real-world applications that mimicked that of professionals, there was no one right answer for how to make the game accessible, and students' personal connection to the task may have been influenced by watching videos of visually impaired players play through popular commercial games, like Zelda. In fact, students in the accessibility lecture watching the blind gamer play Zelda writhed in their seats, moaned when the player fell of cliffs, clasped each other's hands, and made sympathetic exclamations on how hard it appeared to play in this way. As in other studies previously discussed [16, 22], videos appeared effective in connecting learners with the subject matter and possibly impacting the quality of their work after.

Participants receiving the lecture may have also been influenced by the discussion on universal design, as they made more comments in their reports for how their sonifications could benefit players of many kinds of abilities. The abilities of humans are changing constantly over our lifespans, from our ability to see without aid to short-term memory capabilities. Although universal design may not be possible in totality, there are examples where it can benefit many kinds of people (e.g. the Curb Cut Effect [33]) and these can be powerful anecdotes to change the way learners navigate and think about the interactions they have with digital media.

6.1 Recommendations for Instructors of Accessible Game Design

The contribution of this paper is to provide some recommendations for instructors on teaching accessible game design – particularly if resources or time only allow for small pedagogic interventions. As elucidated in the previous research on accessible design in HCI and computer science, leveraging authentic learning theory to generate a deeper connection in learners appears effective also in students learning about accessible game design.

There exists a vocal and active community of gamers with disabilities online that spend considerable time providing documentation on modified hardware/software solutions, research into accessible games, and review and experiences with commercial games specific to their abilities. We recommend instructors to, at the least, encourage students to reach out to these communities to learn about their unique needs, wants, and accessibility recommendations. Platforms, like Twitter, and popular forums, like Reddit, are helpful for learners to communicate with these communities online. Additionally, current professionals in these fields would benefit from dialogue with these communities, and can also utilize the structured guidelines and heuristics provided by advocacy groups like AbleGamers [34].

Perhaps even more effective for learning is to invite individuals with disabilities to act as stakeholders and mentors for student projects. Indeed, this was found to be particularly effective for raising accessibility awareness and increasing social interactions comfort in students [23]. As found in this study, supplementing instruction with first-hand accounts and experiences – even those as passive as a YouTube video – may be effective in influencing learners on accessibility design in games.

As stated by other researchers, accessibility design should be interwoven in all of an undergraduate HCI or computer science student's curriculum. Per the professional codes of ethics by computing organizations, like the Association of Computing Machinery (ACM [35]), our profession emphasizes the ethical design of technology that includes all people regardless of ability or status. Instilling this sentiment in the next generation of computing and design professionals is paramount.

7   Conclusions and Future Work

Ultimately, participants that received the lecture produced a more accessible game product that not only communicated more information to the player through sound, but also indicated that the designer had thought more deeply about the target player's needs. Even one 60-min lecture influenced these students' work and thought-processes on design, and provoked deep empathetic feelings on what challenges disabled gamers face playing even simple games, like *Bubble Trip*. Students receiving the lecture reacted strongly to lecture-provided videos of gamers with disabilities playing commercial games and made more comments indicating they had imagined what it would be like to have a visual impairment. The kinds of errors that lecture-receiving participants made could be typified by less appropriate hedonistic sound design, while creating an appropriate level of game design accessibility.

This is early and exploratory work examining how pedagogic interventions may impact the thoughts and final products of game design accessibility in undergraduate students – an area currently lacking in academic research. These results suggest promoting deeper engagement with the content itself, such as through videos, may produce a higher sense of empathy with disabled players, leading student designers to create more accessible interactive media. Stand-alone lectures or courses should be the minimum provided for higher education, but the contribution of this paper is some further understanding for a minimum pedagogic intervention influencing accessible game design for undergraduate students. We hope to build on this work with future cohorts of students to further understand the beneficial impacts of these kinds of interventions on accessible game design.

Acknowledgements. This work was funded through grants from the National Institute on Disability, Independent Living, and Rehabilitation Research (NIDILRR), NSF #0905127, and ACT, Inc.

References

1. Cole, H., Griffiths, M.D.: Social interactions in massively multiplayer online role-playing gamers. Cyberpsychol. Behav. **10**(4), 575–583 (2007)
2. Staiano, A.E., Calvert, S.L.: Exergames for physical education courses: physical, social, and cognitive benefits. Child. Dev. Perspect. **5**(2), 93–98 (2011)
3. Granic, I., Lobel, A., Engels, R.C.: The benefits of playing video games. Am. Psychol. **69**(1), 66 (2014)
4. Colzato, L.S., et al.: DOOM'd to switch: superior cognitive flexibility in players of first person shooter games. Front. Psychol. **1**, 8 (2010)
5. World Health Organization: Ageing and Health (2018). https://www.who.int/news-room/fact-sheets/detail/ageing-and-health
6. Centers for Disease Control: CDC: 1 in 4 US adults lives with a disability (2018). https://www.cdc.gov/media/releases/2018/p0816-disability.html. Accessed 13 Feb 2019
7. AbleGamers: AbleGamers and gamers outreach partner to help children with disabilities in need (2017). https://ablegamers.org/ablegamers-and-gamers-outreach-partner-to-help-children-with-disabilities-in-need/. Accessed 8 Oct 2018
8. Microsoft, I.: Xbox Adaptive Controller (2018). https://www.xbox.com/en-US/xbox-one/accessories/controllers/xbox-adaptive-controller. Accessed 13 Feb 2019
9. Zhang, F., Kaufman, D.: The impacts of social interactions in MMORPGs on older adults' social capital. Comput. Hum. Behav. **51**, 495–503 (2015)
10. Williams, D., et al.: From tree house to barracks: the social life of guilds in World of Warcraft. Games Cult. **1**(4), 338–361 (2006)
11. Trepte, S., Reinecke, L., Juechems, K.: The social side of gaming: how playing online computer games creates online and offline social support. Comput. Hum. Behav. **28**(3), 832–839 (2012)
12. Keates, S.: A pedagogical example of teaching Universal Access. Univ. Access Inf. Soc. **14**(1), 97–110 (2015)
13. Deibel, K.: Studying our inclusive practices: course experiences of students with disabilities. In: ACM SIGCSE Bulletin. ACM (2007)
14. Benavídez, C., Fuertes, J.L., Gutiérrez, E., Martínez, L.: Teaching web accessibility with "contramano" and hera. In: Miesenberger, K., Klaus, J., Zagler, W.L., Karshmer, A.I. (eds.) ICCHP 2006. LNCS, vol. 4061, pp. 341–348. Springer, Heidelberg (2006). https://doi.org/10.1007/11788713_51
15. Waller, A., Hanson, V.L., Sloan, D.: Including accessibility within and beyond undergraduate computing courses. In: Proceedings of the 11th International ACM SIGACCESS Conference on Computers and Accessibility. ACM (2009)

16. Kurniawan, S.H., Arteaga, S., Manduchi, R.: A general education course on universal access, disability, technology and society. In: Proceedings of the 12th International ACM SIGACCESS Conference on Computers and Accessibility. ACM (2010)

17. Rosmaita, B.J.: Accessibility first! A new approach to web design. ACM SIGCSE Bull. **38**(1), 270–274 (2006)

18. Putnam, C., et al.: Best practices for teaching accessibility in university classrooms: cultivating awareness, understanding, and appreciation for diverse users. ACM Trans. Access. Comput. **8**(4), 1–26 (2016)

19. Rule, A.C.: The components of authentic learning. J. Authent. Learn. **3**(1), 1–10 (2006)

20. Keith, S., Whitney, G., Petz, A.: Design for all as focus in European ICT teaching and training activities (2009)

21. Keith, S., Whitney, G.: Bridging the gap between young designers and older users in an inclusive society. In: Proceedings of the Good, the Bad and the Challenging: The User and the Future of ICT (1998)

22. Carmichael, A., Newell, A.F., Morgan, M.: The efficacy of narrative video for raising awareness in ICT designers about older users' requirements. Interact. Comput. **19**(5–6), 587–596 (2007)

23. Ludi, S.: Introducing accessibility requirements through external stakeholder utilization in an undergraduate requirements engineering course. In: 29th International Conference on Software Engineering, 2007. ICSE 2007. IEEE (2007)

24. Harrison, S.M.: Opening the eyes of those who can see to the world of those who can't: a case study. In: ACM SIGCSE Bulletin. ACM (2005)

25. University of Cambridge: Inclusive design toolkit. http://www.inclusivedesigntoolkit.com/tools_simulation/. Accessed 14 Feb 2019

26. Silverman, A.M., Gwinn, J.D., Van Boven, L.: Stumbling in their shoes: disability simulations reduce judged capabilities of disabled people. Soc. Psychol. Pers. Sci. **6**(4), 464–471 (2015)

27. Levy, L., et al.: Method in the madness: the design of games as valid and reliable scientific tools. In: Proceedings of the 13th International Conference on the Foundations of Digital Games. ACM (2018)

28. Levy, L., et al.: Grouches, extraverts, and jellyfish: assessment validity and game mechanics in a gamified assessment. In: 1st Joint Conference of Foundations of Digital Games (FDG) and the Digital Games Research Association (DiGRA), Dundee, Scotland, UK (2016)

29. Levy, L., et al.: Actions speak louder than words: an exploration of game play behavior and results from traditional assessments of individual differences. In: Foundations of Digital Games. Pacific Grove, CA (2015)

30. Burns, E.M.: Circularity in relative pitch judgments for inharmonic complex tones: the Shepard demonstration revisited, again. Percept. Psychophys. **30**(5), 467–472 (1981)

31. MegaTGarrett: True blind: let's play Zelda, listening in 3D inside the Deku Tree. YouTube (2011). https://www.youtube.com/watch?v=nmmqarQRSSE&t

32. Ashton, M.C., Lee, K.: The HEXACO-60: a short measure of the major dimensions of personality. J. Pers. Assess. **91**(4), 340–345 (2009)

33. Blackwell, A.G.: The Curb-Cut Effect. Stanford Social Innovation Review (2017). https://ssir.org/articles/entry/the_curb_cut_effect. Accessed 13 Feb 2019

34. AbleGamers, I.: https://ablegamers.org/

35. ACM: ACM Code of Ethics and Professional Conduct (2018). https://www.acm.org/code-of-ethics. Accessed 14 Feb 2019

An Investigation on Sharing Economy Mobile Service Adoption: How Perceived Risk, Value, and Price Interact?

Shu-Ping Lin and Ya-Hui Chan[✉]

Department of Banking and Finance,
CTBC Business School, Tainan, Taiwan (R.O.C.)
splin0210@gmail.com, yahui0219@gmail.com

Abstract. Originally developing from redistribution of idle resources, the sharing economy has expanded rapidly since its emergence because it enhances the efficiency of asset utilization through paid rentals of surplus resources, creating a win-win situation between users and re-source owners, and the subversive business opportunities brought by its business model attract global attention. However, related research on discussing user's adoption towards sharing economy mobile services (M-services) is still lacking.

As we know, a solid understanding of user perception enables a more robust definition of better market alignment. The contribution of this study is to discuss the key elements of sharing economy M-service adoption by including contingencies in which low and high user experience existed. We applied three theories – perceived risk (including security uncertainty and performance uncertainty), perceived value (perceived usefulness), and perceived price – and hypothesized that each had a different effect on sharing economy M-service adoption. The hypotheses were tested by multi-group SEM approach with 509 responses in Taiwan.

Our findings verified that users' perceived usefulness is a major driver to the widespread adoption of sharing economy M-services for both low and high-experienced contingencies. Also, the effects of security uncertainty and performance uncertainty are both mediated by perceived usefulness for high experienced users; while the mediated effect of perceived price does not exist. In addition, there were significant differences in the influence of perceived price on adoption intention in low and high-experienced contingencies, and thus illustrated different strategies have to be proposed for sharing economy M-service marketing. Implications and future research is suggested.

Keywords: Perceived risk · Perceived value · Perceived price · Sharing economy mobile services · Moderating effect

1 Background and Motivation

Originally developing from redistribution of idle resources, the sharing economy has expanded rapidly since its emergence. It enables individuals to use resources at a lower cost, while resource owners can more or less receive some benefits in return.

© Springer Nature Switzerland AG 2019
M. Antona and C. Stephanidis (Eds.): HCII 2019, LNCS 11572, pp. 312–325, 2019.
https://doi.org/10.1007/978-3-030-23560-4_23

The sharing economy functions through the concept of utilizing an online third-party platform to temporarily transfer, and further enable resources to be shared and reused, and this mechanism can be seen in examples of sharing of scooters for public and vacant rooms for tourists. The sharing economy enhances the efficiency of asset utilization through paid rentals of surplus resources, creating a win–win situation between users and resource owners, and the subversive business opportunities brought by its business model attract global attention. The overall profit generated by the sharing economy is estimated to be around $40.2 billion in 2022, with at least $18.6 billion estimated for platform providers in 2017, as stated in Juniper's *Sharing Economy: Opportunities, Impacts & Disruptors 2017–2022*.

Sharing economy business is highly integrated with mobile applications that can be used anytime and anywhere, which further impacts traditional B2C and B2B2C service models. Because the third-party platform acts as a matchmaker and guarantees the supplies quality by crowdsourcing mechanism, the concern of risks derived from this condition has great influence on realizing the transactions between supply and demand sides. As illustrated in the Transaction Cost Theory (TCT), the concept of transaction cost explains how both parties of a transaction consider risk will determine the realization of transaction, which means that when transactions are under high uncertainty and complexity, both transaction parties will tend to be more conservative, resulting in the failure of transaction. Besides, for the sharing economy mobile services (M-services), most processes are based on mobile networks. Everything from identity verification, transaction records and payment procedures will all be documented by platform operators. With the possibilities of individual data being disclosed for usage, users may adopt an even stricter approach to assess the risk of the sharing economy M-services. In fact, for users, their adoption of sharing economy M-services is supported by reduced transaction costs. That is to say, users are willing to accept the M-services if the operator can provide easy access to the information of the sharing economy M-services and make sure high quality and on time delivery of their orders with a guarantee of the enforcement of the transaction contract through mobile network connectivity.

On the other hand, the Signaling Theory proposed by Spence (1973) stated that if online transaction markets are not mature enough, serious information asymmetry will occur between the transaction parties, and the delivery of information quality will have certain degree of influence. That is to say, even under the condition of information asymmetry, if sellers can establish a high quality signal through some form of activity to rationalize the compensation buyers get from the activity and further induces buyers' willingness to make additional payments, a transaction can be realized (Lankton and McKnight 2011). For example, when the sharing economy market is still at the early development stage, its M-service has an unstable price-performance ratio because users have lower degree of familiarity with it, which makes price and quality become the major factors of realizing the transaction. In other words, when users' concern for risks outweighs the use value of the sharing economy M-services, users' early adoption intention may be affected, and they may even start to slowly reject the continuous adoption of that services. This also means that delivery of value can help improve users' level of tolerance for risk. The concept of perceived value is also introduced by Davis (1989) in his Technology Acceptance Model (TAM), which has been widely applied by many researchers in the information systems (IS) setting. The common conclusion is that the willingness to adopt IS services for buyers who tend to avoid a high level of uncertainty might be enhanced through their perceived value of how relevant features can improve performance, even though they are likely to consider IS as risky and uncertain (Perez-Alvarez and Paterson 2014). In short, perceived value and perceived price are two factors that may affect the influence state of perceived risk on adoption behavior.

Understanding the engagement and behavior of users is important for the success of businesses offering sharing economy M-services. Especially sharing economy M-services still in the early stages of development, knowing about the motivation of users will enable businesses to build a more detailed user profiling, devise more precise marketing strategies and design adaptive services. However, related research is still at a premature stage in the sharing economy M-services field. Even though existing literature has looked at the impact of perceived price, perceived value, and perceived risk on users' adoption of various IS services, the discussion about how these three factors influence users on adopting IS in the sharing economy is still rather scarce. Hence, this study focuses on integrating the theories on perceived price, value, and risk to establish a relational sharing economy M-services adoption model to analyze the important motives for users to continue to adopt services by including contingencies in which low and high user experience existed.

In the following sections, we first explore how past research and theories look at perceived risk, perceived value, perceived price, and user adoption intention. Next, we propose possible hypotheses and illustrate the methodology used in this research, followed by the results of this study. Finally, we conclude this paper with a discussion section identifying the implications and limitations of our findings as well as possible directions for future research.

2 Theoretical Background

2.1 Perceived Risk

TCT was proposed by Coase (1937). It emphasizes that the realization of a transaction is determined by consideration of risks, which means when a transaction is under high uncertainty and high complexity, it's difficult to draw up a long term contract that includes all possible situations, and hence leads to market failure. Williamson (1975, 1979) later expanded Coase's original theoretical framework and proposed that market and vendors are the mechanisms that realize transactions. That is to say, when transaction cost doesn't exist or is very low, an economic agent will prefer market governance. On the contrary, if the cost is higher than the costs and benefits of production in the market, the economic agent will prefer internal organization. Hence, market failure explains why vendors exist. Market failure is not only based on behavioral assumptions (i.e., bounded rationality and opportunism), but is also influenced by the specificities of transactions, including asset specificity, uncertainty, and frequency of transaction.

Although TCT was first used to discuss market and vendor governance, more and more research later also explains user behavior based on TCT and consider user behavior as an issue of exchang between sellers and buyers. In addition, uncertainty is considered as a main specificity of transactions influencing users' strategic decision making in the realm of strategic management research (e.g., Belkhamza and Wafa 2014; Castaño et al. 2008; Maduku 2014; Perez-Alvarez and Paterson 2014; Teo and Yu 2005). Because of the breakthrough guarantee mechanism from crowdsourcing and asymmetry of information towards sharing economy M-services, it's difficult to predict the behaviors of the other transaction party, and further results in uncertainty. Users' transaction costs may escalate with the increase of uncertainty because users will be required to be engaged in time-consuming activities such as gathering information about vendors, products and services as well as paying attention to transaction process (Teo et al. 2004). Especially at the early stage of the sharing economy M-services, information asymmetry means that users need to take on more uncertainty. Hence, when information delivery and communication fail to efficiently reduce users' concerns of uncertainty, the possibility of realizing the sharing economy M-services will dramatically decrease.

2.2 Perceived Value

Users' motivation of behavior is mainly determined by their perception of benefits. Especially when users are more unfamiliar with new services or products, less experienced, or lack of knowledge, subjective value judgment becomes the basis of users' decision making. The theoretical base most commonly adopted by scholars is the TAM introduced by Davis (1989), which mainly explains users' behavioral model of adopting new IS using the ideas of perceived usefulness and perceived ease of use. Perceived usefulness refers to the subjective perception of users have in believing their work efficiency can be enhanced if they use certain systems. Especially in IS services, technology functions need to fulfill the task users expect from them, and provide users with appropriate feedback and assistance through operating with accuracy continuously (Lankton and McKnight 2011). Perceived ease of use refers to the degree to which an individual believes that using a particular IS would be free of effort. Thus, when users consider that system to be easy to use, they will believe it can improve their efficiency.

In recent years, many researchers (e.g., Godoe and Johansen 2012; Rahman and Sloan 2017) pointed out that perceived usefulness can be the key factor that leads to differentiation, and is often proved to be the most important variable in the model, while perceived ease of use has an inconsistent conclusion. Therefore, this study considered perceived usefulness as the crucial element constituting perceived value.

2.3 Perceived Price

In the context of information quality in Signaling Theory, perceived price can be interpreted as the important element. This is especially true in an immature online service. In this scenario, in addition to sending signals to users to enhance their confidence through marketing strategies such as return and exchange guarantee, privacy protection, and branding, the keys to more effectively and directly impact transactions under information asymmetry are building signals that convey a reasonable price-performance ratio of the product or service to make users agree on the product or service quality reflected in its price, or even be willing to pay a higher price to obtain this product or service. There are two paradigms that define perceived price. The first paradigm is the objective monetary price, referring to the actual cost of buyers' purchase (Dillon and Reif 2004). The second paradigm is the encoded price of the purchase perceived by buyers. Because online services continue to adopt new pricing strategies for matching and selling services, users' perceived price is vital for sharing economy M-services. If sellers implement a good price matching strategy, there would be a decrease in competition for price because competitors will fail to gain profits from lowering prices, which is similar to well-designed price-matching policies (Srivastava and Lurie 2001).

3   Research Hypotheses

3.1   The Effect of Perceived Risk on Adoption Intention

In accordance with TCT, this study used uncertainty to explain how users evaluate the risk of adopting sharing economy M-services. A large amount of research employing TCT stresses how uncertainty impacts decisions with regard to the scope of the enterprise, focusing on the decision of online services. For example, Teo and Yu (2005) used TCT to propose a model for explaining users' online purchase behavior and conducted empirical testing with Singaporean users. Their study found that perceived transaction cost could be used to explains users' willingness to make online purchases, and can be explained by uncertainty, dependability and purchase frequency. In other words, users are more likely to make online purchases if they consider the online store to have higher dependability, see online shopping as having lower uncertainty, and have more online experiences. Utilizing data from users engaged in e-banking services offered by four main retail banks in South Africa, Maduku (2014) also found out that the most important determinant for users to adopt mobile banking and online services is their trust in the e-banking system, which implies that reducing users' uncertainty in these systems can speed up their adoption of online and M-services on a larger scale.

Many IS researchers define uncertainty as a multi-faceted structure and favor the elements in examining uncertainty. Cunningham (1967) originally proposed six uncertainty dimensions to form the perceived risk: (1) performance, (2) financial, (3) opportunity/time, (4) safety, (5) social and (6) psychological loss. A rich stream of literature supports the usage of this measurement to understand e-service evaluations and adoption (e.g., Featherman and Pavlou 2003; Luo et al. 2010). According to Grewal et al. (1994), performance uncertainty is posited to be the most critical because it presents the overall possibility of "the product malfunctioning and not performing as it was designed and advertised and therefore failing to deliver the desired benefits." Their research adopted the performance uncertainty and further advanced the study on perceived risk by including security/privacy uncertainty. Luo et al. (2010) stated that transaction security/privacy uncertainty has to be considered in e-service investigation. The security/privacy uncertainty is defined as "potential loss of control over personal information" by Featherman and Pavlou (2003). Obviously, the concern about the security/privacy is a threat that is often theorized as a cause of user's self-protective behavior, and this argument has been evidenced by many other e-service research. Hence, this study proposes the following hypotheses:

Hypothesis 1: Users with high "performance uncertainty" will perceive low adoption intention toward sharing economy M-services.

Hypothesis 2: Users with high "security/privacy uncertainty" will perceive low adoption intention toward sharing economy M-services.

3.2 The Effect of Perceived Value on Adoption Intention

The TAM is a popular IS theory that models how users come to accept and use an IS service. The TAM has been continuously studied and expanded because it has been evidenced with strong behavioral elements and assumes that when someone forms an intention to act, they will be free to act without limitation. The TAM suggests that when users are presented with a new IS service, two factors influence their decision about how and when they will use it are perceived usefulness and perceived ease of use. Especially, a large number of studies stress the importance of the role perceived usefulness occupies in predicting the IS services usage and acceptance of users. Using a model built on TAM and TRI, Godoe and Johansen (2012) analyzed the reason users reject a system even if they are positive toward technology in general, and concluded that a low degree of perceived usefulness and perceived ease of use could contribute to users' rejection of a system in spite of their optimistic attitude toward the technology. Additionally, in their study conducted in Bangladesh, Rahman and Sloan (2017) also identified perceived usefulness to be the determinant factor of users' adoption of mobile commerce, and concluded that companies should continue to optimize their technologies and services to facilitate users in meeting the demands of contemporary ever-changing lifestyle. Hence, this study proposes the following hypothesis:

Hypothesis 3: Users with high "perceived usefulness" will perceive high adoption intention toward sharing economy M-services.

3.3 The Effect of Perceived Price on Adoption Intention

Perceived price is pointed out in several studies focusing on how it influences user behavior. For instance, Varki and Colgate (2001) investigated the relation between price, user behavioral intentions, and perceived value in the finance industry and found out that perceived price is the major determinant of value perceptions and has a stronger influence on user behavioral intentions, more than their mediated outcome via perceived value. Jiang and Rosenbloom (2005) also analyzed how satisfaction and price influence customer retention in various stages, and found that online retailers should focus on the quality of post-delivery services and improving customers' price perceptions to attain a higher customer retention rate.

Moreover, looking at how perceived price affects customers' decision on buying mobile communication services in the mobile and combined customer segment, Munnukka (2008) reached a conclusion that customers' buying intentions and perceived price are positively and significantly related. Another study exploring the influence of fairness and transparency of price on customer behavior by Rothenberger (2015) also discovered that customers will consider their offer to be superior if they perceive higher price fairness from the clarity of information they receive about product or service price. This results in a more positive attitude and satisfactory reaction of the customers about recommending or repurchasing the services or products. In conclusion, perceived price is considered as an important factor impacting buyers' decision making and a valid equivalence of economic expenditure that customers need to sacrifice to participate in a transaction of purchase. Hence, this study proposes the following hypothesis:

Hypothesis 4: *Users with positive "perceived price" will perceive high adoption intention toward sharing economy M-services.*

3.4   The Relationship Between Perceived Risk, Value, and Price

Businesses need to enhance consumers' level of confidence and assist them with reducing their concerns about uncertainty to ease their anxiety when making transactions through online third-party platforms. In their cross-level research that investigated how national culture and social institutions relate to the way users perceive the usefulness of the IS services, Parboteeah et al. (2005) found that users' perceived usefulness is significantly influenced by the degree of social inequality, industrialization, masculinity, and avoidance of uncertainty. To understand how online user behaved when they adopted e-commerce service, Babin et al. (2009) discovered that the intangible quality of online transaction is what contributes to online users' anxiety. Hence, uncertainty decreases the usefulness users attain from online shopping. They also found that uncertainty has a significant influence on how users perceive the value of the way their needs of information are satisfied, which means that how users perceive the value of standards is decided by the cause of uncertainty. Ntsafack et al. (2018) also pointed out in their research that well-structured services are needed to decrease the level of anxiety in a culture that is characterized with high uncertainty avoidance, which could be explained by the impact of uncertainty on reducing users' perceived usefulness and decreasing users' adoption intention. Hence, this study proposes the following hypotheses:

Hypothesis 5: *Users with high "performance uncertainty" will negatively affect "perceived usefulness" toward sharing economy M-services.*

Hypothesis 6: *Users with high "security/privacy uncertainty" will negatively affect "perceived usefulness" toward sharing economy M-services.*

Previous studies considered risk as influential for consumers' price perception. For instance, Tellis and Gaeth (1990) suggested that if consumers have a higher level of uncertainty about product quality, they are likely to be price-seeking, suggesting underweighting of price, or price-averse, suggesting over-weighting of price. This implies that the accessibility of quality information will influence consumers' sensitivity of price. Recent research by Demirgüneş (2015) also pointed out that the perceived risk of consumers has vital impacts on their willingness to pay a higher price, and concluded that there's a smaller chance for consumers to pay more for the service or product if they perceived uncertainties with it. They also proposed that offering consumers more information will enable enterprises to decrease their perceived uncertainty and thus lead to a higher profit. Hence, this study proposes the following hypotheses:

Hypothesis 7: *Users with high "performance uncertainty" will negatively affect "perceived price" toward sharing economy M-services.*

Hypothesis 8: *Users with high "security/privacy uncertainty" will negatively affect "perceived price" toward sharing economy M-services.*

4   Research Results

4.1   Measurement and Psychometric Properties

The objective of this study was to understand user's adoption behavior from three theories: perceived risk (measured by security/privacy uncertainty (SUN) and performance uncertainty (PUN)), perceived value (measured by perceived usefulness (PU)), and perceived price (PP) in the context of sharing economy M-services. A survey was conducted to obtain primary data with the survey questionnaire comprising 17 items measured on a 7-point Likert scale (where 1 = extremely disagree, 2 = disagree, 3 = somewhat disagree, 4 = neither disagree nor agree, 5 = somewhat agree, 6 = agree and 7 = extremely agree). The data was collected from Taiwan. The online sampling method was used, and a total of 509 questionnaires were completed and returned.

In this study, the multi-item scale was used to assess the various constructs. According to the judgment criteria proposed by Hair et al. (2006), the internal consistency of latent constructs, the factor loading of each observed item, and the average extracted variance (AVE) are the main methods used to evaluate reliability and validity. Specifically, Cronbach' α and composite reliability (CR) are used to represent internal consistency of latent constructs. A higher composite reliability value means that true variance accounts for a higher percentage of the total variance, with its value suggested to be above 0.6. The square of the factor loading of each observed item can be used to represent the explanatory power latent constructs have on the observed item, and is the basis of evaluating convergent validity, with its value suggested to be above 0.7. AVE is the total explanatory power the latent constructs have on the observed items. According to Fornell and Larcker (1981), if the AVE value presents the degree of association in latent constructs to be above 0.5 and higher than the degree of association between latent constructs, it indicates the discriminant validity of measured variables. Finally, the multi-group SEM approach was adopted to examine the moderating effects of contingencies of different user experiences.

Table 1 shows the results of reliability statistics. In terms of reliability, the values of Cronbach's α for the latent constructs were between 0.688 and 0.882 with all the values of CR above 0.69. As for validity, the samples had a factor loading above 0.6 between each measured variable, while all the AVE value were above 0.5 and larger than the square of correlation coefficients between other latent constructs, showing the convergent and discriminant validity of this study.

Table 1. Measurement and reliability statistics

Measurement	Means	FL
Technology uncertainty (Cronbach's α = 0.882; CR = 0.883)		
Car sharing services' security and privacy	4.90	0.83
Car sharing services' mobile payment assurance	5.00	0.83
Car sharing services' network control security	4.96	0.85
Car sharing services' personal data protection	5.00	0.73
Supplies uncertainty (Cronbach's α = 0.733; CR = 0.739)		
Car sharing services' maintenance and replacement management	5.14	0.60
Car sharing services' outdoor safety management	5.22	0.81
Car sharing services' battery charge management	5.27	0.67
Perceived usefulness (Cronbach's α = 0.859; CR = 0.858)		
Car sharing services help save transportation cost	5.31	0.74
Car sharing services help solve parking issues	5.14	0.68
Car sharing services help save on maintenance costs	5.25	0.73
Car sharing services can provide customized services through big data	5.46	0.78
Car sharing services help environmental protection	5.69	0.77
Price perception (Cronbach's α = 0.688; CR = 0.696)		
Charging of car sharing services is reasonable	4.10	0.68
Willing to pay a higher price for car sharing services	3.80	0.77
Adoption intention (Cronbach's α = 0.855; CR = 0.851)		
The design philosophy of car sharing services is good	5.55	0.73
Willing to try car sharing services	5.27	0.84
Willing to recommend car sharing services to friends and family	5.01	0.86

4.2   Results of Structural Equation Modeling

Fit of the Full Structural Model

First of all, clustering analysis was used to classify the samples into groups with different user experience levels for contingency analysis. Based on the k-means method, the whole sample was classified into two groups: low- and high-experienced users, and the F-value revealed that there were significant differences among the two groups on attribute scores. Next, this study adopted the structural equation modeling (SEM) to estimate the structural model using the maximum likelihood (ML) method. The results showed that the chi-square statistics for low- and high-experienced users were 297.81 ($df = 110$) and 243.99 ($df = 110$) separately, and the p-values were less than 0.001, so the model failed to fit in an absolute sense. However, because the chi-square test was known for its sensitivity to sample size (Hair et al. 2006), even a good fitting model (i.e., only small discrepancies between observed and predicted covariance) could be rejected. Thus, researchers recommend complementing chi-square with other goodness-of-fit measures. As noted previously, GFI = 0.86 and 0.91, CFI = 0.86 and 0.91 met the 0.85 cutoff, and the point estimate of RMSEA = 0.088 and 0.065 was less than 0.1. Also, the parsimonious fit measure χ^2/df = 2.71 and 2.22 were under the recommended threshold limits (< 5) for this measure (Jöreskog 1970). Thus, the overall proposed structural model was sufficiently supported.

Hypotheses Testing
This study adopted the multi-group SEM to test the direct and indirect effects of antecedent variables (SUN, PUN, PU, and PP) on adoption intention of sharing economy M-services in different user experiences contingencies. Figure 1 – (1) indicated the path coefficients and their significance for each hypothesis. Overall, two out of the eight hypotheses were significant by low-experienced users: the direct effects of PUN and SUN on adoption intention were nonsignificant, while the main construct - PU (0.67, p-value < 0.01) and PP (0.29, p-value < 0.01) had positive direct effect on adoption intention; therefore, H3 and H4 was supported but H1 and H2 were not supported. Moreover, all the effects of PUN and SUN on PU and PP were nonsignificant. Thus, the results didn't support PU and PP to be the mediator of the structural model. Therefore, H5, H6, H7, and H8 were not supported.

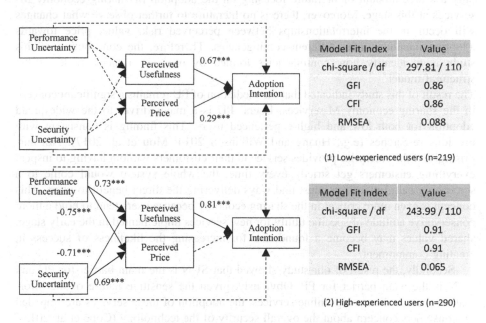

(1) Low-experienced users (n=219)

(2) High-experienced users (n=290)

Fig. 1. Multi-group structural equation modeling results

However, it is worth noting that the high- and low-experienced users had great differences in structural relationships. Figure 1 – (2) showed that six out of the eight hypotheses were significant by high-experienced users: the direct effects of PUN, SUN, and PP on adoption intention were nonsignificant, while PU (0.81, p-value < 0.01) had positive direct effect on adoption intention; therefore, H3 was supported but H1, H2, and H4 were not supported. It was interesting to find that the effect of PUN on PU (0.73, p-value < 0.01) being positive while the effect of SUN on PU (−0.71, p-value < 0.01) being negative. Conversely, the effect of PUN on PP (−0.75, p-value < 0.01) was negative while the effect of SUN on PP (0.69, *p*-value < 0.01) was positive. Thus, the results supported mediated roles of PU on the relationship between PUN, SUN, and adoption intention. However, because of the negative hypotheses of PUN and SUN on PU and PP, H6 and H7 were supported, but H5 and H8 were not supported.

5 Conclusion

Management and Practical Implication

The sharing economy opened up new ways of accessing goods and services in sustainable ways. It required a new level of thinking and creativity, disrupting traditional habits of doing things. Even though the concepts of perceived risk, value, and price have long been central components of a number of theories of user behavior, there is only a scarce amount of literature focusing on the adoption of sharing economy M-services at this stage. Moreover, there is no literature to further observe what changes will occur in the interrelationships between perceived risk, value, price towards adoption intention under different contingencies. Therefore, the contribution of this study is to identify how contingencies formed by user experiences moderate the structural model.

The result of this study indicated that the mediation of PU remains a significant concern in the sharing economy M-services. Users' PU is a major driver to the widespread adoption for both low and high-experienced users. This finding is consistent with previous researches (e.g., Huang and Wilkinson 2014; Mou et al. 2017). Not surprisingly, if the enterprise provides service to their customers without having to inspect everything customers get strictly every time, the whole system would come to a screeching halt. Enterprises must find ways delivering the direct benefit to users. This concept is even more critical in the sharing economy because users tend to hold a more conservative attitude of specific utility for new services implemented in the early stage, shared values may become a foundation for increasing the likeliness of success in creating commitment.

Secondly, the result of our study showed that SUN is the main barrier for PU and PUN is the main barrier for PP. Obviously, given the sensitive nature of the information shared when using online services, the adoption of these services are impeded by consumers concern about the overall security of the technology (Cope et al. 2013). Sharing economy M-services providers therefore need to ensure that online systems are sound with state-of-the-art safety management in place to minimize potential risks that end-users may be exposed to. To decrease users' SUN in sharing economy M-services, enterprises will also need to comply with legal structures to provide transparent guarantees if any dispute occurs. These risk control activities should be part of a communication strategy aimed at instilling trust in users regarding the services (Maduku 2014). On the other hand, the results showed that the higher the PUN, the lower the PP. This demonstrated that compared to the security uncertainty caused by technology, consumers believe that the uncertainty of supplies quality is more controllable by suppliers, and therefore, when PUN is increased, the consumer's tolerance for price is lower.

The third observation in this study was that there is a distinct discrepancy in the price judgment of sharing economy M-services between low and high-experienced users. For the low-experienced users, the price is a driver to determine user's intention towards adopting sharing economy M-services. In comparison, when user experience is increased to a certain level, the consideration of price ceases to significantly influence users' adoption behavior. The practical implications of the findings refer to the fact that the use of pricing schemes needs to not only take service life cycle stages into consideration, but also enhances users' judgment of price reasonableness through delivering signals of service value to prevent pricing schemes from becoming the obstacle of adoption behavior. In their study of pricing objectives over the service life cycle, Avlonitis et al. (2005) also pointed out a similar concept and considered the stage of services' life cycle and the sector of operation to have an influence on the pricing objectives pursued. Managers could have much to gain by taking a "situation specific approach" when they set prices. Therefore, various objectives of pricing need to be determined when a service moves from one life cycle stage to the next, and different services also require a different pricing strategy.

Limitations

Our results and findings should be interpreted in light of the following limitations that are inherent in this research. First, the survey respondents in this study are 20–40 age group; hence, caution should be exercised in generalizing these results to the general population. Second, the research model is designed to discuss the influences on perceived risk, value, and price in adopting sharing economy M-services by using Taiwan users. Future research can further explore the cross-culture investigation to obtain insights for users' continuous adoption.

References

Avlonitis, G.J., Indounas, K.A., Gounaris, S.P.: Pricing objectives over the service life cycle: some empirical evidence. Eur. J. Mark. **39**(5/6), 696–714 (2005)

Babin, G., Kropf, P., Weiss, M. (eds.): MCETECH 2009. LNBIP, vol. 26. Springer, Heidelberg (2009). https://doi.org/10.1007/978-3-642-01187-0

Belkhamza, Z., Wafa, S.A.: The role of uncertainty avoidance on e-commerce acceptance across cultures. Int. Bus. Res. **7**(5), 166–173 (2014)

Castaño, R., Sujan, M., Kacker, M., Sujan, H.: Managing consumer uncertainty in the adoption of new products: temporal distance and mental simulation. J. Mark. Res. **45**(3), 320–336 (2008)

Coase, R.H.: The nature of the firm. Economica **4**(16), 386–405 (1937)

Cope, A., Rock, A., Schmeiser, M.D.: Risk perception, risk tolerance and consumer adoption of mobile banking services (2013). https://ssrn.com/abstract=2048565

Cunningham, S.M.: The major dimensions of perceived risk. In: Cox, D.F. (ed.) Risk Taking and Information Handling in Consumer Behavior. Harvard University Press, Boston, MA (1967)

Davis, F.D.: Perceived usefulness, perceived ease of use, and user acceptance of information technology. MIS Q. **13**(3), 319–340 (1989)

Demirgüneş, B.K.: Relative importance of perceived value, satisfaction and perceived risk on willingness to pay more. Int. Rev. Manag. Mark. **5**(4), 211–220 (2015)

Dillon, T.W., Reif, H.L.: Factors influencing consumers' e-commerce commodity purchases. Inf. Technol. Learn. Perform. J. **22**(2), 1–12 (2004)

Featherman, M.S., Pavlou, P.A.: Predicting e-services adoption: a perceived risk facets perspective. Int. J. Hum. Comput. Stud. **59**, 451–474 (2003)

Fornell, C., Larcker, D.: Evaluating structural equation models with unobservable variables and measurement error. J. Mark. Res. **18**, 39–50 (1981)

Godoe, P., Johansen, T.S.: Understanding adoption of new technologies: technology readiness and technology acceptance as an integrated concept. J. Eur. Psychol. Stud. **3**, 38–52 (2012)

Grewal, D., Gotlieb, J., Marmorstein, H.: The moderating effects of message framing and source credibility on the price-perceived risk relationship. J. Consum. Res. **21**, 145–153 (1994)

Hair, J.F., Black, W.C., Babin, B.J., Anderson, R.E., Tatham, R.L.: Multivariate Data Analysis, 6th edn. Prentice-Hall, Upper Saddle River (2006)

Huang, Y., Wilkinson, I.F.: A case study of the development of trust in a business relation: implications for a dynamic theory of trust. J. Bus. Mark. Manag. **7**(1), 254–279 (2014)

Jiang, P., Rosenbloom, B.: Customer intention to return online: price perception, attribute-level performance, and satisfaction unfolding over time. Eur. J. Mark. **39**(1/2), 150–174 (2005)

Jöreskog, K.G.: A general method for analysis of covariance structures. Biometrika **57**, 239–251 (1970)

Lankton, N.K., McKnight, D.H.: What does it mean to trust facebook? Examining technology and interpersonal trust beliefs. ACM SIGMIS Database DATABASE Adv. Inf. Syst. **42**(2), 32–54 (2011)

Luo, X., Li, H., Zhang, J., Shim, J.P.: Examining multi-dimensional trust and multi-faceted risk in initial acceptance of emerging technologies: an empirical study of mobile banking services. Decis. Support Syst. **49**, 222–234 (2010)

Maduku, D.K.: Customers' adoption and use of e-banking services: the South African perspective. Banks Bank Syst. **9**(2), 78–88 (2014)

Mou, J., Shin, D.-H., Cohen, J.: Understanding trust and perceived usefulness in the consumer acceptance of an e-service: a longitudinal investigation. Behav. Inf. Technol. **36**(2), 125–139 (2017)

Munnukka, J.: Customers' purchase intentions as a reflection of price perception. J. Prod. Brand Manag. **17**(3), 188–196 (2008)

Ntsafack, F.W., Kamdjoug, J.R.K., Wamba, S.F.: Exploring factors affecting mobile services adoption by young consumers in Cameroon. In: Rocha, Á., Adeli, H., Reis, L.P., Costanzo, S. (eds.) WorldCIST'18 2018. AISC, vol. 746, pp. 46–57. Springer, Cham (2018). https://doi.org/10.1007/978-3-319-77712-2_5

Parboteeah, D.V., Parboteeah, K.P., Cullen, J.B., Basu, C.: Perceived usefulness of information technology: a cross-national model. J. Glob. Inf. Technol. Manag. **8**(4), 29–48 (2005)

Perez-Alvarez, C., Paterson, W.: Uncertainty avoidance, IT perceptions, use and adoption: distributed teams in two cultures. J. Acad. Bus. Ethics **8**(1), 1–8 (2014)

Rahman, M.M., Sloan, T.: User adoption of mobile commerce in Bangladesh: integrating perceived risk, perceived cost and personal awareness with TAM. Int. Technol. Manag. Rev. **6**(3), 103–124 (2017)

Rothenberger, S.: Fairness through transparency—the influence of price transparency on price fairness perceptions. CEB Working Paper (2015). https://dipot.ulb.ac.be/dspace/bitstream/2013/200240/3/wp15008.pdf

Spence, M.: Job market signaling. Q. J. Econ. **87**, 355–374 (1973)

Srivastava, J., Lurie, N.: A consumer perspective on price-matching refund policies: effect on price perceptions and search behavior. J. Consum. Res. **28**, 296–307 (2001)

Tellis, G.J., Gaeth, G.: Best value, price-seeking and price aversion: the impact of information and learning on consumer choices. J. Market. **54**, 34–45 (1990)

Teo, T.S.H., Wang, T.P., Leong, C.H.: Understanding online shopping behaviour using a transaction cost economics approach. Int. J. Internet Mark. Advert. **1**(1), 62–84 (2004)

Teo, T.S.H., Yu, Y.: Online buying behavior: a transaction cost economics perspective. Omega **33**(5), 451–465 (2005)

Varki, S., Colgate, M.: The role of price perceptions in an integrated model of behavioral intentions. J. Serv. Res. **3**(3), 232–240 (2001)

Williamson, O.: Markets and Hierarchies, Analysis and Antitrust Implications: A Study in the Economics of Internal Organization. Free Press, New York (1975)

Williamson, O.: Transaction cost economics: the governance of contractual obligations. J. Law Econ. **22**(2), 233–261 (1979)

The Promotion of Empathy for the Experience of Users with Visual Impairment in the Game Design Education

Isabel Cristina Siqueira da Silva[✉]

Laureate International Universities, Porto Alegre, RS 90840-440, Brazil
isabel.siqueira@gmail.com

Abstract. People are constantly seeking new experiences through perceptions that involve practical and subjective aspects such as usability, efficiency, satisfaction, and accessibility. The advent of digital inclusion has encouraged the software development with support for accessibility, which is proposed to promote the improvement of the quality of life of people with some type of disability, although also reflects positively with people without disabilities. In this sense, accessible digital games constitute a growing demand and, among the different solutions that have been proposed, the audiogames propose to offer a differentiated user experience, with the exploration of different sound stimuli that complement the visual stimuli. Thus, audio features are explored with the aim of guiding the player about the game universe based on different sounds and such features are significant for the experience of visually impaired players. However, the development of audiogames that are really accessible and provide a satisfying interaction for visually impaired users is still a challenge for game designers, who need to develop empathy for their target audience by understanding their needs and expectations. This article presents an experience report involving the development of audiogames that, though considering the accessibility to visually impaired, focus on the experience provided to game designers without visually impaired so as to awaken in these the empathy for games accessible through the understanding of how sound stimuli can compensate for lack of vision.

Keywords: Digital accessibility · Game design · User experience

1 Introduction

The digital inclusion promoted in the last decades encouraged the development of software with digital accessibility support, which began to explore resources such as voice recognition, text reading, inclusion of subtitles, pounds and others. In this sense, assistive technology contributes to providing or enhancing functional abilities of people with some kind of disability and helping to promote a more independent and inclusive life [1]. According Schirmer et al. [2], this technology proposes to solve, with creativity, functional problems in a perspective of developing human potentialities, valuing desires, abilities, positive expectations and quality of life.

© Springer Nature Switzerland AG 2019
M. Antona and C. Stephanidis (Eds.): HCII 2019, LNCS 11572, pp. 326–341, 2019.
https://doi.org/10.1007/978-3-030-23560-4_24

Considering the different digital solutions with accessibility features, we have the accessible games, which are a growing demand, but still at an early stage in interest of developers and game market. Among the different solutions proposed, so-called audiogames can be specially designed for users with visual impairment (VI), whether moderate or severe (blindness), although they can also be played by people without VI since audiogames present a complete auditory interface and can be played without the use of graphics.

For gamers without VI, the audiogames propose to offer a differentiated user experience, with the exploration of different sound stimuli that complement the visual stimuli. On the other hand, for gamers with VI, the audio features are explored with the aim of guiding the player about the game universe, mechanics, and interaction.

Valente et al. [3] indicate five major benefits in the audiogames design and development:

- Inclusion of players with VI to the target audience;
- Gameplay innovation, exploring sound feedback incorporated into the game environment;
- Exploration of other senses beyond sight, such as audio and touch;
- Creation of personalized and creative experiences;
- Promotion of new creative experiences in games.

Gerente et al. [4] point out that, in the absence of vision, a spatial reaction is the result of the convergence of auditory, proprioceptive, vestibular, and tactile afferences. People with severe VI (blindness) mainly use a hearing and order to store information about space, especially an object location. The auditory perception unites itself to individual interpretations and experiences.

According Santos [5], although the relationship between the sound stimulus and the reactions of the nervous and conscious systems is physiological, the mental process establishes subjectivity in its interpretation of sound. The ears perceive the sound, the surrounding sound environment, the sound context of production and the capture of the provoked stimulus.

Rober and Masuch [6] talk about the balance between the functionality and the aesthetics of sound in audiogames. The graphical interface of the game must present functionality and usability necessary for the player to complete his tasks and, at the same time, not present excessive information. In this sense, selecting the correct number of sounds is challenging and requires more art than science, since only one sound is perceived over time. Thus, the temporal design is fundamental in order that the audio as a whole is functional for the game and promotes the desired experience to the player.

However, the development of audiogames that are really accessible and provide a satisfying interaction for VI users is still a challenge for game designers. Audiogames require a balance between the functionality of the game and the aesthetics of sound. In order to approach game designers of users with serious VI, so that the first group understands the needs of the second, it is necessary to develop empathy between them.

According Del Prette and Del Prette [7] and Hoffman [8], empathy corresponds to the capacity to understand and to feel what one feels in an interaction of affective demand, i.e., is about the ability to put oneself in the other's place, to assume their perspective in a given situation. Thus, users with VI can actively participate in the main stages of the development of audiogames, while game developers must consider the main needs of these potential users of their products.

This work addresses the need for empathy in relation to players with blindness by game designers so that the latter are able to design audiogames really accessible to VI users. In parallel, it is expected that audiogames will also be challenging for non-VI players, awakening in them the empathy regarding the presence of accessibility in digital games.

In order to investigate how this theme is treated by future professionals in the field of game design, a case study was carried out with students of the final semesters of an undergraduate games course. The main objective was the development of audiogames and the study of how they impact on players without VI who try to play them without seeing the scenario, being guided solely by the audio. In the end, the students/developers became the role of users of the audiogames developed by the peers in order to arouse the empathy of the target audience and the awareness of the importance of digital accessibility.

The remainder of the paper is organized as follows. Section 2 briefly reviews related work. Section 3 presents the methodology employed in this study as well as the proposed audiogames, describing their features. Section 4 present the results obtained and discussion and, finally, the Sect. 5 contains the conclusion and final comments.

2 Related Work

Different approaches have been conceived for the development of audiogames coupled with digital accessibility and/or assistive technology. This section discusses works that address the development of audiogames, especially those that consider players with VI as a target audience.

In 2004, Friberg and Gardenfors [9] discussed the potential of developing audiogames, noting that they not only benefit blind users but also enrich the experience of users without disabilities. The authors highlight advantages that the use of sound resources can offer, so that game designers explore the various layers of information the audio provides, resulting in more multi-faceted play and more attractive to users.

This system can help the designers of the auditory interfaces to visualize the various types of information that sound objects can transmit. By reaching more than one listening mode, sounds can contain multiple layers of information, resulting in a more multifaceted and attractive game audio content.

Goldsmith [10] brings a proposal for assistive technology related to data development for analog role-playing games (RPG) in the RPG project dice for the visually impaired. The project starts from the observation of the difficulty that people with severe VI had to play RPG in its original form (analog). This observation generated empathy in the author who proposed a complete data set (d4, d6, d8, d10, d12 and d20), with braille characters on each face. The data is created from the use of 3D printers.

Araújo et al. [11] raise the question of game designers not being sufficiently familiar with the special needs of users with disabilities to the point of developing truly affordable digital games. The authors present a study of the existing guidelines for the design of digital games accessible from recommendations from six international and national guidelines. From this study, a manual instrument was created to evaluate the accessibility of mobile audiogames, which was applied in audiogames evaluation tests based on digital accessibility. The authors analyzed the results and concluded that the analyzed games were not fully accessible, indicating the complexity of drawing an evaluative standard for accessible mobile digital games, mainly in relation to the variety of devices and systems.

Kleina [12] presents an account of an initiative by the City Hall of Curitiba to use a digital game as a tool for a campaign related to the dissemination of the routines of people with disabilities in order to promote empathy for people without disabilities. In the game, the character must walk through a forest and at each stage has a specific deficiency (cognitive, motor, perceptive, etc.) resulting in a different sensory experience, put into practice through sounds, graphics and gameplay. The game explores visual and auditory features and was originally developed for the web platform.

Monteiro et al. [13] analyze the audio game "Blindside" as an objective to understand the fear-stimulating experience that a game of terror causes in a player in the absence of visual elements. The study points out that the absence of visual stimuli coupled with sound effects and trail contribute to immersion and fear in the players, especially among the less experienced. The sound ambiance and audio and track effects are features that can strengthen narrative, immersion and permanence in the game, assisting mainly users with serious VI.

Dall Agnol [14] presents the game "The Adventures of Joca Valente", developed to assist the rehabilitation of people with VI through the simulation of an external environment. The plot of the game is based on an external environment, using exploitative ludemas, performance physical and cognitive that present the proposed challenges. The game presents to the user sounds of daily life, exercising the spatial notion in relation to the represented virtual environment. Questions about empathy are not addressed.

"Frontiers" [15] is a 3D online multiplayer game that began to be developed in 2007 and addresses issues relating to the flight of refugees from Africa to Europe, with the aim of promoting players' empathy for the refugee cause. In the game, the player may experience a refugee or, on the other hand, a soldier who oversees the borders and is responsible for preventing the refugees from passing it.

Borges and Campos [16] approach recommendations for the development of audiogames so that they really present accessibility when they aim for it. The authors carried out a state-of-the-art research related to proposing recommendations for accessible games and listed thirty-one recommendations, which were used in the analysis of ten audiogames. The authors observed that games involving the constant generation of stimuli from the exploration of different sound resources provided a more immersive experience.

Table 1 presents a synthesis of the analysis of the works discussed in this section.

There are still few academic papers that focus on the role of the game designer when designing accessible audiogames and the experience they provide to their users. Outside the academy, there is still no relevant market movement in relation to the

Table 1. Comparison between related paper.

Work	Audiogames	Accessibility	UX	Empathy in developers
[9]	X	X	X	–
[10]	–	X	X	–
[11]	X	X	X	X
[12]	X	X	X	–
[13]	X	X	X	X
[14]	X	X	X	–
[15]	X	X	X	–
[16]	X	X	X	X

development of accessible digital games as well as in understanding the different needs of its general public.

Regarding VI, for example, Chin [17] points out that the most common type of color blindness, for example, is deuteranopia that affects about 5% of men and makes it difficult to distinguish between red and green, complementary colors that are often used in digital games to distinguish elements. In company, for example, the authors of "Grand Theft Auto" games [18] circumvent this problem using different shapes as well as different colors on the map of the game. While EA Dice [19] offers four pre-selected color schemes in the Star Wars Battlefront game, only one of which is for players without VI; the other three treat people with protanopia, deuteranopia, and tritanopia (which correspond to the difficulties of people who feel red, green, and blue light, respectively).

Thus, it is perceived that it is necessary to develop a multidisciplinary view of game developers, both serious and purely entertaining, in order to meet the demands that become effective in society.

3 Methodology

This section presents an experience report involving the design, development and evaluation of audiogames whose target audience is formed by users with severe VI (blindness). Although the games were tested by different groups of users, both with VI and without VI, it focuses on the students' evaluation of an undergraduate games course without VI that, at the end of game development, evaluated the games of his colleagues by put themselves in the shoes of players with VI. It is intended, therefore, to awaken in future professionals the empathy for the public with VI, which grows every day and is increasingly included digitally, crying for accessibility and innovations in the area of technology.

Next, details of the methodology used to carry out the case study will be presented.

3.1 Subjects

Twenty-three students attending the human-computer interaction (HCI) class of final semesters of an undergraduate games course participated in this experiment. In this group of students, there were only two women, and the ages ranged from nineteen to twenty-five years (see Fig. 1).

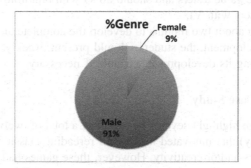

Fig. 1. Percentage of the subjects' genres.

It is also worth noting that 70% (seventy percent) of the students had never had contact with audiogames - neither as a player nor as a developer, and more than 80% (eighty percent) considered themselves an experienced player. Regarding platform preference, 90% (ninety percent) play on personal computers, 73% (seventy-three percent) play on consoles, 36% (thirty-six percent) play on the web platform and 46% (forty-six percent) of these play on mobile devices. These data are summarized in Fig. 2.

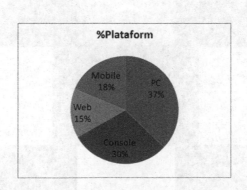

Fig. 2. Percentage of platform preference.

To this group of students, it was proposed the development of functional audio-games, of free theme, being able to be both serious games and games for pure enter-tainment. Thus, students were free to define the genre of the game, the platform, the dimensionality (2D/3D), the type of interaction, the plot and the narrative.

The games could present graphic or non-visual scenarios, and it is mandatory to exploit sound resources so that the interaction can only be based on these. The games should be challenging and interesting in terms of experience for both serious VI players (blindness) and players without VI.

Students could develop the games individually or in groups of two or three components. It was not reported, however, that at the end of game development, the peers themselves would be game testers and should do so with blindfold in order to promote empathy towards users with VI.

The students had about two months to develop the complete and functional games. Throughout the development, the students should present, weekly, report and analysis of evolution, adjusting its development schedule if necessary.

3.2   Games and Case Study

In this subsection, we highlight seven games (out of a total of twelve games developed during the case study) that innovated in terms of rereading classic analog games, plot, gameplay, mechanics and/or creativity. However, these games had some limitation, as will be described below.

The first game to be presented is IGenius, a 2D game of memorization and sequencing, based on a traditional analog game called *Genius*. As in the analog game, in this proposal of accessible digital game the player should reproduce sequences of lights and sounds. The sequences to be memorized and played back are based on both illumination and stereo sound where the right, left, up and down indications are verbalized. On computers, the interaction with the game occurs through directional keys, directly mapped, while on mobile devices the interaction occurs by touching the screen in bounded regions. The initial screen of the game can be seen in Fig. 3.

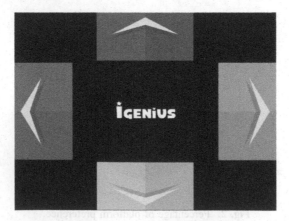

Fig. 3. IGenius game home screen.

Still considering games related to human memory, the game Memories Sound (Fig. 4) is a digital version of a traditional game where it is necessary to find pairs of cards. These hide images with music bands logos and, when a card is selected, the logo is displayed and a song from the related band plays. The game is for PC (personal computer) platform, is 2D and the interaction occurs with keys mapped according to the layout of the cards. Different levels of difficulty are proposed from the increase in the number of cards presented. Such levels and interaction are initially narrated to the player along with the interaction instructions.

Fig. 4. Memories Sound game home screen.

The Balance game (Fig. 5) proposes the player's challenge to be able to balance his avatar by walking on a rope stretched between two tall buildings of a city in a 3D scenario. As the avatar crosses over the rope, bursts of wind constantly unbalance it, arising randomly from right to left and vice versa, indicated by stereo sound. In PC, the player must use the mouse, clicking and dragging in the direction of the wind to help the avatar to balance again and try to reach his goal. On mobile devices, the mouse replaced by touch and slide the finger on the screen. The game does not present initial instructions on gameplay and interaction, so the player must explore the game in order to understand its mechanics.

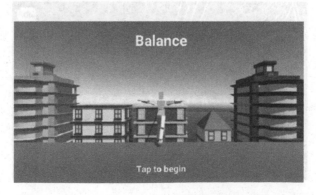

Fig. 5. Balance game home screen.

The PC game of Fig. 6 (Turret Attack) employs the shooter style and, through stereo sound effects, indicates the side where the enemy will appear in order to attack the player. When the enemy enters the scene, the player has a certain amount of time to calibrate his weapon, to aim at this one and to shoot shots against the same until it disintegrates. If the enemy strikes the player before receiving shots, the computer screen shakes by means of simulated camera shake accompanied by effects that indicate this behavior. As in Memories Sound, this 2D game features initial instructions regarding its gameplay and user interaction.

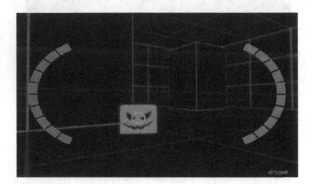

Fig. 6. Turret Attack game home screen.

The PC game In the Darkness (see Fig. 7) brings the proposition of a maze where the player is challenged to find the exit door only by means of sound stimuli. Different from the proposals discussed previously, it does not present visual graphics, and is based entirely on sound resources. These features indicate, through stereo sound, the proximity in reaction to the exit door, collision with walls and attacks by one or more enemies. The game has ten stages with increasing levels of difficulty. Initially, the player can choose to start the game immediately or receive instructions on their plot, gameplay and interaction.

Fig. 7. In the Darkness game home screen.

Figure 8 shows the initial screen of the PC game Maneuvers Simulator whose scenario is a ship flying in a 3D space with obstacles. As the player advances with the ship, obstacles appear on the way and the proximity to them is indicated by stereo sound and rhythm. The interaction is given by the directional keys and the only instructions given to the user are the commands to start the game and exit the game.

Fig. 8. Maneuvers Simulator game home screen.

Finally, the game Explorer (Fig. 9), like In the Darkness, presents a maze to the player, which is guided by sounds to get out of it. In this game, there are no enemy attacks, and for users without VI, the view of the scenery is limited like the sight of a flashlight in a dark setting. As in previous games, the interaction takes place through directional keys in PC.

Fig. 9. Explorer game images.

In addition, other point-and-click style games, shooter, runner and sound-based interaction were proposed, but were not finalized properly within the time frame established for this study.

3.3 Procedure

The seven games selected for this study were evaluated both by users with blindness and by users without VI. However, the focus of this work is the results of user/developer testing without VI, considering only the student group of the HCI class as mentioned at the beginning of this section. In this way, as the testers considered in this analysis were the same colleagues in the class where the case study was proposed, the number of evaluators ranged from 20 (twenty) to 22 (twenty-two), according to the number of students) that were part of the group that had the game evaluated.

Usability tests for game validation started with a pre-test, where information such as gender, age, semester, platform preference was collected, followed by a period of free play exploration, and the post-test, where players answered a questionnaire composed by 5 (five) statements and a five-point Likert scale of agreement ("Fully Agree", "Partially Agree", "Undecided", "Partially Disagree" and "Fully Disagree").

The statements contained in the evaluation form are listed below:

1. *The game interface follows usability heuristics;*
2. *The game is accessible to blind players;*
3. *Sound feedback is suitable for blind players;*
4. *The mechanics of the game are easy to understand for blind players;*
5. *The initial instructions make clear the purpose of the game for blind players.*

Other statements could be proposed, but the present study is based only on these five commons to all groups. The results, suggestions and criticisms are commented in the next section.

4 Results and Discussion

From the results of the tests, it should be noted that the responses to such statements were similar for the seven games evaluated, since the vast majority were between "fully agree" and "partially agree" (see Fig. 10).

For the assertive (1), it is observed that all the players indicated agreement, and the game Balance was the only game to present a low percentage of disagreement. This fact can be due to the characteristics of the same in innovating in terms of mechanics, since an innovative posture is not always easy. However, it was noticed that the interface and the interaction with the game Balance were not intuitive. Already the game Explorer presents 30% of indecision, since its interface is extremely simple, not featuring HUD (Heads-Up Display).

The assessment of statement (2), as the statement (1), presents a high index of evaluators indicating agreement, except for the game Explorer, which obtained 40% indecision and 20% disagreement. For this game, the users indicated that the sounds should have been better worked, fact also reflected in the statement (3) in which the game presents a 40% disagreement.

The Balance game also had a relevant disagreement index of 35%. In this game, the interaction of the mouse movement to balance the avatar got critics regarding the lack of indication of the amplitude, which was fundamental to balance the avatar according

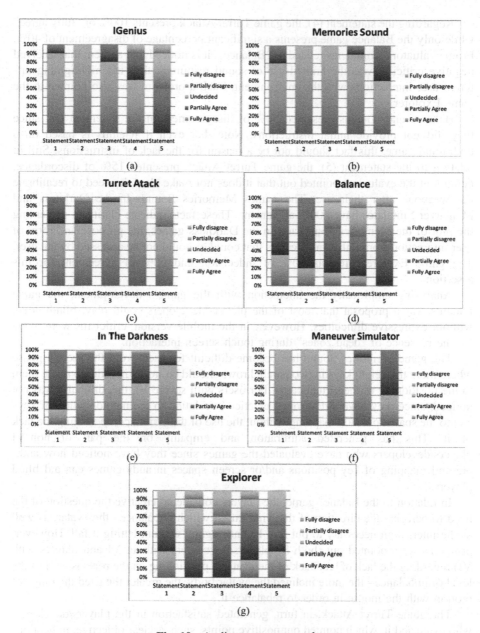

Fig. 10. Audiogames tests results.

to its level of imbalance. According to the tilt of the avatar, a greater range of the mouse movement must be performed to balance it. Another aspect pointed out as negative by the users was the lack of sonorous feedback related to the distance traveled by the avatar on the rope. Still in relation to the statement (3), we can notice for the other games with high percentage of agreement.

Regarding the statement (4), the game Turret Attack presents 100% of "fully agree" while only the Balance game presents a significant percentage of disagreement of 40%. From evaluators' comments related to "Balance", it is noticed that an item that received negative criticism was the limited use of sound resources, thus not highlighting different user interactions with the environment. Such a problem was also pointed to the game Explorer.

Balance and IGenius presented 50% of disagreement in the statement (5), since they did not provide initial instructions. Note that even if IGenius is based on a traditional game, this fact should not be a reason for the lack of instructions. Still in relation to the statement (5), the game Turret Attack presented 15% of discordance, being that the evaluators pointed out that it does not make clear the need to recalibrate the weapons after their use. The games Memories Sound, In the Darkness and Maneuver Simulator have 100% agreement. These facts indicate clarity in presenting the plot of the Memories Sound and In the Darkness games, the purpose and form of user interaction from initial instructions that could or could not be accessed by the user. The game Explorer presents 40% of indecision and 60% of agreement for this assertion.

Analyzing empirically the interaction with the game's development, the game IGenius was a proposal that most of the players/developers could play, blindfolded, without expressive difficulties. However, in the mobile version, criticisms were made for the presence of "dead zones" during touch screen interaction.

The game Memories Sound has become difficult for users from the second phase where more than eight keys in two parallel rows should be stored in order to relate them to the positioning of the virtual cards. For users with severe VI, this difficulty was not noticed, since they have a developed practice in relation to the memorization of keys and to the spatial position mapping without the use of the vision, compensating the lack of it. This has generated admiration and empathy on the part of non-VI players/developers who have evaluated the games since they have noticed how audible and mapping of key positions and/or screen spaces in audiogames can aid blind players.

In relation to the Balance game, the players considered creative the question of the need to perceive the direction of the wind gusts, which unbalanced the avatar, as well as the interaction necessary to put it in balance again, without letting it fall. However, problems were pointed out (both by players/developers without VI and players with VI) regarding the lack of feedback of the avatar's positioning on the rope as well as the level of imbalance - the more inclined the avatar body, the greater the need the range of motion with the mouse in order to rebalance it.

The game Turret Attack, in turn, generated satisfaction in the players/developers who evaluated it, which pointed out positive points, such as clear objective, indications of the enemy's position and elimination of it. However, the players were unanimous in pointing out as a negative point the lack of feedback regarding the need to recalibrate the ammunition of the weapon whenever it ended. Only in the visual scenario version was there an indication of the amount of ammunition available.

The game In the Darkness was considered the most challenging and the best that promoted immersion by the evaluators/developers, since it did not have visual scenarios. Thus, the testers did not have to close their eyes or be blindfolded, which challenged them by allowing them to play with all their active senses, as in their day to day life, but with the breakdown of the visual game paradigm.

In the game In the Darkness, visual scenarios could never be accessed, a fact that encouraged players/developers to play the game several times, trying to build mentally the scenarios of the different phases. At certain times, the players felt psychological terror, indicating immersion in the universe of the game. Clearly the empathy for players with severe VI was promoted, and the evaluators were surprised to see how difficult it was to play such a game, which has ten phases and whose degree of difficulty gradually increases.

The game Maneuver Simulator, like the IGenius, presented a mechanics of easy understanding, being the initial challenge to map the rhythm of the sound to the proximity of the obstacles. Already the game Explorer was criticized for not using audio features according to its simple mechanics, making it difficult to interact in some parts of the game.

At the end of this study, it was noticed the exchange of experiences between the developers and the indication that, even with the end of the case study, they would continue to improve their games and carry out new tests in order to have a final quality product. By putting themselves in the place of players with serious VI, student developers/evaluators come to understand a little more about the difficulties and potentialities that audiogames can offer, developing empathy for the target audience and issues of digital accessibility. Many even performed self-assessment, indicating the evolution in thinking about players with severe VI and their special needs.

5 Conclusions

Digital games have their popularity increasing significantly each day. Such popularity attracts new professionals to the games industry as well as new users and their different needs and expectations. To do so, it is necessary to propose technologies, constant innovation and high potential for creativity. The need to integrate multidisciplinary aspects with a careful look at the heterogeneity of its users makes the development of games a challenging task.

Besides, digital inclusion promoted in the last years drives the demand for the development of accessible digital games that consider different types of special needs. Considering that games are highly visual, to develop games whose plot, mechanics, and gameplay work independently of graphic scenarios and with a focus on sound resources, is an important mission for game designers in audiogames. In this sense, Lemos [20] indicates that the difficulty in designing audiogames is the absence of conventions common to the visual universe, since the audio employed should be easy to learn and memorize, providing an effective experience to the player who has VI.

Archambault et al. [21] highlights that designing games for players with special needs is a challenge: a matter of practical and social research needed. Considering specifically audiogames, these contain specific emotional components and patterns that can be perceived through empathy, which can be experienced by both the game developer and non-VI players.

This paper investigated how developers of digital games, without VI, would behave in the role of blind users, testing games of their colleagues developed during the present study. Considering the proposals developed, seven main ones were discussed in this work according to the type of gameplay, mechanics, interaction and accessibility. In an empirical way, it could be noted that the students who participated in the experiment demonstrated, for the most part, the development of empathy for players with DV as they researched their main needs. Immersion in a virtual world described only by sounds broke the paradigm of visual games, awakening students to the importance of seeing a public that has special needs and that grows every day.

It is hoped, therefore, to contribute to the area of development of accessible digital games in a time of strong appeal for digital inclusion based on empathy.

References

1. Ministério da Educação: Saberes e práticas da inclusão: desenvolvendo competências para o atendimento às necessidades educacionais especiais de alunos cegos e de alunos com baixa visão, 2nd edn. MEC, Secretária de Educação Especial, Brasília (2006)
2. Schirmer, C.R., Browning, N., Bersch, R., Machado, R.: Formação Continuada a Distância de Professores para o Atendimento Educacional Especializado - Deficiência Física. SEESP/SEED/MEC. Gráfica e Editora Cromos, Curitiba (2007)
3. Valente, L., Souza, C.S., Feijó, B.: Turn off the graphics: designing non-visual interfaces for mobile phone games. J. Braz. Comput. Soc. 15(1), 45–58 (2009)
4. Gerente, J.G.S., Pascoal, A.G., Pereira, M.L.: Localização especial de estímulos sonoros em indivíduos cegos congênitos: estudo comparativo da posição tridimensional da cabeça em adultos cegos congênitos e indivíduos videntes. Revista brasileira de educação especial 14 (1), 111–120 (2008)
5. Santos, O.C.: Uma paisagem de sons: a influência dos estímulos sonoros para o gênero dramático no rádio. Intercom – Sociedade Brasileira de Estudos Interdisciplinares da Comunicação. XII Congresso Brasileiro de Ciências da Comunicação da Região Sudeste – Juiz de Fora – MG (2007)
6. Rober, N., Masuch, M.: Leaving the screen new perspectives in audio-only gaming. In: Proceedings of ICAD 05-Eleventh Meeting of the International Conference on Auditory Display, Limerick, Ireland (2005)
7. Del Prette, A., Del Prette, Z.A.P.: Psicologia das Relações Interpessoais. Vozes, Petrópolis (2001)
8. Hoffman, M.: Empathy and Moral Development: Implications for Caring and Justice. Cambridge University Press, New York (2000)
9. Friberg, J., Gärdenfors, D.: Audio games: new perspectives on game audio. In: Proceedings of the 2004 ACM SIGCHI International Conference on Advances in Computer Entertainment Technology (ACE 2004). ACM, New York, pp. 148–154 (2004)
10. Goldsmith, J.: RPG dice for the visually impaired. Kickstarter (2015). https://www. kickstarter.com/projects/1704875037/rpg-dice-for-the-visually-impaired/description. Accessed Jan 2019
11. Araújo, M.C.C., Facanha, A.R., Darin, T., Viana, W.: Um Estudo das Recomendações de Acessibilidade para Audiogames Móveis. In: Proceedings do XIV Simpósio Brasileiro de Jogos e Entretenimento Digital (SBGames), Teresina (2015)

12. Kleina, N.: Game da Prefeitura de Curitiba põe você na pele de pessoas com deficiência. Tecmundo (2016). https://www.tecmundo.com.br/jogos/106402-game-prefeitura-curitiba-poe-voce-pele-pessoas-deficiencia.htm. Accessed Julho 2017
13. Monteiro, C., Araújo, A., Correia, I.: Imersão e medo em jogos de terror: análise das estruturas de áudio e efeitos sonoros do jogo Blindside. In: Proceedings do XV Simpósio Brasileiro de Jogos e Entretenimento Digital (SBGames), São Paulo (2016)
14. Dall Agnol, A: Audiogames: jogos acessíveis para pessoas com deficiência visual. Centro Tecnológico de Acessibilidade, IFRS (2017). http://cta.ifrs.edu.br/noticias/visualizar/126. Accessed Jan 2019
15. Frontiers Game: Life on the verge of hope. http://frontiers-game.com. Accessed Julho 2017
16. Teixeira Borges, O., de Borba Campos, M.: "I'm blind, can I play?" Recommendations for the development of audiogames. In: Antona, M., Stephanidis, C. (eds.) UAHCI 2017. LNCS, vol. 10278, pp. 351–365. Springer, Cham (2017). https://doi.org/10.1007/978-3-319-58703-5_26
17. Chin, W.: Around 92% of people with impairments play games despite difficulties. Game Accessibility (2017)
18. Rockstar Games (2018). https://www.rockstargames.com. Accessed Jan 2019
19. EA Dice (2018). http://starwars.ca.com/pt_BR/starwars/battlefront. Accessed Jan 2019
20. Lemos, E.D.J.: Audiogames: jogos digitais sonorous. Intercom – Sociedade Brasileira de Estudos Interdisciplinares da Comunicação. XXXIX Congresso Brasileiro de Ciências da Comunicação (2016)
21. Archambault, D., Gaudy, T., Miesenberger, K., Natkin, S., Ossmann, R.: Towards generalised accessibility of computer games. In: Pan, Z., Zhang, X., El Rhalibi, A., Woo, W., Li, Y. (eds.) Edutainment 2008. LNCS, vol. 5093, pp. 518–527. Springer, Heidelberg (2008). https://doi.org/10.1007/978-3-540-69736-7_55

Perceivability of Map Information for Disaster Situations for People with Low Vision

Siv Tunold[1] , Jaziar Radianti[2] , Terje Gjøsæter[1(✉)] ,
and Weiqin Chen[1]

[1] Oslo Metropolitan University, Oslo, Norway
tergjo@oslomet.no
[2] CIEM, University of Agder, Grimstad, Norway

Abstract. Digital maps have become increasingly popular in disaster situation to provide overview of information. However, these maps have also created barriers for many people, particularly people with visual impairments. Existing research on accessible maps such as tactile and acoustic maps focuses on providing solutions for blind persons to be able to perceive the information digital maps present. For people with low vision, who often rely on magnifier, good contrast and good navigation support, current digital map solutions present many challenges. In this paper we have studied two types of digital maps and their related surrounding text in the home page of disaster applications. The study focused on perceivability of the information provided by the maps. To investigate this, we have adopted a mix-method approach and performed heuristic testing combined with expert testing by a user with low vision. Based on the evaluation we have made a number of recommendations to improve the perceivability, which can further enhance the accessibility of the maps.

Keywords: Maps · Universal design · Perceivability ·
Emergency management · Low vision

1 Introduction

Maps (both paper and digital maps) and geospatial technologies in general are very crucial for efficient and timely responses in all stages of the emergency management life cycle stages; preparedness, alert, response, relief/recovery and mitigation. In either stage, no actions can be done without knowing the locations. In the preparedness stage, resource inventory, logistic and evacuation planning, as well as in the alert stage such as monitoring, scenario identification, early warning e.g. [1] – all should be made with the help of geospatial technologies. In the response stage, the map is even more critical as it is used for mapping the crisis, conducting situation analysis [2], providing information of evacuation path and shelters [3], dispatching resources and performing search-rescue operations [4, 5]. While in the relief stage, again geospatial information plays a role on informing the emergency organizations on the location of logistics and delivery of the relief supply [6], as well as assessing the early damages [7]. In the recovery stage, maps can be used for spatial re-planning such as infrastructure, housing, transport, water and so on [8]. In the mitigation phase, maps are very

© Springer Nature Switzerland AG 2019
M. Antona and C. Stephanidis (Eds.): HCII 2019, LNCS 11572, pp. 342–352, 2019.
https://doi.org/10.1007/978-3-030-23560-4_25

important to support assessment activities such as risk assessment, vulnerability, hazard and threat analysis [9]. In short, the needs for geospatial information on maps in emergencies are evident, regardless of its form, as agreed by many scholarly articles.

Although the digital maps cannot fully replace the paper-based maps in emergencies, they have been adopted more and more. Even todays' paper versions of updated maps during the emergencies often are prepared and produced digitally, and can then be shared both electronically or in printed forms.

The geospatial information is not only a key point for the emergency services in the field, but also the operators and decision makers sitting and collecting data in Emergency Operation Centers (EOCs). Moreover, maps provide the quickest way to share information with public on updated information of the crisis, such as location of established posts. Besides, we also need to take into consideration the contributions of the digital volunteers in collecting information related to the emergencies [10] which would not be valuable for all without being shared quickly through digital maps. Recent trends of the involvement of the digital volunteers in emergencies, show extensive use of maps to collect and share information.

However, the accessibility of such map systems is not well evaluated, especially when it comes to the people with disabilities. Cardonha et al. [11] share the same concern and have conducted preliminary analysis on accessible maps. However, the focus of that article is to suggest better accessible route on the map, and not about how to deliver accessible map online so that people with visual impairments, for example, can still navigate the map. Thus, there are still limited works dedicated for developing evaluation methodology of the accessibility of the digital emergency management maps, especially also by involving people with visual impairment as evaluators. Keep in mind that in the emergencies, even people without physical and cognitive barriers could experience a sort of temporary or situational disabilities [12] which would further reduce the usefulness of the emergency maps, if we have not considered universal design and especially the accessibility factor [10].

A number of techniques have been developed for making accessible maps for blind persons. For example, tactile maps [13] and acoustic maps [14]. However, for people with low vision also reply on magnifiers, good contrast and navigation support, current solutions in digital maps present many challenges [15].

The goal of this research is to study and evaluate the accessibility of selected digital map applications for people with low vision. We do not differentiate the maps based on the functions of different stages of emergency management cycles. We have selected two different digital maps with relevance for emergency management to be evaluated in terms of their accessibility. One map is used for sharing social media twitter information, and the other map is used for monitoring tsunamis and earthquake including providing alerts.

This paper is organized into six sections. Section 2 is literature review where we present some related works and highlight our contributions compared to previous works. Section 3 contains the method, where we describe the map sources for the analysis and the analysis procedures. Section 4 comprises the use cases and the tasks to analyse the accessibility of the digital maps. In Sect. 4 we present the results of our tests, and discuss them further in Sect. 5. Section 6 is our concluding remarks.

2 Literature Review

As mentioned earlier, the digital maps have been used in the different stages of emergency managements and will continue to be used even more in the future as more technologies can support digital maps, and more people can access these. But many of future directions of the maps focus on the technicalities of the map itself. Bocardo [16] e.g., list some user requirements such as the ability to handle large numbers of data, interoperability, meta data, consistent and self-explanatory maps, accuracy. The requirements also consider the feature extraction algorithms for digitizing satellite imageries, visualize sensor data, and operational services such as provide users an access to data in real time. The term of access is used to refer to "a way or means to make use of the data", instead of the accessibility in relations to the people with disabilities, as we have defined in the introduction.

Previous studies also have discussed the accessibility issues of the maps. Cardonha et al. [11] for example, point out that people with disabilities physically face challenges to find a route from A to B due to flooding, potholes and defective sidewalks. Thus, the "accessibility map" is more about outdoor accessibility map that include accessibility challenges that may be encountered in a city. It classifies and visualize the accessibility needs using voluntary citizen sensing technique which would register their reports on the map, e.g. "the regions have no side walk at all", "sidewalk with obstructing objects" or "sidewalks with steps". While the web accessibility is superficially discussed and is taken for granted, assuming today's web technologies are getting better and taking into account web accessibility. Wang et al. [17] has used tactile audio map for accessibility. They study a technology that can detect and segment text from a map image and generate a Scalable Vector Graphics file that integrate the text and graphical information as an assistive technology. The navigation function can be useful, but it requires several supporting devices (printer, touchpad, enhancer), which would be very unpractical in emergencies. The evaluation of the system in this work is done using user experience survey. Fenandes et al. [18] suggest a slightly more advanced digital map solution for navigation over smartphone intended for people with impaired vision, but the accessibility itself as we have defined was not a part of the solution.

When it comes to emergency management, accessible maps are very limitedly discussed and evaluated. Hence the contributions of this paper are to fill the gaps both in the web accessibility inspection and the evaluation method of the maps with a person with low vision.

3 Method

In the study we have chosen two maps. One is the Disaster Alert map in Pacific Disaster Center (PDC) (see Fig. 1) which is used for monitoring tsunamis and earthquake including providing alerts. The other one is the #onemilliontweetmap (see Fig. 2) which is used for visualizing social media twitter information.

In the evaluation of the two maps, we focused on the maps themselves and the surrounding text and evaluate whether the information provided by the maps and the surrounding text is perceivable for people with visual impairments.

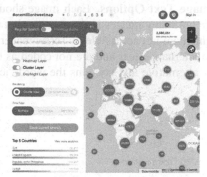

Fig. 1. PDC Disaster Alert map.   **Fig. 2.** #Onemilliontweetmap.

We have used heuristic evaluation based on WAIs10 Easy Checks [18]. In addition, an automatic tool for colour contrast checking (Colour Contrast Analyser version 2.2a) was used to determine whether the colour contrast satisfied the success criteria in WCAG 2.1.

Furthermore, we have invited an expert user with low vision to test the perceivability of the maps, based on Web Content Accessibility Guidelines (WCAG) 2.1 focusing on the Perceivable principle. The expert user is category 3 on the World Health Organization's International Classification of Disease (ICD) [19]; *severe vision impairment*. The user interacted with the web sites by keyboard and a screen reader (JAWS Professional 18). All these evaluations were conducted on browser Google Chrome version 72 on an Asus laptop. In addition, the sites were tested with the browser Safari using the VoiceOver screenreader on an iPad.

The evaluation by the expert user consisted of carrying out the following two tasks:

1. On the #onemilliontweetmap (#1Million), search for #earthquake and #tsunami in the search field [20].
2. On the Disaster Alert map (PDC), find hazards in Indonesia and details about one hazard in the list [21].

4   Results

4.1   Results from 10 Easy Checks

The 10 Easy Checks provided by the Web Accessibility Initiative at W3C [22] covers the basic accessibility barriers of main elements in a web page including page title, image description, text, interaction and general content such as multimedia and basic structure. These two web sites fail on nine out of WAI's ten checks.

Page Title. The title of the application window is sufficient and briefly describes the content of the page. Both sites have well-formed page titles, but none of them reflect the last search which was done. Showing the search terms in the title could be useful to distinguish multiple simultaneous instances of the map.

Image Text Options. Each image should have an appropriate alternative text. There are not many images in these pages, but the main parts of the pages are graphical maps which are not accessible by screenreader. There are some image buttons, but they have no alternative text and are not coded as buttons (Fig. 3). The play-icon is a button and its alternative text contains the word "icon" which is unnecessary information.

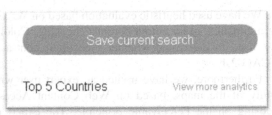

(a)PDC: The Hazards button is nameless and the tooltip text is not accessible by screenreader.

(b) #1Million: The "Save current search" looks like a button or a link, but not coded as either a button or a link. It is thereby not read by screenreader.

Fig. 3. Examples of inaccessible buttons.

Headings. The heading hierarchy is important for navigating web pages. The pages evaluated have hardly any headings at all. #1Million has no headings in the main page, nor does it have headings in the pop-up windows which include many text and links (Fig. 4). PDC has one that looks like a heading, but it is not coded as one. This makes it very difficult to navigate in the page, you have to read the entire page top-down.

> \5.9-magnitude #earthquake hit Gilan-e Gharb in
> Cermanshah, #Iran, on Sunday, January 6, injuring at least
> 00 peo... https://t.co/p8PvvcXuVn
> om @saramokhtar71 at 13.1.2019 10:25:01
> entiment: 0.167 feeling: Negative

Fig. 4. #1Million: a pop-up window with a lot of details, but no heading.

Contrast Ratio ("Colour Contrast"). Web pages should have a minimum contrast. For normal size text a contrast ration should be at least 4.5:1 (Level AA). Both sites fail

WCAG 2.1 AA requirement, especially the maps. Even using high contrast configuration on the screen had no effect on the maps at all.

Contrast Testing of #1Million. Nearly everything on #1Million's start page fail the WCAG requirements for colour contrasts. For example, the contrast between the sea and land is not sufficient as shown in Fig. 5.

The icons shown in Fig. 6 are the main information carriers on the page. They are continually changing, showing that something is going on. The size of the icon, the number in the icon and the red dots all carry information. The contrast between icon and red dots fails to comply to the requirement, and the number in the icon only pass the AA requirement if a particularly big font size is used,

Fig. 5. The contrast between the sea- and land colour fail.

Fig. 6. Icons showing an active event.

Contrast Testing of PDC. There is a lot of information given by colour in this map and the details are quite tiny, like the icons shown in Fig. 7. The icons contain much orange and red colours and fail the contrast check, although the thin white frame helps a bit to distinguish these. Notice also the white text on the coloured map shown in Fig. 8, here the contract obviously fails. In fact, most colour checks fail at WCAG AA-level, including contrast between water and land, and also between sea/land and colours indicating weather conditions.

Fig. 7. Example of a mess of different icons with colour information.

Fig. 8. Map with white text and weather information.

Magnification of the Page. Both pages have separate zooming functionality in the maps. But if you have a pop-up window on the screen when zooming you lose it or the pop-up window was opening up outside the screen. Horizontal and vertical scrolling is done by dragging (click, hold and move the cursor) in the maps. Zooming in the browser affect the whole page. None of the pages can handle 200% magnification. Not all buttons, form fields and other controls are visible and usable at that zoom level. If zooming more than 200% in the #1Million page, the content will wrap, but scrolling to see all content is not possible.

Keyboard Access and Visual Focus. We checked if the keyboard focus was visible and if it did follow a logical sequence through page elements. No keyboard traps were experienced, but the tabbing order was not always correct. It was not possible to tab to all elements on the screen. The active element did not have any visual focus. Visual focus (the blinking circles) were only used to show ongoing events/tweets in the map. The size of the map-pins (bullets) are too small according to WCAG 2.5.5 Target Size (Level AAA): The size of the target for pointer inputs should be at least 44 by 44 CSS pixels.

Forms, Labels, and Errors. There are no input forms in these pages except the search input. So, no error handling is necessary in these pages.

Multimedia (Video, Audio) Options. The weather time progress is playable as a video. The buttons are not labelled correctly and there are no alternative text telling what is happening if you push the play button.

The Basic Structure. The requirements for checking the basic structure, are to look at the application window's images, styles and layout. On these sites use of high contrast colours on the screen didn't have any effect at all. The information was not read in the order in which they are displayed. The alternative texts on some icons/buttons do not provide sufficient information to the models. There were no clear headings at all, navigating content by using headings is not possible.

4.2   Results from Expert Testing

Navigation. The maps are only accessible by mouse, it is difficult to point at and click on the map pins (bullets), because of their small size. The maps would be easier to use if the focus was on the search functionality and not on the map. The first tab should be to the search field. The map and navigating in it by clicking in the map would make more sense to a low vision user as an extra bonus functionality, not the main functionality.

Dynamic Features. The use of blinking icons or running numbers are other issues. Dynamically changing details on the pages can be confusing, and it steals attention.

Colour Contrast. The contrasts are too low, the two sites do not even pass WCAG's AA. This is in particular a problem on the maps themselves. Some persons with stronger visual impairments might not even see that it is a map and be able to see the difference between sea and land. To investigate this further, we have performed automatic contrast testing with Colour Contrast Analyzer against *WCAG 1.4.3 Contrast* *(minimum) - level AA* and *1.4.6 Contrast (Enhanced) - level AAA*, for both of the sites. We also tried the page with high contrasts and it did not have any effect. The map is the main information-carrying part of the screen and thereby also representing a major barrier.

5 Discussion and Recommendations

As mentioned above, our main focus has been the persons who has low vision, it is interesting to see that the 10 easy checks do catch many of the barriers experienced by the expert user.

To summarise: The maps are difficult to use. The main drawbacks in these sites are the colour contrasts, the tabbing order, headings, links and size of icons, the maps not being accessible with keyboard, and the use of pop-up windows for extra information of the events.

For people with low vision, it is preferable to be able to access maps using keyboard or by voice commands rather than mouse. Navigation and zoom are two main challenges in this case. We further suggest that the map pins should be numbered so it is possible to choose them by number, or coded as links so it is possible to navigate to them by tabbing or by link lists.

Furthermore, it is essential that all information shown in the map should have text description somewhere. This is not only beneficial for people with low vision, but also for blind users who will rely on the search function, event result list and detailed information about the events when using the maps.

5.1 Search and Result List

It should be possible to do a free text search within the geographic area displayed in the map on your screen. When the search is done and the results are shown, the user should be notified. The result-lists could show a list of most important recent disasters (PDC)/ events (#1Million).

It would be useful to have a list of ongoing and/or last events, for example a list of the ten most recent events. It would also be nice to have the possibility to easily choose between floods, earthquakes, volcanoes and so on. If you search for a geographical place, as an example Indonesia, both the map and disaster list should reflect this search.

An advanced search setting could be provided. For example, users should be able to search for country or disasters type within the last fifty years.

When selecting an event in the search result-list, it is important to position the cursor in the map, use a lower scale in the map if it is a small spot/town that is displayed and to show some information about the search result selected in the left sidebar.

Detailed information about the selected event should expand in the list of elements, preferably integrated in the page and not as a pop-up window, which is difficult to access with a screenreader. More detailed information could be displayed in a separate tab in the browser. In addition, a proper heading structure is also important for showing the detailed information about events.

5.2   Focus and Zoom

The application should set the focus in the middle of the map when the user is activating it, or done by positioning the cursor with a search first or by positing the cursor directly in the map. When double-clicking on the map, the entire map should be zoomed by 200% each time. Users should only zoom the map within the screen so they do not have to drag the map left or right with the cursor. Expanding the map to cover the entire screen could also be an option.

5.3   Keyboard and Voice Commands for Navigation

Users should be able to navigate in the map by addressing 3 × 3 named squares, by using compass directions as shortcuts such as a combination of a chosen **map key + a letter.** For example, **Map key + X** to the center square of the map and starting point for further navigation, **Map key + N** to the top row, **Map key + W** to the top left corner, **Map key + E to** the top right corner, **Map key + X** and **Map key + S** to the last row.

Another option is to navigate by using the arrow keys to tab through the squares after the user has activated the map and found the centre of it.

All navigating in the map done by the keyboard should also be available by voice commands. Users should be able to navigate by addressing it by 3 × 3 named squares, by using compass directions as "**go North-West**", "**go North**" and "**go North-east**" and "**go centre**".

6   Conclusion

In this paper we present the evaluation of two digital maps and the surrounding text for disaster situation focusing on the perceivability of the information to people with low vision. A mix-method approach was adopted including heuristic evaluation and expert user testing. Many accessibility barriers have been identified that can hinder users to perceive the information provided by the maps. Based on the evaluation we have made a number of recommendations to improve the perceivability, which can further enhance the accessibility of the maps.

In this paper our focus is on making maps in disaster situations accessible for people with low vision. Therefore, colour contrast, zoom, keyboard and voice commands for navigation are important. For blind users, the search function, the event result-list and detail information are more important, all information given in the map should be described by text.

Our general impression from the evaluation shows that maps used in disaster situations have not taken into considerations the accessibility principles and guidelines such as WCAG, although the accessibility of web content is covered in the discrimination laws and regulations in many countries. Access to information is essential in disaster situations and it concerns life and death. Through our study we have found that little research has focused on the evaluation of accessibility of digital maps, and in particular when it comes to maps for use in emergency management. We argue that more knowledge and research are necessary to ensure that digital maps are accessible to all users in disaster situations.

References

1. Huang, H., et al.: Web3DGIS-based system for reservoir landslide monitoring and early warning. Appl. Sci. 6(2), 44 (2016)
2. Clarke, A.E., Friese, C., Washburn, R.: Situational Analysis in Practice: Mapping Research with Grounded Theory. Routledge, Abingdon (2016)
3. Yamamoto, K., Li, X.: Safety evaluation of evacuation routes in Central Tokyo assuming a large-scale evacuation in case of earthquake disasters. J. Risk Financ. Manag. 10(3), 14 (2017)
4. Doeweling, S., et al.: Support for collaborative situation analysis and planning in crisis management teams using interactive tabletops. In: Proceedings of the 2013 ACM International Conference on Interactive Tabletops and Surfaces. ACM (2013)
5. Ganz, A., et al.: Urban search and rescue situational awareness using DIORAMA disaster management system. Procedia Eng. 107, 349–356 (2015)
6. Chen, A.Y., Peña-Mora, F., Ouyang, Y.: A collaborative GIS framework to support equipment distribution for civil engineering disaster response operations. Autom. Constr. 20(5), 637–648 (2011)
7. Miura, H., Midorikawa, S., Matsuoka, M.: Building damage assessment using high-resolution satellite SAR images of the 2010 Haiti earthquake. Earthq. Spectra 32(1), 591–610 (2016)
8. Giardino, M., et al.: GIS and geomatics for disaster management and emergency relief: a proactive response to natural hazards. Appl. Geomat. 4(1), 33–46 (2012)
9. Freire, S.: Modeling of spatiotemporal distribution of urban population at high resolution – value for risk assessment and emergency management. In: Konecny, M., Zlatanova, S., Bandrova, T. (eds.) Geographic Information and Cartography for Risk and Crisis Management. Lecture Notes in Geoinformation and Cartography, pp. 53–67. Springer, Berlin (2010). https://doi.org/10.1007/978-3-642-03442-8_4
10. Radianti, J., Gjøsæter, T.: Digital volunteers in disaster response: accessibility challenges. In: HCII 2019. Springer, Orlando (2019, in press)
11. Cardonha, C., et al.: A crowdsourcing platform for the construction of accessibility maps. In: Proceedings of the 10th International Cross-Disciplinary Conference on Web Accessibility. ACM (2013)
12. Gjøsæter, T., Radianti, J., Chen, W.: Universal design of ICT for emergency management. In: Antona, M., Stephanidis, C. (eds.) UAHCI 2018. LNCS, vol. 10907, pp. 63–74. Springer, Cham (2018). https://doi.org/10.1007/978-3-319-92049-8_5
13. Klaus, H., et al.: AccessibleMap. Springer, Heidelberg (2012)
14. Zeng, L., Weber, G.: ATMap: annotated tactile maps for the visually impaired. In: Esposito, A., Esposito, Antonietta M., Vinciarelli, A., Hoffmann, R., Müller, Vincent C. (eds.) Cognitive Behavioural Systems. LNCS, vol. 7403, pp. 290–298. Springer, Heidelberg (2012). https://doi.org/10.1007/978-3-642-34584-5_25
15. Szpiro, S.F.A., et al.: How people with low vision access computing devices: understanding challenges and opportunities. In: Proceedings of the 18th International ACM SIGACCESS Conference on Computers and Accessibility, pp. 171–180. ACM, Reno (2016)
16. Boccardo, P.: New perspectives in emergency mapping. Eur. J. Remote Sens. 46(1), 571–582 (2013)
17. Wang, Z., et al.: Instant tactile-audio map: enabling access to digital maps for people with visual impairment. In: Proceedings of the 11th International ACM SIGACCESS Conference on Computers and Accessibility. ACM (2009)

18. Fernandes, H., et al.: Providing accessibility to blind people using GIS. Univers. Access Inf. Soc. **11**(4), 399–407 (2012)
19. WHO: ICD-11 for Mortality and Morbidity Statistics. 9D90 Vision Impairment Including Blindness. WHO (2018)
20. Maptimize: #onemilliontweetmap (2017). http://www.onemilliontweetmap.com/
21. DPC: Disaster Alerts (2019). https://disasteralert.pdc.org/disasteralert/
22. WAI: W.A.I. Easy Checks - A First Review of Web Accessibility (2019). http://www.w3.org/WAI/test-evaluate/preliminary/

Multi-faceted Approach to Computer Simplification via Personalization and Layering

Gregg C. Vanderheiden[(✉)] and J. Bern Jordan

University of Maryland, College Park, MD 20779, USA
GreggVan@umd.edu

Abstract. Our society is rapidly incorporating digital interfaces into all aspects of our lives. Those who cannot access and use digital technologies will not be able to participate in the society that is evolving. Yet many cannot due to barriers related to disability, literacy, and digital literacy. Solutions exist but solutions for the area of cognitive, language, and learning disabilities, digital literacy and cognitive aspects of aging lags significantly. Those solutions that do exist are often buried in the settings, hard to find and difficult to understand and use. To address this a strategy combining personalization and layering is being used to simplify both computers and the presentation and operation of features intended to help simplify their use. The combination seeks to make features more discoverable, lower the cognitive load needed to explore and employ them, and have them show up automatically on any computer the individual encounters. It also seeks to stabilize the interfaces experienced by users with cognitive or learning disabilities so that they are not always changing as companies update their software. Using layering – the approach provides better fits for people of different abilities and provides both a simpler interface while still allowing access to full functionality if it is needed. A fully functioning prototype is described that is moving to release following pilot testing in American Job Centers, libraries and a Community College.

Keywords: Morphic · Personalization · Simplification · Digital literacy · Accessibility

1 Introduction

1.1 Need for Simplification

Our society is rapidly incorporating digital interfaces into all aspects of our lives; books, appliances, travel, education, employment, telework, and daily living. Soon those who cannot access and use digital technologies will not be able to learn, work or live independently. Yet many cannot use technology effectively or at all due to barriers related to their disability, literacy, digital literacy or age. Solutions exist – but solutions for people with cognitive disabilities or even just limited digital literacy are far behind other types of barriers. In addition, many of the solutions for other disabilities assume high cognitive and digital literacy skills in order to use them. Finally, many solutions

M. Antona and C. Stephanidis (Eds.): HCII 2019, LNCS 11572, pp. 353–364, 2019.
https://doi.org/10.1007/978-3-030-23560-4_26

are so buried, hard to find, or hard to apply that even those who could use them, do not know of them or know of them but they are too hard to use or to activate or set up.

Some examples to illustrate:

– Very few people were aware that you can change the language that Windows uses (including those from other countries using mobile devices and seeing Windows for the first time).
  - Or change the screen scaling to make everything on screen larger (without needing to scroll in all directions)
  - Or change contrast
  - Or most all of the other accessibility and usability features build into Windows.
– One grandparent, who was using computers for email, chat, social networking and to arrange meet ups with friends stopped using the computer when she heard her grandchildren commenting in the other room "The computer is all messed up for gramma again". She told us that she stopped because she had had her time, and this was their time – and she was unable to set the computer up for herself each time or change it back.
– Another woman reported that she could not use the computer anymore because she needed large print and didn't know how to set it up – and her husband complained when it was large print when he wanted to use it. When told that Windows would change settings for different people when they logged in, she reported that that was too complicated for them.

Those of us with high intelligence or high digital literacy often completely miss the difficulties or lack of transparency in the interfaces we design. For example:

– In creating a QuickStrip of easy to find and use functions (described more below) several people suggested that putting the Volume Control on the strip would be important. When we pointed out that the button to open the QuickStrip was just an inch from a control that already opened up a volume control in Windows, the room went silent. We found (and found repeatedly – even with colleagues) that a surprising number of people who use Windows every day were completely unaware of the fact that clicking on the little speaker icon on the taskbar would bring up a volume control. It never occurred to them; not even to long-time computer users (Fig. 1).

Fig. 1. Image showing mouse cursor over speaker icon that opens up a volume slider in MS Windows (and located 1 inch from chameleon shaped icon for Morphic QuickStrip)

– Another requested feature was a button to open up a USB drive – or to bring it to the top. People in libraries and even the community college who had just begun using Windows recently, would insert the USB and then be unable to find it. They just wanted to update a resume and did not know how to find (or re-find) the window that would show them their files on their USB so they can view or edit them.

– Very few who needed to make text larger knew how to do so using CTRL-+ or CTRL-scrollwheel, or even knew that it was possible to do so. This was especially true for people who were losing acuity gradually and did not know of or encounter people trained in "accessibility" features. Others heard of such people and "assistive technologies", but did not consider themselves to have a disability so would never think of going to such a person. "I don't have low vision, I just have old eyes. Can they just print things bigger?"

Many of us use MS Word, and others are required to for school or work. None of us need all of the controls in the ribbons and many of us need relatively few of them. Yet removing features from the ribbons to simplify them or reduce their number is more complicated than using the ribbons.

1.2   Many Dimensions of Simplification

Simplification is needed across several dimensions:

1. Content
2. Standard Interface
3. The accessibility/simplification features themselves (which are often complicated).
4. The steps needed to activate – and deactivate – access and simplification features.

Most work focuses on #1 and #2. Less has focused on #3 and #4. Yet, we posit that doing only #1 and #2 will severely limit what can be done. Simplification must not be done in a way that all people must use the simplified content/interface since simplification more than a certain amount, necessarily leads to loss of information or function. And adding options to simplify things often adds to the complexity of the product and its settings panels (which are often more complicated than the interface being simplified). It is also a problem on multi-user devices, to require people who have trouble with simplification to have to be able to simplify the device themselves, and then change it back for others.

All four dimensions need therefore to be addressed for practical use of simplification on common or shared technologies (of any type).

2   Strategies for Simplification

There are many strategies for simplification. Good summaries of them can be found in Lewis [1, 2] the MasterList of Accessibility Strategies [3], "Making Content Usable for People with Cognitive and Learning Disabilities" [4] the ETSI Guide EG 203 350 on "Guidelines for the design of mobile ICT devices and their related applications for people with cognitive disabilities" [5].

Many of these deal with creating content or interfaces that are simpler in their basic or original form. Most of them cannot be applied to all content or interfaces, or are not necessarily even good for all types, degrees and combinations of cognitive disabilities. In trying to create guidelines that can be applied to all types of content and interfaces, only a limited subset of them have been identified – even though decades of work have been carried out by multiple international working groups and cognitive accessibility task forces. These can be found in standards and regulations such as the Web Content Accessibility Guidelines (WCAG), the Section 508 and 255 accessibility standards, and the European/International counterpart of the 508 guidelines (EN 301 549). All of these standards and regulations contain language acknowledging the limitations on what can be included when restricted to only approaches that qualify as requirements (are testable and generally applicable).

In this paper we focus on three fundamental approaches to simplification that can be applied generally, that do not interfere with use by any user while greatly increasing the usability for people with a wide range of ability from average to more severe cognitive ability. The three basic strategies are:

1. Personalization (and auto-personalization in particular)
2. Layering
3. Layered, gamified, path to discovery (that is not labelled accessibility)

2.1   Personalization (and Auto-Personalization)

By personalization, we refer to the changing of an interface to match the particular needs and preferences of an individual. By auto-personalization, we refer to the ability to have this done instantly and automatically in a manner that does not require the individual to either understand how to carry out the personalization themselves, or to have the physical, visual, auditory, or cognitive abilities to make the changes.

Ideal personalization would:

1. instantly identify the person whenever they approached a device
2. change the device's interface and content to match their needs and preferences
   a. any device, computer, thermostat, television, microwave, self-driving car, check-in kiosk, vending machine, smartphone, etc.
3. be able to present the interface they are familiar with when they encounter any other similar devices
4. be able to present the interface they are familiar with – when vendors 'update' their products with new, improved, but different interfaces from the one they know
5. allow users to have different preferences that they can invoke at different times, for different circumstances or for different tasks (e.g. tired, leisure reading, complex editing, in public, etc.)
6. be able to suggest settings for the user to try whenever they encountered a new device or interface
   a. based upon their previous preferences for other devices and on settings for this device that are used by people who have settings similar to their settings on other devices
7. store all of the information on users' needs and preferences in a fashion that cannot be used for data mining, advertising, or ways that either commercially exploit the information or use it to change how the user is treated (insurance, employment, care, regard, etc.)

2.2   Layering

By layering, we refer the gradual presentation or exposing of the interface or content in layers of increasing complexity and detail. Users are able to begin with a simpler version of the interface for example, but have all of the functionality of the interface available in additional layers beyond.

Ideally people are able (through personalization) to start at the level of complexity that matches their abilities or preferences at the moment.

Also through personalization, some users could have higher levels of complexity never appear, except on request, simplifying their interface and making it less likely they will accidentally fall into a level they cannot handle.

2.3   Layered, Gamified, Path to Discovery

A key problem of people who need simplification or any other special accommodation (larger text, contrast, etc.) is that they are unaware that such features exist. When they hear of them, they are buried and often have so many settings that they cannot find them or deal with their options.

By a layered, gamified path to discovery, we refer to a path where the user is introduced to basic features in a basic fashion. Quick discovery and ability to quickly invoke and understand features that are helpful gets them onboard and with quick rewards. A "more" or similar button can be used by them when they are comfortable and feeling more explorative to find a second layers of features or more settings for the features they already are using.

Using successive layers – and the ability to pull desired features from a lower layer up to a higher – easier to get at – layer can provide the individual to live in a safe, familiar and easy to handle layer, and dip down when they want to explore or to access a less often used but needed function. Guided tours that they can select from, can also give them a safe way to explore new capabilities.

This approach can be used for interfaces, accessibility/usability features, and for content.

3   An Example Implementation of These 3 Strategies – Applied to Interfaces – Morphic

3.1   Morphic

Morphic is an extension to the operating system that provides a number of these and related functions for both simplification and general accessibility and usability. Morphic is designed to be used for anyone facing barriers or even hinderances to computer use, including the majority of mainstream users. It also has some particular features designed specifically for users of assistive technologies.

Morphic is the result of 8 years of research, testing and user input. Most of the features of Morphic were not envisioned when the effort began, but emerged in discussion and use of prototypes by users. Many of the features would not have occurred to us, except through either suggestions from users, or descriptions of problems faced by them that we would not have predicted.

The core capabilities of Morphic include:

1. **Preference portability** – the ability to capture uses' settings and preferences, store them in a secure private vault in the cloud, and then use them to set up any other device the way the user needs/prefers it
2. **Feature discovery** – the ability to more easily discover features in the operating system or software that make the computer easier for people to use and understand
3. **Quick simple access** – making features that individuals use much easier to find in layered fashion and arrange to be faster to use
4. **Installation on demand** – the ability to have software the users need show up on any computer they sit down at, when at school/library/work (Under development)
5. **Simple, focused environments** – ability to simplify a teaching/study/work environment on their PC by providing just what they need in one place and nothing else. It can also remove some features that should not be there during testing (e.g. spell checker during spelling test, or translator during foreign language or ESL test.)

3.2   Preference Portability

Morphic is able to capture all of the settings of compatible Assistive technologies and the usability and accessibility features of the operating system. These are then stored in a cloud "Vault" that only the user has access to. The Vaults are identified with a long anonymous number (a UUID). When the user comes up to a machine, the UUID is passed to the Morphic cloud system and used to look up the person's preferred settings. A MatchMaker in the cloud looks at their preferences and the computer and then sends down commands to launch software, activate features on the computer and set them all up to match the user's needs and preferences. When the person is done using the machine, Morphic automatically changes all of the settings back to what they were – and turns off any features and software it invoked.

The settings for each person can be individualized. For example, one person using JAWS can have it start up talking very fast and in Spanish and with verbosity (punctuation level, etc.) voice and intonations as they prefer. Another less-experienced user could sit down to the same computer and have it start out in slower English with settings appropriate for them.

Either person, sitting for a standardized test, could sit down to a sterile computer in a test center with a screen reader installed and set to factory settings and have it instantly change to a form identical to what they use every day (filtered of any place where information could be stored) and be able to take the test in that way – similar to allowing people to take a test with glasses with their proper prescription.

The users' preference information is all stored secure cloud storage operated by a non-profit organization (Raising the Floor) and overseen by a Data Security Council being composed of individuals nominated by international human rights and data privacy organizations to ensure that the privacy of the information.

The preference portability can also allow users to easily move to new computers. This could be used if their computer fails and they need to set up a new one.

At companies that simply replace computers that malfunction with a new one each time, this can save weeks of setup for some users with multiple accommodations. One company stopped taking users with disabilities in their internship program because, by the time the person was set up on their computers, they were either too far behind the other interns or, in one case, the internship was over. The ability for users to show up and have their computer set up on day 1, or even hour 1, for an internship or job can be a game changer.

Keys

There are a wide variety of methods for the individual to cause their UUID to be passed up to the Morphic MatchMaker. They can use a USB key with the UUID on it or they can have the key (UUID) associated with their log in or other means of identification. At school the UUID can be associated with their computer log in – and sent automatically to the Morphic cloud (without exposing the user's identity). At a library where users log in with library card it can similarly be automatic as they log in. Facial recognition, voice or other forms of ID including 3rd party two-factor devices can be used. The face, voice, etc. (for example for elders in a residence who would lose keys and forget user names or passwords) can be sent to a remote processing location or processed locally and only the UUID sent to Morphic. Any of these and other techniques can be used to trigger the transformation of the interface (Fig. 2).

Fig. 2. Key shaped USB flash drive with user's UUID on it.

Key to the success of the auto-personalization, is:

- that it be instant or take seconds,
- that it not require the user to understand how to find or operate the settings,
- and that it return the device to its original setup when done.

Multiple Preference Sets

In addition, Morphic allows users to have multiple preference sets. They can thus set up a device to have different settings when they are performing differently (e.g. tired), doing different tasks (ready, writing/editing, doing math), or in different contexts (home, school, in public) where they may need more or fewer features and where they may want to show more or less about themselves.

3.3   Feature Discovery

Some users already have assistive technologies set up for them. Some others know about the settings they need on their computers. Both of these groups can use the preference portability directly.

However, most people who have trouble using computers, or who's use of computer can be made easier, do not know that such features even exist for them. The most common comment we get from user's is "I didn't know the computer could do that" when referring to features built-into the OS. Others may know about features but find it too hard to find them, or find them too complicated to invoke or set up.

To address these issues, Morphic has recently added a QuickStrip of common features and functions. It includes mainstream features, features for people who have different first languages and are learning computers, features for people who are very early computer users and struggling, and features for people with disabilities. The QuickStrip has a sampling of features to engage all types of users – and get them to a) understand that there are features that can make the computer easier for different types of users – mainstream and those with barriers. It then has a second layer of features under the MORE button to allow them to easily explore a second layer. Additional layers and methods for exploration are provided from there. The QuickStrip can also be customized by sites and users to put the features they are interested in on the Quick-Strip (Fig. 3).

Fig. 3. Morphic QuickStrip above Morphic Icon (chameleon) in the Windows Tray

The QuickStrip serves several purposes

1. To have people discover that the computer **can** be easily adapted to different users.
2. To make it easy for users to try different features and settings – and to have the computer instantly respond and change in some dramatic ways.
3. To provide a layered path of discovery that is very simple and engaging (with instant reward) but also allow them to progress further to find the features that best match them.
4. To allow them to have key functions they want/need immediately available to them – one click away.

The More button on the QuickStrip opens a window with additional function buttons, help links and buttons to allow customization of the QuickStrip and exploration of still more features and functions of the Operating System and software that can make the computer easier to use.

3.4 Quick Simple Access

Morphic provides two methods for quick, simple access to personalization features.

First is the QuickStrip which puts features of the user's choosing just a click away. Ordinarily these features are buried deep in the control panels of the computer – or require the user to remember hot-key combinations.

Second – Morphic allows users to have multiple preference sets that they can call up to change multiple settings and launch different programs all with one selection. When they have multiple sets, the blank button in the upper right corner of Fig. 3 above would say "Pref Sets" and be used to choose between them.)

3.5   Installation on Demand (IoD)

Installation on Demand allows users to invoke software that is not currently installed on a computer. Usually at a library or other location that provides public computers, only one or two computers in one room have any assistive technologies on them, and then it is usually only a few programs. If they user wants to participate in an activity in another location, they may not be able to participate if the software they need is not present, or they do not know how to use what is installed there.

With IoD, Morphic will have not just what is on the computer to work with, but also what is available on the IoD server. When the person sits down, Morphic looks up what they need using their stored preference file, and, if the software is not on the computer, downloads it over the LAN from the local Morphic IoD server and installs it on the computer, and then configures it for the user. Only software for which a valid license exists for the user or location is launched.

With IoD, people can use any computer in any room and have the accommodations they need appear on that computer – configured for them.

3.6   Simple Focused Environments

The personalization, and the preference sets, can be used to create focused environments for users. Different preference sets can bring just the apps the individual needs for a task to them. Different preference sets can bring different apps, and different settings. One can turn off all notifications to allow users to focus. Another can turn them back on when they are done.

Employers can use it to provide different environments for different workers or tasks. This can also be useful when hoteling is used at the office.

3.7   Layering with Morphic

In the descriptions above, the use of layering in Morphic itself was described. Here we will describe an example of how layering is being applied to the interface of a popular word processing program Microsoft Word to simplify its use.

Word in its standard configuration has over 10 ribbons with over 250 function and feature buttons distributed across them. This is daunting for many users some of whom cannot find what they need given all the options. Moreover, the icons and how they are displayed and nested can change from one month to the next as updates come out (Fig. 4).

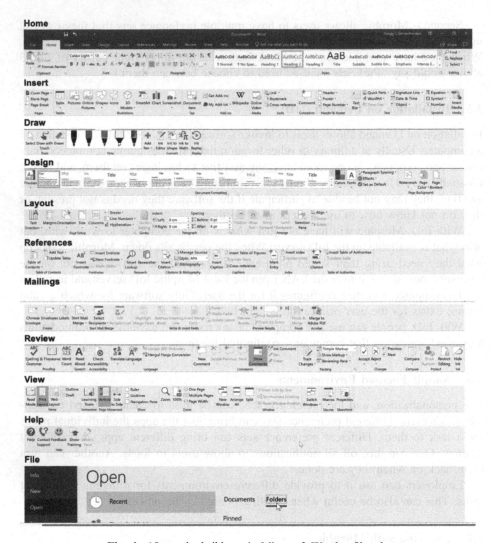

Fig. 4. 10 standard ribbons in Microsoft Word + file tab.

These menus can be customized to simplify them if a user desires, but the ability to do this is not known to most users, is too complicated for those that would need it, and would be lost as soon as one logged out of a public computer.

Morphic allow users to select from among simplified ribbons at different levels. One is designed for very simple Word use by some who need just minimal functionality but would be using say a family or library computer (Fig. 5).

Fig. 5. Very Simple Ribbon for very basic user.

A basic menu adds additional functions and provides all of the capabilities for most basic writing functions including basic formatting and tools for people who face vision, language and learning barriers (Fig. 6).

Fig. 6. A single ribbon with all of the basic writing functions.

For those needing more formatting options, a more complicated single ribbon brings all the capabilities together (Fig. 7).

Fig. 7. A single ribbon with most of the function needed by most writers

Finally, for someone who needs to do editing and chartwork, a single ribbon brings together functions normally found on multiple ribbons together on one ribbon where they can be found more easily. In addition, as different version of the standard ribbons come out arranging things differently and adding functions, this ribbon (and the ones above) stay stable (Fig. 8).

Fig. 8. Ribbon with additional features for tracking edits and inserting charts and shapes.

In keeping with the layered approach all can be provided in addition to (and not replacing) the standard menus so that users can always access all of the other functions should they ever need them – and so that advanced users can show the user where to find any special functions not on their simplified ribbon. Later, they will be able to more easily bring these down to their ribbon to customize them, or have them customized to meet their specific needs. Morphic can capture this new custom menu ribbon and have it show up on any other computer they sit down at.

4 Conclusion

By combining auto-personalization and layering it has been possible to make computer interfaces easier for people with cognitive, language, and learning disabilities to use, by making basic features of the computer and the software designed to make computer simpler easier to discover and configure, and automatically configure new computers the person encounters. The system is currently in pilot testing on Windows computers in American Job Centers, libraries and a Community College, with planned release within the year. The plan is to first move across computer platforms and eventually to other products with digital interfaces. The goal is all products with digital interfaces would automatically configure themselves to each individual that they encounter, based on the needs and preferences of that individual. More information is available at http://morphic.world.

Acknowledgements. This research was funded by the Rehabilitation Services Administration, US Dept of Education under grant H421A150006 (APCP), by the National Institute on Disability, Independent Living, and Rehabilitation Research (NIDILRR), US Administration for Independent Living & US Dept of Education under Grants H133E080022 (RERC-IT) and H133E130028/90RE5003-01-00 (UIITA-RERC), by the European Union's Seventh Framework Programme (FP7/2007-2013) grant agreement n° 289016 (Cloud4all) and 610510 (Prosperity4All). The opinions and results herein are those of the authors and not necessarily those of the funding agencies.

References

1. Lewis, C.: Cognitive disabilities. In: Stephanidis, C. (ed.) Universal Access Handbook, pp. 101–112. Lawrence Erlbaum Associates Inc, Mahwah (2008)
2. Lewis, C.: Simplicity in cognitive assistive technology: a framework and agenda for research. Univ. Access Inf. Soc. **5**, 351–361 (2007). https://doi.org/10.1007/s10209-006-0063-7
3. Vanderheiden, G. (ed.): Accessibility Masterlist (2019). https://ds.gpii.net/learn/accessibility-masterlist. Accessed 26 Jan 2019
4. Seeman, L., Cooper, M. (eds.): Making Content Usable for People with Cognitive and Learning Disabilities. https://www.w3.org/TR/2018/WD-coga-usable-20181211/. Accessed 26 Jan 2019
5. ETSI Guide EG 203 350: Guidelines for the Design of Mobile ICT Devices and Their Related Applications for People with Cognitive Disabilities. https://www.etsi.org/deliver/etsi_eg/203300_203399/203350/01.01.01_60/eg_203350v010101p.pdf. Accessed 26 Jan 2019

On Online Banking Authentication for All: A Comparison of BankID Login Efficiency Using Smartphones Versus Code Generators

Ellen Opsahl Vinbæk[1], Frida Margrethe Borge Pettersen[1],
Jonas Ege Carlsen[1], Karl Fremstad[1], Nikolai Edvinsen[1],
and Frode Eika Sandnes[1,2(✉)] (iD)

[1] Department of Computer Science, Faculty of Technology, Art and Design,
Oslo Metropolitan University, P.O. Box 4 St. Olavs Plass, 0130 Oslo, Norway
frodes@oslomet.no
[2] Institute for Technology, Kristiania University College, Postboks 1190
Prinsens Gate 7-9, Sentrum, 0107 Oslo, Norway

Abstract. Authentication is an essential component of any digital service. In Norway, such authentication is often relying on BankID using either mobile BankID or a code generator. This study set out to explore the efficiency of these authentication user interfaces. A mixed experiment involving 20 users was conducted. The results show that the code generator is faster, but for individuals with a preference for mobile BankID the difference is insignificant. Individuals with a preference for code generators take significantly longer time to use BankID.

Keywords: Accessibility · Authentication · Security · Usability ·
User diversity · Online banking · BankID

1 Introduction

The banks in Norway offers the authentication platform BankID for online banking. BankID is also used for accessing governmental services such as revenue and tax return, digital health services and digital mail services. To use BankID, the customers first need to identify themselves with their 11-digit personal ID-number following a Norwegian standard [1]. The next step is performed using either a smartphone or a code generator. The code generator is a simple small device with a single button and a 6-digit LCD display (see Fig. 1). To use the code generator the user simply presses the button and the code generator displays a disposable 6-digit code that the user inputs in the login form followed by a personal password. To use mobile BankID with a smartphone, the user is asked to enter the mobile phone number during the login procedure. Next, a dialogue is displayed on the phone where the user inputs a personal PIN code comprising 4–8 digits (see Fig. 2).

M. Antona and C. Stephanidis (Eds.): HCII 2019, LNCS 11572, pp. 365–374, 2019.
https://doi.org/10.1007/978-3-030-23560-4_27

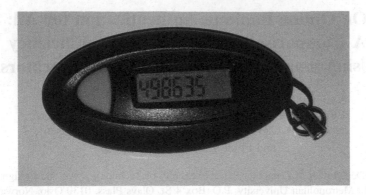

Fig. 1. BankID code generator

Both procedures are simple, but they are different. The code generator involves the copying of 6 arbitrary digits, while mobile BankID involves the input of at least 8 familiar digits making up the phone number, followed by a fixed pin of 4 to 8 digits.

The code generator requires fewer actual keystrokes, yet the task of copying an arbitrary sequence of digits is cognitively and visually more demanding than recalling 8 to 16 digits from memory. Opinions vary about which of the two is the best. This study therefore set out to determine which of the two methods is the fastest to use, and what method users prefer.

2   Background

There has been much research into the relationship between security and usability [2, 3], also in terms of online banking [4–6]. As citizens are expected to use digital services the need for accessibility and usability are more demanding. Internet banking is one such service and online banking has received quite some attention among researchers [7–9]. Olsen [10] documented a case in Norway where the bank automatically appended zeros to incorrectly inputted account numbers. This malpractice led to economic consequences for customers. The Norwegian invoice system requires many digits to be input [11], and better use of mnemonic aids have thus been proposed as one possible remedy [12].

The login procedure is particularly critical. It must be both secure and easy to use. The Norwegian BankID system has received some attention in the research literature [13] and several studies have addressed security issues [14, 15]. BankID has also received some criticism for not being accessible by blind individuals [16]. This questionnaire-based study looked at electronic banking in a wide sense, including Automatic Teller Machines (ATMs), and found that many of the target users have practical IT-skills including that of installing and updating software [16]. This was particularly relevant in the early years of BankID as it required a Java browser plugin capable of running Java applets. The Java-applet oriented solutions have since been replaced with more generic javascript solutions that run in the browser and does not require any browser plugins. Moreover, according to the study [16] many of the services were considered inaccessible yet the level of inaccessibility varied among the services. Most participants reported using several passwords, while the older participants were more likely to always use the same password for different services.

Fig. 2. Smarthpone BankID (Landkreditt Bank AS)

It is especially the BankID web solutions that has been criticized for not been compatible with screen-readers. A screen-reader is a device that allows blind computer users access computer output via synthetic speech or Braille [17]. Screen readers are also used by some dyslexic computer users [18]. Moreover, many banks do not offer code generators with synthetic speech [19] for its visually impaired and dyslexic customers. Recent Norwegian legislature [20] has been introduced to ensure that digital services aimed at the general public are universally accessible to all including individuals with variations in sensory, cognitive or motor functions.

There is a vast body of research that has addressed the general phenomenon involved in man-machine interaction such as output and reduced senses, cognition and memory [21, 22] and input [23]. Several HCI researchers have also addressed banking specifically. For instance, Kaye et al. [24] collected data about monetary and financial patterns of 14 individuals in the San Fransisco Bay Area at both personal and family levels. Vines, Dunphy and Mond [25] studied how technology plays a part in the finances of low-income families and issues related to trust was found to be of importance. A study of users' decision making related to security found that users tended to base their assessment on their perceptions and relationships with the various companies and not the actual privacy characteristics of a service or app [26]. The subjective measurement of trust has also been addressed by the means of Likert scales and semantic differentials [27].

Password credential sharing has been found to be a common practice although it is not allowed by banks [28]. For families, and couples, the sharing of accounts is often practical. A study in Australia [28] showed that especially in low-income communities credential sharing was sometimes the only way to transfer money. The researchers conclude that banking security mechanisms must be flexible enough to facilitate peoples' need to share accounts. Similarly, a study of culture connected password credential sharing showed that users in the Kingdom of Saudi Arabia shared their credentials within families as a token of trust and against the advice of banks [29] leading to certain problems related to accountability and abuse.

Nilsson, Adams and Herd [30] studied how various authentication mechanisms affect trust. Their questionnaire and interview-based approach revealed that users found login procedures involving random passwords generated with a password box more trustworthy than traditional fixed passwords. If these results generalize it could also be that BankID gives user an increased sense of trustworthiness. Security issues such as phishing has received much attention and a literature on counter measure can be found in Purkait [31].

Kim and Moon [32] studied how interfaces can be designed to evoke certain emotions thereby affecting the users trust where online banking was used as a case. Research studying other aspects of banking interaction includes Medhi, Gautama and Toyama [33] who conducted an ethnographic study of the usability of mobile banking solution for urban areas of India with a larger sample of non- and semi-literate users. Their results showed that prototypes of non-textual interfaces, that is, interfacing relying on images or speech were preferred over a text-based interface prototype. Rich multimedia designs led to higher completion rates while speech-based designs led to faster completion times and less need for assistance. Kumar, Martin and O'Neill studied the general deployment of mobile banking in India [34].

Ravendran, MacColl and Docherty [35] found that the usability in terms of SUS-scales where improved when banking interfaces where tag-based, that is, that various elements could be tagged with user-selected names. Vines and colleagues [36] reported on a prototype of a digital cheque book designed for older users that were accustomed to paper-based cheque books. The concept was as follows: the digital cheque book was visually similar to a traditional paper-based cheque book where the user fills in the cheques with a pen. The authors reported on how they worked with the mass media through press releases to get the local banking industry interested in the project.

One approach that avoids the difficulties associated with technological payment systems is UbiPay which goal is to allow payments to be done implicitly using contextual information as part of everyday interactions [37]. Inspired by wallet phones, that is, the use of a phone to make small purchases by placing a smartphone next to a reader payments may for instance be made automatically for single fare tickets when a passenger enters a metro station. Near field communication (NFC) technology is now widely used for simple transactions. Participatory methods with focus groups involving older people has also been used to bring new insight to the design of banking services [38].

To the best of our knowledge there are no existing empirical studies comparing the usability of mobile BankID and BandID code generators.

3 Method

3.1 Experimental Design

A mixed experimental design was chosen with task-completion-time as dependent variable, and authentication device and preferred device as independent variables. Authentication device was a within-groups factor with the two levels smartphone and code generator. Device preference was a between-groups factor with the same two levels, namely smartphone and code-generator.

3.2 Participants

All the 20 participants recruited ranged in age from 15 to 75 years. They were all regular users of BankID. Of these, 6 participants preferred the code generator and 14 participants preferred the smartphone version of BankID.

The participants were asked to use their personal bank-account for the experiment which raises obvious ethical dilemmas. The participants were thus recruited among friends and family to ensure that the participants trusted the experimenters and that no sensitive information would be recorded. Moreover, it would be challenging to recruit arbitrary people in the street as people usually do not carry their code generators around. No personal information, or information that could be used to detect the participants, was recorded. The participation in the experiment was therefore fully anonymous.

3.3 Task

Each participant was asked to log into their Internet bank portal by using both a mobile BankID and by using a code generator. The experiment was balanced to prevent learning effects by randomizing the order of the two authentication devices.

3.4 Procedure

Prior to the observation session the experimenters ensured that the participants had access to their code generator and had activated Mobile BankID. First, each participant was briefed about the experiment. The participants were then asked to sign a consent form which clearly indicated that participation was voluntary, the results are anonymous and that they could withdraw from the experiment at any time. The consent form also asked the participants about their preferred authentication device.

The experiments were conducted in a quiet room with only two of the authors present at in addition to the participants to facilitate the experiment, observe and record the time. The experimenters positioned themselves in such a way as not to pry on the participants sensitive banking details. Each session was run with just a single participant.

After the experiment the participants where asked if they had changed their preferences. None of the participants had changed their BankID preference after the experiment. Each session lasted between 5 to 10 min including briefing.

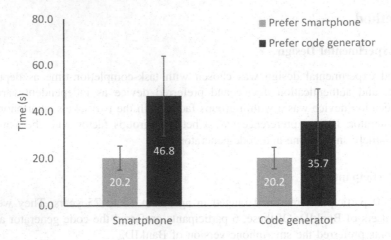

Fig. 3. Results of the authentication experiment. Error bars show standard deviation.

3.5 Measurements and Analysis

A stopwatch was used for recording the task completion times. The time from after the participants had inputted their personal ID-number until they had successfully logged into the Internet bank was recorded manually using pen and paper. None of the participants personal information were recorded. The data were analyzed using the open source statistical software package JASP 0.8.6.0 [39]. The experiments were conducted during the autumn of 2017 before the introduction of the General Data Protection Regulation (GDPR).

4 Results

The results (see Fig. 3) reveal that the code generator was faster to use in seconds ($M = 24.8$, $SD = 10.9$) than the smartphone ($M = 28.2$, $SD = 15.8$) although a majority (70%) of the participants preferred the smartphone. The spread of the measurements using the code generator was also smaller than the measurements observed with the smartphone. Figure 3 shows the results of the experiment also according to the participants preferences. These results reveal that the variation in the observations are related to the participants preferences, as participants who preferred the code generator generally took longer than the participants who preferred the smartphone. The participants who preferred the code generator also performed the task faster with the code generator in seconds ($M = 35.7$, $SD = 13.9$) compared to the smartphone ($M = 46.8$, $SD = 17.1$). This difference between the two authentication devices is significantly different ($F(1, 18) = 13.0, p < .002$).

The results obtained for the participants who preferred the smartphone are significantly different from those who preferred the code generator ($F(1, 18) = 24.9$, $p < .001$). There is also an interaction effect between authentication device, and the preference ($F(1, 18) = 12.9, p = .002$). The participants who preferred the smartphone performed the task slightly faster using the code generator ($M = 20.15$, $SD = 4.61$) compared to the smartphone ($M = 20.21$, $SD = 5.09$). However, a paired t-test revealed that this difference is not statistically significant ($t(13) = 0.039$, $p = .97$). Moreover, the spread in the observations of participants who preferred the smartphone is much smaller than for those who preferred code-generators. These small spread signals a more consistent usage pattern and indicates that these participants have more developed technology skills.

5 Discussion

The results show that the code generator is faster to use than the smartphone. This is not surprising as the code generator is a special-purpose device while the smartphone is a general-purpose device. Generally, users prefer familiar environments and if a user regularly uses a smartphone, the smartphone may be more positively perceived than the code generator. By operating in an environment perceived positively, the user may not actually notice that the task may take longer. However, although all the users solved the tasks faster with the code generator this difference was not significant for those preferring the smartphone.

Participants who preferred the code generator generally took longer time and exhibited a larger variation in performance. This is a sign that this group is less experienced with technology. One may speculate that a preference for the smartphone is related to the technological skills of the users, while less skilled users prefer the simplicity of the code generator with its single button and simple interaction steps.

There may also be situations where technologically savvy users prefer the code generator, such as privacy and security. A smartphone that is constantly connected to the Internet and used for many of the user's daily tasks is vulnerable. The code generator on the other hand may be perceived as safer as it is not connected to the Internet.

5.1 Limitations and Future Work

Conducting observational studies of users conducting sensitive computer operations is challenging as one needs to ensure the privacy of the participants while also ensuring their trust. Consequently, the current study is based on a relatively small sample ($N = 20$) and only one simple dependent variable was observed (completion time). With a larger sample of users from distinct user groups more concrete patterns may be found. For instance, distinct age groups could perhaps be used as a between-groups independent variable to assess the effect of age which has been found to have effects on banking patterns [16].

Moreover, given more elaborate measurements achievable by employing keyboard loggers and screen capturers one may be able to perform more sophisticated analysis of the interaction between users and the banking system. However, detailed logging requires especially stringent steps to ensure privacy and careful ethical considerations.

The study of online banking habits from 2013 [16] did not include smartphone-based BankID. It would thus also be relevant to run a similar study on blind and visually impaired users in context of smartphone-based authentication. Smartphones hold the potential of providing accessibility support when the smartphone apps are implemented to support the built in accessibility facilities such as built-in screen readers such as TalkBack on Android or VoiceOver on IOS.

6   Conclusions

This study explored the difference between BankID authentication using code generators and smartphone solutions from a usability perspective. The results show that the majority prefer the smartphone over the code generator. The code generator is faster to use than the smartphone, but this difference is insignificant for the technology confident participants. Yet, it is expected that all citizens are to use these authentication systems to perform key duties as citizens. Since a large fraction of the population are not interested in or confident using technology, or even wants to use smartphones, it seems sensible to continue with both mobile BankID and the code generator although the smartphone version is both more popular and probably a cheaper alternative for the banks.

References

1. Selmer, E.S.: Personnummerering i Norge: Litt anvendt tallteori og psykologi. Nordisk matematisk tidsskrift **12**, 36–44 (1964)
2. Gunson, N., Marshall, D., Morton, H., Jack, M.: User perceptions of security and usability of single-factor and two-factor authentication in automated telephone banking. Comput. Secur. **30**, 208–220 (2011)
3. Braz, C., Robert, J.M.: Security and usability: the case of the user authentication methods. In: Proceedings of the 18th Conference on l'Interaction Homme-Machine, pp. 199–203. ACM (2006)
4. Casalo, L.V., Flavián, C., Guinalíu, M.: The role of security, privacy, usability and reputation in the development of online banking. Online Inf. Rev. **31**, 583–603 (2007)
5. Pikkarainen, T., Pikkarainen, K., Karjaluoto, H., Pahnila, S.: Consumer acceptance of online banking: an extension of the technology acceptance model. Internet Res. **14**, 224–235 (2004)
6. Smith, A.D.: Exploring security and comfort issues associated with online banking. Int. J. Electron. Finance **1**, 18–48 (2006)
7. Yeow, P.H., Yuen, Y.Y., Tong, D.Y.K., Lim, N.: User acceptance of online banking service in Australia. Commun. IBIMA **1**, 191–197 (2008)
8. Sohail, M.S., Shanmugham, B.: E-banking and customer preferences in Malaysia: an empirical investigation. Inf. Sci. **150**, 207–217 (2003)
9. Laforet, S., Li, X.: Consumers' attitudes towards online and mobile banking in China. Int. J. Bank Mark. **23**, 362–380 (2005)
10. Olsen, K.A.: Customer errors in internet banking. In: Proceedings of Norsk Informatikkonferanse. Tapir Academic Publishers (2008)
11. Sandnes, F.E.: Effects of common keyboard layouts on physical effort: implications for kiosks and Internet banking. In: Sandnes, F.E., Lunde, M. Tollefsen, M., Hauge, A.M., Øverby, E., Brynn, R. (eds.) The Proceedings of Unitech2010: International Conference on Universal Technologies, pp. 91–100. Tapir Academic Publishers (2010)

12. Sandnes, F.E.: A memory aid for reduced cognitive load in manually entered online bank transactions. In: Proceedings of Norsk informatikkonferanse, pp. 273–276. Tapir Academic Publishers (2012)

13. Wangensteen, A., Lunde, L., Jorstad, J., Thanh, D.: A generic authentication system based on SIM. In: International Conference on Internet Surveillance and Protection 2006 (ICISP'06), pp. 24–24. IEEE (2006)

14. Gjøsteen, K.: Weaknesses in BankID, a PKI-substitute deployed by Norwegian Banks. In: Mjølsnes, S.F., Mauw, S., Katsikas, S.K. (eds.) EuroPKI 2008. LNCS, vol. 5057, pp. 196–206. Springer, Heidelberg (2008). https://doi.org/10.1007/978-3-540-69485-4_14

15. Espelid, Y., Netland, L.H., Klingsheim, A.N., Hole, K.J.: A proof of concept attack against Norwegian Internet Banking Systems. In: Tsudik, G. (ed.) FC 2008. LNCS, vol. 5143, pp. 197–201. Springer, Heidelberg (2008). https://doi.org/10.1007/978-3-540-85230-8_18

16. Tjøstheim, F.I.: Undersøkelse om autentisering, innlogging og tilgjengelighet blant medlemmer i Norges Blindeforbund. Technical report DART/12/2013, The Norwegian Computing Center (2013)

17. Lazar, J., Allen, A., Kleinman, J., Malarkey, C.: What frustrates screen reader users on the web: a study of 100 blind users. Int. J. Hum. Comput. Interact. 22, 247–269 (2007)

18. Evett, L., Brown, D.: Text formats and web design for visually impaired and dyslexic readers —clear text for all. Interact. Comput. 17, 453–472 (2005)

19. Subashini, K., Sumithra, G.: Secure multimodal mobile authentication using one time password. In: Proceedings of the 2nd International Conference on Current Trends in Engineering and Technology (ICCTET), pp. 151–155. IEEE (2014)

20. Whitney, G., et al.: Twenty five years of training and education in ICT Design for All and Assistive Technology. Technol. Disabil. 23(3), 163–170 (2011)

21. Berget, G., Sandnes, F.E.: Do autocomplete functions reduce the impact of dyslexia on information searching behaviour? A case of Google. J. Am. Soc. Inf. Sci. Technol. 67, 2320–2328 (2016)

22. Sandnes, F.E., Jian, H.-L.: Pair-wise variability index: evaluating the cognitive difficulty of using mobile text entry systems. In: Brewster, S., Dunlop, M. (eds.) Mobile HCI 2004. LNCS, vol. 3160, pp. 347–350. Springer, Heidelberg (2004). https://doi.org/10.1007/978-3-540-28637-0_35

23. Sandnes, F.E.: Evaluating mobile text entry strategies with finite state automata. In: Proceedings of the 7th International Conference on Human Computer Interaction with Mobile Devices & Services, pp. 115–121. ACM (2005)

24. Kaye, J.J., McCuistion, M., Gulotta, R., Shamma, D.A.: Money talks: tracking personal finances. In: Proceedings of the SIGCHI Conference on Human Factors in Computing Systems, pp. 521–530. ACM (2014)

25. Vines, J., Dunphy, P., Monk, A.: Pay or delay: the role of technology when managing a low income. In: Proceedings of the SIGCHI Conference on Human Factors in Computing Systems, pp. 501–510. ACM (2014)

26. Binns, R., Zhao, J., Van Kleek, M., Shadbolt, N., Liccardi, I., Weitzner, D.: My bank already gets this data: exposure minimisation and company relationships in privacy decision-making. In: Proceedings of the 2017 CHI Conference Extended Abstracts on Human Factors in Computing Systems, pp. 2403–2409. ACM (2017)

27. Rieser, D.C., Bernhard, O.: Measuring trust: the simpler the better? In: Proceedings of the 2016 CHI Conference Extended Abstracts on Human Factors in Computing Systems, pp. 2940–2946. ACM (2016)

28. Singh, S., Cabraal, A., Demosthenous, C., Astbrink, G., Furlong, M.: Password sharing: implications for security design based on social practice. In: Proceedings of the SIGCHI Conference on Human Factors in Computing Systems, pp. 895–904. ACM (2007)

29. Flechais, I., Jirotka, M., Alghamdi, D.: In the balance in Saudi Arabia: security, privacy and trust. In: CHI2013 Extended Abstracts on Human Factors in Computing Systems, pp. 823–828. ACM (2013)

30. Nilsson, M., Adams, A., Herd, S.: Building security and trust in online banking. In: CHI2005 Extended Abstracts on Human Factors in Computing Systems, pp. 1701–1704. ACM (2005)

31. Purkait, S.: Phishing counter measures and their effectiveness–literature review. Inf. Manag. Comput. Secur. **20**, 382–420 (2012)

32. Kim, J., Moon, J.Y.: Emotional usability of customer interfaces: focusing on cyber banking system interfaces. In: CHI1997 Extended Abstracts on Human Factors in Computing Systems, pp. 283–284. ACM (1997)

33. Medhi, I., Gautama, S.N., Toyama, K.: A comparison of mobile money-transfer UIs for non-literate and semi-literate users. In: Proceedings of the SIGCHI Conference on Human Factors in Computing Systems, pp. 1741–1750. ACM (2009)

34. Kumar, D., Martin, D., O'Neill, J.: The times they are a-changin': mobile payments in India. In: Proceedings of the SIGCHI Conference on Human Factors in Computing Systems, pp. 1413–1422. ACM (2011)

35. Ravendran, R., MacColl, I., Docherty, M.: Tag-based interaction in online and mobile banking: a preliminary study of the effect on usability. In: Proceedings of the 10th Asia Pacific Conference on Computer Human Interaction, pp. 35–40. ACM (2012)

36. Vines, J., Thieme, A., Comber, R., Blythe, M., Wright, P.C., Olivier, P.: HCI in the press: online public reactions to mass media portrayals of HCI research. In: Proceedings of the SIGCHI Conference on Human Factors in Computing Systems, pp. 1873–1882. ACM (2013)

37. Lehdonvirta, V., Soma, H., Ito, H., Kimura, H., Nakajima, T.: UbiPay: conducting everyday payments with minimum user involvement. In: CHI2008 Extended Abstracts on Human Factors in Computing Systems, pp. 3537–3542. ACM (2008)

38. Vines, J., Blythe, M., Lindsay, S., Dunphy, P., Monk, A., Olivier, P.: Questionable concepts: critique as resource for designing with eighty somethings. In: Proceedings of the SIGCHI Conference on Human Factors in Computing Systems, pp. 1169–1178. ACM (2012)

39. JASP Team: JASP (Version 0.9) [Computer software] (2018). https://jasp-stats.org/

Universal Access to Learning and Education

Audiovisual Design for Generative Systems: A Customized Audiovisual Experiment

Valdecir Becker[✉], Rafael M. Toscano,
Helder Bruno A. M. de Souza, and Edvaldo de Vasconcelos

Audiovisual Design Research Group, Informatics Center,
Federal University of Paraíba, João Pessoa, PB, Brazil
`audiovisualdesign@lavid.ufpb.br`
`valdecir@ci.ufpb.br`

Abstract. The production of audiovisual content has become an increasingly complex activity as new features of interaction, sharing, different screens and forms of visualization are becoming popular. The architecture of Audiovisual Design arises as a theoretical-methodological instrument for analysis and creation of digital audiovisual content. The purpose of this article is to describe the process of building an audiovisual system based on individuals' data to establish a personalized content enjoyment, using the Audiovisual Design method. The construction of the system revealed that elements available in Audiovisual Design, as designing lines, roles and triggers are potential aspects for creation of modern audiovisual content.

Keywords: Audiovisual Design · Human Computer Interaction · Generative Systems

1 Introduction

The development of audiovisual content has become an increasingly complex activity as new features of interaction, sharing, different screens and forms of visualization are becoming popular. The audiovisual experience, which has been mostly occupied by film and television, now becomes more comprehensive, ranging from Internet research to complex algorithms of recommendation, collaboration and content adaptation. One feature of this scenario is the presence and use of software to compose the experience of enjoyment of audiovisual workpieces. Expansion of computers processing power and increased access to stable network connections enable a scenario where audiovisual content producers are increasingly close to programmers, interaction designers, and data scientists.

An online video, a movie, digital games or even soap operas are examples of how representation media (audio and video) can be used to build an aesthetic and communicational experience. On the one hand, we have the discussions about technologies of capture and representation stimulated by Computer Science, on the other hand we

M. Antona and C. Stephanidis (Eds.): HCII 2019, LNCS 11572, pp. 377–388, 2019.
https://doi.org/10.1007/978-3-030-23560-4_28

have discussions in the field of Communication and Arts about values and meanings generated by content being exposed and watched.

From this computational and complex media context it is possible to identify discussions and experiments that dialogue with the capacity to generate audiovisual narratives from data collected from audiences. In the first cinematographic and television productions it was impracticable to think about construction of content adapted to individual interests or small groups due to the high cost of production and distribution. Nowadays, with the increase of computational processing and internet reach, this scenario becomes increasingly viable.

Based on this complex context of audiovisual media usage arises the theoretical-methodological discussion of Audiovisual Design (AD). Initially proposed by Becker, Gambaro and Ramos [1], the AD integrates aspects of Media and Reception from the Communication Science field to Human Computer Interaction (IHC) tools and concepts, with the purpose of assisting in description, analysis and creation of audiovisual systems. In a second publication the AD is characterized by the authors as an architecture of content and interaction capable of attending contexts of historicity and generativity, scenarios in which both the interaction and the user data are used by the system in offering contents [2].

This work proposes the experimental application of Audiovisual Design as the architecture and method of a generative project, a system that integrates user data and interaction for generation of new customized content. All videos are available on line and compose workpieces accessible in an interactive museum. This study is being carried out by researchers from the Audiovisual Design Research Group at the Laboratory of Interaction and Media (LIM) in the scope of a project for the State of Paraíba Court of Accounts.

2   Theoretical and Conceptual Bases

The development of computational processing capacity as well as the emergence of new sensors have enabled software to innovate ways of capturing and interpreting data to better understand what information is being captured, processed and reproduced [3–6]. Parallel to Computer Science studies it is possible to identify an increasing discussion about different ways of interaction and enjoyment, present in the community of researchers of the Media Studies field. There are scenarios of multiple means and forms of reception [7] in which systems also act as discourse partners [8] and reveal the emergence of new standards and conventions in the process of communication, representation and audiovisual enjoyment [9]. Just as computational studies approach the semantic value of digital data, producers and artists of audiovisual medium are also incorporating and using data and diverse contexts of interaction to improve their narrative and communicational premises.

2.1   Adaptation, Customization and Personalization

The terms customization, adaptation and personalization are outlined in literature in slightly different ways. The logic of customization appears in contexts of offering resources to individuals so they can adjust pre-established elements according to their interests. Adaptation is delimited mostly to technical contexts such as adaptation to network requirements, screen size or accessibility. Finally, the idea of personalization is usually associated with filtering information about audience to recommend, reposition, insert, delete, display certain content or mode of interaction [10–15].

After comprehending the idea of personalization, it becomes necessary to understand what can be personalized. The study [6] conceptualize generation of elements for personalization of audiovisual narrative experience goes through different structural levels. The most general element is the narrative, a precisely form or expression found to present a story. Story is a set of elements constitute a linear relationship. The stories are composed by plots, which are composed by dramatic events. A story can be told from a variety of narrative forms, just as the same story can have variable plots allowing the audience for different perceptions. This structuralist approach helps to understand levels at which digital systems can act in a way that impacts content and enjoyment of individuals.

3 Methodological Procedures

The architecture of Audiovisual Design (Fig. 1) is the conceptual and methodological basis of this study. The AD essentially describes four functions, or roles, individuals can assume while consuming audiovisual content: Audience, which represents a passive enjoyment of content; Synthesizer, where individuals organize, share and comment content on social networks; Modifier, which corresponds to individuals who appropriate contents and modify them; and Producer, which represents the individuals, companies and software that generate new content. Each role has its improved levels, described as Player, when individuals engage and use all available resources, or even completely change the purposes of content and system.

In the Audiovisual Design framework interactions and relations with content occur through four Designing Lines: (a) Content; (b) Identity, which bases the personal relationship with content; (c) Motivation, which leads to engagement; and (d) Experience, which relates enjoyment to advanced use of resources, providing practical or symbolic experience with content and interfaces. This Lines are described to assist the developer of audiovisual system (content and software) to design the interactions, engagement and content of production from variables that impact the enjoyment of individuals.

Another relevant concept to AD architecture are triggers, which arise from the Designing Lines. A trigger is any element added throughout the fruition, or interaction, in order to stimulate individuals' actions. They can come as sound or visual elements, graphic interface, interactions or even action calls done by audio or video content.

AD will be used to describe and create this project. It proposes a set of relational variables or layers that should be considered by content producers within a context of complex media use. In general, the steps that make up the development from the architecture of Audiovisual Design are:

- Identify purpose, main uses of the system and personas;

- Delimit Designing Lines;
- Design Triggers and Affordances;
- Develop the system (content and interface)[1];
- Test the system.

The following sections detail the application of these concepts in the construction of the generative audiovisual system.

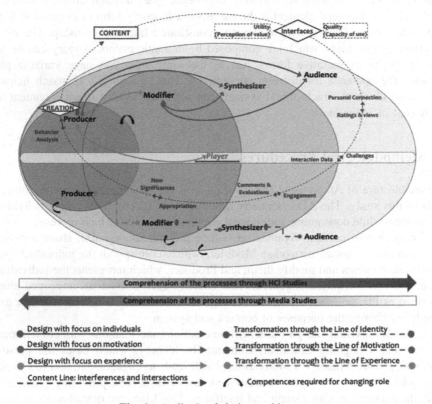

Fig. 1. Audiovisual design architecture.

4 Results

The system described in this paper is part of a project that integrates high school students into a set of activities during classes, such as video production, visit and engage in State of Paraíba Court of Accounts (in Portuguese, TCE-PB) actions. Students are invited by teachers to produce videos about success stories or inefficient aspects in their school community. The audiovisual content is published in TCE-PB's Facebook page. To publish the videos, each student describes the school's name, city

---

[1] In this step are used processes and tools common to video production and software engineering.

and uses predetermined hashtag to inform about the content present in each video. After this stage, conducted by students, teachers review the contents, identified by the system via the GRAPH API[2], as shown in Fig. 1.

This data collection (video, user name and school) serves two systems: Advanced and Collaborative Visualization System via Paraíba State Map and the Support System for Lectures, also called as a Custom Video Generator.

4.1 Advanced and Collaborative Visualization System

The contents are visualized in the Collaborative Map (Fig. 3), which can be accessed on the web or viewed on the Interactive Table in the Museum. On the web, a video gallery presents the students' productions and information about which schools are producing content. Already in the Museum, a touch-sensitive screen contains only the map. In it the teacher defines videos to be presented and chooses a photo of the school. At the end, the system generates a personalized video, opening with images from the school, followed by the students' videos and respective credits. The video can be shared with a QR Code, the last image of the video.

4.2 The Custom Video Generator

TCE-PB receives visits from high school students to know its physical structure and carried out social actions. One strategy to integrate these visitors in themes such as social control and fiscal education, a system of lecture support was developed to integrate institutional audiovisual products into the collaborative production of students, with the purpose of personalizing the experience of each class that visits the TCE-PB.

Applying the Audiovisual Design architecture in the development of this system, we have the following proposal: from an institutional video, which defines the Content line and conceptualizes people's importance in supervision and monitoring public matters, videos produced by students are inserted as integral elements of the narrative (Line of Identity and Motivation), according to Fig. 2.

Fig. 2. Management panel

<hr />

[2] API provided by Facebook to use information from external web services.

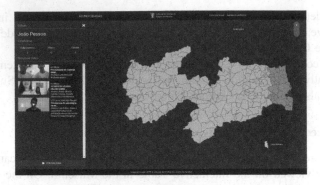

Fig. 3. Collaborative map

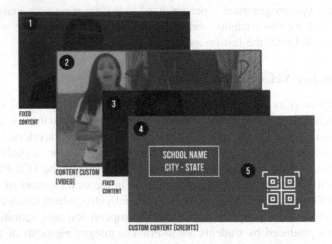

Fig. 4. Abstraction of narrative personalization.

The personalized video, generated based on students' data has the following structure (Fig. 4):

Part 1: Contextualization on aspects of mismanagement and corruption, and how popular participation is important in combating and monitoring failures in public management. Following the AD architecture, in this stage of video narrative resources (rhythm of editing, soundtrack, forms of expression, among others) have to be coherent with students spectating in such a way to stimulate the attention and interest about the subject.

Part 2: Examples of social control attitudes based on student videos. Following the architecture of the AD, the use of students' videos acts as a Trigger and stimulus to attention and formation of Identity and affinity with the content.

Part 3: Experts explain students acts represent social control, a fundamental role in whole society. Following the architecture of the AD, this stage of the video uses the principles of the Content and Identity Line, since the participation of the students is handled at the content level, as a partner of the TCE-PB.

Part 4: Movie credits with names of participants (experts, school and students). This step is also a Trigger, it acts as a stimulus to attention and formation of Identity and affinity with the content.

Part 5: Providing QR code for video sharing. Following the architecture of the AD, this step acts as an Action Trigger, forming the Identity to stimulate the student (Audience) to switch the role to Synthesizer, by sharing the material in their own social media.

Other Designing Lines can be impacted by the system are Motivation and Experience. Since this personalized material from individuals' data is made available in a file format compatible with social media (Youtube, Facebook or WhatsApp) it is possible to enable scenarios in which students can modify, edit or even remix the content.

To guarantee a scenario of enjoyment and interaction, the following functional requirements for the system were delineated: stablish connection with Facebook via API Graph; Incorporate hashtag, video, student name and school from a public post on Facebook; Insert imported data into the video project "Social Control"; Render all material (fixed institutional videos, customizable and data) to generate a single video file compatible with HTML5 and services like Youtube and Vimeo.

5 Analyzing Proposed Interactions

To detail the strategies of interaction and engagement, a system usage scenario based on a persona student named Wellyngton is described below. Use scenarios are verbal narratives objectively situated, with contextual details, aiming to characterize the context of interaction and define relationships of individual with technology. They are useful in design to visualize uses of the system in development. Personas are archetypes that represent a set of users for whom the design is done [16, 17]. The focus of the scenario lies in students because it is through them the general objective of the project, related to citizen and fiscal awareness, will be reached.

5.1 Persona Student

Wellyngton studies in second year of high school, has lessons weekly about History, owns a prepaid internet access smartphone he uses while the daily data limit lasts. In addition, he connects to the internet using wi-fi from school, where he spends the day. Wellyngton has accounts in several social networks, but mainly uses Instagram, Youtube and Facebook. He thinks all politicians are corrupt, but is intrigued because the history teacher, Cida, spoke during a class it is everyone's responsibility to monitor and control public spending, including those at school.

5.2 Use Scenario

In School: During the class History teacher Cida presents the Portal Aluno Cidadão[3] (ToA 1), which has a Map of State of Paraíba with municipalities and schools. Wellyngton is very interested in videos produced by students from other schools about

---

[3] The portal can be accessed at this link: http://controlesocial.tce.pb.gov.br/.

public management, enforcement and denunciations about unfinished public works. When teacher finishes showing videos, he asks if their class also wants to produce and include videos in the Portal. Cida then shows a movie about how to record and share videos on Facebook (ToA 2), which will then be included into Aluno Cidadão Portal.

Wellyngton creates a group with his friends and records two videos, one on an unfinished bridge on the way home and the other on abandoned ground next to the school where people throw garbage. They share the videos on Facebook, with hashtags describing the content and the name of the school (ToA 3).

In the next class, teacher opens the Aluno Cidadão Portal, clicks on the Alagoa Grande municipality, in the name of the school, Josué Gomes da Silveira, and all videos procied by the class are listed (ToI 1). The class attends and discusses the origin of the problems, responsibilities and how to solve them. To compare, the teacher shows videos of students from Padre Hildo Bandeira State School, from the neighborhood, who also recorded a video on the unfinished bridge of Wellyngton's group.

Scenario of Use Visiting the Interactive Museum
The school receives an invitation to visit the TCE-PB facilities, through the School and Citizenship Project. Wellyngton is elated to know TCE, which he has only heard about on television. At TCE students are received with snacks and juices and invited to enter the auditorium (ToI 2). A lecture begins on recycling garbage, with a TCE professional speech. During the lecture, video clips are shown, among them those produced by school students, such as Wellyngton's, relevant to the subject (ToA 4) and incorporated into the presentation by the speaker.

At the end of the lecture a QR Code appears on the board (ToA 5). The speaker explains that by photographing it students have access to the whole video, can copy it or share it on social networks. Wellyngton immediately photographs the QR Code and shares it in social media, commenting that his video has appeared in a TCE event.

The speaker then invites Wellyngton's class to visit the TCE Interactive Museum, where Cida begins by showing the games, virtual reality, the coworking space, and a theater to watch movies. The class goes close to a touch-sensitive monitor, which contains the same Aluno Cidadão Portal Map (ToA 6). The teacher again selects the municipality and the school. But this time does not appear the list of all the videos produced by the class: the best videos act as "symbolic affordance" (ToA 6) and are assembled in a unitary workpiece. Cida elucidates she chose the videos about public works and explains the responsibility on roads and bridges can be as much of the city hall as of the state and federal governments. She selects "play videos" (ToI 3), which now start with a photo and name of the school. When the video ends, teacher's name and the students who recorded the videos also appear on a black background, such as on TV. A QR Code offers the option to share the video (ToA 7). Wellyngton leaves TCE-PB talking to his colleagues about themes of next videos they will record.

6   Trigger Definition and Analysis

Methodologically, according to the Audiovisual Design framework, once established the objective to be reached with the content, the Designing Lines are defined, according to an utility perception of each role. Considering purpose and utility, media affordances are developed, resulting in triggers to promote notions of system quality, thus guaranteeing good experiences of individuals. Each Designing Line provides tools to achieve the individual's goals.

Every change of role begins with the perception of a media affordance and is performed using triggers, which may correspond to action or to inertia. In the case of Aluno Cidadão, there are changes of roles proposed by the system, and the persona Student will alternate among Audience, Synthesizer and Producer. Modifier actions are focused on teachers and speakers. Table 1 describes the Triggers of Action (ToA) and Inertia (ToI) designed to change roles using the four Designing Lines: Identity (LI), Motivation (LM), Experience (LE) and Content (LC).

Considering the purpose of this project, specifically raising awareness about social control and involving society in actions to combat corruption, individuals together play a key role. It is considered that high school students have a central role in medium and long term in this process. The main Designing Line that guides audiovisual enjoyment is Identity. Allied to the Content Line, this Line represents the contact of the individual with the premise of awareness. The stimulus to share is materialized through the Motivation Line, focused on the role played by Synthesizers.

From the theoretical point of view, the Audience, when creating the identity with the theme, is encouraged through Triggers of Action to change to the role of Producer. In this role, production and sharing take place (remembering by describing the DA in the form of sets, the Producer has the abilities of all antecedent roles). By enjoying the videos in the classroom (Trigger of Inertia), the student, who acted as a Producer, returns to the role of Audience. It is important to consider the change from the role of Audience to Producer goes beyond engagement through identification. The stimulus to active participation is part of life experience, which, as a citizen, leads to produce contents relevant to this context. Likewise, we cannot ignore that Identity Line will also be fundamental for students who do not produce, for, identified as citizens, to be motivated to at least watch the videos.

Table 1. Triggers for Aluno Cidadão.

ToA/ToI	D.L.	Description	Goal	Role change
ToA 1	LI and LE	Access to Aluno Cidadão portal, whose content is based on collaboration	Awakening the Audience's attention to record	Audience for Producer
ToA 2	LI and LE	Teacher encourages students to produce video	Motivate the Audience to produce	Audience for Producer
ToA 3	LM	Students use hashtags when sharing videos	Develop identity and generate new engagements	Producer for Synthesizer
ToI 1	LI	Students watch and discuss videos in classroom	Reinforce identity	Producer for Audience
ToA 4	LE	Teacher modifies the students' videos, concatenating several productions, professional and amateur, to compose the presentation	Enable presentation assembly options to the Speaker (Modifier)	Audience for Modifier
ToI 2	LI	Students attend lectures	Reinforce identity	Producer for Audience

(continued)

Table 1. (*continued*)

ToA/ToI	D.L.	Description	Goal	Role change
ToA 5	LM	Students share the content of the lecture	Create identity on social networks	Audience for Synthesizer
ToA 6	LE	Teacher concatenates various productions by entering information about the school and the students	Enable content to be assembled for school representation in the system	Audience for Modifier
ToI 3	Li	Students watch the video	Reinforce identity	Producer for Audience
ToA 7	LM	Producer Design to create identity in social networks	Create identity in social networks	Audience for Synthesizer

At this point, the teacher is a mediator between objectives of the system (defined by TCE-PB) and Audience, serving as a trigger, both of action in the first moment and of inertia in the second. Already when the teacher moderates videos that compose the Portal and creates the playlist of personalized videos in the Museum, he himself acts as a Modifier. In the case of moderation, Modification happens at a macro level, since the teacher changes the whole system by selecting which videos compose the Map; in the Museum this Modification happens at a micro level, generating a video with data of the students.

A similar relationship can be established when the Audience watches the contents in the Auditorium and in the Museum. In both cases, a modified content is offered to the Audience with a trigger to share at the end (Synthesizer), represented by the QR Code. By photographing the QR Code and sharing the video, the student moves from Audience to Synthesizer.

The media affordances prevail in defining triggers of this system are symbolic. Calls for action or for inertia are part of the teacher-student relationship within the classroom and in the Museum, as well as speaker and audience, in the auditorium. In addition, there are elements of awareness, central objective of the project, that lead to the action of the Audience. This process of awareness takes place at psychological and motivational levels, where perception of a possible agenda for the video can also become a Trigger of Action (as is the case of the unfinished bridge of the use scenario). The QR Codes, used in two moments, correspond to visual media affordances, centered on the video graphical interface.

7   Conclusions

This article describes how the methodological process of Audiovisual Design was used in the production process of customized audiovisual contents for an Interactive Museum. The development of Interaction Triggers was described, based on the museum's objectives and the profile of the visiting public. Each role described in the Audiovisual Design model has associated affordances for Triggers of Action (ToA) or of Inertia (ToI). Role change is a central part in the production of content for complex audiovisual systems.

A methodological course was designed starting from the objective to be reached with the content, considering different possibility of fruition of the individual. From the objective relevant Design Lines were defined, aiming to awake the notion of system utility (audiovisual content, interfaces and interaction). From this logical construction, relevant medium affordances have been defined, which lead to Triggers. All these steps should result in system quality, central element of usability for the satisfaction of individuals.

The research on the construction of generative audiovisual systems is still undergoing. The next parts are user tests for validation of usability and engagement. As future activities, this research has two actions. The first one, theoretical and conceptual, is related to an extended description of the relationship between tools needed in each Design Line with development of media affordances and triggers. The second action consists of evaluations of software development quality and usability tests with students, teachers and employees of TCE system users. In this way, we intend to validate the development described in this article, specially aspects related to the Motivation Line, with development of engagement.

References

1. Becker, V., Gambaro, D., Ramos, T.S.: Audiovisual Design and the Convergence Between HCI and Audience Studies. In: Kurosu, M. (ed.) HCI 2017. LNCS, vol. 10271, pp. 3–22. Springer, Cham (2017). https://doi.org/10.1007/978-3-319-58071-5_1
2. Toscano, R., Becker, V., Ferreira, L., et al.: Arquitetura de design colaborativo para imersão temporal e espacial em vídeos de altíssimas resoluções e HFR. In: O futuro da videocolaboração: perspectivas, pp. 13–53. Sociedade Brasileira de Computação (SBC), Porto Alegre (2017)
3. Hanjalic, A., Li-Qun, Xu: Affective video content representation and modeling. IEEE Trans. Multimed. 7, 143–154 (2005). https://doi.org/10.1109/TMM.2004.840618
4. Havaladar, P., Medioni, G.: Multimedia Systems: Algorithms, Standards, and Industry Practices. Course Technology, 1st edn. CENGAGE Learning, Boston (2010)
5. Hughes, J.F., Van Dam, A., Mcguire, M., et al.: Computer Graphics: Principles and Practice, 3rd edn. Addison-Wesley, Reading (2014)
6. Kybartas, B., Bidarra, R.: A survey on story generation techniques for authoring computational narratives. IEEE Trans. Comput. Intell. AI Games 9, 239–253 (2017). https://doi.org/10.1109/TCIAIG.2016.2546063
7. Jenkins, H., Ford, S., Green, J.: Cultura da conexão: Criando valor e significado por meio da mídia propagável. Aleph, São Paulo (2014)
8. Manovich, L.: Software Takes Command: Extending the Language of New Media. Bloomsbury Academic, London (2013)
9. Murray, J.H.: Inventing the Medium: Principles of Interaction Design as a Cultural Practice. Mit Press, Cambridge (2011)
10. Amy, S.: Video usability. In: Nielsen Norman Gr. Evidence-Based User Exp. Res. Training, Consult (2014). https://www.nngroup.com/articles/video-usability/. Accessed 7 Jul 2018
11. Barbosa, S.D.J., da Silva, B.S.: Interação Humano-Computador, 1st edn. Elsevier, Rio de Janeiro (2010)
12. Elmagarmid, A.K.: Smart Video Text : An Intelligent Video Database System (1997)
13. Guerrini, F., Adami, N., Benini, S., et al.: Interactive Film Recombination. ACM Trans. Multimed. Comput. Commun. Appl. 13, 1–22 (2017). https://doi.org/10.1145/3103241

14. Meixner, B.: Hypervideos and interactive multimedia presentations. ACM Comput. Surv. **50**, 1–34 (2017). https://doi.org/10.1145/3038925
15. Xu, M., Jin, J.S., Luo, S.: Personalized video adaptation based on video content analysis. In: Proceedings of the 9th International Work Multimedia Data Mining Held Conjunction with ACM SIGKDD 2008—MDM 2008, pp. 26–35 (2008). https://doi.org/10.1145/1509212.1509216
16. Lowdermilk, T.: User-Centered Design: A Developer's Guide to Building User-Friendly Applications. O'Reilly Media, Inc., Newton (2013)
17. Preece, J., Rogers, T., Sharp, H.: Design de Interação—Além da Interação Homem–computador, 3rd edn. Bookman, Porto Alegre (2013)

How to Design an Intervention to Raise Digital Competences: ALL DIGITAL Week – Dortmund 2018

Manuela Becker[1], Alexandra Benner[1], Katrin Borg[1], Jan Hüls[1],
Marina Koch[1], Annika Kost[1], Annabelle Korn[1],
Marie-Christin Lueg[1], Dominique Osthoff[1], Bastian Pelka[2(✉)],
Carina Rosenberger[1], and Helene Sattler[1]

[1] Faculty of Rehabilitation Sciences,
TU Dortmund University, Dortmund, Germany
{Manuela.becker, Alexandra.benner, Katrin.borg,
Jan.huels, Marina2.koch, Annika.kost, Annabelle.korn,
Marie-christin.lueg, Dominique.osthoff,
Carina.rosenberger, Helene.sattler}@tu-dortmund.de
[2] Social Research Centre Dortmund,
TU Dortmund University, Dortmund, Germany
pelka@sfs-dortmund.de

Abstract. The article describes and evaluates a local campaign to support digital skills of marginalized persons. Due to the increasing digitization which is taking place all over the world, it becomes necessary to support the expansion of people's digital competences and close the "digital gap" that causes multiple disadvantages for certain groups of people. In March 2018, eleven students of Rehabilitation Science at University of Dortmund (Germany) conducted five different courses for disadvantaged persons in Dortmund. The courses lasted around two hours and aimed at raising awareness for the potentials and pitfalls of digital tools used in the everyday life of people from different target groups. In total, 417 people attended these courses, mostly 6 to 10 participants per course. The article describes the best practices in designing, developing, conducting and evaluating these courses. An extensive survey (338 participants) is used to analyze successful means in delivering courses on IT topics to diverse target groups. The student activities were linked to the "ALL DIGITAL Week", a pan-European campaign that organizes courses in 25 countries with more than 92,460 participants. The "Get Online Week" Dortmund 2018, which is part of the European "ALL DIGITAL" campaign and carried out in Germany, is listed as an example in this article, to show how a project to raise digital competences can be designed and what is essential for a successful implementation. The article closes with recommendations for conducting alike interventions in other circumstances.

Keywords: Digital inclusion · Digital gap

© Springer Nature Switzerland AG 2019
M. Antona and C. Stephanidis (Eds.): HCII 2019, LNCS 11572, pp. 389–407, 2019.
https://doi.org/10.1007/978-3-030-23560-4_29

1   The Societal Problem Situation on Digital Inclusion

Within the last years, there has been a vast development within the world of digital media that has fundamentally influenced and changed our society and everyday life, resulting in a new type of society - the information society [1–3]. The information society in the European context is characterized by increasing economic growth as well as a broad modernization on the most diverse levels. The main reason for this development is the use of modern information and communication technology such as smartphones [4]. Such devices are easily accessible, can be carried close to the body due to their size and are therefore permanently available [5]. Also, their functions multiply continuously within a process of media convergence [6] leading to a changed consumer behaviour. However, the increasing use of digital devices is not only developing due to the media convergence, but it is also a consequence of the ever more digitizing society, which affects all our areas of life [7]. The term "digitization", on the one hand referring to the technical transfer of information from analogue to digital storage [8] which allows editing with the computer [9], is also referring to changes semantic layers [10], as it also refers to the process of introduction of digital technologies or application systems based on them. Following this approach, the ever-digitizing society represents the main cause for the rapid digitization of areas that were previously unrelated to the digital world. For example, 61% of Europeans use online banking, while 72% of them access the news online [11]. With 81% of Europeans using the internet at least once per week and 72% going online every day [12], the internet has become an integral part of the everyday life [5]. Also, the digitization of the social and recreational area leads to many advantages. Nowadays, digital participation is strongly connected with social participation, since the use of digital media allows changes within society and provides opportunities for new connections between people [10].

While millions of people in Europe, but also worldwide frequently use the internet, 13% of the Europeans have never dealt with it [12]. Within Germany, 19% do not even use the internet from time to time [13]. These people can be described as "offliners" and their existence refers to the still unequal distribution of internet usage. The differing use of digital media often results in different participation opportunities within important and scarce social resources [14]. Wealth, education, (social) security, health as well as individual autonomy can be assigned to these resources. These social inequalities have far-reaching consequences which affect the social participation of each individual.

The efficiency of access is, according to Wilson [15], characterized by a variety of factors, including access to digital media, the ability to use them, costs, design, self-initiative, potential language barriers and public internet access [28]. All of this contributes to the broadening of the so called "digital divide" within our society [16]. As the concept of social inequality only includes socially anchored forms of favoritism or pre-emption and therefore does not refer to physical heterogeneity or different biological systems [14], it cannot be used to fully explain the digital divide. To include other aspects and to ascertain which factors influence the differences in digital media usage, countless studies, such as the "Digital Economy and Society Index" (DESI Index) [11] as well as the "D21 Digital Index" [13], have researched the correlations between sociodemographic data and individual media usage. The latter, which is based on a large representative survey among 20,500 Germans aged 14 years and older, annually provides information on the digitization of the German society on a federal level. The current report from 2017/2018 e.g. states, that young people with a high level of education have a much higher degree of digitization, that high levels of income and education correlate with high levels of digitization and, that professionals are more digital than those who are not working [13].

What is particularly striking about the results of the index is that people with disabilities are not counted as one of the risk groups threatened by digital exclusion. This does not seem to be plausible, as especially for this group of people, the internet is of greater relevance and allows them to participate in social, cultural and professional life in a self-determined manner, thus suggesting an increased degree of independence [17]. Also, the right of complete accessibility is assured in federal laws like the Disability Equality Act [18] as well as the Convention on the Rights of Persons with Disabilities [19] and includes aspects like the full availability and usability of infrastructure and equipment [18] – which also includes information and communication devices [19]. In the context of digitization, this means that everyone, regardless of physical or mental limitations, should be able to participate equally within our social system.

However, digital devices and media can lead to new barriers and confront users with challenges [20] and especially the group of people with disabilities often faces insurmountable barriers when using the Internet. These are as diverse as the types of disabilities themselves and are linked to these as well as to their individual age. Numerous studies therefore differentiate between blindness, visual impairment, hearing loss, deafness, motor impairment, reading and spelling impairment and learning and mental disabilities [21]. Overall, the studies showed that significantly more people with impaired vision, hearing and physical activity use the Internet than people in the subgroup with learning difficulties [22]. Also within the subgroup of people with an disability, age is a significant negative factor correlating with internet usage – however, "in every age group, fewer respondents with disabilities regularly use the internet than the average population" (own translation) [22].

On the basis of these findings, which show that people with disabilities represent a risk group and are particularly affected by digital exclusion, it is necessary to dissolve at least the environmental barriers in order to guarantee all people unlimited participation in the media offerings. Consequently, environmental barriers for digital participation of people with disability as a risk group of digital exclusion have to be dismantled. The ever-changing application and use of the internet demands an ongoing re-experiencing and valuing of opportunities and risks. It seems to be crucial to intervene at an early stage and prevent people with disabilities from not participating due to their material, social or attitudinal environment. Competitions for good barrier-free websites like the "Bee Competition" [21] are one possibility; however, it is also possible to address the level of end-users – not just people with disabilities but all people at risk of digital exclusion. Since interest in further training in the digital sector is low, a systematic acquisition of knowledge through training does not take place on national level [13]. Thus, despite years of progressive digitization, Germany fails to achieve its goal of enabling all people to connect to the digital society.

2 The Intervention

The annual campaign "ALL DIGITAL Week" (ADW), first held as "Get Online Day" in 2010 in the UK, is one of the measures to counteract the progressive digital divide. It digitally empowers people and challenges Europeans to learn, participate, share and create. The campaign is organized by the pan-European non-profit association "ALL DIGITAL" which represents around 25,000 organizations in the field of digital education in Europe. Its main focus lies in supporting Europeans with insufficient levels of digital skills. Every year thousands of different events and activities that support the digital transformation are held all over Europe within one specific week in March – the "ALL DIGITAL Week". In 2017 about 170.000 first time internet users in Europe were reached by the event [23]. Behind the European structure of the campaign are the national partners that organize events in the member states. For Germany, "Stiftung Digitale Chancen" (SDC) organized the "ADW" in 2018 for the sixth time and coordinated 69 digital competence centers who participated by conducting different events and workshops focused on digital inclusion. Important for the realization of the single initiatives is the "European Digital Framework for Citizen" (DigComp) [24], which provides a common understanding of planning such initiatives topic as well as a guideline "ALL DIGITAL" created for adapting the framework [25].

In 2018, as in the previous three years, eleven students from the "Faculty of Rehabilitation Studies" at the "Technical University Dortmund" organized local events in Dortmund as part of the national "ADW" in Germany. They implemented five different concepts on developing digital skills, organized various local events and evaluated them afterwards [23]. To guarantee a successful process, their work was guided professionally by Dr. Bastian Pelka from the "Sozialforschungsstelle Dortmund". The time frame of the project extended over nine months, beginning in October 2017 and ending in July 2018, starting with a phase of planning and designing, leading to the implementation of the courses and ending with the phase of evaluation. The realization of the project was possible by working together with different institutions like schools, libraries, a penal institution, workshops for people with disabilities, rehabilitation centers and others which were often already known for their participation in previous years. The courses took place in the premises of the participating institutions and they were the ones who enlisted the participants, who were interested in the courses. The telecommunications provider "DOKOM21" was an official sponsor, who helped the participants getting access to the internet during the courses by supplying hotspots.

All courses were free of charge and took two hours each. This time frame was set so that the courses could be a short introduction of the topic and induce a further follow up with the content that was part of the respective course. This method was chosen so that as many courses as possible could take place and a large number of participants could be reached. Another reason is that the main aim was to raise the participants' interest, to close a first gap and give an opportunity to connect to the field of digital media. Most of the addressed target groups were chosen because they have a greater need to improve their digital skills and are more likely threatened by digital exclusion. In some institutions, the length of the course was shortened to 90 min due to the ability of the participants to concentrate. In the first phase of the organization of the "GOW", six different concepts for courses concerning the improvement of digital skills for various target groups were designed. Each concept had its own theme and aim and was conducted by two or three members of the project group. To present the course ideas and by that obtain cooperation partners for the project, a contact day that took place in December was organized. Various institutions that came into question for realizing the "GOW" 2018 in cooperation with the students were invited in writing. Employees from 25 different institutions attended this event and made appointments for courses they wanted to offer to their clients. After the contact day, it was decided to realize five out of the six concepts due to the interests and requirements that were shown by the institutions during the event:

- **"Sexual Education with help of Digital Media":** The course aimed to show students, people with disabilities, parents and educational professionals how to use websites on Sexual Education.
- **"Facebook, Instagram and Co. - How can I deal with hate on the Internet?":** The course contained information on how to behave respectfully in social networks and mainly addressed adolescents (12 years and older) as well as people with mental disorders.
- **"What does my child do on the internet? The digital world easily explained."** contained preventive educational exercises focused the contents children come across while surfing the internet. Target group were parents and educational professionals.
- **"Get ready for your future! - Job and Apartment Search online"** addressed job and apartment search on the web. It included digital research competences and e.g. writing an online application and addressed students, refugees and people in disadvantaged situations (e.g. prisoners, people with a mental illness, homeless).
- **"From dial to touchscreen - Lead-in to the media use of tablets, smartphones and computer"** aimed to provide a first contact with the named devices as well as a basic knowledge on digital communication. The target group included seniors and people with disabilities.

3   Methodology

The following section is going to introduce the methodology, which was used to investigate to what extent the course concepts were successfully implemented. In addition, a description of the sample will be presented which gives an overview of the survey participants

3.1   Research Design

To evaluate the courses scientifically, a combination of qualitative and quantitative research methods was used. After every course, a questionnaire was filled in by all the participants. The questionnaire was constructed and pretested by the project group. A month after the project week, members of the participating institutions were interviewed about the sustainability of the course content. The aim of these research methods was to find answers to the three established research questions which are determined to be decisive for the research process:

1. To what extent does the participants' interest increase in integrating the course topics into their everyday life?
2. How can digital competences be improved sustainably by participating in a course during the "Get Online Week"?
3. How can the satisfaction of all participants and institutions be achieved?

The main goal was to assess, if the courses that took place were able to improve digital skills for the participants sustainably and by that formulate recommendations for other following projects with similar aims. This research target is based on the assumption that a successful campaign will work if it reaches the interest, sustains the competencies sustainably and reaches the satisfaction of the participants. The appropriate methods for this purposes can either be qualitative or quantitative as well as a combination of both, depending on the context. Therefore, quantitative and qualitative research are not contradictory and hence can be used complementary [26]. The decision to combine those two methods harbors different advantages and disadvantages, which are both research-practical and of substantive nature. For those who cannot focus on a long interview or feel comfortable with it, questionnaire surveys are more useful. They include a distance to the researcher and minimize his influence, are more anonymous, easier to carry out, to evaluate and to compare [27, 28]. On the other hand, qualitative surveys are more suitable for people who are willing to verbalize their thoughts [27]. For example, a guided interview can provide room for the respondent to articulate individually and the resulting qualitative material is much richer and detailed and uncovers detailed interrelations [27]. It is however problematic that guided interviews require more time, as fewer people can be interviewed. Moreover, the individual utterances of the respondents are harder to compare than within the results of a questionnaire [27]. The questionnaire mainly aims to collect the demographic data of the participants in order to create a picture of the target group and to evaluate the experiences of the participants and the individual evaluation of the courses. In addition to that, the expert interviews aim to assess the satisfaction of the participating institutions and to gain insights into possible sustainability and an increase of competences. By including all perspectives into the analysis, a meaningful evaluation of the course is to be created.

With the conducted interviews and the questionnaire, information concerning the category "course evaluation" was gathered, which contains six subcategories: course structure, presentation, content, time management of the courses, expert knowledge of the instructors and topic relevance for the participants.

The following subchapter showcases the sample of the questionnaire.

3.2   Description of the Sample

During the "Get Online Week" 2018 in Dortmund, 417 participants took part within at least one of the 43 courses, from which 338 filled out a questionnaire. The gender distribution of the sample proofed to be balanced with 52.7% women, 46.7% men and 0.6% alternative genders (4 participants did not provide information on their gender).

However, the distribution of disabilities and age show some conspicuities: Nearly half of the participants had an disability (49.2%) – with the most prevalent kind being speed impediment with 59 participants - and the average age was 28 years with the age group "younger than 16" being the biggest (see Fig. 1). As the concepts of the courses offered during the "GOW" aimed to reach specific target groups and the involved institutions also had distinct clientele, this distribution was however also expectable. Also, a comparison between the 5 courses shows, that the characteristics of the participants strongly vary. For example, the participants of the course on tablets, smartphones and computers had an average age of 60.7 years – as this course specifically addressed seniors. Low proportions of people with a disability were e.g. reached in the courses on Sexual Education (35%) and "Job and Apartment Search online" (36.8%).

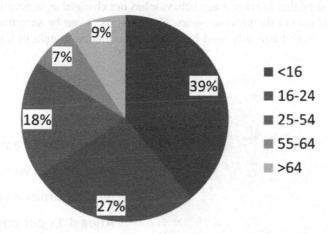

Fig. 1. Distribution of participants (own illustration). N = 338, missing values = 4

The young age of the participants may also explain why – despite the aim of the event to reach "onliners" and "offliners" – the prevalence of internet use was relatively high among them: The results showed that 97.6% of them already used the internet before and only 8 participants (2.4%) stated that they had never used the internet so far – while the share of offliners within the German population lies at 19% [13]. 68% of the surveyed people use the internet several times a day (see Fig. 2).

In addition to the frequency of internet use, the spread of various digital devices also reflects a clear trend. Among the participants, the smartphone is a permanent fixture at 87.9% and is – like on federal level with 70% [13] – the most common terminal. The percentage also has risen by over 10% compared to the participants of the "GOW" 2017 [29]. The mobile devices laptop (55.9%) and tablet (49.4%) followed up, while only 41.7% of the participants used a classical computer. Like on federal level, where also only 47% use such a device [13], the use of digital media seems to be increasingly tied to its independence of time and place. Additionally, users are also more and more using more than one device – in Germany, in average than two terminals per person [13]. Considering the high frequencies of the single devices, this obviously also applies to the sample. Regarding the reasons for using the internet, for most of the participants (73.1%), communications seems to be an important motivation just like the use of digital media for entertainment purposes (72.8%). The connected motivation "playing online games" applies to just 41.4% of the participants, but the proportion has almost doubled since 2015, when 26.6% of the course participants indicated the use of online games. In addition to the Internet applications already listed, searching for information online is another key aspect of using the internet. 79.3% use the internet to access important information. Based on the described internet use purposes, the participants have not only assigned themselves to one category. This is perfectly legitimate and serves to give a comprehensive picture of the range of activities they carry out via the internet. Many students have indicated three (36.7%) or even four ways of using the Internet (25.1%). Taking into account the information provided, it can be emphasized that Internet usage behavior has not changed significantly compared to the collected data of the previous years. Nevertheless, it can be seen that the digital devices, which were frequently used before, have continued to gain in importance.

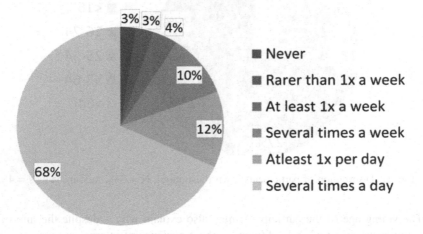

Fig. 2. Frequency of internet usage per week (own illustration). N = 338, missing values = 8

4   Evaluation Results

Within the following chapters, the evaluated data from the questionnaire and the conducted interviews will be assigned to the three research questions and an evaluation of the "Get Online Week" will be carried out on this basis.

4.1   Sustainability and Increase of Competences

An important part of the questionnaire dealt with the increase of digital competences for the participants through the contents of the different courses. Herewith the research question "How can digital competences be improved sustainably by participating in a course during the 'Get Online Week'?" will be subsequently answered within the next paragraph. Four different statements were part of the questionnaire before and after the course and their answers were analyzed depending on their change. The statements were "I know how to use a mobile terminal", "I am able to search information on the web", "I know how to upload and share content on social media" and "I trust myself with assessing if the information I find on the web are reliable and correct". We speak of an increase in competences if the average of the answers to all four of these statements is positive. For 46.2% of the participants it can be said that the reported level of competences have increased after participating in the course (see Table 1). For 33.1% of the participants no change was registered and for 20.7% a lower level of competences was detected. That can be explained by the fact that the participants might have changed their view on their own competences during the course by finding out that they know less than they thought before, so their self-assessment decreased after the course compared to the one at the beginning of the course. People with disabilities seem to have a bigger profit concerning the improvement of their competences. 58.8% of the participants with a disability stated a higher level of competences than they did before. Regarding age, the most positive result can be found in the category of people older than 64 years, where for 85.0% an increase of the perceived competences were captured, followed by people aged 55 to 64 years with 70.0%. This corresponds with the high increase of competences among the predominantly senior participants of the course "Lead-in to the media use of tablets, smartphones and computers" (63-. A high increase of competences could also be detected at the course "What does my child do on the internet? The digital world easily explained." with a rate of 56.1%. After the course, it was additionally asked, if the participants feel like their amount of knowledge is higher after the course – 38.9% and 30.1% rather agreed to this statement, while only around 9% fully or rather disagreed. Again, the courses on child digital media use and digital devices were rated particularly successful in this regard (with 52.6% and 49.1% fully agreeing).

Table 1. Change in competences divided in categories of age (own table).

Age	Increase	Neutral	Loss	Total
Under 16	44.0% (51)	29.3% (34)	26.7% (31)	38.8% (116)
16 to 24	40.0% (34)	40.0% (34)	20.0% (17)	28.4% (85)
25 to 54	37.9% (22)	44.8% (26)	17.2% (10)	19.4% (58)
55 to 64	70.0% (14)	20.0% (4)	10.0% (2)	6.7% (20)
Over 64	85.0% (17)	5.0% (1)	10.0% (2)	6.7% (20)
Total	46.2% (138)	33.1% (99)	20.7% (62)	100.0% (299)

Regarding the sustainability of the courses, a high interest to follow up with the covered content after course is crucial, as the courses are designed to be only an incentive for further activities. 80.7% of the participants feel motivated to follow up the covered contents. 63.5% stated additionally that the course was a suggestion to think about and discuss the topic critically afterwards. Female participants feel a little more motivated (85.5%) compared to male participants (75.2%). A similar result can be found in the second statement. 70.1% of the female participants and 55.7% of the male participants feel compelled to think about the topic critically afterwards. Also, older people agreed surpassingly strong to these standings to these statements.

The high increase of the participants' competences as well as their interest in the contents could be validated by the interviewed experts, from whom most stated that the courses encouraged the participants to deal with the course topics, either in group discussions or on their own. The experts think that making the access to different digital topics possible for the participants can contribute to their digital inclusion. The processed topics of the course "Job and Apartment Search online" tempted the participants to do some research on the internet by themselves, like one expert stated: "It was searched for jobs and possibilities for an internship. They did that without any guidance and dealt with it on their own without asking me before."[1] The cooperating institutions speak of an increase in competences as a noticeable effect of the courses and some want to continue the course in their institution. For example "the cybermobbing-course [...] became part of the German-lessons [...]" in one of the schools and the course about sexual education offered the teachers further inspiration for the instructional design of their biology lessons. By that we can identify a good base for a sustainable uptake of the courses and their content.

4.2   Satisfaction of Participants and Cooperating Institutions

Within the following section, the results of both the questionnaires and expert interviews on the topic of satisfaction of the participants and institutions are discussed. Herewith the research question "How can the satisfaction of all participants and institutions be achieved?" will be subsequently answered within the next paragraph. First, the satisfaction of the institutions will be evaluated on the basis of the expert interviews. The contact day, which took place in December 2017, was rated as good and informative by all experts both on the organizational as well as the executional level. The content and the structure of the "GOW" had become clear only through the contact day: "[...] we were informed very comprehensively. Especially the presentation of the course offers by the course instructors was helpful" one expert reported. Some interviewees even stated that they would not have booked any of the courses without the contact day. Insofar, the contact day can be described as an indispensable component to attract participating institutions for the courses. The interviews also indicate that almost all institutions selected the courses according to their clientele. For example, the participating schools did not conduct the course concerning the topic of how to use a smartphone, but rather courses that already require an understanding of media literacy. It also shows, that digital competences already occur in elementary schools. Especially students "[...] are all trained online, that means [...] [they are] represented on Facebook, on Instagram [...]". In addition, all partner organizations were especially interested in the clarification of the opportunities and dangers that the internet, but also mobile devices imply.

The courses were perceived as well and professionally designed by the interviewees. Especially the practical oriented building blocks were highly valued. One

---

[1] The interviews were conducted in German. For this publication, required quotation were translated into English.

institution e.g. positively mentioned the opportunity to try out things, as the participants "simply could continue using the electronic devices on their own". Another positive aspect was the presentation of various websites and additional materials. The contents of the handouts e.g. were highly valued as well as the possibility to use these materials in the future to further deal with the course contents. That the courses lasted mainly about two hours, was also perceived as beneficial, mainly because the concentration of the participants was not strained. Despite that, the instructors often described a "lack of time" as their main struggle, which led to cuts in the content, although none of the participants and experts seemed to be affected. In terms of content, all of the courses were perceived positively by the interviewed experts of the participating institutions. In addition to the successful course concepts, the content was seen as detailed and appealing. In some courses however, the imparting of information did not always proceed smoothly: In one course, the high diversity and abundance of information, which could have been supplemented by active methods, was criticized. And in yet another course, most participants were able to grasp the overall context, but "the smaller details were not always understood". Some institutions also mentioned, that handouts should have been distributed at an earlier stage and criticized the required media literacy. This however could, as stated by interviewers, be based on the respective claim or special need of the participants - which suggests, that – despite a convincing course concept – a special adjustment to the specific needs of the clients is crucial. To detect these needs, target groups have to be pre-examined carefully, for example through an internship.

The instructors were – beneath the (positively mentioned) intensive preparation of the course, a "reasonable group size" and a "great interest in the topic" – one of the most frequently mentioned aspects of the courses. Especially, the possibility of (spontaneous) exchange within a group setting was mentioned favorably. In addition, the personality and warmth of all instructors, who contributed to a pleasant course climate and partly also to the concentration and motivation of the participants, were valued. Expertise, theoretical competence as well as the imparting of theoretical knowledge of the instructors were rated as adequate and extensive and it was emphasized that answers to (current) questions were always given immediately. Most interviewees stated, that the instructors had "pleasure in communicating the content" and "thanks to the good preparation" "flexible, individual and spontaneous work within the courses" could easily be implemented. An example for this could also be found at the penal institution, where the instructors used their professionalism and flexibility to work through the prevailing internet-free space, which was especially appreciated.

More than half of the interviewees stated, that they had already participated in the "GOW" one or more times, thus it had become an integral part of their annual planning. The annually participating institutions thus form an important cornerstone when it comes to acquiring participants for the "GOW". All eleven interviewed cooperation partners stated that they would like to attend the "GOW" again next year. The conduction of the courses by young students provided a good source of inspiration for all employees and supervisors within the participating institutions for their own offers and teaching designs. However, the course content would be decisive for some cooperation partners to select a course and annually participate within the "GOW". Of eleven interviewees, five gave an overall positive feedback. Commitment devotion as well as the personal and professional competences of the course instructors were highly. Furthermore, it was appreciated, that the courses were carried out at the participating institutions. While comparing the interviews with the course reflections, which were written down by the instructors themselves to express their personal feeling on the successful execution of the "GOW", it can be said that both success and criticisms were often perceived by both sides. From this it can be concluded that the course ideas, the associated concepts and implementation contributed to the highest satisfaction of all participating institutions, the participants as well as instructors and thus to a successful "GOW".

Within the questionnaire, the participants were asked to evaluate themselves with the aid of an evaluation tool called "target". The collected data can be used to evaluate both the content and design of the courses as well as the impact of the course instructors. The "target" was embedded within the questionnaire and all participants were given eight different statements which they could rate on a 5-level scale from "I disagree" to "I agree". Following, the collected data from the questionnaire, which was completed by 338 participants, will be presented to evaluate the satisfaction of the participants.

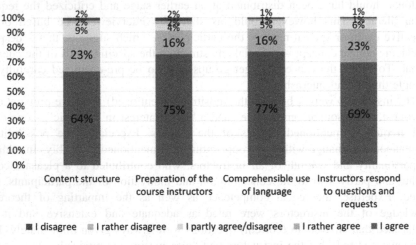

Fig. 3. Target evaluation method part 1 (own illustration). N = 274

All eight items received predominantly positive ratings (see Figs. 3 and 4). This applies especially to the assessment of lingual comprehensibility of the instructors (76.8% fully approval), the preparation of the courses (75.2%) as well as the instructors responds to questions and requests (69.3%). Also, the content structure was well received (63.5% fully approval). The amount of full disapproval was accordingly low with rates ranging from 0.7 to 2.2%.

The participants were the least satisfied with the personal relevance of the course contents, so that merely 49.8% fully agreed with them. While still a large majority fully or partly agreed with the statement (76%) and nearly all respondents (95%) assumed at least a neutral position, a more detailed analysis shows, that the disapproval rates were in some courses particularly high, e.g. in the course "Sexual Education with help of Digital Media" with 10.3% of the participants fully disagreeing and 2.6% rather disagreeing. When stated that the course was designed in an interesting way and that the content was comprehensively communicated, 56.9% and 63.4% of the participants fully agreed. The last statement focused on whether the practical examples helped to better understand the course content. Most of the participants (57.5%) fully agreed, while merely 0.7% disagreed.

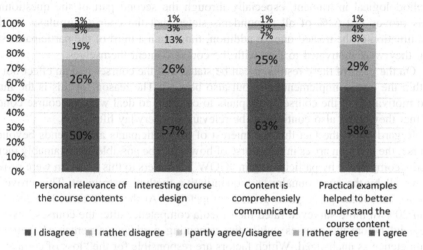

Fig. 4. Target evaluation method part 2 (own illustration).

In addition to the "target" method, the participants were asked to give a statement on what they liked the most and what they liked the least about the individual courses they attended. The participants mainly noted the practical aspects of the courses as positive, for example, the topics of tablet and mobile phone use as well as games and videos. Furthermore, the detailed information transfer as well as the intensive response to questions and requests from the instructors were rated positively by the participants. Lastly, education about different topics such as social media and sexual education was named positively. Within the negative aspects, the participants mainly noted that all of the courses seemed short on time and that they would appreciate a follow-up course to intensify the course contents. The majority of the participants had nothing to complain about and stated that they are all in all satisfied. A few have noted critically that it was too long, as they already knew a lot and that they did not like the research on the computer.

All in all, most of the participants were satisfied and therefore the conduction of the "GOW" can be rated as highly successful.

5 Conclusion

Within this chapter, the decisive results that have contributed to answering the research questions are compiled.

The first research question deals with the interest of the participants to integrate the treated topics into their everyday life. According to the project group, the decisive factor for the further use of the course contents was both the critical analysis of the course participants with the topics dealt with and their motivation to continue to deal with them. The extent to which the courses were able to call for continuous integration of the course content into everyday life could be determined as a quantitative methodological instrument, especially through the second part of the questionnaire. This proves that 64% of all respondents stated that the course stimulates a critical examination of the treated one. In addition, more than a third of the participants stated that they were motivated to deal with the course content themselves.

On the basis of these results, it can be stated that the courses had an effect not only within the course implementation, but also beyond. The reason for this is the interest and motivation of the course participants to continue to deal with the course contents, so that they could also continue to be relevant in everyday life.

Regardless of the fact that the interest of the participants also extends beyond the course, the question arises in the course of how it can be possible to sustainably increase media competence by participating in "GOW". Answers to this question were provided above all by the questionnaire as a quantitative method instrument. This proves that almost half of the participants gained competence. At the same time, however, more than 20% of those surveyed rated their media competence after the courses lower than they did before the courses, while the remaining participants perceived their media competence as unchanged. Which factors are responsible for the "loss of competence" cannot be fully clarified. However, it is possible that the awareness of the participants was trained to the effect that they have experienced that their media competence has not been developed to the extent that they initially assumed. According to this it can be assumed that the course participants had already assessed their knowledge and competences disproportionately high before the course was held, but noticed during the course that this assessment did not correspond to reality. Nevertheless, the increase in competence achieved is a benefit for all parties involved. As proven by the qualitative method instrument, the increase in competence mentioned above lies in the creation of points of contact and a professional course design.

The third research question dealt with the satisfaction of all persons and institutions involved in "GOW". Both qualitative and quantitative methods showed that the vast majority were extremely satisfied with the process. Thus 80% gave a positive rating. The satisfaction of the cooperation partners is reflected in the fact that all of the respondents would participate again and materials were also exchanged. The decisive factor for the 80% satisfaction of the respondents and participating institutions seemed to be the contact day in December 2017. A positive aspect is that it is possible to get an overview of the campaign and current course topics. In addition, it is also possible to get a first impression of the course leaders. One of our cooperation partners was so convinced of the contact day that he told us that without it he would not have taken part in the "GOW". The flexibility and willingness of the course leaders to compromise with target groups, as well as the main topics and premises, had also contributed to the satisfaction of the participants. All this attracted the positive attention of the cooperation partners. In order to keep the campaign and the courses and their content up to date, an analysis of the digitization trend at both international and national level is required prior to the course conceptualization. This makes it easy to adapt the course topics to the current situation of the company.

Compared to the 2017 project group, the project group has therefore focused primarily on serving online users. This corresponds to the progressive digitization trend. Thus 87% of Germans are online [13]. With regard to course design, "[…] easy handling combined with target-group-specific topics and applications from everyday life can increase the attractiveness of the Internet as a medium for the majority of offliners" [13].

6   Recommendation

Within this last section, various recommendations based on the experience gathered during the "GOW", which contribute to the successful implementation of such an intervention, will be presented. The respective recommendations are subdivided into the phases of the preparation, implementation and evaluation.

6.1   Preparation

At the beginning, it is essential to choose which topic content should be discussed fundamentally within the courses or webinars. In order to select the topics, it is useful to examine the current societal situation with regard to the digital transformation as well as the current topics and interests of the participating institutions and organizations and to define the main topics based on the findings. Currently, a topic like e.g. cybersecurity is more important as the basic use of media, which becomes increasingly outdated due to the progressive development towards a digital society. Furthermore, it should be discussed which topics are of interest to the participants and which topics have already been discussed in the various institutions in order to avoid repetition. To ensure a successful completion, the key topics also have to be adjusted to the knowledge and interests of the instructors. Key topics have to be determined previously by an intensive examination of the course contents. If the topics are to be adapted to the interests of the students and the wishes and expectations of the institutions, a previous internship is necessary. Thus, on site the participants can be acquainted and an overview of the available rooms and resources can be made. Afterwards it can be decided, whether the course can be performed at the facility or if it may need to be moved to an alternative location. An internship has also the advantage of adapting the course content to the different target groups and their strengths and weaknesses. Thus, the problem to overwhelm the participants with the course content, the problem that the topic content is of no relevance to the participants and that the duration of the attention span does not correspond with the time structure can be solved. This leads to a successful intervention and therefore to an overall satisfaction of all participants, as everyone gets the chance to fully participate and increase their competences. Another important step during the preparation is to acquire cooperation partners for your own course concept as well as institutions in which the courses can be held. The project group has therefore decided to invite different institutions and organizations within the region to a so-called contact day. During an afternoon, the individual course contents were presented and the visitors had the opportunity to talk with the instructors about the contents and to exchange their own wishes and expectations. Based on the experiences of this year it can be said, that it makes sense to design such a day to attract a large number of cooperation partners and thus to acquire a heterogeneous group of participants. It was proved as helpful to hand out flyers with the most important information about the individual courses, which the institution could further use to acquire participants.

6.2   Implementation

Once the cooperation partners and the topic content of the course have been determined, the course concept can be developed and thus the course content be finalized. It is easier to work with a homogeneous audience within the course. This ensures that all participants can follow the course content equally. Still, most of the groups are very heterogeneous and a one hundred percent adjustment to the respective target group cannot succeed. Therefore, when creating the concept, it is essential to keep in mind to focus on a rough framework rather than a detailed plan. This allows both alternative processes during implementation and a high degree of flexibility which leads to being able to respond to all eventualities. All arrangements made between the course instructors and all participating institutions during the course design should be recorded and communicated both verbally and in writing. In order to achieve a successful implementation, it is necessary to constantly exchange information in order to meet the expectations of all those involved. Based on the gathered experience, it can be said that an optimal group size consists of ten participants. However, the size of the group should always be adapted to the individual needs of the participants as well as to the context of the institution – in a school an entire class can attend the course, but within a penal institution it was only possible to work with a group of six participants, based on their current situation. Nevertheless, the size of the group should always be such that individual questions can be addressed in order to give the participants the chance to extend their competencies. It has been found that this can best be achieved if the courses are run by two course instructors. Thus, the instructors can support each other and give individual attention to the participants during the practical exercises and answer questions which may arise. Within this year's "GOW", a time frame of 90–120 min was chosen, which proved to be sufficient for a short intervention. However, depending on the course content it may be advisable to extend or shorten the course duration to the individual resources of the participants so that all relevant information can be conveyed. If during the execution, it should prove that it is not possible to provide all relevant information within the set time frame, the content of the course should be shortened. An extension of the course to convey all information should be avoided in order not to strain the attention of the participants. Hereby, the importance to be able to act spontaneously and the planning of the course with a rough framework becomes clearer. Therefore, a variety of different methods should be used, both on a practical and an informational level. Conducting the courses can cost the instructors a lot of energy. Therefore, care should be taken not to perform too many course interventions in one day. The project group has determined that a maximum of three courses a day is possible – summing up to six hours of intervention. To lighten the course a bit and consolidate the course content, a variety of different practice exercises should be implemented. In this way, all participants have the opportunity to implement the course contents correctly and to examine whether they still have questions or require more intensive help. If it is planned to reach disabled people with the courses, the courses should be created as barrier-free as possible and address many senses. At the end of the course – or at the beginning- different visual aids and handouts can be given to the participants, which provide them the opportunity to engage with the content beyond the courses respectively to access all information gathered during the course when questions or problems arise afterwards. Furthermore, various teaching materials or topic-specific additions can be forwarded to the institutions, so that the course contents can be further discussed. This contributes above all to the sustainability of the short interventions.

6.3   Evaluation

In the context of the evaluation of the individual course concepts, it has been found useful to link qualitative and quantitative surveys. Thus, a wide range of information can be obtained, which promote the subsequent evaluation and further development of the concepts and the course contents. Furthermore, the project group decided to use the same questionnaire to evaluate all courses. To gain more specific insights, e.g. regarding course content and gain in competences, it could be beneficial to develop individual course questionnaires in future inquiries. Retrospectively, however, it turned out that it would have been better to adapt the questionnaire to the individual courses in a specific and individual way. Within the qualitative survey it was decided to conduct a guideline interview with representatives of the participating institutions. The aim was to be able to make statements on the sustainability of the course content based on the assessment of the educational staff and their observations. The project group decided against an observation while conducting the courses, as in this way the facilitators could better focus on the participants and would have been overwhelmed with simultaneously observing and documenting the specific situations. As mentioned earlier, the survey has identified three different objectives. On the one hand the goal was to examine the extent to which the competencies of the participants were increased and on the other hand to examine how high the achieved sustainability of the course interventions could be assessed. Another goal was to evaluate the satisfaction of all the participants. The questionnaire as a quantitative survey method has proven to be effective for the collection of sociodemographic data as well as to give an overview of the participants' heterogeneity and media usage behavior. In addition, the questionnaire provided information on competence acquisition and participant satisfaction. The interview was used to review the sustainability and to query the satisfaction of the participating institutions. Furthermore, while conducting the interview the possibility arose to specifically evaluate the different courses and course concepts which weren't possible with solely the questionnaire. Herewith it can also be seen that the two survey methods complement each other well. In addition, it can be said, that it has proved to be most effective to use different measurement times. The project group decided to run the questionnaire directly during the "GOW" at the beginning and end of the course. Thus, it was possible to avoid the problem that some institutions and participants opted not to participate in the questionnaire or that the time of the survey was too long ago and the participants were unable to answer the questions. The guided interview was deliberately carried out a few weeks after the "GOW" to examine the sustainability. The representatives of the institutions were asked, for example, to what extent the participants dealt with the topics beyond the courses content. In conclusion it can be stated that in order to achieve an even greater success in organizing an event like the "GOW", in future there should be a closer exchange between the instructors and the participating institutions as well as a better reconcilement of the course contents and the specific needs of the participants. Alternatively, the courses could also be planned in such a way that they address only one specific target group and thus be able to respond even more explicitly to their need. This would be particularly advantageous and interesting for institutions for mentally ill people.

References

1. Steinbicker, J.: Informationsgesellschaft. In: Mau, S., Schöneck, N.M. (eds.) Handwörter-buch zur Gesellschaft Deutschlands, pp. 408–421. Springer, Wiesbaden (2013). https://doi.org/10.1007/978-3-531-18929-1_27
2. Richier, A.: Digital Skills for Future Wor (2016). https://teannualconference2014dotinfo.files.wordpress.com/2014/06/an-dre-richier_keynote.pdf
3. De Croo, A.: Digital Belgium (2014). https://teannualcon-ference2014dotinfo.files.word press.com/2014/06/alexander-de-crook-eynote.pdf
4. Federal Agency for Civic Education: Informationsgesellschaft und Europa (n.d.). http://www.bpb.de/nachschlagen/lexika/das-euro-palexikon/177055/informationsgesellschaft-und-europa
5. Krotz, F., Hepp, A. (eds.): Mediatisierte Welten: Beschreibungsansätze und Forschungs-felder. VS Verlag für Sozialwissenschaften, Wiesbaden (2012)
6. State Chancellery of North Rhine-Westphalia: IM BLICKPUNKT: Medienkonvergenz (2008). https://imblickpunkt.grimme-institut.de/wp/wp-content/uploads/2014/12/IB-Medien konvergenz.pdf
7. Initiative D21 e.V.: D21-DIGITAL-INDEX 2016: Jährliches Lagebild zur Digitalen Gesellschaft (2016). https://initiatived21.de/app/uploads/2017/01/studie-d21-digital-index-2016.pdf
8. Bengler, K., Schmauder, M.: Digitalisierung. Z. Arb. Wiss. **70**, 75–76 (2016). https://doi.org/10.1007/s41449-016-0021-z
9. Hippmann, S., Klingner, R., Leis, M.: Digitalisierung—Anwendungsfelder und Forschungs-ziele. In: Neugebauer, R. (ed.) Digitalisierung, pp. 9–18. Springer, Heidelberg (2018). https://doi.org/10.1007/978-3-662-55890-4_2
10. Federal Agency for Civic Education: Digitale Teilhabe als Voraussetzung für soziale Teilhabe (Hamburg, 11 May 2017): Keynote zum DIVSI-Bucerius Forum in Hamburg (2017). http://www.bpb.de/presse/248495/digitale-teilhabe-als-voraussetzung-fuer-soziale-teilhabe-hamburg-11-mai-2017
11. European Commission: Use of Internet and Online Activities (2018). https://ec.europa.eu/digital-single-market/en/use-internet
12. European Commission: Human Capital: Digital Inclusion and Skills. Digital Economy and Society Index Report 2018 (2018). http://ec.europa.eu/newsroom/dae/document.cfm?doc_id=52247
13. Initiative D21 e.V.: D21 DIGITAL INDEX 2017/2018: Jährliches Lagebild zur Digitalen Gesellschaft (2018). https://initiatived21.de/app/uploads/2018/01/d21-digital-index_2017_2018.pdf

14. Zillien, N.: Digitale Ungleichheit: Neue Technologien und alte Ungleichheiten in der Informations- und Wissensgesellschaft, 2nd edn. VS Verlag für Sozialwissenschaften, Wiesbaden (2009). https://doi.org/10.1007/978-3-531-91493-0
15. Wilson, E.J.: The Information Revolution and Developing Countries. MIT Press, Cambridge (2004)
16. Van Dijk, J.A.G.M.: A theory of the digital divide. In: Ragnedda, M., Muschert, G.W. (eds.) The Digital Divide: The Internet and Social Inequality in International Perspective, pp. 29–51. Routledge, Abingdon (2013)
17. Hojas, R.: Behinderte Menschen und das Internet (2004). https://www.barrierefreies-webdesign.de/spezial/multimediale-inhalte/behinderung-und-internet.html
18. Disability Equality Act North Rhine-Westphalia (2016)
19. Federal Ministry of Labour and Social Affairs (2011). UN Konvention. [Online]. Verfügbar unter: http://www.bmas.de/SharedDocs/Downloads/DE/PDF-Publikationen/a729-unkonven tion.pdf?blob=publicationFile. 14 May 2018
20. Kubicek, W., Welling, S.: Vor einer digitalen Spaltung? Annäherung an ein verdecktes Problem von wirtschafts- und gesellschaftspolitischer Brisanz. Medien & Kommunikationswissenschaft **48**, 497–517 (2000)
21. Berger, A., et al.: Web 2.0/barrierefrei: Eine Studie zur Nutzung von Web 2.0 Anwendungen durch Menschen mit Behinderungen (2010). https://www.digitale-chancen.de/transfer/downloads/MD967.pdf
22. Haage, A.: Studie: Wie behinderte Menschen die Medien nutzen. https://leidmedien.de/aktuelles/studie-wie-behinderte-menschen-die-medien-nutzen/
23. Telecentre Europe: GOW 2017 (2017). http://getonlineweek.eu/wp-content/uploads/2017/05/GOW17_Report.pdf
24. European Comission: DigComp: Digital Competence Framework for citizens (2018). https://ec.europa.eu/jrc/en/digcomp
25. Kluzer, S.: Guidelines on the adoption of DigComp (2015). https://all-digital.org/wp-content/uploads/2015/12/TE-Guidelines-on-the-adoption-of-DIGCOMP_Dec2015.pdf
26. Baur, N., Blasius, J. (eds.): Handbuch Methoden der empirischen Sozialforschung. Springer VS, Wiesbaden (2014). https://doi.org/10.1007/978-3-531-18939-0
27. Bortz, J., Döring, N.: Forschungsmethoden und Evaluation für Human- und Sozialwissenschaftler, 4th edn. Springer, Heidelberg (2006). https://doi.org/10.1007/978-3-642-41089-5
28. Häder, M.: Empirische Sozialforschung: Eine Einführung, 2nd edn. VS Verlag für Sozialwissenschaften, Wiesbaden (2010). https://doi.org/10.1007/978-3-531-92187-7
29. Pelka, B., et al.: Get Online Week 2017: Eine Woche zur Verbesserung der digitalen Teilhabe in Dortmund. TU Dortmund, Dortmund (2017). http://www.sfs.tu-dortmund.de/sfs-Reihe/Band_198.pdf

3D Interaction for Computer Science Educational VR Game

Santiago Bolivar[1]([✉]), Daniel Perez[1], Armando Carrasquillo[1],
Adam S. Williams[2], Naphtali D. Rishe[1], and Francisco R. Ortega[2]

[1] Florida International University, Miami, FL, USA
{sboli001,dpere103,acarr009}@fiu.edu, ndr@acm.org
[2] Colorado State University, Fort Collins, CO, USA
{adamwil,fortega}@colostate.edu

Abstract. We propose a full immersion 3D environment in the form of a video game. The environment offers the player the opportunity to explore basic Computer Science (CS) concepts without removing any of the entertaining aspects of games. We believe in creating a software that can be enjoyed by anyone regardless of age and at the same time can increase CS awareness. We developed a complete 3D game emulating an Escape Room. We aim to capture the attention of not only teenagers but also adults. The solution to each room is presented as puzzles based on the background concepts of computer science. These concepts are in the form of every day decisions to bring familiarity into the game play. The games aim is to be inviting and fun. Ultimately, giving each player the opportunity to be engaged into computer science concepts as they go thought the game and sparking interest towards CS.

Keywords: Virtual Reality · Education · Computer science education

1 Introduction

Every year more and more companies are in search for individuals that can understand and write code. Big companies like Google, Microsoft, Facebook, Code.org and others, support the creation of programming courses as early as middle school [1]. The Department of Education has also joined the efforts to bring Computer Science into the classrooms [2]. However, even with all these combined efforts from society, companies, the work force, and the government, the question still remains as of why we don't see a substantial increase on the amount of students enrolling and graduating from higher education institutions with a degree in Computer Science or related fields. In recent years, statistics show that even though there has been a surge of students registering for CS majors, the graduation rate is much lower [3]. Moreover, the diversity of the field is minimal, bringing minorities to the lowest proportion of the population on universities. Accounting for one-fourth of all the enrolling students on the field [4].

© Springer Nature Switzerland AG 2019
M. Antona and C. Stephanidis (Eds.): HCII 2019, LNCS 11572, pp. 408–419, 2019.
https://doi.org/10.1007/978-3-030-23560-4_30

Even with the advance of technology, higher education institutions still offer traditional stand up and deliver methodologies when teaching CS courses. Every year, more and more diverse students fill the classrooms, this diverse population requires a deeper approach for delivering meaningful education. Some of these students may require extended time, visual and/or hearing aids, one on one tutoring, or other options. These are options that traditional techniques do not offer [5]. Computer Science requires that students develop skills such as problem-solving, math literacy, ability to understand abstract concepts, heavy science background, and adaptability to ever-changing field. These among other skills can still be taught to and learned by students, but at the same time these same skills scare away students from enrolling in science, technology, engineering, or mathematics (STEM) majors [6]. If we go a step backwards, many K-12 schools offer free education but this not a guarantee that the students will graduate with a high school diploma, moreover this also does not ensure that students who actually graduate, will pursue or commit to higher education such as college or university [7].

Many individuals have started to come into CS majors thanks to all the incentives from companies and society. However, it is still important to create a sense of care and desire to pursue a career. As many more graduates start to feel proud of their education, it is important to translate this message towards younger generations. With the continuous growth of technology and the internet, it is important to denote that new ways of learning have emerged. Online learning has taken classrooms and moved learning into virtual rooms with the chance to reach even greater audiences. Virtual Reality (VR) and Augmenter Reality (AR) devices have enhanced the experience of learning by bring new visuals along with the regular theory. All these tools considerably enhance learning by using visuals rather than standard text and narrative [8].

Students that take CS classes get discouraged by the constantly "difficult" labeled classes. Areas such as calculus, physics and programming. Many of the students become afraid of CS not because its is difficult on its own but because of the high complexity portrayal that is given to it by scholars and the media. However, when looked at with a different scope, in a more simplistic and individualized scenario, computer science is very graspable. Originally, computers were designed as an extension of human capacity and are always seen as the human mind. In other words, computers function in a similar way as the human brain functions; Actions triggered by decisions [9]. The game seeks to demonstrate this idea to the user. This idea that a casual environment can embody several Computer Science concepts [10].

1.1   What Is the Difference with CScape?

Alchemist Escape is the completed version of CScape. The software consists of a total of four levels, achievement system, menu, keyboard and game-pad controls, and metrics. Since we wanted the game to be as inclusive as possible, we used an environment that resembled a medieval house, also we made sure that the game can be played by anyone by providing different control modes, and lastly,

We ported the system into Virtual Reality. In this version, the software ensures the player experience is as smooth as possible by providing hints, clear user interface, challenge messages, reset buttons and sound effects. In comparison with the first version, the completed version presents a full software that allows us to use it for the original purpose of increasing Computer Science awareness in minorities [11].

1.2 Motivation and Challenges

High school graduation rates are low when compared to the total students that start. Moreover, the amount of students that pursue higher education is even lower. By taking a deeper look in those statistics, we can recognize that many of the students steer away from STEM majors. Looking even deeper into the distribution of students that choose CS (or any related fields) as their major, we can see minimal representation of minority groups.

When selecting a major, the early identification what they want could help future steps towards success. Not only the classes to take, but also the motivation to continue thought-out the major [12]. When looking for a suitable medium to generate interest, we recognized the motivational power that video games have on children, teenagers and young adults [13].

2 Background

When looking at education and even educational standards, many times they are associated with money and socioeconomic status. As high school students approach their senior year, they start to look for opportunities to help build their careers. At the same time they face the reality of expensive education and in some cases, not being able to afford it. Lastly, when you add the lack of learning or little interest to pursue the career, there is even smaller chances that the individual would successfully finish the major after enrolling. Ultimately, affecting graduation rates from universities as a whole [10].

Even though video games have carried stigma for influencing children and teenager into abnormal behaviors and sometimes even addiction due to the release of dopamine in the brain [14]. Recent research actually shows that they are beneficial for motor skills, concentration, and multitasking. Another important skill developed when playing game is quick decision making and improvement on problem solving skills. It can be seen that even with the many games being released constantly, the average player can play with ease new games, with a minimal learning curve, showing adaptation to change. Furthermore, games have been used in the medical field, rehabilitation, psychology, and training individuals [15]. By utilizing video games and including learning tools into them without compromising the games entertainment, we would not only be helping the individuals but also starting to change the stigma that games have [16].

It is also important to denote that video games are not strangers to the classroom. Many systems have been created to spark an interest in learning. Systems in the form of simulators or tutorial driven platforms that teach many of these concepts. Even though it's a good a approach to the use these technologies, it does lack in one of the most important values brought by industry games: entertainment. The heart of every game is the ability to discover, have fun, get rewards, and be challenged. The sense of discovering something new, challenging and even sometimes surreal, is what drives many players to spend their time in a game. In other words, its paramount to maintain any and every entertainment factor that the video game industry brings to the table [17].

In the USA, the average house hold has access to computers, smart phones, and if the family has children, a high chance of owning a console or gaming device. Hence, by making a software that does not force the purchase of a new device (eg. VR headsets, Gaming computers, Projectors and sensors) there is a good chance to reach a large audience. Introducing CS concepts and the notion of how to use them from an early age, can spark more interest into the major as they grow older [18]. It is also proven, that children that are engaged and determined to pursue a "hobby" from early on, become stronger professionals in the same field on later stages of their lives [19].

3   Alchemist Escape: Discover CS by Playing

3.1   Objective

We developed a video game in the style of a escape room. Every game rewards the players efforts by providing some type of incentive. Alchemist Escape features a total of three different rooms. The player needs to solve a different kind of puzzle in each room, not only to proceed but also to finally reach the final room and to be able to finish the game. The concept of an escape room was adapted due to the popularity of it. Moreover, the urge to escape a room provides a better setting for problem solving and decision making [20] (Fig. 1).

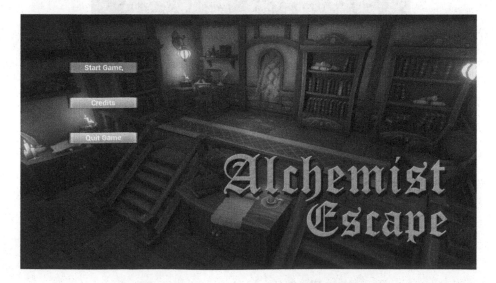

Fig. 1. Alchemist Escape - main screen screenshot

3.2 Concept

The game was developed using Unreal Engine 4 as the game engine and Visual Studio as the IDE. For the logic of the system a combination of C++ and Unreal Engine Blue print system were utilized. The game is divided into a total of four consecutive rooms. The first 3 rooms hold locked doors that can only be opened by solving each rooms puzzle. The last room holds the reward for opening all the doors and then the game ends. Since the player is immersed in a 3D environment, there are also ambient effects that can help the player acknowledge when the doors have been unlocked. Lastly, with the use of the Unreal Engine, in-game physics are very close to real-world physics, giving the player a even more realistic experience when playing the game.

Prior to developing the game, a small survey was conducted to decide the proper theme for the game. The survey showed two different possible scenarios to be played (See Fig. 2). Scenario A was a highly realistic environment that mimics a modern home. Scenario B was a less realistic yet still detailed home that also displayed "magical" scenery in a sci-fi setting. The results showed that people would opt to play a game with Scenario B over Scenario A. This results also reflect one of the reasons many players want to play video games and it is to escape reality and unwind from society [21].

Fig. 2. Surveyed scenarios

Each room is equipped with a legend that aims to guide the player into solving the puzzle (See Fig. 3). The script on each room is cryptic enough to bring a challenge into the puzzle but not to the level of making the puzzle unsolvable. In case that the player feels the need of help, the system is also equipped with a help sub-menu that elaborates into the hint given at first. There is not a limit to the amount of times each puzzle can be tried. We are not looking for performance or efficiency, just for the experience.

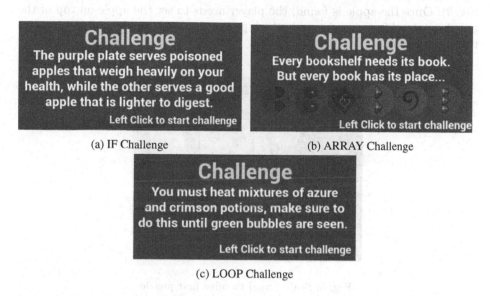

(a) IF Challenge   (b) ARRAY Challenge

(c) LOOP Challenge

Fig. 3. Room challenge legends

When a player successfully completes the puzzle, a achievement badge is displayed on the screen. The badge can also be clicked and it shows what he or she has unlocked (See Fig. 4). on this screen the player can see the explanation of the puzzle and the logic that sits behind the puzzle. The achievement explanation helps reinforce the puzzle's CS concept.

Fig. 4. Achievement badges

3.3 Puzzles

The first room is a two part puzzle. Both parts require the use of the same concept: IF STATEMENT.

On the first part of the puzzle, the player needs to move around the room and look for the apple that weights the most from the bunch (See Fig. 3a). There is a total of seven apples in the room but only one weights more than the others. The room has an old scale that the user can utilize to solve the puzzle (See Fig. 5). Once the apple is found, the player needs to set the apple on top of the purple plate. After completing both steps the first door opens giving access to the second room.

Fig. 5. Scale - used to solve first puzzle

The second room consists of a single puzzle that is divided on 3 sub puzzles. This puzzle concept is ARRAYS.

The player needs to arrange a set of books on the pattern that is shown in the hint as he or she enters the room. each sub puzzle has a verification mechanism, once the correct books have been set on the bookshelves, a green light will illuminate the shelf, if not a red light will show instead. Once the three shelves have been correctly solved the door to the next room will be opened (See Fig. 3b). This room also offers the option to reset the puzzle, allowing the player to start from the beginning. The reset feature also sets the books on its original position as how they where once the player entered the room.

The third room consists of a single puzzle. The concept behind the puzzle is LOOPS.

As the player enters the room, the player is confronted with a cauldron and a total of eight potions. Four potions are blue and the remaining four are red color (See Fig. 3c). As the hint reads, the player needs to proceed to put the correct potions into the cauldron in a set order. Even though the action seems similar to the previous room, this time around he has to repeat the same action on the same medium. As the player places the correct potions, the cauldron sparks change color progressively.

Once the last puzzle has been solved, the final door opens to show the player the prize and finally exiting the game. The player screen is also equipped with a room counter. At the top right corner, the player can see a counter of 0/3. As the player progresses to the rooms and successfully solve the puzzles, this counter will increase. By adding this feature, the player can keep track of his or her achievements and how close the goal is.

3.4   Controls

The current system offers the player the ability to play with either a keyboard or a game-pad. Both of these devices are very well known among players. We also took into consideration any new players. By keeping the amount of interactions and controls needed for the user to choose from down. For the keyboard W Key and Up-arrow move forward, S Key and Down-arrow key move backward, A Key and the Left-Arrow key to move to the left and D Key and the Right-Arrow key to move to the left (See Fig. 6). If the user decides to use the game-pad, for the movement the player only need the left D-pad to control the same motions as the keyboard.

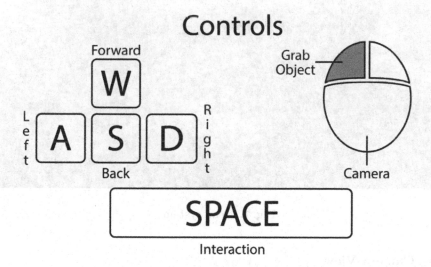

Fig. 6. Basic keyboard control system

To maintain the simplicity of the system and ease-of-use for the player, only limited actions are required to interact with the system. The Grab action allows the player to freely move objects from its original position to the new desired position. Grab can be activated using right click with the mouse if the player is using the keyboard setting, or by pressing X button on the game pad. The next action is the Activate action, it can be used by pressing space-bar in the keyboard and left trigger on the game pad. This action allows to reset the puzzles or activate the props throughout the game. The last key is the Escape key on the keyboard and the start button on the game pad. This option lets the player access the Menu system. Note that the HTC Vive controllers are also available.

3.5 Menu System

The game contains a simple menu system with a total of five buttons: Resume, Controls, Hints, Achievements, Quit Game (See Fig. 7). Resume and Quit Game are a single action buttons that allow the player to go back into the game or quit the game respectively. Controls, Hints and Achievements are a single screen options that displays the information of each menu respectively. We designed the menu system with the same style as the controls, by keeping the options to a minimum the user experience is enhanced, specially to a first a time player.

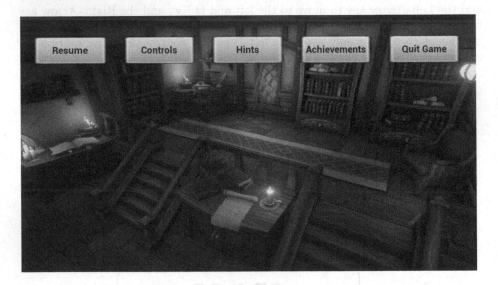

Fig. 7. Menu system

3.6 Camera View

The camera chosen for the game was set to first-person. When in first person, the player can have a greater immersion into the game. At the same time, the settings for camera movement in the game are set to low to minimize any motion sickness or motion blur caused by moving the character. At the same time, this camera can be reused for the VR version of the game. The current version is created for desktops/laptops so everyone that has access to a computer can play the game. VR systems do increase interest into games by their novelty, but they also limit the amount of people that can use it due to its current market value.

3.7   Metrics

The system is equipped with a simple metric collection method. As the player goes through the game, the game collects the movement path coordinates. Also, the time the player takes to solve each puzzle, from the moment he or she crosses the door until the next door is opened. No personal data such as gender, name, nationality, or level of education is collected.

4   Virtual Reality Mode

Even thought having access to virtual reality headsets is still difficult due to the steep prices. We realized that by porting the system into VR, we will have a greater reach. With the increase of technology people are drawn to test and explore the new devices being created [22]. VR mode gives the player an even more full immersion. Aside from the first person camera provided by the headset, the game remains the same as the desktop version. We utilized the HTC Vive device, and the controls were kept to only grab and teleport. Since the headset controls the camera, the player does not need to worry about pressing many buttons to move around the map. Ultimately, we kept the system as simple as possible so it can be played by anyone.

5   Future Work

In future work, we first want to run an experiment to evaluate the success of the system. We want to see if the system does spark interest into CS when played by people without any prior CS knowledge. After conducting the experiment, we would like to use the feedback collected from the users to enhance the system. After running the initial experiment, we will run a control group with CS students and will use the results to compare the metrics between both groups.

Furthermore, we want to see the how the game contributes towards the inclusion of minorities. Mainly if the game sparks interest into considering CS as a major by women. Current women representation on STEM fields is low [23], Also women population is known to not be interested on playing video games as much as men do [24].

6   Repository

The final version of this game is freely available at (including source code) at: https://github.com/OpenHID/VRForEducation.

7   Conclusion

We propose a video game themed as a escape room. This game is designed to spark interest into Computer Science. With the combination of simple game play along with an inviting game mode, The player will not only be enjoying the experience just like any other game, but subconsciously will be learning concepts of Computer Science. Each achievement reached by the player, will present a new concept of Computer Science. It is the purpose of the software to create interest into Computer Science in as many people as possible. Effectively reaching High School students pursuing a higher education, and also minorities, specially women.

Acknowledgments. This material is based in part upon work supported by the National Science Foundation under Grant Nos. I/UCRC IIP-1338922, III-Large IIS-1213026, MRI CNS-1429345, MRI CNS-1532061.

References

1. Kalelioğlu, F.: A new way of teaching programming skills to k-12 students: Code.org. Comput. Hum. Behav. **52**, 200–210 (2015)
2. DOE: Office of innovation and improvement - computer science - department of education (2018)
3. USDL: Computer and information technology occupations, January 2018
4. NCES: Bachelor's degrees conferred to females by post secondary institutions, by race/ethnicity and field of study: 2014–15 and 2015–16, August 2017
5. Rasul, S., Bukhsh, Q., Batool, S.: A study to analyze the effectiveness of audio visual aids in teaching learning process at uvniversity level. Proc. - Soc. Behav. Sci. **28**, 78–81 (2011). World Conference on Educational Technology Researches - 2011
6. Rheingold, H.: Virtual Reality: Exploring the Brave New Technologies. Simon & Schuster Adult Publishing Group (1991)
7. NCES: Public high school graduation rates, April 2017
8. Felder, R.M., Silverman, L.K.: Learning and teaching styles in engineering education. Eng. Educ. **78**, 674–681 (1988)
9. Von Neumann, J.: The Computer and the Brain. Yale University Press, New Haven (2012)
10. Carter, L.: Why students with an apparent aptitude for computer science don't choose to major in computer science. SIGCSE Bull. **38**, 27–31 (2006)
11. Bolivar, S., Ortega, F.R., Zock-Obregon, M., Rishe, N.D.: 3D Spatial gaming interaction to broad CS participation. In: Antona, M., Stephanidis, C. (eds.) UAHCI 2018. LNCS, vol. 10908, pp. 39–47. Springer, Cham (2018). https://doi.org/10.1007/978-3-319-92052-8_4
12. Kashdan, T.B., Silvia, P.J.: Curiosity and interest: the benefits of thriving on novelty and challenge. Oxford Handb. Posit. Psychol. **2**, 367–374 (2009)
13. Papastergiou, M.: Digital game-based learning in high school computer science education: impact on educational effectiveness and student motivation. Comput. Educ. **52**(1), 1–12 (2009)

14. Gentile, D.: Pathological video-game use among youth ages 8 to 18: a national study. Psychol. Sci. **20**(5), 594–602 (2009). PMID: 19476590
15. Barko, T., Sadler, T.D.: Practicality in virtuality: finding student meaning in video game education. J. Sci. Educ. Technol. **22**, 124–132 (2013)
16. Funk, J.B.: Reevaluating the impact of video games. Clin. Pediatr. **32**(2), 86–90 (1993). PMID: 8432085
17. Cummings, A.H.: The evolution of game controllers and control schemes and their effect on their games. In: The 17th Annual University of Southampton Multimedia Systems Conference (2007)
18. DeJarnette, N.: America's children: providing early exposure to stem (science, technology, engineering and math) initiatives. Education **133**(1), 77–84 (2012)
19. DeRidder, L.: The impact of parents and parenting on career development (1990)
20. Nicholson, S.: Peeking behind the locked door: a survey of escape room facilities. White Paper (2015). http://scottnicholson.com/pubs/erfacwhite.pdf
21. McGonigal, J.: Reality is Broken: Why Games Make Us Better and How They Can Change the World. Penguin, London (2011)
22. Blascovich, J., Bailenson, J.: Infinite Reality: Avatars, Eternal Life, New Worlds, and the Dawn of the Virtual Revolution. William Morrow & Co, New York (2011)
23. Falkner, K., Szabo, C., Michell, D., Szorenyi, A., Thyer, S.: Gender gap in academia: perceptions of female computer science academics. In: Proceedings of the 2015 ACM Conference on Innovation and Technology in Computer Science Education, ITiCSE 2015, pp. 111–116. ACM, New York (2015)
24. Funke, A., Berges, M., Mühling, A., Hubwieser, P.: Gender differences in programming: research results and teachers' perception. In: Proceedings of the 15th Koli Calling Conference on Computing Education Research, Koli Calling 2015, pp. 161–162. ACM, New York (2015)

A Flexible Assessment Platform
for Middle School Supported
on Students Goals

Pedro J. S. Cardoso[1]([✉])(iD), Roberto Lam[1](iD), Rui Penha Pereira[2](iD),
Nuno Rodrigues[2], and Cláudia Herdeiro[3](iD)

[1] LARSyS, University of the Algarve, Faro, Portugal
{pcardoso,rlam}@ualg.pt
[2] ISE, University of the Algarve, Faro, Portugal
{rpper,a4571}@ualg.pt
[3] AEJD, Faro, Portugal
claudia.cardoso@aejdfaro.pt

Abstract. Rooted in many education system, assessment by written exams in a live only time evaluation is a traditional way to judge the student learnings. This live only time evaluation method leads to dysfunctionalities such as high levels of stress and the assumption, by the students and by some teachers, that exams reflect the educational goals. This paper presents the Assessment Centers in Schools (ACiSs) project which aims to mitigate some of the identified problems. The final goal of the ACiSs system is a web platform which allows students to have an out of class assessment system, reducing factor like stress by granting the possibility to complete more than one examination and consequent approval per module of the studied subjects. The ACiSs system is comprised by a dataset of questions, properly categorized, which allows the automatic generation of exams wordings for summative and formative assessment. In the latter case, exams can be generated in order to mitigate individual weaknesses in the subject's curricular goals.

Keywords: Assessment Centers in Schools · Curricular goals ·
Exams generation

1   Introduction

Traditional assessment methods (e.g., written exam, quizzes, and presentations) enable teachers to make judgments about the students learnings, translated in the assignment of grades. These methods of assessment can have a direct impact on the quality of student learning as many of them assume that the focus of exams and assignments reflects the educational goals most valued by an instructor, directing their learning and studying accordingly (McKeachie and Svinicki 2013). Changing this view is somehow difficult since it is rooted in many teaching systems. However, alternatives to the traditional class assessment can try to mitigate some of those problems.

© Springer Nature Switzerland AG 2019
M. Antona and C. Stephanidis (Eds.): HCII 2019, LNCS 11572, pp. 420–432, 2019.
https://doi.org/10.1007/978-3-030-23560-4_31

Assessment Centers in Schools (ACiSs) is a pilot research project in the area of school education that aims to investigate the possible improvement of learning outcomes and stress reduction, by modifying the traditional processes of summative and formative assessment of students in middle schools – although applicable to any level of education. These centers, supported in an information technology (IT) system, will be managed by teachers who do not necessarily teach students in class. Students can, individually, request a written evaluation exam on a certain subject module, choosing between summative or formative examination. Furthermore, students will also be scrutinized through a conversation with the teacher who evaluates their knowledge in the great context of the contents, understanding-relationally a wider area of knowledge. It is intended to bring the teacher back in class, to the role of master teacher that is no longer in opposition with the student, lowering the intense interpersonal comparison and stress, commonly linked to traditional assessments in class. It is also believed to contribute to the improvement of dysfunctionalities such as indiscipline, bullying and violence at school, which can benefit the most disadvantaged and create opportunities to reduce early school leaving (Noel et al. 2015).

The objective is, therefore, to have a more rigorous and demanding assessment, to increase the success of learning for a larger number of students, to increase the quality and quantity of the different potentialities of each student, to increase the possibility of such potentialities to flourish asymmetrically adjusting to different students, and at the same time, as already mentioned, reducing the intense interpersonal comparison and stress.

The technical request behind the operation and implementation of a ACiSs are very low as it requires a server and a, possibly devoted, classrooms equipped with some mean of access (e.g., computers) to the exams wordings. In an extreme case, tablets or smart-phones owned by the students can also be used to access the exams.

This paper describes the efforts being made to build such a system. The platform will manage users, subjects, subject chapters and curricular goals (CG), questions, exams, grades, etc. Teachers upload questions to the platform (namely, question wording, subject, chapter, CG involved in its resolutions, resolution time estimation, degree of difficulty, and one or more answers). Then, exams (formative or summative) are generated taking into consideration those attributes (e.g., subject, CG, solving time, degree of difficulty, etc.). Upon solving an exam, students upload their solutions to the system, to be classified by a teacher which will mark the CG successfully attained by the students. The exams can latter be retrieved given an identifier, which allows to associate exams to students. In this context, exams can also be semi-automatically generated by manually adjusting automatically generated exams. Beside being used to maintain the users' grades and assessment, CG attainment by the students are used to generate exams adequate to the student, implementing the formative assessment.

This paper is divided as follows The next section presents the motivation, context and background of the problem. Section 3 makes a brief description of the ACiSs system. Section 4 outlines the assessment platform and some examples of the required set up. The final section presents a conclusion and future work.

2   Context and Background

2.1   Pedagogy for Well-Being – Comprehensive-Relationship (PWb–CR)

The ACiSs project arises in the context of previous research carried out at the Institute of Education of the University of London and the University of Algarve, within the framework of an education centred on well-being, inspiring a Pedagogy for Well-being (PWb).

The Education for Well-being, departs of current views (White 1990), coupled with those of the classical age, as summarized in (Williams 1981, pp. 20), which are the following: (i) The purpose of life is to live it in well-being, whereas education is the complex process of learning to live the good life and in well-being; (ii) Well-being is a reflective tranquility; (iii) Such reflexive tranquility originates in the autonomy of the person (self-sufficiency); (iv) Autonomy is the greater capacity to be with one's neighbor, originated in the capacity of the person to be alone with himself and in reflective tranquility; (v) But there are important aspects that are not under the control of the person, being of the domain of luck and affected by the contingent enemies of the reflexive tranquility, provoking disorder in the person. (vi) Such disorder may be, for the purposes of practical guidance in schools, summarized in the complex and interrelated action of the following seven forms of disorder (FDs), here postulated as follows: (vi.1) Intense interpersonal comparison through competition, envy, jealousy, vanity, prestige, relationships of superiority and inferiority, podiums of winners and losers, comparisons of physical, artistic, intellectual, or industrial capacities; (vi.2) Corruption of intention; (vi.3) Dependence on substances, persons, objects, organizations and traditions; (vi.4) Division by nationalities, regions, languages, professions, sexual orientation, "races", social classes, religions, gender, ethnic tribalism, physical or mental impaired and not impaired, old and new people, human and nonhuman animals, etc.; (vi.5) Fear, prominent in schools, like fear of examinations, fear of showing ignorance in public, fear of student to teacher, fear of teacher to students, fear of colleagues and of the culture of cruelty and humiliation of mobs in the classroom or in the corridors, fear of public speaking, etc.; (vi.6) Self disintegration for lack of basic goods for the body, such as shelter, clothing, food, but above all, caused by affectations of the mind that can be inscribed under the title of neuroses, such as depressions and anxieties; (vi.7) Violence that can take forms of oppression by domination, power, exploitation, greed, hatred, punishment, and humiliation.

That is, the person in the absence of these forms of disorder, can enjoy autonomy with reflexive tranquility, being the educated person. Thus, education can be seen as a complex process of learning to live a life in well-being that promotes an environment in the absence of the forms of disorder and the sensitivity to it, so as to let flourish the autonomous person, enjoying reflexive tranquility.

A pedagogy inspired by an education for well-being is especially sensitive in creating learning environments that are focused on removing or mitigating the presence of forms of disorder, fitting in the double purpose of preparing students for the life of work, and being an active contributor to the social cohesion. With this fundamental background, PWb aims at:

Forms of Disorder. Creation of learning environments in the absence of the seven forms of disorder;

Luck, Interdependence and Forms of Disorder. Sensitize students to the prominence of luck in the origin and unfolding of personal life and to the prominence of interdependence between all people, in the conditioning of our lives, and to the occurrence of a myriad of complex situations where forms of disorder occur.

Greater Framework. Provide the student with opportunities of a greater framework, helping him/her throughout his/her evolution, to position himself/herself, threefold: before the universe, before society and before his/her neighbor, as a reflection of his positioning with himself;

Outside Order and Inner Order. To seek to harmonize the inquiry by the search for the truth of the external order in nature and society, science, with the inquiry of the search for the truth of the inner order of the student, namely, for example, by "mindfulness", or others spiritual inquiries.

Comprehensive-Relationship (CR) in the Curriculum Comprehensive - Relational learning of curricular subjects, with great attention to the power of "concept words". Permanently, in double movement, goes from the particular to the general framework, and vice versa, being especially careful with key words and symbols. This is in the sense that one does not manipulate only the word mimetically, but rather touches more closely the reality that it is supposed to represent. Such movement must be done even within the topic matter, vertically, and still with the other topics under study, horizontally, comprehensively and relational. This is a permanent effort to broaden the great frameworks of the outer order as currently described by the sciences and the humanities. For example, the study of mathematical equations may, vertically, require a careful explanation of algebra, the origin of the word and history, the explanation of the branches of mathematics and their relation to the sciences, and the enquiring of what is a science. Horizontally it can lead to the key concept of energy in physics and mathematics there used, or to the quantitative study of racism in society.

Soft Skills. Provide and encourage opportunities for the acquisition and training of soft transversal skills, such as: creativity and entrepreneurship, verbal communication in public, orientation of meetings, financial literacy, debate of ideas, etc.

PWb contrasts with the criticized "exam pedagogy," too focused on mechanical answers to the most likely exam questions. For example, it is usually not surprising that in a mathematics examination questions are asked about what is Algebra, its history, its framing with other chapters of mathematics, its relation with the great framework in the investigation by the external order, on the part of diverse Sciences. The student solves the restricted problem of equations by solving them, but tends not to enjoy the broader understanding of their relational understanding of the world. Thus PWb-CR assumes at its heart a concern for a more holistic approach, at the levels of the outer and inner order of the person.

2.2   The Discomfort in Schools, Absolute Superiority, and Two Paths of Solution

Schools, in general, are currently the scene of several dysfunctions widely reported in the literature, as very serious: indiscipline, bullying and various types of violence that can exceptionally escalate to bloody shootings. Such disturbances are believed to potentiate problems that are also widely reported, such as early school leaving, school failure, the discrimination of the most disadvantaged, which end up being the most affected.

What is assumed here as the cause of such dysfunctional behaviours is that, unconsciously, by tradition and in the eagerness to help students acquire the indispensable instrumental knowledge for their performance and success in this "knowledge society," families and schools, adopt intense but subtle practices, permeated by FDs. Thus, they seriously erode students' emotional robustness and self-confidence, weakening them to success at work and in life for well-being. More directly, student violence, in and against school, is seen here as a response to what they feel to be, unconsciously and emotionally, the violence of the school over them.

As prominent FDs in school, one can point to intense interpersonal comparison and fear. Hume (1992, pp. 594) gravely credits this type of comparison with the removal of sympathy, making us feel pain with the happiness of the other, and feeling happiness in his pain. Focusing on school, da Silva (2000, pp. 235) states that "the student is especially educated to keep his work to himself, to" shine "at the expense of others, if necessary; The machine of notes and podiums of honours, of vigilance in the tests and of the lessons recited, leads, although perhaps not for this purpose, to an almost monstrous development of selfishness; The child is accustomed to not helping anyone." And further on (da Silva 2000, pp. 270), "comparative praise," "medals," and "the notes given much less to know of individual value than to grade the whole class and to make the differences between students very clear."

Note that da Silva (2000) stresses that the problem is not notes and exams *per se*. It would be absurd not to make gauges, to encourage students to improve and succeed in blossoming their potential, or to want to level them all underneath. What is called "monstrous" is the use of grades, to install an intense interpersonal comparison that generates certain dominant feelings of superiority in some, and dominant feelings of inferiority in others. These are not feelings of superiority-inferiority, morally and emotionally innocuous. It is normal for any student to have relative superiority, for example as to competence in mathematics, compared to others. Having such an advantage, it can keep the humanity of the contact, helping their peers. So the problem is not the superiority relative to functionalities, in the sciences, arts, sport, etc. The crucial problem is when the complex, because it frustrates any complete description, interaction of school and social devices generate and attribute to some students an "absolute superiority", making them believe to be better and more deserving human beings than others. And, making others, the majority, feel symmetrical negative feelings, believing themselves less valuable and incompetent, eroding their self-confidence and self-esteem. As Macmurray (2004, pp. 151) points out, "If the inequalities of functional life are not subordinated to the deeper equality of human fellowship, they become absolute and community perishes."

Conscious of this central problem of the disruptive violence of human fellowship, contained in the absolute superiority-inferiority in which the school community perishes, and where the different dysfunctional violent reactions such as indiscipline and bullying emerge, two solutions present themselves. First, the Finnish solution, which removed exams from pre-university schools, as argued by White (2014) in the book "Who Needs Examinations?". But, in some social and political traditions, the examinations occupy a very important place to dethrone, so we are taken to the second solution. Second, the implementation of ACiSs that, keeping grades, further increase the number of possible exams and their rigor, reinforcing confidence for the success of learning, but mitigating the intense interpersonal comparison and fear, as described ahead, in the context of PWb-CR.

3   Brief Description of the ACiSs

ACiSs are conceptualized as spaces within the school, having teachers assigned to it exclusively or as a complementary task to teaching, intervening in the assessments of students who do not attend their classes. Using predominantly an IT system to generate tests/exams wordings from questions in a database, with generosity of time to reduce fear/stress, students can make written exams in a particular subject modules, at their request. These written exams can have the form of summative or formative evaluation, being the latter generated to improve the students competences according with the subject's CG. However, in addition to this written assessment, the student should have an oral evaluation (CR conversation) with the teacher, to ensure that he/she masters the great concepts of knowledge framing, avoiding the strong incidence of a "predominant pedagogy for exams", in which some questions/problems can be solved, in writing, without really knowing the main concepts.

The minimal initial requirements is a room, equipped with computers. Supported by a teacher, the student can individually request the assessment in the ACiSs, for a comfortable number of times, so as to remove as much stress as possible from "single occasion exams." Among other benefits, the following are listed: (1) Mitigate the fears linked to the stress of evaluations, allowing the students to access the center a comfortable number of times; (2) To free the teacher, who teaches in the classroom, of the burden of summative evaluations and to facilitate their establishment as the master-friend who helps the disciple to overcome the evaluation in the center. Thus, ceasing their state of opposition and becoming in communion. (3) Freeing the learning system from a strong "predominant examination pedagogy" and inaugurating the predominance of a PWb-CR; (4) Facilitate student progression by evaluating shorter modules of the syllabus; (5) Mitigate interpersonal comparison by increasing exam opportunities, further trivializing the grades and creating the student's private area, where all data is stored and access reserved. The grades are no longer published or displayed in public places; (6) Mitigate the intense interpersonal comparison, since the evaluations are not done at the same time in the class where results are also disclosed, tending to make this whole process more personal and diffuse; (7) Mitigate the interpersonal comparison, in the long term, by facilitating a future new school organization that will put an end to the permanent and exclusive connection of a student to the same class during the school, allowing the enrollment of the student in several modules of the various subjects, in different classes. This will facilitate the progressive implementation of a system that, in parallel with a compulsory curriculum, will open more to an offer of options for free choice by students, referred to a credit system. It is intended to facilitate the disappearance or reduction of incidence of the class-tribe, creating situations of greater socialization of students, because it is more diversified and makes even more diffuse comparisons of grades and other skills. (8) Facilitate the possibility of different degrees of progression of pupils according to their abilities, by allowing them, at their request, to perform exams more quickly and with greater difficulty.

The next section is devoted to the presentation of the ACiSs technological platform.

4   ACiSs Technological Platform

4.1   ACiSs Flow

The ACiSs will be supported on a web platform accessible from any browser, given the proper credentials. The platform will manage users, subjects, subject chapters and CG, questions, exams, grades, etc. In a general description (see Fig. 1), teacher will upload questions to the platform, including the wording, the subject chapter and CG involved in its resolutions (see Sect. 4.2), the resolution time estimation, the degree of difficulty, and one or more answers.

Upon request, exams are generated taking into consideration the subject chapter or the required CG to solve the questions (i.e., users can request an exam from a particular chapter or simply focusing in some particular CG), a maximum solving time estimation, and the degree of difficulty. Then students solve the exam and upload their solutions to the system, answer by answer or bulk, to be classified by a teacher. The teacher will then classify the student's resolutions and simultaneously mark the CG which where attained by the students.

As IT system should be approved by the users (namely, teachers and students), key elements in the system design, the authors decided to use a mix of Data Flow Diagram (DFD) and Use Cases diagrams to present the system's specifications, see (Yourdon , 2000; Kulak and Guiney , 2004) and also the arguments of Millet and Nelson (2007). On the other hand, the object/class concept of Unified Modeling Language (UML) was not used for describing the IT system due to its complexity and the fact that many teachers are not used to object oriented concepts. Use Case diagrams is used to describe the interaction of actors (Teachers and Students) with the IT system, see Fig. 1. A context DFD shows the data flow between the IT system and external entities, see Fig. 2 showing most important data flows. The interaction of a teacher with ACiSs system, in an exam creation, is showed in an activity diagram, see Fig. 3. Figure 4 shows the different processes that will be responsible of perform actions, to achieve the goals described in the next 2 paragraphs.

In this context, users management includes personal data, actions log and, in the particular case of the students, information about the taken exams, attained CG and corresponding grades.

Exams generation refers to the definition, automatically or manually, of sets of questions to form an exam. As expected, the automatic version depends on the subject's chapter/CG, degree of difficulty, and an estimated resolution time. Furthermore, exams' questions should be diversified within the defined subject chapter or set of CG, as exams are not a collection of questions. If the exam is formative, its generation will also take into consideration student's data, that is, it will use questions related with the student's CG difficulties. The exams can latter be retrieved given an identifier, which allows to associate exams to students. In this context, exams can also be semi-automatically generated, e.g., an automatically generated exam can be reformulated (delete and/or add questions) or, on the opposite way, from a fixed set of questions the system can be asked to complete the exam with other questions from the database. As so, beside being used to maintain the users' grades and assessment, CG attainment are used to generate exams adequate to the student. Other functionalities are also in study, such as automatically sending exams by email to the students to prepare them for scheduled summative examinations.

Out of the scope of this paper is the automatic exam generation algorithm. Nevertheless, the problem has already been studied by some authors in different context and with different complexities. For instance, Nalawade and Ramesh (2016) propose a somehow similar system which automatically generates a question paper from a semantically tagged question repository. This system offers flexibility by supporting four tags (cognitive level, difficulty level, type of question, content/topic for defining a question). However, the system does not generate exams according with the students difficulties, i.e., to prepare them for summative assessments. González and Muñoz (2006) proposed a web-based tool, known as e-status, which allows students in introductory courses to solve exercises in probability and statistical inference. The proposed solution is dynamic in the sense that every problem presents new sample data that is generated randomly, i.e., the student could do the same exercise again but the data (and the solution) would be different. Other examples of similar projects

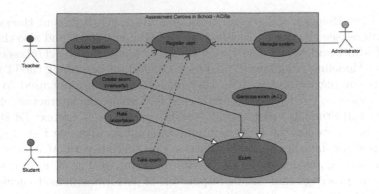

Fig. 1. Main actors in ACiSs system.

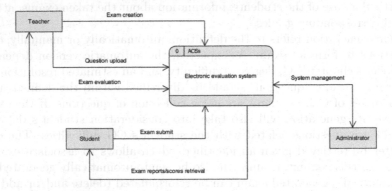

Fig. 2. Context diagram showing the most important data flows between the ACiSs system, teachers, students and administrator.

can be seen in (Soler et al. 2012; Rashad et al. 2010). Also out of the scope of this paper is automated grading, already essayed in works such the ones from Ramalingam et al. (2018) where an automated essay assessment system was defined by use of machine learning techniques, by classifying a corpus of textual entities into small number of discrete categories, corresponding to possible grades. Zesch et al. (2015) investigated which features are task-independent and evaluate their transferability on English and German datasets. This approach tries to solve the complicated problem of transferring a system trained on one task to another.

4.2   The Curricular Goals Approach

To be more precise on how CG work, this section considers the set of CG of the "Mathematics A" subject that students from the "Sciences and Technology" and "Socio-economic Sciences" courses must undertake during their Secondary Education in the Portuguese education system (Diário da República 2012; Ministério da Educação 2015). The overall objectives, complemented with more

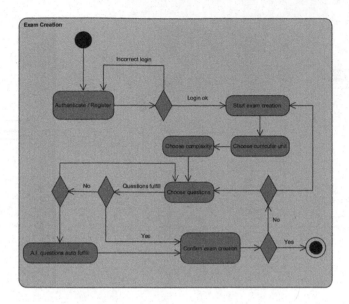

Fig. 3. Activity diagram of a teacher in an exam creation process.

precise descriptors/CG, are organized in each education year, by domains and sub-domains, according to the following structure:

Domain
  Sub-domain
    1. *General objective*
      (a) *Descriptor (CG 1)*
      (b) *Descriptor (CG 2)*
      (c) *etc.*

The different descriptors/CG are written objectively, in strict language to the teacher, and the teacher must select an appropriate teaching strategy. Furthermore, the precise meaning of certain verbs with which some descriptors/CG begin are accurately defined as: *Identify/Designate/Refer* – the student should correctly use the designation of the concept presented as indicated or equivalent; *Recognize* – the student must present a coherent argument, even if possibly more informal than the explanation provided by the teacher; *Know* – the student must know the result, without being required any kind of justification or verification; *Prove/Show/Demonstrate* – the student must present a mathematical demonstration as accurate as possible; or *Justify* – the student must justify the wording in a simple way, evoking a property already known. These prerequisites are not detailed in the text, and the teacher must identify them according to the need, the pertinence and the characteristics of each group of students.

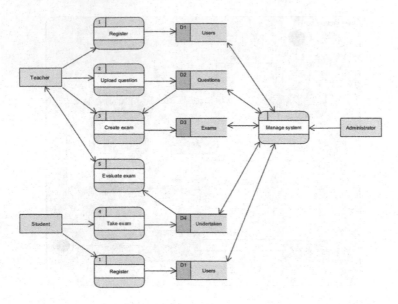

Fig. 4. DFD Level 1, interaction of the Teachers and Students with processes in ACiSs system. The data flows descriptions are omitted to simplify the understanding.

The remaining section introduces some examples, liable of being presented in an exam of the 10th Grade for the Portuguese Schools System. The chosen domain is Algebra and the sub-domain is Radicals. For the Radicals sub-domain eleven CG are defined. By way of example, the first three are:

Algebra
  Radicals
   1. *Defining and performing radicals operations.*
       a. *Recognize, given two real numbers a and b and an odd number $n \in \mathbb{N}$, that if $a < b$ then $a^n < b^n$.*
       b. *Recognize, given two real numbers a and b and an even number $n \in \mathbb{N}$, that if $0 \leq a < b$ then $0 \leq a^n < b^n$ and if $a < b \leq 0$ then $a^n > b^n \geq 0$.*
       c. *Know, given a real number a and an odd number $n \in \mathbb{N}$, that there is a real number b such that $b^n = a$, prove that it is unique, designate it by root index, and represent it by $\sqrt[n]{a}$.*

In this context, the wording of two exercises evaluating the CG 1a and 1b can be stated as follow:

Exercise 1. Let a and b be two real number such that $0 \leq a < b$.

(a) Prove that $a^2 < b^2$ and $a^3 < b^3$.
(b) Prove that if $a^n < b^n$ for a given $n \in \mathbb{N}$ then $a^{n+1} < b^{n+1}$.

Exercise 2. It is known that if x and y are two real number such that $0 \leq x < y$ and n is a natural number then $x^n < y^n$. Prove that if $a < b < 0$ then, $a^n < b^n$ if n is odd and $a^n > b^n$ if n is even.

The previous questions should be uploaded to the system separately and the student's resolution should then be evaluated taking into consideration the attained CG. To upload the questions, the teacher uses a Microsft Word template allowing him/her to upload complexly composed exercises (e.g., containing with tables, figures, mathematical formulas, chemical equations, etc.). Furthermore, the template helps to maintain a congruent design, e.g., in terms of font type and size. Then the ACiSs software will concatenate a header with a set of those word upload documents to generate a final document which can be in several formats, such as HTML, open document formats for office applications (such as, docx or odt), or Portable Document Format (pdf).

5 Conclusion

ACiSs is a pilot research project that suitable to be used in the majority of the subjects present in any level of education. In its core, the system is composed of a dataset of question associated to the CG defined for that subject. Those questions are then used to generate exams to perform formative and summative evaluations. The students resolutions are evaluated in accordance with the attained CG, being this information maintained in the system and latter used to generate appropriate exams. I.e., if a formative evaluation is being performed then, besides CG, resolution time and degree of difficulty, questions will take into consideration the user's previous answers. The ACiSs platform is in an embryonic stage where simple interfaces were developed and are being tested to their usage.

In the future, the authors intend to study the influence of the ACiSs system by applying it to different classes of the same year while maintaining control classes, i.e., classes using the traditional assessment of exams in the classroom. A comparative analysis of the learning outcomes in both groups will, hopefully, prove the usefulness of the ACiSs. Furthermore, other actions will be taken to measure the stress and concentration of students during the exams using biometric devices, inquiring of their satisfaction, interviewing teachers and school directors.

Acknowledgments. This work was supported by the Portuguese Foundation for Science and Technology (FCT), project LARSyS (UID/EEA/50009/2013).

References

da Silva, A.: Textos pedagógicos (Pedagogic Papers I). Editora Âncora (2000). (in Portuguese)

Diário da República (2012). Decreto-lei n.139/2012. Diário da República, 1.a série - N. 129–5 de julho de 2012. (in Portuguese)

González, J.A., Muñoz, P.: E-status: an automatic web-based problem generator-applications to statistics. Comput. Appl. Eng. Educ. **14**(2), 151–159 (2006)

Hume, D.: A Treatise Of Human Nature. Prometheus Books (1992)

Kulak, D., Guiney, E.: Use Cases: Requirements in Context, 2nd edn. Addison-Wesley (2004)

Macmurray, J.: John Macmurray: Selected Philosophical Writings, vol. 4. Imprint Academic (2004)

McKeachie, W.J., Svinicki, M.: Assessing, testing, and evaluating: grading is not the most important function. In: McKeachie's Teaching Tips, 14th edn., pp. 74–86. Cengage Learning (2013)

Millet, I., Nelson, R.: Student perceptions of data flow diagrams vs. use cases. Int. J. Inf. Commun. Technol. Educ. (IJICTE) **3**(1), 94–102 (2007)

Ministério da Educação: Programa e metas curriculares - matemática a (program and curriculum goals - mathematics a) (2015). (in Portuguese)

Nalawade, G., Ramesh, R.: Automatic generation of question paper from user entered specifications using a semantically tagged question repository. In: 2016 IEEE Eighth International Conference on Technology for Education (T4E), vol. 00, pp. 148–151 (2016)

Noel, C., Timmerman, C., Macedo, E., Rocha, C., Araújo, H.: Early school leaving and beyond. Educação, Sociedade Cultura **45**, 7–12 (2015)

Ramalingam, V., Pandian, A., Chetry, P., Nigam, H.: Automated essay grading using machine learning algorithm. J. Phys. Conf. Ser. **1000**, 012030 (2018)

Rashad, M.Z., Kandil, M.S., Hassan, A.E., Zaher, M.A.: An arabic web-based exam management system. Int. J. Electr. Comput. Sci. IJECS-IJENS **10**(01), 48–55 (2010)

Soler, J., Prados, F., Poch, J., Boada, I.: ACME: an e-learning platform including desirable features for engineering courses. Formacion Universitaria **5**(3), 3–16 (2012)

White, J.: Education and the good life: beyond the national curriculum. Kogan Page (1990)

White, J.: Who Needs Examinations: A Story of Climbing Ladders and Dodging Snakes. Institute of Education Press, London (2014)

Williams, B.: Moral Luck: Philosophical Papers 1973–1980. Cambridge University Press, Cambridge (1981)

Yourdon, E.: Modern Structured Analysis, 2nd edn. Prentice Hall PTR, Upper Saddle River (2000)

Zesch, T., Wojatzki, M., Scholten-Akoun, D.: Task-independent features for automated essay grading. Proceedings of the Tenth Workshop on Innovative Use of NLP for Building Educational Applications, pp. 224–232 (2015)

A Delphi Study on the Design of Digital Educational Games

Panagiota Chalki(✉), Tassos Anastasios Mikropoulos,
and Angeliki Tsiara

University of Ioannina, Ioannina, Greece
pahalki@uoi.gr

Abstract. The biggest challenge for the Digital Educational Games Design refers to how to integrate game mechanics and learning mechanics into the gameplay in order to enhance motivation and engagement and improve learning outcomes. This study is the pilot phase of a Delphi method that proposes guidelines for the design of Digital Educational Games. The participants of the Delphi study were academic experts from the scientific field of Digital Educational Game Design. In the first round of the study, a questionnaire of six open-ended questions was sent. The second round questionnaire consisted of 46 closed-ended questions in order to estimate agreement between the participants. The third round questionnaire consisted of one open-ended question. According to the results of the study, the learning and game mechanics elements that have been suggested by the participants as the most important elements are those that promote constructivism, authentic learning environments, personalized learning, and fun. The experts mentioned as very important and challenging element, the way learning mechanics should be integrated into the context of the gameplay. What is proposed to achieve the learning objectives and bring the maximum extent of engagement into the game, is that the learning objectives should be included in activities that do not clearly reveal the learning objectives themselves but incorporate them into symbolic representations of everyday life experiences and examples, that are fun for the users and motivate them for high interaction during the gameplay.

Keywords: Digital educational games · Design guidelines · Delphi method

1 Introduction

In recent years, research in the field of Digital Educational Games has shown positive contributions to learning as far as K12 education, higher education, elderly people, and training are concerned [1]. The positive contribution mainly refers to motivation, engagement and learning outcomes in terms of skills of the 21st century [2]. However, much work has still to be done in order to learn how to better design, and evaluate digital games across different learning contexts and target audiences [3].

The basic features of a digital game can firstly be divided into two main categories, the Learning Mechanics (LM) and the Game Mechanics (GM). LM includes all the concepts related to learning principles, instructional models and teaching techniques,

M. Antona and C. Stephanidis (Eds.): HCII 2019, LNCS 11572, pp. 433–444, 2019.
https://doi.org/10.1007/978-3-030-23560-4_32

learning objectives, skills development, etc. [4]. GM includes all the elements that structure a game and describe the gameplay such as avatars, 2D/3D environments, virtual money, points, timers, feedback (reward, penalty, etc.), narrative (story), rules, goals, competition, levels, cut scenes etc. [5].

Most of the educational games that have been designed are based on the considerations relevant to the traditional learning context. There is a lack of the use of modern learning theories and models such as exploratory learning, problem-based learning and active learning [4]. However, digital educational games support features such as high user interaction, feedback, personalized teaching, teamwork, authentic learning frameworks that do not match with traditional learning [1].

What is more, educational games do not document the design they follow (learning theories, learning objectives, learning techniques etc.) [5].

This suggests that appropriate design models are needed in order to facilitate and guide educational game designers to work more efficient.

2 Related Work

Several studies have been conducted in the context of creating models, methodologies and conceptual frameworks for the design of digital educational games [1, 4–34]. The biggest challenge for the design of the games refers on how well the models can describe the relationships between the different components that consist the digital educational games. This challenge actually includes the ways LM and GM integrate into learning activities through gameplay in order to create learning environments to enhance motivation and engagement and improve learning outcomes.

A review of the literature concerning the models, methodologies and conceptual frameworks for the design of digital educational games shows that the researchers [1, 4–34]:

- Propose general guidelines based on pedagogical approaches without using their corresponding instructional strategies in the gameplay.
- Do not describe the connection between the game elements and the learning objectives of the game.
- Do not describe how to integrate the LM elements into the gameplay.
- Describe the learning and game elements per se, but not the relation between them.
- Do not classify the individual components of a game.
- Do not incorporate an explicit guide for the game design.
- Approach the game design only from a game developer perspective.

Moreover, in most of these studies the methodology is based on empirical data where users are the participants who they are called to design or/and evaluate a given model or methodology or conceptual framework. The users do not have the scientific background to support the design evaluation as they come from different scientific fields. In few cases, game designers are also used as participants. Similar issues apply in this situation, too. Game designers seem that do not transfer the scientific expertise of the necessary instructional design for an educational game to evaluate the game design.

This study proposes guidelines for the design of digital educational games by using the Delphi method, where academic experts of the specific scientific field participate. The guidelines proposed by this pilot Delphi study refer to the LM and GM that educational games should include as well as the ways that learning activities should be integrated into the gameplay.

3 Methodology

The Delphi study was conducted online via questionnaires in Google forms and included three rounds. Five academic experts in the field of Digital Educational Game Design participated. The participants had a period of two weeks to fill in their responses to the questionnaires. Consensus was equaled with 70% agreement among the respondents.

In the first round, a questionnaire of six open-ended questions was sent. The questions were related with the LM and GM that should be incorporated in the games, suggestions about the way that learning activities should be integrated into the gameplay and about the procedure and the challenges of the game design. The participants were asked for at least six opinions per question. The data collected from this initial round followed the content analysis technique. The data were analyzed by grouping similar opinions/items together after the process of determining the most important issues between them.

Subsequently and based on the analysis of the first round answers, a second round questionnaire consisting of 46 closed-ended questions, was configured. The questionnaire included the participants' answers from the first round in order to be rated about their importance through a 9 point Likert scale (1 = no importance, 2 = very low importance, 3 = low importance, 4 = slightly important, 5 = neutral, 6 = moderately important, 7 = high importance, 8 = very high importance, 9 = extremely important). This was followed by the collection and analysis of the second round questionnaire's answers, according to quantitative techniques in order to estimate the agreement between the participants' responses.

According to those results, the questionnaire of the third round was prepared. The third round questionnaire consisted of one open-ended question were participants were asked to describe an exemplary snapshot of an educational digital game for any age or subject of their preference, which combines learning and game mechanics. Data collected from the third round followed the content analysis technique as in the initial round.

4 Results

4.1 First Round

Concerning the LM elements that participants considered that should be included in digital educational games, their answers are summarized below:

- Actions/tasks, challenging activities, competition, problem solving, because the student gets more motivated and engaged.
- Appropriate, constructive feedback, because the student needs it in order to learn from his/her actions.
- Experimentations, because the student should have opportunities to form hypotheses and test them through experimentation, being an active way of learning.
- Exploration, Discovery, because the student gets more engaged and motivated when he/she takes part in active learning.
- Role-playing, because the student gets more empathy, critical and social skills.
- Simulations, because they transfer real-life phenomena that are difficult to otherwise explore, but crucial in constructing meaning and understanding.
- Discussions, social interactions, collaboration activities, because the student can learn interacting with others.
- Assessment, because the student needs to self-monitor his/her performance and gets motivated when he/she progresses.

Moreover, investigation of learners' previous knowledge test and scaffolding activities were also mentioned. Overall, the participants mentioned that LM must be always selected according to the learning objectives of the game.

Referring to the GM elements that participants considered they should be included in games, the answers are summarized below:

- Rules of the gameplay: rules provide a constraining and support strategy necessary for learning and playing.
- Cut scenes: they can easily situate the student within the game narrative and the tasks that he/she is called to undertake, and they can offer information that are relevant to the game's learning objectives.
- Scoring mechanism (e.g. action points), visible progress and levels: gathering action points or unlocking a new level can be very motivational for the student. Furthermore, designing various levels offers the student variety and enables a better organization of the game's learning activities.
- Collecting and interacting with objects: exploring a digital environment in order to discover interactive objects that offer opportunities for experimentation can support active learning. Collecting objects can also be motivational.
- Challenges: motivational well-designed challenges that are in accordance with the game's learning objectives are at the core of an educational game.
- Appropriate, constructive feedback: the student needs it in order to learn from his/her actions.
- Multiplayer capabilities: social interactions may foster learning.
- Simulations: they can bridge the gap between the real world and the game's world.
- Movement in the digital environment, sensation of exploration, realism: students usually like to be situated within a digital environment that consists of various spaces, which they can explore. In addition, this 'spatial metaphor' can help the game designer to better organize the challenges that he/she will embed in the game.

In addition, the adaptation to the learner's needs (learning style, misconceptions) was mentioned. The participants mentioned that the appropriate GM would depend on the entertainment and fun goals of the game.

As far as the ways that learning activities should be integrated into the gameplay, this could be managed by converting learning activities into challenges that the student has to resolve and by meaningfully integrating those challenges in the context of the game with relevant GM into an engaging and fun narrative. In addition, the results show that the learning activities should be integrated in the context of the game by authentic learning approach, by incorporating real world problem-solving activities. That means that the connection between learning and GM should be so well made that the learner typically will not be consciously aware of the learning objectives of the game until he or she is already highly engaged. The participants also mentioned that the integration of learning activities into the gameplay depends on the specific game by considering the specific high level educational and entertainment requirements.

Regarding the procedure (stages/steps) for the design of digital educational games, the answers are summarized below:

- Take into account modern pedagogical approaches, e.g. constructivism, multiple intelligence theory, social theories of learning.
- Take into account basic game-based learning principles.
- Define the learning objectives and sub-objectives.
- Connect the learning objectives and sub-objectives with the acts of the game.
- Define the scoring mechanism as well as the game's levels.
- Define the possible actions that the player can take within the digital environment and the corresponding feedback that he/she can get.
- Design the scaffolds that the player will be offered.
- Evaluate the game with experts (teachers and usability experts).
- Evaluate the game by using real students.
- Redesign the game after evaluation.

As far as it regards the challenges during the game design, the main challenges according to the participants' answers were as follow:

- To transfer the basic aspects of modern pedagogical approaches into educational game-design principles.
- To create appropriate challenges in accordance with the specific learning objectives.
- To create an interesting, persuasive narrative.
- To create appropriate challenges that are motivational and not explicitly didactic.
- To incorporate feedback by using the appropriate GM.
- To have different professionals (e.g., graphic designers, game designers, programmers, educators) cooperating in order to design and develop the game.

4.2 Second Round

Figure 1 shows the results of the second round. The results concern the importance of the LM that should be included in digital educational games.

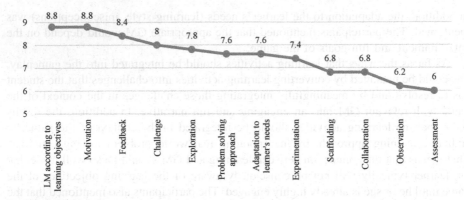

Fig. 1. Average of importance rate about which Learning Mechanics elements should be incorporated into a digital educational game (1 = not at all important, 9 = extremely important)

The participants mentioned assessment, observation, collaboration and scaffolding as least important LM elements. They commented that these four elements depend only on the learning objectives, and not on the game design.

Figure 2 shows regarding the results concerning the importance of the GM elements that should be included in the games.

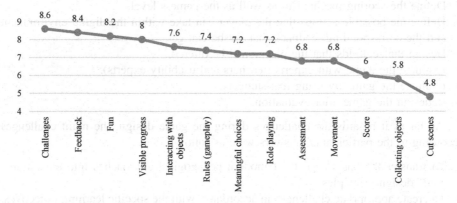

Fig. 2. Average of importance rate about which Game Mechanics elements should be included in a digital educational game (1 = not at all important, 9 = extremely important)

Movement is the least important element, as participants said that it depends on the game and should only be used only if required by the learning and game objectives. Score mentioned to be not so important because the progress could be indicated in other more meaningful ways. Collecting objects is also not important because it depends on the game's learning objectives and should be used if it is required for experimentation, problem solving, or rewards. Finally, cut scenes are not so important because their use should depend on the game and it is not necessary for every game.

As far as the importance of the stages/steps that should be parts of the procedure for the design of digital educational games, the results are follow in Fig. 3.

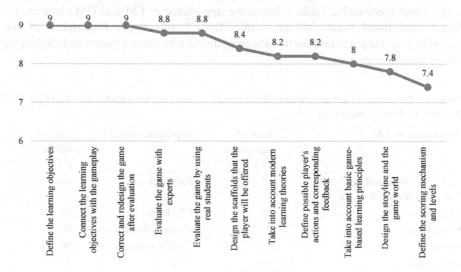

Fig. 3. Average of importance rate about the stages/steps that should be parts of digital educational game design (1 = not at all important, 9 = extremely important)

The results show that the highest and maximum rate is related to the learning objectives themselves, that is the connection of the learning objectives with gameplay, and the evaluation of the game. The lowest rate concerns the design of the storyline and the game environment and defining the scoring mechanism as well as the game's levels.

Figure 4 shows the importance of the challenges that designers face during the game design.

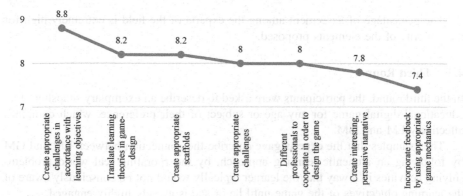

Fig. 4. Average of importance rate concerning the main challenges during the digital educational game design (1 = not at all important, 9 = extremely important)

In the highest rate of all challenges is the design of the appropriate challenges according to the learning objectives

Tables 1 and 2 show the percentages of agreement between the participants of the study. More specifically, Table 1 shows the importance of LM and GM elements for digital educational games design, while Table 2 shows the importance of the stages/steps of the procedure for the design of digital educational games and challenges during the game design.

Table 1. Percentage of agreement among the experts concerning the importance of LM and GM elements in digital educational games

Importance of LM	Rate of agreement (%)	Importance of GM	Rate of agreement (%)
LM selected according to the learning objectives of the game	95	Feedback	93
Motivation	95	Challenges	93
Observation	93	Meaningful choices	90
Feedback	93	Visible progress	90
Challenge	85	Fun	88
Exploration	85	Assessment	88
Assessment	83	Collecting objects	83
Experimentation	78	Interacting with objects	75
Adaptation to the learner's needs	78	Rules (game play)	73
Scaffolding	75	Movement in the virtual environment	73
Problem solving approach	75	Role playing	73
Collaboration	73	Score	63
		Cut scenes	63

The percentage of agreement among the experts of the field is extremely high for the majority of the elements proposed.

4.3   Third Round

In the third round, the participants were asked to describe an exemplary snapshot of an educational digital game for any age or subject of their preference, which combines effectively LM and GM.

The examples that the experts gave describe the connection between LM and GM by following an authentic learning approach, by incorporating real world problem-solving activities in a way that the learner typically would not be consciously aware of the learning objectives of the game until he or she is already highly engaged.

Table 2. Percentage of agreement among the experts concerning the importance of the stages/steps of the procedure for the design of digital educational games and challenges during the game design

Importance of stages/steps of the procedure for the design of educational digital games	Rate of agreement (%)	Important challenges during the game design	Rate of agreement (%)
Define the learning objectives	100	Create appropriate challenges in accordance with learning objectives	95
Connect the learning objectives with the gameplay	100	Create appropriate scaffolds	95
Correct and redesign the game after evaluation	100	Incorporate feedback by using the appropriate GM	93
Evaluate the game with experts	95	Different professionals to cooperate for the design of the game	85
Evaluate the game with students	95	Transfer pedagogical approaches in game-design	83
Design the scaffolds	88	Create appropriate challenges	83
Take into account modern pedagogical approaches	83	Create an interesting, persuasive narrative	80
Define possible player's actions and corresponding feedback	83		
Take into account basic game-based learning principles	78		
Design the storyline and the game world	75		
Define the scoring mechanism as well as the game's levels	70		

5   Discussion

This Delphi study proposes the pilot phase of a study that proposes guidelines for the design of digital educational games.

Our results show that the most important elements for the design of digital educational games is the clear description of the learning objectives and their integration into the context of the game by selecting the appropriate constructive LM elements and approaches as well as the GM elements that promote active learning. The LM and GM elements that have been suggested by the experts as the most important elements are those that promote constructivism, authentic learning environments, personalized learning and fun.

The experts mentioned the way the LM elements should be integrated into the context of the gameplay as the most important and challenging point for the design of the digital educational games. The learning objectives should be included in activities that do not clearly reveal, but incorporate them into symbolic representations of everyday life experiences and examples that are fun for the users and motivate them for high interaction into the gameplay.

This study is the first attempt to approach the field of digital educational games design by using the Delphi method. Our immediate future plan is the redesign of the Delphi study based on the outcomes of this pilot phase in order to get the more specific guidelines possible for the design of digital educational games for all ages.

Acknowledgments. This research/project is implemented through/has been co-financed by the Operational Program "Human Resources Development, Education and Lifelong Learning" and is co-financed by the European Union (European Social Fund) and Greek national funds.

References

1. Annetta, L.A.: The "I's" have it: a framework for serious educational game design. Rev. Gen. Psychol. **14**(2), 105 (2010)
2. Bellotti, F., Berta, R., De Gloria, A.: Designing effective serious games: opportunities and challenges for research. Int. J. Emerg. Technol. Learn. (iJET) **5**(2010), 22–35 (2010)
3. Shaffer, D.W., Squire, K.D., Halverson, R., Gee, J.P.: Video games and the future of learning. Phi Delta Kappan **87**(2), 104–111 (2005)
4. Arnab, S., et al.: A serious game model for cultural heritage. ACM J. Comput. Cult. Herit. **5** (4), 1–27 (2012)
5. Carvalho, B., et al.: An activity theory-based model for serious games analysis and conceptual design. Comput. Educ. **87**, 166–181 (2015)
6. Akilli, G.K., Cagiltay, K.: An instructional design/development model for the creation of game-like learning environments: the FIDGE model. In: Pivec, M. (ed.) Affective and emotional aspects of human–computer interaction – game-based and innovative learning approaches, pp. 93–112. IOS Press, Amsterdam (2006)
7. Amory, A.: Game object model version II: a theoretical framework for educational game development. Educ. Technol. Res. Dev. **55**(1), 51–77 (2007)
8. Björk, S., Holopainen, J.: Patterns in Game Design. Charles River Media, Boston (2004)
9. Buchinger, D., da Silva Hounsell, M.: Guidelines for designing and using collaborative-competitive serious games. Comput. Educ. **118**, 133–149 (2018)
10. Capdevila Ibáñez, B., Marne, B., Labat, J.M.: Conceptual and technical frameworks for serious games. In: Proceedings of the 5th European Conference on Games Based Learning, pp. 81–87. Academic Publishing Limited, Reading (2011)
11. de Freitas, S., Oliver, M.: A four dimensional framework for the evaluation and assessment of educational games. Paper accepted for Computer Assisted Learning Conference 2005 (2005)
12. de Lope, R., López Arcos, J.R., Medina-Medina, N., Paderewski, P., Gutiérrez-Vela, F.L.: Design methodology for educational games based on graphical notations: designing Urano. Entertain. Comput. **18**, 1–14 (2017)
13. Echeverría, A., et al.: A framework for the design and integration of collaborative classroom games. Comput. Educ. **57**, 1127–1136 (2011)

14. El Mawas, N.: An architecture for co-designing participatory and knowledge-intensive serious games: ARGILE. In: Proceedings of the International Conference on Collaboration Technologies and Systems (CTS 2014). Minneapolis, USA (2014)
15. Gunter, G.A., Kenny, R.F., Vick, E.H.: Taking educational games seriously: using the RETAIN model to design endogenous fantasy into standalone educational games. Educ. Technol. Res. Dev. **56**(5–6), 511–537 (2007)
16. Huynh-Kim-Bang, B., Labat, L.-M., Wisdom, J.: Design patterns in serious games: a blue print for combining fun and learning (2011). http://seriousgames.lip6.fr/DesignPatterns/designPatternsForSeriousGames.pdf. Accessed 17 Sep 2018
17. Kelle, S., Klemke, R., Specht, M.: Design patterns for learning games. Int. J. Technol. Enhanced Learn. **3**(6), 555–569 (2011)
18. Kiili, K.: Digital game-based learning: towards an experiential gaming model. Internet Higher Educ. **8**, 13–24 (2005)
19. Kordaki, M.: A 7-step modeling methodology for the design of educational constructivist computer card games: results fron an empirical study. Special Issuc of Recent Patents on Computer Science on "Technology-Centered Higher Education: Best Approaches and Practices in Technology Integration" (2015)
20. Lim, T., Louchart, S., Suttie, N., Ritchie, J.M., Aylett, R.S., Stanescu, I.A., et al.: Strategies for effective digital games development and implementation. In: Baek, Y., Whitton, N. (eds.) Cases on Digital Game-Based Learning: Methods, Models, and Strategies, IGI Global, pp. 168–198. Information Science Reference, Hershey (2013). https://doi.org/10.4018/978-1-4666-2848-9.ch010
21. Lindley, C.A.: Game taxonomies: A high level framework for game analysis and design. Gamasutra **2003**(10), 03 (2003)
22. Marne, B., Wisdom, J., Huynh-Kim-Bang, B., Labat, J.-M.: The six facets of serious game design: a methodology enhanced by our design pattern library. In: Ravenscroft, A., Lindstaedt, S., Kloos, C.D., Hernández-Leo, D. (eds.) EC-TEL 2012. LNCS, vol. 7563, pp. 208–221. Springer, Heidelberg (2012). https://doi.org/10.1007/978-3-642-33263-0_17
23. McMahon, M.T.J.: The DODDEL model: a flexible document-oriented model for the design of serious games. In: Connolly, T., Stansfield, M., Boyle, L. (eds.) Games-Based Learning Advancements for Multi-Sensory Human Computer Interfaces: Techniques and Effective Approaches. Information Science Reference, Hershey (2009)
24. Moreno-Ger, P., Martínez-Ortiz, I., Sierra, J.L., Fernández-Manjón, B.: A content-centric development process model. Computer **41**(3), 24–30 (2008)
25. Moya, S., Tost, D., Grau, S., von Barnekow, A., Felix, E.: SKETCH'NDO: a framework for the creation of task-based serious games. J. Vis. Lang. Comput. **34–35**, 1–10 (2016)
26. Plass, J.L., Homer, B.D.: Educational game design pattern candidates. J. Res. Sci. Teach. **44**, 133–153 (2009)
27. Arnab, S., et al.: Mapping learning and game mechanics for serious games analysis. Br. J. Educ. Technol. **46**(2), 391–411 (2015)
28. Salen, K., Zimmerman, E.: Rules of Play: Game Design Fundamentals. MIT Press, Cambridge (2004)
29. Sanchez, E.: Key Criteria for Game Design. A Framework. MEET Project. European Commission (2011)
30. Sicart, M.: Designing game mechanics. Int. J. Comput. Game Res. **8**(2), 1 (2008)
31. van Staalduinen, J.P., de Freitas, S.: A game-based learning framework: linking game design and learning outcomes. In: Khyne, M.S. (ed.) Learning to Play: Exploring the Future of Education with Video Games, pp. 29–54. Peter Lang, New York (2011)

32. Westera, W., Nadolskl, R.J., Hummel, H.G.K., Woperels, I.G.J.H.: Serious games for higher education: a framework for reducing design complexity. J. Comput. Assist. Learn. **24**, 420–432 (2008)

33. Wouters, P., Oostendorp, H.V., Boonekamp, R., Spek, E.V.D.: The role of Game Discourse Analysis and curiosity in creating engaging and effective serious games by implementing a back story and foreshadowing. Interact. Comput. **23**(4), 329–336 (2011)

34. Yusoff, A., Crowder, R., Gilbert, L., Wills, G.: A conceptual framework for serious games. In: Aedo, I., Chen, N.S., Sampson, K.D., Zaitseva, L. (eds.) Proceedings of ICALT 2009, 9th IEEE International Conference on Advanced Learning Technologies, pp. 21–23. University of Southampton, Southampton (2009)

Visualizing Student Interactions to Support Instructors in Virtual Learning Environments

André Luiz de Brandão Damasceno$^{(\boxtimes)}$, Dalai dos Santos Ribeiro$^{(\boxtimes)}$,
and Simone Diniz Junqueira Barbosa$^{(\boxtimes)}$

Pontifical Catholic University of Rio de Janeiro, Rio de Janeiro, RJ, Brazil
{adamasceno,dribeiro,simone}@inf.puc-rio.br

Abstract. Online education has broadened the avenues of research on student's behavior and performance. In this paper, we shed light on how make visualizations to better support the instructors in the analyses of students interactions on VLE. We conducted a study in order to identify which data the instructors take into account and their visualization preferences. As result, even though instructors were presented different types of the visualization, the ones they selected the most and evaluated better are in line with they already used.

Keywords: Learning analytics · Educational data mining ·
Visualization · Virtual Learning Environments · VLE · Logs ·
Interviews · eLearning · Student · Teacher · Behavior · Interaction

1 Introduction

Distance Learning (DL) is no longer a novelty. From the records of correspondence courses in Brazil in the 19th century [1], to the rise of computers and evolution of the Internet, instructors and students have experienced novel ways of teaching and learning. In particular, improvements to multimedia technologies have contributed to the creation of online courses in Virtual Learning Environments (VLEs). One of the reasons for the popularity of online courses is that students can decide their own study pace and participate in courses regardless of geographic distance limitations [2]. Moreover, VLEs are not exclusive to DL. There is evidence of their usage together with face-to-face learning (*aka* blended learning) [3].

Students' interactions with VLEs are often stored in logs. The analysis of these logs can predict the students' performance, evaluate their learning achievement in a course, and even identify behavior patterns [4,5]. Instructors usually get information from observing what students say and do on a VLE. Some challenges regarding this analytical process are the following: the instructors often do not have time to analyze these logs in depth; they are not statistics experts; or they have not received training to extract key information from VLE logs,

M. Antona and C. Stephanidis (Eds.): HCII 2019, LNCS 11572, pp. 445–464, 2019.
https://doi.org/10.1007/978-3-030-23560-4_33

as those logs are not always very readable. For instance, Damasceno et al. (2018) conducted interviews with instructors and found evidence that several instructors do not have any analytic tool or information besides the student access logs [3]. According to the instructors interviewed, they are very often already overwhelmed by the time and effort needed to prepare their classes, to prepare and assess coursework, and to evaluate students.

Furthermore, Damasceno et al. uncovered requirements and proposed guidelines for what tools should help to analyze in VLEs [3]. For instance, this requirements are based on papers showing that (i) student engagement in the online environment can be measured by materials accessed on the environment [6–8]; and (ii) students can be clustered into different groups based on their access or interaction patterns, such as, with which resources they interact first, how long they stay or what times they usually access the VLE [9–11]. In general, the instructors interviewed reported that they intend to identify patterns related to (a) student access (*e.g.*, login, materials, forum) and (b) student performance. They also claim that a dashboard providing such student information could support them in spending their time more efficiently, adopting new teaching methods, and preparing better course materials.

The purpose of this paper is to identify instructors' preferences regarding the visualization of either student access or performance in courses using VLEs. To achieve our goal, we elaborated a survey about which visualizations answered efficiently a set of questions that are relevant to instructors, according to Damasceno et al. [3]. The visualizations in the survey were developed to support the analysis of the logs from students' interactions with VLEs and to provide insights to instructors. Then, we asked instructors from Brazilian education institutions to respond to the survey and analyzed the collected data. The main outcome of the study are the types of visualization to show certain VLE data, the instructors' visualization preferences, and their evaluations of each type of visualization.

This paper is structured as follows. Section 2 shows the design process of VLE data visualization. Section 3 describes the exploratory study performed with instructors about their visualization preferences. In Sect. 4 we discuss the results of the study. Lastly, Sect. 5 presents some final considerations.

2   Proposed Visualizations

Damasceno et al. described 38 requirements and 18 guidelines for tool support for analyzing VLE logs [3]. The guidelines were compiled from the literature and the requirements resulted from the instructors' interviews. However, 15 requirements were not related to student access or performance, and were therefore removed from the study reported in this paper.

After selecting the relevant requirements and guidelines, we arranged them in 11 visualization groups (VGs) with common VLE data logs and elaborated questions to be answered for each VG[1]. For instance, VG-05 is related to correlations between students' grades and activity logs (*e.g.*, access, assignments

---

[1] In this paper, visualization groups are identified in the format VG-99.

completed, forum posts). Table 1 presents the visualization groups, their corresponding questions and visualization task. This last one is based on the taxonomy of visualization tasks proposed by Amar et al. [12].

Table 1. Visualization groups and the questions related to them.

VG	Questions
VG-01	Task: Filter and Retrieve Value.
	Q-01: Which students completed the assignments?
	Q-02: Which assignments were completed by the students?
VG-02	Task: Filter and Retrieve Value.
	Q-01: Which students accessed the materials?
	Q-02: Which materials were most accessed by the students?
VG-03	Task: Filter and Retrieve Value.
	Q-01: How many student accesses, posts, and likes were there?
VG-04	Task: Determine Range
	Q-01: For how long did the students watch each video?
VG-05	Task: Cluster, Compute Derived Value and Correlate
	Q-01: What is the relation between students' grades and VLE access?
	Q-02: What is the relation between students' grades and materials access?
	Q-03: What is the relation between students' grades and assignments completed?
	Q-04: What is the relation between students' grades and forum access?
	Q-05: What is the relation between students' grades and forum posts?
	Q-06: What is the relation between students' grades and forum replies?
	Q-07: What is the relation between students' grades and forum threads?
VG-06	Task: Cluster, Compute Derived Value and Correlate.
	Q-01: What is the relation between students' age and VLE access?
	Q-02: What is the relation between students' age and forum access?
	Q-03: What is the relation between students' age and forum posts?
	Q-04: What is the relation between students' age and forum replies?
	Q-05: What is the relation between students' age and forum threads?
VG-07	Task: Cluster, Compute Derived Value and Correlate.
	Q-01: What is the prediction of students' grades and dropout?
VG-08	Task: Cluster, Compute Derived Value, Correlate, Determine Range.
	Q-01: How many students' accesses were there each day?
	Q-02: How many students' accesses were there per week?
VG-09	Task: Determine Range.
	Q-01: What are the statistics of interactions with video (*e.g.* play, seek)?
VG-10	Task: Filter and Retrieve Value.
	Q-01: Which videos were understood by students?
VG-11	Task: Cluster, Compute Derived Value and Correlate.
	Q-01: What were the students' navigation patterns on the VLE?

Next, based on the information visualization literature (*e.g.*, [13–15]) and online data visualization catalogues[2], we designed visualizations in order to handle the different kinds of data (*e.g.*, numerical, categorical, time series), their

---

[2] For instance: https://datavizcatalogue.com and https://www.data-to-viz.com.

cardinality (*e.g.*, 1, 2, ... N), and the task supported by the chart (*e.g.*, compare, correlate) used by each VG. For the development of the visualizations we used Dash[3], a Python Framework for building data visualization applications. In the Appendix, Figs. 3, 4, 5, 6, 7, 8, 9, 10, 11, 12 and 13 show a sample of all types of visualizations designed for each VG. These visualizations present different ways to view the same data. Although the data depicted in the figures are fictional, they are in line with actual study results presented by Damasceno et al. [3] (*e.g.*, number of clusters presented in Fig. 7, student access patterns in Fig. 10). In addition, each figure is assigned to one VG question (*i.e.*, questions in blue shown in Table 1). Even though different VG questions may use the same type of visualization, they have distinct parameters or axis values. For instance, Fig. 10 presents visualizations related to VG-08's second question (*i.e.*, related to student access per week), whereas VG-08's first question uses the same visualization type, but presents data access per day instead of week.

3 Study Procedure

Although instructors are domain experts, they do not necessarily know how to use information visualizations to answer their questions [16]. It is necessary to identify which questions they take into account and how those questions can be answered through graphical means. To achieve this goal, we developed an online survey using all types of chart designed for each VG. This survey was designed to assess just what is relevant for our study. It included fields for the instructors to identify themselves (*e.g.*, name, age, institution) and to answer questions about their experience with VLE, meaningful student information, VLE data logs, data visualization, and their visualization preferences. We also presented all the questions of Table 1 asked them which questions they found relevant to them. Next, the survey displayed all the VG charts related to the questions they selected. As illustrated in Fig. 1, for each chart, a Likert scale ranging from 1 (strongly disagree) to 7 (strongly agree) was presented for the instructors to evaluate how efficiently the chart answers the corresponding question. To break possible ties, the instructors then were asked to select the chart that, in their opinion, better answers the question. The charts presented in the survey were related to questions shown in blue in Table 1.

4 Results

The survey was online between December 2018 and January 2019. We sent emails inviting the participation of 88 instructors and 15 universities from different Brazilian regions. The survey was responded by 21 instructors (15 men and 6 women) from institutions located in eight Brazilian states (Amazonas, Ceará, Maranhão, Paraíba, Paraná, Piauí, Rondônia, and São Paulo).

---

[3] https://dash.plot.ly.

How many student accesses, posts, and likes were there?

Chart 2

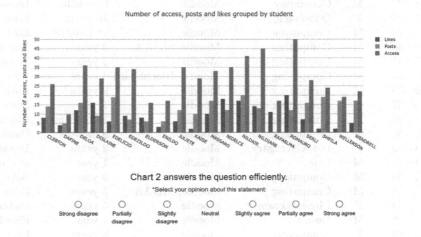

Number of access, posts and likes grouped by student

Chart 2 answers the question efficiently.

*Select your opinion about this statement:

○ Strong disagree   ○ Partially disagree   ○ Slightly disagree   ○ Neutral   ○ Slightly sagree   ○ Partially agree   ○ Strong agree

Fig. 1. A fragment of the online survey.

Table 2 shows an overview of the instructors' profiles[4]. They all have experience with Virtual Learning Environments: 10 had taught courses that were entirely at a distance, 1 a blended learning course, and 10 both categories. In total, the instructors mentioned having worked with three different VLEs (*i.e.*, Blackboard, Moodle, SIGAA), and Moodle was the most often cited one (by all the instructors). In regard to educational roles performed, most had experience as teacher or tutor (except I-06) and four of them reported experience as coordinator (I-04, I-06, I-09, I-17). Most of the instructors have a computing degree, and two other instructors have programming experience (I-03, I-18).

Table 3 shows an overview of the students' age and educational background provided by each instructor. Most of them had taught students between 18 and 50 or more years old. In particular, some instructors reported that their students had various educational backgrounds, without specifying them. However, like the instructors, most of the students had a computing background.

All of the instructors claimed to use some VLE communication resource (*i.e.*, chat, forum); most of them reported the use of videos (except I-06, I-09, I-10, I-11, I-18) and 7 mentioned they used e-books (I-02, I-04, I-04, I-11, I-12, I-13, I-16, I-20). They also mentioned other resources, such as text (I-05, I-15, I-19), audio recording (I-15), questionnaires (I-14, I-17), poll (I-19), badges (I-18), and wikis (I-19). Only one mentioned he/she oversaw student access (I-07). Nevertheless, when we asked how they monitor the students and what student data they analyze, most of the instructors reported student access (except I-01,

---

[4] In this paper, instructors are identified in the format I-99.

Table 2. Overview of the instructors' profiles.

I	Age	Gender	Scholarship area	VLEs	Using VLEs	Mode
I-01	45	M	Philosophy	Moodle	5 years	Both
I-02	52	F	Pedagogy	Moodle	6 years	Both
I-03	37	M	Geography	Moodle	6 months	Distance
I-04	35	F	Odontology	Moodle	10 years	Both
I-05	29	M	Computing	Moodle	18 months	Both
I-06	40	M	Computing	Moodle, SIGAA	2 years	Distance
I-07	35	M	Computing	Moodle	2 years	Distance
I-08	30	M	Computing	Moodle, Blackboard	4 years	Both
I-09	37	M	Computing	Moodle	9 years	Both
I-10	37	F	Computing	Moodle	1 year	Distance
I-11	28	M	Computing	Moodle	14 months	Distance
I-12	30	M	Computing	Moodle	9 months	Distance
I-13	42	F	Ind. Chemistry	Moodle	2 years	Distance
I-14	28	M	Law	Moodle	1 year	Distance
I-15	33	M	Computing	Moodle	9 years	Both
I-16	39	M	Computing	Moodle, SIGAA	5 years	Both
I-17	34	F	Physiotherapy	Moodle	5 years	Distance
I-18	29	M	Design	Moodle	1 year	Blended
I-19	46	F	Computing	Moodle	8 years	Both
I-20	31	M	Computing	Moodle	3 years	Distance
I-21	31	M	Computing	Moodle	2 years	Both

I-06, I-11, I-14, I-16, I-17, I-18, I-20). In addition, they also oversaw the student completion assignments (except I-02, I-06, I-07, I-14, I-16, I-18) and forum usage (except I-04, I-06, I-13, I-14, I-15, I-16, I-17, I-18, I-21).

We asked how the VLE log data are presented to the instructors. Most of them said through tables (I-02, I-04, I-07, I-08, I-11, I-13, I-19, I-21) and graphical means (I-02, I-03, I-04, I-07, I-08, I-10, I-11, I-13, I-15, I-20), such as Bar Chart (I-11, I-15, I-20), Histogram (I-10), Line Graph (I-07) and Pie Chart (I-02). Some instructors mentioned that the VLE shows reports (I-09, I-14, I-21) without specifying their presentation. In particular, I-06 said that the VLE does not show these data and I-17 claimed to use a resource called course progress (also without specifying the data presentation).

In regards the periodicity of reading and interpretation of charts, 6 instructors said to realize this activity more than once per week (I-01, I-05, I-06, I-11, I-15, I-16), 7 once per week (I-03, I-04, I-08, I-09, I-10, I-14, I-20), 3 once per month (I-13, I-17, I-21) and 5 seldom (I-02, I-07, I-12, I-18, I-19), whereas the periodicity of making charts was reported by 4 as once per week (I-03, I-08, I-10, I-11), 8 as once per month (I-01, I-04, I-05, I-06, I-09, I-13, I-16, I-20), 7 as seldom (I-02, I-14, I-15, I-17, I-18, I-19, I-21) and 2 as never (I-07, I-12).

Table 4 presents the questions grouped by VG that instructors take into account or would like to take. The questions related to VG-01 and VG-03 were the most chosen by them. Except for VG-06, at least one question of each VG

Table 3. Overview of the students' ages and educational background, per instructor.

I	Range of age	Scholarship area
I-01	23 to 65	Miscellaneous
I-02	18 to 60	Education and Health
I-03	30 to 55	Public administration
I-04	23 to 60	Health
I-05	18 to 50	Computing
I-06	18 to 60	Computing
I-07	18 to 28	Computing
I-08	25 to 60	Agronomy, Computing, Economy, Forest Engineer and Mathematics
I-09	13 to 45	Computing
I-10	18 to 50	Computing
I-11	20 to 30	Does not know
I-12	25 to 40	Computing
I-13	18 to 50	Agronomy, Business administration, Chemistry, Computing and Health
I-14	25 to 45	Miscellaneous
I-15	18 to 60	Computing
I-16	18 to 30	Computing and Health
I-17	25 to 60	Health
I-18	18 to 60	Miscellaneous
I-19	15 to 50	Computing
I-20	18 to 50	Business administration and Computing
I-21	22 to 60	Computing

was selected by most instructors. In other words, most instructors do not (or would not) take into account the correlation between students' age and their VLE interactions, even though they had said they taught students between 18 and 50 or more. We also ask what other questions they take into account and how they prefer that such questions be answered. In the first question, only three were mentioned: (i) why the students did not access the VLE, (ii) why the students did not meet the assignment deadline, and (iii) what the relation of both students grades and interaction in presential classroom is. In regard to the second question, almost all the instructors (except I-12, I-16, I-18, I-19) said through table (I-01, I-02, I-08, I-09, I-11, I-13, I-17, I-21) and graphical means (I-01, I-03, I-04, I-05, I-06, I-07, I-08, I-09, I-10, I-11, I-13, I-14, I-15, I-17, I-20, I-21), such as Bar Chart (I-01, I-07, I-11, I-13, I-14), Line Graph (I-07) and Pie Chart (I-15, I-21). I-16 and I-19 did not answer, I-12 said what he wants to see without specifying how and I-18 mentioned that he wants to receive by e-mail. Moreover, Table 4 shows the type of visualization most often selected by them. Most instructors chose Table (VG-02, VG-05, VG-06, VG-08, VG-11) or

452   A. L. de Brandão Damasceno et al.

Multi-set Bar Chart (VG-01, VG-03, VG-04, VG-10) as a way of data presentation. Only in the case of VG-07 (Scatterplot) and VG-09 (Stacked Area Graph) another way of data presentation was selected by most of them.

Figure 2 shows the instructors' evaluation of each VG chart. Only in 5 VGs (VG-02, VG-05, VG-08, VG-09, VG-10) the charts with the best evaluations are the same as the selected one. However, the other charts are among the 3 best evaluated. In line with the instructors' visualization preferences, data presented in Tables, Bar Chart, Multi-set Bar Chart, Stacked Bar Chart and Lollipop receive good evaluations, whereas the use of Bubble Chart, Flow Chart, Heatmap and Violin Plot received poor evaluations. In general, the charts used to show both data distribution and variation, Box & Whisker Plot received more good evaluations. Another interesting point is in all Heatmap charts with good evaluations had the corresponding data values presented in each cell.

Table 4. Overview of both the questions chosen and visualization style more selected by the instructors.

I	VG-01 Q-01	VG-01 Q-02	VG-02 Q-01	VG-02 Q-02	VG-03 Q-01	VG-04 Q-01	Q-01	Q-02	Q-03	Q-04	VG-05 Q-05	Q-06	Q-07	Q-01	Q-02	VG-06 Q-03	Q-04	Q-05	VG-07 Q-01	VG-08 Q-01	VG-08 Q-02	VG-09 Q-01	VG-10 Q-01	VG-11 Q-01
I-01																								
I-02																								
I-03																								
I-04																								
I-05																								
I-06																								
I-07																								
I-08																								
I-09																								
I-10																								
I-11																								
I-12																								
I-13																								
I-14																								
I-15																								
I-16																								
I-17																								
I-18																								
I-19																								
I-20																								
I-21																								
Total	20	17	14	15	17	14	11	15	13	13	12	13	6	5	5	8	8	7	13	8	15	12	11	16
Selected	j		a		b	h				a						a				b	a	c	k	a

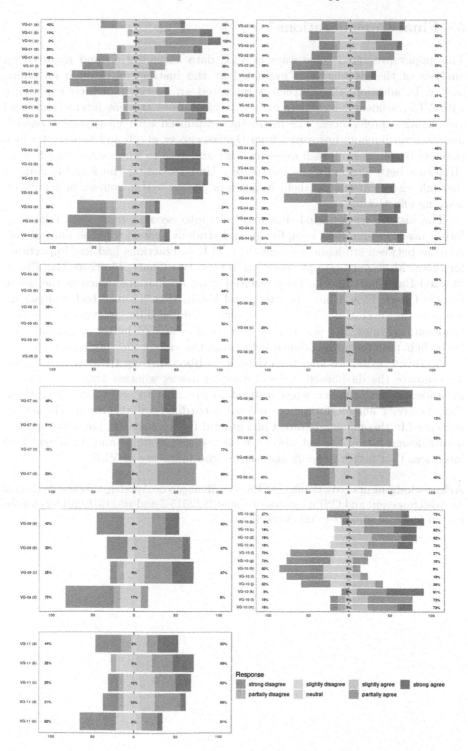

Fig. 2. Results of the evaluation of each group of visualizations.

5   Final Considerations

This paper presented some ways of VLE data visualization and reported an analysis of the visualizations evaluated by the instructors through an online survey. In addition, the instructors presented an overview of their experience with VLE, students, how they make analyses about student interactions, and visualization preferences. The instructors evaluated each visualization regarding the requirements uncovered from Damasceno et al. [3] and to report which chart(s) better answer each question. Our aim was to understand which visualizations better support the instructors. Understanding the learning process through visualizations can help instructors design better courses and improve learning effectiveness.

The instructors reported that they take into account more data related to forum usage, assignment completion, and student access, whereas data of correlation between students' age and their VLE interactions had less importance for them. Moreover, data presented in Tables, Bar Chart, Multi-set Bar Chart, Stacked Bar Chart and Lollipop received good evaluations, whereas the use of Bubble Chart, Flow Chart, Heatmap and Violin Plot received bad evaluations. We note that even though instructors were presented different types of the visualization, the ones they selected the most and evaluated better are in line with both their preferences mentioned before and the charts they already used.

As future work, we plan to develop a dashboard using those visualizations. To evaluate the dashboard, we will want to assess whether there are changes in students' performance when instructors are able to see information about their behavior and performance, and act accordingly. Furthermore, the results presented in this paper can direct and ground future research, not only on dashboard design for VLEs, but also on recommender systems and intelligent user interfaces that better support instructors who make use of VLEs.

Acknowledgments. We thank CAPES, Coordenação de Aperfeiçoamento de Pessoal de Nível Superior, and CNPq (processes #309828/2015-5 and #311316/2018-2) for the partial financial support to this work.

Appendix: Visualizations used in each VG

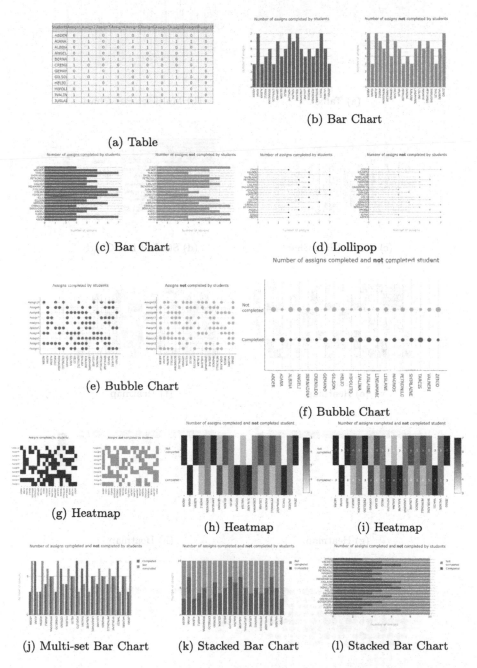

Fig. 3. Sample of visualizations used in VG-01 question: "Which students completed the assignments?"

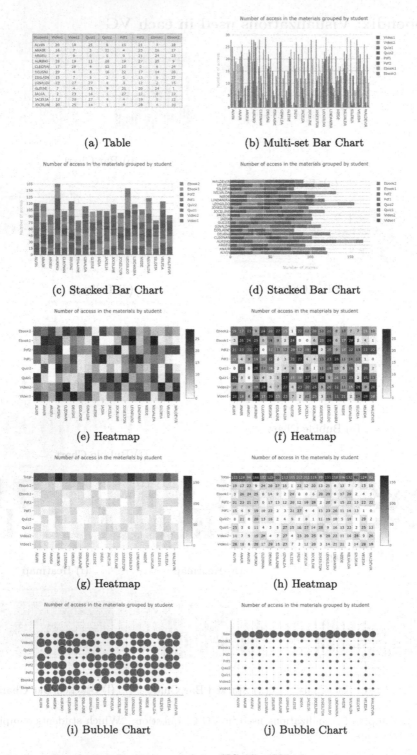

(a) Table

(b) Multi-set Bar Chart

(c) Stacked Bar Chart

(d) Stacked Bar Chart

(e) Heatmap

(f) Heatmap

(g) Heatmap

(h) Heatmap

(i) Bubble Chart

(j) Bubble Chart

Fig. 4. Sample of visualizations used in VG-02: "Which students accessed the materials?"

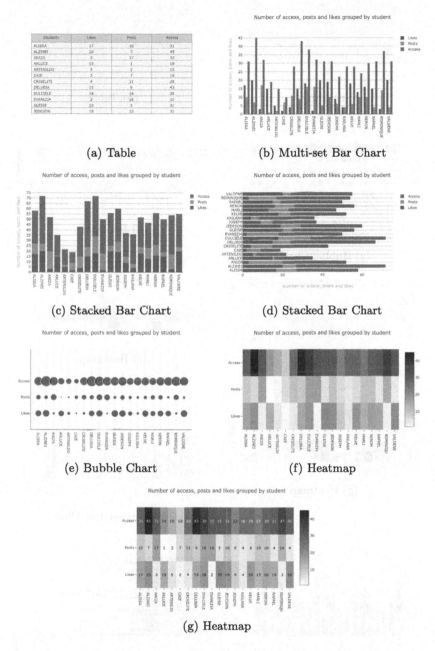

Fig. 5. Sample of visualizations used in VG-03: "How many student accesses, posts, and likes were there?"

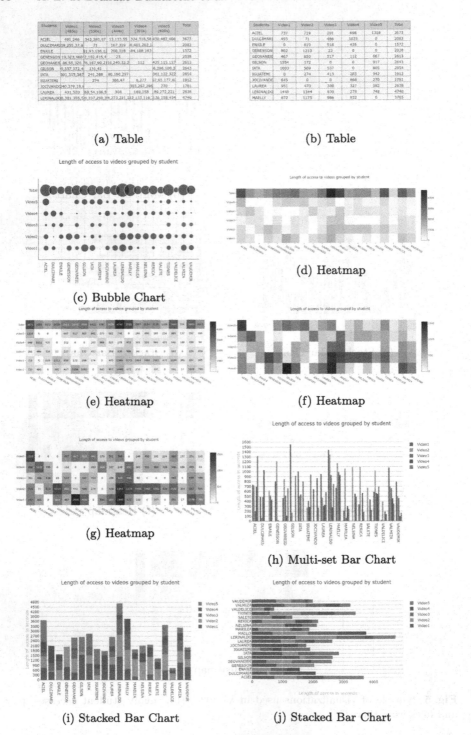

Fig. 6. Sample of visualizations used in VG-04: "For how long did the students watch each video?"

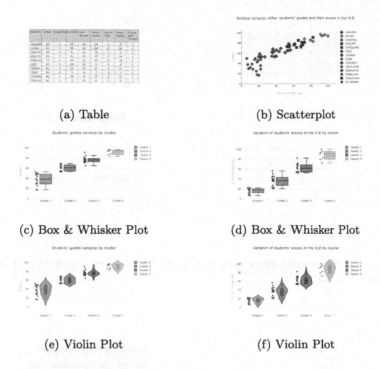

(a) Table

(b) Scatterplot

(c) Box & Whisker Plot

(d) Box & Whisker Plot

(e) Violin Plot

(f) Violin Plot

Fig. 7. Sample of visualizations used in VG-05: "What is the relation between students' grades and VLE access?"

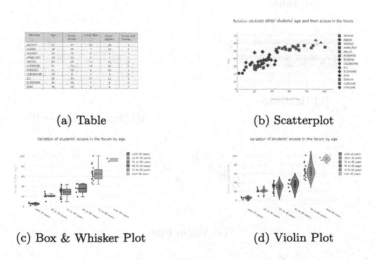

(a) Table

(b) Scatterplot

(c) Box & Whisker Plot

(d) Violin Plot

Fig. 8. Sample of visualizations used in VG-06: "What is the relation between students' age and forum access?"

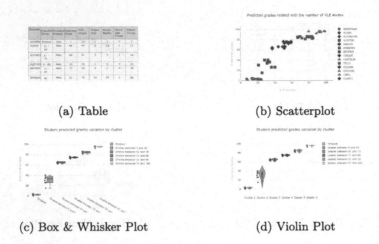

(a) Table

(b) Scatterplot

(c) Box & Whisker Plot

(d) Violin Plot

Fig. 9. Sample of visualizations used in VG-07: "What is the prediction of students' grades and dropout?"

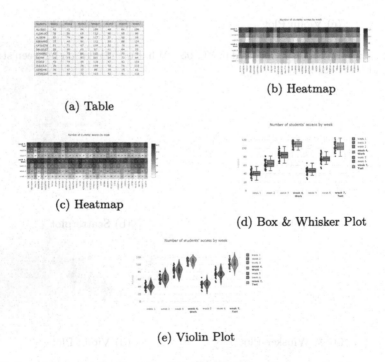

(a) Table

(b) Heatmap

(c) Heatmap

(d) Box & Whisker Plot

(e) Violin Plot

Fig. 10. Sample of visualizations used in VG-08: "How many students' accesses were there per week?"

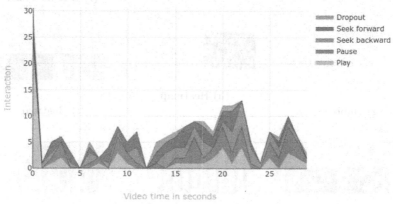

(a) Table   (b) Table

Number of interaction by video time

(c) Stacked Area Graph

Interactions of seek forward and seek backward by time

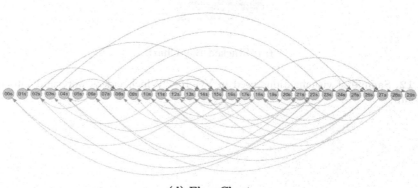

(d) Flow Chart

Fig. 11. Sample of visualizations used in VG-09: "What are the statistics of interactions with video (e.g. play, pause, seek)?"

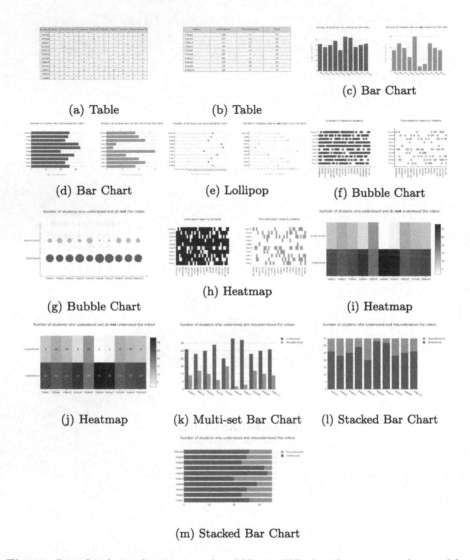

(a) Table

(b) Table

(c) Bar Chart

(d) Bar Chart

(e) Lollipop

(f) Bubble Chart

(g) Bubble Chart

(h) Heatmap

(i) Heatmap

(j) Heatmap

(k) Multi-set Bar Chart

(l) Stacked Bar Chart

(m) Stacked Bar Chart

Fig. 12. Sample of visualizations used in VG-10: "Which videos were understood by students?"

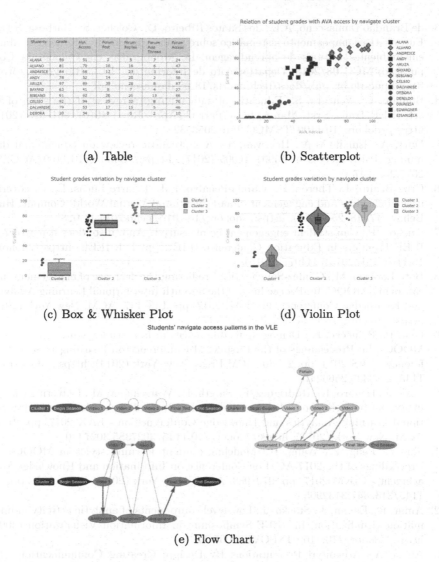

(a) Table

(b) Scatterplot

(c) Box & Whisker Plot

(d) Violin Plot

(e) Flow Chart

Fig. 13. Sample of visualizations used in VG-11: "What were the students' navigation patterns on the VLE?"

References

1. Saraiva, T.: Educação a distância no Brasil: lições da história. Em Aberto **16**(70), 17–27 (1996). http://emaberto.inep.gov.br/index.php/emaberto/article/view/2076
2. Seaton, D.T., Bergner, Y., Chuang, I., Mitros, P., Pritchard, D.E.: Who does what in a massive open online course? Commun. ACM **57**(4), 58–65 (2014). https://doi.org/10.1145/2500876

3. de Brandão Damasceno, A.L., dos Santos Ribeiro, D., Colcher, S., Barbosa, S.D.J.: Entrevistas e mapeamento sistemático sobre análise de logs de interação de alunos em ambientes virtuais de aprendizagem. In: Monografias em Ciência da Computação, MCC 08/2018, Departamento de Informática, PUC-Rio (2018). ftp://ftp.inf.puc-rio.br/pub/docs/techreports/18_08_damasceno.pdf
4. Romero, C., Ventura, S.: Educational data mining: a review of the state of the art. IEEE Trans. Syst. Man Cybern. Part C (Appl. Rev.) 40(6), 601–618 (2010). https://doi.org/10.1109/TSMCC.2010.2053532
5. Dutt, A., Ismail, M.A., Herawan, T.: A systematic review on educational data mining. IEEE Access 5, 15991–16005 (2017). https://doi.org/10.1109/ACCESS.2017.2654247
6. Cruz-Benito, J., Therón, R., García-Peñalvo, F.J., Pizarro Lucas, E.: Discovering usage behaviors and engagement in an Educational Virtual World. Comput. Hum. Behav. 47, 18–25 (2015). https://doi.org/10.1016/j.chb.2014.11.028
7. Samson, P.: Can student engagement be measured? And, if so, does it matter? In: IEEE Frontiers in Education Conference (FIE), pp. 1–4. IEEE. https://doi.org/10.1109/FIE.2015.7344077 (2015)
8. Bote-Lorenzo, M., Gómez-Sánchez, E.: Predicting the decrease of engagement indicators in a MOOC. In: Proceedings of the Seventh International Learning Analytics and Knowledge Conference on - LAK 2017, pp. 143–147. ACM, New York (2017). https://doi.org/10.1145/3027385.3027387
9. Guo, P., Reinecke, K.: Demographic differences in how students navigate through MOOCs. In: Proceedings of the First ACM Conference on Learning @ Scale Conference - L@S 2014, pp. 21–30. ACM Press, New York (2014). https://doi.org/10.1145/2556325.2566247
10. Park, J., Denaro, K., Rodriguez, F., Smyth, P., Warschauer, M.: Detecting changes in student behavior from clickstream data. In: Proceedings of the Seventh International Learning Analytics and Knowledge Conference on - LAK 2017, pp. 21–30. ACM, New York (2017). https://doi.org/10.1145/3027385.3027430
11. Shi, Y., Peng, Z., Wang, H.: Modeling student learning styles in MOOCs. In: Proceedings of the 2017 ACM on Conference on Information and Knowledge Management - CIKM 2017, pp. 979–988. ACM, New York (2017). https://doi.org/10.1145/3132847.3132965
12. Amar, R., Eagan, J., Stasko, J.: Low-level components of analytic activity in information visualization. In: IEEE Symposium on Information Visualization (2005). https://doi.org/10.1109/INFOVIS.2005.24
13. Abela, A.: Advanced Presentations By Design: Creating Communication That Drives Action. Wiley, Hoboken (2008)
14. Kirk, A.: Data Visualization: A Successful Design Process. Packt Publishing Ltd., Birmingham (2012)
15. Munzner, T.: Visualization Analysis and Design. CRC Press, Boca Raton (2014)
16. Cox, K., Grinter, R.E., Hibino, S.L., Jagadeesan, L.J., Mantilla, D.: A multi-modal natural language interface to an information visualization environment. Int. J. Speech Technol. 4(3), 297–314 (2001). https://doi.org/10.1023/A:1011368926479

A Place to Discover, Imagine, and Change: Smart Learning with Local Places

Dalit Levy[1], Yuval Shafriri[2(✉)], and Yael Alef[3]

[1] Zefat Academic College, Community Information Systems, Zefat, Israel
dalitl@zefat.ac.il
[2] Tel Aviv University, Tel Aviv, Israel
yuval.shafriri@gmail.com
[3] Bar Ilan University, Ramat Gan, Israel
yaelalef@gmail.com

Abstract. Following the results of a study focusing on the unique affordances of mobile technologies that support their informed integration in learning, a novel pedagogical model has been developed. This model was tried out within the context of geography and cultural heritage in four different cases. The first part of this paper briefly presents the main findings of the study and sketches the emergent uniqueness profile of mobile apps for learning. The second and main part outlines the DICE model (Discover, Imagine, ChangE) that was developed for designing place-based learning activities with the assistance of mobile apps, and presents its main characteristics through data gathered from the four cases. Through participating in DICE activities, learners uncover the invisible in familiar places and become more aware of their surroundings, while the place becomes a powerful object to learn with.

Keywords: Blended spaces · Environmental knowledge · Mobile learning · Place-based learning

1 Introduction

The concept of 'place' is known to be simple and complicated at the same time, while "no-one quite knows what they are talking about when they are talking about place" [1, p. 1]. According to one definition, a place is a meaningful location. This definition encompasses the engagement of people with placemaking and the human need for a 'sense of place' [1, 2]. The consolidation of the web, the mobile and locative media [3], and the internet of smart things (IOT) [4], opened new possibilities of interaction between the individual, her or his community, and their places of living, working, and visiting. Technologies such as mobile field survey, AR, location-based games and digital objects embedded in the place, enable strengthening the attachment to the place for both individuals and communities. Such technologies help in making places and their values more accessible while creating new formal and informal learning opportunities [5, 6]. As a result, the processes of giving meaning to places have also changed. These processes not only document and teach about the place in which the community operates, but also act and interact within the place. The variety of interactions might

© Springer Nature Switzerland AG 2019
M. Antona and C. Stephanidis (Eds.): HCII 2019, LNCS 11572, pp. 465–480, 2019.
https://doi.org/10.1007/978-3-030-23560-4_34

change both the relations with the place and the meaning given to it, in addition to actual changes (physical and digital) in the environment. The paper discusses these new possibilities through the pedagogical lens of "Discover, Imagine, Change" abbreviated as DICE. This is an educational process formulated as an implication of a recent study on the uniqueness profile of educational mobile applications [7].

The educational use of mobile applications is thought to have significant learning potential. Smartphones are already massively embedded in daily life but integrating mobile technologies within learning environments is a complex and challenging mission which requires innovative pedagogical thinking and strategic changes, beyond merely implementing e-learning methods with the aid of mobile devices. In recent years, much research has been conducted on the integration of mobile apps into educational settings [8, 9]. However, the task of identifying the unique features and affordances of mobile technologies has been a complex one [10]. The research from which DICE has emerged sought to focus solely on learning processes and outcomes that are possible only when using mobile apps, and to identify their unique and exclusive affordances. Within this framework, a unique educational mobile application has been defined as an application that has learning affordances attributed exclusively to mobile devices and apps, with benefits that are unattainable in outdoor learning environments, when no digital technologies are involved. As Fig. 1 suggests, the term MUC has been used to label such a unique mobile app.

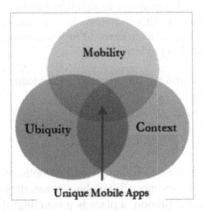

Fig. 1. MUCs - unique mobile apps selected for the study

While both the "M" (mobility) and the "U" (ubiquity) imply independent learning anytime and anywhere, the "C" (context) suggests some dependency on the decisions and actions of the instructional designer and the learner. The distinctiveness of MUCs thus lies in their ability to be deployed at any time and in any location, while nevertheless being sensitive to the context - the environment, the user, and the learning activity. This combination is what makes mobile apps unique for learning purposes.

The next section of this paper sketches the analytic process conducted as part of a study of more than two hundred mobile applications for learning, focusing on selected MUCs. The third section outlines the DICE idea - a novel pedagogy based on collaborative mobile and place-based learning using MUCs, developed and tried out in four different communities of learners in Israel. Through participation in such mobile-enhanced activities, learners not only discover the place they live in but might also contribute to its change. Section 4 discusses the lessons learned from implementing the DICE model in these four cases. The last section summarizes the significant educational values of the model and concludes that learners can develop a deeper understanding of their environment as an outcome of the *Discover → Imagine → ChangE* process.

2 Constructing the Uniqueness Profile of MUCs

When discussing and studying mobile learning [11], three types of affordances are often mixed: (1) affordances attributed to non-mobile desktop applications, including complex design systems such as AutoCAD; (2) universal applications operating both on non-mobile and mobile computing devices, thus available anywhere and anytime; and (3) affordances attributed exclusively to mobile apps. While many studies focus on learning with mobile applications as part of using a broader technology-enhanced learning toolbox, the study briefly presented in this section sought to focus solely on those learning processes and learning outcomes that are made possible only when using mobile apps and to identify those unique and exclusive affordances.

The analytic process was conducted as part of a more extensive study of more than two hundred mobile applications for learning [7]. Most of these apps have been available for free use by any teacher or learner, on any conventional mobile device, and did not require special hardware or external gadgets. Two research questions directed the study: first, what makes mobile apps unique for educational purposes? And second, what are the unique affordances of mobile technologies that support their informed integration in learning environments? The gradual qualitative analytic process began in 2015 and resulted in five emergent themes of uniqueness of mobile apps, organized into three levels, as is shown in Fig. 2.

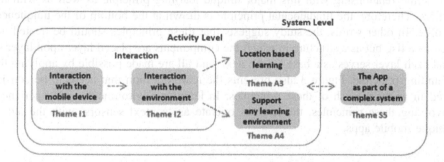

Fig. 2. The emergent categorical system

Common to these emergent categories is the experience of learning in blended spaces [12, 13]. This primary pedagogical principle led to additional principles such as embodied cognition, the device as a discovery machine, and open playful design.

Taken together, these principles draw a uniqueness profile for MUCs that supports system thinking and deep understanding of the environment in which the unique mobile app is used. The emergent profile of uniqueness encircling these principles is drawn in Fig. 3.

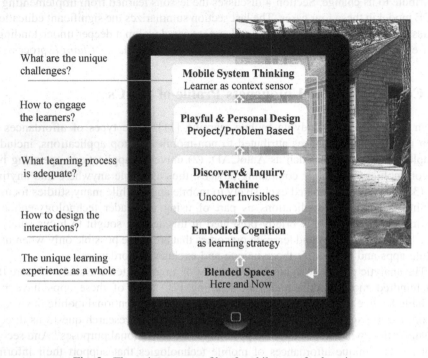

What are the unique challenges?

Mobile System Thinking
Learner as context sensor

How to engage the learners?

Playful & Personal Design
Project/Problem Based

What learning process is adequate?

Discovery& Inquiry
Machine
Uncover Invisibles

How to design the interactions?

Embodied Cognition
as learning strategy

The unique learning experience as a whole

Blended Spaces
Here and Now

Fig. 3. The uniqueness profile of mobile apps for learning

According to the results of the study, the overall uniqueness profile stems from the fundamental principle Blended Space – *Here and Now*, while each additional principle has some relationship with this major unique learning principle as well as with the others. Therefore, the fundamental principle is drawn at the bottom of the uniqueness profile. In other words, the study suggests that these principles should be treated not just as a list, but as a structure in which the components are placed layer upon layer so that each layer serves as a base for the next, and all are made possible by applying the founding principle. Figure 3 also presents the main question that needs to be considered in applying each of these principles. In learning environments and experiences involving these principles, the learners operate as 'context sensors' with the aid of unique mobile apps.

3   DICE: Smart Learning with Local Places

The uniqueness profile facilitates the use of the pedagogical principles for a deep understanding of the environment and promotes new literacy of mobile system thinking. To enable such use, mobile place-based learning activities should integrate innovative technologies and pedagogies that allow the learners to perform as a "context sensor" of their environment [14, 15]. This section outlines DICE (*Discover, Imagine, ChangE*) as a novel pedagogy for dealing with such integration.

The proposed model serves as an implementation of place-based learning with the assistance of mobile and other 'smart' technologies [5]. It aims to use the uniqueness profile [7] in such a way that the student becomes more aware of the surrounding while the place becomes a powerful or 'smart' object to learn with.

The pedagogical process includes elements of mobile inquiry and discovery, mapping and documentation using locative media, location-based games, and knowledge sharing. These elements are based on the results of the research presented in Sect. 2 and on the uniqueness profile of mobile applications for learning (Fig. 3). As will be exemplified in the following four cases (Subsects. 3.1–3.4), the DICE model can be implemented in diverse communities considering their unique cultural heritage and places, taking into account specific needs and local themes.

The DICE pedagogical model involves three components or learning phases; each answers a different question.

1. *Discover*: *What was here, and what is here now?*
   Activities at this phase include inquiry into the place ontology - its past, and its present. Such activities enable learners to reveal and express the unique "sense of the place" [2], and to document, map and share knowledge and findings. This component can be implemented as a standalone learning activity and might incorporate a field survey using mobile inquiry apps and archeological, historical or environmental survey.
2. *Imagine*: *What might be done here in the future?*
   Learners are asked to think creatively about the future of the place and to make suggestions for future communal projects and interventions, based on the knowledge they created in the first phase.
3. *Change*: *How to intervene in the place?*
   This phase refers to physical "placemaking" projects as well as virtual interventions, as an implementation of the designs from the *Imagine* phase. The *Change* might be in the form of increased public awareness or/and improved accessibility to the place. Such changes are also a result of sharing information and knowledge at the *Discover* phase.

The DICE model has been developed and tried out within geographical and cultural heritage context in four different communities of learners in Israel. In two of them, the activity was connected to an ongoing conservation project. The activities took place in rural and urban settings, with learners' age ranging from sixth graders to students in academic project-based courses. The rest of this section details these four case studies.

3.1   DICE as Part of the Excavation of an Ancient Galilean Synagogue

The first case tells the story of implementing the DICE pedagogical model by an elementary school in the Galilean community of Yesod Hama'ala, in collaboration with the Israel Antiquities Authority. The project was part of the excavation and conservation of the ancient synagogue and Crusaders sugar factory remains found near the village of Yesod Hama'ala. The school children and teachers participated in the excavation during three successive years (2016–2018).

During the first year, in addition to the excavation, the children also explored the historic part of their village that was established in the 19th century. The exploration was done as a mobile inquiry activity using a dedicated mobile app (Fig. 4b). In this *Discover* first phase of the DICE model, the learners surveyed historic houses and courtyards in the village, with the help of the house owners. Their task was to search and document the locations and properties of historic artifacts and antiquities that can serve as evidence for different periods at the village. The result was an online map of the artifacts that the children shared with the community (Fig. 4a). Then, they continued to study the artifacts and used them to design a 'treasure hunt' game for and with the broader village's community.

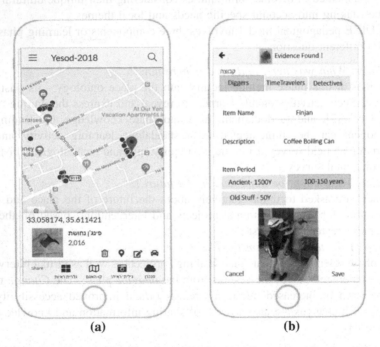

(a)   (b)

Fig. 4. (a) The shared artifacts map. (b) The mobile app used for the survey

Following the first DICE phase, the elementary school students were also engaged in the second *Imagine* phase when the thought about future archaeologists visiting their village. They decided to prepare a time capsule for these future visitors and explorers. The capsule consists of personal seals the children prepared, as well as a memory stick with the artifact's pictures and description from the survey. The children buried the time-capsule in the archaeological site (see Fig. 5c), thus contributed to a minor but meaningful *Change* of their place.

The second year of the project was centered around the idea of a placemaking design process, in the archaeological site. The first *Discover* phase included mobile inquiry of the immediate surrounding of the ancient site they excavated previously, where they searched for evidence of the lost Hula lake that was drained seven decades ago. The children also documented their impressions from the site's 'sense of place' [1, 2].

Then, as part of the Imagine phase, they were asked to envision the site in the future and to design their intervention to conserve and develop the site for the benefit of the community. Finally, one proposal from the Imagine phase was implemented as part of the last Change phase: an original seating area was constructed onsite (Fig. 5d). At that seating area, the children embedded a small digital object that refers to a website detailing the story of the site and the project.

Fig. 5. (a) Example from the *discovery* phase: documenting artifacts. (b) Example from the *Imagine* phase: planning a sculptures garden. (c) Example from the *Change* phase: burying the time capsule. (d) Example from the *Change* phase: construction of the sitting area

As is illustrated in the details of the Yesod HaMa'ala case, the principle of using mobile apps as an inquiry and discovery machine plays a key role within the DICE model. The principle was implemented through an open and playful learning activity, of reviling and mapping local pieces of evidence of the history of the village (Fig. 5a). The children were enthusiastic about the mobile inquiry, the immediate "here and now" results on the online map, and the ability to share their discoveries with the community.

Another implication regards the power of imagination in the learning process. The second *Imagine* phase of the DICE model has proved to serve as a powerful trigger for students' engagement with the project (Fig. 5b). They approached it with fun and intrinsic motivation, probably due to both their involvement with the place in the previous *Discover* phase and the opportunity to express their ideas and influence their environment in later phases.

The Yesod HaMa'ala case also raises the issue of the complexity of making physical changes in a place. A physical change has a significant educational value, but at the same time, it also has some practical and administrative limitations. One recommendation to consider is therefore to involve virtual changes such as mobile geocaching, Google 360° documentation, and mapping of a place in creating the change within a blended space [12]. Indeed, throughout the different DICE phases in this case, we noted the relevance of the fundamental principle of blended. For example, a group of children proposed to create an augmented reality gaming activity with IOT objects for visitors in the archaeological site. Such ideas might reflect that young learners nowadays experience blended spaces as part of their culture.

3.2   DICE in a Community College: Making Peripheral Places More Accessible

The second case is related to a short-term project that took place as part of a social media course in the CIS department (Community Information Systems) at Zefat Academic College. The college is located in the northern periphery of Israel, in the heart of the ancient city of Zefat. The city is one of the most important historic cities in Israel with unique cultural significance. However, it lacks documentation, and many of its sites are neglected and deteriorating. The CIS program seeks to prepare and grow local Information Systems workforce by advancing understanding of computing, design, HCI, digital culture, entrepreneurship and other subjects regarded as critical to developing the needed workforce for the 21st century. Since mobile system thinking is regarded as one of these essential skills, it seemed valuable to implement the DICE model with CIS students.

The academic project focused on the first and the last components of the DICE model. During the *Discover* phase, students were asked to select a special place in the college area[1] or elsewhere in the Galilee and to document it using the Google 360° mobile app. A collaborative shared map containing all of the students' contributions has been constructed, updated and distributed within the college (Fig. 6 brings a partial map of the chosen places). A *Change* activity was also implemented using Geocaching - hide and seek. A cache was hidden in the Crusader citadel of Zefat[2], adjacent to the college, and was followed by a cache seeking gaming activity with the students. The cache became available for the public to discover, imagine, and change as well.

In addition to the principle of using mobile apps as a discovery machine, the Zefat case highlights the unique principle of Embodied Cognition (see Fig. 3 above). That principle was implemented through the physical actions needed for a successful recording of a panoramic picture of the place using the mobile app. For creating an

---

[1] See a link to the college's library on Google Street View, created by one of the CIS students https://goo.gl/maps/g4r5qw9KFCA2.

[2] The Zefat Citadel geocache: https://www.geocaching.com/geocache/GC7FQZG.

impressive and accurate 360° panoramic object, the creator must be fully aware of the details of his or her surroundings, while turning around slowly. Such use raises students' awareness of environmental elements as well as to their physical presence within the frame. Furthermore, when a 360° panoramic object is recorded and uploaded successfully, it can make a real contribution to the accessibility of unique and remote places. In some of the remote places documented by the college students, their contribution was the only 360° street view documentation on Google map in the area. As a result of such authentic acts of crowdsourcing, the visibility of those sites has been raised, and the accessibility to peripheral locations has been improved. One example is the Circassian village of Rihaniya shown in the center of the map in Fig. 6. The panoramic view of a place at the historic center of Rihaniya was chosen and recorded by a student living in that village. As it turned out, it has been the first and only documentation of that place in Google Maps[3] since the villages in this remote area were not documented by Google except for the main roads.

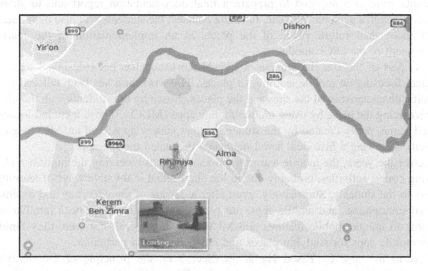

Fig. 6. Changing the online map of Rihaniya

The Zefat case also demonstrates Geocache as IOT placemaking. The *Change* component of the DICE model, in this case, has been mostly viable through non-physical terms such as increased awareness and accessibility to the place. However, the experience of Geocaching also contributes to a small physical change, that requires mobile system thinking, and environmental awareness. Interestingly, even after the DICE implementation has ended, the Department of Community Information Systems took responsibility for maintaining the cache in its area. This has also an educational value related to the department's goals.

---

[3] The Rihaniya historic center on street view: https://goo.gl/maps/nPEbWQ2Rvst.

3.3   DICE as Part of the 'IT Applications for Studying a Place' Course and the 'Uncovering the Invisible in the Familiar' Effect

Both the third and the fourth cases were carried out at the Department of Geography and Environment at Bar-Ilan University. The university is located in Ramat Gan, a city adjacent to Tel Aviv, within the largest metropolitan area of Israel.

The BA course titled "IT applications for studying a place" has been offered by the Department of Geography and Environment for the last couple of years, using project-based learning (PBL) approach. Recently, the DICE model has been integrated within the course, when students have been requested to select a place according to their interests and to conduct an inquiry in and about the place throughout several *Discover* activities. Those included exploring the 'sense of the place' as well as engaging in historical and geographic documentation, collecting field data and mobile mapping. Like in the Zefat case described in Sect. 3.2, each Bar-Ilan student recorded a 360° panorama of his or her selected place and uploaded it into Google Street View. The students were also required to prepare a final documentation report and to share it online through a personal web site. In future courses, the students will also be requested to propose their future vision of the place, as an implementation of the *Imagine* component of the DICE model.

As part of the Bar-Ilan course, a special workshop has been designed and conducted, focusing on mobile learning of places. The workshop has been tailored to the specific characteristics of the sites and the places chosen by the students with the aim of experiencing the place by using unique mobile apps (MUCs). Those included location-based game, partly created by the students; street survey apps; and an AR navigation activity following a historical aerial map on a dedicated mobile app.

Over the years, the mobile learning workshop keeps receiving the highest ranking among course activities, probably due to the playful and innovative ways of learning it offers to the students. Surprisingly, even after a decade of the everyday and extensive use of smartphones and mobile apps, our typical students have not been familiar with regards to unique mobile features and MUC apps in general, nor were they familiar with mobile apps for studying places and environments in particular.

As in the case of Yesod Hama'ala (Sect. 3.1), the principle of the discovery machine played a key role in the current case. Even when the students were familiar with the place, they often revealed new and unexpected features of it. The discovery phase was assisted by 'here and now' blended-space objects such as AR historical maps. This blended-spaces experience brought about curiosity to gain a deeper understanding of the place. The excitement of re-discovering has been noticed in students' feedback when they described how surprised they were to find out new and meaningful characteristics of familiar places they thought they had known well. Therefore, we suggest naming this effect "uncovering of the invisible in the familiar". Students also testified that the mobile inquiry helped in strengthening their attachment to their studied place. For some of Bar-Ilan Geography students, it even served as a trigger for further independent exploration (after the course itself has ended). Therefore, the *Discovery* phase of the DICE model might have a lasting effect on lifelong learning of places and environments.

3.4   DICE in the Context of the Old City of Jaffa Conservation Survey

The last case is also a project-based learning course offered at the Department of Geography and Environment at Bar-Ilan University. This MA course is a part of the program for Preservation and Development of Landscape and Cultural Assets. The students, guided by professionals in the field, conduct an urban conservation survey in an area under planning processes. In the *Discover* phase, students survey the area, collect data and produce a report with the findings. In the *Imagine* phase, the students are asked to propose suggestions for a conservation plan. The report is made available to local authorities, and in some cases, it might inform their conservation plan, and thus might have an actual effect on the *Change* of the place.

The focus of the 2018 survey has been on the northern slopes of the Old City of Jaffa. The students recorded and mapped hidden historical elements in the area, through a dedicated *Discover* mobile app. The app enabled the students to locate themselves on historic aerial maps, to record the historic elements they discovered, and to locate them on the map. In Fig. 7 below, the app interface is displayed, showing the mapping of remains found by the students together with a picture of one student standing in the present location where according to the 1936 aerial map the small 'Hammam' (a Turkish bath) used to be.

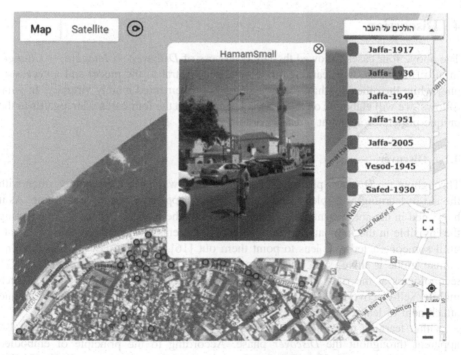

Fig. 7. Using a mobile app for multilayered mapping of remains in a conservation survey

The "uncovering the invisible in the familiar" effect has been particularly evident in the Jaffa survey, because of the multi-layered complex nature of its heritage. In the survey area, the historic buildings were destroyed, and in later years a garden was planted over the rubbles. The garden today is very popular among locals and is well known to tourists. Although the MA students were familiar with it too, they were surprised to discover that the historical remains in the garden which they never noticed before. Until they were required to be engaged in a *Discover* mobile inquiry activity, those remains, and some other parts of the Old City's past, were transparent to the students. In that sense, the unique mobile app together with the DICE learning activities might contribute to discovering such a multi-layered place, incorporating various and conflicting narratives that are not easily accessible to the typical visitor.

The Jaffa case also serves as an example for dissolving boundaries between the classroom and the world, which is one of the main implications of the uniqueness profile described previously [7, 16, 19]. The area is undergoing re-evaluation for planning, and the mobile inquiry app allows to document and share the survey findings. Such digital mapping also serves as a reference point to the *Imagine* phase in the course and the *Change* phase that takes place in the authentic planning process, outside the framework of the student's project. In this case, the *Change* component has a relatively high potential.

4 Discussion

The above four cases followed the DICE process of *Discover* → *Imagine* → *Change*. In all of them, the first learning phase has been central to the model and a necessary one, while the other two have been sometimes implemented mainly virtually. In what follows, we will elaborate on the lessons learned from the four cases with regards to the unique principles apparent in each learning phase.

4.1 Discover

Throughout the *Discover* phase learners come to know the place they study, often with the aid of learning principles such as using mobile apps as a discovery machine. As it happened in the abovementioned cases, this creates the powerful effect of "uncovering the invisible in the familiar", while transparent elements had been invisible in the site until someone acted as a lens to point them out [16]. In many cases, when there no human guide is there, such uncovering can only be achieved using mobile or IOT technologies at the right time and in the right place. The immediate effect of such mobile self-discoveries is of primary importance in creating the connection and attachment of learners to the place.

Other learning principles contained in the uniqueness profile of MUCs were also apparent throughout the *Discover* phase. According to the principle of embodied cognition, the understanding of a place is constructed through the experience of being in it and moving around it [17]. The ability to place and show local findings from the site on an online map also contributes to creating a blended space experience. Naturally, open and playful learning design has also been used in the *Discover* activities.

The *Discover* component serves as a basis for the other two components. Its outcomes activate the imagination by connecting the question of "what was/is here" of the first phase to the question of "what can be here in the future" of the second phase. At the same time, the findings from the inquiry constitute the understanding of the characteristics of the place as a basis for the *Change* phase.

4.2   Imagine

The rationale for the *Imagine* component of DICE derives both from architectural design practices and from constructionist approaches for learning by design [18].

In the abovementioned case studies, the *Imagine* component played an essential role in motivating the learners while the question "what can be here in the future" led to unlimited directions and ideas. For example, while one team in Yesod HaMa'ala built a model for an ancient playground, another proposed an outdoor art gallery. Other idea suggested a kinetic sculpture operated by actual visitors or from afar, using IOT-enhances placemaking. The outcome of the imagination phase depends mainly on the discovery findings and the instructions for the *Change* component. Knowing that the proposed designs might have a real impact on a place has been both challenging and motivating, allowing for an authentic yet creative process.

In the *Imagine* phase, the use of mobile applications has not been as significant as in the *Discover* phase. However, design applications, or VR applications of an existing place with the addition of VR/AR imaginary 3D elements to it[4], can indeed be used to spark the imagination further. Furthermore, mobile apps for collaborative idea sharing and the use of the 'wisdom of the crowd' using social media apps might have additional potential for the *Imagine* phase.

4.3   Change

The component of *Change* in DICE comes in different modes, from a physical intervention at the end of the design process to a change in public awareness. *Change* can also be in the form of creating virtual access to a remote location, or access to place-based information "here and now" for visitors on site.

Listed below are the different modes of *Change* in the place and in its context that were identified in the abovementioned case studies.

1. Physical intervention in the site can be implemented using a placemaking approach at the end of DICE's overall process. Making a physical change can be complicated as it naturally depends on various constraints, but it is recommended to include even a small portion of physical change due to its high educational value.
2. A proposal for a physical change in a place. Even without an actual intervention, the proposal in itself might be significant both in its contribution to the community and in deepening the learners' understanding of the place. For example, in the case of Bar-Ilan conservation survey, the actual *Change* was not a part of the course

---

[4] Platform for creating AR/VR objects linked to real places: https://edu.cospaces.io/Studio.

framework, but it did inform the local authorities in their actual planning for the Jaffa garden on the slope.

3. Creating blended space objects that connect a virtual domain to a physical one. For example, *Change* can be achieved by adding a physical geocache onsite or by burying a time capsule that relates to the findings from the *Discover* phase. Hiding a geocache requires real-world considerations, such as the knowledge about the local population, social norms and the values of the place. Being aware of such considerations has by itself a significant educational value.

4. Virtual change of the place's accessibility and meaning. For example, by documenting and mapping interesting elements on an online map during the mobile inquiry, and by sharing the online map with the broader community through social media channels, the place is made more accessible, visible, and familiar. Although virtual, such change impacts the meaning of the place for the learners as well as for the wider community.

5   Conclusions

The Uniqueness Profile (Fig. 3) suggests that mobile devices and apps might serve as the context sensors of a discovery machine in different environments and places, enabling embodied cognition interactions through sensory affordances like AR, GPS or 360° panoramas. MUC apps and learning activities also enable constructing smart blended space artifacts in context, documenting sensations, and sharing it between near and distant actors in an open and playful approach.

As part of the overall DICE pedagogical model described in this paper, learners can develop a deeper understanding of their environment, through learning activities based on the Uniqueness Profile principles. Blended space objects, e.g., mapping invisible items, geocaches, location-based games or time capsules, can be created by learners themselves as an outcome of the *Discover* → *Imagine* → *Change* process. This, in turn, leads to an enhanced mobile system thinking, which includes improved environmental and contextual awareness.

Two additional educational values are noteworthy. First, the unique principle of discovery machine on which the DICE's first phase is based supports the effect of "uncovering the invisible in the familiar". This effect might be one of the reasons for the growing sense of attachment reported by users involved in a mobile inquiry of familiar places. Interesting potential for further research grows out of this, especially in light of the common perception of mobile technology as an agent of disconnection from ourselves and our environment. Second, mapping and sharing mobile inquiry findings might also contribute to learning processes outside of the classroom. This is how the boundaries between the educational realm and other social institutions like municipalities might be dissolved. Furthermore, with MUC apps we can now annotate our environment [19], so that the places become like books and the world turn into a library.

Although the *Discover* phase can standalone, the *Imagine* and *Change* components are very important, even in a small portion or in virtual mode. These phases of the DICE model serve as an intrinsic trigger to an authentic and more engaged process. When adding the *Imagine* and *Change* components to the *Discover* phase, the world might become more than 'just' a library as it turns into a laboratory or a "Construction Kit", when "it is re-seeing the world as something that can be re-made that is the goal" [16].

In this article, we described the implementation of four DICE cases that were different in their goals, places, and learners' characteristics. Some were done in cooperation with the authorities in the context of planning and conservation projects. All cases have been conducted in educational institutions. However, further implementation can be made by place-based organizations that can adopt the DICE model in the context of community projects and cultural initiatives. Additionally, a global open online course for "learning a place" can be developed based on the DICE model, where students undertake a learning project in their area and share their findings and ideas in the online system. Such a global initiative will enable discussion and dialogue with students and mentors around the globe. An academic course of this type may be relevant to the study of various environmental disciplines and activities in urban and rural environments.

To summarize, when participating in mobile-enhanced DICE activities, learners not only discover the place they live in but might also contribute to its actual change. The learners in such activities are a small step ahead of being just mobile consumers and even producers of digital information. The DICE model suggests using unique mobile affordances in conjunction with non-mobile and analog activities. In this way, learners become more aware of their surroundings, while the place becomes a powerful object to learn with.

A major challenge in applying the affordances of MUC apps is by using these unique mobile applications not merely as 'context sensor' extensions of the human body and mind. It is rather the way for the learners themselves to become 'context sensors', curious and aware of their surroundings. It is especially important as mobile apps already serve as a digital interface to the world; the world itself is increasingly turning digitized, and objects are becoming more connected and 'smarter.' This fascinating combination generates new objects to think with, new blended spaces to live in, and may also generate new ways of being, experiencing and learning.

References

1. Cresswell, T.: Place: A Short Introduction, 2nd edn. Wiley, Hoboken (2014)
2. Massey, D.: Space, Place, and Gender. University of Minnesota Press, Minneapolis (1994)
3. Farman, J. (ed.): The Mobile Story: Narrative Practices with Locative Technologies. Routledge, London (2013)
4. Borda, A., Bowen, J.: Smart cities and cultural heritage: a review of developments and future opportunities. In: Electronic Visualization and the Arts (EVA 2017), London, UK, 11 July–13 July 2017. BCS (2017)
5. Zimmerman, H.T., Land, S.M.: Facilitating place-based learning in outdoor informal environments with mobile computers. TechTrends **58**(1), 77–83 (2014)
6. Dunleavy, M., Dede, C.: Augmented reality teaching and learning. In: Spector, J., Merrill, M., Elen, J., Bishop, M. (eds.) Handbook of Research on Educational Communications and Technology, pp. 735–745. Springer, New York, NY (2014). https://doi.org/10.1007/978-1-4614-3185-5_59

7. Shafriri, Y., Levy, D.: What are the unique characteristics of integrating mobile applications in learning? J. Interact. Learn. Res. **29**(3), 271–299 (2018)

8. Hirsh-Pasek, K., Zosh, J.M., Golinkoff, R.M., Gray, J.H., Robb, M.B., Kaufman, J.: Putting education in "educational" apps: lessons from the science of learning. Psychol. Sci. Public Interest **16**(1), 3–34 (2015)

9. Notari, M.P., Hielscher, M., King, M.: Educational apps ontology. In: Churchill, D., Lu, J., Chiu, T.K.F., Fox, B. (eds.) Mobile Learning Design. LNET, pp. 83–96. Springer, Singapore (2016). https://doi.org/10.1007/978-981-10-0027-0_5

10. Woodill, G.: Unique Affordances of mobile learning. In: Udell, C., Woodill, G. (eds.) Mastering Mobile Learning. Wiley, Hoboken (2014). https://doi.org/10.1002/9781119036883.ch15

11. Pegrum, M.: Future directions in mobile learning. In: Churchill, D., Lu, J., Chiu, T.K.F., Fox, B. (eds.) Mobile Learning Design: Theories and Applications, pp. 413–431. Springer, Singapore (2016). https://doi.org/10.1007/978-981-10-0027-0_24

12. Benyon, D.: Presence in blended spaces. Interact. Comput. **24**(4), 219–226 (2012)

13. O'Keefe, B., Benyon, D.: Using the blended spaces framework to design heritage stories with schoolchildren. Int. J. Child-Comput. Interact. **6**, 7–16 (2015)

14. FitzGerald, E., Ferguson, R., Adams, A., Gaved, M., Mor, Y., Thomas, R.: Augmented reality and mobile learning: the state of the art. Int. J. Mob. Blended Learn. **5**(4), 43–58 (2013)

15. Kamarainen, A., Metcalf, S., Grotzer, T., Dede, C.: EcoMOBILE: designing for contextualized STEM learning using mobile technologies and augmented reality. In: Crompton, H., Traxler, J. (eds.) Mobile Learning and STEM: Case Studies in Practice, pp. 98–124. Routledge, New York (2015)

16. Silver, J.: Lens × Block: World as Construction Kit, p. 9 (2014) https://dspace.mit.edu/handle/1721.1/95590

17. Farman, J.: Embodiment and the mobile interface. In: Mobile Interface Theory. pp. 16–34. Routledge, London (2013)

18. Resnick, M.: Sowing the seeds for a more creative society. Learn. Lead. Technol. **35**(4), 18–22 (2008)

19. Brown, E.: Introduction to location-based mobile learning. In: Brown, E. (ed.) Education in the Wild: Contextual and Location-Based Mobile Learning in Action. STELLAR Alpine Rendez-Vous Workshop, pp. 7–9. Learning Sciences Research Institute, University of Nottingham, Nottingham (2010)

A Learning Management System Accessible for Visual, Hearing and Physical Impairments

Marcos Nascimento[1]([✉]), Thiago Oliveira[2], Nelson Lima[2], Renato Ramos[2], Lidiane Silva[2], Francisco Oliveira[2], and Anarosa Brandão[1]

[1] Universidade de São Paulo, São Paulo, SP, Brazil
marcos.devaner@usp.br
[2] Universidade Estadual do Ceará, Fortaleza, CE, Brazil

Abstract. Accessible web-based learning (E-learning) has been an research agenda for a long time, being inadequate learning material and interfaces the main responsible for that. In addition, poorer education often means lower quality of life. In this text we present an accessible learning management system (LMS) built on accessibility guidelines and a participatory design, including people with disabilities (PwD) from design to validation process. The real use of our LMS has presented good results with average range of 92% acceptance and 53% in relation to the formation of PwD and non-PwD, thus the results show that an accessible LMS may be a toward to inclusive learning.

Keywords: E-learning · Accessibility · Learning Management System

1 Introduction

According to the World Health Organization (WHO), 15,6% of the world's population have some type of disability, of which 2.2% face significant difficulties in carrying out their daily activities [17]. Among them, there are people with several types of impairment: visual (VI), hearing (HI) and physical (PI). Many difficulties faced by these people are related to the fact that the environment is not accessible for them. As stated by the United Nations (UN), accessibility occurs when a person with some disability has the independence to act in an environment, whether it physical or virtual [17].

Some initiatives have been taken for accessibility in physical and web-based environments, and the universal design [18] is one of them. For physical environments the universal design proposes a series of design guidelines so that it meets the needs of the people with disabilities (PwD) [22]. For web-based environments, W3C an international community where member organizations, a full-time staff, and the public work together to develop Web standards proposes accessibility guidelines through the Web Content Accessibility Guidelines 2.0 (WCAG) aiming to make web-based environments more accessible [7]. Despite such initiatives,

© Springer Nature Switzerland AG 2019
M. Antona and C. Stephanidis (Eds.): HCII 2019, LNCS 11572, pp. 481–493, 2019.
https://doi.org/10.1007/978-3-030-23560-4_35

studies show that accessibility in Learning Management Systems (LMS) has still been a major challenge [4,6,9]. In fact, the most adopted open source LMS does not have accessibility among its main features [8].

These challenges motivated our research group[1] to create an accessible LMS, called **AccessLearning**. Our LMS was created to meet the needs of people with visual, hearing and physical impairment. In this work we present its accessibility features as well as the sketch of its development, testing and validation models with the aim of supporting future research in accessibility on LMS.

The AccessLearning applies the concept of ergonomics, adapting itself to the user profile [11]. Its accessible interface and features are related to the disability profile. Therefore, HI, VI, and PI have different forms of visualization and accessibility features. These profiles include the roles of student, tutor and administrator in the system. An interpreter profile for sign language has been created, as it arose from a demand of HI students.

In addition to the web system, students also have an App (Android and IOS) that allows to carry out various activities using a smartphone or tablet [15]. The two versions of AccessLearning, web-based and App, have been developed according to the accessibility requirements established by WCAG 2.0. All learning objects (LO), educational resources to support students in teaching and learning [12], available within the environment were also developed by following the same accessibility standards.

For the development of our LMS, the incremental process was applied by a multidisciplinary team that includes PwD such as hearing impairment, visual impairment and physical impairment, besides the support of architects, software developer and specialists in distance education and accessibility. The most important task of PwD was to test and validate the features, interface and types of interaction with the system. Before coding, interaction and validation tests of functional prototypes were performed. We were able to validate user journeys according to each user profile and make the necessary adjustments for each of them. Given the composition of the team, it was possible to test the environment with an heterogeneous group of users enabling the creation of efficient interfaces and interactions for several user profile concerning heir associate disabilities.

Several distance learning courses were offered using AccessLearning, in partnership with some public and private institutions. Among them are courses of Introduction to programming logic and Fundamentals and Object Oriented Programming. The attendance was composed of higher education students, with and without disabilities. Despite all accessible features present in AccessLearning, all courses count with tutors (to help students concerning the learning content); support team (to help students to interact with the system); and an interpreter of the Brazilian Language of Signal (LIBRAS).

Questionnaires were applied at the end of each course to evaluate the students' degree of satisfaction while interacting with AccessLearning. In addition, each student who had been approved in the course received a formal certificate

---

[1] Distance Education Laboratory for People with Disabilities (LE@D) - http://projetolead.com.br/en/about-us.

from the educational institution. Most of PwD students that had attended the courses were certified. The results of questionnaire application result in average range of 92% acceptance and 53% in relation to the formation of PwD and non PwD. Thus, it indicates that he use of an accessible platform can be an alternative for promoting learning opportunities for all. Accessibility features break interaction barriers, facilitating the use of the tool and allowing students to address their cognitive effort in understanding the content rather than in the interaction with the platform.

This paper is organized in 5 sections. In Sect. 2 we discussed accessibility in LMS, and present some related work (Moodle, Canvas and OLAT) pointing out some accessibility problems of them. The AccessLearning is presented in Sect. 3. In addition, the real courses application as well results of pedagogical questionnaire are presented in Sect. 4. Finally, conclusion and future work are pointed in Sect. 5.

2 Background and Related Work

E-learning can be a way for PwD access adequate vocational education. Assistive technologies associated with pedagogical strategies may result in an accessible education. The combination of e-learning with assitives technologics can provide the same learning opportunities for all [19]. On the other hand, although e-learning modality has a great potential to bring education to the PwD, many of the most adopted LMS do not have accessibility resources among their main functionalities [8]. As a consequence, PwD faces several problems during navigation, interaction, and didactic content access [1].

Since each disability type presents specific needs, it is important to provide adaptations to the environment considering disability profile. Nevertheless, adaptation must consider that the same resource that support an specific disability profile, may even hinder interaction for users with other disabilities [10]. For instance, a VI using a screen reader to navigate over a LMS should be confused whenever it finds pre-recorded videos content in sign language while browsing. In this case, such confusion could be given by not knowing if the video content is something relevant to their purpose in the learning environment. This problem is also identified in face-to-face teaching. In fact, in a class where deaf and blind students are in the same environment and pedagogical model, great challenges would be faced, turning impractical the teaching and learning of these individuals [13].

Universal Design for Learning (UDL) is a model that proposes an adapted learning environment and strategies, taking into consideration each person, his limitations and abilities. The same strategy applied to LMS may produce positive effects, mitigating accessibility barriers [10,21]. Likewise, an LMS adapted with resources to provide accessibility may positively impact the teaching and learning of PwD, giving them a chance of training in equity regardless of their limitations and abilities [2]. LMS widely used such as Moodle, Canvas and OLAT [8] have initiated the implementation of accessibility features, however some aspects still need to be improved to really support any PwD.

Moodle is an open source LMS, constantly upgraded. It provides several tools that enable educators to offer and manage courses. Widely used by universities and schools for distance learning, Moodle can also support face-to-face courses. Studies have shown that Moodle is used in 223 countries with more than eighty million users [8]. Although Moodle has many features and a large scale of use, it is still not considered accessible for people with disabilities such as VI, DI and PI [5,19].

Canvas is an LMS available as a web service, widely used by universities. It also has different versions designed for the specific needs of K12 education. In addition, it offers accessibility resources, while implementing the WCAG 2.0 guidelines and having Gold Certified compliance certifications from the National Federation of the Blind [8]. Although Canvas implements some customization that facilitate access by PwD, it does not have accessibility features that support PwD during interaction, such as font resize, high contrast, among others. In addition, it does not adapted interface and resources for other disability profile, as a consequence people with other disabilities may find some barriers during interaction with Canvas [10].

Another important and widely LMS used, OLAT is an open source Web-based LMS. It is geared towards teaching, learning, assessment and communication. It has a sophisticated modular toolkit, provides a range of possibilities for didactic applications. Like Moodle, it does not have accessibility features and does not implement the accessibility guidelines proposed by WCAG [3].

Based on OLAT, the OpenOlat[2] is a web-based e-learning platform for teaching, learning, assessment and communication that provides modular toolkit for courses. OpenOLAT allows individually extended installation and adaptation to organizational needs, besides integrated into existing Information Technologies infrastructure.

In this work, it is presented, AccessLearning, an accessible and adaptive LMS, that implements resources of OpenOlat. It have many interaction and learning resources, furthermore several accessibility resources allows adaptation based on the type of disability (VI, HI or PI). The interface can be adapted according disability profile, thus each disability profile has specific features for its needs, as it is shown in Sect. 3.

3   An Accessible LMS for Visual, Hearing and Physical Impairments

AccessLearningis an affordable LMS, based on OpenOlat, developed by Le@d in cooperation with the Universidade Estadual do Ceará and Dell Computers in Brazil. The use of web services allows AccessLearningto implement OpenOlat resources such as database, learning tools, chat and tools to interact with each other. Although, many of these resources it have been totally modified to turn accessible.

---

[2] https://www.openolat.com.

The AccessLearningprovides several features to support VI, HI, and PI during interaction with the system and to access learning content. In addition to applying the guidelines proposed by WCAG, each feature can be triggered by disability profile, since a different interface is available for each profile. Thus, each disability profile has characteristics and features adapted to its needs. A screenshot of The student area AccessLearningis presented in Fig. 1.

Fig. 1. Student home page

As it has shown in Fig. 1, the student area was divided in four areas:

1. It is the accessibility bar with all accessibility resource further language option and editor profile;
2. It presents a menu of tools available for student such as my courses, calendar, mail, my grades, conference, glossary ans settings;
3. It presents status of the courses that a student is enrolled as well a link to access the course;
4. The student can visualize in a panel your agenda and notices posted by tutor.

Different role of users such as student (impaired and non-impaired), tutor, system administrator, pedagogical coordination and interpreter of sign language are available. Each user has a specific role into LMS, these roles are:

– **Student:** It represents students who are enrolled in a course. A user with student role can access classes, interact with classmates and tutors. In addition, it has access to performance report (grades, frequency and average grades), being able to follow his/her performance during a course. All pages are structured to support screen readers, allowing blind to access content and achieve good browsing experience.

- **Tutors:** This role represents a user who supports students in doubts, evaluation and motivations within learning environment. They have the same tools and resources available to students, besides a set of features specific for them as shown in Table 1.
- **Pedagogical Coordinator:** This role represents a user who supports tutors and students in learning process. They can generate reports of classes, create and apply questionnaires of courses evaluation, besides to have a vision of the environment as a student.
- **System Administrator:** This role represents a user who have complete control over the system, configuring classes, posting content, enrolling students, setting deadlines for activities. In addition to the features related to a course, the administrator can also open a selection of students for a course, defining deadlines and configuring of evaluations application.
- **Interpreter:** This role represents a user who mediates communication between HI and non-HI. The Interpreter receives the request from students or tutors for translation of mails (messages) and forums. When the Interpreter answer a request, the student or tutor receives in his forum or mail the translation in sign language or text automatically.

In Table 1 are present AccessLearningresources available for each user role.

Table 1. Access Learning Tools and Resources by user role

Tools and resources	Student	Tutor	Pedagogical coordination	Sign language interpreter	Administer of system
Lesson	X	X	X	X	X
Forum	X	X	X	X	X
Exercises	X	X	X	X	X
Assessment	X	X	X	X	X
Workshop	X	X	X	X	X
Chat	X	X	X	X	X
Simulator	X	X	X	X	X
Sing language (LIBRAS) glossary	X	X	X	X	X
Video conference	X	X	X	X	X
Grade report	X				
Calendar					
Notifications	X	X	X	X	X
Student follow-up reports		X	X		X
Pedagogical usability questionnaire	X		X		X
Translation request				X	
General AccessLearning configurations					X

The development process involved a multidisciplinary team of system architects and software developers as well as specialists in distance education. In addition, an heterogeneous (different age, sex and instruction degree) group of VI, HI, PI and non-impaired participated in the entire process of designing, testing and validating accessibility features available. The incremental development model, allowed tests with PwD and arrangements before release to final user. As a consequence, VI, HI and PI, besides non-impaired people, could have access to resources previously validated, increasing satisfaction with the resources and interface. The preformed satisfaction evaluation was by final users applying a pedagogical usability questionnaire during courses application using AccessLearning.

3.1   Adapting to Student Profile and Accessibility Resources

Several tools and resources are available so that students can interact with the environment as shown in Table 1. Standard resources such as learning objects, exercises, workshops, forum and others are configurable by System Administrator, thus helping the Pedagogical Coordination to implement courses according pedagogical model planed.

The profile of the student is defined after the first login into AccessLearning, thus adapts for his/hers general interaction needs. The accessibility resources are previous configured for VI, HI and PI. The Fig. 2 presents possible accessibility resources available. Despite previous configuration resources by type of disability, it is possible to select all resources, in case of user interest.

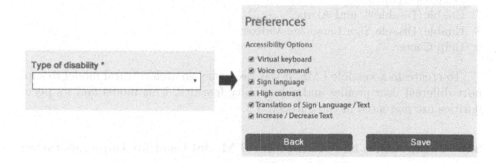

Fig. 2. Selecting accessibility resources

In addition to the available accessibility features, AccessLearninghas several implementations of guidelines suggested by WCAG. The accessibility resources previous configured as well implementations of guidelines by type of disability are:

1. **For hearing impaired:** all content in Portuguese and Libras (Brazilian sign language), request translation of mail and forum messages and sing language glossary(LIBRAS);

2. **For the visually impaired:** Adapted interface, audible alerts, audio description, font resizing, high contrast, shortcut keys and voice commands;
3. **For the physically disabled:** adapted icons and interface, voice commands and shortcut keys.

After to define a student profile and preferences, a menu with accessibility shortcuts becomes available, as shown in Fig. 3.

Fig. 3. Accessibility resources

In the menu presented at Fig. 3 described according to shortcuts and number:

- K: is a Shortcut to Content;
- A: to Accessibility Menu;
- Q: to Navigation Menu.

1. List of hot keys and voice commands;
2. Enable/Disable Virtual Keyboard;
3. Enable/Disable High contrast;
4. Increase Font Size;
5. Restore Font Size;
6. Decrease Font Size;
7. Enable/Disable Sound Alerts;
8. Enable/Disable Sign Language Videos;
9. Help Center.

To create an accessible LMS, it was necessary an architectural model to support different user profiles and accessibility features. This model and its peculiarities are presented in the Subsect. 3.2.

3.2 Technologies and Architectural Model Used for Implementation

AccessLearning was conceived and developed as a large distributed system with several modules that interact with each other. Following this concept, the modules run on different servers, avoiding overhead on a single server, ensuring greater scalability to the system. Figure 4 shows these different modules that run on different servers. AccessLearning, as the main application, could consume the services of other applications via webservice REST. Openolat, for example, is used as a repository of courses and didactic materials, as well as managing AccessLearning classes [16].

As it shown in Fig. 4, AccessLearning also connects via REST to the CHAT module, which runs on a separate server, to allow students and tutors to talk

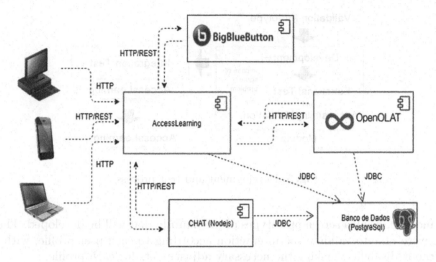

Fig. 4. Architecture and modules

to each other in real time. The BigBlueButton[3] is used for video conferencing and is managed through AccessLearning. All of these applications use postgresql as the database and each has its own database. In addition to these modules, a Mobile version of AccessLearning has been developed, which works for both Android and iOS devices. Through this application, students will be able to perform various class activities, giving students greater flexibility [15].

All modules are managed independently through AutoScaling technology. This technology allows the modules to operate in a scalable and elastic way, increasing and reducing the number of servers as needed. By using Load Balance technology, load balancing is performed between the servers that support a given application [14].

This distributed architecture aims to ensure better maintainability and adaptability of the applications. With several smaller applications, it becomes simpler to maintain and evolve each module in isolation. As the future intention is to provide new accessibility features, this architecture allows adding new functionality and modules without having to refactor the entire system.

3.3   Development and Tests Process

The development of AccessLearninghas an iterative process composed by three environment: development environments: development, test and user environment. The Fig. 5 shows this process and the performed tests in each environment.

Before include a module for development of code, it is performed a test of screen prototypes, in this case, testers PwD and non-PwD validate a simulation

---

[3] https://bigbluebutton.org/.

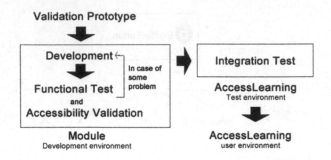

Fig. 5. Development and test process

of module, using a screen prototypes of the module that will be developed. Thus, we were able to validate the interaction according to each user profile, with or without disability, making the necessary adjustments for each profile.

In development environment is implemented the code, besides apply tests of functionality and accessibility, verifying whether a functionality have errors or accessibility problems. The accessibility problems are verified using AccessMonitor[4] an automatic validator that verifies the application of accessibility guidelines, according WCAG 2.0 in the HTML contents. In case of some functionality problem, it is back to development in order to adjustments.

The validation is performed in test environment, during this process testers PwD and non-PwD validate the module integrated with the AceesLearning. This validate is made through usability tests. Finally, after validation the module is integrated into AccessLearning final user version.

4   AccessLearning Use in a Real Setting

AccessLearning was adopted to deliver a training track for Java software development. This training was offered in partnership with private and public institutions of São Paulo, Brazil. The courses were offered in the years 2017 and 2018. In 2018 there were two 2018.1 and 2018.2 offers, as shown in Table 2. The students had six months to complete all the tracks, the course was including distance learning modality. The student had the support of tutors, besides sign language interpreter for deaf students. All courses were well-attended both by PwD and Non-PwD. To take the course, students had to take a test of Portuguese, logic and LIBRAS (only for deaf candidates).

To evaluate courses, students were asked to answer a questionnaire upon completion. An ergo-pedagogical questionnaire which is used as a tool for the ergo-pedagogical evaluation of the Computerized Educational Products, called MAEP [20]. Some adjustments were made for usability and accessibility evaluation. MAEP was used to a five dimension evaluation: didactic-pedagogical organization, faculty and tutorial, infrastructure, accessibility and mobility.

---

[4] http://www.acessibilidade.gov.pt/accessmonitor.

Results show that the level of satisfaction is between 89% and 93%, indicating that all aspects were well evaluated by PwD and non-PwD. It is also possible to realize that although PwD presents little representativeness with just 10% and 50% student in courses. In general, it can be inferred that courses offered and AccessLearningmay support PwD and non-PwD. Considering that AccessLearningwas successfully used in the real setting, we can advocate that.

Table 2. Quantitative courses results

Year	Total students non-PwD	Total students PwD	Total approved	Satisfaction level
2017	1028	50%	55%	89%
2018.1	249	10%	59%	93%
2018.2	406	19%	43%	93%

5   Conclusion and Future Work

This article has exposed the great need for adaptive courses for PwD. Given this, a platform was developed that fills a space that other tools had not yet occupied, focusing on the wide access, having several accessibility features and interface adapted to each profile of disability. In its implementation, we use modern technologies, which guarantee a good structure for its use, and follow consolidated agile methods to manage its development. Platform assessment presents good results, with several students already impacted, being a good part of them PwD themselves.

The results show that the use of an accessible platform can be an alternative to egalitarian training and promote learning opportunities for disabled and non-disabled people. Although the use of AccessLearning shows good results, they are not enough to verify how accessibility features allow the elimination of access barriers for each user profile, therefore, more applied accessibility disability studies are required.

In addition to specific research on the accessibility of the platform, we intend to research and develop solutions that cover other types of disabilities, such as autism, making access to the platform as broad as possible. Furthermore, we intend to develop an application for the tutor, which allows the monitoring of students with greater mobility and practicality through the use of smartphones. With this, we will have an increasingly accessible LMS and mobility, making teaching and distance learning increasingly efficient for different types of users.

Acknowledgments. This study was an initiative of Dell Computers, Universidade Estadual do Ceará and Universidade de São Paulo. In addition, financed in part by the Coordenação de Aperfeiçoamento de Pessoal de Nível Superior - Brasil (CAPES) - Finance Code 001.

References

1. Al-Mouh, N.A., Al-Khalifa, A.S., Al-Khalifa, H.S.: A first look into MOOCs accessibility. In: Miesenberger, K., Fels, D., Archambault, D., Peñáz, P., Zagler, W. (eds.) ICCHP 2014. LNCS, vol. 8547, pp. 145–152. Springer, Cham (2014). https://doi.org/10.1007/978-3-319-08596-8_22
2. Alves, G.M., Aguia, Y.P.C.: Acessibilidade e tecnologia assistiva no ambiente educacional: Mapeamento sistemático. In: Anais do Workshop de Informática na Escola, vol. 20, p. 16 (2014)
3. Arnold, S., Fisler, J.: OLAT: the swiss open source learning management system. In: International Conference on e-Education, e-Business, e-Management, and e-Learning, IC4E 2010, pp. 632–636. IEEE (2010)
4. Batanero, C., et al.: Accessible platforms for e-learning: a case study. Comput. Appl. Eng. Educ. **25**(6), 1018–1037 (2017)
5. Calvo, R., Iglesias, A., Moreno, L.: Is moodle accessible for visually impaired people? In: Filipe, J., Cordeiro, J. (eds.) WEBIST 2011. LNBIP, vol. 101, pp. 207–220. Springer, Heidelberg (2012). https://doi.org/10.1007/978-3-642-28082-5_15
6. Calvo, R., Iglesias, A., Moreno, L.: Accessibility barriers for users of screen readers in the moodle learning content management system. Univ. Access Inform. Soc. **13**(3), 315–327 (2014)
7. World Wide Web Consortium, et al.: Web content accessibility guidelines (WCAG) 2.0 (2008)
8. Elabnody, M.R.: A survey of top 10 open source learning management systems. Int. J. Scient Technol. Res. **4**(8), 7–11 (2015)
9. Hersh, M.: Accessibility and usability of virtual learning environmemts. In: Eighth IEEE International Conference on Advanced Learning Technologies, 2008. ICALT 2008, pp. 1038–1039. IEEE (2008)
10. Janeth Lancheros-Cuesta, D., Carrillo-Ramos, A., Pavlich-Mariscal, J.A.: Content adaptation for students with learning difficulties: design and case study. Int. J. Web Inform. Syst. **10**(2), 106–130 (2014)
11. Karwowski, W.: International Encyclopedia of Ergonomics and Human Factors, vol. 3. CRC Press, Boca Raton (2001)
12. Kurilovas, E., Kubilinskiene, S., Dagiene, V.: Web 3.0-based personalisation of learning objects in virtual learning environments. Comput. Hum. Behav. **30**, 654–662 (2014)
13. Lancaster, P.: Universal design for learning. Colleagues **3**(1), 5 (2008)
14. Li, L.E., Woo, T.: Dynamic load balancing and scaling of allocated cloud resources in an enterprise network. US Patent App. 12/571,271, 31 March 2011
15. Nascimento, M.D., et al.: Aprendizado acessível. In: Anais dos Workshops do Congresso Brasileiro de Informática na Educação, vol. 6, p. 110 (2017)
16. Neumann, A., Laranjeiro, N., Bernardino, J.: An analysis of public rest web service APIs. IEEE Trans. Serv. Comput. (2018)
17. World Health Organization, et al.: World report on disability (2011)
18. Preiser, W.F., Ostroff, E.: Universal Design Handbook. McGraw Hill Professional, New York (2001)
19. Shawar, B.A.: Evaluating web accessibility of educational websites. Int. J. Emerg. Technol. Learn. (iJET) **10**(4), 4–10 (2015)
20. e Silva, C.R.D.O.: MAEP: um método ergopedagógico interativo de avaliação para produtos educacionais informatizados. Ph.D. thesis, Universidade Federal de Santa Catarina, Centro Tecnológico. Programa de Pós ... (2002)

21. Simsik, D., Galajdova, A., Onofrejova, D.: Some aspects in e-learning for persons with disabilities. In: 2017 15th International Conference on Emerging eLearning Technologies and Applications (ICETA), pp. 1–7. IEEE (2017)
22. Story, M.F.: Principles of universal design. Univ. Design Handb. (2001)

Expressing the Personality of a Humanoid Robot as a Talking Partner in an Elementary School Classroom

Reika Omokawa[1], Makoto Kobayashi[2], and Shu Matsuura[3(✉)]

[1] Setagaya Elementary School Attached to Tokyo Gakugei University,
4-10-1 Fukasawa, Setagaya, Tokyo 158-0081, Japan
[2] Tokyo Gakugei University Oizumi Elementary School, 5-22-1 Higashioizumi,
Nerima, Tokyo 178-0063, Japan
[3] Faculty of Education, Tokyo Gakugei University, 4-1-1 Nukuikita,
Koganei, Tokyo 184-8501, Japan
shumats0@gmail.com

Abstract. A humanoid robot NAO was introduced as a talking partner of teaching AI and robot to the elementary school students to stimulate empathy for the intelligent machines. Two dialog types were defined. First, the query type dialog was defined as a robot's answer to human questioning. Second, the phatic type dialogs were defined to express the personality of the robot. While the former type dialog is initiated by formulated questioning, the latter type response can even be induced by misrecognition of human speech.

Applying this simple method, the same unit sessions for each of the three classrooms on AI and robot were conducted. During the sessions, students' burst of laughter was induced at 83% of the phatic type dialog, and the laughing response was found at 44% of the query type dialogs. By this representation, it became easier for the students to empathize with the robot.

After this session, a questionnaire survey on the preference of robot pet, on what the students wanted to talk with the robot that dreams at night, and on their view of life if AI robots replaced human workers was conducted. The results suggested that the students got to imagine a virtual subjectivity of the intelligent machines and considered a better life for the human with them.

Keywords: Humanoid robot · Phatic dialog · Empathy · Elementary school

1 Introduction

Mechanisms of the emergence of consciousness in the human brain are a fundamental and attractive problem of brain science [1–3]. On the other hand, modeling of consciousness of intelligent robots is of engineering importance [4–6]. Also, humor and empathy are known as essential elements to build a friendly communication [7]. This may be true between human and intelligent machines. Empathy is regarded as the ability to figure out things from the other one's self [8]. If we seek to have an in-depth insight into the intelligent sociable robot, it might be unsatisfactory to understand the robot simply as a mechanical system governed by an artificial algorism.

© Springer Nature Switzerland AG 2019
M. Antona and C. Stephanidis (Eds.): HCII 2019, LNCS 11572, pp. 494–506, 2019.
https://doi.org/10.1007/978-3-030-23560-4_36

In this study, fifth-grade elementary school students who learn Artificial Intelligence (AI) and its influence on society have a classroom session to ask questions about AI and robots to one of the authors. The students surveyed AI and robots individually before the session. The teacher had a lecture based on the students' questions in the first half of the session and answered the students' questions directly in the rest of the time. In this session, the teacher introduced a humanoid robot NAO (Softbank Robotics) as a talking-partner. The robot had explanation type talks and phatic type small talks [9]. The latter phatic type dialog conveyed a humor personality and stimulated students' laughing responses. The laughing response is known to enhance empathy [10]. In our previous study, we found the development of thought on life through the projection of their consciousness onto the robot partner in the successive classroom sessions of second-grade elementary students [11].

The purpose of this study is to observe that a humorous personality of a talking partner robot stimulates elementary school students' empathy to the intelligent machines. We expect the empathy leads in-depth thinking on the intelligent machines that will exert a great impact on the future human life. Students' thinking is surveyed by a simple description type questionnaire.

2 Method

2.1 Classroom and Humanoid Robot

Ninety-three fifth-grade male and female students in three classrooms participated in a pilot subject "research" that consisted of the learning on "Society 5.0, a super smart society" [12], home study on AI, AI-related technologies in the daily life and presentation, asking questions to one of the authors, visiting a museum of high technology, discussing on what were understood on AI, and having presentations on the impact of deep learning AI. The sessions studied in this paper for the above three classes were held in January 2019. The sessions of three classes were conducted successively in the same day. Each session duration was 45 min consisting of the time for teacher and robot's explanation and the time for students' questions.

A sociable humanoid robot used in this study as the talking partner of the lecture was NAO V5 (Softbank Robotics) [13] with the NAOqi operating system (version 2.1.4.13). The purpose of use of NAO robot is to let students have a feeling of being with a sociable robot that intervenes in human's talk. The development environment was the Choregraphe version 2.1.4. NAO represented an interface of the intelligent machine that played a sociable behavior. During the classroom, the speech recognition threshold was set to 55% avoiding over responses caused by the frequent misrecognition. Also, NAO was set to talk in a sitting position on a teacher's desk in front of the blackboard.

2.2 Data Acquisition

Before the session, a response card survey of the students' questions on AI was conducted for two classes. Each student wrote down one question of their own. To detect the students' responses to NAO's talk, the sounds of the classrooms were recorded.

After the session, a questionnaire survey was conducted to extract an emotional aspect, and students' feelings imagined as being along with AI or robots. The questions were as follows:

(1) Do you like a robot that resembles human and animals? Please describe why do you like or not.
(2) Imagine you have a robot that dreams at night. What do you talk to your robot?
(3) In the future, robots will work for the people. If the robot workers replace the human workers, what do you like to do? If you still like to work yourself, what kind of job do you like to do? What do you like to do other than the job?

The above question (1) implies the life with an intelligent machine and empathy for it. Question (2) intends students to notice the inner side of their mind. Question (3) orients the students' minds again to the public world and consider the relationship between intelligent machines and them. Students answered these questions writing short sentences. The texts were categorized on the basis of broader_narrower association [14].

3 Results and Discussion

3.1 Students' Questions on AI

Students' questions on AI was collected in two classrooms before the session. The total number of students who wrote their questions was 54 in the two classrooms. Some of the students' writings included more than one question so that we collected 59 individual questions in total. These questions were categorized into four sub-categories and two super-categories as shown in Fig. 1 and Table 1.

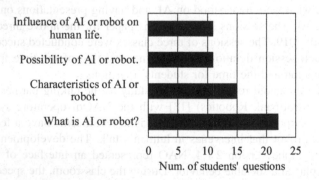

Fig. 1. Categorized questions on AI

Many of the students have a vague understanding of AI and have a will to understand the definition and its fundamental character, although they previously studied AI-related technologies that can be found in their personal life. At the same time, since the students studied the applications of AI to the daily life apparatus, they showed substantial interest in the possibility of AI and how it would change human life.

Table 1. Students' questions on AI to the teacher. The left two columns show the sup- and sub-category names of questions. The right column shows the instance names of the questions. Numbers in parentheses are the number of actual questions (text instances). The words written in Italic imply the students' sense of humanity.

Super-category	Sub-category	Types of questions (number of text instances)
Emergence of AI	What is AI or robot? (22)	What is AI (13)? The significance of AI (5). What can the robot do (3)? Difference between human and AI (1)
	Characteristics of AI or robot (15)	*Does it have a heart* (6)? What is AI's weakness (5)? Does it fail (1)? *Can it take responsibility* (1)? Does it have questions (1)? What is the lifetime of the robot (1)?
Humanity and AI	The possibility of AI or robot (11)	Does AI exceed humans (4)? Is human-like AI possible (3)? Does AI develop further (2)? Does AI alone superior to the others (1)? Is non-human made program possible (1)?
	Influence of AI or robot on life (11)	Does it change human life (3)? What kind of work to increase with AI (3)? Will AI be a disaster for human (3)? *What is required of human in an AI society* (2)?

Table 1 shows the categorized types of students' questions. The students questioned what AI was and what would happen with AI. At first glance, their questions seem biased towards knowledge about AI, rather than the questions from their mind. They might not have full reality on AI or life with robot support enough for holding inspiration, sympathy or a network of meanings for them. However, the questions represented in italic in Table 1, such as "does AI have a heart?" "does AI can take responsibility?" and "What is required of human in the AI society?" implies that the students sensitively consider an extension of humanity to the machine. These questions have significance in considering human life with the support of AI or robots, rather than in attaining knowledge of them.

3.2 Types of Dialogs

In the sessions of the classrooms, the humanoid robot NAO was used as a knowledge source. The teacher asked NAO a question on the intelligent machine from time to time in the session. Then NAO answered the question.

The dialogue can be written in the following form by using human utterance and robot response, as,

$$u:(\sim utteraces) \sim responses,$$

where, "utterances" is a set of utterances, and "responses" is a set of responses, respectively.

Dialogs were categorized into two types, namely a query type and a phatic type. The query type is a question-and-answer type, in which the relationship between the utterance and response are determined by their contexts and independent on the situation. However, some of the explanations were based on the view of machines as a "robot's personality." For example, NAO asks the students, "We have algorisms inside, what kind of algorism do you have?" Also, the utterances are shaped in a formulated style by using interrogative words. No abbreviation was used in these utterances. These conditions led the sentences relatively long so that the robot spoke the response sentence only when the utterance sentence was fully recognized.

The phatic type dialog is a more casual response that is spoken as a heart movement, such as the expression of feeling, acceptance or refusal, confirmation or embarrassment, muttering and nodding, small talks, etc. The dialog of this type is not the necessary condition of the knowledge transfer but may affect the human mind in the sense of empathy. A fixed "personality" of the robot was assumed for the classroom session. We assume that a "virtual personality" may be expressed by a function f as,

$$f(\text{phatic type utterances}) = \text{phatic type responses}.$$

For the present session, an encouraging personality was considered, and a set of responses that has encouraging and humorous words was prepared for f.

Further, many of the above phatic type utterances consisted of short words. As a result, the misrecognition of undefined words as the defined phatic words was likely to occur even at the level of speech recognition threshold of 55%. Thus, the occasional phatic type response can often be evoked by the misrecognition of the human's short utterances. In the classroom sessions described below, occasional recognitions evoked 88% of the robot's phatic responses unexpectedly.

3.3   Students' Responses to the Robot's Replies in the Classroom Session

Within the session talks of three classrooms, NAO expressed query type responses 16 ± 1 (average $\pm$ standard deviation) times led by the instructor's utterances, and showed phatic type responses 11 ± 3 times for each session, as shown by the black bars in Fig. 2. They are compared with the number of the subsequent reaction of the students, particularly laughing, as 7 ± 3 for query type and 9 ± 2, respectively. This means 44% vs. 82% is laughing for query vs. phatic reactions, respectively.

As seen in Fig. 2, laughter took place to 82% of the robot's phatic responses. Many of the cases were burst out laughing. The students listened particularly to the robot's answers to the previous questions summarized in Table 1. Still, the students showed some responses to nearly half the robot's query talks. Students' friendly responses even to the query dialog are supposed to be related with the personality making in the corresponding dialog as well as the friendly appearance and voice of NAO.

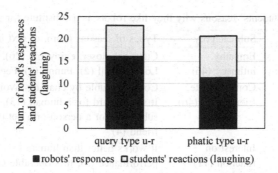

Fig. 2. Stacked bar chart to compare the average number of robot's response and the subsequent students' reaction voices in the cases of the query type and phatic type dialogs.

3.4 Students' Acceptance of Robot and AI

As mentioned in Sect. 3.1, the students' interests were mainly directed to the knowledge of AI. This was also expected from the original lesson plan. Then, we conducted an experimental session of this study with NAO as a talking partner. In this section, we discuss the students' acceptance and empathy with the intelligent machines after the session by analyzing the results of the questionnaire survey.

Figure 3 shows the results of the question of whether the student likes a robot that resembles human and animals. 73% of students answered that they like it, and 23% of them do not like it. In the classroom session, the students did not discussion this topic, and the results are expected to reflect individual preference directly.

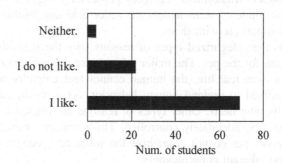

Fig. 3. The number of students who like or not like human-like or animal-like robot.

The session with NAO might have affected the students' acceptance of intelligent machines through the anthropomorphism of the robot. Table 2 shows the reasons why the students like the robot as a substitute for the pet animals. Students' answers were summarized into four categories to make the tendency of awareness clearer. Table 2 shows hierarchically categorized types of reasons that the students listed. The students wrote one or more reasons. The numbers in the parentheses are numbers of written instances of reasons. Also, Fig. 4 shows the numbers of written instances for each reason type.

Table 2. Students' reasons why they like robots as a substitute for pet animals.

Sup-category	Sub-category	Types of reasons (num. of text instances)
(a) Intuitive and anthropomorphism	Empathy, intimacy (46)	Cute, get closer, enjoyable (26). Healing (15). Love animal (2). Funny (2). Feel resemblance (1)
	Communicate, friendliness (46)	Communicable by chatting, avoid loneliness (24). It works hard for a human (13). It can be a substitute for a person or a pet (5). It can be a friend (4)
(b) Objective	Interest on function (11)	It works better than human (3). Mechanism and performance (3). It is operable (1). The general-purpose AI is expectable (1). Expect its future (1). The difference between intelligent machines and human (1). I prefer the typical robot (1)
	Necessity (4)	I cannot feed an animal. As such, the robot is a good substitute to a pet (3). Good for those who have an allergy to animals (1)

As seen in Table 2 and Fig. 4, the intuitive and anthropomorphism type reasons are overwhelming and 86% of the comments of those who like robot pets. These types of reasons suggest that the students who accept robot pets might instead expect the technology as a friend and a partner of life. Viewing of personality interface of NAO presentation possibly induced this trend of awareness of the students. Before the session, AI and robots were the subjects that the students wanted to know about. During the session, the sociable intelligent machine became a subject of emotion.

The "communicate, friendliness" category particularly suggests emotional factors of communication. Students seem to feel the robot cute and to thank it if the robot works hard to communicate with them.

Table 3 shows the categorized types of reasons why the students do not like the robot as a substitute for the pet. The major criticism of the robot pet is that since the machine does not have real life, the human cannot feel empathy with it. Also, the robots are programmed to pretend human behavior. As a result, one cannot see an expression from its own heart. Other types of reasons are related to the danger of a machine that cannot be adequately controlled. These reasons show that the students who dislike the robot pet do not empathize the robot and recognize it merely as a machine having no inherent consciousness.

Considering all of the super categories from (a) to (d) in Tables 2 and 3, the category (a) intuitive and anthropomorphism means that the students empathize the pet robot that may evoke richness in their heart. The percentage of the reason text instances of category (a) was 65%. This percentage is smaller than the percentage of students who answered they like the robot pet, as shown in Fig. 3. Thus, some of the students like the robot pet because of its objective function or mechanism. The robot moves and speaks by its algorithm. The response it makes and let the students feel funny comes from an algorithm. The majority of the students pay attention to the state of their mind of forming the impression.

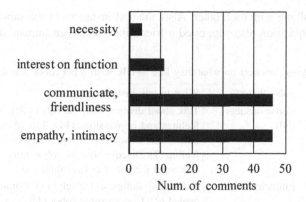

Fig. 4. Numbers of students' written instances of reasons categorized into four supertypes of reasons why they like human- and animal-like robot.

Table 3. Students' reasons why they do not like robots as a substitute for pet animals.

Sup-category	Sub-category	Types of reasons (num. of text instances)
(c) Resemblance but no-living	No real life, no empathy (12)	I prefer real living things (7). I do not feel empathy (3). It is only an information-processing machine (1). The program does not think of human (1)
	Artificial pretension (10)	No more than the pretension (5). Congruity in resemblance (4). Speak artificial response, not the robot's own words (1)
(d) Fear on machine	Danger and Fear (8)	Fear of mechanical things (4). Fear on the out-of-control machine (1). Dangerous (1). It might attack human (1)
	Spoil human (5)	Machine replaces human work (2). Humans degenerate (2). The machine answers everything (1)

3.5   What Do the Students Want to Talk with the Robot that Dreams at Night?

Question (2) described in Sect. 2.2 assumes that dreams come from continuously working brain that unifies many latent elements of wishes. The students who feed pets experience that many of the pet animals look dreaming while sleeping. Elementary students can find out many similarity or analog between human and humanoid robot [11]. Although dreaming seems common in human and animals, dreaming remains not required a function for the robots. Therefore, this question was intended to let the students consider the robot that might have subjectivity and consciousness in addition to sensing. Note that the teacher did not explain this intention to the students.

Table 4 shows a hierarchical arrangement of categorized students' answer types. The supercategory (a), the inner side, means that the students attempt to talk to the robot's heart. Figure 5 shows a comparison of the numbers of text instances. The inner side talk was 53% of all text instances. The robot's subjectivity and consciousness are of interest in talking with each other. Also, the text instances of the sub-category of the information acquisition also suggested a friendliness between human and robot.

Table 4. Students' answers on what they like to talk with a pet robot that dreams at night.

Sup-category	Sub-category	What to talk-instances
(a) The inner side	Consciousness (60)	Talk about dreams with the robot (30). Talk about feelings and impressions (14). Talk about what dream each wants to see (7). Want to consult if it has the feeling (7). Discuss how the robot thinks of humans (1). Ask what the robot always thinks (1)
	Empathy (16)	Talk funny things and laugh (13). Communicate and is healed (2). Cheer up the robot (1)
(b) Informational	Information acquisition (26)	Talk about the hobby and about what I like (10). Talk about various things (4). Talk about the school (4). Ask about what I cannot understand (4). Learn from the robot about what I want to know (3). Talk with the robot about my house (1)
	Future, virtual, fantasy (21)	About future robot and AI (9). About if the human worker is replaced by AI (5). About the future of society and me (3). About fantasy world (2). About virtual stories like "if something happened,..." (2)
(c) Role of the robot	Relation with the robot (17)	What can the robot do? Does the robot exceed human (8)? About what AI is useful (5). The relation between robots and human (4)
	Function of the robot (4)	I want to be taken care of by the robot (2). Let the robot reproduce the memory of dream (1). I want to do theater with the robot (1)

In the categories (b) informational and (c) role of robot, there found the questions on the future, possibility, or risk of the intelligent machines. If the robots do not have consciousness and subjectivity, these questions were not asked to the intelligent machines. Instead, the students would ask the questions to the developer or planner. The present session was meant for asking questions on AI to the teacher that develops the robot program.

Although the number was only two, the students wrote that they want to be taken care by the robot. This means if the robot dreams at night and has a subjectivity they will admit the intelligent machine as a life supporter. One can make use of the machines that do not have subjectivity or consciousness. However, when it comes to being taken care of oneself, one may be anxious if the machine is no more than an algorithm. One may hope essentially to empathize with the machine feeling the machine's consciousness.

Expressing the Personality of a Humanoid Robot as a Talking Partner 503

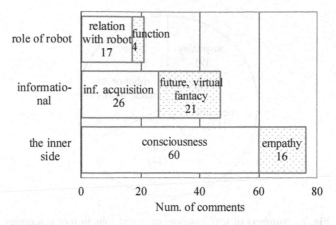

Fig. 5. Categorized topics students want to talk with the robot that dreams at night.

3.6 Future Life with Robots

The last question (2.2-3) asked what the students are interested in doing under a situation that the human is not always obliged to work. Overall, education in Japan is meant to develop young people to be an autonomous and subjective citizen that works or contributes to society. The teacher explained the possibility of a robot with a general-purpose AI, which can work flexibly like a human. More people might choose freely to work or not by one's will under such a circumstance. At this time of the session, the students can assume the subjectivity of intelligent machines as an essence of the human-machine interface (Fig. 6).

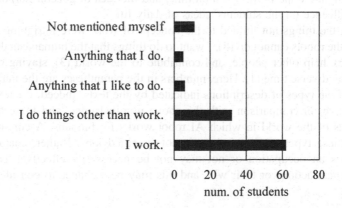

Fig. 6. Students' answers on what they want to do if the robots work for them.

Before the session, as shown in Table 1, the students' questions were mainly technical. The questions related with humanity, as shown in italic in Table 1 were nine in all 59. As a result of the questionnaire survey, those who clearly stated that they like to work was 45% after the session. The breakdown of what jobs they want to obtain was shown in Fig. 7.

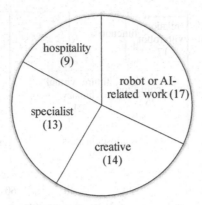

Fig. 7. Numbers of text instances of actual jobs in four categories.

The students were quite positive in working. Notably, 32% of those who want to work stated they want to develop, drive, or manage the AI robots by themselves. This tendency may be invoked through this curriculum.

26% of them preferred creative works such as the designer, architecture, town planner, writer, chef, pâtissier, artists, and broadcaster. 24% of the students preferred to be specialists, such as prosecutor, lawyer, police, teacher, sports player, game player, or the jobs in which communication is quite essential. 17% of the students preferred to have jobs of hospitality, such as animal feeder, animal-related works, doctor, nurse, or shoppers. These jobs are considered to be the students' ordinary dreams.

On the other hand, things that the students like to do other than jobs were, for instance, as follows: leisure, play, hobby, travel, cooking, home keeping, games, etc. These usually are done in the vacation time, and the idea of general-purpose AI robot has little influence on the students' ideas of daily life.

Instead, the things not limited to the concept of work were intriguing as follows, things that the robots cannot do (8), I want to do things that the human can do (6), AI as a partner (6), help other people, and contribute to the world (3), staying comfortable (1), spending diverse time (1). Here, numbers in the parentheses are the number of text instances of the types of descriptions indicated by the texts. Indeed, the text instances are descriptive, in comparison with the above nominal ones, and these texts reflect imaginations of the world in which AI robot works for humans. A common characteristic of these types of descriptions is not specified jobs. Rather, characteristic of whether it is an occupation or not may not be necessarily effective. The students describe human actions or their will, and this may be a chance to consider how they like to live.

4   Concluding Remarks

This paper presented a case study of a classroom session on the AI and a robot with a humanoid robot NAO talking-partner for fifth-grade elementary school students. The students surveyed on AI before the session and prepared the questions on AI individually. To construct dialogs, the query type dialog for providing knowledge and the phatic type dialog for occasional small talks with personality effect was created. During the sessions, laughter occurred at 82% of the phatic type response. Meanwhile, laughter occurred at 44% of the query type dialog.

The students' questions prepared for the session were mainly on the knowledge of AI. Whereas a few questions were on an extension of humanity to the machines. After the session with NAO, the students wrote answer texts to three questions. The answer texts were categorized and summarized into type hierarchy tables.

First, it was found that although they had an objective impression on AI and robot, many of them obtained subjective views through the image of the robot as a pet and can feel richness in emotion by the empathy on the robot pet.

Second, the students considered a dialog with an intelligent machine which has subjectivity. The students' texts implied that they expect communication between human and robot's subjectivity.

Third, as for a future society in which the general-purpose robots work in place of humans, a majority of students expected they would do their favorite jobs or free time activities. However, it was notable that other students described how they could spend better time as a human.

This case study implies that personality designing affected the students' emotions and let them imagine conscious intelligent machines. The students noticed that if they could recognize a machine's subjectivity, they can communicate with it, beyond the knowledge of it, and consider better life with it as the humans.

Acknowledgments. We would like to thank Masaru Tashiro and Ryo Sugimoto, Tokyo Gakugei University Oizumi Elementary School for providing us an opportunity to have classroom sessions. This work was partly funded by a Grant-in-Aid for Scientific Research (C) 15K00912 from the Ministry of Education, Culture, Sports, Science and Technology.

References

1. Dehaene, S.: Consciousness and the Brain: Deciphering How the Brain Codes Our Thoughts. Penguin, London (2014)
2. Massimini, M., Tononi, G.: Nulla di più grande. Baldini & Castoldi, Milan (2013)
3. Koch, C., Massimini, M., Boly, M., Tononi, G.: Neural correlates of consciousness: progress and problems. Nat. Rev. Neurosci. **17**, 307–321 (2016)
4. Kubota, N., Kojima, F., Fukuda, T.: Self-consciousness and emotion for a pet robot with structured intelligence. In: Proceedings of Joint 9th IFSA World Congress and 20th NAFIPS International Conference, vol. 5, pp. 2786–2791 (2001)
5. Takeno, J., Akimoto, S.: A conscious robot to perceive the unknown. In: 2010 IEEE International Conference on Systems, Man and Cybernetics, pp. 1375–1379 (2010)
6. Komatsu, T., Takeno, J.: A conscious robot that expects emotions. In: 2011 IEEE International Conference on Industrial Technology, pp. 15–20 (2011)
7. Wu, S.-R.: Humor and empathy: developing students' empathy through teaching robot to tell English jokes. In: 2nd IEEE International Conference on Digital Game and Intelligent Toy Enhanced Learning, pp. 213–214 (2017)

8. Edirisinghe, C., Nakatsu, R., Widodod, J.: Empathy as a factor for a new social contract. In: 2013 International Conference on Culture and Computing, pp. 161–162 (2013)
9. Bilandzic, M., Filonik, D., Gross, M., Hackel, A., Mangesius, H., Kremar, H.: A mobile application to support phatic communication in the hybrid space. In: 2009 Sixth International Conference on Information Technology: New Generations, pp. 1517–1521 (2009)
10. Egawa, S., Sejima, Y., Sato, Y., Watanabe, T.: Laughing-driven pupil response system for inducing empathy. In: Proceedings of the 2016 IEEE/SICE International Symposium on System Integration, pp. 520–525 (2016)
11. Omokawa, R., Matsuura, S.: Development of thought using a humanoid robot in an elementary school classroom. In: Antona, M., Stephanidis, C. (eds.) UAHCI 2018. LNCS, vol. 10908, pp. 541–552. Springer, Cham (2018). https://doi.org/10.1007/978-3-319-92052-8_43
12. Cabinet Office Government of Japan. https://www.gov-online.go.jp/cam/s5/eng/index.html. Accessed 12 Feb 2019
13. Softbank Robotics. https://www.softbankrobotics.com/emea/en. Accessed 12 Feb 2019
14. Matsuura, S.: Development of a trans-field learning system based on multidimensional topic maps, linked topic maps. In: Fifth International Conference on Topic Maps Research and Applications TMRA 2009, University of Leipzig, Institute fur Informatik, vol. 19, pp. 83–89 (2009)

Evaluation of User-Interface Designs for Educational Feedback Software for ASL Students

Utsav Shah, Matthew Seita, and Matt Huenerfauth$^{(\boxtimes)}$

Rochester Institute of Technology, Rochester, NY 14623, USA
{ups9461,mss4296,matt.huenerfauth}@rit.edu

Abstract. Facilitating students learning American Sign Language (ASL) promotes inclusion and communication for people who are Deaf, yet students learning ASL face challenges. In a classroom setting, instructors are limited in how frequently they can provide feedback on student's work, typically with many students submitting videos of their signing. Thus, we investigate software to analyze videos of ASL students' signing and provide immediate, albeit limited, feedback about aspects of a student's movements that are *likely* errors. In this study, we have conducted an investigation of a wide variety of designs for the presentation of feedback to ASL students, with a focus on the students' subjective judgments and preferences for any specific features and whether or not the feedback provided is easily understood. As part of an interview-based study, we conducted 3 rounds of iterative re-designs with 24 participants. At each round, a static design prototype was shown to 8 participants, who provided qualitative feedback. Open-ended interview questions asked for opinions on the visual appearance of feedback messages and the language used to convey errors. At each round, common themes were extracted from the data, and changes were made to the designs. We found that participants were comfortable in suggesting specific design modifications and in requesting additional features, which were incorporated into the designs shown in the prototypes used in the subsequent round. The contribution of this research is to provide guidance on the future development of language-learning feedback systems for sign-language.

Keywords: User-interface design · Educational feedback · American Sign Language

1 Introduction

American Sign Language (ASL) is now the third most popular foreign language studied in U.S. universities [2], and there are many people who would like to learn ASL for a variety of personal reasons: It is estimated that there are 28 million people in the U.S. who are deaf or hard of hearing [6, 7]. More than 80% of deaf children are born to hearing parents. In a study by Henderson et al. [3], the authors state that deaf individuals who acquire ASL skills at a very young age have superior ASL skills and are more capable of learning a second language than students who have picked up ASL later. A study conducted by Strong [8] showed that there is a relationship between ASL

© Springer Nature Switzerland AG 2019
M. Antona and C. Stephanidis (Eds.): HCII 2019, LNCS 11572, pp. 507–525, 2019.
https://doi.org/10.1007/978-3-030-23560-4_37

skill and English literacy. While many parents of deaf children attempt to learn ASL, they face several challenges due to the lack of tools that would allow them to practice ASL on their own. The students could benefit from a method of practicing and receiving feedback on their signing in a time-flexible manner.

Currently, ASL instructors must provide feedback to students in person (during class) or analyze the videos submitted by their students as homework assignments. The human ASL instructors must go through every video and make sure they provide quality feedback that the student can use to improve his or her learning. However, this imposes a heavy workload on the instructor, and it limits the amount of feedback an individual student can receive during a semester. We are investigating how to provide feedback when students use software that provides immediate, albeit limited, feedback of ASL students' signing that are likely errors. This is not a complete sign language recognition software, rather the software can recognize certain pre-defined errors and give immediate feedback that can then be further supplemented by feedback from the instructor. The goal of this project is not to replace human ASL instructors (who can provide sophisticated feedback about a student's signing), but rather to allow students to obtain some idea of how well they are signing in a timelier manner. To help with this, this study aims to find the best ways to provide this immediate feedback using a graphical user interface, based on users' subjective preferences.

2 Prior Work

Most of the previous work in automatic sign language recognition and analysis is focused on the computer vision techniques necessary to analyze human movements. Little research has examined how this technology could be incorporated into a useful system for providing educational feedback to students. Some prior studies on multi-modal educational technologies have also shown that the overall system design and the presentation of feedback can have a significant impact on the user experience [1]. Thus, it is critical to ensure that the method of providing feedback to students is easy to use and understand.

In an *ASSETS '15* paper [4], our laboratory presented a study with 8 ASL students. In this study, we compared three different prototype designs for how a future system might give feedback to ASL students about errors in their signing: video, notes, and popup. As shown in Fig. 1, the 'video' condition consisted of replaying the student video for them to watch. The 'notes' condition consisted of displaying a written message to indicate any errors identified in the video (or correctly performed linguistic elements). The 'popup' condition consisted of replaying the video with messages that 'popup' on the video when the system identifies linguistic errors.

The students in the study recorded a video while attempting an ASL homework assignment on one day, and then humans analyzed their video to look for errors. Video mock-ups of the three feedback conditions were produced (with a third of each student's videos produced in each condition). The students returned to the lab during the following week, and after viewing each feedback video, the student re-attempted the homework assignment. The student answered a survey about their experience and opinion of each feedback condition, and an ASL instructor graded the quality of the

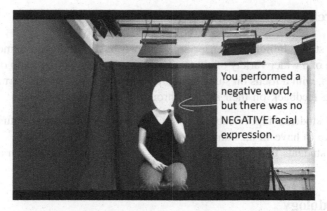

Fig. 1. Feedback overlaid on a student's own video, from our prior work [5].

student's signing their first and their second attempt at each homework item. In this way, the team was able to look for differences in subjective preferences and in the actual impact on students' signing skills for each feedback condition.

In [5], our lab reported the results from a second round of experimental studies in which we compared three different forms of feedback for students – popup, simple and photo. As shown in Fig. 1, the 'popup' condition consisted of displaying messages that appear as 'pop-ups' when a linguistic error is identified. The 'simple' condition was identical to the 'popup' condition, but any linguistic jargon contained within the pop-up messages was replaced with simpler text. The 'photos' condition was identical to the 'simple' condition except that photos were added to the on-screen feedback to illustrate specific aspects of ASL grammar. The students in the study were presented with an ASL homework assignment and were given 20 min to prepare to record a video of themselves. Video mock-ups of the three feedback conditions (popup, simple or photos) were presented to the participants after which they attempted their homework assignment. At the end of the study, participants were asked subjective questions regarding their experience about each of the three feedback conditions. Participants indicated higher subjective preference for the 'photos' condition as compared to the 'simple' condition. Unlike the previous study [4], where ASL experts graded the students' homework, this study [5] focused only on the subjective preferences of the participants.

While our lab has conducted some prior work to investigate how to provide feedback to ASL students, because a resource-intensive experimental study methodology was used in the prior design prototyping studies, our research team was only able to consider a limited set of design options. To address this limitation, in this paper, we discuss a project to investigate a wider set of design parameters (involving the language used in error messages and the visual appearance of the messages – including the use of photos or videos of correct usage) to determine some optimum design mock-ups for how the system should provide feedback to ASL students.

3 Research Questions

In this new study, building upon prior work, we have conducted a more thorough investigation of a wider variety of alternative designs for the presentation of feedback to ASL students, with a focus on students' subjective judgments about alternative designs for providing feedback on their signing through video. We investigate:

1. Do ASL students report subjective preferences for particular features that they would like to have in an immediate feedback system?
2. Do ASL students understand the feedback reported from using such a tool?

4 Methodology

To investigate alternative designs for the presentation of feedback to the students (e.g. about how they should improve their ASL signing), we conducted a study with 3 rounds of iterative re-designs and with a total of 24 participants. The participants consisted of 23 females and 1 male, and all were students at Rochester Institute of Technology who had at least 6 months of experience learning ASL.

Each round of the study included 8 participants who provided qualitative feedback on some designs. At the end of each round, themes were identified from their feedback and changes were made to the designs. Suggestions for changes or addition of new features became the test hypotheses for subsequent rounds of interviews.

Participants were first briefed that our lab was interested in understanding how they currently received feedback on their ASL assignments. They were then asked about their current experience of receiving feedback, the problems they faced and what changes they would like to see in the way they currently received feedback. The participants were then introduced to the idea of an automated feedback system that would provide feedback in real time. After explaining the scenario where such an automated system might be helpful, we presented the participants with non-interactive design mock-ups (some including videos of ASL) and asked them to provide feedback on the designs. We asked them some open-ended interview questions regarding their opinion about the visual appearance as well as the language used to convey the error message. The following sections discuss the prototype features shown to participants in each round, and the feedback they provided, which led to changes in the design.

5 Iterative Design – Round 1

Before showing participants any of our designs, we first asked them to describe how they currently receive feedback on their video assignments. As a follow up question, they were asked the kind of problems they faced receiving feedback. We learned that students typically received feedback through either an online feedback system called GoReact (used by RIT students learning sign language to submit their videos to the instructor and receive feedback comments) or through individual one-on-one feedback during weekly tutoring meetings with a human instructor. The feedback provided via the GoReact website would include either video or typed English comments.

The participants faced several problems with their current methods of receiving feedback. Technical video problems included frozen video, files getting corrupted, and blurry videos. P4 pointed out that the current method of "feedback is not quick enough" as it required the students to wait for the faculty to review and provide feedback.

The students also faced difficulties understanding what the professor was trying to convey in the feedback or if the professor used signs that they were not familiar with (P8, P6). This would lead the participants to watch the feedback with their friends to make sure they were getting the right message (P7). P4 described that it was difficult to "apply written comments to a visual language" while P1 indicated difficulties in translating between written English feedback and ASL.

For the first round of iterative testing, we started with testing four design features, which we presented to the participants. These features are as follows:

1. **Smiley Timeline versus Pointer Timeline** – As discussed in [4], our system will automatically identify moments in a video when a student is making an error (of a specific, limited set) or moments when they have done something that is clearly correct. The timeline bar on the 'My Video' column had 2 variations of visual markers illustrating the occurrence of an error and a correct instance (Figs. 2 and 3). We wanted to understand whether students preferred seeing a cartoon face (or smiley) or some other marker. In the first variation, a straight face was used to denote an error and a happy face for a correct instance. The second variation featured red and green dashes on the timeline to denote an error and a correct instance respectively.

Fig. 2. Screenshot of a design variation shown in Round 1. Label "1" indicates the smiley pointer timeline, "2" indicates presence of visual markers and "3" indicates font size of 21px (Color figure online).

Fig. 3. Screenshot of a design variation shown in Round 1. Label "1" indicates the green and red pointer timeline, "2" indicates lack of visual markers and "3" indicates font size of 17px (Color figure online).

2. **Arrows and No Arrows** – The designs also featured two separate variations with the feedback images (illustrating a correct ASL performance) having an arrow pointing to relevant facial expression or movement – or a version without any arrows (see Figs. 2 and 3). We wanted to know whether such arrows helped students understand the error (or a correct instance) that had occurred.
3. **Font** – In this first version, Slabo27px, a free Google Serif font, was chosen to display feedback text. To identify a suitable font size for reading feedback text, two variations of the font size, 17px and 21px, were presented to the participants.
4. **Image and Video** – In the "Feedback" region on the right side of the designs in Round 1, we presented either static images or video clips in which a signer demonstrated correct ASL performance. The variations were used to learn whether a static image would convey enough information about the error, or whether a video demonstrating the error would be preferable to students.
5. **Alternative Design** - An alternative design featuring both the 'My Video' and 'Feedback' columns on a white background was also presented to the participants at the end of the study (Fig. 4). This variation was incorporated to understand if the participants preferred a certain background color.

5.1   Feedback on Round 1 Designs

- **Feedback Video Structure.** The participants found the feedback videos to have incomplete information as it only indicated the error type that was found. Participants expressed that the feedback video should show "what was wrong, how to correct it and give an example" (P6). P3 described that a feedback video that said, "You did this, but this is how you're supposed to do it" would provide complete information to the student receiving feedback. This is important as P8 pointed out that sometimes "I don't see what I did wrong" and having the video showing

Fig. 4. Screenshot of a design variation shown in Round 1, with white backgrounds.

exactly what they did wrong and how to fix it would help them understand the error and learn how to improve their signing. Further, P6 described that students may learn to sign by copying the movements in the video. This explains why participants preferred having the feedback video show the correct way to sign for the errors. The participants P6 and P7 also mentioned that the feedback video should have a light or a plain background with the person wearing contrasting colors so that there are no distracting background elements and they can clearly understand the feedback being provided.

- **Video and Text Feedback.** Participants were very enthusiastic about the possibility of having the combination of video (or an image) and text feedback as it provided more information to understand the error made. While certain participants reported a preference for video feedback over static images (P5 and P2), P6 indicated that videos aren't necessary for all the 21 errors. This finding was supported by P1 who described that videos would be necessary for more "conceptual ideas" and P7 who stated the need for videos when "movements are involved".
- **Video Timeline.** Participants reported a preference for green/red markers on the timeline as compared to the smiley faces. P4 and P5 stated that they did not understand what the smileys represented. While P6 encouraged the idea of smileys as markers on the timeline but added that the straight face (which was used to represent the case in which an error occurred) was unclear. According to the participants, the other reason for the preference of red/green markers on the timeline was that it looked "more professional."
- **Participant Impressions about Arrows.** Arrows pointing to the relevant facial expression or movement were included in the designs to understand if they help to make sense of the error. It was learned that arrows on static images made understanding the error easier in certain cases (P6). While P2 had a strong opinion on the

arrows describing it as "confusing" and "not helpful", other participants supported the idea of having arrows and described it as helpful.

- **Alternative Designs.** The alternative test design condition featured the 'My Video' and 'Feedback' columns on a plain white background. P6 described the alternative design as "clean and clear" while P8 and P2 stated that the alternative design did not have a clear separation between the 'My Video' and 'Feedback' columns and thus made it difficult to visually identify which column denoted which section.

Participants in Round 1 also requested several features:

- Participants asked for a way to "save thoughts or questions that a student might have" (P7). Participants wanted to save tips or comments for themselves that might remind them when they were viewing the feedback. Participants also mentioned that if the software picked up a certain error, they wanted a way to mark the error that was picked up and show it to their professor to get more details on the error.
- P5 stated that a way to read aloud the feedback text would be an additional feature to consider as this would allow for another way for understanding the error. Participants also reported features such as the ability to enlarge videos and control the speed of the videos (both My Video and Feedback). Since ASL is a visual language, a student might have to replay the movements to fully understand what was being communicated. In the case when the signer is fingerspelling too fast, it would allow the students to able to view the videos at different speeds to better understand the feedback. Moreover, being able to view the videos full screen would allow the participants a better view of the feedback video or their own video.
- P4 suggested that their own video should stop playing the moment the error had occurred and the feedback video should pop up, P1 stated that having the control to individually view their own video and the feedback video was preferable.

Participants suggested several changes in the feedback text used in Round 1 (i.e. the text displayed on the screen that communicated to the user the nature of their ASL error or what they had done correctly). In addition to some of these messages appearing on the visual prototype designs, participants were also shown a document that listed approximately 30 text messages that the system may display.

- One of these messages indicated that the student had made an error when using a "question facial expression," participants asked for the system to be more specific in its error message – since there are two major types of question facial expression used in ASL ('WH' questions and 'yes/no questions'). As the signer should move their eyebrows differently for each type of question, participants felt that an error message referring to "question facial expression" was too vague.
- Additionally, participants suggested incorporating the following terms into the feedback messages: "sign prosody, non–manual markers, eye gaze and role shift." These terms are often used when describing ASL grammar in ASL courses, and such terms are especially well known among more advanced ASL students. The participants in Round 1 had higher level of ASL skills (second year or higher) and believed even beginner students would be able to understand these jargon terms. Their suggestion was to replace 'facial expression' by 'non-manual markers' and replace longer sentences with these jargon terms. For instance, they recommended

that a feedback text about "usage of proper body movement," could be replaced by a text about 'role shift,' and they recommended that a feedback text message about looking at a location should be replaced with a text using the term 'eye gaze.'

Based on this feedback from participants, we revised the text of the on-screen text feedback in our prototype designs. And we used the new version of the text feedback messages in Round 2.

6   Iterative Design – Round 2

For the second round of iterative prototype testing, new design features, discussed below, were presented to the participants based on feedback received during Round 1.

1. **Notes** – Multiple Participants in Round 1 suggested including the ability to save thoughts, comments, or tips in a form that would be easily accessible. For this reason, in the designs presented in Round 2, a 'Notes' feature was introduced that would allow the students to be able to save some textual notes about their thoughts or questions. Two design variations were considered: The first version shown in Fig. 5 allowed users to drag a sidebar from the left. The second version (Fig. 6) had a text box immediately below the 'My Video' timeline that allowed for directly typing thoughts and comments. Half of the designs that were presented to the participants made use of version one and the other half used version two.

Fig. 5. Screenshot of a design variation shown in Round 2. This image shows the different visual variations with 'Feedback' on dark background. Label "1" indicates the notes panel sliding from the left, "2" indicates presence of visual markers to denote errors and "3" indicates serif font. (Color figure online)

Fig. 6. Screenshot of a design variation shown in Round 2. This image shows the different visual variations with 'Your Video' on dark background. Label "1" indicates the notes panel at the bottom of the student video, "2" indicates absence of x marks on the top left corner, "3" indicates sans serif font and 4 indicates Read Aloud feedback icon (Color figure online).

2. **Video Player controls** – The designs in Round 1 had used static images to represent where a video could be shown in the 'Feedback' column, and the design lacked video controls that would be needed to play such a video. Further, participants had suggested including a feature to control the speed of the video or enable full-screen display of the video. Therefore, the designs in Round 2 incorporated these ideas.

3. **Read Aloud Feedback** – In Round 2, the concept of 'Read aloud' feedback was incorporated (based on suggestions in Round 1) to learn if students would like comments to be read aloud through speech synthesis software. In this prototype design in Round 2, a sound icon with a thin gray stroke in the bottom right corner of the feedback text box was used to represent the Read Aloud feature.

4. **Sans Serif and Serif fonts** – In Round 1, participants indicated that a font size of 21 pt. was comfortable to read. In Round 2, fonts were varied by their family – serif and sans serif to explore participant's preferences. For the tests, Open Sans (a Sans Serif font) and Playfair Display (a Serif font), both 21pt. in size were presented as possible alternatives to the participants for displaying feedback text. The decision to switch to Open Sans was because of the speed of loading time. Slabo 27px had a 11 ms delay loading the font when compared to Open Sans which is the fastest. Further, the font 'Slabo 27px' is fine tuned for use at the pixel size in the name. For the reasons, we switched to Open Sans as the Sans Serif font.

5. **Additional Visual Cues** – Participants in Round 1 suggested using shapes such as a red "X" mark and a green "check mark" to distinguish between an error occurrence and a correct instance. The designs in Round 2 incorporated such additional cues.

These cues were positioned on the top left corner of the feedback images. An equal number of screens were designed that had these additional visual cues (and those that did not) to understand how participants rated the benefits of having them.

6. **Alternative dark backgrounds** – Participants in Round 1 disliked the design with white backgrounds for both columns. For the designs in Round 2, we explored which of the two columns (My Video or Feedback) participants preferred having a dark background. Participants were presented with an equal number of design screens with 'My Video' on the dark background (and 'Feedback' on a light background) and 'Feedback' on the dark background (and 'My Video' on the light background).

As in the first round, before we showed any of our design prototypes in Round 2, we asked participants to describe issues they faced with the current method of receiving feedback from their instructor on homework assignments in which they submit a video of themselves signing. Participants described several issues they faced with GoReact. P3 expressed that it was difficult to understand how 'edit video' functionality works on GoReact. Moving videos to separate folders took a while for P1 to figure out. P3 also mentioned that the rubric-style feedback they received from their instructor about their ASL homework assignments did not provide enough specific information on how to sign better. P7 described that it was difficult to know what part of their video the instructor was specifically referring to in their feedback message – saying that sometimes "you don't see what mistake you made." P2 had a specific issue with understanding video-based feedback from their instructor in which the instructor used some fingerspelling in their signing, as the instructor's speed was very fast. P8 described another anecdote about a time when the instructor's feedback on a homework assignment mentioned "You could have used a different sign." The problem was that P8 did not know what other options were available (what other sign they should use). Finally, P7 mentioned that when making a video recording for a homework assignment, if it was necessary to pause and then resume the recording process, the resulting video may have an awkward pause.

After viewing the designs shown in Figs. 5 and 6, participants in Round 2 provided some feedback:

- **First Impressions.** Participants mentioned that they liked the layout of two columns showing both (My Video and Feedback video) side by side. P8 added that the title for two columns helped differentiate the two videos. Participants had diverse opinions about the background colors for the two videos. For the Round 2 designs, each participant was presented with 2 screens with 'My Video' on dark background and 2 screens with 'Feedback' on dark background. In the former case, the feedback text box had a dark background with white text while in the latter the feedback text box had a white background with black text. This was done to have contrast between the elements in the design. P1, P5, P7 and P8 preferred having 'My Video' on the dark background and 'Feedback' on a white background while P2, P3, P4 and P6 preferred the 'Feedback' video on the dark background.

- **Visual Cues.** A red X mark and a green check mark was placed on the left corner of the feedback images to distinguish errors and correct instances. P7 pointed out that having such visual cues helped "emphasize what had happened". P4 and P6 also described having such visual cues as a very helpful feature. P3 suggested that the visual cues be made thicker as they blended into the background making it difficult to see. The green/red markers on the video timeline was found to be more professional by participants in Round 1. Therefore, no changes were made to the markers. P3 suggested using bubbles instead of dashes as markers on the video timeline. P5 and P6 that the green/red markers were helpful in distinguishing the occurrence of errors and correct instances picked up by the system.

- **Impressions about Arrows.** Participants P1, P2, P6 and P7 indicated that having the arrows pointing to facial expressions would be helpful on static images.
- **Video Controls.** Participants described the ability to enlarge the video as a helpful feature (P3, P4 and P8). Controlling the speed of the videos was described as a requirement by the participants in Round 1. Therefore, speed control for both 'My Video' and 'Feedback' was incorporated in the designs for Round 2. Participants in Round 2 described that the speed control for their own video was not helpful and unnecessary (P2, P3).
- **Notes.** The feature to save thoughts and comments was described by the participants as a very helpful feature. However, the icon representing 'Notes' was described by participants as "not clear" (P7). They suggested that changing the icon to pen and paper. Two separate designs for the 'Notes' feature was shown to the participants. The first version had the 'Notes' sliding out from the left sidebar while the second version featured a text box below the 'My Video.' P1, P2, P3, P6 and P7 preferred the second version wherein the 'Notes' were placed right below 'My Video.' They elaborated that the second design version of 'Notes' allowed them to see their video while typing (P6), was easily accessible (P7), and did not require additional steps according to P3.
- **'Read aloud' feedback.** The feature to read aloud the feedback text was described as "not helpful" by P7, P8 and P3, "unnecessary" by P2 and P3. Participants also described that the icon for the 'read aloud' feedback was not clear and that the icon color did not have a strong contrast to be noticed by them.

Based on the feedback received in Round 1, the text for all the error messages that we anticipate using in this software were revised, e.g. to add more technical terminology about ASL linguistic concepts. This updated version of text feedback messages shown to participants in Round 2. Participants in Round 2 indicated that the feedback messages were still not specific enough as to what the student should do to improve their signing. For instance, one error message indicated that the student should "use a yes/no facial expression," but the message did not explain to students that such a facial expression requires that they raise their eyebrows as their tilt their head forward. Further, 3 participants who were ASL beginners pointed out that the technical terms 'eye gaze', 'non-manual markers' and 'role shift' did not make sense to them, and they rejected the notion of including such words in the feedback text. (These jargon terms had been introduced into the text in this round, based on suggestions in the Round 1 study).

6.1 Features Desired by Round 2 Participants

Participants suggested that if the software were to display both video-based and a text-based feedback to them about an error in their signing, it would be better if the student were shown the video (of someone signing in ASL to convey the error message) prior to seeing the English text version of this message. Students believed that it would be more educational if they had to try to understand the ASL video message first, before seeing the English text. P7 and P8 suggested hiding the feedback text under a 'Hint' button which when clicked would show the error message.

In our prototype, when a student was replaying their video to see if there were any error messages, the video of their own performance would pause whenever the system had some feedback for them – and then the feedback message (shown in the video region on the right side of the GUI) would play the feedback message. P8 requested that the feedback video should not always pop up and pause their own video; this participant wanted an option to disable the presentation of feedback messages so that they could re-watch the video of their own performance completely – without interruption.

For feedback videos in which a signer conveys in ASL some comment about an error in their signing, participants suggested that the videos should have a neutral backdrop (P1, P2 and P4) so that there are no distracting background elements in the video. In our prototype, the sample feedback videos consisted of an ASL signer who used ASL to communicate an error message to the student, and each video began with the sign WRONG/ERROR. P1 indicated that having the message begin with WRONG/ERROR may be disheartening. This participant also preferred messages that conveyed "what you were doing wrong versus what you're supposed to do."

P7, who had indicated that students sometimes need to pause and resume while they are making a recording, asked for a feature in which the student could replay what they had just recorded, so that they could more naturally and quickly resume recording the rest of their ASL message. P7 indicated that such a feature may help to reduce the "awkward pause" or discontinuity that may result when a student pauses the recording process and resumes mid-message. P6 suggested incorporating a 'Mute' button to eliminate background noise when recording videos.

P8 suggested having a system that would calculate the total number of error messages (perhaps grouped by different categories of mistakes in the students signing) so that students could more easily notice if there was a pattern as to what types of errors they make more frequently in their signing.

P4 requested that if a student types any text in the "Notes" region, then the software should note the time duration in the student's own video recording when the 'Note' region had been clicked – so that it would be possible to later review their notes in a time-synchronized manner with their own video.

7 Iterative Design – Round 3

For the third and final round, the following design alternatives were presented to the participants based on feedback received from the previous round.

1. **Color-coded Error Categories** – Round 2 participants suggested using color-coded error categories and that the interface should indicate the count of errors in each category. In our Round 3 designs, this information was included in a 'Summary' section below the 'My Video' timeline. The error categories in the 'Summary' section featured an expandable sub-section that listed the occurrence of error and duration of feedback in a tabular form. Two separate visual variations were explored: The first variation utilized flags (Fig. 7) while the second variation made use of diamonds (Fig. 8) on the video timeline and on the 'Summary' section.

2. **Hint Button** – Participants in Round 2 indicated that the feedback text should not always be present on the screen as it would not encourage the students to learn from the feedback videos presented. However, they indicated that having a way to toggle the feedback text would be helpful. The designs in Round 3 incorporated the changes by placing a 'Hint?' button below the 'Feedback' timeline which when clicked would display the error message.

3. **Notes feature** – The icon used to represent the 'Notes' feature in Round 2 was described as unclear by the participants. Therefore, the icon was changed to pen and paper for the designs in Round 3. The 'Notes' feature in Round 3 was designed as a sidebar drawing in from the right. This would allow the 'My Video' to be visible even when 'Notes' were being typed. It would also test whether having the 'Notes' slide out from the right would cause the students to face any problems or not. Additionally, the 'Notes' were organized by the time code highlighted on the top left corner to draw attention to the time code. The individual notes also featured a trash can icon to delete any notes that the students no longer needed.

4. **Sidebar Navigation** – The left sidebar navigation was designed to provide the users with easy access to the system features. Participants had suggested including a way to organize their notes, see the videos they submitted to the system and a help button. Additionally, the system had to have a way to Record video and toggle Settings if necessary. Hence, the designs in Round 3 had the left sidebar always accessible that would make the system easy to use.

5. **Segoe UI** – The results in Round 2 showed that participants described a Sans Serif font more easily readable than a Serif font. However, the Sans Serif font used in Round 2 (Open Sans) had a relatively loose kerning between characters causing uneven spaces to appear between letters. The result was that the text did not look visually pleasing. Hence, another Sans Serif font – Segoe UI (21pt. font size) was used for the feedback text in Round 3.

6. **Mute background noise** – Participants in Round 2 pointed out problems of having background noise in their video recordings. Hence, the designs in Round 3 included a 'Mute Background noise' button on the recording screen that allowed participants to toggle the background noise being recorded in the video.

7. **Pause – Resume Recording Feature** – One of the pressing problems that the participants described was having an awkward pause in their resulting video when needed to pause and resume during their recording process. Participants wanted the ability to view what was last signed to avoid relying on their memory to decide how to proceed. In the light of this issue, the resume recording feature was designed such that it would play the previous 10 s of what was signed so that there was a visual confirmation of the point where the recording was paused (Fig. 9).

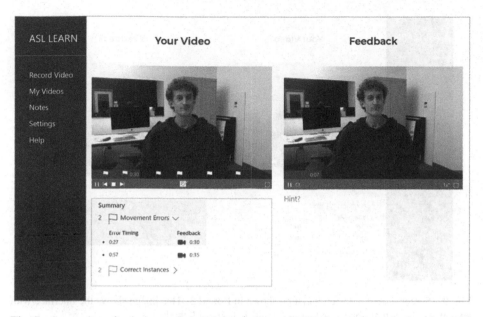

Fig. 7. Screenshot of a design variation shown in Round 3. This image shows the interface with flags as markers and summary of errors recognized by the system.

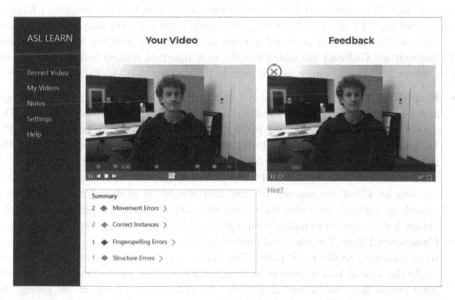

Fig. 8. Screenshot of a design variation shown in Round 3. This image shows the interface with diamonds as timeline markers to denote summary of errors and visual markers to illustrate error.

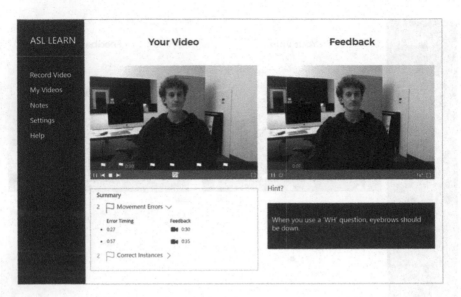

Fig. 9. Screenshot of a design variation shown in Round 3. This image shows the interface with textual feedback that appears when the 'Hint' button is clicked.

Participants described their first impression of the interface as 'simple', 'organized' and 'easy to use.' P3 mentioned that the interface was so simple that "you don't have to guess anything." P1 described that the color palette used was very easy on the eyes and the fonts looked clear and good. P2 pointed out similarities between the interface and the pre-existing GoReact but added that the new interface looked simpler. P2 and P4 also appreciated the 2-column layout used to display the two videos side by side.

- **Recording.** The record button in red instantly attracted the participants' attention and they described the functionalities of the interface 'very clear' (P3, P4). The option to mute background noise in the video was described very helpful by P3, P5, P6 and P7. The feature that allowed participants to view previous 10 s of the recording before resuming recording was acknowledged by the participants as a good feature to have. However, P5 and P8 suggested having a manual setting that allowed to adjust the amount of time that would be replayed before resuming recording. Further, they also added that the student should be presented with the option if they wanted to replay what was last signed or continue recording anyway.
- **Color-coded flags.** For the visual markers on the video timeline, 2 design variations were presented to the participants. The first variation had flags as visual markers while the second had diamonds as visual markers. The participants described the color-coded flags as "clear" and "easy" to understand. However, on seeing the second variation, P1 described that the diamonds were "easier to see." P5 described another problem wherein the flags might crowd the video timeline making it harder to distinguish between individual flags. Overall, the 'Summary' section indicating errors by category was found to very helpful by the participants.

- **Notes.** The designs for the 'Notes' was described by the participants as clear and simple. P1 and P5 pointed out that the highlighted timestamps on the individual notes was helpful.
- **Background Color.** According to the participants, the white background used for designs in Round 3 was clean, clear and a more user-friendly design as compared to the dark background color.
- **Feedback Text.** The idea that the feedback text would not be always visible was described by P2 as a good learning practice. While P1 and P6 found the term 'Hint' to be vague, P5 described that it wouldn't be difficult to know what 'Hint' did, once a student used the system.

Participants in the Round 3 study commented on several design features they would like to see added to the software:

- Participants requested was that the system have a countdown timer before beginning to record a video of their signing. Five participants had suggestions of this nature, indicating that having a countdown timer would allow them enough time to know that the system is ready to record. Further, P1 recommended that the system prompt the user if they want to stop recording in case the user accidentally pressed the stop recording button.
- P1 found the icon for muting background noise as distracting and suggested using a neutral color for the button to keep the focus on the record video button.
- The 'Summary' section consisted of expandable error categories listing errors and feedback duration in a tabular form. P1 recommended renaming the column heading from "Feedback" to "Feedback Duration" to clarify what the column represented.
- For the 'Notes' feature, participants expected that the system would pick the timestamp when the note button was clicked (P5) but the students should also have the ability to change the timestamp later. Further, P2 added that the video timeline should include visual markers that indicate a note had been added at that time. P6 added that bright colors highlighting the timestamp were not necessary and could be replaced by the timing in bold. P1 suggested making use of 'User Profiles' that would allow students to log in and see their individual feedback and notes in one place. P5 suggested replacing the 'Summary' tab with 'Notes' when clicked to be able to view both videos at the same time while taking individual notes.
- While participants in Round 2 had suggested that a speed control for when a student is re-watching their own video recording was not necessary, the participants in Round 3 requested a speed control for their own video. P4 and P5 described that when watching a long video that had multiple errors and correct instances, they would like the ability to change the speed of their video once they understood what had gone wrong. Additionally, P5 pointed out that the recording time of the video should be overlaid on the video as it is can be distracting. While P5 suggested having the recording time next to the 'Stop' button, P7 suggested having the time on top side of the video and P8 suggested having it near the video recording controls.

8 Limitations of This Work

The designs for the interface were presented to participants in this study as non-interactive visual prototypes; therefore, this study as not able to investigate participant's opinions about any time delays that would be involved when the system processes the feedback (for instance, if the system needed a few minutes to process the student's video prior to providing feedback, this delay time was not simulated in this study). A progress-bar or other indicator of "wait time" might be necessary if students need to wait for their videos to be processed.

Further, in this study, the system did not actually allow the participant to record and re-watch their own signing. Instead, when shown a visual design of a "rewatch your video and see feedback" page, a sample video of an ASL student's signing performance was shown on the prototype. These example videos of student signing were all short clips, e.g. one or two sentences in length. Thus, this study did not investigate how participants would react to designs when viewing feedback on a longer video that had been submitted, e.g. a long paragraph for which there would be multiple feedback messages may need to be displayed to the student. If the system needed to provide users with multiple videos containing feedback information about their video, then some list or sequence of such videos would need to be provided.

Additionally, the participant gender demographics were imbalanced, with 23 female and 1 male participant. It is not possible to predict what effect that this gender imbalance might have had on the studies, but it would be helpful to conduct future studies with a more balanced participant demographic.

9 Conclusion

The goal of this research was to design an interface for an automated ASL system that would provide real time feedback to students who are learning sign language. The effectiveness of this automated tool lies in its ability to provide and communicate the feedback to the students. Hence, it was important to understand the visual requirements of the interface and the language that should be used to present the feedback.

Three rounds of iterative re-designs were conducted to understand the important factors that would help students in understanding the feedback provided by the system. After every round, the interface design incorporated the feedback given by the participants and subsequent changes were made. These changes were based on the common themes that emerged across a round of interviews. The study was aimed at understanding the visual requirements –and the language/wording to be used in text messages on the system that convey feedback to students.

We found that participants wanted to see a summary of errors as identified by the system so that they could understand what they need to focus on improving the most. Further, participants encouraged that if feedback is conveyed in the form of a video message (of an instructor or someone performing ASL explaining the error) and as an English text message explaining the error, then the *video* feedback should be the primary focus of the interface, with the feedback text secondary. Participants (all students enrolled or recently enrolled in ASL courses) indicated that this is because

ASL is a visual language and having the text always visible would discourage the students from practicing their skill at watching and understanding ASL. Additionally, visual markers that indicate an error or correct usage presented on a timeline below a video were described as helpful by the participants. We also found that technical words such as "prosody, non-manual markers, etc." should not be used in the feedback text as beginner students might not be familiar with such terms. The participants also wanted the video feedback to have a structure that would tell them what they did wrong, how to correct the mistake, and to show an example of the correct way to sign.

One of the limitations of the study was that it did not consider the time delays that would be involved while the system processes the feedback. Furthermore, this study did not investigate the issue of accuracy – as we are developing an automatic system that would give feedback to students, this prototype presented an ideal scenario wherein the system always identified the what the error was. Future work could investigate additional higher fidelity prototypes that consider the delays involved and also consider the scenarios wherein a system incorrectly identified a sign as incorrect and how students could flag them as errors.

While this current set of studies primarily gathered subjective feedback which was evaluated qualitatively, we would also like to take a quantitative approach to this problem for future work, including asking participants to rate their preferences using Likert-scale questions or testing how well they understand the feedback that is displayed. In future work, as we develop an actual working system, we would also like to test our prototypes in a real-world setting where ASL students use it for their courses.

Acknowledgements. This material is based upon work supported by the National Science Foundation under award number 1400802 and 1462280.

References

1. Alharbi, R., Alharbi, D., Alharbi, A.: An investigation on the role of multimodal metaphors in e-feedback interfaces. Interact. Technol. Smart Educ. **8**(4), 263–270 (2011)
2. Goldberg, D., Looney, D., Lusin, N.: Enrolments in languages other than English in US institutions of higher education, fall 2013. Modern Language Association (2015)
3. Henderson, V., Lee, S., Brashear, H., Hamilton, H., Starner, T., Hamilton, S.: Development of an ASL game for deaf children. In: Proceedings of Interaction Design and Children, Boulder, CO (2005)
4. Huenerfauth, M., Gale, E., Penly, B., Pillutla, S., Willard, M., Hariharan, D.: Comparing methods of displaying language feedback for student videos of American Sign Language. In: Proceedings of ASSETS 2015 ACM SIGACCESS Conference on Computers and Accessibility, pp. 139–146 (2015)
5. Huenerfauth, M., Gale, E., Penly, B.S., Willard, M., Hariharan, D.: Designing tools to facilitate students learning American Sign Language. In: Poster presented at effective access technologies conference, Rochester, New York, USA, 10 November 2015
6. Lin, F.R., Niparko, J.K., Ferrucci, L.: Hearing loss prevalence in the US. Arch. Intern. Med. **171**(20), 1851–1852 (2011)
7. Mitchell, R., Young, T., Bachleda, B., Karchmer, M.: How many people use ASL in the United States? Why estimates need updating. Sign Lang. Stud. **6**(3), 306–335 (2006)
8. Strong, M., Prinz, P.M.: A study of the relationship between American Sign Language and English literacy. J. Deaf Stud. Deaf Educ. **2**(1), 37–46 (1997)

HCI Methods and Practices for Audiovisual Systems and Their Potential Contribution to Universal Design for Learning: A Systematic Literature Review

Rafael M. Toscano(✉) , Helder Bruno A. M. de Souza ,
Sandro G. da Silva Filho , Jaqueline D. Noleto ,
and Valdecir Becker

Audiovisual Design Research Group, Informatics Center,
Federal University of Paraiba, João Pessoa, Brazil
audiovisualdesign@lavid.ufpb.br

Abstract. Audiovisual production, which was previously mostly investigated by film and television studies, now becomes more comprehensive and can involve aspects of psychology, pedagogy, neuroscience and especially computing. In parallel to this evolution, studies on Universal Access or Universal Design have been expanding their scope for services, technologies and learning processes. This article presents a systematic literature review with the objective of investigating the main uses and applications of Computer Human Interaction (IHC) theories and methods related to the development of audiovisual systems and their possible contributions to Universal Design for Learning (UDL). The review contemplates articles from four databases in the period from 2010 to 2018. All 31 articles are classified by the context of the research problems and solutions proposed using principles of the grounded theory, that is, the codification of data through hierarchical categorization, establishment of relation and creation of central categories. These works are divided into three main groups of problems (user interfaces, theoretical and behavioral bases and system application) and solutions (theories and methods, design and evaluation of interactive systems and case studies). HCI state of the art productions and methods using audiovisual systems, i.e. audio and video, multimedia, hypermedia or even multimodal systems, has revealed a scenario of products, devices and interaction methods that have evolved and become more complex over the years. While not working directly with the Universal Design context, the various solutions present results that can benefit the development of learning support systems.

Keywords: HCI · Audiovisual systems · Universal Design for Learning

1 Introduction

Audiovisual production, which in early days was mostly investigated by film and television studies, now becomes broader involving aspects of psychology, pedagogy, neuroscience and especially computing [1]. The term audiovisual, according to [2]

M. Antona and C. Stephanidis (Eds.): HCII 2019, LNCS 11572, pp. 526–541, 2019.
https://doi.org/10.1007/978-3-030-23560-4_38

refers to works that mobilizes at once, sounds and images. This general definition does not, in turn, include the existence of more complex products or experiences. In this context, we present the compound term audiovisual system, understood by us as a merging of any elements of software, hardware and content that compose an artifact in order to provide solutions for entertainment, health, art, education, and many other subjects.

In parallel to this evolution, studies on Universal Access and Universal Design have been expanding their scope for services, technologies and educational processes [3]. This revealed the opportunity to survey fields previously mentioned and seek eventual interconnections. Although universal design discussion has an interdisciplinarity that involves guidelines for the fields of architecture, product design and software, we do not find a systematization of such principles that contributes for the construction of audiovisual systems focused on education.

This paper presents a systematic literature review (SLR), which objective is to research Human Computer Interaction (HCI) theories and methods main usage and applications related to audiovisual systems developments and possible contributions to the Universal Design for Learning (UDL).

Present work is structured as follows: section two presents general concepts about UDL; section three details systematic review and its methods; section four categorizes research results into perspectives of problems and solutions; section five shows analyses and discussion results; the 6th and last section bestows this paper's conclusion.

2   Background

Universal Design for Learning proposed by [4] splits its framework into three networks that toils on different features belonging to strategies used in content production regarding the act of teaching. Each UDL network has its own specific goal, which considers apprentices individual capacities and their different previous experiences, promoting multiple ways of engagement, representation, action and expression for learners.

The Affective Network is branched into grids, and its objective is to make learning purposeful and motivating for the apprentice. This network is known as the "WHY" of learning and is sorted into three categories or lines of treatment for teaching content called: access, build and internalize. The access line is concerned in providing options to recruit interest, which can be done by optimizing individual choice and autonomy, optimizing content relevance, value and authenticity and minimizing threats and distractions. The build line suggests options to sustain learners efforts and persistence, vary demands and resources to optimize challenges, foster collaboration, community and increase mastery-oriented feedbacks. The internalize line recommends options for self-regulation with topics to promote expectations and confidence by optimizing motivation, facilitating coping skills, strategies and developing self-evaluation and reflection.

Recognition and Strategic Networks lines are also divided into tables with the same access, build and internalize grids, working respectively with aspects of "WHAT" and "HOW" of learning. Their goals are focused on learners who are resourceful and purposeful (Recognition Network), strategists and more objective (Strategic Network). In the access line of the Recognition Network, the Perception grid suggests topics of perception, offering means to customize the display of information and alternatives for audible and visual information. The build line proposes options for the grid of Language and Symbols in topics that recommends treatment on vocabulary and symbol clarity, clear syntax structure, text decoding support, mathematical notations and symbols, the promotion of understanding between languages and demonstrations through different media. The internalize line indicates needs in the Comprehension grid to activate and supply background knowledge, highlight patterns, critical features, great ideas and relationships.

In the Strategic Network, the access line suggests Physical Action, with topics including the variation of methods for response and navigation and the optimization of access to tools and assistive technologies. In the building line we have the Expression and Communication grid with topics suggesting the use of multiple media for communication, multiple tools for construction, composition and construction of fluences with graduated levels of support for performance practices. The internalize line offers a grid that indicate needs for options of Executive Functions in topics of: appropriate goal-setting guidance; support planning and strategic development; information and resource management facilitation; monitoring progress capacity enhancement.

3   Methods

This review includes articles from three different databases and classifies the results from problems and solutions proposed by the analysed papers. For this SLR, we adopted the PICO (Population, Intervention, Comparison and Outcomes) protocol for initial organizing. Population comprises primary studies on HCI theories and methods. Intervention indicates theories or reports on use, development and evaluation of audiovisual systems. For Comparison and Outcomes it was sought to see which studies were directly involved with UDL principles or had potential contribution to the development of audiovisual systems aimed at the universal design for the learning field. Based on these topics, the following questions were raised: what is discussed about audiovisual systems at HCI, what are the main technologies and methods used for systems development, and what practices or recommendations converge with UDL principles.

3.1   Search Protocol

The string used for the article gathering at Springer, ACM Digital Library and Scopus was "('Audiovisual System' OR 'audiovisual' OR multimedia OR hypermedia) AND ('Human Computer Interaction' OR 'User experience') AND 'Design Method'". These bases were chosen because they are the most relevant for the topics of computing, multimedia and interdisciplinarity. In addition to the search string, the following filters were added: articles published exclusively in English language, complete articles published in periodicals or conferences, articles referring to human computer interaction sub discipline or group of areas of computation and applied social sciences and temporal filter with articles published between 2010 and 2018.

3.2   Inclusion and Exclusion Criteria

All articles were reviewed considering inclusion (I) and exclusion (E) criteria. Studies were included in the systematic review by meeting the following conditions: I1, only primary study; I2, available for full access; I3, include the elements of the string in title, abstract or keywords; I4, and deal objectively with theories or methods of development and /or use of audiovisual systems. Regarding exclusion conditions (E), the studies were rejected when: denying criteria I1, I2 and I4; or if the paper has been duplicated, thus being considered only the most recent publication.

3.3   Studies Selection and Classification

Applying this search protocol to mentioned databases, we obtained 336 articles for review (Table 1).

Table 1. Application of search criteria.

Base	Return	Criteria			
		Duplicated	Irrelevant	Unavailable	Approved
ACM	14	0	12	0	2
Scopus	3	0	0	1	2
Springer	319	0	292	0	27
Result	336	0	304	1	31

At the end of the review, 31 articles followed the conditions proposed by the scope of this research. The results were: two articles at ACM database, two at Scopus and 27 at Springer. Only one article was unavailable for access.

The approved articles were classified by the context of the research problems and solutions proposed using principles of the grounded theory, that is, the codification of data through hierarchical categorization, establishment of relation and creation of central categories. Initially the 31 articles were organized by affinities in order to find patterns between the themes. After this first organization general groups were created. The coding occurred in two cycles, one for the research problems (P) and the other for the proposed solutions (S).

4   Results

In this section, we present the results of the systematic review.

4.1   Problems

Research questions were classified in this review from three large groups. The first group is related to interfaces possibilities and includes new affordances (P1) and optimization and redesign (P2) categories. The second group contains discussions about theoretical bases and individual behaviors from scenario inspection (P3) and scientific gaps and theoretical limitations (P4) categories. The third and final group refers to diversified use of audiovisual, multimedia or multimodal systems, which includes categories of artifact development (P5) and special needs (P6).

User Interfaces
Studies [5–13] within this group range from investigations on creation of minimalistic graphic interfaces to complex multimodal experiments that establish new modes of interaction between individual-system and individual-individual.

New affordances (P1): issues related to new modes of systems interaction and perception are in such themes as the poetic exploration of location-based narratives [5]; variables that stimulate immersion in panoramic media [6]; user data snatching to generate new requirements and symbols for interaction [7]; spatial and visual inter-action dynamics that integrates visitors in the same enjoyment experience [8].

Optimization and redesign (P2): the work on improvement or reconfiguration of projects is an issue addressed in studies in contexts of language aspects optimization, layout and narrative to facilitate the awareness of children about sexual violence [9]; navigation problems in systems with complex and extensive information generates cognitive overload [10]; interaction with Head Mounted Displays [11]; content pro-duction in virtual reality [12]; information consumption while watching television [13].

Theoretical and Behavioural Bases
Search problems of the second category includes articles [14–23]. Studies range from theoretical researches to surveys about consumption habits, perception and reception of technology, and conceptual discussions on demands for new routines and standard-ization processes.

Scenario inspection (P3): the understanding of scenarios comprehend studies from themes such as interface development for children from 9 to 11 years old using electronic games [14]; how do children perceive and interact with interfaces visual elements [15]; generation of informative content on treatments for cancer on toddlers [16]; the unfolding of gender demography in the scenario of development and use of electronic games [17]; the teaching of affordance concept within interaction design [18].

Scientific gaps and theoretical limitations (P4): discussions and comparisons on methodological practices are present in methods to evaluate and support emotion and affectivity aspects in interface design [19]; absence of application development guides in the context of body interactions [20]; lack of foundation to describe and foster the development of complex audiovisual systems [21], teaching skills and abilities with focus on children with Autism Spectrum Disorder [22] and procedural content gen-eration in games [23];

Systems Application
This category include studies [24–35]. The research questions of these studies incor-porate the development of solutions for diverse contexts and targets.

Artifacts development (P5): studies indicated the interest in artifacts production in contexts such as content teaching on marine animal species using augmented reality [24]; content adaptation interface for engaging students in learning [25]; simulation of classroom situations to improve teacher education and decision making [26];

audiovisual production to compose exhibition environments [27]; game for Brazilian Sign Language learning [28]; engagement in informal learning activities in the museum [29]; multisensory environment for reinforcement in offline stores [31];

Special needs (P6): issues related to the development of artifacts for individuals or contexts are framed in topics of autonomy of people with intellectual disabilities [32]; development of interfaces for the elderly in hybrid TV systems [33]; Degradation of spatial visualization capacity by elderly people [34]; Limitations in rehabilitation therapies for stroke patients [35];

4.2 Solutions

All 31 articles approved in the review were also classified according to the proposed solution. The result of this process defined three general groups: theories and methods, design and evaluation of interactive systems and case studies.

Theories and Methods

The first group is related to a proposition of notes, guidelines or theoretical reviews on production, use, and analysis of audiovisual systems. This set is divided into the categories of new modes of interaction (S1), development tools (S2) and methods and frameworks (S3).

New modes of interaction (S1): the proposition of new interfaces or affordances is present in topics such as the insertion of audio to establish interaction feedback in spatial and 3D information systems [10]; in the creation of an interactive gestural language that allows individuals to communicate with character on a second screen while accompanying a main narrative on a television [14];

Education in HCI (S2): The central idea of this category is the discussion about work processes for designers and developers. There is only one work related to this theme. The study proposes teaching the concept of "affordance" through the contextualization of the limitations and comorbidities of individuals with autism spectrum disorder [18];

Methods and frameworks (S3): the absence of design guides, implementation and conceptual bases capable of describing certain processes motivated the studies of this category to investigate topics such as the creation of a framework for the development and evaluation of poetics in narratives based on location [5]; pervasive media framework and augmented reality as a focus on integrating experience into multiple spaces [30]; framework that integrates aspects of media and learning particularities of autism for the development of audiovisual systems focused on teaching skills and abilities [22]; method to analyze emotions and motivations to design affective user interfaces [19]; method of interaction integrates multimodal and affective elements to use Virtual Reality systems [11]; method to design multimedia interfaces for m-learning [25]; model of creation and analysis of complex audiovisual systems that considers multiple levels of identity, motivation, content and experience from the convergence of concepts of human computer interaction with studies of media and audience [21]; a method that works on personalizing difficulty levels of games as a way to expand the potential of m-learning applications [35]; architecture that assists the development of multimodal interfaces for TV use by the elderly [33]; agile methods for applications development in the context of corporal interactions [20];

Design and Evaluation of Interactive Systems

The second group of researches consists of the following articles [6, 8, 13, 16, 17, 23, 24, 26–29, 31, 32, 34]. This set is divided into the categories of educational tools (S4), assistive technology (S5) and experimental artifacts (S6).

Educational tools (S4): issues related to development of artifacts for educational processes or activities is the focus of this category. The studies cover topics such as the development of an educational game that teaches entrepreneurship principles geared towards female players demographics [17]; the production of an interactive audiovisual system to broaden the engagement of museum visitors [27]; development of a multimedia and interactive environment designed to help young patients understand cancer-related medical treatments from language and age-appropriate representations of these individuals [16]; development of an augmented reality educational system with the ARToolkit library [24]; development of a dialog-based game where teachers can simulate teaching and learning situations in classroom [26]; development of a guessing game for listening users learn sign languages [28];

Assistive technology (S5): the development of artifacts for individuals in specific contexts is the focus of this category involving two studies: the creation of an augmented reality spatial visualization training system to reduce or delay the loss of the ability of elderly in perception of space surrounding them [34]; development of a collaborative communication and localization system for people with intellectual disabilities and their caregivers on daily commutes [32].

Experimental artifacts (S6): this category focuses on unconventional systems, interfaces and solutions. Studies that integrate item (S6) presents themes such as the development of immersion from three-dimensional audio applied in omnidirectional movies [6]; prototype of an android application that detects the program being watched on TV and provides real-time information in a contextualized way [13]; tool that assists the generation of procedural content for game design [19]; development of a visit support system that integrates augmented reality with the social content and geolocation of the public [8]; audiovisual system integrating the experience in museums from the virtual abstraction of the operation of the objects on display [29]; multisensory experiment for store environments [31].

Case Studies

The last group of solutions (S7) involves studies [7, 9, 12, 15]. These articles have in common the development of studies on the understanding of the use, reception and impact of the proposed artifacts. The works that integrate this group present the following themes: production and verification of an experiment that involves aspects of presence, disorientation, sense of control, pleasantness, exploration and vertigo for the experience of immersion with virtual reality [12]; study of usability and engagement for contents generated by the collection and recommendation of multimedia data in social media [7]; comparative study on design improvements [9]; organization of a participatory design process with children to raise requirements as they interact with aspects of color, layout and visual perception [15].

5 Analysis and Discussion

In this section the results obtained in the systematic review will be discussed and related to the theoretical framework of this research.

5.1 General Analysis

Studies identified within this review vary from methodological expositions to diverse levels of complexity and support technical experiments. It is possible to identify the use of technologies such as head-mounted displays [11, 12]; motion and odor sensors [19]; cybergrasp data glove [31]; computer tables [35]; Eye-Tracking, Set-top box [33]; smartphones [12–14, 32] and computers [24, 34, 35] in contexts as virtual and augmented reality [6, 11, 12, 30, 34]; web application [7, 15, 26]; embedded systems [13, 33], digital games [17, 28] and wearable and tangible interfaces [18].

The classification proposed by this review between research problems and solutions allows an insight into how researchers have directed the themes of their studies. Analyzing Fig. 1 we can see the predominance of the category of problems in the item development of artifacts (P5) and the strength of the category of Theories and Methods (S3). This scenario reflects a typical approach of HCI to be concerned as much with the particularities of the artifacts development in certain themes or scenarios as the organization of knowledge, processes and standards in theories and methods to assist designers and developers.

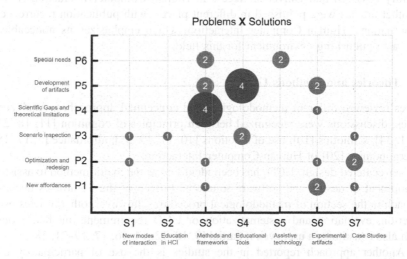

Fig. 1. Relationship between categories

The research question with the greatest recurrence among the studies is the production of artifacts (P5). In response to this theme, the studies propose two methods and frameworks to increase engagement on young people (S3); four systems aimed at teaching marine animals, history, sign language and improvement of teacher didactics

(S4); and two experiments on the development of multisensory artifacts for exposure environments (S6).

Yet the solution with greater recurrence is the item of methods and frameworks (S3). The proposition of processes, recommendations or development models is related to five of the six research questions in this review. Solution S3 is presented in the questions, use of poetics in location based narratives of the new affordance category (P1); improvements in the experience of using Head Mounted Displays of the Optimization and Redesign category (P2); theoretical limitations to describe and assist the development of complex audiovisual systems, absence of guides for the development of applications in the context of corporal interactions, use of emotion in the design of interfaces and absence of approaches to help the use of audio and video technologies for children autistic patients of the Scientific Gaps and Theoretical Limitations category (P4); interfaces for increased engagement in museums and learning from the Development of artifacts category (P5); therapies in patients suffering from stroke and television interfaces for the elderly special needs category (P6).

In relation to studies temporal occurrence, two works were published in 2018, eight in 2017, two in 2016, five in 2015, five in 2014, four in 2013, one in 2012 and four in 2011. Regarding its publications, studies are divided in four periodical papers and 27 conference papers, published as book chapters or as a unity at conference proceedings. International Human Computer Interaction event went out as the highlight between publishing databases, containing 12 papers out of 31. These 12 articles are divided between event's main track and affiliated conferences: Design, User Experience, and Usability (DUXU) and Universal Access in Human Computer Interaction (UAHCI). The other articles were published in different places, with publication recurrence only at International Human Computer Interaction, which emphasizes its noticeable relevance as a publishing environment for this field.

5.2 Theories and Methods Used

Studies reviewed different methodological and conceptual approaches. Analyzing the articles, discussions were recognized between principles of cognition [11, 18, 21, 22, 25, 31, 34]; semiotics [10], use of emotions [10, 11, 19, 35]; affordance [5, 17, 18, 22] and ergonomics [20] of Human Computer Interaction.

User-centered design (UCD) has been identified as the major method to assist in the development of design and software solutions. Fifteen of the 31 articles declare this approach in the section of methodological procedures, however, other articles use data collection, evaluation and systematization of UCD requirements in their processes, which also constitutes a use, even if partial [9, 10, 12, 14, 16, 17, 19–21, 28–30, 32, 33, 35]. Another approach reported in the studies is the use of participatory design, sometimes associated to the UCD or other concepts, as a way of approaching individuals in the development of the proposed solutions [5, 8, 15, 18, 23, 32]. Besides these two central topics, there are references in the studies to the concepts of color, layout and visual structures from the principles and methods of User Interface Design. There is also the use of the task analysis technique to understand the scenario of the proposed artifacts [10, 17, 20, 25, 34, 35].

Evaluating the use and proposition of methods by the chronology of publication of the studies, we can notice the predominance of UCD and participatory design in the years 2010 to 2013. From 2014 it is possible to identify other methodological and conceptual perspectives among the studies. For example, in the year 2015 Universal Instructional Design is applied associated with the UCD [35]. In 2016, UCD is used in conjunction with agile methods of project management to build a game focused on the particularities of young girls [17]. As early as 2017 the UCD appears related to the concepts of multimodal systems design and affective computing [11]. In the same year the study [19] works on the expansion of user-centered design for analysis of scenarios and affective contexts and the study [21] propose a new theoretical methodological model that integrates general principles of HCI to media studies, denominated Audiovisual Design (AD). Finally, in 2018 we have the study [22] that starts from AD to generate a sort of adaptation of the method to the context of educational products aimed at autistic children.

Synthesizing theoretical foundations of the studies and their propositions, a table was assembled with methods and frameworks that present a potential contribution to the development of audiovisual systems to support learning (Table 2). Although the studies of category (S3) have proposed several models or frameworks, only the researches [19, 21, 22] are configured as potential theoretical-methodological approaches, since they are not restricted to guides or exclusively technological recommendations. Contributions from other studies will be elaborated in Sect. 5.4 of this review.

Table 2. Methods to artifacts development.

Used by	Method	Potential	Limitations
[9, 10, 12, 14, 16, 17, 19–21, 28–30, 32, 33, 35]	UCD	Methodology with tools and practical instruments for software development assistance	Generalist scope and does not provide educational context
[19]	Emotions in UCD	Use of emotions in an interactive project building	No validation and scope are restricted to analyze scenarios
[21]	Audiovisual Design	Media approaches to content, identity, engagement, and experience factors	No validation, generalist scope and does not provide for educational context
[22]	Audiovisual system for ASD	Media approaches to learning in cognitive, affective and psychomotor skills	No validation and scope are initially restricted to autism

The first table item is user-centered design. UCD is a widely consolidated method in software development studies. Its use in parallel to Universal Design can occur in a variety of ways, for example, in the construction and validation of personas and scenarios from the learning requirements and common points between users that have turned into design and software solutions. Although the UCD does not directly provide educational solutions, the method offers a set of practical tools to assist in the development of any kind of software. These instruments, together with UDL guidelines, can enable artifacts aimed at educational purposes.

The second item is the method proposed by study [19]. The work adds the traditional perspective of user-centered design (UCD) theories of motivation and emotion. Incorporating a taxonomy of 22 emotions to the UCD the study propose a method to initially help the construction of interaction scenarios solely. As in the previous item, there are no particularities of the educational context incorporated in the method. However, the increase of the emotional aspect expands the potential of the UCD as a method to support the creation of audiovisual systems, since the creator of the system will have more information to design the content according to the audience.

The third table item is the theoretical methodological model named Audiovisual Design (AD) proposed by [21]. The study incorporates central discussions on Human Computer Interaction as utility and quality of use issues, identity and motivation of media studies. The model defines four possible levels of interaction and states that the alternation between them occurs through four design lines: content, identity, motivation, and experience. Audiovisual Design is not necessarily contrary to the UCD approach; while the UCD is a method of supporting any type of software, the AD is directed specifically to the interaction project of audio and video systems. Like the previous items the AD does not mention learning in its scope. However, its understanding of interaction levels and design lines is a potential practice for the creation of education systems when combined with the UDL guidelines.

The fourth and final item of the table is a framework for the development of audiovisual systems for children with autism. Study [22] is an application of the model developed by [21]. The framework for autistic children incorporates the aspects of media and interaction of audiovisual design into the taxonomy of educational objectives. This arrangement is positioned to particularities of individuals as an instrument that comprises levels of interaction and learning in cognitive, affective and psychomotor domains. Among the methods and models, this is the only one that incorporates the learning process. Nevertheless, its scope of use is initially centered on the particularities of individuals with Autism. The systematization of these recommendations, together with the UDL guidelines, is a potential approach for the construction of educational systems for broad access.

It is not the intention of this work to point out a definitive solution to build audiovisual systems based on the UDL principles. The table is only intended to organize identified approaches and to reflect on their potential aspects and limitations. The perceived proposals vary in two perspectives of UCD and AD as general methodological proposals to the development of computational and audiovisual systems that can be applied in several contexts and two more specific approaches one for the analysis of scenarios and the other for autistic children. These approaches have been shown as potential practices that can be harnessed in other classes of problems outside of their initial proposition. Comprovations and checkings on the effectiveness of the methods may be verified on future studies with this purposes.

5.3   Contribution to UDL

This review gathered a total of 31 different works. From these studies, a total of six articles were compatible with the UDL principles: the Affectivity (I), Recognition (II) and Strategic (III) networks. From the total, twenty-seven articles presented some development potential for audiovisual systems focused on education.

Studies [14, 15, 17, 19, 22, 28] presented direct relationship with UDL principles, since they work on issues such as: the varied experiences of the individual during learning; the different ways of executing a specific activity; the best forms of content representation, considering the medium in which it is inserted and the forms of representation itself (audio, text, images, etc.) [25]; use of pictorial language to increase apprentices engagement and broaden learning necessities [14]; aspects of game development to motivate girls in entrepreneurship, taking gender features into account [18]; facilitation of sign language teaching from appropriate representations [28]; survey of requirements for the construction of interfaces that improve aspects of representation, engagement and expression for children and their learning characteristics [15]; the proposal of building interactive artifacts based on cognitive, affective and psychomotor domains related to media enjoyment and learning focused on children with Autistic Spectrum Disorder [22];

Although 24 articles from the total have no direct connection with the principles of the UDL, 20 of them showed solutions with some potential to help the development of audiovisual systems oriented to education, thus forming a total of 27 works (those 20 added to the other 7 with direct relation with UDL) that may contribute in some way to the development of these systems [5–8, 10–17, 19–22, 25–35]. The contributions identified are systematized in Table 3.

Table 3. Potential contribution to UDL.

Article	Type	Potential contribution	Network
[12]	Strategy	Ux Dimensions to increase immersion in virtual reality	I, II, III
[5]	Technical	Generating content from the location of individuals	III
[25]	Method	Guidelines for creating m-learning content	II
[35]	Method	Designing difficulty levels of games in m-learning	II
[10]	Technical	Use of audio as interaction feedback in 3D environments	II, III
[21]	Method	Media approaches to identity, engagement, and experience factors.	I, II, III
[30]	Strategy	Multisensory representation of content	II
[20]	Method	Develop body tracking based applications	I, III
[34]	Technical	Use of system based in AR for spatial visualization training	II, III
[13]	Technical	Multi-screen information consumption	I, II
[27]	Technical	Use metadata Collector for create Interactive system	II
[14]	Strategy	Pictorial interaction language creation for interface development	I, II, III

(*continued*)

Table 3. (*continued*)

Article	Type	Potential contribution	Network
[16]	Strategy	Age-specific interactive hypermedia environment	I, II
[33]	Technical	Multimodal interaction interface development for accessibility	I, II, III
[17]	Strategy	Particularities for the development of games for young girls	I, III
[8]	Technical	Visiting system development to integrate visitors	I, III
[30]	Technical	Framework design for visiting engagement	I, III
[11]	Method	Affective multimodal interaction design for VR	I, II
[6]	Method	Immersive experiment development on panoramic media	I, II, III
[28]	Strategy	Presentation of content in game format	I, II
[29]	Strategy	Multiple means of visual representation	II, III
[26]	Strategy	use of game to simulate decision making	I, III
[32]	Technical	Collaborative system to support educational mediation	I, II, III
[7]	Technical	Use of data to generate new interface requirements	I, II, III
[19]	Method	Use of emotion for designing user interfaces	I, III
[15]	Strategy	Inspect children interface perception	I, II, III
[22]	Method	Planning of audiovisual systems from educational objectives	I, II, III

The contributions presented in Table 3 are divided into ten technological resources to enable systems and interfaces of interaction, eight conceptual recommendations and seven strategies to use systems to achieve results such as engagement and learning. The influence of these studies vary according to their impact on UDL networks. Nineteen studies contribute to the goals of the affectivity (I) and recognition network, while 18 studies contribute to the Strategic (III) network. Only four studies have direct collaborations with all UDL networks. The integration of these approaches to UDL principles is seen by this review as a potential contribution to the development of new audiovisual learning systems.

6   Conclusions

This article presented a systematic literature review with the objective of investigating main uses and applications of theories and methods from Human Computer Interaction (HCI) related to the development of audiovisual systems and their possible contributions to Universal Design for Education (UDL). HCI's state of the art productions and methods using audiovisual systems, i.e. audio and video, multimedia, hypermedia or even multimodal systems, has revealed a scenario of products, devices and interaction methods that have evolved and become more complex over the years. While not working directly with the educational context, the various solutions present results that can benefit the development of learning support systems.

Among these 31 studies there are researches that highlight the most varied technical solutions that extend the way in which the systems perceive better the interaction of the individuals, in real time or not, in such a way as to return adequate solutions to their cognitive, motor and affective capacity. Although none of the identified studies propose a totally direct relation of their results to the context of universal design, it is possible to recognize that the lessons learned can be systematized and attributed to a context of greater benefit of individuals. For example, studies that have worked on understanding forms of content representation and interaction for the elderly, autistic, and children have pointed to the same premise of the need for direct communication that avoids mental overload (excessive use of colors, shapes and movement) and approaching more natural interaction interfaces. Another example of this relationship are the several studies that highlight the variation in the interfaces of representation and interaction as a way of guaranteeing to the public new forms identification and engagement for the execution of some activity.

Finally, it is believed that audiovisual system production can benefit by incorporating already consolidated discussions such as intelligent tutoring or smart learning, virtual learning environments and video lectures.

References

1. Meixner, B.: Hypervideos and interactive multimedia presentations. ACM Comput. Surv. **50**, 1–34 (2017)
2. (2006) Dictionary of Media Studies. A & C Black, London
3. Smith, K.H., Preiser, W.F.E.: Universal Design Handbook. McGraw-Hill, New York (2011)
4. Gordon, D., Meyer, A., Rose, D.: Universal Design for Learning: Theory and Practice. CAST Professional Publishing, Wakefield (2016)
5. Millard, D.E., Hargood, C.: A research framework for engineering location-based poetics. In: Proceedings of the 2015 Workshop on Narrative and Hypertext – NHT 2015, Guzelyurt, Northern Cyprus, pp. 13–16. ACM Press (2015)
6. Kondo, Kazuaki, Mukaigawa, Yasuhiro, Ikeda, Yusuke, Enomoto, Seigo, Ise, Shiro, Nakamura, Satoshi, Yagi, Yasushi: Providing Immersive Virtual Experience with First-Person Perspective Omnidirectional Movies and Three Dimensional Sound Field. In: Shumaker, Randall (ed.) VMR 2011. LNCS, vol. 6773, pp. 204–213. Springer, Heidelberg (2011). https://doi.org/10.1007/978-3-642-22021-0_23
7. Spiliotopoulos, D., Tzoannos, E., Stavropoulou, P., Kouroupetroglou, G., Pino, A.: Designing user interfaces for social media driven digital preservation and information retrieval. In: Miesenberger, K., Karshmer, A., Penaz, P., Zagler, W. (eds.) ICCHP 2012. LNCS, vol. 7382, pp. 581–584. Springer, Heidelberg (2012). https://doi.org/10.1007/978-3-642-31522-0_87
8. Huang, W., Kaminski, B., Luo, J., Huang, X., Li, J., Ross, A., Wright, J., An, D.: SMART: design and evaluation of a collaborative museum visiting application. In: Luo, Y. (ed.) CDVE 2015. LNCS, vol. 9320, pp. 57–64. Springer, Cham (2015). https://doi.org/10.1007/978-3-319-24132-6_7
9. Kim, D., Kwak, J., Sung, Y., et al.: Enhanced user interface for a sexual violence prevention education app. In: Park, J.J., Jin, H., Jeong, Y.-S., Khan, M.K. (eds.) Advanced multimedia and ubiquitous engineering, pp. 635–639. Springer, Singapore (2016). https://doi.org/10.1007/978-981-10-1536-6_82

10. Absar, R., Guastavino, C.: Nonspeech Sound Design for a Hierarchical Information System. In: Kurosu, M. (ed.) HCD 2011. LNCS, vol. 6776, pp. 461–470. Springer, Heidelberg (2011). https://doi.org/10.1007/978-3-642-21753-1_52

11. Kang, J.: Affective multimodal story-based interaction design for VR cinema. In: Chung, W., Shin, C.S. (eds.) Advances in Affective and Pleasurable Design, pp. 593–604. Springer, Cham (2017). https://doi.org/10.1007/978-3-319-41661-8_58

12. Kauhanen, O., Väätäjä, H., Turunen, M., et al.: Assisting immersive virtual reality development with user experience design approach. In: Proceedings of the 21st International Academic Mindtrek Conference on - Academic Mindtrek 2017, Tampere, Finland, pp. 127–136. ACM Press (2017)

13. Chuang, Y.-L., Liao, C.-W., Chen, W.-S., Chang, W.-T., Cheng, S.-H., Zeng, Y.-C., Chan, K.-H.: Use second screen to enhance TV viewing experiences. In: Rau, P.L.Patrick (ed.) CCD 2013. LNCS, vol. 8023, pp. 366–374. Springer, Heidelberg (2013). https://doi.org/10.1007/978-3-642-39143-9_41

14. Endrass, B., Hall, L., Hume, C., Tazzyman, S., André, E.: A pictorial interaction language for children to communicate with cultural virtual characters. In: Kurosu, M. (ed.) HCI 2014. LNCS, vol. 8511, pp. 532–543. Springer, Cham (2014). https://doi.org/10.1007/978-3-319-07230-2_51

15. Tengku Wook, T.S.M., Salim, S.S.: Exploring children's requirements for the graphic design of WebOPAC. In: Jacko, J.A. (ed.) HCI 2011. LNCS, vol. 6764, pp. 627–636. Springer, Heidelberg (2011). https://doi.org/10.1007/978-3-642-21619-0_75

16. Gansohr, C., Emmerich, K., Masuch, M., Basu, O., Grigull, L.: Creating age-specific interactive environments about medical treatments for children and adolescent patients diagnosed with cancer. In: Göbel, S., Wiemeyer, J. (eds.) GameDays 2014. LNCS, vol. 8395, pp. 141–152. Springer, Cham (2014). https://doi.org/10.1007/978-3-319-05972-3_15

17. Heath, Corey D.C., Baron, T., Gary, K., Amresh, A.: Reflection on assumptions from designing female-centric educational games. In: Marsh, T., Ma, M., Oliveira, M.F., Baalsrud Hauge, J., Göbel, S. (eds.) JCSG 2016. LNCS, vol. 9894, pp. 25–41. Springer, Cham (2016). https://doi.org/10.1007/978-3-319-45841-0_3

18. Yantaç, A.E., Esin Orhun, S., Ünlüer Çimen, A.: A challenging design case study for interactive media design education: interactive media for individuals with autism. In: Marcus, A. (ed.) DUXU 2014. LNCS, vol. 8520, pp. 185–196. Springer, Cham (2014). https://doi.org/10.1007/978-3-319-07638-6_19

19. Sutcliffe, A.: Designing user interfaces in emotionally-sensitive applications. In: Bernhaupt, R., Dalvi, G., Joshi, A., K. Balkrishan, D., O'Neill, J., Winckler, M. (eds.) INTERACT 2017. LNCS, vol. 10515, pp. 404–422. Springer, Cham (2017). https://doi.org/10.1007/978-3-319-67687-6_27

20. Breyer, F., Reis, B., Vasconcelos, L.A., Cavalcanti, A., Teixeira, J.M., Kelner, J.: Design methodology for body tracking based applications - a kinect case study. In: Marcus, A. (ed.) DUXU 2013. LNCS, vol. 8014, pp. 227–236. Springer, Heidelberg (2013). https://doi.org/10.1007/978-3-642-39238-2_25

21. Becker, V., Gambaro, D., Ramos, T.S.: Audiovisual design and the convergence between HCI and audience studies. In: Kurosu, M. (ed.) HCI 2017. LNCS, vol. 10271, pp. 3–22. Springer, Cham (2017). https://doi.org/10.1007/978-3-319-58071-5_1

22. Toscano, R., Becker, V.: Audiovisual design of learning systems for children with ASD. In: Antona, M., Stephanidis, C. (eds.) UAHCI 2018. LNCS, vol. 10907, pp. 613–627. Springer, Cham (2018). https://doi.org/10.1007/978-3-319-92049-8_45

23. Craveirinha, R., Roque, L.: Studying an author-oriented approach to procedural content generation through participatory design. In: Chorianopoulos, K., Divitini, M., Hauge, J.B., Jaccheri, L., Malaka, R. (eds.) ICEC 2015. LNCS, vol. 9353, pp. 383–390. Springer, Cham (2015). https://doi.org/10.1007/978-3-319-24589-8_30

24. Martono, K.T., Fauzi, A.: Design of learning media for fish classification with augmented reality technology. In: 2017 4th International Conference on Information Technology, Computer, and Electrical Engineering (ICITACEE), Semarang, pp. 270–275. IEEE (2017)

25. Nagro, S., Campion, R.: A method for multimedia user interface design for mobile learning. In: 2017 Computing Conference, London, pp. 585–590. IEEE (2017)

26. Nordvall, M., Arvola, M., Samuelsson, M.: Exploring simulated provocations. In: Zaphiris, P., Ioannou, A. (eds.) LCT 2014. LNCS, vol. 8524, pp. 182–193. Springer, Cham (2014). https://doi.org/10.1007/978-3-319-07485-6_19

27. Damnjanovic, U., Hermon, S., Roitman, A., Hazan, S., Deutscher, T., Scheffer, H.: Bringing new life to video narratives for exploring cultural heritage. In: Nesi, P., Santucci, R. (eds.) ECLAP 2013. LNCS, vol. 7990, pp. 1–12. Springer, Heidelberg (2013). https://doi.org/10.1007/978-3-642-40050-6_1

28. Moura, G., et al.: Luz, Câmera, Libras!: how a mobile game can improve the learning of sign languages. In: Marcus, A. (ed.) DUXU 2013. LNCS, vol. 8013, pp. 266–275. Springer, Heidelberg (2013). https://doi.org/10.1007/978-3-642-39241-2_30

29. Narumi, T., Ohara, H., Kiyama, R., Tanikawa, T., Hirose, M.: Switching the level of abstraction in digital exhibitions to provide an understanding of mechanisms. In: Yamamoto, S. (ed.) HCI 2014. LNCS, vol. 8522, pp. 567–576. Springer, Cham (2014). https://doi.org/10.1007/978-3-319-07863-2_54

30. Kahl, T., Iurgel, I., Zimmer, F., Bakker, R., van Turnhout, K.: RheijnLand.Xperiences – a storytelling framework for cross-museum experiences. In: Nunes, N., Oakley, I., Nisi, V. (eds.) ICIDS 2017. LNCS, vol. 10690, pp. 3–11. Springer, Cham (2017). https://doi.org/10.1007/978-3-319-71027-3_1

31. Bie, B., Zhang, Y., Fu, R.: Study on display space design of off-line experience stores of traditional handicraft derivative product of ICH based on multi-sensory integration. In: Marcus, A., Wang, W. (eds.) DUXU 2018. LNCS, vol. 10920, pp. 459–470. Springer, Cham (2018). https://doi.org/10.1007/978-3-319-91806-8_36

32. da Silva, D.M.A., Berkenbrock, G.R., Berkenbrock, C.D.M.: An approach using the design science research for the development of a collaborative assistive system. In: Gutwin, C., Ochoa, Sergio F., Vassileva, J., Inoue, T. (eds.) CRIWG 2017. LNCS, vol. 10391, pp. 180–195. Springer, Cham (2017). https://doi.org/10.1007/978-3-319-63874-4_14

33. Hamisu, P., Heinrich, G., Jung, C., Hahn, V., Duarte, C., Langdon, P., Biswas, P.: Accessible UI design and multimodal interaction through hybrid TV platforms: towards a virtual-user centered design framework. In: Stephanidis, C. (ed.) UAHCI 2011. LNCS, vol. 6766, pp. 32–41. Springer, Heidelberg (2011). https://doi.org/10.1007/978-3-642-21663-3_4

34. Chang, K.-P., Chen, C.-H.: Design of the augmented reality based training system to promote spatial visualization ability for older adults. In: Shumaker, R., Lackey, S. (eds.) VAMR 2015. LNCS, vol. 9179, pp. 3–12. Springer, Cham (2015). https://doi.org/10.1007/978-3-319-21067-4_1

35. Hocine, N., Gouaïch, A., Cerri, S.A., et al.: Adaptation in serious games for upper-limb rehabilitation: an approach to improve training outcomes. User Model User Adapt. Interact. 25, 65–98 (2015)

Virtual and Augmented Reality in
Universal Access

Analysis of Biofeedback Through Heartbeat Obtained by Exposure to Phobia Through Virtual Reality

Edvaldo de Vasconcelos[1](✉)🆔, Amaro Neto[2]🆔,
Lillian dos Santos[3]🆔, and Paula Ribeiro[4]🆔

[1] Audiovisual Design Research Group, Informatics Center,
Federal University of Paraíba, João Pessoa, PB, Brazil
edvaldorpg@gmail.com
[2] Informatics Center, Federal University of Paraíba, João Pessoa, PB, Brazil
Amaro.euclides@gmail.com
[3] Technology Center, Federal University of Paraíba, João Pessoa, PB, Brazil
lila.dosantos@gmail.com
[4] Center for Communication Tourism and the Arts,
Federal University of Paraíba, João Pessoa, PB, Brazil
paularibeiro.16@hotmail.com

Abstract. This article aims to analyze the biofeedback (result obtained, through an analysis made based on data of human aspects through some method of evaluation) of deaf individuals male and female listeners by means of Beats Captured through a smart watch (a device that measures heart beats with a certain accuracy). This analysis was possible by conducting an experiment, where individuals with acrophobia or fear of heights were exposed to it, through two videos, representing places with a certain level of height, but with different perspectives through Virtual Reality (VR) technology. At the end of the experiment, a database was organized, and from that, some analyses were presented that we can draw from the gathered data, in addition, some curiosities are presented about this new type of technology aimed at the treatment of Phobias by means of exposure therapy through virtual reality (Vret), subsequently, some comparisons of (Vret) with other existing therapies that do not use virtual reality technology (VR) are made and describing the benefits and advantages of Use of the (Vret).

Keywords: Biofeedback's · VRET · Virtual Reality

1 Introduction

Virtual Reality (VR) has been used in a wide range of contexts; Having its efficiency accepted in the health area, using more varied technology with experimental purposes in the treatment of phobias [1]. It is possible to observe the use of (VR) in a broad context in mental health, as an example the treatment of anxiety disorders, anorexia and bulimia nervosa, support for diagnosis and psychotherapeutic counseling [1].

M. Antona and C. Stephanidis (Eds.): HCII 2019, LNCS 11572, pp. 545–554, 2019.
https://doi.org/10.1007/978-3-030-23560-4_39

This new VR utilization paradigm is responsible for the profound social and technological transformations observed in the last decade. In the United States, Canada, Italy, Belgium and other countries that developed VR applications, it is observed the use of technology employed even for professional training [1]. These experiments simulate, for example, the interaction between the physician and the patient, phobias scenarios and situations that compromise the normal state of the individual.

Products and services related to VR virtual reality have been applied in several contexts, including Vret virtual reality therapy for clinical support in the treatment of phobias, among others. The use of this technology in the sessions is mainly associated with the patient's report and the therapist's careful observation and the use of this therapy works with the focus of a cognitive and emotional education for the individual to deal better with the Phobias. In order to investigate (a) the use of heart rate monitoring as biofeedback, that is, a biological indicator of the individual's experience and (b) the difference in reception between hearing and non-hearing individuals, this paper proposes an experiment with adults who present the clinical picture of acrophobia, a phobia popularly known as "fear of height".

In this article, virtual reality (VR) will be used to design a scenario of the individual's discomfort object, such as acrophobia due to being a necessarily common phobia and to offer a low impact /risk and to verify its biofeedback and to assemble through the data collected a statement of emotional and physical stress levels.

2 Theoretical and Conceptual Bases

In this section, we present the theoretical bases of this study.

2.1 Virtual Reality

The age of virtual reality comes in full force. For years, science fiction productions, whether in the movies, video games, books, comics, used and abused "super" characters who have used virtual reality devices for various reasons, then in the year 2016, some glasses (VR) are released with this vision of science fiction and has become increasingly popular among technology fans, allowing you to see the virtual world in a different way and sensations.

The term virtual reality refers to an immersive experience based on a set of three-dimensional images or recordings. One of the goals of this technology is to enable the user to enjoy an equally satisfying feeling equally for the real world. To provide this sense of presence in the "real" world VR integrates sophisticated devices such as sensors in the headset and motion sensors that must be kept with one's hands or just with one. and several others that can be docked. A person using an equipment VR along with their sensors can interact with the items, move around and look around in the artificial world. This effect is commonly created by virtual reality equipment, for example headphones and movements; The headset consists of two small screens that are and face the user's eyes, but there is also how to recreate the effect in larger rooms, designed with several large screens replacing the glasses and giving 3D vision through these screens.

Other equipment helps in immersion, such as systems known as Haptic, which recaptures sensations such as touch, applying forces, vibrations or movements to the user, thus giving a greater sensitivity of the virtual world that overflowed the "new experience" as a very rewarding thing.

2.2 Definition of Fear and Phobia

Fear is an emotional behavior that has phylogenetic (unconditional) and ontogenetic (conditional) origin. According to the Darwinian model of natural selection, stress behaviors are selected throughout evolution and are typical of a large part of the species. In addition to unconditional fear, a large part of the animal species, as well as man, presents behaviors of fear that are acquired during life (Ontogenetic), through conditioning of the respondent type (Pavloviano) and operant type.

It is good to highlight that fear, like other behaviors, can be developed without any pairing between neutral stimulus and unconditional stimulus, this is an individual may never have made contact with the aversive stimulus that he avoids. When this occurs, the behavior may have been established by (a) behavior of a model (Bandura 1969), (b) rules formulated from the behavior of the model or taught by the model (Albuquerque et al. 2013; Catania et al. 1990), (c) transferência de função; A complex process that happens when equivalence classes are formed between arbitrary stimuli (Dack et al. 2012).

Fear can acquire highly harmful functions for the individual and thus generate what in the literature is called "phobia". Phobia is a type of anxiety disorder characterized by persistent fear or repulses of an object or situation. If she is unable to avoid the objects or the situation, the person begins to show signs of distress, such as faint, or panic attacks. In these cases, beyond behavior there may be other alterations such as insomnia, feelings of guilt, pessimism, inability to concentrate and total lack of interest in something that relates to phobia. It may be a generalized or specific fear, private or public, being characterized as a simple discomfort or something extremely harmful to your physical or mental health (American Psychiatric Association 2013).

2.3 Casual Psychological Interventions

Traditional treatment of people with specific phobias or fears is done through psychological or pharmacological intervention. Meanwhile, Baldwin et al. (2005) recommended only to consider pharmacological intervention with the use of selective serotonin reuptake inhibitors or benzodiazepines when clients exhibit disabling phobias and considerable distress and did not respond to less invasive psychological approaches.

2.4 Phobia Treatment Using Virtual Reality

In addition to the evolution that psychotherapies for fear and phobias have presented regarding their methods of intervention, they are being modified by the introduction of computational technologies. Techniques such as exposure to the object of discomfort underwent an enormous modification when virtual reality technologies emerged, thus having a safe and controlled form of the results of the reactions of the individuals, with, for example, the use of simulators, which made the exposure would be increasingly explored and applied to the area of Health and Psychology. The influence and updating of techniques that use virtual reality.

In 1993 there were no publications in the area of Health, on virtual reality and 6 years later (1999) 53 articles were located. However, when comparing this data with what we have today, the difference is very great: a new search made in the PUBMED database, returned 8,852 references, by typing the keyword "virtual reality".

3 Method

The evaluation was made with 10 different individuals, where we asked the participants a few questions, the participants were male and female listeners and deaf people over 18 years of age with the same phobia; among the asked questions, one of them was about what each felt after the experiment and opinions about Virtual Reality technologies.

The participants of this study were chosen through a set of 30 people by a psychologist from the Federal University of Paraíba. Taking into consideration the aspects of the individuals for better analysis and data capture for the experiment. The experiment was carried out under the supervision of the psychologist and during the experiment there was no contact with the individual so that there were no changes in the data and in the immersion of the individuals. The participants and the psychologist did not know themselves, so that it is the first time that all participants and the psychologist met together, thus avoiding some analysis bias due to already knowing each other.

3.1 Experiment Description

It was presented two videos A and B. The former consisted of a scene where there was a bridge located above a lake, and the goal was to reach the other side of the bridge; with the immersion of the virtual reality stimulating vision, and through wind and birds sounds from the headphones, the participant could move his view to any angle (side), so that it was all dynamic (360°) while the video was playing, showing the displacement to the other side of the bridge, it was the participant's responsibility to control the direction he could look . The later video was incorporated by a passenger into a roller coaster trolley where the same presented dynamic in the 360° view video A was composed, and the sounds of people screaming, and more ambient sounds; we utilized a precision clock of precise beats during the experiment; before and after the experiment a professional heartbeat was used and the same intelligent clock the two gave very similar values.

3.2 Equipment

It was used a video game PlayStation 4 Fat, the player of the videos that was used was the Youtube application, the interface of visualization was the Sony Virtual Reality glasses from the PlayStation itself of the following specifications Display: 5.7, "OLED, field of view 100°, Graphics: 1080p RGB (960xRGBx1080 per eye; 90–120 Hz refresh rate), Sound: 3D audio, via TRS connector and microphone input available; Input: Positional tracking of 9 LED's via Playstation Camera; Connectivity: PlayStation 4 connection via HDMI (with a size of 3 m), an Earphone: Samsung Brand, Model: In-Ear Stereo IG935, PlayStation Camera with two lenses (cameras) to check the 9 Sensors of the (VR), with a resolution of 1280 × 800 pixels (with lenses having a f 2.0, with 30 cm focus distance, and 85° field of view). With the dual camera configuration, the camera can operate in different modes, depending on the application destiny. The two cameras can be used together for the perception of depth of objects in their field of vision, or only one can be used for motion tracking and another for recording videos, the Tv playback of the images for observation was a Tv 60 in., LG LCD.

3.3 Equipment

The environment used was a room of size 5 × 3 m with totally free space for the movement of individuals at 2.5 to 3 m from the video capture camera and recording motion sensors to have a good average movement space of the space was isolated so that there was no disturbance of external lighting.

3.4 Results and Discussion

We asked a series of 20 questions about the experience of exposure to phobia with VR, such as whether people already had contact with this kind of technology, if they had any negative aspect after its use, if they could tell the difference between virtual and real, whether the sound mattered or not in the experience, among other questions. All participants had notoriously a great experience due to the encounter with a technology they had never used. Aside the questions, we also created tables with the levels of variation of the beats and we have also separated the sex of the person and whether or not he was a listener so that we can verify in his subsets the data whether or not there was any coherence between the same subsets.

An important part was the analysis of the experiment in the aspect of sound, because, as the research was conducted on listening and deaf participants, sound was a fundamental part, and certainly the biggest difference between the two sets of partic-ipants, and ended up making the greater curiosity between the aspects of the partici-pants, because the sound really made a difference between the listeners and the deaf. The listeners had a greater reaction to the fear of height in relation to the deaf. In addition, deaf people had an average change in heart rate less than the listeners heart rate, showing the uncontrolled situation or lack of immersion or real understanding of the situation or simply a natural reaction of the functions thus, showing greater control in terms of phobia in height. It is worth mentioning that the two minor variations were deaf; Showing in this study that the sound in the view of our current virtual reality (VR) technology and according to the videos A and B presented and the analyzes done with the established points were more effective with sound.

The following tables named Tables 1, 2, and 3 show the summary of what was done in the experiment where we analyzed the participant's results one by one, placing the pulse reader on his wrist, thus storing the heartbeat before the tests and give with the smartwatch on his arm, during the experiment every 2 s he calculated the heart rate again, the intelligent clock sent the calculation to the computer through his application (pre-established by the watch manufacturer) in the case "Background Wear" after saving the heart rate soon after performing the experiment we do another check of the beats without the virtual reality apparatus and headphones of the experiment and we move on to the questions about the experience with the experiment, catalog the data and move on to the next individual to shut down people, Table 1 consists of a table of the 10 individuals selected in general, deaf people and listeners where we can see their variations and the observations of the experience as well as their sex Tables 2 and 3 result in a separate analysis only to confirm that we did tests before with listeners and with sound and without sound so that we can really know the importance of the sound in the experiment and giving an even greater security to the data and final conclusion of the test.

Table 1. Table of general results listeners and deaf.

Individual	H.Before	H.During	H.After	Variation	Sex	Condition	Note
1	83	90	96	15	F	Listener	Little fear
2	72	85	78	13	F	Listener	Fear
3	86	92	90	6	F	Deaf	Happiness
4	102	110	105	8	F	Deaf	Dizziness
5	94	100	98	6	M	Listener	Dizziness
6	76	82	80	6	M	Deaf	Curiosity
7	92	98	90	6	M	Listener	Distrust
8	84	87	80	3	M	Deaf	Curiosity
9	85	89	87	4	M	Deaf	Anxiety
10	100	127	105	27	M	Listener	Fear

Table 1 shows the data of the hearing and deaf individuals doing the test, the listeners made the headset test by emitting sound from the respective videos A and B, as shown in the subsequent tables, which are the Tables 2 and 3 the listeners when exposed to the test without the sound showed results of very low immersion, different from when it was with the sound, showing the immersion data much more expressive, the three tables were placed so that any questioning that may be made can be answered, for example: Why did not they test with soundless listeners? then Tables 2 and 3 may respond.

We put as general table in the case the Table 1 a new experiment of deaf and hearing with results different from the Tables 2 and 3 by the factor that we repeated the experiment with the listeners to give the certainty of the greater immersion due to the video with the sound of any form can if we observe the similarity of data from both Tables 1 and 3 that are experiments with sound listeners.

Table 2. Experience without sound.

Individual	H.Before	H.During	H.After	Variation	Sex	Condition	Note
1	88	92	90	4	F	Listener	–
2	90	88	92	-2	F	Listener	–
3	90	95	94	5	M	Listener	–
4	100	98	94	-2	M	Listener	–
5	105	108	98	3	M	Listener	–

Table 3. Experience with sound.

Participant	H.Before	H.During	H.After	Variation	Sex	Condition	Note
1	83	98	96	15	F	Listener	–
2	72	85	78	15	F	Listener	–
3	94	100	98	6	M	Listener	–
4	92	98	90	6	M	Listener	–
5	100	127	105	27	M	Listener	–

Table 2 shows how the results of the Variation were low, this is the experience without sound for listeners showing no immersion in the experiment.

In the table we separated the subjects from 1 to 5, the beats before the procedure the average sum of the beats during the video, and the beats after the video, we calculated their variations in the difference of beats before the experiment and during the experiment, we also show the sex and the condition, which in the case of this table were all listeners, Table 2.

Table 3 shows the great variation of the heart beats of the experiment with sound to the listeners, thus showing the great difference between Tables 2 and 3, showing the sound function for a greater immersion in the experiment.

In the table we separated the subjects from 1 to 5, the beats before the procedure the average sum of the beats during the video, and the beats after the video, we calculated their variations in the difference of beats before the experiment and during the experiment, we also show the sex and the condition, which in the case of this table were all listeners, Table 3.

The technologies that exist today in VR are not totally geared towards equality between deaf people and listeners. There is a great disparity between these sets, this is what this article also shows, that a technology like RV is a breakthrough in many areas such as health, education, entertainment, thus demonstrating great flexibility in many ways, to be desired when it comes to the fairness of satisfaction and /or immersion of the two sets of participants studied, i.e. deaf and hearing, this may be due to the low demand of buyers who are deaf compared to hearing buyers, or to participants who consume products in general do not need such drastic changes because of the custom of having only a median rather than a maximal experience or someone whose disability does not fully immerse, thus making people with specific disabilities out of the target public of companies that produce for this technology.

4 Conclusion

There were some limitations in the research due to a few points. The main one was the exclusive use of a single virtual reality glasses model, which was PlayStation VR, so there would be no way to analyze and see the data that were based on other virtual reality glasses, such as Gearvr or Sansung HMD Odyssey. The fact that this technology is still very expensive and we couldn't afford it, that everyone in this test should have the same phobia /fear containing something that was equal to all participants and it could be that the data were with a variation of much higher beats are available from a more immersive environment, obtaining a greater reality in the experiments, like a Digital cave.

With the data extracted from this evaluation through biofeedback and the questions asked, we can evaluate that VR draws attention, due to its interaction but efficient response to human body actions, with almost instantaneous response of its movements through its sensors. Also, the participants ability is embedded in the scenario of interaction due to his set of lenses to give the 3d look, in the case of this work, the immersion was of his phobias and /or fears of height, as shown in videos. A and B, where it was collected from the cardiac variation, thus leading us to understand that even with the deafness deficiency and the set of participants being eclectic all had a similar behavior of increased anxiety before the display of the point of discomfort, shown that yes virtual reality resembles the real world; With some participants more intensity and others with less intensity, as shown in Tables 1, 2 and 3 of tests. In any case we have to have a greater discussion, due to the immeasurable possibility of the evolution of this technology of Virtual Reality VR in the area of health as well as in the area of entertainment and studies thus giving a huge range of experiments that can be done and studied so that with the advancement of studies.

We need to open up more discussion space to the technological aspects, taking into account people with disabilities, we have to take the technology to the people who are unable to have, or at least appreciate such technology making the VR technology a force of union, not of segregation, we have to create technologies and technological advances that can be inserted in any group of people, and we do not segregate people by their differences; this work then shows that it does have the possibility of finding a junction of factors because the data are similar between deaf and hearing all the two sets tend to have an increase in the beat before the exposed of their phobias showing the importance of terms that advance in the technology through the study of the most varied cases, with or without special needs with the most varied individuals, and of different types of forms.

One part that became peculiar in the test was the aspect of sound because as the research was done over listeners and deaf, the sound eventually became a fundamental part and it certainly is the biggest difference between the two sets of individuals. This was something that was not expected among the proposed aspects due to being a joint thinking team that would not make the sound difference due to the fear of height seemingly to be almost all visual, however the sound really made a difference between listeners and deaf. Listeners presented a greater reaction to fear when exposed to fear along with sound as shown in Table 1 (general) and the notorious difference in Tables 2 and 3 that was presented while the deaf.

Deaf people had a lower average heart rate (measured by the smart evaluation clock) than the hearing loss. In addition, the two worst heart rate variations were deaf people, we considered the higher the heart rate variation, but the individual would be anxious and more immersive to the experiment treating the virtual world as real hence the more anxious the greater response to the experiment we can then classify the people who had the most reaction to the experiment when separated showed that the set of people with more reaction were the listeners; showing in this study that the sim sound in the vision of our current Virtual Reality technology and according to the videos A and B presented were more effective with sound, this raises a hypothesis will be that we are not forgetting to create a truly inclusive technology of parameters equal to all? and how can we do this analysis? and really understand the reality of every great group in society how can we create something egalitarian for the use of all?.

We tried to perform a more effective treatment of Phobias and /or fears to confront in an immersive way and compare with the existing treatments for such purpose using virtual reality. We created a more interactive environment not only in the video part but rather that individuals can, through moving controls, interact with the proposed scenario. We conducted a test with more people of different aspects to expand the scope of future research findings. We created a model of study that will progress in the future to a method that in addition to measuring the stress in some way, will calm the individual through something stimulus that makes the scenario more comfortable.

Acknowledgments. We thank the MSc. Diógenes Galdino Gondim and Rafael M. Toscano for the support in the development of this research.

References

Wendt, G.W.: Tecnologias de interface humano-computacional: realidade virtual e novos caminhos para pesquisa. Arch. Clin. Psychiatry (São Paulo) **38**(5), 211–212 (2011)

Robles-De-La-Torre, G.: International Society for Haptics: Haptic technology, an animated explanation. Isfh.org (2010). Archived from the original on 2010-03-07. Accessed 26 Feb 2010

Banaco, R.A., Zamignani, D.R.: An analytical-behavioral panorama on the anxiety disorders. In: Grassi, T.C.C. (ed.) Contemporary Challenges in the Behavioral Approach: A Brazilian Overview, pp. 9–26. ESETec, Santo André (2004)

Baldwin, D.S., et al.: Evidence-based guidelines for the pharma- cological treatment of anxiety disorders: recommendations from the British Association for Psychopharmacology. J. Psychopharmacol. **19**, 567–596 (2005). https://doi.org/10.1177/0269881105059253

Simão, M.J.P.: Terapia comportamental cognitiva. Técnicas para o tratamento de transtornos ansiosos. In: Wielenska, R.C. (ed.) Sobre comportamento e cognição: questionando e ampliando a teoria e as intervenções clínicas e em outros contextos, pp. 248–255. ESETec, Santo André (2001)

Albuquerque, L.C., Paracampo, C.C.P., Matsuo, G.L., Mescouto, W.A.: Variáveis combinadas, comportamento governado por regras e comportamento modelado por contingências. Acta Comport. **21**, 285–304 (2013)

American Psychiatric Association: Diagnostic and Statistical Manual of Mental Disorders, 5ª edn. American Psychiatric Publishing, Washington (2013)

Dack, C., McHugh, L., Reed, P.: Transfer of judgments of control to a target stimulus and to novel stimuli through derived relations. Learn. Behav. **40**, 448–464 (2012). https://doi.org/10.3758/s13420-012-0066-6

Bandura, A.: Modificação do Comportamento. Interamericana, Rio de Janeiro (1969)

Laboratório de Sistemas Integráveis, USP. http://www.lsi.usp.br/interativos/nrv/caverna.html

Using Digital Puppetry to Prepare Physicians to Address Non-suicidal Self-injury Among Teens

Kathleen Ingraham[1]([✉]), Charles E. Hughes[1], Lindsay A. Taliaferro[1],
Nicholas J. Westers[2], Lisa Dieker[1], and Michael Hynes[1]

[1] University of Central Florida, Orlando, FL, USA
kingraham@ucf.edu
[2] University of Texas Southwestern Medical Center
and Children's Medical Center, Dallas, TX, USA

Abstract. Research has shown that adolescents that engage in non-suicidal self-injury (NSSI) are at an increased risk of suicidal behavior. Primary care providers can help identify NSSI behaviors and assess suicide risk; however, many physicians report feeling underprepared to do so in a clinical environment. Thus, this simulated training experience was built to create an authentic practice interview environment. Two adolescent cases have been modeled using avatars and a digital puppetry system that allows for complex and nuanced non-verbal behavior. After several iterations, a combination of gesture based puppetry, real-time head tracking, and triggered automated animation sequences was found to provide suitable control to create subtle and appropriate non-verbal behaviors in the context of the interview. Data is currently being gathered from pilot groups of medical residents and physicians to evaluate the authenticity of the simulated environment and to explore whether this simulated interview training changes physician behavior in a way that may help prevent adolescent suicide.

Keywords: Non-suicidal self-injury (NSSI) · Virtual learning environments · Digital puppetry · Interpersonal skill training · Physician education

1 Introduction

Suicide now ranks as the second leading cause of death among adolescents [1]. Though non-suicidal self-injury (NSSI; deliberate destruction of body tissue without suicidal intent and not socially sanctioned) remains distinct from a suicide attempt [2, 3], over time, NSSI increases risk of suicidal behavior [4, 5]. The National Institute of Mental Health (NIMH) recognizes that enhancing clinicians' ability to identify persons considering suicide could help prevent more suicides [6]. A high priority area for mental health professionals involves reducing the burden and mortality associated with suicidality through research on early detection, assessment, and interventions [7]. Identifying youth who engage in NSSI and adequately assessing and managing self-injury represents a strategy to prevent suicidal behavior among adolescents. Non-mental health care providers, including primary care providers (PCPs), are positioned to lead such important public health interventions to prevent youth suicide [8]. However,

© Springer Nature Switzerland AG 2019
M. Antona and C. Stephanidis (Eds.): HCII 2019, LNCS 11572, pp. 555–568, 2019.
https://doi.org/10.1007/978-3-030-23560-4_40

research has shown that only about 1 in 4 PCPs routinely inquires about and addresses NSSI among youth [9]. Further, relative to other areas of mental health care, pediatric PCPs feel least prepared to address and want more training on NSSI [9].

To address gaps in training, this simulated training is aimed at non-mental health clinicians and involves developing and validating the efficacy of training in a realistic virtual environment enhanced with tools for reflective learning. Ultimately the goal is to help reduce NSSI and suicidal behavior among adolescents. We propose the training intervention will improve clinicians' skills in identifying youth who engage in NSSI and increase the frequency and thoroughness with which they assess NSSI and suicide risk. Upon completion of the prototype simulated environment, a large-scale controlled clinical trial will be designed to validate the effectiveness of the training intervention in reducing NSSI and suicidality.

2   Study Design

Residents within two pediatric residency programs in Florida will complete the didactic training and simulation practice. Residents in one pediatric residency program in Texas will participate in the didactic training only. We will collect pre-training and 1-month post-training assessments from all residents regarding their knowledge, attitudes, skills, behavioral control and intentions, and behavior changes. In addition, a subset of residents will complete 3- and 6-month follow-up assessments to determine preliminary longitudinal effects of the training. Data collection using additional methods that supplement provider self-reports will occur in Florida. We hypothesize that training in the proposed virtual learning environment (VLE) will result, on average, in improved attitudes and increased knowledge and behavioral control and intentions, leading to positive behavior changes among clinicians and, ultimately, decreased incidence of NSSI and suicidal behavior among youth. Analyses will be based on before-after comparisons via paired t-tests for demonstrating benefits of the training, as well as generalized multiple regression with random and fixed effects.

2.1   Suicidality and NSSI Among Adolescents

Suicide rates for adolescent males and females in the U.S. have steadily increased since 1999 [1]. In 2014, 5504 adolescents aged 10 to 24 died by suicide, which represented more deaths than the next eight leading causes of death combined [1]. The rates of suicidal behavior among youth heighten the public health significance of the problem. Suicidal ideation and suicide attempts increase precipitously during adolescence, peaking during mid-adolescence (15 to 18 years) [10, 11]. For every death by suicide, 100 to 200 adolescents attempted to take their own lives, compared to a rate of 4 attempts to 1 death among the elderly population [12]. In 2015, almost 18% of high school students seriously considered attempting suicide, and 9% actually attempted suicide during the previous 12 months [13].

NSSI and suicide attempts differ, yet sometimes co-occur [3]. Repetitive NSSI increases risk of suicide by reducing fears of pain and injury over time, removing a barrier to completing suicide [3, 4, 14]. Prior research involving team members found that NSSI represented the most important factor to distinguish youth from the general community who attempted suicide from those who only considered suicide [5]. Approximately 18% of adolescents have engaged in NSSI, [15] with an age of onset usually between 13 and 15 [16]. Adolescents most often engage in NSSI to regulate overwhelming, negative emotions such as anger, anxiety, or frustration [17–19]. NSSI reduces negative emotions, making this coping behavior highly reinforcing [20]. Many adolescents who self-injure report weekly episodes of behaviors such as cutting, burning, scraping, or erasing the skin [21]. Factors distinguishing NSSI from a suicide attempt include intent or purpose, frequency, interpersonal and intrapersonal consequences, severity or lethality of methods used, number of methods used, and cognitive state during self-harm [3]. Still, some adolescents engage in NSSI as a strategy to avoid/suppress suicidal thoughts [22]. Thus, we hypothesize that addressing NSSI and suicidal ideation will represent highly effective strategies for preventing youth suicide.

2.2 Clinician Education, Perceptions, and Behavior

Despite increased awareness of suicide and NSSI as major public health problems, many healthcare professionals who have frequent contact with high-risk patients lack adequate training in specialized assessment techniques and treatment approaches [23]. The Joint Commission stated: "Clinicians in emergency, primary, and behavioral health care settings particularly have a crucial role in detecting suicide ideation and assuring appropriate evaluation" [24 (p. 1)]. However, clinicians' knowledge, comfort, and skills determine their ability to provide appropriate care to distressed adolescents [25]. The Commission and U.S. government's National Strategy for Suicide Prevention recommend educating all staff in patient care settings to identify and respond to patients with suicidal ideation toward a goal of "zero suicides" [24, 26]. Researchers, including members of this team, also have highlighted the need for clinician training on NSSI [9, 27, 28].

As discussed in a review article [23], healthcare providers with pediatric patient populations encounter distressed and suicidal adolescents, and thus can play a major role in NSSI and suicide prevention. Research shows that 20% to 41% of adolescents who present to PCPs have high levels of emotional distress and/or suicidal ideation, yet PCPs identify less than half (24%–45%) of these young people [29–31]. Given the prevalence of NSSI, non-mental health care providers will likely confront self-injurious behavior among adolescents [9]. Therefore, they would benefit from enhanced skills related to engaging youth in conversations about NSSI; assessing the history, context, and functions of the behavior; and referring patients to mental health specialists [9, 27, 28]. Research suggests non-mental health clinicians are often unprepared to address NSSI, and thus need additional training [32–34]. Research also suggests medical staff may feel more frustrated, burdened, impatient, and unsympathetic toward patients who engage in NSSI, compared to other patients [35]. Applying Weiner's Attributional Model of Helping Behavior [36], members of the research team found that clinicians attributed more control, stability, and internal locus to a self-injuring patient, resulting in less willingness to help [35]. Unhelpful attitudes of healthcare providers toward individuals who self-injure remain common [37–39]. For example, Friedman et al. [40] found that 77% of emergency clinicians felt NSSI was about seeking attention.

These researchers also found that just 13% of clinicians strongly agreed healthcare providers should consider people who engage in NSSI at risk of suicide, and 92% thought training in managing NSSI was important [40]. Further, these attitudes likely contribute to adolescents' fears of being labeled as an "attention seeker," "stupid," or "crazy" and their reluctance to seek help [41]. Negative attitudes held by clinicians, and a lack of confidence and competence to address self-injury, may compromise a therapeutic relationship with an adolescent and increase risk of suicide [42]. Receipt of care among adolescents who self-injure remains low [41, 43–45]. However, training clinicians to screen for and assess NSSI should facilitate increased NSSI self-disclosure and receipt of needed care [9].

3 Virtual Learning Environments and NSSI

The virtual environment research used for this study augments existing didactic training that is already implemented in programs of study. Residents will apply the knowledge they acquired during the didactic session and practice new skills (e.g., identifying and assessing NSSI) by engaging with an adolescent patient avatar who self-injures within the NSSI_VLE (Virtual Learning Environment) simulation. At the end of each practice session, residents will receive feedback on their interactions. Some feedback will be automated, e.g., time the resident talked versus listened and time he/she displayed negative nonverbal interactions; some will be human-based annotations, e.g., was the dialogue empathetic or did it shut down communications. This feedback, built into the VLE, can be used for either self- or guided-reflection with the goal of improved interactions when working with patients [46]. Each resident will have 10–15 min to interact with the patient avatar, followed by a 5- to 10-minute feedback session. The simulation is easily portable – the participant can use a PC, Linux or Mac laptop computer; the subject matter expert observes and tags events and the human-in-loop guiding the avatar's behaviors can be anywhere in the world. Moreover, the experience is intense and contextually correct in terms of avatar appearance and behaviors. Thus, the NSSI_VLE has the potential for greater dissemination and impact on clinical practices than does the use of real standardized patients and the employment of programmed, rather than human-guided, behaviors in computer simulations.

The underlying technology and paradigm for the NSSI_VLE were designed and developed over the last decade by an interdisciplinary team of faculty members, research staff, and students from computer science, education and modeling & simulation [47]. The system can create and deliver an interactive virtual reality-based learning experience – all systems built in this environment run with and without a head-mounted display (HMD). The initial and dominant use of the system we will adapt involved preparing pre-service teachers and honing the skills of in-service teachers. At present, the system is deployed at universities and school districts across the United States and internationally. In this context, the teacher enters a room that looks like a classroom, including props, whiteboards, and students [48]. However, students are avatars in a virtual classroom typically projected on a TV monitor or laptop screen (other options include full surround displays and low-cost HMDs such as the Vive). As evidenced in prior studies, delivering experiences on a laptop places no constraints on a user's sense of immersion, nor on the learning that occurs. The students represent a range of personalities, from passive to aggressive and dependent to independent. Avatar students are "puppeteered" by a single trained human operator, which makes the experience realistic, as the operator can adapt to specific actions of the teacher [49].

The efficacy and effectiveness of the underlying system has been demonstrated in a series of studies funded by the Bill & Melinda Gates Foundation from 2012 to 2016. Studies show that rehearsing skills in the simulated classroom can change targeted behaviors, these learned behaviors transfer to the real world and, in the case of teaching, behavior changes have positive effects on student success [50, 51]. The broader impacts of the paradigm have been demonstrated in law enforcement preparation (interviewing and de-escalation skills), protective strategies for students (resisting peer pressure and providing support for others to do the same) [52], social skills for children with autism, peer tutoring, and job interviewing (as interviewer and interviewee).

3.1 The VLE Paradigm

In the existing paradigm, there are three kinds of users: *interactors*, *participants* and *observers*. A scenario is chosen by a participant or their coach and then initiated by a primary interactor, whose role is to provide genuine human interaction that is mediated by virtual characters. While multiple interactors, one primary and the others helpers, are supported by the software, we rarely use more than a single interactor. That interactor, trained in improvisation, controls one of more avatars (typically between one and six) using gestures to initiate behaviors and their own voice, morphed to match that of the currently inhabited avatar, to enable genuine human-to-human conversations. The second type of user is a participant who is the learner, interacting with the avatar(s). As with interactors, there can be multiple participants but the vast majority of times we have just one or two. The third class of user is an observer who can be passive or active. An active observer is a subject-matter expert (SME) who annotates events that are captured in a video that shows the avatars and the participants. Those annotations, also called tags, can be simple built-in phrases such as "Elicits a Personal Response" or "Does Not Appear to Display Empathy" each of which is associated with the beginning of a sequence of relevant frames in the video. Such annotations can be made on-line (as the events occur) or off-line (as part of after-action review) or even as a combination where on-line annotations might be altered, expanded with comments, or removed upon further examination. All such annotations are hopefully based on objective criteria but have the potential for bias based on the SME's subjective opinions. Other annotations can be objective and involve no human input. In previous teacher training applications, these have included teacher versus student talk time and percentage of teacher-student interaction time spent with each individual student. All such annotations should be made for the purpose of learning, either through self- or guided-reflection.

3.2 Pilot NSSI Simulation Application

In preparation for this development effort, we have worked with clinical psychologist Dr. Nicholas Westers, from Children's Medical Center Dallas, who has pioneered the development and begun to evaluate a didactic training program on adolescent NSSI for pediatric residents. Our current effort is a small study funded internally to test the NSSI_VLE concept using two patient avatars to enhance clinicians' capacity and willingness to engage in helpful conversations with youth about NSSI and assess suicide risk. Results of this study are preliminary but demonstrate the promise as participants report that they feel they are better prepared and will be more comfortable in dealing with NSSI than prior to the training. Figures 1 and 2 show the two scenes that are being used in this pilot study. In keeping with our paradigm, we develop detailed profiles of these subjects including their family situations and the stressors that may make them prone to NSSI behaviors. The following are brief summaries of those profiles.

Fig. 1. NSSI Interview with Kasi

Fig. 2. NSSI Interview with Alex

Figure 1 shows Kasi, a 17-year-old female in the 12th grade at a private school. She typically earns A's and B's, but has been struggling this year academically, earning B's and C's and failing one or two classes. She lives with her biological parents and four other siblings (she is the oldest). She has used alcohol and marijuana in the past, having gotten drunk on a few occasions, often in the context of her NSSI. She is sexually active with her boyfriend and feels guilty about this. Her Patient Health Questionnaire (PHQ-9) score is a 22 (i.e., severe depression) and she also experiences significant levels of anxiety. Although she has thought about suicide, including sometimes when she self-injures, she has never acted on these thoughts (i.e., she has never attempted suicide). She first started to self-injure because some of her friends disclosed their own NSSI as a coping strategy, so she tried it for herself and realized it worked well to cope with her emotions or punish herself.

Figure 2 shows Alex, a 14-year-old male in the 8th grade at a public school. He typically earns mostly B's with occasional A's. He lives with both biological parents and his 8-year-old sister. He has denied ever having used any alcohol or drugs, has never had sex, and does not exhibit symptoms of an eating disorder. His PHQ-9 score is an 8 (i.e., mild depression). His girlfriend since 7th grade broke up with him five months ago.

As is evident, the cases are quite different and, if these youths self-injure, the frequency and the means of doing so are likely to be different. Moreover, their responses, including openness to share, may be quite different. This situation can be intimidating for a PCP who is primarily trained to deal with more objective medical matters. The goal, as stated, is to provide experiences through which they can hone their skills much as a pilot does, gaining confidence even for situations that occur rarely in their practice, but are nonetheless important to their performance as first-line health professionals.

Regarding this approach, researchers have suggested the need to include virtual patients in medical education to support competency-based education [53], and have shown equivalent improvements in skills after trainings with virtual patients as compared with live standardized patients [54]. Interactive trainings prove most effective in changing clinicians' behavior [55, 56]. Role-playing with feedback allows clinicians to practice skills and enhances clinicians' capacity to address diverse adolescent health issues [57, 58], including suicidality [59, 60]. This project builds on identified best practices for enhancing clinicians' knowledge, skills, and behaviors by incorporating an interactive VR experience using role-playing and feedback with patient avatars.

4   Digital Puppetry Development

Given the complexity of communication in these adolescent interview cases, creating a digital puppetry interface that would allow interactors to perform nuanced non-verbal behavior was a significant challenge which required multiple iterations to achieve the necessary granularity of expression and control. Multiple combinations of technologies were tested to find a solution that allowed for precision control and quality performance across distributed networks.

4.1   Gross Body Movement

Initial iterations of the digital puppetry system assumed a one-to-one real-time motion tracking paradigm using a combination of infrared head tracking and a Microsoft Kinect Device [61] to control gross body movement and posture of the virtual avatar. However, sending the motion capture data in real time over a distributed network created visual quality issues. Lack of precision in tracking and lag combined with imperfect occlusion models in the environment created a high frequency of instances where avatar gross body motion appeared unnatural. In worst cases avatar limbs would spasm, jerk, or extend through inanimate objects in the environment. Efforts to constrain possible motion to avoid those visual errors were unsuccessful in that those efforts limited the range of motion in a way that made performance of nuanced non-verbal expression inconsistent and difficult to achieve. Thus, the one-to-one real-time motion tracking paradigm was abandoned and replaced by a gesture-based puppetry paradigm.

In the gesture-based puppetry paradigm, the full range of motion for each avatar was pre-defined, modeled, and mapped to geographic triggers that the interactor can use to manipulate the body posture of the avatar in real-time without motion capture. The range of motion for each avatar was defined as a body pose palette which was collaboratively designed by SMEs, interactors, and an animator using video reference materials from clinical case studies. Examples from the body pose palettes of Kasi and Alex can be seen in Figs. 3 and 4.

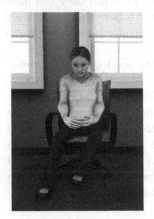  

Fig. 3. Body pose palette samples for Kasi

Fig. 4. Body pose palette samples for Alex

The virtual environment allows the interactor to calibrate the geographic trigger for each body pose. Thus, while limited to a defined set of pre-determined poses, the interactor can customize the trigger points to suit individual preferences and physical requirements which allows for more natural and intuitive motion control while avoiding the visual errors produced by motion capture. However, even improved, this paradigm was found to be insufficient to produce the desired level of natural motion. Using the geographic trigger method, we found that ten to twelve poses were the upper limits of what interactors could reliably navigate for each avatar. Interactors quickly became frustrated with the limitations of the palette and expressed a need for more subtle motion between more communicative larger pose choices.

To address the need for these more subtle and transitional body postures, three key frames of animation were added to each body pose in the palette along with gesture pacing controls. Using the pacing control, interactors are now able to scroll through a range of motion within each body pose. We've found that this subtle motion contained within the body pose range allows for more authentic conversational movement. Additionally, the head controls for the avatar were separated from the body poses and returned to use one-to-one infrared tracking based on real-time interactor head movement. In this way, interactors could use head position to alter emotional and status cues of the body poses to expand the expressive potential of the set. Motion controls were also set on the head tracking to prevent avatar head motions that would not be physically possible. If incompatible tracking data is sent to the system, the head position reverts back to body pose defaults and thus prevents most visible errors. Thus, the gesture-based body pose control system in combination with infrared head tracking and key frame animation control was found to be optimal for precision puppetry of the avatars.

4.2 Facial Expressions

Similar to the development process for gross body poses, the development cycle for a digital puppetry system for facial expression transitioned from a one-to-one motion capture paradigm to pre-defined range of triggered expressions. Initially we attempted to use direct motion capture using facial markers. Unfortunately, we experienced the same issues of lack of precision control, instances of tracking failure, and lag. Next, an attempt was made to design generalized facial expressions based on theories of universal facial expression characteristics with the hopes that this set could be applied to all avatars in the system and that could be triggered using a joystick control. While the joystick control was found to be much more reliable than the motion capture control and eliminated the lag and visual errors, we found the resulting facial expressions to be insufficient to communicate nuanced emotional states required by the interview situation. Thus, instead of creating a general set of universal facial expressions, we developed specific facial expression palettes for individual avatars to cover the range of expression expected in these interview situations. Examples of the facial expression palettes can be seen in Fig. 5.

The effect of using these standardized palettes for body and facial expression is that the performance of the human interactor is contained within these standardized physical expressions while allowing the interactor the freedom to respond to interview cues

Kasi   Alex

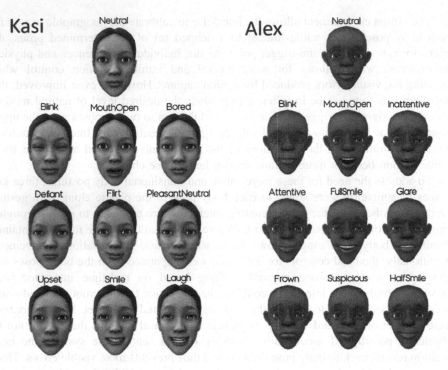

Fig. 5. Facial expression palettes for Kasi and Alex

from the learner. This feature provides an added benefit over motion capture techniques in that the puppetry performance can be both responsive and standardized. The interactor has sufficient precision to respond authentically to the learner, and yet responses are bounded within a standardized set of expressions that can be based upon authentic sources and input from SMEs.

5   Conclusion

When addressing complex interpersonal situations such as conversations between physicians and adolescents engaging in NSSI, using gesture-based digital puppetry provides a way to create a responsive virtual environment for authentic rehearsal. We foresee VLEs enhancing the capacity of clinicians who must communicate effectively about sensitive topics and build trusting relationships with young people. This paradigm can be used to better prepare physicians through scenario rehearsal that approximates real practice and via informed reflection that identifies types of interaction, reinforcing those SMEs deem as effective ones and highlighting what these SMEs view as ineffective ones.

This project also is taking advantage of research we are carrying out on the affective states of participants. Initial work has focused on body posture and separately on facial gestures with studies investigating alternative means of feedback regarding body poses

[62] and the challenges posed by hand to face occlusions [63]. We have also studied various late versus early fusion strategies for multimodal data, typically involving vocalizations (sounds) but not verbalizations (words). This work is still ongoing but shows great promise for reflective feedback and even automated changes to avatar behaviors.

References

1. Heron, M.: Deaths: Leading Causes for 2014. National Vital Statistics Reports 56(5). National Center for Health Statistics, Hyattsville (2016)
2. Kerr, P., Muehlenkamp, J., Turner, J.: Nonsuicidal self-injury: a review of current research for family medicine and primary care physicians. J. Am. Board Family Med. 23, 240–259 (2010)
3. Muehlenkamp, J., Kerr, P.: Untangling a complex web: how non-suicidal self-injury and suicide attempts differ. Prev. Res. 17, 8–10 (2010)
4. Joiner, T., Ribeiro, J., Silva, C.: Nonsuicidal self-injury, suicide behavior, and their co-occurrence as viewed through the lens of the interpersonal theory of suicide. Curr. Dir. Psychol. Sci. 21, 342–347 (2012)
5. Taliaferro, L., Muehlenkamp, J.: Risk and protective factors that distinguish adolescents who attempt suicide from those who only consider suicide in the past year. Suicide Life Threat. Behav. 44, 6–22 (2014)
6. National Institute of Mental Health.: Suicide prevention: how can suicide be prevented. http://www.nimh.nih.gov/health/topics/suicide-prevention/index.shtml. Accessed 20 July 2016
7. National Institute sof Mental Health. Division of Services and Intervention Research (DSIR): areas of high priority. http://www.nimh.nih.gov/about/organization/dsir/index.shtml. Accessed 20 July 2016
8. American Academy of Child and Adolescent Psychiatry: Improving mental health services in primary care: reducing administrative and financial barriers to access and collaboration. Pediatrics 121, 1248–1251 (2009)
9. Taliaferro, L., et al.: Nonsuicidal self-injury among adolescents: a training priority for primary care providers. Suicide Life Threat. Behav. 43, 250–261 (2013)
10. Gould, M., Greenberg, T., Velting, D., Shaffer, D.: Youth suicide risk and preventive interventions: a review of the past 10 years. J. Am. Acad. Child Adolesc. Psychiatry 42, 386–405 (2003)
11. Rueter, M., Kwon, H.: Developmental trends in adolescent suicidal ideation. J. Res. Adolesc. 15, 205–222 (2005)
12. Drapeau, C., McIntosh, J.: U.S.A.: Suicide 2015: Official Final Data. American Association of Suicidology, Washington, D.C. (2016)
13. Centers for Disease Control and Prevention: Youth risk behavior surveillance-United States, 2015. Morb. Mortal. Weekly Rep 65, 1–180 (2016)
14. Whitlock, J., Knox, K.: The relationship between self-injurious behavior and suicide in a young adult population. Arch. Pediatr. Adolesc. Med. 161, 634–640 (2007)
15. Muehlenkamp, J., Claes, L., Havertape, L., Plener, P.: International prevalence of adolescent non-suicidal self-injury and deliberate self-harm. Child Adolesc. Psychiatry Mental Health 6, 1–9 (2012)
16. Ross, S., Heath, N.: A study of the frequency of self-mutilation in a community sample of adolescents. J. Youth Adolesc. 31, 67–77 (2002)

17. Klonsky, E.: The functions of deliberate self-injury: a review of the evidence. Clin. Psychol. Rev. **27**, 226–239 (2007)
18. Klonsky, E.: The functions of self-injury in young adults who cut themselves: clarifying the evidence for affect regulation. Psychiatry Res. **166**, 260–268 (2009)
19. Nock, M., Prinstein, M., Sterba, S.: Revealing the form and function of self-injurious thoughts and behaviors: a real-time ecological assessment study among adolescents and young adults. J. Abnorm. Psychol. **118**, 816–827 (2009)
20. Nock, M., Prinstein, M.: A functional approach to the assessment of self-mutilative behavior. J. Consult. Clin. Clin. Psychol. **72**, 885–890 (2004)
21. Lloyd-Richardson, E., Perrin, N., Dierker, L., Kelley, M.: Characteristics and functions of non-suicidal self-injury in a community sample of adolescents. Psychol. Med. **37**, 1183–1192 (2007)
22. Klonsky, E., Muehlenkamp, J.: Self-injury: a research review for the practitioner. J. Clin. Psychol. **63**, 1045–1056 (2007)
23. Taliaferro, L., Borowsky, I.: Physician education: a promising strategy to prevent adolescent suicide. Acad. Med. **86**, 342–347 (2011)
24. The Joint Commission: Detecting and treating suicide ideation in all settings. Sentin. Alert Event **56**, 1–7 (2016)
25. Shain, B., Committee on Adolescence: Suicide and suicide attempts in adolescents. Pediatrics **138**, e1–e11 (2016)
26. U.S. Department of Health and Human Services (HHS) Office of the Surgeon General and National Action Alliance for Suicide Prevention: National Strategy for Suicide Prevention: Goals and Objectives for Action. HHS, Washington, DC (2012)
27. Klonsky, E., Weinberg, A.: Assessment of nonsuicidal self-injury. In: Nock, M.K. (ed.) Understanding Nonsuicidal Self-Injury: Origins, Assessment, and Treatment, pp. 183–199. American Psychological Association, Washington, D.C. (2009)
28. Miller, A., Muehlenkamp, J., Jacobson, C.: Special issues in treating adolescent nonsuicidal self-injury. In: Nock, M.K. (ed.) Understanding Nonsuicidal Self-Injury: Origins, Assessment and Treatment, pp. 251–270. American Psychological Association, Washington, D.C. (2009)
29. McKelvey, R., Davies, L., Pfaff, J., Acres, J., Edwards, S.: Psychological distress and suicidal ideation among 15–24 year-olds presenting to general practice: a pilot study. Aust. N. Z. J. Psychiat. **32**, 344–348 (1998)
30. Ozer, E., et al.: Are adolescents being screened for emotional distress in primary care? J. Adolesc. Health **44**, 520–527 (2009)
31. Pfaff, J., Acres, J., McKelvey, R.: Training general practitioners to recognize and respond to psychological distress and suicidal ideation in young people. Med. J. Aust. **174**, 222–226 (2001)
32. Crawford, T., Geraghty, W., Street, K., Simonoff, E.: Staff knowledge and attitudes towards deliberate self-harm in adolescents. J. Adolesc. **26**, 619–629 (2003)
33. Jeffery, D., Warm, A.: A study of service providers' understanding of self-harm. J. Mental Health **11**, 295–303 (2002)
34. Cooke, E., James, V.: Self-harm training needs assessment of school nurses. J. Child Health Care **13**, 260–274 (2009)
35. Marion, A., Muehlenkamp, J., Taliaferro, L.: Attitudes toward deliberate self-injury and elective cosmetic surgery patients in emergency department and urgent care settings. In: Poster Presented at the International Society for the Study of Self-Injury Annual Meeting. Vancouver, British Columbia
36. Weiner, B.: A cognitive (attribution)-emotion-action model of motivated behavior: an analysis of judgments of help-giving. J. Pers. Soc. Psychol. **2**, 186–200 (1980)

37. Saunders, K., Hawton, K., Fortune, S., Farrell, S.: Attitudes and knowledge of clinical staff regarding people who self-harm: a systematic review. J. Affect. Disord. **139**, 205–216 (2012)
38. Harris, J.: Self-harm: cutting the bad out of me. Qual. Health Res. **10**, 164–173 (2000)
39. McAllister, M., Creedy, D., Moyle, W., Farrugia, C.: Nurses' attitudes towards clients who self-harm. J. Adv. Nurs. **40**, 578–586 (2002)
40. Friedman, T., et al.: Predictors of A&E staff attitudes to self-harm patients who use self-laceration: influence of previous training and experience. J. Psychosom. Res. **60**, 273–277 (2006)
41. Fortune, S., Sinclair, J., Hawton, K.: Help-seeking before and after episodes of self-harm: a descriptive study in school pupils in England. BMC Public Health **8**, 369 (2008)
42. Patterson, P., Whittington, R., Bogg, J.: Testing the effectiveness of an educational intervention aimed at changing attitudes to self-harm. J. Psychiatr. Mental Health Nurs. **14**, 100–105 (2007)
43. Baetens, I., Claes, L., Muehlenkamp, J., Grietens, H., Onghena, P.: Non-suicidal and suicidal self-injurious behavior among Flemish adolescents: a web-survey. Arch. Suicide Res. **15**, 56–67 (2011)
44. Nixon, M., Cloutier, P., Jansson, S.: Nonsuicidal self-harm in youth: a population-based survey. Can. Med. Assoc. J. **178**, 306–312 (2008)
45. Whitlock, J., et al.: Nonsuicidal self-injury in a college population: general trends and sex differences. J. Am. Coll. Health **59**, 691–698 (2011)
46. Barmaki, R., Hughes, C.: Providing real-time feedback for student teachers in a virtual rehearsal environment. Paper presented at the international conference on multimodal interaction. Seattle, Washington (2015)
47. Nagendran, A., Pillat, R., Kavanaugh, A., Welch, G., Hughes, C.E.: A unified framework for individualized avatar-based interactions. Presence Teleoperators Virtual Environ. **23**(2), 109–132 (2014)
48. Dieker, L.A., Hughes, C.E., Hynes, M.C., Straub, C.: Using simulated virtual environments to improve teacher performance School University Partnerships. J. Nat. Assoc. Prof. Dev. Schools **10**(3), 62–81 (2017)
49. Hughes, C.E., Nagendran, A., Dieker, L.A., Hynes, M.C., Welch, G.F.: Applications of avatar mediated interaction to teaching, training, job skills and wellness. In: Brunnett, G., Coquillart, S., van Liere, R., Welch, G., Váša, L. (eds.) Virtual Realities. LNCS, vol. 8844, pp. 133–146. Springer, Cham (2015). https://doi.org/10.1007/978-3-319-17043-5_8
50. Dieker, L., Delisio, L., Bukaty, C.: Tuning in with technology. In: Scott, W.W., Scott, K.L. (eds.) What Really Works in Elementary Education: Research-Based Practical Strategies for Every Teacher. Corwin Press, Thousand Oaks (2015)
51. Dieker, L.R., Rodriguez, J.A., Lingnugaris-Kraft, B., Hynes, M., Hughes, C.: The potential of simulated environments in teacher education: current and future possibilities. Teacher Educ. Spec. Educ. **37**, 21–33 (2014)
52. Norris, A.E., Hughes, C., Hecht, M.L., Peragallo, N.P., Nickerson, D.: Randomized trial of a peer resistance skill-building game for His-panic early adolescent girls. Nurs. Res. **62**(1), 25–35 (2013)
53. Berman, N., Durning, S., Rischer, M.H., Triola, S.M.: The role for virtual patients in the future of medical education. Acad. Med. **91**, 1217–1222 (2016)
54. Triola, M., et al.: A randomized trial of teaching clinical skills using virtual and live standardized patients. J. Gen. Int. Med. **21**, 424–429 (2006)
55. Johnson, M., May, C.: Promoting professional behaviour change in healthcare: What interventions work, and why? A theory-led overview of systematic reviews. BMJ (2015). https://doi.org/10.1136/bmjopen-2015-008592

56. Mostofian, F., Ruban, C., Simunovic, N., Bhandari, M.: Changing physician behavior: what works? Am. J. Manage Care **21**, 75–84 (2015)
57. Lustig, J., et al.: Improving the delivery of adolescent clinical preventive services through skills-based training. Pediatrics **107**, 1100–1107 (2001)
58. Ozer, E., et al.: Increasing the screening and counseling of adolescents for risky health behaviors: a primary care intervention. Pediatrics **115**, 960–968 (2005)
59. Fallucco, E., Seago, R., Cuffe, S., Kraemer, D., Wysocki, T.: Primary care provider training in screening, assessment, and treatment of adolescent depression. Acad. Pediatr. **15**, 326–332 (2015)
60. Fallucco, E., Conlon, M., Gale, G., Constantino, J., Glowinski, A.: Use of a standardized patient paradigm to enhance proficiency in risk assessment for adolescent depression and suicide. J. Adolesc. Health **51**, 66–72 (2012)
61. Kinect for Windows. https://developer.microsoft.com/en-us/windows/kinect. Accessed 30 Jan 2019
62. Barmaki, R., Hughes, C.E.: Embodiment analytics of practicing teachers in a virtual rehearsal environment. J. Comput. Assist. Learn. **34**(4), 387–396 (2018)
63. Nojavanasghari, B., Hughes, C.E., Baltrusaitis, T., Morency, L-P: Hand2Face: automatic synthesis and recognition of hand over face occlusions. In: Proceedings of Affective Computing and Intelligent Interaction (ACII 2017) San Antonio, TX, 23–26 October 2017, pp. 209–215 (2017)

Using Virtual Reality to Create an Inclusive Virtual Drumming Environment

Jacob Jewel and Tony Morelli[(⊠)]

Central Michigan University, Mt Pleasant, MI 48859, USA
{jewel3ja, morella}@cmich.edu.com

Abstract. Upon doing research in the realm of physical disability, a common occurrence that was found was people missing the ability to take part in passions they had when they were without any disability. Two areas that were targeted in particular were those affected by paralysis by unnatural causes and those dealing with multiple sclerosis. Accounts of paralysis stem from injuries such as car accidents or sports injuries, while multiple sclerosis is a disease in which the immune system attacks the protective covering of the nerves. In order to find solutions to these lost abilities we attempted to find a way allow people to play music again. The research presented in this paper describes an interactive virtual drumming environment for people who do not have the use of their arms and it also contains a visual representation of the drum rhythms for people who are not able to hear. Players play the drums by moving their head and the audio is played through speakers and through a DMX lighting system. Twenty-five people played the virtual drums and their feedback was recorded and used to make suggestions about improvements.

Keywords: Accessibility · Vision · Mobility

1 Background

Drums come in a variety of types and sizes. For example, Japanese Taiko drums are played on very large drums that are meant to be played in a group setting. Similarly, African drums such as the djembe or conga are also played in a group setting. Each drummer is playing a specific drum and a specific tone. These types of drums have only one basic tone and could be simulated by a foot pedal. In this case a foot pedal could be hit to generate the sound, and the intensity of the sound could follow the amount of pressure the foot hit the pedal with. A drummer in these types is rarely playing two different drums at the same time.

Looking at more complicated drum arrangements like a modern day rock drum set, the simulation of these sounds and rhythms without the use of arms and hands becomes more difficult. A simple drum kit contains a snare drum, two toms, a floor tom, a hihat cymbal and a crash symbol as well as a bass drum. Simulating all of these with foot movements is difficult as the hihat and bass drum typically are played using two different foot pedals leaving the arms to do the rest of the work.

Rick Allen is one of the most famous drummers who does not use both arms. He is the drummer for the rock band Def Leppard and due to a car accident had his left arm

M. Antona and C. Stephanidis (Eds.): HCII 2019, LNCS 11572, pp. 569–577, 2019.
https://doi.org/10.1007/978-3-030-23560-4_41

amputated in 1984. Despite this setback, he has remained the band's drummer and has played with a modified drum kit. He has a mostly electronic kit with additional pedals used to generate the sounds and tones previously done by his left arm. He has four pedals for his left foot that play the hihat, bass drum, snare drum, and floor tom. These modifications allow him to continue to play drums at a very high level of skill and consistency [13].

Another drummer, Cornel Hrisca Munn, was born without forearms. He is able to play the drums by attaching the sticks to his arm with a band, moving his arm at the shoulder to create the motion necessary to hit the drum heads while also using his feet to hit the pedals [14]. Alvin Law, is a drummer who was born without arms. Throughout his life he has learned to use his feet as arms in a variety of situations, including playing the drums [15].

As described above, playing the drums without arms is possible, however playing the drums also requires the neurological capability to quickly play within the desired rhythm. Some people may not be able to do that. Music has shown to be useful in the treatment of Parkinson's disease. However playing music can prove to be difficult for someone with a disease such as Parkinson's. Parkinson's Disease whose symptoms include tremors and bradykinesia. Bradykinesia is the slowness of the body to react physically to mental commands. Tasks such as finger tapping, or buttoning shirts become difficult. Foot movement issues like shuffling or dragging feet when walking are common. These types of issues make it difficult for someone with Parkinson's Disease to keep a rhythm by using physical drums even if foot pedals are used. A person with Parkinson's Disease might also have tremors, which are involuntary muscle movements. A Parkinson's tremor is typically a resting tremor as it occurs when the body is at rest. A person may attempt to hide the tremors by moving limbs on purpose and that could also have an effect on a person attempting to drum.

A virtual reality based drumming system has been created before [2], however the participants in that study played a real physical drum while in virtual reality. The study was examining the users interpretation of the virtual world. Virtual avatar based drummers have also been created [3]. Virtual reality has been shown as an effective method for rehabilitation [4, 8, 9], and in this case we seek not to rehabilitate the body, but to rehabilitate the mind and bring back an enjoyable experience to someone who can no longer play the drums. As shown in [5], a virtual drumming type of environment can be measured by watching for accelerometer values, however attaching controllers to a person's arms or limbs would not be an effective method when a person no longer has functioning arms. Making accessible instruments has been done for things such as virtual guitars [12].

2 Implementation

The development technology used to create a solution to losing the ability to play the drums with a user's arms was the Oculus Rift and the Unity game development program. The Oculus Rift is used in this application by taking advantage of its positional tracker and headset. The positional tracker is set in a position that faces the headset. Then the tracker monitors a series of infrared LEDs embedded in the headset. This allows the Oculus to know the position of the user's head which is essential for locating where the user is looking in the application.

Target acquisition in virtual reality can be done a variety of ways [10, 11]. In this case the gaze detection was used as found in similar approaches [1, 7]. Unity's Raycast function was used which triggers and returns a true boolean whenever it intersects with a game object collider. The Raycast casts a ray from an origin point, the user's first-person camera, for a set distance in a direction straight out from the user's perspective. Each drum in the environment has an individual collider which will return the game object's name when the user's Raycast intersects it.

The application itself, utilizes two different modes in an attempt to find the most effective environment for someone without mobility below the neck to play the drums with head movements. In both environments the user is placed in a small virtual soundproof room and is placed in front of a drum set.

The first environment created involves a free play mode in which the drum that is looked at will play automatically. In order for the user to know which drum is being played, the piece that is being intersected by the Raycast will be highlighted with a blue circle. After being highlighted, a script will play the corresponding sound. In order to play the next beat the user must look away from the current piece and either look back at it or to a different piece. The user could choose between a crash or ride cymbal, bass drum, snare drum, and 3 types of toms Floor, High and Middle (Fig. 1).

Fig. 1. Open play.

Upon initial tests with drummers it was found that this limitation, although easy to understand how to play, was limiting. Many drum patterns involve hitting multiple drums at the same time. And using the glance method did not allow for multiple drums to be played at the same time. Several design options were considered, but it was decided to implement a time line type of a feature where a user would select one or more drums, and then increment a time pointer.

The second application mode is a more involved interaction as the user composes a sheet of music by looking at the drum set and then plays it all upon completion. For clarity, a music sheet is placed in front of the user in the interface. As the user selects the beats by looking at the different drum pieces, notes will appear on the music sheet. Within the environment, there is also a button placed in the center of the room for the user to select the pacing of the music by looking at it. A run through of this environment would involve the user looking at drum pieces to be played together, then setting the pacing, then looking at the next button to the user's left, and then repeating this process until the user has queued up the desired music sheet. Then upon looking at the play button to the user's right the entire sheet will play (Fig. 2).

The last object will play automatically. In order for the user to know which drum is being played, the piece that is being intersected by the Raycast will be highlighted with a blue

Fig. 2. Incrementing the time pointer.

This method was found to allow users to create somewhat complex drum patterns and play them back. It was found that different types of drummers preferred different methods of interactions.

To properly display the graphics in this environment the user needs to have a computer with at least 8 Gigs of RAM, an Nvidia 1060, and an i5-4590. Player interaction was done completely through head movements using the Oculus Rift Virtual Reality Headset. The rift as 2 OLED displays each with a resolution of 1080 × 1200, a

90 Hz refresh rate, contains sensors for positional and rotational tracking, and has support for 3 dimensional audio. The rift ships with a Constellation sensor that tracks the position of the head and any motion controllers through infrared sensors. Oculus provides motion controlled touch controllers. These controllers' motion are sensed with an additional infrared Constellation sensor. In the specific usage here, the motion controllers were not used and neither was the second Constellation sensor.

3   Public Demonstration and Feedback

In the public area of a University, students and faculty were invited to test out the VR Drummer. As this was in a public area, no formal data was collected, however many items were observed. As users walked up to the demonstration table, a VR drummer would give a quick explanation of how things worked and start the application by using a mouse. Then the user was given the virtual reality headset and all further controls were done using head movements.

It was found that the glance method was much easier for people to understand. When a person would first start to play with the system, he was shown how to use the glance method. This gave immediate satisfaction to the person as wherever the head was moved a corresponding drum sound was being played. The display gained a lot of attention as the user was doing a lot of head bobbing and the drum set was on display on a large screen. After a few minutes the player would be tapped in the shoulder and informed of the second method of play – composition.

Players understood the composition mode, but through anecdotal evidence, only people with previous drumming experience had any interest in continuing on with this method. The composition method required planning and some sort of knowledge of what sounds good when as well as the patience to finish off a complete piece of drumming music before playing it back. When shown this method, many users requested to go back to the glance method and just have fun making noise.

Discovered during this public play was the lack of additional audio cues. Observers could see what the player was doing by watching the external screen, however the audio was only available to the player through the virtual reality headset. The built-in head phones provided the required amount of the audio for the user, however for the observers they were left to guess what was happening with the audio. This also could have been a good thing because for people to experience the full atmosphere it was required to be in virtual reality. If the observers were provided with both audio and video it may have prevented people from actually participating in the virtual reality experience. However with the audio missing, observers understood that they were missing a large component of the experience and wanted to try it out.

Overall feedback on the system was good. Suggestions included allowing for the user to import other audio such as guitar backing tracks or vocals to play along with. Also users requested a method to export the drumming track audio. As this was a proof of concept demonstration, there was no way to export anything created within the experience (Fig. 3).

Fig. 3. Press play.

As an added feature to this application we have added a light system that changes colors upon the user playing different beats [6]. This is meant to add inclusiveness for the deaf community. Utilizing the drums in VR provided an environment for someone to play the drums but it also prevented others from hearing the sounds of the drums. This can be fixed by splitting the audio from the headset to also go into an external amplifier, but it also brought up the question about how a person who is deaf would get any enjoyment out of this application. Without seeing arms going up and down or any vibration or motion from the cymbals or the kick drum it would be very difficult for someone who is deaf to understand what is going on.

As a common solution to these types of issues, sensory substitution can be used. That is converting the items that would normally be perceived by a specific sense into another sense that can perceive the same data. For example a person who is blind may have visuals converted to audio. In this case the audio information would need to be transposed into a different sensory modality. Vision is an alternative, however vision requires focus from the user. Unlike audio that can be heard from multiple directions at once, vision requires the focus of the user on the signals, for example looking at a teleprompter or video display. In order to overcome this, a much larger scale lighting can be used. For example lighting up an entire room to different colors can create an ambient secondary visual cue.

An example of a beat pattern to be represented as video could be bright white flashes for the kick drum sound, blue for the toms, and red for the cymbals. Although only one color could be visible at a time (assuming 1 light source) the order of priority for controlling the light was used in order to optimize the information space. For most drum patterns, the bass or kick drum is relatively constant as is the cymbal pattern. As a result, the kick drum was given the lowest priority. A user could get a feel for the overall beat of the music through this cue. Next up on the priority list was the cymbals. Much like the kick drum cymbals keep the beat with occasional accents. The highest priority was given to the toms as they add the characteristics to the songs.

Two different lighting styles were investigated: consumer grade smart bulbs and professional stage lighting. The interface was implemented in Unity as that is where the logic for the hit detection was done. It was then translated into either of the two supported lighting options.

There are many different smart bulb models and manufacturers, here the Philips Hue bulb was investigated. From a smart phone app a user can change the brightness and the color of a bulb. In order to do this through software, open source libraries can be used. It is required to have a Philips Hue Hub. This hub contains a physical network interface and communicates to the smart bulbs. All communication to the light bulbs from any kind of device must travel through this hub. The hub will be assigned an ip address on the network and all communication is through TCP/IP. The open source library phue was utilized to send commands. The protocol using phue is pretty straight forward. The developer is required to connect to the hub, then query for the number of bulbs connected to the hub, then send instructions that set the brightness or color to the desired bulb (Fig. 4).

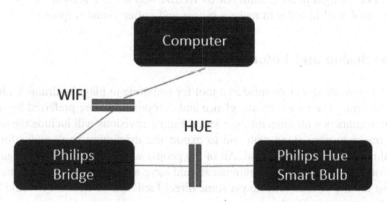

Fig. 4. Philips Hue smart bulb architecture.

After running this first application, it was found that the latency was unusable. It was in the order of seconds for the lights to respond to any commands. This may be due to the involvement of the Hue Bridge, or some underlying issues within the phue python library, but whatever the reason it was essentially unusable. The delay not only misrepresented what was going on to observers but confused the active player as indirect light might leak into the headset and not be in beat with what was going on causing confusion for everyone. Because of this a more responsive lighting solution was sought out (Fig. 5).

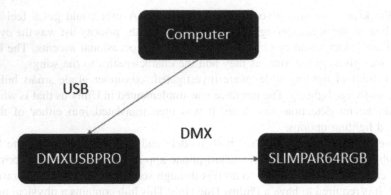

Fig. 5. DMX controller architecture.

DMX512 is the standard for communication between a controller and lighting equipment. In order to control DMX light sources from a computer, a USB interface is required. For this experiment, the ENTTEC DMXUSB PRO 70304 was used. It is supported on Windows and on OSX, and is supported by open source software. Using this setup, the response time dropped to be sub-second and the system worked as desired. For the light itself, a SlimPAR 64 RGBA was used. The light was pointed at a white painted wall in order to make a bigger and softer visual response.

4   Conclusion and Future Work

The VR Drummer shows promise as a tool for someone to play the drums without the use of the arms. The two methods, glance and composition were preferred by different types of drummers with different experience. Future revisions will include the ability to import tracks to play along with and to export the drumming track audio for use in external utilities like Garage Band. All of the people who played through the game had the use of their arms. The VR Drummer should have a study done with drummers who have lost the use of their arms to get some direct feedback on how they would like the application to be modified.

References

1. Holland, A., Morelli, T.: Dynamic keypad – digit shuffling for secure pin entry in a virtual world. In: Proceedings of HCII 2018. Virtual, Augmented and Mixed Reality: Interaction, Navigation, Visualization, Embodiment, and Simulation, July, pp 102–111. HCI International, Las Vegas, NV (2018)
2. Kilteni, K., Bergstrom, I., Slater, M.: Drumming in immersive virtual reality: the body shapes the way we play. IEEE Trans. Visual Comput. Gr. **4**, 597–605 (2013)
3. Kragtwijk, M., Nijholt, A., Zwiers, J.: Implementation of a 3D virtual drummer. In: Computer Animation and Simulation 2001, pp. 15–26. Springer, Vienna (2001)

4. Larson, E.B., et al.: Virtual reality and cognitive rehabilitation: a review of current outcome research. NeuroRehabilitation **34**(4), 759–772 (2014)
5. Morelli, T., et al.: Pet-N-Punch: upper body tactile/audio exergame to engage children with visual impairments into physical activity. In: Proceedings of Graphics Interface 2011. Canadian Human-Computer Communications Society (2011)
6. Roberge, B., et al.: Lighting methods and systems. U.S. Patent No. 7,178,941, 20 Feb 2007
7. Špakov, O., Miniotas, D.: On-line adjustment of dwell time for target selection by gaze. In: Proceedings of the Third Nordic Conference on Human-Computer Interaction. ACM (2004)
8. Subramanian, S., et al.: Virtual reality environments for post-stroke arm rehabilitation. J. Neuroeng. Rehabil. **4**(1), 20 (2007)
9. Subramanian, S.K., et al.: Arm motor recovery using a virtual reality intervention in chronic stroke: randomized control trial. Neurorchabil. Neural Repair **27**(1), 13–23 (2013)
10. Vanacken, L., Grossman, T., Coninx, K.: Exploring the effects of environment density and target visibility on object selection in 3D virtual environments. In: IEEE Symposium on 3D User Interfaces. IEEE (2007)
11. Ware, C., Lowther, K.: Selection using a one-eyed cursor in a fish tank VR environment. ACM Trans. Comput. Human Interact. **4**(4), 309–322 (1997)
12. Yuan, B., Folmer, E.: Blind hero: enabling guitar hero for the visually impaired. In: Proceedings of the 10th International ACM SIGACCESS Conference on Computers and Accessibility. ACM, New York (2008)
13. Tour of Rick Allen's Drum Kit. https://www.youtube.com/watch?v=YS53IJAqquw
14. Anna Molly - Incubus drum cover. https://www.youtube.com/watch?v=b3pxcQtQh7Y
15. Alvin Law Change the Label: Break free of the labels that bind you and live the life you deserve. https://alvinlaw.com/about/

Visual Issues on Augmented Reality Using Smart Glasses with 3D Stereoscopic Images

Masaru Miyao[1]([⊠]), Masumi Takada[2], and Hiroki Takada[3]

[1] Nagoya Industrial Science Research Institute,
Yotsuya-Dori, Nagoya 4640819, Japan
miyao@yc4.so-net.ne.jp
[2] Yokkaichi Nursing and Medical Care University,
Kayoucho, Yokkaichi 5128045, Japan
[3] University of Fukui, Bunkyo, Fukui 91058507, Japan

Abstract. Recently, binocular see-through smart glasses have become available. These glasses stereoscopically overlay a virtual image on a real world image and are used as a form of augmented reality (AR). We aimed to quantitatively estimate the efficiency of information seeking when using these smart glasses. We employed Route Tracking Test (RTT). With the help of 143 volunteers participating, we evaluated the ease and accuracy of an information seeking task. We also measured the lens accommodation while the user was viewing the virtual guide through the smart glasses. A comparison was made between using and not using the smart glasses. Also, we measured their accommodation when they watched 2 targets of real and virtual images. We found that the smart glasses significantly increased the ease and accuracy of the task. We propose the following guideline for good visual recognition with binocular see-through 3D smart glasses. 1. In AR work guidance, these glasses stereoscopically overlay a virtual image so that the workers can see the operating field and the guidance simultaneously. 2. The inter-pupillary distance (IPD) of the smart glasses should be suitable for most users and controllable. 3. The luminance of the virtual guidance images and real operating fields should be similar. 4. The speed of computer image processing should be fast enough.

Keywords: Binocular see-through smart glasses · Augmented reality · 3D stereoscopic images · Accommodation · Ergonomic guideline

1 Introduction

The public generally understands that, during stereoscopic vision, accommodation and convergence are mismatched and that this is the main reason for the visual fatigue caused by 3D. But, from our previous study, during 3D vision, while accommodation is fixed on the display showing the 3D image, convergence of both eyes crosses at the location of the stereo image. We will explain this fact based on our experiments [1].

© Springer Nature Switzerland AG 2019
M. Antona and C. Stephanidis (Eds.): HCII 2019, LNCS 11572, pp. 578–589, 2019.
https://doi.org/10.1007/978-3-030-23560-4_42

Recently, binocular see-through smart glasses have become available. These glasses stereoscopically overlay a virtual image on a real world image. They are used as a form of augmented reality (AR). We measured accommodation when people watched 2 targets of real and virtual images. People can utilize these devices in many ways, including in industrial environments. But, at present, there are many troublesome smart glasses, which the users cannot see well. We aimed to quantitatively estimate the efficiency of information seeking when using these smart glasses. And at last, we propose the guideline of ergonomic use of smart glasses with 3D stereoscopic images.

In 1997, Azuma defined augmented reality (AR) as an environment where the real world was supplemented by computer-generated virtual objects. At present, the stream of development of Internet of Things (IoT) which includes "wearable computing devices" is expanding greatly. With 3D see-through smart glasses, the real world is seen through semi-transparent screens placed in front of the user's eyes and is optically merged with computer-generated virtual information. When wearing smart glasses, observers can see additional information embedded in real environments. The advantage is that they give hands-free capability for various applications especially in industrial environments, medical surgery, and so on. The devices provide instructions and other information to workers without disturbing their current work process. However, the major disadvantage would be visual problems which may occur from a conflict with counter-intuitive depth perception cues that occur between the 3D real world image and the 2D virtual image overlaid in the flat displays. The conflict is known as visual rivalry. In contrast, such a conflict can diminish in a suitable environment in wearing binocular 3D devices. We expect that a virtual image overlaid at an appropriate depth position upon an intended location in the real world image can be naturally perceived.

The aim of final experiment was to estimate how much binocular 3D see-through smart glasses can increase the efficiency of information seeking as a work assisting device. See-through smart glasses have the advantage of leaving the view of the real world almost intact.

2 Methods of Experiment 1

According to the findings presented in our previous report, however, such explanations are wrong. We found that lens accommodation for 3D images is in fact consistent with convergence among young men.

We carried out the experimental 1 designed as Figs. 1, 2, 3 and 4. We could measure the accommodation, convergence and pupil diameter, simultaneously.

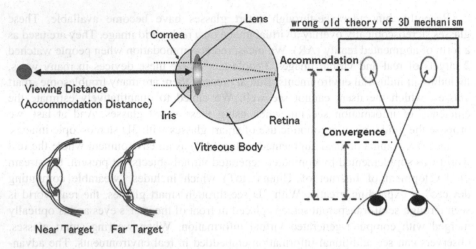

Fig. 1. Principle of lens accommodation and inconsistency between lens accommodation and convergence. This is wrong old theory of 3D mechanism.

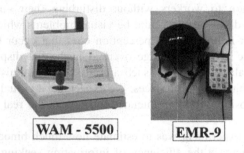

Fig. 2. We developed an original machine by combining WAM-5500™ and EMR-9 ™.

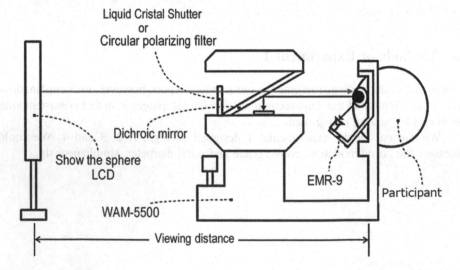

Fig. 3. We Schematic diagram of experiments. We measured accommodation using WAM-5500 (accommodation-refractometer) and convergence with EMR-9 (binocular eye movement measuring machine), simultaneously.

Fig. 4. A virtual sphere moved the range from 1.0 to 0.5 m in 10 s in front of participants who were asked to gaze at the center of the sphere.

3 Results of Experiment 1

We could measure the accommodation and convergence with pupil diameter change when the participant gazed the virtual sphere moved the range from 1.0 m to 0.5 m in 10 s.

From Fig. 5, we can recognize that participant's eyes worked as synchronized movements among virtual sphere movement, accommodation, convergence, and pupil diameter fluctuations.

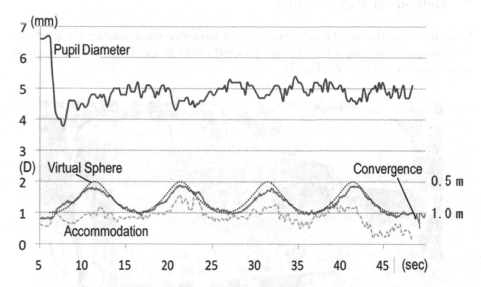

Fig. 5. An example of the measurements for 50 s of pupil diameter, accommodation, and convergence when the participant gazed a virtual sphere moved the range from 1.0 to 0.5 m in 10 s in front of participant. The curve of accommodation was similar to that of convergence.

Figure 6 shows that both the accommodation and convergence of participants changed in a coordinated way. The experiment included six healthy young men (age: 20–37 years).

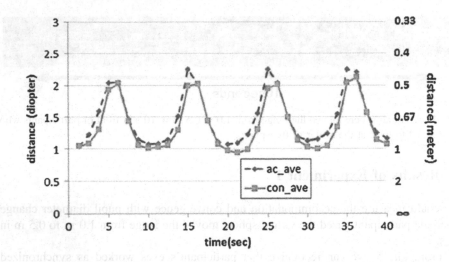

Fig. 6. Average of simultaneous measurement of lens accommodation and convergence in all participants for 3D video clips.

4 Methods of Experiment 2

Recently, binocular see-through smart glasses have become available. These glasses stereoscopically overlay a virtual image on a real world image. They are used as a form of augmented reality (AR) (Fig. 7).

Fig. 7. See-through smart glasses and virtual work-guide. The worker can easily understand assembling ways using the superimposed work-guide in front of the work field.

We measured accommodation when people watched 2 targets of real and virtual images. People can utilize these devices in many ways, including in industrial environments. We aimed to quantitatively estimate the efficiency of information seeking when using these smart glasses (Fig. 8).

We measured accommodation while gazing virtual images of participants who wore 3D see-through smart glasses. The virtual distances were 3.33 m (0.30 Diopter), 1.25 m (0.80 Diopter), and 0.70 m (1.43 Diopter) (Fig. 10).

Fig. 8. Binocular see-through smart glasses of EPSON MOVERIO Pro BT-2000.

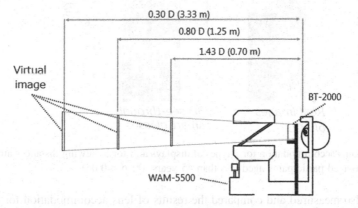

Fig. 9. One-hundred and twenty-eight participants were asked to gaze the 3 distances of virtual images using smart see-through 3D glasses. (66 males and 62 females)

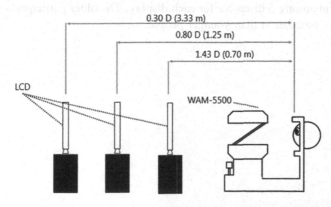

Fig. 10. We also measured accommodation while viewing real images of participants. The target distances were same as Fig. 9. They gazed the targets without smart glasses.

5 Results of Experiment 2

We measured and compared the results of lens accommodation for 2 types of displays and for 3 viewing distances among 58 young and middle-aged participants aged less than 45 years. The results are Fig. 11. There was no significant differences between two types of displays. The accommodative power levels were significantly different among 3 distances for each display.

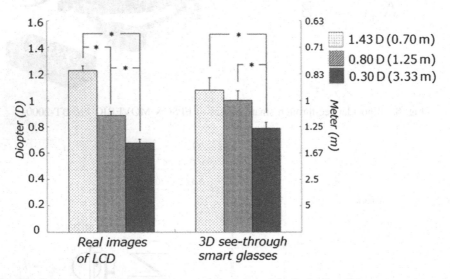

Fig. 11. Lens accommodation for 2 types of displays and for 3 viewing distances among young and middle-aged participants aged less than 45 years. (*: $p < 0.05$)

We also measured and compared the results of lens accommodation for 2 types of displays and for 3 viewing distances among 70 senior and elderly participants aged older than 45 years. The results are Fig. 12. There was no significant differences between two types of displays. The accommodative power levels were partly significantly different among 3 distances for each display. The older participants showed less power of accommodation than younger people.

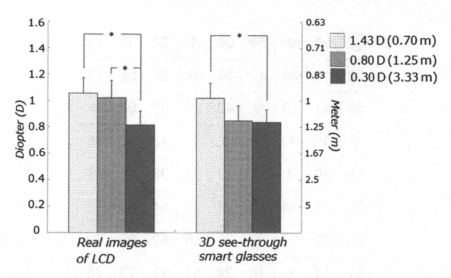

Fig. 12. Lens accommodation for 2 types of displays and for 3 viewing distances among senior and elderly participants aged older than 45 years. (*: $p < 0.05$)

6 Methods of Experiment 3

We investigated the work performance carrying out visual search tasks. We used binocular smart glasses (EPSON MOVERIO Pro BT-2000) where virtual information was projected in 3D (at an appropriate depth position) in the real environment through the glasses. As a visual search task, we used the Route Tracking Test (RTT), a uniquely developed test that allows 3D imaging and AR technologies to evaluate the ease and accuracy of operational work. The RTT possibly replicates visual perception process of the instructions given to the worker who is to move promptly to the next operation such as identifying the location.

Experimental Task. The "virtual" path guidance (red figures) is overlaid (superimposed) on the "real" numerical table (black grid with random numbers) through the smart glasses. The pathway guidance consists of a circle (start), arrows (tracking directions) and a square (goal) (Fig. 13).

Experimental Condition. Participants sit down 70 cm apart from the display. There is a real numerical matrix on the display, square of 20 cm × 20 cm. The participant can use tracking pathway (paper guide or smart glasses guide. In case of smart glasses, at the virtual distance of 70 cm, the guide is seen as a square of 20 cm × 20 cm). We gave them two types of pathway. The order of pathway was changed for each person randomly (Fig. 14).

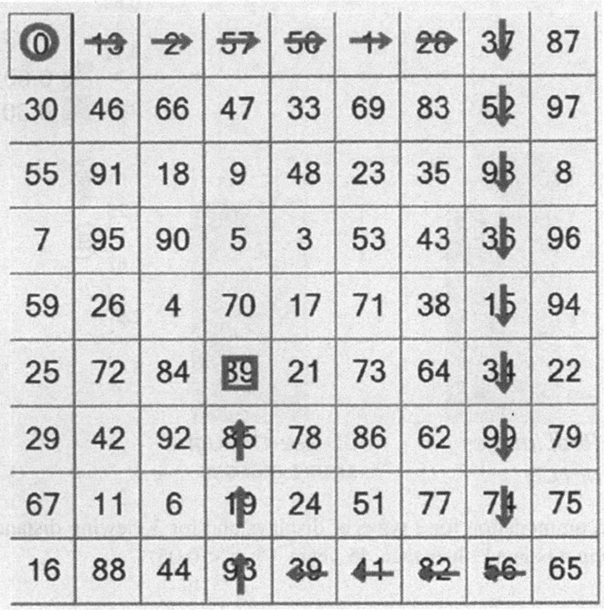

⓪	13	2	57	50	1	20	3	87
30	46	66	47	33	69	83	52	97
55	91	18	9	48	23	35	93	8
7	95	90	5	3	53	43	36	96
59	26	4	70	17	71	38	15	94
25	72	84	39	21	73	64	34	22
29	42	92	85	78	86	62	99	79
67	11	6	19	24	51	77	74	75
16	88	44	93	39	41	82	56	65

Fig. 13. The concept of Route Tracking Test (RTT) (colour figure onlie).

Fig. 14. The experiment 3.

7 Results of Experiment 3

Figure 15 shows the results of experiment 3. The search time is shorter using smart glasses than using paper guide. There were significant differences between two ways of work guide.

Figure 16 shows the comparison of accuracy. The correct answer rate is better using smart glasses than using paper guide. There were significant differences between two ways of work guide.

Most of the participants said that the Rout Tracking Test (RTT) is much easier when using smart glasses than using paper guide except elderly participants.

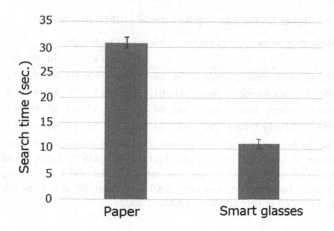

Fig. 15. Comparison of search time using average values of 142 participants.

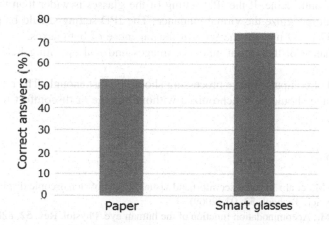

Fig. 16. Comparison of accuracy (correct answer rate (%) of 142 participants.

8 Discussion

For smart glasses, the inter-pupillary distance (IPD) should be taken into account. According to the percentile on Table 1, IPD values between 57 mm to 69 mm covered 95% of people and those between 55 mm to 71 mm covered 99% of people irrespective of age and sex.

We propose the following guideline for good visual recognition with binocular 3D see-through smart glasses.

1. In AR work guidance, these glasses stereoscopically overlay a virtual image so that the workers can see the operating field and the guidance simultaneously. The viewing distance of the virtual guidance should be the same as or a little closer to the user than the operating objects. Otherwise, the glasses cannot superimpose the guidance and working field.

Table 1. The inter-pupillary distance (IPD) distribution[a]

Measuring items	Unit	n	Mean	S.D.	Percetile				
					1	5	50	95	99
IPD of youth male	mm	56	64.1	3.0	60	60	64	69	71
IPD of youth female	mm	61	61.7	2.7	57	58	62	65	68
IPD of eldaerly male	mm	100	64.4	3.0	57	60	65	69	71
IPD of eldaerly female	mm	100	61.1	2.6	55	57	61	66	67

[a]The database consists of original data obtained by National Institute of Advanced Industrial Science and Technology (AIST), Japan. Head dimension of Japanese people was measured for about 120 young people in between Nov. and Dec., 2001 and about 200 elderly people aged over 60 in between Jan. and Mar., 2002.

2. The inter-pupillary distance (IPD) of the smart glasses should be suitable for most users and controllable. If the IPD setting of the glasses is wider than that of users, they cannot recognize the virtual guidance. The IPD setting should be controllable between 57 to 69 mm for the 95% of the Japanese of both sexes.
3. The luminance of the virtual guidance images and real operating fields should be similar.
4. The speed of computer image processing should be fast enough. The real image and virtual image should be synchronized without strange or discomfort feeling.

References

1. Lambooij, M., et al.: Visual discomfort and visual fatigue of stereoscopic displays: a review. J. Imaging Sci. Technol. **53**, 03 (2009)
2. Toates, F.M.: Accommodation function of the human eye. Physiol. Rev. **52**, 828–863 (1972)
3. Toates, F.M.: Vergence eye movements. Doc. Ophthal. **37**, 153–214 (1974)
4. Cho, A., et al.: A study on visual characteristics binocular 3-D images. Ergonomics **39**(11), 1285–1293 (1996)
5. Sierra R. et al.: Improving 3D imagery with variable convergence and focus accommodation for the remote assessment of fruit quality. In: SICE-ICASE International Joint Conference, pp. 3554–3558 (2006)
6. Hoffman, D.M., et al.: Vergence–accommodation conflicts hinder visual performance and cause visual fatigue. J. Vis. **8**(3), 1–30 (2008)
7. Ukai, K., Howarth, P.A.: Visual fatigue caused by viewing stereoscopic motion images: background, theories, and observation. Displays **29**(2), 106–116 (2008)
8. Miyao, M., et al.: Visual accommodation and subject performance during a stereographic object task using liquid crystal shutters. Ergonomics **39**(11), 1294–1309 (1996)
9. Patterson, R.: Human factors of stereo displays: an update. J. SID **17**(12), 987–996 (2009)
10. Campbell, F.W.: The depth of field of the human eye. Int. J. Opt. **4**(4), 157–164 (1957)
11. Ogle, K.N., Schwartz, J.T.: Depth of focus of the human eye. J. Opt. Soc. Am. **49**, 273–280 (1959)

12. Wang, B., Ciuffreda, K.J.: Depth of focus of the human eye: theory and clinical applications. Surv. Ophthal. **51**, 75 (2006)
13. Azuma, R.: A survey of augmented reality, presence: teleoperators and virtual environments. MIT Press **6**(4), 355–385 (1997)
14. Furht, B. (ed.): Handbook of Augmented Reality. Springer, Berlin (2011). https://doi.org/10.1007/978-1-4614-0064-6
15. Billinghurst, M., Clark, A., Lee, G.: A survey of augmented reality. Found. Trends Hum. Comput. Interact. **8**(2–3), 73–272 (2015). https://doi.org/10.1561/1100000049
16. Bajura, M., Fuchs, H, Ohbuchi, R.: Merging virtual objects with the real world: seeing ultrasound imagery within the patient. In: Proceedings of the 19th Annual Conference on Computer Graphics and Interactive Techniques, ACM Press, pp. 203–210 (1992). https://doi.org/10.1145/142920.134061
17. Ockerman, J.J., Pritchett, A.R.: Preliminary investigation of wearable computers for task guidance in aircraft inspection. In: Proceedings of the 2nd International Symposium on Wearable Computers (ISWC 1998), pp. 33–40 (1998)
18. Azuma, R., Baillot, Y., Behringer, R., Feiner, S., Julier, S., MacIntyre, B.: Recent advances in augmented reality. IEEE Comput. Graphics Appl. **21**(6), 34–47 (2001). https://doi.org/10.1109/38.963459
19. Baird, K.M., Barfield, W.: Evaluating the effectiveness of augmented reality displays for a manual assembly task. Virtual Real. **4**(4), 250–259 (1999). https://doi.org/10.1007/BF01421808
20. State, A., Ackerman, J., Hirota, G., Lee, J., Fuchs, H.: Dynamic virtual convergence for video see-through head-mounted displays: maintaining maximum stereo overlap throughout a close-range work space. In: Proceedings of the IEEE and ACM International Symposium on Augmented Reality, pp. 137–146 (2001). https://doi.org/10.1109/ISAR.2001.970523
21. Sielhorst, T., Bichlmeier, C., Heining, S., Navab, N.: Depth perception—a major issue in medical AR: evaluation study by twenty surgeons. In: Larsen, Rasmus, Nielsen, Mads, Sporring, Jon (eds.) MICCAI 2006. LNCS, vol. 4190, pp. 364–372. Springer, Heidelberg (2006). https://doi.org/10.1007/11866565_45
22. Huckauf, M.H. et al.: Perceptual issues in optical-see-through displays. In: Proceedings of the 7th Symposium on Applied Perception in Graphics and Visualization, pp. 41–48 (2010). https://doi.org/10.1145/1836248.1836255
23. Wade, N.J.: Descriptions of visual phenomena from aristotle to wheatstone. Perception **25**(10), 1137–1175 (1996). https://doi.org/10.1068/p251137
24. Shiomi, T., et al.: Simultaneous measurement of lens accommodation and convergence in natural and artificial 3D vision. J. Soc. Inf. Disp. **21**(3), 120–128 (2013). https://doi.org/10.1002/jsid.156
25. Kimura, R., et al.: Measurement of lens focus adjustment while wearing a see-through head-mounted display. In: Antona, M., Stephanidis, C. (eds.) UAHCI 2016. LNCS, vol. 9738, pp. 271–278. Springer, Cham (2016). https://doi.org/10.1007/978-3-319-40244-4_26

Automation of Box and Block Test in Virtual Reality and Augmented Reality

Kouki Nagamune$^{(\boxtimes)}$ and Yujiro Tsuzuki

University of Fukui, Fukui, Japan
nagamune@u-fukui.ac.jp

Abstract. This study focuses on virtual rehabilitation (VR) and augmented reality (AR). In previous study, the effect of improving the function of rehabilitation by VR has been shown. It is useful for stroke survivors as what can be done at home. This study examin usefulness of box and block test (BBT) with VR and AR. Out final goal of this study is to make it possible to do rehabilitation at the home with virtual rehabilitation test, and we create an environment where each person can maintain and improve their own performance at own home, so that rehabilitation can be continued in daily life.

Keywords: Stroke · Virtual reality · Augmented reality · Rehabilitation · Automation

1 Introduction

In Japan now, the number of people suffering from stroke continues to increase. the mortality rate in Japan is fourth and many people suffer from stroke [1]. From 1960 to 2004 due to medical progress, the survival rate continues to increase [2]. However, even if they survive from stroke, they suffer from sequelae [3, 4]. After stroke, the stroke survivors suffer from sequelae such as motor dysfunction, hemiplegia, speech disorder. To return to daily life, they need to perform functional improvement and rehabilitation that are important for stroke survivors to perform after stroke.

Rehabilitation for improvement mainly do at the hospital in many cases because it needs medical instruments, large space and staff. In addition, there are limitations on the number of occupational therapists in hospitals. Thus, stroke survivors who receive tests of exercise for rehabilitation or improvement are limited. There is such a problem with the rehabilitation. In recent years, a new rehabilitation based on VR (Virtual Reality) has appeared to solve conventional problem and encourage improvements in exercise function for people with upper limb dysfunction among stroke survivors [5, 6]. In previous studies, it has been shown that there is utility for improving motivation for subject's rehabilitation and improving motor function in some tests [7, 8], the rehabilitation using VR shows a solution to the problem of the limitation of conventional physiotherapy. To verify this usefulness, we focused on virtual rehabilitation [9, 10]. In previous study, the effect of improving the function of rehabilitation by VR has been shown [11–16]. It shows that it is useful for stroke survivors as what can be done at home. From that point onwards, we consider that it can be expected that greater effects

M. Antona and C. Stephanidis (Eds.): HCII 2019, LNCS 11572, pp. 590–600, 2019.
https://doi.org/10.1007/978-3-030-23560-4_43

can be expected by rehabilitation in more realistically environment in VR rehabilitation testing from our previous research we focused on augmented reality (AR). It is considered that this AR can rehabilitate the stroke survivors more realistically by projecting virtual objects. However, as the number of researches on AR is small, we thought that it is necessary to verify whether the exercise of the finger is different from the rehabilitation at the time of AR, when it is used, as in the case of VR. Therefore, we reproduce the Box and Block Test (BBT) that was virtualized in the previous research with AR. From there we show usefulness by comparing real, VR and AR. We consider that the final goal of this study is to make it possible to do rehabilitation at the home with virtual rehabilitation test, and we create an environment where each person can maintain and improve their own performance at own home, so that rehabilitation is not burdensome.

2   Preliminaries

2.1   Stroke

Cerebrovascular disorders that develop suddenly are called stroke [17]. It damages for our brain and causes local or general disfunction. Stroke can be classified, cerebral hemorrhage, subarachnoid hemorrhage (cerebral blood vessel break) and cerebral infarction (cerebrovascular accident). Stoke patients are counted as 1 million. It is the fourth leading cause of death in Japan. Major symptoms of stroke sequelae are motor dysfunction and cognitive dysfunction [17].

2.2   Sequelae

When surviving after a stroke occurs, many stroke survivors cause sequelae to the body due to damage to the brain. As this sequelae has damaged to the brain, obstacles often remain at the distal part of the body and sensation, often interferes with daily living.

Paralysis is most common sequelae after subjects survive in stroke. Paralysis is usually on the other side of the brain that was damaged by a stroke. It affects the entire face, arm, foot or body full side. This paralyzed stroke subjects becomes difficult to grasp and walking. It causes difficulties in daily life. Damage to the lower part of the brain or cerebellum effects the ability to adjust body movement. Its disorders called ataxia, which leads to problems of body posture, gait, and balance [18].

Stroke survivor will lose the ability to feel touch, pain, temperature or their own position. Sensory disorder also hinders the ability to recognize object that subjects are holding and they will loss off recognition of one's own limb.

2.3   Rehabilitation Test

Subjects perform rehabilitation test to know their own status and recover for stroke sequels. In this section, we explain the rehabilitation tests that are commonly used as Wolf motor Function Test (WMFT) and Box and Block Test (BBT).

Wolf Motor function test (WMFT) is one of the evaluation methods of upper limb movement function in hemiplegic stroke. Subjects perform with 6 exercise and 9 items goods operations. It is evaluated score that the required time (second) and quality of action in 6 levels, 0 (no movement at all) to 5 (operation close to healthy). The total number of seconds and the total point are calculated as the final point [19, 20].

We explain about the procedure and scoring method of Box and Block Test [21, 22]. It is one of evaluation methods to evaluate upper limb or finger dexterity. This method evaluates the dexterity of one hand on the relative evaluation. We can evaluate finger dexterity with simple and short time (Fig. 1).

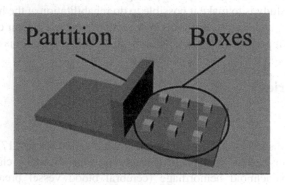

Fig. 1. Device of BBT

We show contents of the test as follows: We prepare a box divided into two by a partition. The size of the divided space is the same. There are one hundred cubes that the scale is 5 cm in one side on the dominant hand side of the subject. The subject is evaluated of the number of cubes can be moved to the other side within 60 s. The test observer sits down on the other side of the subject to observe the test performance. The subjects move cubes to the other side and get points when they over the partition. The subjects drop or bounce cubes beyond the partition to compartment. Even if one or more cubes are simultaneously moved, it is evaluated as one movement. For the evaluation method, the higher the score, the more dexterity of the hand is evaluated, and the scoring table for entering the score includes the question of the dominant hand, the date, the score of the dominant hand, and the score of the not dominant hand.

2.4 Virtual Reality

VR creates an environment that stimulates the sense that includes the user's five senses, such that the essence as a function is not the actual thing but the similar as the function is realized technology and its system. In the old days, novels, paintings, theaters and television also have the function of VR as much as possible [23].

2.5 Augmented Reality

AR system supplements the real world with virtual (computer-generated) objects that appear to coexist in the same space as the real world. It creates virtual objects in the real world, adds information, deletes, emphasizes, and attenuates information [24–26].

3 Methods

3.1 Overview of Measurement

This section explains mainly the principle of the measurement system and analysis methods. We measure same test in three ways that we use different devices in each way. Imitation way used sensors and an imitation device, VR way used sensors, Leap Motion, and Unity, and AR way used sensors, Meta2, and Unity. Figure 2 shows devices are used for measurement in each way.

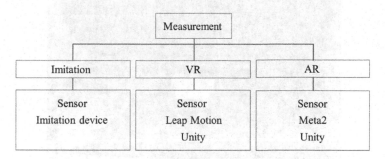

Fig. 2. Overview of measurement

3.2 Structure of Measurement Device

We developed a wearable measuring device for finger angles. This measurement device used gyro sensor MPU6050 (GY-521: Invensense). Gyro sensors arranged on the glove. In addition, we used two micro controllers to get the angular velocity by gyro sensors. It has the serial interface such as Serial Peripheral Interface (SPI) and Inter-Integrated Circuit (I2C) functions to communicate sensor module and micro controller. The obtained data are logged on microSD (CK-40, Sunhayato) card. The sampling rate of this system is 45 Hz. Overview of the developed device is shown in Fig. 3.

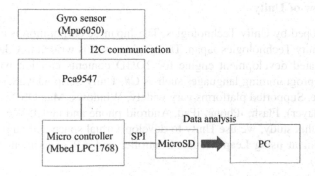

Fig. 3. Developed measurement device

To measure flexion angles of fingers, we decide that a reference point is the back of the hand. We use two sensors each finger. We use five sensors (Ch0-4) for reference points in each finger and 5 sensors (Ch5-9) for tips of five fingers. Figure 4 shows the measurement environment in the imitation device. We develop the imitation device with reference to BBT. We show the scale of the imitation device on Table 1. In the figure, cubes of 2 cm and 5 cm are shown. The cubes are the objects that the subject moves in this imitation device.

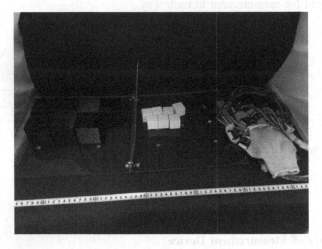

Fig. 4. Imitation environment

Table 1. The scale of imitation device.

Vertical	25.9 [cm]
Width	51.4 [cm]
Height	10.0 [cm]

3.3 Overview of Unity

Unity is developed by Unity Technologies. The Japanese corporation is a joint venture company of Unity Technologies Japan. This engine itself is written in C language/C++. It is an integrated development engine for 2D/3D contents creation which supports three kinds of programming languages such as C#, Unity Script (JavaScript), Boo as a script language. Supported platforms vary widely, Windows, Mac OS X, Web browser (Unity Web player), Flash, iPhone, iPad, Android phone and tablet, Wii, Wii U, PS 3, Xbox 360. In this study, we use Unity to develop virtual space and augmented reality for VR experiment using Leap Motion Controller and AR experiment using Meta 2 (Figs. 5 and 6).

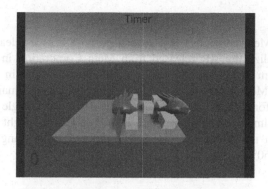

Fig. 5. Unity in VR

Fig. 6. Unity in AR

3.4   Leap Motion Controller

Leap Motion (Leap Motion, Leap Motion Inc) is a sensor specialized in the detection of fingers released from Leap Motion Inc. (Fig. 7). It was released in general in July 2013 [16]. The size is 30 mm in length, 80 mm in width, and 12.7 mm in thickness. It uses on a desktop. In this study, we use version (4.0.0 + 52173) of Leap Motion. Leap Motion consists mainly of three infrared LEDs and two stereo cameras.

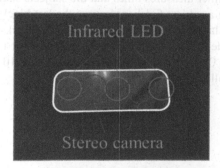

Fig. 7. Leap Motion controller

3.5   Meta 2

Meta 2 (Meta 2: Meta company) is a general-purpose device released in July 2013 as a device to realize the AR released from Meta Corporation in the US (Fig. 8). The size is 300 mm in length, 185 mm in width, and 127 mm in thickness. In this research, we used Meta 2 software version 2.7. Meta 2 consists mainly of five stereo cameras. It is comfortable to use in left and right 30° as view angle and in the sitting position. The maximum recognition angle is 50° of left and right. It has the range of −12° to 20° in up and down. The maximum recognition angle in the vertical direction −40° to 60°.

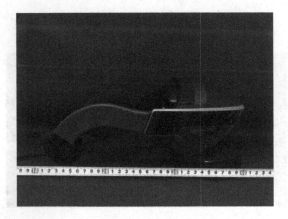

Fig. 8. AR glasses

3.6   BBT Automation in VR

We use Unity to reproduce BBT of VR/AR. In this section, we show the BBT in the VR environmental. For the movement distance of the block, the same scale as the imitation device is reproduced on Unity. It is set to 514 mm which is the same as the actual movement distance.

An example of VR display for BBT is shown in Fig. 9. A timer is set at the top of the game screen. This timer measures times that the subjects start to move. Unity show performance time when a subject finishes to move the last block. Score label is shown at lower left. The score label shows the current number of blocks. When subjects move one block from one side to the other side, score in lower left number decreases. The number is expressed as 0, when all cubes are moved. Figure 10 shows hands detected by Leap Motion controller.

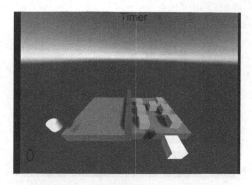

Fig. 9. Display of VR for BBT

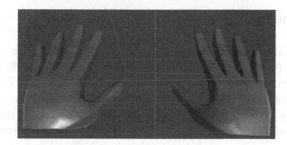

Fig. 10. Hand detected by Leap Motion controller

3.7 BBT Automation in AR

We use Unity to reproduce BBT of VR/AR. We show the BBT in the AR environmental. For the movement distance of the block, the same scale as the imitation device is reproduced on Unity. It is set to be 514 mm which is the same as the actual movement distance (Figs. 11 and 12).

Fig. 11. Display of AR for BBT

Fig. 12. Hand detected by Meta 2

4   Experiments

This chapter mainly explains the contents of the experiment. We measured finger flexion/extension in BBT on three situations (imitation device, VR device and AR device). We describe the following situations in the next section. The subjects were three healthy young men (23 years old). Subjects grasp cubes of 2 cm and 5 cm in each device. We conducted a total of six experiments for one person. In this measurement, we move seven cubes and do not evaluate the first and last movements.

5   Results

Figure 13 shows the number of grasping mistake. This figure shows AR shows the highest number for grasping mistake. It means the difficulty of BBT in AR for the subjects. While BBT in VR seems to be close to BBT of imitation device. Naturally, BBT imitation device shows no mistake, because the subjects can feel the objects directly.

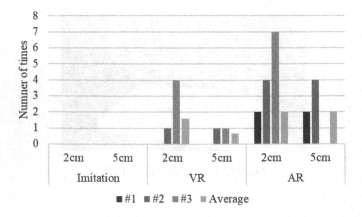

Fig. 13. The number of grasping mistake

6   Conclusion

We measured three kinds of devices, imitation, VR and AR to measure BBT to verify virtual reality availability. We measured BBT in these devices with our developed measurement system consisted of ten gyro sensors and two microcontrollers. From the results, BBT in AR shows higher difficulty than BBT in VR. However, both of them shows grasping mistake, because there is no physical feedback. Therefore, we need to improve the feeling to overcome the difficulty.

References

1. Ministry of Health, Labor and Welfare Heisei 26: Patient survey overview estimated number of patients (2014)
2. Yoko, M.: Changes in Medical Institution Visit Conditions of Persons with Cerebrovascular Disease, pp. 1–5. NLI Research Institute, Tokyo (2014)
3. Staub, F., Bogousslavsky, J.: Fatigue after stroke: a major but neglected issue. Cerebrovasc. Dis. **12**(2), 75–81 (2001)
4. Lai, S.M., Studenski, S., Duncan, P.W., Perera, S.: Persisting consequences of stroke measured by the Stroke Impact Scale. Stroke **33**(7), 1840–1844 (2002)
5. Schulthcis, M.A., Himelstein, J., Rizzo, A.A.: Virtual reality and neuropsychology: upgrading the current tools. J. Head Trauma Rehabil. **17**(5), 378–394 (2002)
6. Rizzo, A.A., Wiederhold, M., Buckwalter, J.G.: Basic issues in the use of virtual environments for mental health applications. Stud. Health Technol. Inform. **58**, 21–42 (1998)
7. Colomer, C., Llorens, R., Noē, E., Acañiz, M.: Effect of mixed reality-based intervention on arm, hand, and finger function on chronic stroke. J. Neuroeng. Rehabil. **13**(1), 1–10 (2016)
8. Shota, A.: Automation of Simplified Upper Limb Function Test Using Leap Motion Controller. Fukui University Intelligent Systems Engineering Department, Fukui (2016)
9. Tsuzuki, Y.: VR Using Finger Measuring Device and Box and Block Test by Imitation Device. Fukui University Intelligent Systems Engineering Department, Fukui (2017)
10. Sveistrup, H.: Motor rehabilitation using virtual reality. J. Neuroeng. Rehabil. **1**, 10 (2004)
11. Jack, D., et al.: Virtual reality-enhanced stroke rehabilitation. IEEE Trans. Neural Syst. Rehabil. Eng. **9**(3), 308–318 (2001)
12. Lozano-Quilis, J.-A., et al.: Virtual rehabilitation for multiple sclerosis using a kinect-based system: randomized controlled trial. JMIR Serious Games **2**(12), 1–8 (2014)
13. Markovic, M., Dosen, S., Cipriani, C., Popovic, D., Farina, D.: Stereovision and augmented reality for closed-loop control of grasping in hand prostheses. J. Neural Eng. **11**(4), 1741–2560 (2014)
14. Im, D.J., et al.: Utility of a three-dimensional interactive augmented reality program for balance and mobility rehabilitation in the elderly: a feasibility study. Ann. Rehabil. Med. **39**(3), 462–472 (2015)
15. Kato, N., Tanaka, T., Sugihara, S., Shimizu, K.: Development and evaluation of a new telerehabilitation system based on VR technology using multisensory feedback for patients with stroke. J. Phys. Therapy Sci. **27**(10), 3185–3190 (2015)
16. Kanbe, A., Ishihara, S., Nagamachi, M.: Development and evaluation of ankle mobility VR rehabilitation game. Adv. Intell. Syst. Comput. **585**, 325–336 (2017)
17. Persky, R.W., Turtzo, L.C., McCullough, L.D.: Stroke in women: disparities and outcomes. Curr. Cardiol. Rep. **12**(1), 6–13 (2010)

18. Ropper, A.H., Adams, R.D., Brown, R.F., Victor, M.: Adams and Victor's principles of neurology, pp. 686–704. McGraw-Hill Medical Pub. Division, New York (2014)
19. Wolf, S.L., Catlin, P.A., Ellis, M., Archer, A.L., Morgan, B., Piacentino, A.: Assessing Wolf motor function test as outcome measure for research in patients after stroke. Stroke **32**, 1635–1639 (2001)
20. Morris, D.M., Uswatte, G., Crago, J.E., Cook, E.W., Taub, E.: The reliability of the Wolf Motor Function Test for assessing upper extremity function after stroke. Arch. Phys. Med. Rehabil. **82**(6), 750–755 (2001)
21. Mathiowetz, V., Volland, G., Kashman, N., Weber, K.: Adult norms for the Box and Block Test of manual dexterity. Am. J. Occup. Therapy **39**, 386–391 (1985)
22. Canny, M.L., Thompson, J.M., Wheeler, M.J.: Reliability of the box and block test of manual dexterity for use with patients with fibromyalgia. Am. J. Occup. Therapy **63**(4), 506–510 (2009)
23. Steuer, J.: Defining virtual reality: dimensions determining telepresence. J. Commun. **42**(4), 75–93 (1992)
24. Azuma, R., Baillot, Y.: Recent advances in augmented reality. IEEE Comput. Graphics Appl. **21**(6), 35–47 (2001)
25. Mousavi Hondori, H., Khademi, M., Dodakian, L., McKenzie, A., Lopes, C.V., Cramer, S. C.: Choice of human-computer interaction mode in stroke rehabilitation. Neurorehabil. Neural Repair. **30**, 258–265 (2016)
26. Hugues, O., Fuchs, P., Nannipieri, O.: New augmented reality taxonomy: technologies and features of augmented environment. Hand Book of Augmented Reality, version1, pp. 47–63 (2011)

Exploration of Physiological Signals Using Different Locomotion Techniques in a VR Adventure Game

Stanislava Rangelova[1,2($\boxtimes$)], Simon Flutura[2], Tobias Huber[2], Daniel Motus[1], and Elisabeth André[2]

[1] BMW Group, Munich, Germany
{stanislava.rangelova,daniel.motus}@bmw.de
[2] Human Centered Multimedia, Augsburg University, Augsburg, Germany
{simon.flutura,andre}@informatik.uni-augsburg.de, huber@hcm-lab.de

Abstract. In the past few years, Virtual reality gained popularity thanks to advancing technology. Although the consumer head-mounted displays provide affordable access to immersive virtual environments, one of the disadvantages is the induced discomfort during or after exposure, called simulation sickness. Simulation sickness is a condition of physiological discomfort felt during or after exposure to any virtual environment. One of the possible factors inducing simulation sickness could be locomotion, the travel of the user through the virtual space from one point to another. The study presented in this paper aims to expand the knowledge on how the human body responds to different locomotion techniques in a virtual reality environment. A within-subjects design ($n = 9$) was conducted to explore simulation sickness outbreak, sense of presence and physiological responses induced by free teleportation and indirect locomotion in a virtual reality adventure game. The results showed that participants experienced significantly less simulation sickness while using the free teleportation during the game when compared to indirect locomotion. These findings indicate that simulation sickness symptoms can be reduced using free teleportation in a virtual reality adventure game.

Keywords: Locomotion · Simulation sickness · Virtual reality ·
Physiological signals · Adventure game · Presence ·
Head-mounted display

1 Introduction

Virtual reality (VR) environments have certain advantages when it comes to evaluating Human-Computer Interaction (HCI). Modern computation technology and sensors enable immersive testing frameworks which can be accessed using head-mounted displays (HMDs). Thus the interest in VR has been increased. The beginning of the second decade of the twenty-first century marked an intensive hardware and software jump for the computer technology. This jump has

© Springer Nature Switzerland AG 2019
M. Antona and C. Stephanidis (Eds.): HCII 2019, LNCS 11572, pp. 601–616, 2019.
https://doi.org/10.1007/978-3-030-23560-4_44

affected the VR technology as well. With improved hardware and software, VR is widely accepted by researchers and users alike. VR systems offer a safe and fully controlled high fidelity environment which can provide low-cost setups for studies. In other words, an environment can be created which is close to a realistic experience without the liability issues or high costs [39]. In contrast to those advantages, VR has disadvantages as well. One of them which concerns the VR experience and the user's well-being directly is simulation sickness (SiS). SiS is a form of motion sickness which is induced by virtual environments and is also referred to as VR sickness or cybersickness [20]. It is a condition of physiological discomfort felt during or after exposure to a virtual environment. According to Cue conflict theory, the discrepancy between visual and motion cues is one of the assumed reasons for SiS [25]. SiS symptoms such as general discomfort, eye strain and difficulty in concentrating are more likely to be experienced while a user is using a fully immersive virtual environment (e.g. HMD) [12]. For example, eye strain could be experienced due to the close distance between the eyes and the HMD's screen, which could also induce headache. Those symptoms, also known as oculomotor symptoms, are the primary difference between SiS and motion sickness, where the nausea discomfort prevails [6,14,15,37]. The Ecological theory states that persons get sick from a prolonged postural instability during travel [26]. Locomotion, the travel from one point to another, could be one of the factors inducing SiS in VR simulations. Therefore, researchers have investigated which type of locomotion is suitable for VR games and what effect these types of locomotion have on the user [18,31]. The used measures are questionnaires and interviews with the users; however, physiological data were not collected. In this paper, a study which compares two different types of locomotion in a VR adventure game regarding SiS and presence is presented. In particular, physiological data and in-game events are reported as well as subjective data. The first type of locomotion is free locomotion which is known as point and teleport locomotion. The second one is inactive locomotion which mimics the controls of a standard game controller.

In the next section, related work will be provided. The methodology for the user study and the experimental setup will be described in Sect. 3, followed by the results of the trials. This paper concludes with a discussion of the results and shows a way toward future research.

2   Related Work

With the growing body of VR research, the interest in locomotion in virtual environments has expanded as well. Thus, different locomotion techniques have been evaluated. Some of the techniques are: Omni-Directional Treadmill [7], redirected walking [24], walk-in-place [29], and teleportation [2]. An Omni-directional treadmill is a device similar to a treadmill used in the gyms which allows the user to walk in any direction in the virtual world [11,30]. These type of input devices are already on the market. Redirected walking allows the user to move through a large-scale VR area while physically stays in a much smaller workspace.

This gives the opportunity to use VR in a reasonably small space while the simulation presents a different size of space. The virtual camera motion is manipulated in a way that the user's self-motion in the virtual world differs from the movements in the real world [4, 32]. The walk-in-place technique allows the user to continuously walk in place while movements of the body are tracked and analyzed. The early implementations of this technique were based on processing of the head position using a neural network. More recent implementations track the legs position, below the knees, of the user to calculate the virtual locomotion [35, 36, 41]. Teleportation is an instant movement of the user from one location to another in the virtual world [3, 8]. Each of the listed techniques has its advantages and disadvantages which may also depend on the application's objectives.

In general, there are many different ways that a user can travel in VR using the controllers. Frommel et al. [9] investigated the effect of different controller-based locomotion on the player experience in a VR game. In this paper, they pointed out that the most popular type of travels with controllers which are used in VR for entertainment purposes can be narrowed down to four:

- Free teleport locomotion
- Fixpoint Teleport Locomotion
- Indirect Locomotion
- Automatic Locomotion

The results from their studies showed that free teleport locomotion induced the lowest and the indirect locomotion induced the highest SiS scores. Therefore, in this paper, these two types of locomotion are evaluated in a VR adventure game. The free teleport locomotion is a locomotion technique which allows the user to teleport herself freely within the field of view. The user points to the desired direction and an arc is presented which ends with a point where the user's avatar will be teleported. In this paper, the free teleport locomotion will be referred to as free teleportation and additionally includes an avatar model which shows the location of the player after the teleportation. The indirect locomotion is a technique which allows the user to move around the virtual world using a similar input as a standard game controller. The user can move forward by pressing forward on a touchpad (HTC Vive Controller) or a joystick (Oculus Touch).

A recent study introduced a node-based locomotion technique which is using a predefined node position to which the user can travel with rapid, continuous, linear motion [10]. The technique was compared with indirect locomotion and free teleportation regarding SiS and presence. The results showed that the proposed node-based locomotion technique induced less SiS compared to the indirect locomotion. Both nausea and oculomotor clusters, based on the Simulation Sickness Questionnaire (SSQ) [13], were lower for node-based techniques compared to the indirect locomotion technique. However, the results stated that the mean score for nausea cluster of the free teleportation is slightly lower than the mean score of the node-based locomotion. Regarding presence, no differences were found between the conditions.

The two studies [9] and [10] compare different locomotion techniques regarding SiS in a virtual environment using subjective measurements. In this paper, a comparison of locomotion techniques using not only subjective measurements (questionnaires) but also objective measurements (physiological signals) is presented. These measurements give an essential insight into the users' physical response to the virtual world while traveling within the virtual world.

3   Methods

3.1   Setup

The system setup consisted of an HMD with a tracking system, controllers, sensors, and a computer for rendering the VR scene. The HMD was an HTC Vive with a field of view of 110°, a resolution of 1080 × 1200 pixels per eye, and a Dual AMOLED screen. The tracking system was a Vive Lighthouse system consisting of two black boxes which create a 360° virtual space within which the position of the HMD and the controllers are tracked. The controllers are the standard controllers included in the package with the HMD. They have multiple input methods including grip buttons, a dual-stage trigger, and a touchpad. In the adventure game, the grip buttons were used as a trigger for grabbing objects in the virtual world. While the buttons are pressed the user holds the object, on the release of the button, the user drops the held object. The heart rate (HR), skin conductance level (SCL) and respiration rate (RR) signals were collected using Plux sensors [27]. All three signals were recorded with a frequency of 1 kHz. The HR was collected using a blood volume pulse sensor attached to the tip of the ring finger on the left hand with velcro strips. The SCL was recorded through electrodermal activity sensors attached on the third and fourth fingers of the left hand. The RR was collected using piezoelectric respiration sensor attached to the abdomen via an elastic strapped belt. Then the data was sent to the data collection computer via Bluetooth and recorded by the Social Signals Interpretation (SSI) software developed by the University of Augsburg [38]. The experimental setup with the HMD and the Plux sensors is shown in Fig. 1.

The SSI framework offers tools to record, analyze and recognize human behavior in real-time, such as gestures, mimics, head nods, and emotional speech. It supports streaming from multiple sensors and includes mechanisms for their synchronization. To integrate with other applications, SSI features a set of network plugins such as Transmission Control Protocol (TCP), User Datagram Protocol (UDP), User Datagram Protocol, OSC or Websockets. Beneath continuous streams, sporadic events can be recorded in synchronous. Particularly, SSI supports the machine learning pipeline in its full length (pre-processing, feature extraction, and online classification and fusion) and offers a graphical interface that assists a user to collect own training corpora and to obtain personalized models. It also suits the fusion of multimodal information at different stages including early and late fusion. SSI is written in C++ and the source code is available under LGPL. All the data of the study is recorded by SSI which stored the recorded data in its own, simple, text-based data format. This way, the data

Fig. 1. A participant using the experimental setup. The controller is in his right hand while the sensors are attached to his left hand and chest. Behind him is the computer on which VR scene is rendering and the physiological signals are recording.

of all sessions can later be further analyzed using different tools such as data analysis and machine learning features of SSI, Python or Matlab.

3.2 Measures

Blood volume pulse (BVP) is presented by changes in the volume of blood in the vessels. A non-invasive sensor can measure the BVP through light absorption of the skin and tissues and their level of illumination [1]. Usually, the sensor is attached to the non-dominant hand on the tip of the ring finger. From the BVP signal, the HR is calculated by estimating the time interval between the heartbeats, named the interbeat interval measured in seconds [23]:

$$HR = 60 \ seconds/interbeat \ interval \tag{1}$$

Prior studies displayed that immersion in a virtual world increased the HR with prolonged stay in the VR [33] and had a positive relationship with SiS onset [21].

Electrodermal activity (EDA) is a property of the human body that causes continuous variation in the electrical characteristics of the skin. It is measured with sensors which detect the changes in the passing a neglected amount of currency through the skin and the unit is micro-Siemens (uS). There are two main parts of the EDA which can be used to measure the ongoing electrodermal changes. The first one is the tonic level which is related to the background characteristics of the signal and a slower acting change. The second one is the phasic level which is associated with faster changes in the signal. EDA can be measured through the galvanic skin response (GSR), the electrodermal response, the psychogalvanic reflex, the skin conductance response, the sympathetic skin response, and the SCL. Most often the phasic response is used to present the results of the EDA data. However, this is just a part of the EDA complex. Typically the EDA changes when people are under stress which is shown by sweating on the inner side of the hand, the palms and the fingers. Previous research showed a connection between the SiS onset and SCL [19].

Respiration is the process of breathing in (inhalation) and breathing out (exhalation) [34]. The respiratory effort is measured by the number of breaths taken under a certain amount of time, often referred to us as an RR. Frequently this time is measured in minutes and therefore, the RR is given in breaths per minute which can be calculated into a frequency. A higher RR is related to arousal [19]. Furthermore, SiS scores had a significant positive correlation with respiration rate. The higher a participant's RR changes from the baseline, the more the participant reported SiS symptoms [16].

In another study, the RR was used as an objective measurement as well as GSR, HR, and skin temperature, in a flight simulator study comparing the presence in HMD and conventional setups [40]. There was no significant difference in the HR or RR. However, the skin resistance displayed more reactance in HMD condition.

Pre-questionnaire is a self-report instrument in which the participants are asked to answer questions to determine the socio-demographic information, previous gaming and VR experience. The questionnaire consists of seven questions, of which the first three questions were standard socio-demographic (age, gender, and education). The next two questions measured the previous gaming and HMD experience by using the five-point Likert scale (i.e., from strongly agree to strongly disagree). The last two questions checked whether the participants drank coffee or if they are smokers.

Simulation sickness questionnaire (SSQ) was provided to collect information about the participants state of well-being after the experiment. The questionnaire was originally developed by Kennedy and his colleagues in 1993 [13]. It is widely used to measure SiS and was the most suitable instrument for this project. The questionnaire consists of 16 questions where each question has four possible answers e.g. none, slight, average and severe. Each answer reflected the current condition of the participant and at what level each symptom is experienced. Each answer is scored with 0 - none, 1 - slight, 2 - moderate and 3 - severe scores and corresponds to one of the three clusters (Nausea, Oculomotor, and Disorientation). Some of the symptoms such as general discomfort, difficulty focusing, difficulty concentrating, and blurred vision are part of two clusters.

iGroup Presence Questionnaire is a self-report instrument, which was used to gather information about the user's VR experience and enjoyment [28]. It consists of 16 questions where each question could be answered once through a five-point Likert scale (from strongly agree to strongly disagree). The IPQ is based on a presence questionnaire originally developed by Witmer and Singer [42]. A few questions regarding enjoyment [17] were included in the IPQ questionnaire to measure the users' emotional reaction to the VR game.

In-game events are events which were created to track the interactions of the participants with the virtual environment. Some of the events are related to the interaction with the inventory such as "Drop *item name* into inventory" (see Table 1). Others are related to more active interactions with objects (e.g. lockpick, lighter, glass bottle) such as "Pick up *item name*," "Drop *item name*" and "Chop wood." Furthermore, there are events which track the interaction with environmental objects like a car trunk or a light switch. At last, some events to monitor the position of the participant in the virtual environment were added like "Entered water area" or "Spawning to *spawn location*." All the events are recorded through SSI and can be further analyzed together with the synchronized physiological signals.

Table 1. List of the in-game events and their short description which were using during the VR session.

Events	Description
Pick up *item name*	The user picks up an object
Drop *item name*	The user drops the picked object
Drop *item name* into inventory	The user drops an object in the inventory bag
Interact with *object*	The user interacts with an environmental object
Unlock	The user unlocks the shack's door
Chop wood	The user uses an ax to chop wood
Adding wood	The user adds wood to the fire
Enter Area	The user enters a particular area
Spawning to *spawn location*	The user spawns at the given location

3.3 Participants

Nine participants aged between 24 and 32 years (M = 26.44; SD = 2.51) took part in the study. Only three female participated and therefore, gender as a variable was unequally distributed and could not be evaluated. The participants were students or employees of the University of Augsburg, Germany. Five of the participants described themselves as frequent video gamers who play computer or console video games. In respect to previous experience with HMDs, three participants had used an HMD before this trial, one of those participants experienced dizziness during previous VR session.

3.4 Procedure

An adventure exploratory VR game study with a within-subjects design was conducted. Two conditions were presented: free teleportation and indirect locomotion. Each participant took part in both conditions. The experimental design was counterbalanced by alternating the starting condition for each participant. Before starting the VR session, the participants were informed of the procedure and the aim of the study. A consent form was handed to each participant followed by the pre-questionnaire. After that, instructions about the game controls were given and the Plux sensors were attached to the body. With the help of the researcher, the HMD was put on the head. For the first one minute, the participants were instructed not to move, only to rotate the head if he wanted to. During that time baseline data was collected. The game started with the participants spawning in a forest. There they were instructed to walk around and to find a car or a fireplace, whichever she found first (Fig. 2). At the car's location, the participants were able to interact with the car's trunk to open it. Inside of the trunk, there were a few lockpicks and a lighter laying around. These objects could be picked up and stored in the participants' inventory for later usage. After the interaction with the car, the trunk could be closed or left open.

When the participants arrived at the fireplace, they were told to light a fire. To do that they had to grab logs of wood which were placed around the fireplace and had to throw them into the smoldering fire. For each piece of wood, the fire grew larger. There was also an ax placed close to the fireplace. The participants could use this ax to cut the logs into smaller pieces of wood which were also usable in the fire. The aim of this interaction was to make a big fire by using as many pieces of wood as the participant wanted to but always at least three pieces.

After lighting the fire, the participants were instructed to head to a shack located not far away. On the way to the shack, they had to cross a small river by using a bridge or by going the through the water. The shack door was locked, so the participants had to use a lockpick to unlock the door. If they did not pick up the lockpick previously, they had to go back to the car and get a lockpick from the car trunk.

After entering the shack, the participants were able to use the lighter or a light switch to brighten up the dark shack. Here, the participants were free to explore the room and to interact with various objects placed inside of the shack. After that, the participants opened the door to leave the shack and the game was over. All sensors, the HMD, and the controller were removed. Before the session was over, the IPQ and SSQ were given to the participants.

Fig. 2. Two different experimental conditions: free teleportation (on the left side) and indirect locomotion (on the right side).

4   Results

The results showed that there were differences between the HR and SCL baseline and the ones recorded during the game. The participants felt more nauseous and disorientated during the indirect locomotion. However, there were no differences regarding presence and physiological signals between the conditions. The software toolbox used to analyze the data was Biosppy, which is written in Python 3 [5].

The results of the SSQ indicated that there was a significant difference between the free teleportation and indirect locomotion conditions regarding SiS. Paired sample t-test revealed statistically significant differences between the two conditions in Nausea cluster (free teleportation: $M = 9.54$; $SD = 10.67$, indirect locomotion: $M = 29.68$; $SD = 19.34$; $t(8) = -3.59$; $p = 0.007$), Disorientation cluster (free teleportation: $M = 41.76$; $SD = 28.70$, indirect locomotion: $M = 75.79$; $SD = 49.27$; $t(8) = -2.63$; $p = 0.030$), Total score (free teleportation: $M = 298.96$; $SD = 215.25$, indirect locomotion: $M = 548.79$; $SD = 309.60$; $t(8) = -3.85$; $p = 0.005$). These results suggested that free teleportation really had an effect on SiS symptoms from the Nausea and Disorientation clusters and Total score. Specifically, our results suggested that when participants use free teleportation, the SiS onset decreases. The same test revealed not significant difference between the two condition but a trend in Oculomotor cluster (free teleportation: M = 28.64; SD = 24.50, indirect locomotion: M = 41.27; SD = 29.14; t(8) = –2.18; p = 0.06). These results implied that the type of locomotion technique had no effect on SiS symptoms from the Oculomotor cluster. One of the participants stopped the session due to severe discomfort while using the indirect locomotion. The most rated symptoms for the free teleportation condition were "Difficulty focusing," "Blurred vision," and "Eyestrain." For the other condition, Indirect locomotion, they were "General discomfort," "Difficulty focusing," and "Blurred vision." The overall score indicated that the participants felt less discomfort using the point and teleport locomotion technique (Fig. 3).

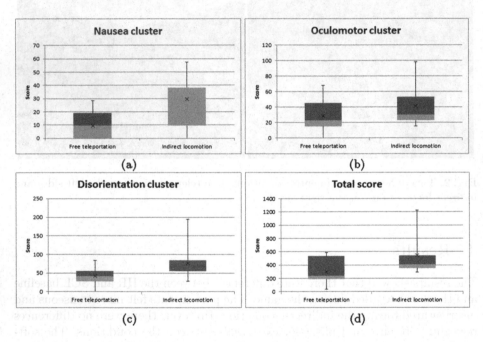

Fig. 3. Nausea (a), Oculomotor (b) and Disorientation (c) clusters as well as Total score (d) for free teleportation and indirect locomotion conditions.

Regarding the sense of presence, there were no significant differences between the free teleportation and indirect locomotion. However, the indirect locomotion was rated slightly higher on the items "In the computer-generated world I had a sense of "being there.""; "I felt like I was just perceiving pictures."; "I still paid attention to the real environment." On the items regarding enjoyment in the VR game, the participants gave positive responses for both conditions which did not yield any differences. The participants with previous gaming experience reported a higher sense of presence.

A paired sample t-test revealed no statistically significant difference between the two conditions in the HR (free teleportation: M = 90; SD = 11.59, indirect locomotion: M = 95; SD = 14.16; t(8) = −1.34; p = 0.218); SCL (free tele-portation: M = 0.48; SD = 0.44, indirect locomotion: M = 0.59; SD = 0.83; t(8) = −0.41; p = 0.689); RR (free teleportation: M = 0.23; SD = 0.03, indirect locomotion: M = 0.23; SD = 0.01; t(8) = 0.22; p = 0.83). The HR shows a trend towards reduced HR in the free teleportation condition. That means that participants had a lower HR. The results are shown in Fig. 4.

However, a comparison between the baseline HR recorded before the game and during the VR game HR revealed a significant difference for the free tele-portation condition (VR game: M = 98; SD = 7.23, baseline: M = 90; SD = 11.6; t(8) = 2.45; p = 0.04). Significant difference was found as well between the baseline and during the VR game SCL for the free teleportation condition (VR game: M = 0.78; SD = 0.74, baseline: M = 0.48; SD = 0.44; t(8) = 0.25; p = 0.039). The same analysis showed no significant difference for the baseline and the VR game RR for the free teleportation (VR game: M = 0.23; SD = 0.01, baseline: M = 0.23; SD = 0.03; t(8) = −0.6; p = 0.57).

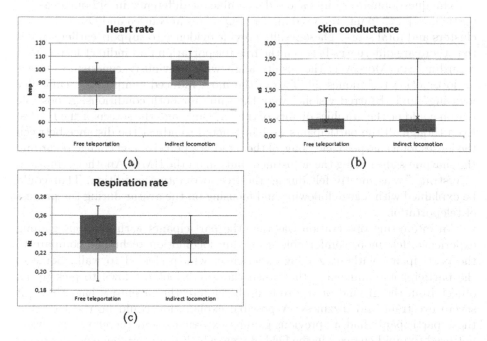

Fig. 4. Heart rate (a), skin conductance (b) and respiration rate (c) for free teleporta-tion and indirect locomotion conditions.

The most recorded in-game events were "Drop *item name*," "Drop *item name* into inventory," and "Chop wood." Due to personal preferences, each participant was more involved with one or another from the events listed above and therefore an overview analysis was conducted. Nevertheless, further analysis is required in order to show whether a correlation between the physiological signals and certain events exists or not.

5 Discussion

The popularity of HMDs among users and researchers has made this medium a valuable evaluation tool in HCI research. However, the technology of VR and in particular HMDs has its disadvantage regarding users' well-being, namely SiS. Prior research has documented the positive correlation between locomotion and SiS onset in VR. Habgood et al. [10], for example, reported that participants felt less SiS during locomotion techniques using rapid continues movements between nodes. However, these studies were evaluating the locomotion techniques via subjective measures such as questionnaires. In this paper two different locomotion techniques, free teleportation and indirect locomotion were tested in a VR adventure game using objective (physiological signals) and subjective (questionnaires) measurements.

The questionnaire results showed a significant difference in SiS outbreak. In particular, participants reported higher SSQ scores in Nausea and Disorientation clusters and total score. These results provide evidence to support earlier studies that there are differences between the free teleportation and indirect locomotion regarding SiS. Moreover, the results align with previously conducted studies on locomotion techniques [9]. Two of the most induced symptoms, "Difficulty focusing" and "Blurred vision," were the same for both conditions. A possible reason could be the graphics quality of the VR game and the screen of the HMDs. Even though all the participants were instructed to adjust the distance between the lenses for a sharper view, some of them did not perceive any change regarding the sharpness after using the adjustment button on the HMD. Another symptom, "Eyestrain," was mostly felt during the free locomotion condition. That could be explained with a gaze following and focusing on the avatar during the process of teleportation.

An interesting observation was that the participants with previous gaming experience, felt more comfortable using any locomotion technique compare to the participants without gaming experience, who preferred to walk. Some of the participants commented that when they were looking down to pick up an object from the ground or to drop an object into the inventory bag, they felt severe eyestrain and dizziness. A possible explanation could be the fact that those participants had no previous gaming experience and therefore, they were not used to rapid changes in the field of view which is a common aspect of many video games.

Regarding the presence and enjoyment during the VR adventure game, no significant difference was found between the free teleportation and indirect locomotion conditions. The participants experienced the same level of presence regardless of the locomotion technique. These findings are consistent with those of Habgood et al. [10] who found no difference comparing three locomotion techniques regarding presence. Furthermore, the participants reported a slightly higher presence in the indirect locomotion. A possible explanation for that could be that this technique is closer to the real world walking. Surprisingly, the participants with the highest SiS score reported that they felt present and had a sense of being in the virtual world. These results did not support a previous research [22] on presence which stated that a lower sense of presence might increase the SiS onset.

The slight decrease in the HR corresponds to the lower score in the SSQ for the free teleportation. One possible explanation of why the signals did not show a greater difference is that the participants had to move in order to interact with the VR environment. This could bring noise to the signal and later is more difficult to compare the signals. The significant difference comparing baseline and VR game data, showed in the previous section, might be due to the participants' movements during the game which can increase the HR and the SCL. In other words, the participants did more movements with the free teleportation than with indirect locomotion. These results differ from previous research [21] where the increased HR was related to increased SiS.

These results must be interpreted with caution because of some limitations of the study. In particular, the small sample size, unequal distribution across gender and age, and the rather short duration of the VR game. Furthermore, the study design did not include familiarization scenario which could help some participants to get acquainted with the controllers.

6   Conclusion

The results presented in this paper support findings in previous research on the observation that a free teleportation technique induces less SiS. Moreover, the results may help to understand the SiS induced by locomotion in VR better. A VR gaming environment with minimal induced discomfort could be a powerful user evaluation tool in the field of HCI.

Considering the findings, a future study might include a different locomotion technique, such as rapid, continuous movement between nodes, and different VR game scenarios. The occurrence of no visible difference in the physiological signals points to larger and diverse sample size and longer exposure time. Further investigation is needed to estimate the influence of locomotion techniques to SiS outbreak in VR games.

References

1. Allen, J.: Photoplethysmography and its application in clinical physiological measurement. Physiol. Meas. **28**(3), R1 (2007)
2. Bowman, D.A., Koller, D., Hodges, L.F.: Travel in immersive virtual environments: an evaluation of viewpoint motion control techniques. In: Virtual Reality Annual International Symposium, pp. 45–52. IEEE (1997)

3. Bozgeyikli, E., Raij, A., Katkoori, S., Dubey, R.: Point & teleport locomotion technique for virtual reality. In: Proceedings of the 2016 Annual Symposium on Computer-Human Interaction in Play, pp. 205–216. ACM (2016)

4. Bruder, G., Lubas, P., Steinicke, F.: Cognitive resource demands of redirected walking. IEEE Trans. Visual Comput. Graphics **21**(4), 539–544 (2015)

5. Carreiras, C., Alves, A.P., Lourenço, A., Canento, F., Silva, H., Fred, A., et al.: BioSPPy: Biosignal processing in Python (2015). https://github.com/PIA-Group/BioSPPy/

6. Cobb, S.V., Nichols, S., Ramsey, A., Wilson, J.R.: Virtual reality-induced symptoms and effects (VRISE). Presence Teleoperators Virtual Environ. **8**(2), 169–186 (1999)

7. Darken, R.P., Cockayne, W.R., Carmein, D.: The omni-directional treadmill: a locomotion device for virtual worlds. In: Proceedings of the 10th Annual ACM Symposium on User Interface Software and Technology, pp. 213–221. ACM (1997)

8. Edeker, A.M., Syomik, A.P., Siyanko, A.: Networked computer system for communicating and operating in a virtual reality environment. US Patent 7,269,632, 11 Sept 2007

9. Frommel, J., Sonntag, S., Weber, M.: Effects of controller-based locomotion on player experience in a virtual reality exploration game. In: Proceedings of the 12th International Conference on the Foundations of Digital Games, p. 30. ACM (2017)

10. Habgood, J., Moore, D., Wilson, D., Alapont, S.: Rapid, continuous movement between nodes as an accessible virtual reality locomotion technique. In: IEEE Conference on Virtual Reality and 3D User Interfaces (VR), pp. 371–378 (2018)

11. Huang, J.Y.: An omnidirectional stroll-based virtual reality interface and its application on overhead crane training. IEEE Trans. Multimedia **5**(1), 39–51 (2003)

12. Jinjakam, C., Hamamoto, K.: Simulator sickness in immersive virtual environment. In: Biomedical Engineering International Conference (BMEiCON), pp. 1–4. IEEE (2012)

13. Kennedy, R.S., Lane, N.E., Berbaum, K.S., Lilienthal, M.G.: Simulator sickness questionnaire: an enhanced method for quantifying simulator sickness. Int. J. Aviat. Psychol. **3**(3), 203–220 (1993)

14. Kennedy, R.S., Lane, N.E., Lilienthal, M.G., Berbaum, K.S., Hettinger, L.J.: Profile analysis of simulator sickness symptoms: application to virtual environment systems. Presence Teleoperators Virtual Environ. **1**(3), 295–301 (1992)

15. Kennedy, R., Berbaum, K., Lilienthal, M., Dunlap, W., Mulligan, B.: Guidelines for alleviation of simulator sickness symptomatology. Technical report, Naval Training Systems Center, Orlando (1987)

16. Kim, Y.Y., Kim, H.J., Kim, E.N., Ko, H.D., Kim, H.T.: Characteristic changes in the physiological components of cybersickness. Psychophysiology **42**(5), 616–625 (2005)

17. Lin, J.W., Duh, H.B.L., Parker, D.E., Abi-Rached, H., Furness, T.A.: Effects of field of view on presence, enjoyment, memory, and simulator sickness in a virtual environment. In: Proceedings of Virtual Reality, pp. 164–171. IEEE (2002)

18. McMahan, R.P., Bowman, D.A., Zielinski, D.J., Brady, R.B.: Evaluating display fidelity and interaction fidelity in a virtual reality game. IEEE Trans. Visual Comput. Graphics **4**, 626–633 (2012)

19. Min, B.C., Chung, S.C., Min, Y.K., Sakamoto, K.: Psychophysiological evaluation of simulator sickness evoked by a graphic simulator. Appl. Ergon. **35**(6), 549–556 (2004)

20. Mousavi, M., Jen, Y.H., Musa, S.N.B.: A review on cybersickness and usability in virtual environments. In: Advanced Engineering Forum, vol. 10, pp. 34–39. Trans Tech Publications Ltd. (2013)
21. Nalivaiko, E., Davis, S.L., Blackmore, K.L., Vakulin, A., Nesbitt, K.V.: Cybersickness provoked by head-mounted display affects cutaneous vascular tone, heart rate and reaction time. Physiol. Behav. **151**, 583–590 (2015)
22. Nichols, S., Haldane, C., Wilson, J.R.: Measurement of presence and its consequences in virtual environments. Int. J. Hum Comput Stud. **52**(3), 471–491 (2000)
23. Peper, E., Harvey, R., Lin, I.M., Tylova, H., Moss, D.: Is there more to blood volume pulse than heart rate variability, respiratory sinus arrhythmia, and cardiorespiratory synchrony? Biofeedback **35**(2) (2007)
24. Razzaque, S., Kohn, Z., Whitton, M.C.: Redirected walking. In: Proceedings of Eurographics, vol. 9, pp. 105–106. Citeseer (2001)
25. Reason, J.T., Brand, J.J.: Motion Sickness. Academic Press, London (1975)
26. Riccio, G.E., Stoffregen, T.A.: An ecological theory of motion sickness and postural instability. Ecol. Psychol. **3**(3), 195–240 (1991)
27. PLUX Wireless Biosignals S.A.: Plux research kit (2018). http://www.biosignalsplux.com/
28. Schubert, T., Friedmann, F., Regenbrecht, H.: The experience of presence: factor analytic insights. Presence Teleoperators Virtual Environ. **10**(3), 266–281 (2001)
29. Slater, M., Usoh, M., Steed, A.: Taking steps: the influence of a walking technique on presence in virtual reality. ACM Trans. Comput. Hum. Interact. (TOCHI) **2**(3), 201–219 (1995)
30. Souman, J.L., et al.: CyberWalk: enabling unconstrained omnidirectional walking through virtual environments. ACM Trans. Appl. Percept. (TAP) **8**(4), 25 (2011)
31. Sra, M., Xu, X., Mottelson, A., Maes, P.: VMotion: designing a seamless walking experience in VR. In: Proceedings of the 2018 on Designing Interactive Systems Conference, pp. 59–70. ACM (2018)
32. Steinicke, F., Bruder, G., Jerald, J., Frenz, H., Lappe, M.: Analyses of human sensitivity to redirected walking. In: Proceedings of the 2008 ACM Symposium on Virtual Reality Software and Technology, pp. 149–156. ACM (2008)
33. Tarvainen, M.P., Niskanen, J.P., Lipponen, J.A., Ranta-Aho, P.O., Karjalainen, P.A.: Kubios HRV-heart rate variability analysis software. Comput. Methods Programs Biomed. **113**(1), 210–220 (2014)
34. Telford, A., Malpeli, R., Whittle, R., Seery, P., Corrie, M.: Physical Education: VCE Units 1 & 2. Thomas Nelson, Australia (2017)
35. Templeman, J.N., Denbrook, P.S., Sibert, L.E.: Virtual locomotion: walking in place through virtual environments. Presence **8**(6), 598–617 (1999)
36. Terziman, L., Marchal, M., Emily, M., Multon, F., Arnaldi, B., Lécuyer, A.: Shakeyour-head: revisiting walking-in-place for desktop virtual reality. In: Proceedings of the 17th ACM Symposium on Virtual Reality Software and Technology, pp. 27–34. ACM (2010)
37. Uliano, K., Lambert, E., Kennedy, R., Sheppard, D.: The effects of asynchronous visual delays on simulator flight performance and the development of simulator sickness symptomatology. Technical report, Essex Corp., Orlando (1986)
38. Wagner, J., Lingenfelser, F., Baur, T., Damian, I., Kistler, F., André, E.: The social signal interpretation (SSI) framework: multimodal signal processing and recognition in real-time. In: Proceedings of the 21st ACM International Conference on Multimedia, pp. 831–834. ACM (2013)

39. Walch, M., et al.: Evaluating VR driving simulation from a player experience perspective. In: Proceedings of the 2017 CHI Conference Extended Abstracts on Human Factors in Computing Systems, pp. 2982–2989. ACM (2017)
40. Wiederhold, B.K., Davis, R., Wiederhold, M.D.: The effects of immersiveness on physiology (1998)
41. Williams, B., Bailey, S., Narasimham, G., Li, M., Bodenheimer, B.: Evaluation of walking in place on a Wii balance board to explore a virtual environment. ACM Trans. Appl. Percept. (TAP) 8(3), 19 (2011)
42. Witmer, B.G., Singer, M.J.: Measuring presence in virtual environments: a presence questionnaire. Presence 7(3), 225–240 (1998)

Editor of O & M Virtual Environments for the Training of People with Visual Impairment

Agebson Rocha Façanha[1](✉), Windson Viana[2], and Jaime Sánchez[3]

[1] Federal Institute of Education,
Science and Tecnology of Ceará (IFCE), Fortaleza, CE, Brazil
agebson@ifce.edu.br
[2] Federal University of Ceará (UFC), Fortaleza, CE, Brazil
windson@virtual.ufc.br
[3] Universidad de Chile (UChile), Santiago, Chile
jsanchez@dcc.uchile.cl

Abstract. The lack of vision increases the complexity of performing tasks that require spatial representation. People with visual impairment face challenges in establishing positions of obstacles in a physical space. It is hard for them to discern their current location or a direction to go. Thus, any information about the ambient characteristics tends to be relevant to the decision-making process of people who are blind. This process involves the creation of a mental representation of the physical space, which is responsible for storing, retrieving, and decoding information about the environment. A mental representation of the space is a key factor for their Orientation and Mobility (O & M) skills. Several studies have investigated the impact of the use of O & M Virtual Environments in the construction of these mental maps. This paper reports the development of an editor for O & M Virtual Environment focusing on generating indoor spaces simulations, called E3 Editor. Differently, from other studies that provide solutions specific to a given space, E3 Editor allows O & M experts to create their virtual indoor maps and applied them in their practical classes with learners with visual impairment, thus favouring the autonomy of these subjects.

Keywords: Editor of virtual environments · Orientation and Mobility · People with visual impairment

1 Introduction

The biggest challenge faced by people with visual impairment when they move around is to know about their position and their surroundings. For instance, it is essential to know what direction they are going and where are the obstacles they need to avoid. In this context, obtaining spatial information is always very relevant to the process of decision making of the movement actions of these individuals need to perform.

A mental map of the space in which they are placed is essential to the efficient development of Orientation and Mobility (O&M) skills for people who are blind.

© Springer Nature Switzerland AG 2019
M. Antona and C. Stephanidis (Eds.): HCII 2019, LNCS 11572, pp. 617–627, 2019.
https://doi.org/10.1007/978-3-030-23560-4_45

A mental map of the space helps them to store, retrieve, and decode information about an existing building or space. It plays a crucial role in improving their autonomy and mobility [2, 11].

Several studies have investigated the impact of the use of O&M virtual environments in the construction of the mental maps of space [5–8]. Frequently, these virtual environments simulate real-world spaces and use 3D audio to guide the interaction [6–8]. Their goal is to train users to improve their real-life navigation skills. Researchers hypothesize that people who are blind exploring the virtual environment will able to transfer such representations to the real world. They combine the use of haptic devices (e.g., joysticks, enhanced canes) and 3D audio to improve user interaction aiming to foster technology acceptance and its cognitive impact.

O&M virtual environments stand out in the process of acquiring spatial information and identifying obstacles in a simulated space. For example, it is possible to reconstruct the most diverse environments and situations (houses, public buildings visits, outdoor spaces) virtually by using 3D sound and haptic resources (multimodal interfaces) [12]. This approach allows people with visual impairment to learn O&M skills in virtual worlds with safety [6, 8].

O&M virtual environments rely on digital maps that describe indoor or, less frequently, an outdoor space. Digital and interactive maps form a system of spatial knowledge, a symbolic representation of external reality. They provide a reference structure to understand and interpret the information on the environment (e.g., obstacles, Pont-of-Interests, rooms). In some solutions, they simulate real-world spaces (e.g., museum, schools) preserving proportions and relative objects position. For people who are blind, O&M environments can improve their understanding of the space, spatial relations among existing objects, and dangerous places and directions to go (e.g., stairs), even before visiting the real space.

Therefore, there is a constant need for maps to stimulate and practice O&M techniques in a safe and low-cost environment. However, most of the studies of the domain have predefined indoor maps. The majority of O&M virtual environments do not enable map customisation by users, which is making their applicability restricted. According to our knowledge, only two works provide tools for map creation. However, the systems do not target O & M teachers, and their map customisation is very rudimentary.

Thus, the primary goal of this research is to design, implement, and evaluate an editor to customise O & M virtual environments with multimodal interfaces. Our focus is to improve spatial cognition in people with visual impairments by offering a way to expand the availability of indoor maps. We propose a Web system, called E3 Editor, which provide features for building 2D maps. The tool follows a tile-design approach. A mobile application reads its indoor map representation and executes an O & M virtual environment with 3D audio and haptic feedback.

The remainder of this paper is organised as follows: in Sect. 2, we present a brief overview of the O & M virtual environments. Section 3 shows the design and development of the E3 Editor, detailing its context of use, and the user-centred design methodology we adopted to develop it. In Sect. 4, we conclude the paper discussing the future research directions of this work.

2   O&M Virtual Environments

2.1   Overview

In a real environment, people with visual impairment can recognise the space with the aid of a cane, applying orientation and mobility techniques (e.g., tracking the perimeter, shifting toward a sound source). The idea of O & M virtual environment is to replicate these navigation and orientation techniques using 3D audio and haptic feedback.

From an investigation of scientific literature, we identified some systems focusing on practices of O & M skills using virtual environments for people who blind [1, 3, 4, 6–8, 12, 13]. In some of the works, researchers study the relationship between the mental representations of space constructed by users and the use of virtual environments. Authors demonstrate that when the O & M virtual environment simulates real-world spaces, users can transfer mental representations of the virtual map they navigated to the real world [6, 12].

For instance, in Audio-based Environment Simulator (AbES) [12], the O & M virtual environment uses a game-based approach. The idea is to promote engagement, and, as a consequence, to increase the chances of a full exploration of the virtual environment map. The player is looking for hidden jewels (random located) in a virtual building. It must remove them from the indoor space; meanwhile, it must avoid roving monsters, which are programmed to take away the jewels and hide them in new locations.

Figure 1 shows an example of such a system. Two people who are blind are using our O&M Environment, called AVER, that uses a head-mounted device. They navigated in a virtual house enriched with 3D audio, which describes walls, doors, and objects. During the session, one user holds the joystick that controls the navigation in the system with one hand and, sometimes, when his avatar is moving in the virtual environment, he was feeling as manipulating a cane in the real world. The other user intuitively does the perimeter scan in the real world with one hand, even though he knows he is walking in a virtual environment.

Fig. 1. O & M virtual environment usage

The people who are blind will build a description of the O & M virtual environment by using these sensations and metaphors. After several interactions, the user becomes aware of the spatial relations of the scene (e.g., using the number of moving steps when walks, counting his avatar rotation degrees). He goes, therefore, identifying the position of walls (using the collision feedback), objects (from the audio cues), obstacles, thus creating a mental map of the space.

2.2   Map Editors

From the investigation of scientific literature, we identified most of the O & M environments propose dedicated solutions with a specific map (e.g., a building). We identified only two works, the BlindAid [7] and the Binaural Navigation Game [1], which offer a tool to edit and expand the maps of the O & M virtual environment. Both are desktop system and use 3D audio for user interaction. Figure 2 shows the interface of these editors. However, none of the applications are available online for download.

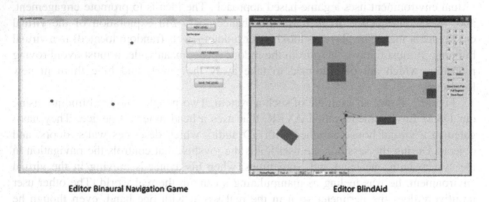

Editor Binaural Navigation Game   Editor BlindAid

Fig. 2. Screenshots of the Binaural Navigation Game Editor and BlindAid, extracted from [1, 7].

In the case of the BlindAid editor, the environment (e.g., house, school) described by the map is modelled using some CAD (Computer-Aided Design) software. The O & M virtual environment designer imports the CAD file into the editor. After some adjustments, end-users can interact with the new map by using the computer keyboard or a Phantom haptic device.

With the Binaural Navigation Game, designers can create a map layout in a straightforward and interactive way. The map designer places a set of points representing objects or obstacles. Green points refer to objects, and the red ones identify obstacles. Users define the locations of these elements by clicking on the editor window in the positions where the system will place the items. The approach limits only five obstacles per map. The data for each level is stored in text files, containing the point type and its 2D coordinate on the map.

The two approaches are a bit different. The Binaural Navigation Game allocates points of interest and obstacles along the map. It is more intuitive and easier to use. However, the tool does not provide O & M expert users with the support to create more elaborate maps. For instance, to add walls or predefined objects is not available in this tool.

As we stated, the BlindAid editor imports CAD files (e.g., first floor of a building). On the one hand, it incorporates all the details of a building plan, for example, keeping its spatial scales. On the other hand, the tool increases the complexity of manipulating the virtual map. The tool users need to be experts for customising the map. In the studies presented by the two editors, we did not find how a user integrates the editing tool results with O & M virtual environments.

3 Design and Development of a Customizable Map Editor

3.1 E3 Editor Approach

The present work investigates the gaps and the real possibilities for the development of a map editor for O & M virtual environments. We are targeting as users the O & M teachers, who want to create virtual environments with audio-haptic interaction for O & M training. In this way, we intended to study the application of this technology as a tool to support O & M classes.

Figure 3 depicts an overview of our approach. We have two main users: O & M teachers and people who are blind. Teachers will create indoor maps and customize their navigation activities. People with visual impairment will execute and navigate in the new virtual map by using a mobile application that runs the O & M virtual environment. The mobile app offers audio-haptic feedbacks during the indoor map exploration.

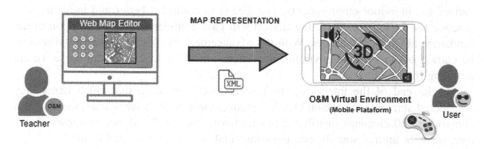

Fig. 3. Proposed approach

3.2 Methodology

To create our editor, we follow the User-Centered Design methodology, which consists of four iterative stages: observation, idealisation, prototyping, and testing. In this methodology, the designer repeats its steps until the desired solution is obtained [9].

The iterative development process was adopted, which included brainstorming sessions, behavioural observation, and contextual exploratory interview. We applied it with a multidisciplinary team composed of O & M specialists, people with visual impairment, and our team of researchers and developers. We follow four main steps: Establish requirements, Idealisation, Prototype, and Evaluation.

3.3 Brainstorming

First, we made Brainstorming sessions with a group of three O & M teachers, all with more than eight years of experience in O & M classes.

The goal was to investigate the real needs for the construction of virtual maps that could help them in their O & M classes. For instance, we discuss how to structure O&M activities carried out with the students with visual impairment in a virtual world. Figure 4 shows drawings made by the teachers. The draws represent a simplification of real environments the teachers use for O&M practice. We also observe a part of a practical orientation and mobility class held with a student with visual impairment.

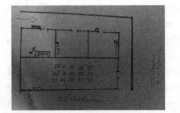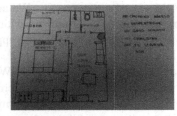

Fig. 4. Representation of three maps of the O & M classes

Teachers stated practical self-protection activities (pre-cane class) are initially carried out in indoor environments. The idea is to control it better and to assure safe practice for the learner. Thus, the student will gain confidence in the execution of the fundamental O&M techniques. With the advancement of training, other activities can be carried out in external environments. These initial O&M classes are those we are targeting in our approach.

At the end of the interview, the teachers were asked to list which items they considered attractive to have on O & M virtual environment. A week later, we had a list containing 120 elements distributed among floor types, walls, doors, windows, furniture, utensils, animal sounds, and environmental noises they desired to use.

3.4 Idealisation

Searching Other Editors

To complement the teachers' demands, we reuse the work of Project ATMAPS [10]. This work specifies objects to be used in audio-haptic maps. We also decided to simplify the development of the map editor by adopting a 2D approach for its design. The manner the teachers create their O & M classes inspired this decision.

In this perspective, we sought to know more about 2D game map editors already existing in the market. We tried to have insights examining their layouts. We used them as references for the construction of the 2D map editor prototype. We selected two of them to better study: the TileMapEditor[1] and the web tool Pyromancers[2].

We highlighted them for being in constant improvements. They have active communities elaborating new maps. We believe these virtual communities could be stimulated to engage in our project in the future. Our prototype has a visual organisation based on two work areas: the map creation (viewport and canvas) and the palette containing the graphic characteristics of the elements. The layout is similar to the reference tools aiming to facilitate the learning, the editor use, and the number of errors committed.

We organised the elements available to be placed in the map into thematic sets, called Tilesets (e.g., Floor, Wall, Door and Window, Furniture, Electro/Electronics, Household Tools and Interactive Elements). This structure has been adopted to facilitate the inclusion of new elements and to help the teacher in their selection.

Our goal is facilitating the learning and the quick location of the items. After all, the presentation of information on the display screen should take into account the cognitive and perceptual characteristics of the users. Therefore, the best understanding/readability of the screen depends, among other things, on the ordering of the objects. The editor layout tries to attend the O & M teachers' expertise. In this case, they have little experience in using the computer and expect a very friendly/intuitive interface.

During the process of making the indoor map, the O & M teacher defines which elements will be placed and their positions. Figure 5 depicts the action of drag and drops the icons from the palette to the canvas. The drop position of the element will correspond to its location on the audio-haptic map in O & M virtual environment.

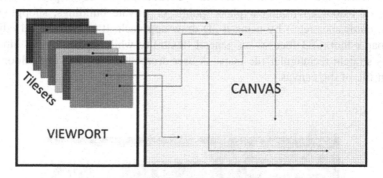

Fig. 5. Drag-and-drop movement examples

[1] http://www.tilemapeditor.com/.

[2] http://pyromancers.com/dungeon-painter-online/.

O & M Teachers Feedback

We verified the first layout of E3 and the idea of dragging and dropping elements to create virtual maps. The teachers well accepted the proposal. They stated the usage of the editor would act better when the user made a pre-planning of the map. For instance, they suggest using child education classroom materials to design a low fidelity map before use our tool. Figure 6 shows two examples of pre-planning they suggest; one uses a checkered sheet of paper and the other employs coloured toy bricks to represent indoor maps.

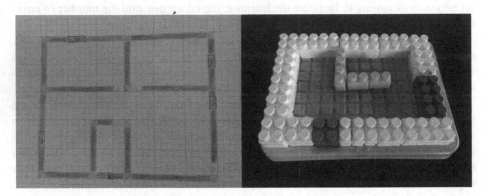

Fig. 6. Checkered Sheet and Toy bricks for pre-planning the virtual map

3.5 First Prototype

Figure 7 shows the Web Editor (HTML + JavaScript) we developed. It allows the creation of indoor environment plans (public or private buildings, shopping malls, airports, companies, etc.) by using a 2D draw approach. It is a tile-based editor like game map editors. E3 focuses on general flexibility while trying to stay intuitive. It supports straight rectangular tile maps. A user drops "wall bricks" and "floor pieces" for each tile of the canvas.

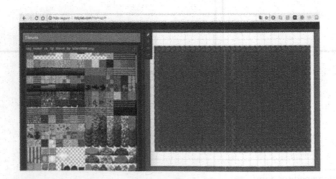

Fig. 7. Editor's main screen and Example of a ready-made map

The E3 Editor export the map generated in the XML format. The mobile app is interpreting this file by using the game engine Unity3D. The application renders at runtime a navigable O & M virtual environment. It generates a 3D model for each element with their associated audios and haptic interactions. For that, we are developing a repository of 3D elements and their respective sounds (e.g., collision audio, audio cues). Such a feature is essential to provide immersion trying to help the construction of the mental map of the real space.

The mobile app has predefined mechanics to able navigation, rotation, wayfinding, and access to tutorial features. All these features use well-defined accessible interfaces, which are based on 3D audio and haptic feedback.

Figures 8 and 9 illustrate this process of map creation and its runtime rendering in the O & M virtual environment. The video available at https://youtu.be/kvgdSks0cuI shows the result of this process. The user draws a simple map with walls and a floor. The E3 Editor represents it in XML identifying the position and element identification of each tile on the map. The mobile app searches these ids to identify the correspondent 3D objects and their audio-haptic interactions.

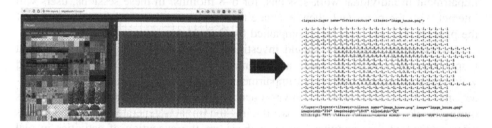

Fig. 8. Web Editor exports the map information into an XML file

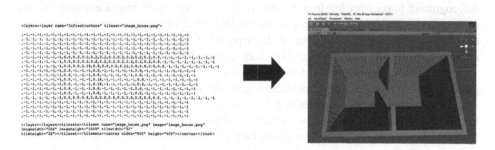

Fig. 9. Mobile application reads XML and renders the environment automatically

4 Final Considerations and Future Directions

The acquisition of O & M skills for people with visual impairment is crucial for their autonomy. In this sense, the use of virtual reality technology should provide these users with new ways of acquiring spatial information and identifying obstacles that guide the locomotion in the various spaces. The present work presents the creation of an editor of audio-haptic maps to be executed in O & M virtual environments. O & M teachers can easily generate useful maps for their classes.

As future work, two more phases are planned for this research: the first consists of a usability assessment with a significant sample of users. We expect to evaluate E3 Editor with a group of experts and O&M teachers. The next phase will deal with the study of the use of the E3 Editor in the practice and teaching of O&M techniques. Our goal is to investigate the cognitive impact resultant of our approach implementation in the context of O&M training.

The usability evaluation of E3 editor approach with end-users (apprentices and O&M specialists) will be performed using questionnaires, direct observation through the analysis of use videos and software to record the interaction with the tool. We aim to assess the user error rate and editor acceptance. We are also planning to carry out a heuristic evaluation of the Web tool to observe the relevance of the interface information and its affordance.

The objective of this phase is to evaluate the initial cognitive impact of the use of the developed maps. We will implement research intervention with users with visual impairment in individual work sessions, for 6–8 months. In these sessions, users will interact with the maps and, then, evaluate their representativeness. As a facilitator of the process, the user may be accompanied by O & M teachers.

In this sense, this work should investigate cognitive processes, such as mental maps, cognitive spatial structures, and orientation and mobility skills, navigation, and wayfinding of people with visual impairment. We aim to analyse the different interactions of these users with the environment, unveiling their limits and possibilities during the development processes, ascertaining the impacts generated. The experiments often performed for cognitive impact analysis are the execution of activities in real environments, the verbal description, and the recreation of the virtual scenario with toy bricks. The execution of activities in the real situation is a common approach to assess the cognitive impact arising from the interaction of users with visual impairment and representative real-world audio-haptic maps. The other recurrent assessment is to ask the participants to provide a verbal description of the map visited virtually. This approach allows for understanding how they constructed the mental map of the space.

Already in the recreation of the virtual scenario experiment, researchers often ask participants to reconstruct a physical/realistic model or schematic diagram of the virtual map. This approach allows assessing the transfer of cognitive knowledge given the location of objects. In the end, we intend to analyse how the maps with such specification facilitate the improvement of the mental representation of the space. We want to measure the increase in the spatial structuring and in the users' navigational abilities.

Acknowledgements. This work was carried out in partnership with the Federal Institute of Education, Science, and Technology of Ceará (IFCE). CNPq funded this research partially, through the Research Project of CNPq, under concession number 458825/2013-1, prepared for execution within the Call MCTI-SECIS/CNPq N° 84/2013' - Assistive Technology. The title of this project is "Research and development of digital solutions for education, culture, and interaction with mobile systems for the people with visual impairment". The project was also funded by FONDECYT 1150898 and by CONICYT's Basal Funds for Centers of Excellence, Project FB0003.

References

1. Balan, O., Moldoveanu, A., Moldoveanu, F., Butean, A.: Developing a navigational 3D audio game with hierarchical levels of difficulty for the visually impaired players. In: RoCHI, pp. 49–54 (2015)
2. Carreiras, M., Codina, B.: Cognición espacial, orientación y movilidad: consideraciones sobre la ceguera. Integración **11**, 5–15 (1993)
3. Cobo, A., Guerrón, N.E., Martín, C., del Pozo, F., Serrano, J.J.: Differences between blind people's cognitive maps after proximity and distant exploration of virtual environments. Comput. Hum. Behav. **77**, 294–308 (2017)
4. Connors, E.C., Chrastil, E.R., Sánchez, J., Merabet, L.B.: Virtual environments for the transfer of navigation skills in the blind: a comparison of directed instruction vs. video game based learning approaches. Front. Hum. Neurosci. **8**, 223 (2014)
5. Ducasse, J., Brock, A.M., Jouffrais, C.: Accessible interactive maps for visually impaired users. In: Pissaloux, E., Velázquez, R. (eds.) Mobility of Visually Impaired People, pp. 537–584. Springer, Cham (2018). https://doi.org/10.1007/978-3-319-54446-5_17
6. Lahav, O., Mioduser, D.: Construction of cognitive maps of unknown spaces using a multi-sensory virtual environment for people who are blind. Comput. Hum. Behav. **24**(3), 1139–1155 (2008)
7. Lahav, O. Schloerb, D.W., Kumar, S., Srinivasan, M.A.: BlindAid: a learning environment for enabling people who are blind to explore and navigate through unknown real spaces. In: Virtual Rehabilitation, 2008, pp. 193–197. IEEE (2008)
8. Merabet, L.B., Sánchez, J.: Development of an audio-haptic virtual interface for navigation of large-scale environments for people who are blind. In: Antona, M., Stephanidis, C. (eds.) UAHCI 2016. LNCS, vol. 9739, pp. 595–606. Springer, Cham (2016). https://doi.org/10.1007/978-3-319-40238-3_57
9. Norman, D.: The Design of Everyday Things: Revised and Expanded Edition. Constellation (2013)
10. Papadopoulos, K., et al.: User requirements regarding information included in audio-tactile maps for individuals with blindness. In: Miesenberger, K., Bühler, C., Penaz, P. (eds.) ICCHP 2016. LNCS, vol. 9759, pp. 168–175. Springer, Cham (2016). https://doi.org/10.1007/978-3-319-41267-2_23
11. Sanabria, L.: Mapeo congnitivo y exploración háptica para comprender la disposición del espacio de videntes e invidentes. TED: Tecné, Episteme y Didaxis 21 (2007)
12. Sánchez, J.: Development of navigation skills through audio haptic videogaming in learners who are blind. Proc. Comput. Sci. **14**, 102–110 (2012)
13. Yu, J., Habel, C.: A haptic-audio interface for acquiring spatial knowledge about apartments. In: Magnusson, C., Szymczak, D., Brewster, S. (eds.) HAID 2012. LNCS, vol. 7468, pp. 21–30. Springer, Heidelberg (2012). https://doi.org/10.1007/978-3-642-32796-4_3

AR Contents Superimposition on Walls and Persons

João M. F. Rodrigues[1]([⊠]) [ID], Ricardo J. M. Veiga[1] [ID], Roman Bajireanu[1],
Roberto Lam[1] [ID], Pedro J. S. Cardoso[1] [ID], and Paulo Bica[2]

[1] LARSyS (ISR-Lisbon) and ISE, University of the Algarve, 8005-139 Faro, Portugal
{jrodrig,rjveiga,rlam,pcardoso}@ualg.pt, romanmsn.com@hotmail.com
[2] SPIC - Creative Solutions, Faro, Portugal

Abstract. When it comes to visitors' experiences at museums and heritage attractions, objects speak for themselves. With the aim of enhancing a traditional museum visit, a mobile Augmented Reality (AR) framework was developed during the M5SAR project. This paper presents two modules, the wall and human shape segmentation with AR content superimposition. The first, wall segmentation, is achieved by using a BRISK descriptor and geometric information, having the wall delimited, and the AR contents superposed over the detected wall contours. The second module, person segmentation, is achieved by using an OpenPose model, which computes the body joints. These joints are then combined with volumes to achieve AR clothes content superimposition. This paper shows the usage of both methods in a real museum environment.

Keywords: Augmented Reality · Wall detection · Human detection · Wall overlapping · Clothes overlapping · HCI

1 Introduction

Augmented Reality (AR) [3] is no longer an emergent technology, thanks mainly to the mobile devices increasing hardware capabilities and new algorithms. As cornerstone, AR empowers a higher level of interaction between the user and real world objects, extending the experience on how the user sees and feels those objects, by creating a new level of edutainment that was not available before. While many mobile applications (App) already regard museums [31,56], the use of AR in those spaces is much less common, albeit not new, see e.g. [21,46,49,58].

The Mobile Image Recognition based Augmented Reality (MIRAR) framework [45] (developed under M5SAR[1] project [49]) focuses on the development of mobile multi-platform AR systems. One of the MIRAR's requirements is to only use the mobile devices RGB cameras to achieve its goals. A framework that

---

[1] Mobile Five Senses Augmented Reality System for Museums, financed by CRESC ALGARVE2020, PORTUGAL2020 and FEDER.

© Springer Nature Switzerland AG 2019
M. Antona and C. Stephanidis (Eds.): HCII 2019, LNCS 11572, pp. 628–645, 2019.
https://doi.org/10.1007/978-3-030-23560-4_46

integrates our presented goals is completely different from the existing AR software development kits – SDK, frameworks, content management systems, etc. [2,11,37].

This paper focuses on two particular modules of MIRAR, namely: (a) the recognition of walls, and (b) the segmentation of human shapes. While the first module intends to project AR contents onto the walls (e.g., to project text or media), the second contemplates the overlap of clothes onto persons. The wall detection and recognition is supported upon the same principles of the object's recognition (BRISK descriptor) but uses images from the environment to achieve it. On the other hand, the human detection and segmentation uses Convolutional Neural Networks (CNN) for the detection (namely, the OpenPose model [9]). The overlapping of contents in the museum environment is done over the area limited by the wall or using the body joints along with clothes volumes to put contents over the persons. The main contribution of this paper is the integration of AR contents in walls and persons in real environments.

The paper is structured as follows. The contextualization and a brief state of the art is presented in Sect. 2, followed by the wall segmentation and content overlapping sub-module in Sect. 3, and the human shape segmentation and content overlapping in Sect. 4. The paper concludes with a final discussion and future work, Sect. 5.

2   Contextualization and State of the Art

AR image-based markers [12] allow adding in any environment easily detectable pre-set signals (e.g. paintings and statues), and then use computer vision techniques to sense them. In the AR context, there are some image-based commercial and open source SDK and content management systems, such as Catchoom [11], ARtoolKit [2] or Layar [37]. Each of the above solutions has pros and cons and, to the best of your knowledge, none has implemented wall and person segmentation with information overlapping.

The ability of segmenting the planar surfaces of any environment continues to be a challenge in computer vision, mainly if only a monocular camera is used. One of the directest approach to an environment's scanning is the use of RGB-D cameras [25] or LiDaR devices [30] to directly acquire a 3D scan of the cameras' reach. A more indirect approach – more based on computation than hardware – is the Simultaneous Localization and Asynchronous Mapping (SLAM) [13]. SLAM's methods for indoor and outdoor navigation has shown new advances either by using the Direct Sparse Odometry [15], or with a feature matching method like the ORB SLAM [42] or even a Semi-Dense [17] or Large-Scale Direct Monocular SLAM [16].

Another usual approach is the cloud of points method or the structure from motion, which is part of the SLAM's universe, relying on multiple frames to be able to calculate a relation in-between the features – 3D points – and the camera's position. There have been developments in the outdoor, or landmark, recognition [4], an also simple objects detection and its layout prediction using the cloud of oriented gradients [48]. Another example, proving the possibilities of a proper environment's layout analysis, is the use of a structure from motion algorithm using the natural straight lines in an environment, through representation, triangulation and bundle adjustment [6].

One of the main novelties is the use of CNN to solve any complex computer vision challenge, including environment's layout prediction [54], although the current state is not useful in runtime. On the other hand, in every common human-based construction there can be found the presence of lines or edges in its geometric perspective. These vanishing lines allows us to predict the orientation and position of planes [26]. It is even possible to compute a relative pose estimation using the present lines in the environment [14]. These techniques, applied to the indoor layouts' prediction, allows us to compute the existence of natural planar surfaces [51], even by using the edges of maps available on any indoor layout [39]. One major advance in the outdoor camera localization is the PoseNet [33], which also uses a CNN. It is important to stress that none of those methods presents the superimposing of contents over an environment know *a priori*, on a monocular mobile device and in runtime.

The second module to be presented in this work focuses on human segmentation and pose estimation, which is also a challenging problem due to several factors, such as body parts occlusions, different viewpoints, or human motion [20]. In the majority of models based on monocular cameras, the estimation of occluded limbs is not reliable. Nevertheless, good results for a single person's pose estimation can be achieved [20]. Conversely, pose estimation for multiple people is a more difficult task because humans occlude and interact between them. To deal with this task, two types of approaches are commonly used: (a) top-down approach [27], where a human detector is used to find each person and then running the pose estimation on every detection. However, top-down approach does not work if the detector fails to detect a person, or if a limb from other people appears in a single person's bounding box. Moreover, the runtime needed for these approaches is affected by the number of people in the image, i.e., more people means greater computational cost. (b) The bottom-up approach [10,20] estimates human poses individually using pixel information. The bottom-up approach can solve both problems cited above: the information from the entire picture can distinguish between the people's body parts, and the efficiency is maintained even as the number of persons in the image increases.

As in the wall detection, the best results for pose estimation are achieved using R-CNN (Regions - CNN) [23] or evolutions, such as the Fast R-CNN [22], Faster R-CNN [47] or the Single Shot MultiBox Detector (SSD) [29]. A comparison between those methods can be found in [29]. The results show that SSD has the highest mAP (mean average precision) and speed. With good results, OpenPose [10] can also be used for pose estimation, being based on Part Affinity Fields (PAFs) and confidence maps (or heatmaps). The method's overall process can be divided in two steps: estimate the body parts (ankles, shoulders, etc.) and connect body parts to form limbs that result in a pose. In more detail, the method takes an input image and then it simultaneously infers heatmaps and

PAFs. Next, a bipartite matching algorithm is used to associate body parts and, at last, the body parts are grouped to form poses. The OpenPose can be used with a monocular camera and run in "real-time" on mobile devices. Additionally, the estimated 2D poses can be used to predict 3D poses using a "lifting" system, that does not need additional cameras [55].

Several methods exist for clothes overlapping. A popular one is Virtual Fitting Room (VFR) [18], which combines AR technologies with depth and colour data in order to provide strong body recognition functionality and effectively address the clothes overlapping process. Most of these VFR applications overlap 3D models or pictures of a clothing within the live video feed and then track the movements of the user. In the past, markers were used to capture the person [1]. In that case, specific joints are used to place the markers, which differ in colours according to the actual position on the body. From a consumer's point of view, a general disadvantage is the time consumed placing the markers and the discomfort of using them. Isikdogan and Kara [32] use the distance between the Kinect sensor and the user to scale a 2D model over the detected person, only depicting the treatment of t-shirts. Another similar approach, presented in [18], uses 3D clothing with skeleton animation. Two examples of the several commercial applications are FaceCake [19] and Fitnect [34].

3 Wall Detection and Information Overlapping

Previously, the authors followed two distinct approaches to solve the environments' surfaces detection [45,50,59,60]. A first approach assumes that the vanishing lines present in the environment follow an expected geometric shape; and a second approach focuses on retrieving the walls' proportions using the features extraction and matching method, followed by the homographies' computation. The methods were then combined in order to achieve a harmonious detection, recognition and localization of the environment, allowing to dynamically superimpose different types of content over the walls, such as images, video, animations, or 3D objects.

As detailed next, the present algorithm is designed to work over regular plane walls, which are known *a priori* through a previously bundle creation phase. Being the purpose of this AR application the ability to run seamlessly on any current monocular smartphones, from which only a RGB image is provided by the camera (i.e., without any additional depth information), it is important to assure an ideal performance using less computational' eager algorithms.

Our current algorithm divides itself in five different stages: (a) the bundle creation, (b) the recognition and localization, (c) corners' adjustment, (d) tracking, and (e) superimposition.

The first stage of the algorithm – the bundle creation (a) – is pre-executed, i.e., not performed during runtime. For this task two distinct types of bundles are generated: a FLANN (Fast Library for Approximate Nearest Neighbours) [41] Index (FI) bundle, and a FLANN Based Matcher (FBM) bundle. This odd combination is due to a better performance being obtained by a hybrid version

Fig. 1. Top two rows, from top left to bottom right: Example of five templates following of the same wall. Bottom row, pre-processing of the templates. Left to right, input image with the complete desired height of the wall, mask applied over removing the wooden frames, features retrieved and computed.

of both FLANN matchers instead of only one, as presented in [60]. Reasons for this choices will be better detailed during the recognition and localization (b) phase.

Museums' environments are full of detail and some of its areas gather enough significant information to be considered keypoints, which can be detected and define by computing its descriptors. In this approach, the BRISK keypoint detector and descriptor extractor [38] is used, due to its capabilities of performing well with image scaling. Images of continuous walls, as can be seen in Fig. 1 top two rows, allow not only to project content, but also retrieve the users' localization through the sparse unique keypoints inside the artworks. The retrieved features are stored during the bundle creation, allowing the comparison during runtime with the ones obtained from the smartphones' cameras.

As observed in [60], the paintings' wooden frames are rich in similar features, which often would lead to cross-matched in between them. To prevent this false matches, the templates are pre-processed before training the FLANN indexes, defining masks where only the features from the artworks could be obtained, as it can be seen on Fig. 1 bottom row. Additional final templates examples can be

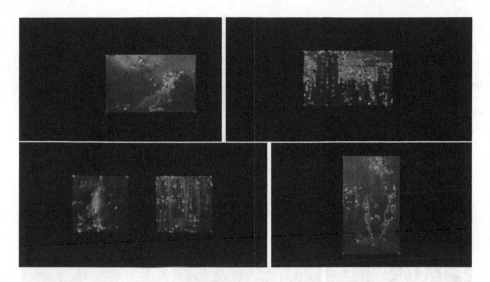

Fig. 2. Example of some of the templates used during the bundle creation stage.

observe on Fig. 2. The motive behind the shape and form of the templates will be explained in detail during the next phases.

Although FBM is built upon FI, previous performance tests showed that the bare FI returns results similar to the ones obtained with FBM, but with an average of 60.66% less processing time [60], which justifies the choice of building an FI bundle. While both methods retrieve the same template index, the FBM also retrieves the matching between features, which is essential for the computation of the homography. Following this necessity, a bundle is created for each matching method, which allows to generate a hybrid FLANN matching method. This method, starts by searching across our templates with the FI bundle and then only process the top retrieved results with FBM, which was proved to be a faster matching method, when compared to using exclusively FBM [60].

Both methods – FI and FBM – used the same index parameters, and the same searching algorithm, the Locality-Sensitive Hashing (LSH), which performs extremely well with non-patent binary descriptors. The LSH used a single hash table with a key size of 12, and only 1 multiprobe level. The addition of a multiprobe to the LSH, allows to reduce the number of hash tables, obtaining a better computational performance without affecting precision. As presented in [60], it was noted an average reduction of 76.56% of processing time across different binary features detectors and descriptors (AKAZE, BRISK, ORB) [53] while using only 1 hash table, versus the 6 hash tables originally recommended.

The runtime computation starts with the recognition and localization stage (b). While no localization information or previous match is available, the retrieved frame from the camera is resized to a resolution of 640 × 480 pixels (px), and processed with the BRISK feature detector through the FI feature matcher, returning a list of probabilities for the index of each template, as can

Fig. 3. Pipeline of the environments' superimposition algorithm. Left to right, top to bottom: input frame, keypoints and descriptor computation, homography's calculation, demonstration of the relation between matches and the homography, Canny edge detection, Probabilistic Hough Transform, vanishing lines post-processing, content superimposed.

be seen on the top-left and top-centre of Fig. 3. Similar to the top-5 rank in CNN, the image with highest probability is not occasionally matched, although one within the top-5 is used. Then the FBM is applied through the top-5 indexes and the results are subjected to the Lowe's ratio test, where only the matches with distances to each other with a relation between 55% and 80% are considered. If at least 20 of these matches are obtained, then the algorithm continues, otherwise it skips this frame's processing. It is also important to stress that in order to achieve a near real-time performance, the previous frame's processing time is correlated with the total amount of descriptors for the current frame, with all being firstly sorted by their response parameter, which correlates the level of similarity between the templates and frames' descriptors.

With the computation of the homography's matrix between the correlated matches of the template and the camera's frame, the perspective transformation of the 2D template can be computed as an object within the 3D world, which can be observe in Fig. 3 – top-right. Normally, the homography only requires 4 matches to be able to calculate but, with the user navigating through out the museum, steady results for this AR application were obtained only when the minimum limit of matches was increased to 20 points. We also discard the bad homographies verifying if the computed matrix presents a possible solution which could match our desired output: direction, proportion, and perspective. A demonstration of this process can be seen in Fig. 3 – centre-left and right.

During the bundle creation stage (a) the templates' shape form where made for a specific purpose: the ability to find the upper and bottom margins of any specific wall, as well the left and right limits when necessary. The current arrangement of templates is divided between two rooms, one regular – cuboid – and one irregular. The aim for the regular room is to be able to localize the exact position and angle that the user is pointing. Furthermore, using the continuous templates from the same wall, as shown in Fig. 1 – top two rows, an automated mixed 3D layout of the museum's room is being designed, with the objective of further exploring the AR applications without the need for advanced 3D calculations. In the irregular room, the walls are used to project any desired content, e.g., a video-documentary related to the artwork exposed on that specific wall without the ability to project over the entire environment's layout.

With the homography already known, the next step is the corner's adjustment stage (c), which is the result of the combination of several methods [45,50,59,60]. The frame's edges are computed by applying a Gaussian filter to blur the frame, followed by a dynamic Canny edge detection [8] using the Otsu threshold [43] to replace the high Canny's threshold, which decides if a pixel is accepted as an edge, while the lower threshold, which decides if a pixel is rejected, varies with a direct proportion of 10% to the higher. The computed edges can be seen on the centre-right of Fig. 3. Afterwards, the Probabilistic Hough Transform [36] is applied in order to retrieve the lines present in the frame, as seen in the bottom-left of Fig. 3.

Next, the obtained lines are filtered by discarding the extremely uneven lines in relation to the horizon line, followed by the calculation of the similar ones, resulting only in the expected environment's vanishing lines. The lines' intersecting points were clustered using a K-means clustering method, where the densest cluster is chosen, and its centroid is considered as the vanishing point of said lines. Considering the original location of the homography's corner points, with the known vanishing point, these corners can be adjusted to existing lines in the environment – upper and lower limit of the wall –, as observed in the bottom-centre of the Fig. 3.

Previously, the application of Kalman filters to the vanishing point and its corresponding corner's coordinates was introduced in [60], allowing for a better perception of the user's movement, and consequently smoothing the transitions of the superimposed content. Although the current state of the present algorithm retains this step, Kalman filters are no longer used for tracking, with its main function being the validation of a proper template's perspective found on the processed frames. More precisely, the Kalman filtering of the coordinates allows to predict their next position and estimate if the ones retrieved behaved as noise or valid inputs. This favors the obtention of more precise coordinates in time with more harmonious trajectories – it is important to refer that the obtained homographies are not perfect and their perspective fluctuates significantly, which leads to noisy coordinates. This probably is due to the recursiveness of the Kalman filters but, there was only the need to adjust the uncertainty matrix to our specific application and no additional past information is required to be able to process in real time. Before advancing to the last two stages of the algorithm, the previous steps are computed again using a mask retrieved from the calculated coordinates. When the Kalman filters stabilizes, the process proceeds to the next stage.

Regarding the tracking stage (d), with the corresponding template's coordinates found, the good features to track within our current frame's mask are computed, using the Shi-Tomasi method [52]. Afterwards, the optical flow between the previous and the current frame is calculated using the iterative Lucas-Kanade method with pyramids [7]. Using this method, a more accurate homography between frames can be computed, which results in a more fluid and smooth tracking using even less computation than our previous approach. It should be noticed some important aspect of this approach such as the fact that the smartphones' cameras are different between brands and models, sometimes even between the operating system versions, which results in different features match across the devices. Through this method, a lighter computational tracking in any device and in multiple conditions was possible. The Shi-Tomasi corners continues to be obtained through the tracking, which enables the visitor to continue walking through the museum without the AR experience – which enables the visitor to explore the content in a higher detail.

Following the previous stage, the superimposition stage (e) can finally processed. With the improved tracking stage, the overlay of content over the environments' previous known walls, allowing the visitors' movement, is possible, without affecting the projected content. The result can be seen in the bottom-right of Fig. 3. Although, it is only presented the projection of content over the corresponding template's shape, it is also possible to use the template's mask and re-purpose the artwork's surrounding empty walls with content without covering the artwork. With the different templates, specific content can be projected on different walls throughout the museum's divisions.

4   Person Detection and Clothes Overlapping

As mention, the goal of the Person Detection and Clothes Overlapping module is to use a mobile device to project AR content (clothes) over persons that are in a museum. On other words, the goal is "to dress" museums' users with clothes from the epoch of the museums' objects. The module has two main steps: (i) the person detection and pose estimation, and the (ii) clothes overlapping. Those steps will be explained in detail in the following sections.

The implementation was done in Unity [57] using the OpenCV library (Asset for Unity). In order to verify the implementation's reliability, computational tests were done in a desktop computer and in a mobile device, namely using a Windows 10 desktop with an Intel i7-6700 running at 3.40 GHz and an ASUS Zenpad 3S 10″ tablet.

Fig. 4. Left to right, example of confusion between left and right ankle, the correct detected pose, and the pose estimation with spatial size of the CNN equal to 368×368 px and 192×192 px. (Color figure online)

The method used for pose estimation was OpenPose (see Sect. 2 and [10, 35]). OpenPose was implemented on TensorFlow [24] and the CNN architecture for feature extraction is MobileNets [28]. The extracted features serve as input for the OpenPose algorithm, that produces confidence maps (or heatmaps) and PAFs maps which are concatenated. The concatenation consists of 57 parts: 18 keypoint confidence maps plus 1 background, and 38 $(= 19 \times 2)$ PAFs. The component *joint/body part* of the body, e.g., the right knee, the right hip, or the left shoulder, are shown in Fig. 4, where red and blue circles indicate the person's left and right body parts. A pair of connected parts, *limb*, e.g., the right shoulder connection with the neck are shown in the same figure, the green line segments.

A total amount of 90 frames of expected user navigation were the input to the CNN. Furthermore, two input sizes images for the CNN were tested: 368×368 and 192×192 px. Depending on the size of the input, the average process time for each frame was 236 ms/2031 ms (milliseconds) and 70 ms/588 ms, respectively in the desktop and tablet. As expected, reducing the input size images of the CNN allow attaining improvements on the execution time, but the accuracy of the results dropped. The pose is always estimated, but the confidence map for a body part to be considered valid must be above 25% of the maximum value estimated in the confidence map (this value was empirically chosen), otherwise is not considered. A missing body part example for a 192×192px image which was detected in the 368×368 px image is shown in Fig. 4, right most image. The same figure also shows an example of error that sometimes occurs in the identification of the right and left hands/legs (left most image).

Besided the presented cases, a stabilization method was needed because pose estimated (body part) can wrongly "change" position, for instance due to light changes. The stabilization is done using groups of body parts from the estimated pose. The body parts selection for each group is based on the change that body parts do when any single one moves, see Fig. 5.

Groups	1st	2nd	3rd	4th	5th
Parts	Neck	Right Hip	Left Hip	Right Elbow	Left Elbow
	Right Shoulder	Right Ankle	Left Ankle	Right Wrist	Left Wrist
	Left Shoulder	Right Knee	Left Knee		

Fig. 5. Pose estimation stabilization groups.

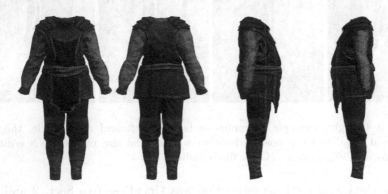

Fig. 6. Examples of volume 2D views.

The stabilization algorithm is as follows: (a) for each one of the 5 groups present in Fig. 5, a group of RoIs (one for each body part), with 2% of the width and height of the frame (value chosen empirically), is used to validate if all the body parts from the group have changed position or not. (b) To allow a body part to change position, all the other group body parts must change, i.e., they must have a position change bigger than the RoIs mentioned before. (c) Depending of the group, if one or two body part(s) have a value bigger than the predefined RoIs, this wrong body part(s) is/are replaced by the correct ones, that was/were estimated in a previous frame.

To solve the incorrect detection of the body parts problem, the estimated pose view is used, i.e., to distinguish between right and left body parts it is necessary to validate if the body is in a front or in a back view. (d) This is done by observing that in a front view, the x coordinates of the right side body parts should be smaller than the ones from the left side. To replace a missing body part from a pose is used the previously estimated pose.

In the second phase, the clothes overlapping methods has as input the estimated body parts. For clothes overlapping, three methods were tested: (i) segments, (ii) textures, and (iii) volumes. The first two methods were presented in [5], showing some lack precision and the limitation of only working in frontal view.

For the third method (volumes), the two main steps are: (a) rotate and resize the volume, (b) project the (clothes) volume over the person.

In the first step, (a.1) a clothe volume was developed in 3DS MAX [40] and (a.2) imported to Unity. Then, (a.3) the volume was rotated horizontally

Views		Body Parts				
		Nose	Right eye	Left eye	Right Ear	Left Ear
	Front	1	1	1	1	1
		1	1	1	0	0
		1	1	1	0	1
		1	1	1	1	0
	Back	0	0	0	0	0
		0	0	0	1	1
		0	0	0	1	0
		0	0	0	0	1
	Right Side	1	1	0	1	0
	Left Side	1	0	1	0	1

Fig. 7. Created views conditions represented horizontally. A detected part is represented by 1 and not detected by 0.

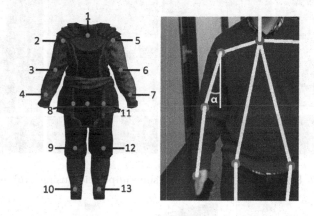

Fig. 8. Left, volume keypoints. Right, example of a limb's angle.

accordingly to four pose views, as presented in Fig. 6 where frontal, back, side right, and side left views of the volume can be seen. (a.4) The views were then associated to the OpenPose detected and non detected body parts (namely: nose, right eye, left eye, right ear and left ear) according with the conditions presented in Fig. 7, where 1 represents a detected body part, and 0 a non detected body part. Additionally, (a.5) to strengthen the assurance of front or back view, the x coordinates distance between right and left hips and shoulders coordinates should be more than 5% of the frame width (this value was empirically chosen). (a.6) A previous view is used if none of the above conditions are met. Finally, (a.7) the volume is resized using the distance between ankles and neck which is an approximation to the person's height.

The resized volume is now project over the detected person (b). To achieve the referred projection, the volume body parts keypoints (see Fig. 8 left) are (b.1) overlapped over the estimated OpenPose pose body part keypoints, and (b.2) rotated accordingly to the angle (α_i) between a vertical alignment and each OpenPose's i-limb, see Fig. 8 right.

Fig. 9. Examples of human shape superimposition using "volumes".

Fig. 10. Examples of both modules working together.

Figure 9 shown results of the overlapped volume in a museum environment. The overlapping volumes over a person takes an average processing time of 6.1 ms/31.4 ms for the desktop and mobile respectively. In general, the overall process takes a mean time of 76.1 ms (70 ms + 6.1 ms) and 590.4 ms (559 ms + 31.4 ms) for the desktop and mobile.

5   Conclusions

This paper presents two modules to be integrated in MIRAR framework [45], namely: the wall segmentation with overlapping of information and the human shapes segmentation with clothes overlapping. Furthermore, the modules were integrated as it can be seen in the examples in Fig. 10.

Regarding the walls' detection and information overlapping, the current results present a functional and fluid experience of content superimposition even with visitors' movements or with acute angles between the camera's position and the superimposed walls. Nevertheless, further tests in different conditions and new environments' implementations are required to improve and evolve the present algorithm into a more broad and stable performance.

For human clothes overlapping in real involvements (museum in this case), the proposed method combines OpenPose body parts detection with volumes overlapping. For better pose estimation accuracy in mobile devices, a stabilization method and the pose views were created. For real-time performances on mobile devices an OpenPose model with a MobileNet architecture was used and two input image sizes were tested (namely, 368×368 and 192×192px). The smallest size is the best option for mobile devices in term of execution time, but it is worse in term of accuracy, nevertheless is a good trade-off for the application.

For future work, a faster and more accurate performance with OpenPose could be achieved by testing new network architectures, new training strategies and other datasets. Another way to get better pose estimation results could be achieved by testing models like PersonLab [44] or others. For this specific module, other way to do pose view estimation is to train a model to do body/foot keypoints estimation and use the foot keypoints position to know the pose view. Additionally, to predict 3D poses by using the estimated 2D poses, the "lifting" system implementation could be done. In the case of the indoor localization through only computer vision is still not resolved, with the necessity of creating a new compatible method to our present tracking system. There is also a need to develop a mixed 3D layout of the regular museums' rooms in order to be able to totally replace the environment if needed. This would also allow, especially with the seamless tracking, the possibility of superimposing advanced 3D models contents that could offer better information, orientation or navigation through the user's visit, fully immersing the visitor in this new era museums' experience.

Acknowledgements. This work was supported by the Portuguese Foundation for Science and Technology (FCT), project LARSyS (UID/EEA/50009/2013), CIAC, and project M5SAR I&DT nr. 3322 financed by CRESC ALGARVE2020, PORTUGAL2020 and FEDER. We also thank Faro Municipal Museum and the M5SAR project leader, SPIC - Creative Solutions [www.spic.pt].

References

1. Araki, N., Muraoka, Y.: Follow-the-trial-fitter: real-time dressing without undressing. In: Proceedings of IEEE Conference on Digital Information Management, London, UK, pp. 33–38 (2008)
2. Artoolkit: ARtoolKit, the world's most widely used tracking library for augmented reality (2017). http://artoolkit.org/. Accessed 16 Nov 2017
3. Azuma, R., Baillot, Y., Behringer, R., Feiner, S., Julier, S., MacIntyre, B.: Recent advances in augmented reality. IEEE Comput. Graph. Appl. **21**(6), 34–47 (2001)
4. Babahajiani, P., Fan, L., Gabbouj, M.: Object recognition in 3D point cloud of urban street scene. In: Jawahar, C.V., Shan, S. (eds.) ACCV 2014. LNCS, vol. 9008, pp. 177–190. Springer, Cham (2015). https://doi.org/10.1007/978-3-319-16628-5_13
5. Bajireanu, R., et al.: Mobile human shape superimposition: an initial approach using OpenPose. In: Proceedings 18th International Conference on Applied Computer Science (2018)
6. Bartoli, A., Sturm, P.: Structure-from-motion using lines: representation, triangulation, and bundle adjustment. Comput. Vis. Image Underst. **100**(3), 416–441 (2005)
7. Bouguet, J.-Y.: Pyramidal implementation of the affine Lucas Kanade feature tracker description of the algorithm. Intel Corporation **5**(1–10), 4 (2001)
8. Canny, J.: A computational approach to edge detection. IEEE Trans. Pattern Anal. Mach. Intell. **8**(6), 679–698 (1986)
9. Cao, Z., Hidalgo, G., Simon, T., Wei, S.-E., Sheikh, Y.: Openpose: real-time multi-person 2D pose estimation using part affinity fields. arXiv preprint arXiv:1812.08008 (2018)
10. Cao, Z., Simon, T., Wei, S.-E., Sheikh, Y.: Realtime multi-person 2D pose estimation using part affinity fields. In: CVPR, vol. 1, no. 2, p. 7 (2017)
11. Catchoom: Catchoom (2017). http://catchoom.com/. Accessed 16 Nov 2017
12. Cheng, K.-H., Tsai, C.-C.: Affordances of augmented reality in science learning: suggestions for future research. J. Sci. Educ. Technol. **22**(4), 449–462 (2013)
13. Durrant-Whyte, H., Bailey, T.: Simultaneous localization and mapping: part I. IEEE Rob. Autom. Mag. **13**(2), 99–110 (2006)
14. Elqursh, A., Elgammal, A.: Line-based relative pose estimation. In: Proceedings IEEE Conference on Computer Vision and Pattern Recognition, pp. 3049–3056. IEEE (2011)
15. Engel, J., Koltun, V., Cremers, D.: Direct sparse odometry. IEEE Trans. Pattern Anal. Mach. Intell. **40**(3), 611–625 (2018)
16. Engel, J., Schöps, T., Cremers, D.: LSD-SLAM: large-scale direct monocular SLAM. In: Fleet, D., Pajdla, T., Schiele, B., Tuytelaars, T. (eds.) ECCV 2014. LNCS, vol. 8690, pp. 834–849. Springer, Cham (2014). https://doi.org/10.1007/978-3-319-10605-2_54

17. Engel, J., Sturm, J., Cremers, D.: Semi-dense visual odometry for a monocular camera. In: Proceedings IEEE International Conference on Computer Vision, pp. 1449–1456 (2013)
18. Erra, U., Scanniello, G., Colonnese, V.: Exploring the effectiveness of an augmented reality dressing room. Multimedia Tools Appl., 1–31 (2018)
19. Facecake: Facecake (2016). http://www.facecake.com/. Accessed 17 September 2018
20. Fang, H., Xie, S., Tai, Y.-W., Lu, C.: RMPE: regional multi-person pose estimation. In: Proceedings IEEE International Conference on Computer Vision, vol. 2 (2017)
21. Gimeno, J., Portales, C., Coma, I., Fernandez, M., Martinez, B.: Combining traditional and indirect augmented reality for indoor crowded environments. A case study on the casa batlló museum. Comput. Graph. **69**, 92–103 (2017)
22. Girshick, R.: Fast R-CNN. In: Proceedings IEEE Conference on Computer Vision, pp. 1440–1448 (2015)
23. Girshick, R., Donahue, J., Darrell, T., Malik, J.: Rich feature hierarchies for accurate object detection and semantic segmentation. In: Proceedings IEEE Conference on Computer Vision and Pattern Recognition, pp. 580–587 (2014)
24. Google: TensorFlow - an open-source machine learning framework for everyone (2018). https://www.tensorflow.org/. Accessed 14 Jan 2018
25. Gupta, S., Arbeláez, P., Girshick, R., Malik, J.: Indoor scene understanding with RGB-D images: bottom-up segmentation, object detection and semantic segmentation. Int. J. Comput. Vis. **112**(2), 133–149 (2015)
26. Haines, O., Calway, A.: Detecting planes and estimating their orientation from a single image. In: BMVC, pp. 1–11 (2012)
27. He, K., Gkioxari, G., Dollár, P., Girshick, R.: Mask R-CNN. In: Proceedings IEEE International Conference on Computer Vision, pp. 2980–2988 (2017)
28. Howard, A.G., et al.: MobileNets: efficient convolutional neural networks for mobile vision applications. arXiv preprint arXiv:1704.04861 (2017)
29. Huang, J., et al.: Speed/Accuracy trade-offs for modern convolutional object detectors. In: Proceedings IEEE Conference on Computer Vision and Pattern Recognition, vol. 4, Honolulu, HI, USA, pp. 3296–3297 (2017)
30. Hulik, R., Spanel, M., Smrz, P., Materna, Z.: Continuous plane detection in point-cloud data based on 3D Hough transform. J. Vis. Commun. Image Represent. **25**(1), 86–97 (2014)
31. InformationWeek: Informationweek: 10 fantastic iPhone, Android Apps for museum visits (2017). https://goo.gl/XF3rj4. Accessed 04 April 2017
32. Isıkdogan, F., Kara, G.: A real time virtual dressing room application using Kinect. Computer Vision Course Project (2012)
33. Kendall, A., Grimes, M., Cipolla, R.: PoseNet: a convolutional network for real-time 6-DOF camera relocalization. In: Proceedings of the IEEE International Conference on Computer Vision, pp. 2938–2946 (2015)
34. Fitnect Interactive Kft. Fitnect (2016). http://www.fitnect.hu/. Accessed 17 Sept 2018
35. Ildoo Kim: tf-pose-estimation (2018). https://bit.ly/2HJxxcq. Accessed 10 April 2018
36. Kiryati, N., Eldar, Y., Bruckstein, A.M.: A probabilistic Hough transform. Pattern Recogn. **24**(4), 303–316 (1991)
37. Layar: Layar (2017). https://www.layar.com/. Accessed 16 Nov 2017
38. Leutenegger, S., Chli, M., Siegwart, R.Y.: BRISK: binary robust invariant scalable keypoints. In: Proceedings IEEE International Conference on Computer Vision, pp. 2548–2555. IEEE (2011)

39. Mallya, A., Lazebnik, S.: Learning informative edge maps for indoor scene layout prediction. In: Proceedings IEEE International Conference on Computer Vision, pp. 936–944 (2015)
40. 3DS MAX: 3DS MAX (2018). https://www.autodesk.com/products/3ds-max/overview. Accessed 3 Dezember 2018
41. Muja, M., Lowe, D.G.: Fast matching of binary features. In: Proceedings 9th Conference Computer and Robot Vision, pp. 404–410. IEEE (2012)
42. Mur-Artal, R., Montiel, J.M.M., Tardos, J.D.: ORB-SLAM: a versatile and accurate monocular SLAM system. IEEE Trans. Rob. **31**(5), 1147–1163 (2015)
43. Otsu, N.: A threshold selection method from gray-level histograms. IEEE Trans. Syst. Man Cybern. **9**(1), 62–66 (1979)
44. Papandreou, G., Zhu, T., Chen, L.-C., Gidaris, S., Tompson, J., Murphy, K.: PersonLab: person pose estimation and instance segmentation with a bottom-up, part-based, geometric embedding model. arXiv preprint arXiv:1803.08225 (2018)
45. Pereira, J.A.R., Veiga, R.J.M., de Freitas, M.A.G., Sardo, J.D.P., Cardoso, P.J.S., Rodrigues, J.M.F.: MIRAR: mobile image recognition based augmented reality framework. In: Mortal, A., et al. (eds.) INCREaSE 2017, pp. 321–337. Springer, Cham (2018). https://doi.org/10.1007/978-3-319-70272-8_27
46. Portales, C., Vinals, M.J., Alonso-Monasterio, P.: AR-immersive cinema at the aula natura visitors center. IEEE MultiMedia **17**(4), 8–15 (2010)
47. Ren, S., He, K., Girshick, R., Sun, J.: Faster R-CNN: towards real-time object detection with region proposal networks. In: Advances in Neural Information Processing Systems, pp. 91–99 (2015)
48. Ren, Z., Sudderth, E.B.: Three-dimensional object detection and layout prediction using clouds of oriented gradients. In: Proceedings IEEE Conference on Computer Vision and Pattern Recognition, pp. 1525–1533 (2016)
49. Rodrigues, J.M.F., et al.: Adaptive card design UI implementation for an augmented reality museum application. In: Proceedings 11th International Conference on Universal Access in Human-Computer Interaction (2017)
50. Rodrigues, J.M.F., et al.: Mobile augmented reality framework - MIRAR. In: Antona, M., Stephanidis, C. (eds.) UAHCI 2018. LNCS, vol. 10908, pp. 102–121. Springer, Cham (2018). https://doi.org/10.1007/978-3-319-92052-8_9
51. Serrão, M., et al.: Computer vision and GIS for the navigation of blind persons in buildings. Univ. Access Inf. Soc. **14**(1), 67–80 (2015)
52. Shi, J., Tomasi, C.: Good features to track. Technical report, Cornell University (1993)
53. Tareen, S.A.K., Saleem, Z.: A comparative analysis of SIFT, SURF, KAZE, AKAZE, ORB, and BRISK. In: Proceedings International Conference on Computing, Mathematics and Engineering Technologies, pp. 1–10. IEEE (2018)
54. Tateno, K., Tombari, F., Laina, I., Navab, N.: CNN-SLAM: real-time dense monocular SLAM with learned depth prediction. In: Proceedings IEEE Conference on Computer Vision and Pattern Recognition, vol. 2 (2017)
55. Tome, D., Russell, C., Agapito, L.: Lifting from the deep: convolutional 3D pose estimation from a single image. In: Proceedings IEEE Conference Computer Vision and Pattern Recognition, pp. 2500–2509 (2017)
56. TWSJ: The wall street journal: best apps for visiting museums (2017). https://goo.gl/cPTyP9. Accessed 4 April 2017
57. Unity: Unity3D (2018). https://unity3d.com/pt. Accessed 10 Jan 2018
58. Vainstein, N., Kuflik, T., Lanir, J.: Towards using mobile, head-worn displays in cultural heritage: user requirements and a research agenda. In: Proceedings 21st International Conference on Intelligent User Interfaces, pp. 327–331. ACM (2016)

59. Veiga, R.J.M., Bajireanu, R., Pereira, J.A.R., Sardo, J.D.P., Cardoso, P.J.S., Rodrigues, J.M.F.: Indoor environment and human shape detection for augmented reality: an initial study. In: Proceedings 23rd Portuguese Conference Pattern Recognition, p. 21 (2017)
60. Veiga, R.J.M., Pereira, J.A.R., Sardo, J.D.P., Bajireanu, R., Cardoso, P.J.S., Rodrigues, J.M.F.: Augmented reality indoor environment detection: proof-of-concept. In: Proceedings Applied Mathematics And Computer Science (2018)

Gaming Background Influence on VR Performance and Comfort: A Study Using Different Navigation Metaphors

Jose L. Soler-Dominguez[1]($\boxtimes$), Carla De-Juan-Ripoll[1], Jorge D. Camba[2], Manuel Contero[1], and Mariano Alcañiz[1]

[1] Instituto de Investigación e Innovación en Bioingeniería (I3B), Universitat Politècnica de València, Camino de Vera s/n, 46022 Valencia, Spain
{josodo,mcontero}@upv.es, {cardejua,malcaniz}@i3b.upv.es
[2] Department of Computer Graphics Technology, Purdue University, 501 Grant Street, West Lafayette, IN 47907, USA
jdorribo@purdue.edu

Abstract. Navigation metaphors in Virtual Reality environments have consistently challenged researchers and developers due to the difficulty of implementing locomotion techniques with high levels of comfort, sense of presence, efficacy and able to fit different narrative environments. In this context, several studies have linked cybersickness to the performance of navigation metaphors, concluding that navigation metaphors based on natural locomotion and with kinesthetic feedback (such as walking-in-place) are more comfortable than those based on indirect locomotion (such as flying). In this paper, we present the results of a study where 41 individuals were asked to navigate a VR environment with two different navigation metaphors. A primary performance metric (karmapoints) derived from the game mechanics introduced in the virtual environment was recorded. Additional subjective metrics about comfort (related to cybersickness) were also recorded through questionnaires. Our results show that participants with a more intense "gamer" background outperform those without such background in both navigation metaphors, regardless of their previous VR experience. Likewise, high level gamers felt less comfortable with the walk-in-place metaphor, which challenges the more accepted explanations of the causes of cybersickness.

Keywords: Virtual reality · Games · Interaction · Navigation

1 Introduction

From the early 2000s, we have witnessed a significant increase in the amount of Virtual Reality (VR) software, devices, and platforms. The scope of this paper is limited to VR systems based on Head Mounted Displays (HMDs).

One of the most challenging design decisions that VR developers face is how users will interact with the Virtual Environment (VE), i.e., the artificial world

M. Antona and C. Stephanidis (Eds.): HCII 2019, LNCS 11572, pp. 646–656, 2019.
https://doi.org/10.1007/978-3-030-23560-4_47

filled with assets designed to host the virtual experience. Even when hundreds of interactions are available (e.g., grabbing an apple from the tree, shooting a tank cannon, etc.), locomotion (the navigation ability of users) remains the most common user action. According to Bowman's taxonomy of interactions in Virtual Reality [1], locomotion can be understood at three different levels:

- Travel: Control of the user's viewpoint and motion in the three-dimensional environment.
- Way-finding: Cognitive process of determining a path based on visual cues, knowledge of the environment and aids such as maps or compasses.
- Navigation: Together, travel and way-finding make up the overall interaction called navigation.

In games and simulators designed for traditional screens, interaction typically occurs through devices such as keyboards, mice, joysticks, game pads or touch screens. Actions performed with these devices are mapped on a quasi-standard set of reactions inside the environment. For example, pushing forward on a joystick, pressing the W key, pressing the UP arrow key or pushing forward on the mini-stick of a pad, are actions typically linked to the forward motion of a character, a vehicle or other virtual avatars. These unwritten assumptions define what is called "an intuitive control schema."

When trying to adapt these intuitive controls (which have been perfected for more than 60 years of gaming and simulation history) to the VR medium, developers found that traditional navigation methods are not entirely suitable to this emerging platform. At the root of the problem is cybersickness, a phenomenon that typically manifests itself as disorientation, eye strain or nausea, among others [12]. Cybersickness is inherent to VR but strongly linked to simulator sickness. It is also common in 3D non-stereoscopic screen environments [11], but has different origins and symptoms [14].

To avoid cybersickness, various locomotion metaphors have been proposed based on natural movements, real or fake, such as redirected walking, walk-in-place or arm swinging. These approaches, far from traditional navigation techniques for games and simulators, are designed to reduce the negative effects of VR. However, as a result of the alternative kinesthetic way of operation, they also reduce performance, mainly in usual gamers, as a collateral effect of the loss of control [13].

In this paper, we compared cybersickness and user performance with two different groups of users: High Intensity Gamers (HIG) and Low Intensity Gamers (LIG). Our results show that both groups of participants experienced higher levels of cybersickness when using a head-bobbing (HB) navigation metaphor. Significant differences were also observed between groups in terms of performance both with natural locomotion (HB) and artificial locomotion (touch-pad based indirect walking, TP).

2   Previous Work: Cybersickness and VR

Cybersickness or VR-induced sickness is a phenomenon derived from the use of Virtual Reality through a Head Mounted Display (HMD) [2,3]. It is a polysymptomatic sickness [4] which means that it causes different symptoms in different people. The most common symptoms include nausea, oculomotor disorders and disorientation [5].

There are several explanations of the causes of cybersickness. The most accepted theory is the Sensory Conflict Theory (SCT). In the words of Mousavi et al. [15], "the theory is based on the premise that discrepancies between the senses which provide information about the body's orientation and motion cause a perceptual conflict which the body does not know how to handle. With cybersickness and motion sickness, the two primary senses that are involved are the vestibular sense and the visual sense. These sensory conflicts arise when the sensory information is not the stimulus that the subject expected based on his/her experience". In cybersickness, those discrepancies come from vection, i.e. the perception of a fake self-movement through visual feedback even when there is no actual movement [16]. By linking vection to interaction, the possibility of "real walking" can be provided through navigation metaphors such as redirected walking, walk-in-place or stepper, among others, which reduces discrepancies between the visual and the vestibular systems [17]. Therefore, the use of traditional game controllers like joysticks or game pads with mini-sticks that simulate indirect walking (similar to flying) should improve vection and consequently, cybersickness [9].

3   Empirical Evaluation

A total of 41 individuals (29 males and 12 females) participated in our study. The average age of the participants was 24.22 years old. Participants included students and staff members from Florida Universitaria, an external campus of the Universitat Politècnica de València in Spain. IRB approval was obtained and all participants gave written informed consent for the study.

3.1   Procedure

In order to determine the influence of locomotion techniques in different psychological and physiological aspects of the user, a Virtual Environment was developed where participants had to navigate and perform various tasks. Data were collected before, during and after the VE session. Since our study involved intra-group comparisons, each individual experienced the virtual environment twice, each with a different navigation metaphor. The order of the conditions was randomized to minimize learning bias.

The experiment was divided into three stages:

1. Pre-VE questionnaires: Collection of demographic data such as participants' gender or age. Additionally, participants had to identify themselves as Hight Intensity Gamers (HIG) or Low Intensity Gamers (LIG) based on how often they played video games, the places where they played, and the gaming devices they owned.

2. Virtual environment. Performance data while experiencing the VR environment (time, distance, etc.)
3. Post-VE questionnaires: Participants completed the ITC-Sense of Presence Inventory questionnaire [7]. The Negative Effects factor was considered as a metric to identify cybersickness symptoms.

3.2   Experimental VE

The VE used in our experiment took the form of a maze filled with karmaspheres (which give the player karmapoints) and various hazards such as fire or poisoned puddles (which take karmapoints away from the player) that "harm" the player unless a shield is activated. The shield is a field of energy that protects the player against any hazard but makes him walk at a slower pace. The goal is to find the exit of the maze within the allotted time (3 min) and the maximum amount of karmapoints.

When first entering the virtual environment, the following audio instructions were played:

Hello and welcome to our maze. You have been selected to participate in a competition where there can only be one winner. You will have 3 minutes to find the exit of the maze and throughout your journey, you must collect as many karmaspheres as you possible. Karmaspheres can be picked up by simply touching them. Each karmasphere you collect will increase your Karma score. But, beware, there are elements that can make you lose karma. Exposing yourself to risks may cause the loss of karmapoints. Fortunately, we will not let you face the hazards of this maze totally unprotected. You have a shield that can protect you from all the risks you may find throughout your journey. While active (by pressing the trigger button at the bottom of your controller), no karma will be lost. However, your shield will slow you down and you will not be able to collect any more spheres. The shield is powered by a battery which is discharged with each use, but recharges automatically when the shield is not in use. If the battery becomes completely empty, you will not be able to activate the shield until it recharges. Before entering the maze, you will have the opportunity to become familiar with how to interact with our virtual space by entering the training area. In this area, you will have to approach three target points marked with lights in the following order: green, yellow and red, and capture your first karmaspheres. Immediately after collecting the last karmasphere at the red light, you will be teleported to the actual maze and the competition will begin.

To explore this scenario you will use:
- *Touchpad. Touch it (gently) to move in the direction of your line of sight*
- *Walk-in-place (Walk on site). The system detects the movements of your head up and down, so, maybe, you should exaggerate your steps slightly.*

*Remember, you must leave the maze before the time runs out, and earn
the greatest amount of karma. Are you ready? Good luck!*

The "Training Room," is a small environment with a neutral and minimalist
design to reduce the user cognitive impact of the first encounter with our virtual
environment (Fig. 1). The room is designed to practice the three basic interactions available in the VE: locomotion, picking up spheres and activating the
shield. Participants were asked to navigate to three different spot lights located
on the floor in a specific sequence: green, yellow, red. This task allows users
to practice the specific locomotion technique assigned to their group. Karmaspheres are included to practice the catching action and the option to test acti-
vation/deactivation of the shield (pressing the trigger button in the controller)
is also available.

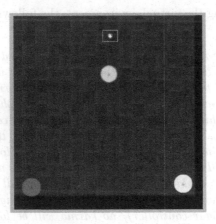

Fig. 1. Top view of the training room (Color figure online)

After completing the training, a new scene is loaded in the VE. The user is
placed in a larger room called the "Risk Room" (Fig. 2). This room has a maze
structure, which makes navigation more challenging. Along the path that leads
to the exit, participants will encounter three different hazards. The hazards are
strategically designed to trigger behavioural presence signals and evaluate risk
perception as the primary goal of our study. A detail of a participant' view with
a fire hazard and some karmaspheres is shown in Fig. 3.

3.3   Hardware Elements

The virtual experiences were implemented on a HTC Vive system [18], composed
of two standard tracking cameras and a headset. The system was supported by
a high performance laptop with Intel i7 CPU, 16 GB RAM and NVIDIA 1050Ti

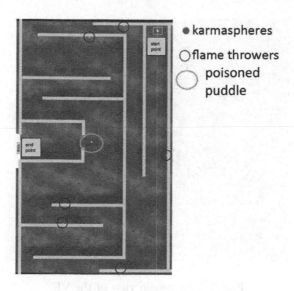

Fig. 2. Top view of the VE

GPU to ensure high graphic performance and avoid the appearance of visual glitches such as rendering delays or similar issues that could affect the users' perception.

The commercial version of the Vive has a refresh rate of 90 Hz. The device uses one screen per eye, each with a display resolution of 1080 × 1200. The headset and the controllers include more than 70 infrared sensors and contain an internal gyroscope and accelerometer. These sensors are used in combination with two stationary "lighthouse" base stations that can track the user's movement with submillimeter precision. The lighthouses emit infrared light and are effective within a 4.6 m × 4.6 m tracking space.

The HTC Vive's headset also has a front-facing camera that allows the user to observe her surroundings without removing the headset. The camera can be used to identify any moving or stationary object in a room. This functionality can be implemented as part of a "Chaperone" safety system, which will automatically display a virtual wall or a feed from the camera to safely guide users away from obstacles or real-world walls.

3.4 Locomotion Techniques Implementation

In our experiment, two different locomotion techniques were implemented: head bobbing and indirect walking. Head bobbing is a technique based on the detection of head movements that an individual makes when walking, even when walking in place. Using HTC Vive's sensors, we were able to accurately detect those movements in the real world and translate them to the locomotion pace of the virtual avatar. Furthermore, since our head moves faster when we run, faster

Fig. 3. First person view of the VE

movements are registered even if user runs in place. Consequently, faster movements are applied to the avatar. Although some commercial implementations of this technique add arm tracking (through the controllers) to provide a more robust input system, it was not considered in our study due to the additional energy consumption and effort required from participants.

Indirect walking is a navigation metaphor that is similar to the way we move in a traditional video game. By pushing down the touchpad in the controller, the users' avatar moves in the direction he is facing (the HMD determines the gaze orientation). This technique has a fixed speed and cannot be increased. We conservatively set it at 2 m/s, based on the results by So et al. [6], which suggest that cybersickness symptoms increase quickly at speeds higher than 3 m/s.

3.5   Metrics

The following parameters were used as performance indicators (values were tracked for both walk-in-place metaphor and indirect walk metaphor):

- Karma (K): The final amount of karmapoints earned (and not lost) by participants. Each karmasphere equals 1 karmapoint.
- Time (T): The time (in seconds) that the individual spent from the beginning of the experience until the exit point was reached.
- Shield (TS): The amount of shield used. It is a factor obtained by multiplying the time (in seconds) that the user keeps the shield active by the intensity of activation (how far the trigger button was pressed).

The ITC-SOPI questionnaire [7] was used to assess cybersickness. The Negative Effects factor in this questionnaire provides a simple alternative to the classic

SSQ [5], including information about adverse physiological symptoms such as "I felt nauseous," "I felt dizzy," "I felt I had a headache," or "I had eyestrain."

Finally, participants were asked to identify themselves as High Intensity Gamers (HIG) or Low Intensity Gamers (LIG), based on how often and for how long they play video games, and the places and the priority of gaming in their lives. We prioritized qualitative over quantitative evaluation to avoid negative social bias.

4   Results

Our sample (n = 41) was split into two main groups: HIG (High Intensity Gamers; n = 30, 73.17%) and LIG (Low Intensity Gamers; n = 11, 26.83%) (Table 1).

Table 1. Demographic variables for each gaming subgroup

Variable	HIG	LIG
Age	22.8 (sd = 6.04)	28.09 (sd = 10.7)
Male	86.66%	27.27%
Female	13.33%	72.73%

4.1   Performance

Karma value was the only factor considered as a performance indicator. Since users had to maximize their activity in the maze to obtain the most karmapoints without going over the 3 min limit, Time and Distance do not necessarily reflect better performance. Our results show that a participant's previous experience in video games generally translates into better performance in the new medium, with alternative interactions. In terms of average karmapoints, the HIG group scored nearly the double amount of points (AVG = 17.13, sd = 6.84) than the LIG group did (AVG = 9.675, sd = 8.96). In terms of the two different navigation metaphors (HB for Head-Bobbing and TP for TouchPad based indirect walking), our results show a similar distribution (see Fig. 4).

All variables were normally distributed (Kolmogorov Smirnov p > .05), and a t-test to both subgroups revealed statistically significant differences for both conditions: HIG KarmaTP and LIG KarmaTP (p = 0.0415) and HIG KarmaHB and LIG KarmaHB (p = 0.0139). No significant differences between karmapoints under each navigation condition were found in intra-group analysis.

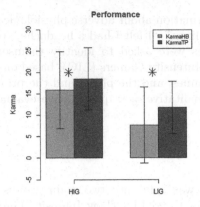

Fig. 4. Karmapoints per intensity of gaming profile and locomotion metaphor

4.2   Cybersickness

As an indicator of cybersickness, we analyzed the Negative Effects dimension (SOPI-NE) of the ITC-SOPI questionnaire. The values in this scale range from 1 (strongly disagree) to 5 (strongly agree). Higher scores are related to a higher sense of cybersickness.

In our study, the HIG subgroup scored slightly lower in the SOPI-NE (AVG = 2.261, sd = 0.86) than the LIG subgroup, SOPI-NE (AVG = 2.371, sd = 0.959). Differences in navigation conditions per subgroup are shown in Fig. 5.

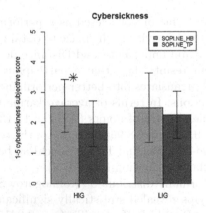

Fig. 5. SOPI Negative Effects per gaming subgroup and navigation metaphor

No significant differences between subgroups were found for the navigation conditions. However, an intra-group analysis revealed significant differences in the HIG group between head-bobbing navigation and touchpad indirect walking navigation (p = 0.006998). The difference is not significant in the LIG group (p = 0.5904).

5   Discussion

In our gamified VE, High Intensity Gamers performed consistently better than Low Intensity Gamers with similar prior VR experience, regardless of the navigation metaphor used to explore the maze. This sheds light on the transferability of gaming skills between different locomotion techniques, which is counter-intuitive since users had never experienced a walk-in-place metaphor before.

Both groups of participants performed better with the more artificial locomotion technique, the indirect walking based on touchpad. Despite being considered less comfortable in terms of cybersickness (caused by vection), this technique offers a better sense of control, as described by Bozgeyikli et al. [8].

Regarding the cybersickness assessment based on the ITC-SOPI Negative Effects factor, no significant differences were found between HIG and LIG, which suggests that prior gaming experience does not prevent cybersickness symptoms. However, by studying each group individually important differences were found in the HIG subgroup between the two locomotion metaphors. Specifically, users felt significantly more uncomfortable with the walk-in-place technique than they did with the touchpad based indirect walking. This result is interesting because it contradicts prior research on cybersickness [9,10] which claims that indirect walking is supposed to cause more vection due to the evident mismatch between visual and vestibular systems. No differences in cybersickness were found between navigation metaphors in the LIG subgroup.

6   Conclusions and Further Work

In this paper, a VE (a maze) with various gamified interactions was implemented to determined the effects of two different navigation metaphors related to the gaming profile of users on cybersickness and performance. Our results show that High Intensity Gamers performed better than Low Intensity Gamers in both locomotion methods. More significant differences were observed between locomotion techniques in the HIG group. Participants in this group reported feeling significantly worse with the walk-in-place technique, even when considered more comfortable than the one based on touchpad. Our findings suggest that prior gaming experience may play an important role in cybersickness, which naturally calls for further studies on gaming background: what genres of games do users play? On which platforms? For how long have they been playing games?

References

1. Bowman, D.A., Koller, D., Hodges, L.F.: A methodology for the evaluation of travel techniques for immersive virtual environments. Virtual Reality **3**(2), 120–131 (1998)
2. LaViola Jr., J.J.: A discussion of cybersickness in virtual environments. ACM SIGCHI Bull. **32**(1), 47–56 (2000)

3. Sharples, S., Cobb, S., Moody, A., Wilson, J.R.: Virtual reality induced symptoms and effects (VRISE): comparison of head mounted display (HMD), desktop and projection display systems. Displays **29**(2), 58–69 (2008)
4. Nichols, S., Patel, H.: Health and safety implications of virtual reality: a review of empirical evidence. Appl. Ergon. **33**(3), 251–271 (2002)
5. Kennedy, R.S., Lane, N.E., Berbaum, K.S., Lilienthal, M.G.: Simulator sickness questionnaire: an enhanced method for quantifying simulator sickness. Int. J. Aviat. Psychol. **3**(3), 203–220 (1993)
6. So, R.H., Lo, W.T., Ho, A.T.: Effects of navigation speed on motion sickness caused by an immersive virtual environment. Hum. Factors **43**(3), 452–461 (2001)
7. Lessiter, J., Freeman, J., Keogh, E., Davidoff, J.: A cross-media presence questionnaire: the ITC-Sense of Presence Inventory. Presence Teleoperators Virtual Environ. **10**(3), 282–297 (2001)
8. Bozgeyikli, E., Raij, A., Katkoori, S., Dubey, R.: Locomotion in virtual reality for room scale tracked areas. Int. J. Hum.-Comput. Stud. **122**, 38–49 (2019)
9. Frommel, J., Sonntag, S., Weber, M.: Effects of controller-based locomotion on player experience in a virtual reality exploration game. In: Proceedings of the 12th International Conference on the Foundations of Digital Games, p. 30. ACM, August 2017
10. Merhi, O., Faugloire, E., Flanagan, M., Stoffregen, T.A.: Motion sickness, console video games, and head-mounted displays. Hum. Factors **49**(5), 920–934 (2007)
11. Davis, S., Nesbitt, K., Nalivaiko, E.: A systematic review of cybersickness. In: Proceedings of the 2014 Conference on Interactive Entertainment, pp. 1–9. ACM, December 2014
12. Biocca, F.: Will simulation sickness slow down the diffusion of virtual environment technology? Presence Teleoperators Virtual Environ. **1**(3), 334–343 (1992)
13. Albert, J.M.: User-centric classification of virtual reality locomotion methods. Doctoral dissertation (2018)
14. Stanney, K.M., Kennedy, R.S., Drexler, J.M.: Cybersickness is not simulator sickness. In: Proceedings of the Human Factors and Ergonomics Society Annual Meeting, vol. 41, No. 2, pp. 1138–1142. SAGE Publications, Los Angeles, October 1997
15. Mousavi, M., Jen, Y.H., Musa, S.N.B.: A review on cybersickness and usability in virtual environments. In: Advanced Engineering Forum, vol. 10, pp. 34–39. Trans Tech Publications Ltd., December 2013
16. Rebenitsch, L., Owen, C.: Review on cybersickness in applications and visual displays. Virtual Reality **20**(2), 101–125 (2016)
17. Llorach, G., Evans, A., Blat, J.: Simulator sickness and presence using HMDs: comparing use of a game controller and a position estimation system. In: Proceedings of the 20th ACM Symposium on Virtual Reality Software and Technology, pp. 137–140. ACM, November 2014
18. HTC Corporation 2018. HTC Vive (2018). https://www.htcvive.com. Accessed 16 Dec 2018

Changes in Eye Movements and Body Sway While Viewing Stereoscopic Movies Under Controlled Consciousness

Akihiro Sugiura[1(✉)], Kunihiko Tanaka[1], and Hiroki Takada[2]

[1] Department of Radiological Technology,
Gifu University of Medical Science, Seki, Japan
asugiura@u-gifu-ms.ac.jp
[2] Graduate School of Engineering, University of Fukui, Fukui, Japan

Abstract. In our previous study, we found that it is possible to have an effect of change in the condition of consciousness (allocation of consciousness) on visually evoked postural responses (VEPRs) and subjective symptoms of visually induced motion sickness (VIMS). Thus, in this study, we verified the effect of controlling consciousness on body sway and eye movements while participants viewed stereoscopic movies. Participants watched a three-dimensional movie consisting of several colored balls that moved sideways sinusoidally at 0.25 Hz for 180 s after pre-instruction. Pre-instructions included "uncontrolled consciousness," "keep a static, upright posture," and "sway body in the same/opposite direction." This study recorded both center of pressure, as body sway, and electrooculography (EOG) data, as eye movements. Recorded EOG data were converted to eye movement velocity. The results clearly showed that (1) the influence of the pre-instruction appeared to be much stronger than that of the VEPRs, (2) the pre-instruction changed the frequency of the saccade, or interquartile range of eye movement, velocity histogram according to each task as measured by changes in retinal slip velocity, and (3) the condition of consciousness that controlled body motion changed the participants' postural instability and eye movement results. Thus, after considering many theories for the origin of VIMS, we concluded that the condition of consciousness controlled VIMS.

Keywords: Visually Evoked Postural Response (VEPR) · Body sway · Visually Induced Motion Sickness (VIMS) · Electrooculography (EOG) · Consciousness

1 Introduction

With recent advances in display or imaging technologies, users can enjoy virtual experiences that provide feelings of presence, defined as a "sense of being there," [1]. However, there has been an increase in the presentation of symptoms similar to motion sickness, often referred to as visually induced motion sickness (VIMS) or cybersickness [2, 3], which are experienced by users during or after virtual activities. Stanney reported that 88% of virtual environment participants developed VIMS when viewing

© Springer Nature Switzerland AG 2019
M. Antona and C. Stephanidis (Eds.): HCII 2019, LNCS 11572, pp. 657–668, 2019.
https://doi.org/10.1007/978-3-030-23560-4_48

virtual reality movies for over an hour [4]. Thus, in their current state, virtual experiences for amusement often become stressors instead.

The origin of VIMS and the reasons for the onset of its complex symptoms are not sufficiently understood. However, one of the major hypotheses involves sensory conflict theory, which suggests that the complex symptoms are caused by the presence of conflicts among the afferent inputs of sensory modalities (vision, equilibrium sense, and somatosensation) and the subject's perception [5, 6]. In particular, VIMS is evoked when the information relayed by the visual system is contradictory to information from the other senses.

Postural responses that are induced by visual information, such as motion or gradients, are collectively called visually evoked postural responses (VEPRs) [7] and are among the body responses to VIMS [8, 9]. Although there are various theories for the appearance of VEPRs, our past study suggested the possibility that VEPRs were a conflict correction response aimed at resolving the information from all the senses [10]. If the conclusions in our past study were correct, suppressing or accelerating the conflict correction response (adjustment of the VEPRs) may be a method of controlling VIMS. Thus, experimental verification for this hypothesis is important to developing a method of preventing VIMS. In our previous study, we found it was possible to affect VEPRs and subjective symptoms of VIMS by changing conditions of consciousness (allocation of consciousness) [11]. In this study, we verified the effect of controlling consciousness on body sway and eye movements in participants while they viewed stereoscopic movies.

2   Materials and Methods

2.1   Participants

Eleven subjects (3 males and 8 females; 21–27-years-old) who did not have vision or equilibrium problems participated in this study. The study was approved by the Research Ethics Committee at the Gifu University of Medical Science. Oral and written consent was obtained from the participants after the purpose and significance of the study and the nature and risk of the measurements were explained. In addition, the study was conducted in accordance with the 1964 Declaration of Helsinki and its later amendments or comparable ethical standards.

2.2   Visual Stimulation

A screenshot of the movie, used for visual stimulation in this study, is shown in Fig. 1. The visual stimulation was delivered via a movie created using the 3ds Max 2017 computer graphics software (Autodesk, San Rafael, CA, USA). The movie consisted of several colored balls displayed at random positions. We generated the horizontal, sinusoidal movement of the balls at 0.25 Hz in the movie by moving camera-simulated ocular globes (the balls themselves did not move). The amplitude of the sinusoidal motion was set to 200, according to the software setting.

The experimental setup utilized in this study is shown in Fig. 2. We performed the experiments in a controlled environment (illuminance: under 10 lx) in order to limit the variations to visual input. The movie was displayed on an LCD monitor that was positioned (42LW5700, LG, Seoul, Korea) 50 cm in front of the participant. The displayed movie size was 93.30 cm × 52.62 cm with a resolution of 1,920 × 1,080 pixels. The participants watched the experimental three-dimensional (3D) movies with peripheral vision using circularly polarized glasses.

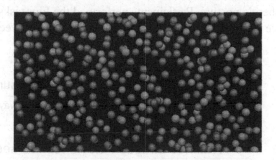

Fig. 1. Screenshot of the movie used in this study. A large number of balls were located at random positions. The balls moved sinusoidally at 0.25 Hz in a horizontal direction in the videos

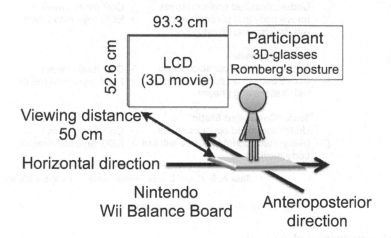

Fig. 2. Diagram of the experimental setup. The movie was displayed on an LCD monitor 50 cm in front of the participant. The participants watched the experimental 3D movies using 3D glasses without restricting peripheral vision. In order to measure the position of the center of pressure (CoP), participants were asked to stand on a Wii Balance Board with Romberg's posture

2.3 Procedure and Design

The study protocol is shown in Fig. 3. A participant stood on the Wii Balance Board with Romberg's posture and watched a static (nonmoving) movie for 180 s as the Pre-task. The study task was divided into four tasks (A, B, C, and D) following different pre-instructions. For Task A ("Uncontrolled consciousness"), participants watched the motion movie for 180 s with uncontrolled consciousness. For Task B ("Same"), participants watched the movie for 180 s after pre-instruction to sway their body in a direction parallel to the ball's movement while maintaining Romberg's posture. For Task C ("Opposite"), participants watched the movie for 180 s based on the pre-instruction to sway their body in a direction opposite to the ball's movement while maintaining Romberg's posture. For Task D ("Controlled Static"), participants watched the movie for 180 s based on the pre-instruction to maintain a static, upright pose while maintaining Romberg's posture. Participants performed the four tasks (Task A to D) in a random sequence to avoid an effect of the order. Interval of between tasks was set at more than 5 min.

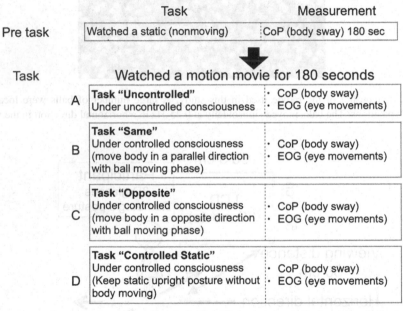

Fig. 3. Study protocol and measurements

2.4   Measurement and Analysis

This study recorded both the center of pressure (CoP), as body sway, and electrooculography (EOG), as eye movements. The CoP was continuously measured by the Wii Balance Board, which was controlled by stabilometry software custom-built into the board, and recorded with WiimoteLib for each Task. The CoP measurements were recorded at 20 Hz, which is the basic setting for sampling in clinical gravimetric tests. The continuous CoP data were separated by intervals of 60 s of viewing time to analyze each time segment. CoP data were analyzed for instability of postural maintenance. Standard deviations (SD) of locus changes in the horizontal direction were calculated as indexes of postural instability and the total locus length in the horizontal direction. Changes in these indexes were induced by visual stimulation from the movie or each pre-instruction. Statistical tests were performed using ORIGIN Pro 8.5 software (OriginLab, Corporation, Northampton, MA, USA) with the two-way repeated measures ANOVA and post-hoc comparisons to confirm differences among each task and time segment.

EOG measures the electric potential changes caused by eye movements [12]. The EOG requires multiple electrodes to be attached to facial muscles. We only measured conjunctive horizontal eye movements in this study because the motion components in the movie were horizontal and sinusoidal, without movement in the vertical direction. Thus, electrodes were placed on the outer corners of both eyes and in the middle of the eyebrows, respectively. Changes in the electric potential were recorded at 200 Hz using LabChart 7.3.7 software (ADInstruments, Dunedin, Otago, New Zealand) after the biological signal was amplified and software-filtered with a hum-filter at 60 Hz with EBA-100 (Unique Medical Co., Ltd., Tokyo, Tokyo, Japan).

Measurement and processing procedures are shown in Fig. 4. Eye movements are generally evaluated by velocity because differences in velocity reflect differences in neural activity. Measured electric potential data must be converted to velocity to determine changes in eye movements. Thus, this study performed four steps for the conversion: (1) Participants looked 30° to the right and to left with each repetition to accrue data, which was then converted to electric potential to degree of visual line. (2) Measured electric potential data converted degree of visual line following pre-measurements. (3) A low-pass filter (LPF) at 50 Hz was applied to data from step 2 to reduce high-frequency noise. Then, in order to obtain velocity data, the data that were filtered with LPF were differentially processed using five measured points in a 0.025 s window. The continuous velocity data were separated by 60 second-intervals of viewing time to analyze each time segment. To analyze velocity, two-way repeated measures ANOVA followed by post-hoc comparisons were used to statistically compare body sway among groups using ORIGIN Pro 8.5.

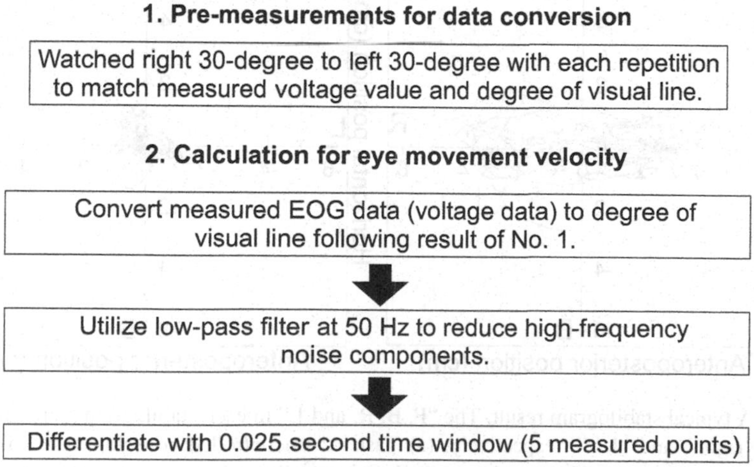

1. Pre-measurements for data conversion

Watched right 30-degree to left 30-degree with each repetition to match measured voltage value and degree of visual line.

2. Calculation for eye movement velocity

Convert measured EOG data (voltage data) to degree of visual line following result of No. 1.

Utilize low-pass filter at 50 Hz to reduce high-frequency noise components.

Differentiate with 0.025 second time window (5 measured points)

Fig. 4. Study protocol and measurements

3 Results

3.1 Results of Body Sway

A typical stabilogram result generated from the CoP data of a 22-year-old female participant is shown in Fig. 5(a–d). Points to the left, or posterior to the CoP, are expressed as negative values. Each panel (a–d) shows a different task. The stabilogram in Fig. 5(a) (Uncontrolled consciousness) shows that the area was relatively small, and the spread of locus was in a horizontal direction. By contrast, the stabilogram in Fig. 5(d) (Controlled Static) shows that area was relatively small but the spread of the locus was not in a horizontal direction. Figure 5(b) (Same) and Fig. 5(c) (Opposite) had stabilograms with a large area and large spread in locus. When comparing Fig. 5(b)

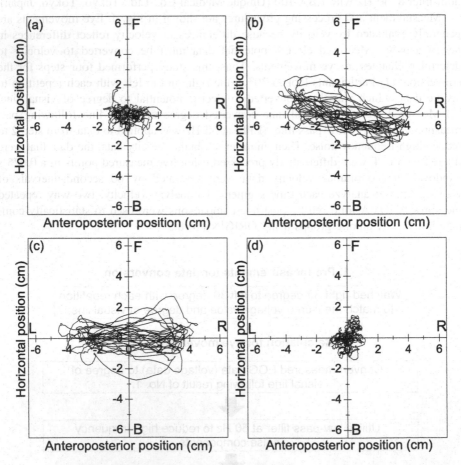

Fig. 5. A typical stabilogram result. The "F, B, R, and L" in each stabilogram represent "front", "back", "right", and "left", respectively. (a) Task A: uncontrolled consciousness, (b) Task B: controlled consciousness (Same task), (c) Task C: controlled consciousness (Opposite task), and (d) Task D: controlled consciousness (Controlled Static)

with Fig. 5(c), the locus changes in the horizontal direction in Fig. 5(b) were larger than those in Fig. 5(c). Based on these results, the VEPRs worked as counter factor in the Opposite task, and worked as additional factor in the Same task. Moreover, these data suggest that the pre-instruction has an especially strong influence, compared to information from the other senses.

Figure 6 shows a summary of changes in postural instability in the horizontal direction in different tasks based on the pre-instruction. Figure 6(a) shows the standard deviation in horizontal locus changes during the tasks, and Fig. 6(b) shows the locus length in the horizontal direction. These results indicated similar tendencies across the groups. The results of both the Same and the Opposite tasks showed significantly high postural instability in the horizontal direction, compared to the Uncontrolled consciousness and Controlled Static tasks (P < 0.01). By contrast, significant changes in stability were not found among the groups following increases in recording time.

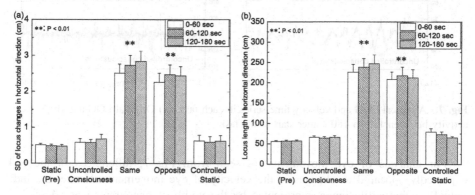

Fig. 6. Summary of changes in postural instability in the horizontal direction with different pre-instructions. (a) Standard deviation of horizontal locus changes, and (b) horizontal locus length

3.2 Results of EOG

Figure 7 shows a typical an original EOG and velocity time series from 120 s to 180 s from a 22-year-old female who is the same individual in the Fig. 5. Figure 7(a) shows the original EOG for each task and Fig. 7(b) shows the velocity time series calculated from differential processing the data. Periodic changes including spike-like high frequency activities were found in all tasks with some differences between conditions. The amplitude of the Same task in Fig. 7(a) was the smallest, while those of the others were approximately similar. The wave form of the Uncontrolled consciousness and the Controlled Static tasks were remarkably regular in pattern. Figure 7(b) presented the velocity of the eye movements to in response to rapidly changing eye movement components. The velocity time series in the Opposite task had much larger peaks, approximately 400 or −400 deg./s greater than that of other tasks, while the other tasks had approximately similar number of peaks.

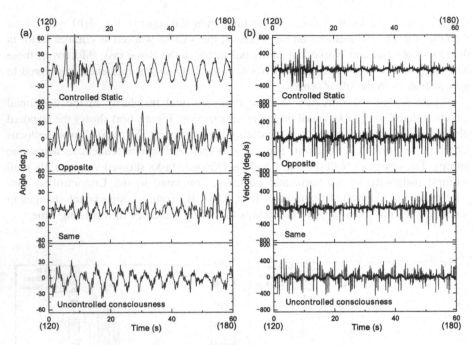

Fig. 7. A typical EOG and velocity time series in each task. (a) Original EOG and (b) Velocity activity between 120 to 180 s after start of the task

For analysis of eye movements, as seen from Fig. 7, differences in the task expectedly appeared as changes in the velocity of eye movements. Hence, the individual's interquartile range, represented by the width of histogram, was adopted as index of the eye movements in this study. Figure 8 summarizes the results of the interquartile ranges during different tasks using a typical histogram and a model of normal distribution. Additional character in Fig. 8 represents different time segment: (a) represents 0 to 60 s, (b) represents 60 to 120 s and (c) represents 120 to 180 s, respectively. The interquartile range increased in the following order: the Same task < the Controlled Static task = the Uncontrolled consciousness task < the Opposite task. This result was promoted visually understanding by Fig. 8(a-2) to (c-2) because the histogram and normal distribution model of the Opposite task were the widest compared to the other tasks. This occurred because fast velocity components increased. As time increased, significant differences between each task became clearly apparent, except for between the Uncontrolled consciousness task and the Controlled Static task (P < 0.05).

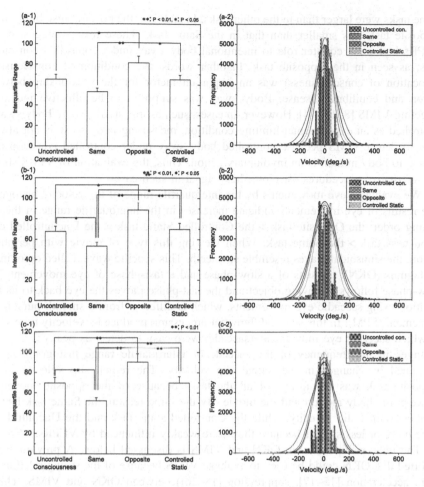

Fig. 8. Summary of the interquartile range results from the different tasks using a typical histogram and a model of normal distribution. Additional character such as (a) to (c) represents different time segment: (a) is 0 to 60 s, (b) is 60 to 120 s and (c) is 120 to 180 s, respectively

4 Discussion

In this study, we verified the effect of controlling consciousness on participants' body sway and eye movements while they watched stereoscopic movies. The balls moved sinusoidally, at 0.25 Hz in a horizontal direction, to evoked VEPRs in the horizontal direction. To control consciousness, we pre-instructed participants to maintain Romberg's posture with different pre-instructions while viewing the experimental movie in each task. The results of stabilogram showed an increase in postural instability in the following order: the Same task > the Opposite task > the Uncontrolled consciousness task = the Controlled Static task. Thus, the influence of pre-instructions appeared to be much stronger than that of VEPRs because postural instability in the Opposite and

Same tasks were larger than in the other tasks. In addition, the postural instability in the Opposite task was smaller than that in the Same task. These results suggested that VEPRs had weak counter role to intentional body sway under controlled consciousness, as seen in the Opposite task. In other words, the condition of consciousness (allocation of consciousness) was an important factor for the relationship between vision and equilibrium sense. Body sway was supposed to be effective index for detecting VIMS [8, 13, 14]. However, in cases, such as this study, where body sway is controlled as an experimental-limiting condition, measuring body sway is not always easy to detect VIMS because controlled body sway under controlled consciousness related to body motion is an involuntary action. Thus, the evaluation of VIMS should use alternative procedures for biomedical signal in such cases.

We evaluated eye movements by the interquartile range of the velocity histogram. The results of eye movements indicate increases in the interquartile range in the following order: the Opposite task > the Controlled Static task = the Uncontrolled consciousness task > the Same task. When viewing this type of movie with peripheral vision, the sinusoidal waves resemble saw teeth. This specific wave, called optokinetic nystagmus (OKN), consists of a slow-phase and a fast-phase of eye movement. The slow-phase follows a moving object and the fast-phase moves the eye back to its first position using saccadic eye movements, which is different from a smooth pursuit eye movement (SPM). In this study, differential processing produced a velocity time series in which saccadic eye movements (saccade) were easy to detect as peaks (Fig. 7(b)). Changes in the frequency of the saccade or interquartile range histogram can be explained by changes in the retinal slip velocity. The retinal slip velocity in the Opposite task was the fastest of all the tasks because of the opposite movement between the body motion and the movie. By the same reason, the Same task had the smallest retinal slip velocity, while the Controlled static task and the Uncontrol task were more or less similar because they were weakly influenced by VEPRs.

The relationship between OKN and VIMS is discussed below. A previous study reported that OKN could be used to evaluate VIMS because of the strong relationship (e.g., acceleration [15–17], suppression [18–20]) between OKN and VIMS. This is based on the eye movement theory that OKN, evoked by moving visual patterns, innervates the vagal nerve and that such innervations lead to VIMS [21, 22]. On the other hand, another previous study reported that VIMS had strong relationship both the vection (the vection is one phenomenon of the VEPRs) and OKN. Then, exclusive condition between the vection and OKN increased the severity of VIMS [16]. The paper suggested that the change in the degree of VIMS was dependent on postural instability (postural instability theory [23, 24]). Many related studies on the mechanisms underlying the appearance of VIMS have had inconsistent conclusions. However, these theories are not necessarily limited or exhaustive, and elements of each theory may be true in certain situations. It is highly possible that we can obtain some beneficial information to address this issue from measurements of each type of controlled consciousness because this study included each quantitative and central index and is based on many theories, such as the OKN and postural instability.

5   Conclusion

In this study, we verified the effect of controlling consciousness on body sway and eye movements while participants viewed stereoscopic movies. The following conclusions can be drawn:

1. The influence of pre-instruction appeared to be much stronger than that of the VEPRs because measurements of the body sway in the Opposite and Same tasks were larger than those in the other tasks. In addition, the postural instability in the Opposite task was smaller than that in the Same task. In this case, the body sway induced by the pre-instruction worked as counter factor to the VEPRs.
2. The pre-instruction changed the frequency of the saccade or the interquartile range of eye movement, as noted by the velocity histogram for each task. This can be explained by changes in the retinal slip velocity.
3. The condition of consciousness that controlled body motion changed the above measurement results. Thus, after considering many theories for the origin of VIMS, we concluded that the condition of consciousness controlled VIMS.

Acknowledgements. We would like to thank the participants of this experimental study. This work was supported by a JSPS KAKENHI Grant-in-Aid for Scientific Research (C) (18K11971, 15K00702 and 17K00715).

References

1. Bowman, D.A., Mcmahan, R.R.P., Tech, V.: Virtual reality: how much immersion is enough? Computer (Long. Beach. Calif) **40**, 36–43 (2007)
2. Kennedy, R.C.S., Drexler, J., Kennedy, R.C.S.: Research in visually induced motion sickness. Appl. Ergon. **41**, 494–503 (2010)
3. Stanney, K.M., Kennedy, R.S., Drexler, J.M., Harm, D.L.: Motion sickness and proprioceptive aftereffects following virtual environment exposure. Appl. Ergon. **30**, 27–38 (1999)
4. Stanney, K.M., Kingdon, K.S., Kennedy, R.S.: Dropouts and aftereffects: examining general accessibility to virtual environment technology. In: Proceedings of the Human Factors and Ergonomics Society Annual Meeting, pp. 2114–2118. SAGE Publications (2002)
5. Oman, C.M.: Motion sickness: a synthesis and evaluation of the sensory conflict theory. Can. J. Physiol. Pharmacol. **68**, 294–303 (1990)
6. Reason, J.T.: Motion sickness adaptation: a neural mismatch model. J. R. Soc. Med. **71**, 819–829 (1978)
7. Bronstein, A.M.: Suppression of visually evoked postural responses. Exp. Brain Res. **63**, 655–658 (1986)
8. Stoffregen, T.A., Smart, L.J.: Postural instability precedes motion sickness. Brain Res. Bull. **47**, 437–448 (1998)
9. Rebenitsch, L., Owen, C.: Review on cybersickness in applications and visual displays. Virtual Real. **20**, 101–125 (2016)
10. Sugiura, A., Tanaka, K., Wakatabe, S., Matsumoto, C., Miyao, M.: Temporal analysis of body sway during reciprocator motion movie viewing. Jpn J. Hyg. **71**, 19–29 (2016). Nippon Eiseigaku Zasshi

11. Sugiura, A., Tanaka, K., Ohta, K., Kitamura, K., Morisaki, S., Takada, H.: Effect of controlled consciousness on sense of presence and visually induced motion sickness while viewing stereoscopic movies. In: Antona, M., Stephanidis, C. (eds.) UAHCI 2018. LNCS, vol. 10908, pp. 122–131. Springer, Cham (2018). https://doi.org/10.1007/978-3-319-92052-8_10

12. Hale, K.S., Stanney, K.M.: Handbook of Virtual Environments: Design, Implementation, and Applications. CRC Press, Boca Raton (2014)

13. Takada, H., Miyao, M.: Visual fatigue and motion sickness induced by 3D video clip. Forma 27, S67–S76 (2012)

14. Smart, L.J., Stoffregen, T.A., Bardy, B.G.: Visually induced motion sickness predicted by postural instability. Hum. Factors 44, 451–465 (2002)

15. Hu, S., Stern, R.M., Vasey, M.W., Koch, K.L.: Motion sickness and gastric myoelectric activity as a function of speed of rotation of a circular vection drum. Aviat. Space Environ. Med. 60, 411–414 (1989)

16. Ji, J.T.T., So, R.H.Y., Cheung, R.T.F.: Isolating the effects of vection and optokinetic nystagmus on optokinetic rotation-induced motion sickness. Hum. Factors 51, 739–751 (2009)

17. Hu, S., Stern, R.M.: Optokinetic nystagmus correlates with severity of vection-induced motion sickness and gastric tachyarrhythmia. Aviat. Space Environ. Med. 69, 1162–1165 (1998)

18. Flanagan, M.B., May, J.G., Dobie, T.G.: Optokinetic nystagmus, vection, and motion sickness. Aviat. Space Environ. Med. 73, 1067–1073 (2002)

19. Webb, N.A., Griffin, M.J.: Optokinetic stimuli: motion sickness, visual acuity, and eye movements. Aviat. Space Environ. Med. 73, 351–358 (2002)

20. Flanagan, M.B., May, J.G., Dobie, T.G.: The role of vection, eye movements and postural instability in the etiology of motion sickness. J. Vestib. Res. 14, 335–346 (2004)

21. Ebenholtz, S.M.: Motion sickness and oculomotor systems in virtual environments. Presence Teleoperators Virtual Environ. 1, 302–305 (1992)

22. Ebenholtz, S.M., Cohen, M.M., Linder, B.J.: The possible role of nystagmus in motion sickness: a hypothesis. Aviat. Space Environ. Med. 65, 1032–1035 (1994)

23. Stoffregen, T.A., Riccio, G.E.: An ecological critique of the sensory conflict theory of motion sickness. Ecol. Psychol. 3, 159–194 (1991)

24. Riccio, G.E., Stoffregen, T.A.: An ecological theory of motion sickness and postural instability. Ecol. Psychol. 3, 195–240 (1991)

Effects of Low/High-Definition Stereoscopic Video Clips on the Equilibrium Function

Masumi Takada[1], Syota Yamamoto[2], Masaru Miyao[3],
and Hiroki Takada[2(✉)]

[1] School of Nursing, Yokkaichi Nursing and Medical Care University,
Yokkaichi, Mie 512-8043, Japan
[2] Department of Human and Artificial Intelligence Systems,
Graduate School of Engineering, University of Fukui, Fukui 910-8507, Japan
takada@u-fukui.ac.jp
[3] Nagoya Industrial Science Research Institute,
2-10-19, Sakae, Naka-Ku, Nagoya 460-0008, Japan

Abstract. Stereoscopic video clips are studied in order to enhance brain activity. Virtual space might enhance brain activity for mild cognitive impairments, which are reported to be on the increase in an aging society. We herein increase the knowledge about the influence of stereoscopic images on the human body, especially on brain activity. The stabilogram and cerebral blood flow are measured in this study. Activity in the ventral and dorsal streams is enhanced. The most suitable cutoff frequency for viewing the effects of the dorsal stream are estimated between 0.1–0.3 Hz in a Fourier-Shuffle surrogate data analysis of the cerebral blood flow.

Keywords: Near-infrared imaging (fNIRS) · Stereoscopic video clips ·
Motion sickness · Equilibrium function

1 Introduction

In recent years, various three-dimensional (3D) video display systems have been developed. Generally, they require 3D glasses, but some recent displays can present binocular and multiaspect autostereoscopic images. However, in either case, there are issues: (1) unpleasant symptoms such as headaches, vomiting, and eyestrain, (2) and a lack of ambience and realism. Especially with Japanese 3D televisions, binocular disparity is set to 1° or less; therefore, dynamic movements cannot be fully expressed. The reason for the eyestrain induced by 3D video viewing is not fully known yet; thus, without an appropriate manufacturing standard for 3D videos and their display systems, excessive measures against visually induced motion sickness (VIMS) have been implemented.

With natural vision, accommodation and vergence are consistent. However, it is generally understood that in 3D video viewing, while the lens is accommodated to the position of the screen that displays the image, the eyes converge at the position of the 3D object (a common reason for eyestrain during 3D image viewing). This discrepancy between the accommodation and vergence is considered to be the reason for the eyestrain from 3D viewing and visually induced motion sickness [1–4].

© Springer Nature Switzerland AG 2019
M. Antona and C. Stephanidis (Eds.): HCII 2019, LNCS 11572, pp. 669–682, 2019.
https://doi.org/10.1007/978-3-030-23560-4_49

We can easily view stereoscopic video clips in daily life; however, it has been reported that symptoms such as headaches, nausea, dizziness, and vomiting occurred from VIMS [5]. It is said that the abovementioned symptom is induced by the vestibulo-vegetative reflex [6]. The vestibulo-vegetative system is closely accompanied by the vestibular nuclei, which is also involved in body balance. Compensatory movements in this equilibrium function are controlled by the vestibule-spinal reflex and the vestibule-ocular reflex. In these, the outputs from the vestibular nuclei are projected to the antigravitational muscles and the extraocular muscle, respectively. Therefore, body sway is affected by motion sickness, although there are some processes that control the antigravitational muscles through other nervous pathways (see [7]).

According to Patterson [8], if the viewing conditions are sufficiently bright, the depth of field of a target has a mean difference on the order of 1.0 D (diopter), and the accommodation-vergence conflict discussed above is a problem unique to proximity displays. Factors associated with the depth of field are the pupil diameter and resolution, and viewing conditions of images influence the pupil diameter. Most previous studies used a deep depth of field to prevent blurriness, resulting in a measurement environment quite different from that of everyday life.

Moreover, distribution of the vergence fusional stereoscopic limits in stereoscopic images is desired [9]. Eighty-four percent of all subjects could see a stereoscopic image of two planar images with a binocular disparity of 2°. The target under such a condition is a single target without a surrounding image. When there is no other parallax image, an accommodation-vergence process that creates an image from a double image is considered to function as a positive feedback system [10].

With developments such as the miniaturization of diagnostic equipment, brain science is developing rapidly, and a variety of brain activities are being defined [11]. Brain functional imaging using near-infrared spectroscopy (NIRS) has been developed in recent years [12]. This technique is known to be a noninvasive measurement of brain activity. The NIRS utilizes the property of a hemoglobin which absorbs near infrared light, and it is capable of noninvasively measuring the blood volume in the body. Applying this to surfaces on the brain, changes in cerebral blood flow (CBF) within a 2–3 cm range from the scalp can be measured, and activated local regions can be detected.

Thus, NIRS is a test capable of noninvasively detecting the time course of the overall reactivity to activation of the cerebral cortex in subjects in a natural state [13–17]. In NIRS, changes in the hemoglobin level are calculated from the values of irradiation and detection lights, but the distance (effective optical path length) that the light actually forwarded in the head tissue is not measurable at present. The generally used unit of measurement for NIRS values is the product of the hemoglobin concentration and length, such as [mM·mm] (hemoglobin concentration length).

It has been confirmed in stabilometry that compared to tracking a target while viewing 3D images, using peripheral vision for the entire screen triggers 3D sickness more readily [18]. Therefore, to elucidate the cause for 3D sickness, we examined the impact of viewing 3D images on brain activities and used functional near-infrared spectroscopy (fNIRS) to measure potential changes in brain activity during tracking. We used peripheral vision for a comparison. In addition, we measured eye movements to confirm whether subjects were tracking or using peripheral vision while viewing images.

Neurovascular coupling refers to the relationship between local neural activity and subsequent changes in the CBF [19]. Tight temporal and amplitudinal linkages between neuronal activity and CBF delivery have been observed for over 120 years [20–22]. The magnitude and spatial location of blood flow changes are tightly linked to changes in neural activity through a complex sequence of coordinated events involving neurons, glia, and vascular cells (see Fig. 1). According to previous studies [23–25], the regional blood flow is likely controlled by multiple mechanisms such as the feedforward involving neural signaling via neurotransmitters and the function to mediate neurovascular coupling, in addition to the feedback mechanisms that are sensitive to variations in the concentration of ionic and molecular metabolic byproducts. The last one is known to be a classical description that the energy supply is controlled by the energy demand. Many vascular-based functional brain imaging techniques such as fNIRS and fMRI rely on this coupling to infer changes in neural activity.

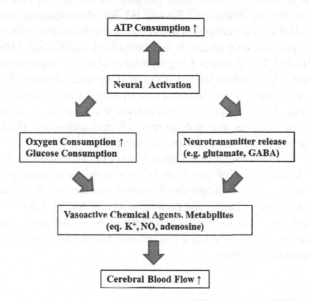

Fig. 1. Summary of physiological changes linking neural and vascular responses.

In this study, we investigated the effects of 3D video clips on the human body. In this experiment, we measured the body sway and recorded a stabilogram from which the severity of the VIMS could be estimated. The brain function, especially in the hemodynamics in the CBF, was also measured.

2 Material and Method

Biometric data were obtained for the center of pressure (CoP), heart rate variability, and hemodynamics on the surface of the cerebrum in 11 healthy young individuals (mean ± standard deviation: 22.6 ± 1.0 years) with no abnormalities in the extremities and no past medical history of ear or nervous system disease. Moreover, the visual acuity of subjects with the naked eye and/or contact lenses had to be greater than 0.8 and capable of stereoscopic vision. The experiment was fully explained to the subjects beforehand, and written consent was obtained. The experiment was approved by the Ethics Committee of the Department of Human and Artificial Intelligent Systems in the Graduate School of the Engineering University of Fukui (No. H2018010).

2.1   Experiment 1

In this study, subjects wore a head-mounted display (HMD) GOOVIS G2 (Lets-co.jp, Nagoya), and the following video clips (VCs) were projected to the HMD:

(VC1) stereoscopic video clip with a resolution of 1080p

(VC2) stereoscopic video clip with a resolution of 360p

A resolution of 1080p (1920 × 1080 px; also known as Full HD (high definition video) or FHD (full high definition 2 K) and BT.709 (broadcasting service television 709) is a set of HDTV (high-definition television) high-definition video modes characterized by 1,920 pixels displayed across the screen horizontally and 1,080 pixels down the screen vertically. The p stands for progressive scan, i.e. noninterlaced [26]. The displayed content was supplied by Sky Crystal (Olympus Memory Works Ltd. Co., Tokyo), which was modified with the company's permission and was used as the visual stimulus in this experiment. A sphere was ambulated in a video clip in a complex manner.

Biometric data such as the stabilogram, electrocardiogram (ECG), and oxy-/deoxygenated hemoglobin concentrations on the cerebrum blood flow were recorded while the participant viewed high-resolution video clip VC1 and low-resolution video clip VC2. Each sway of the CoP was recorded at a sampling frequency of 100 Hz. The subjects were instructed to maintain the Romberg posture during the duration of the trials. The subjects were asked to use peripheral vision for VC1 for the first 60 s and VC2 for the next 60 s, and to stand when there were no images (resting state). The stabilometry was conducted by using a Wii balance board (Nintendo, Kyoto). This trial (Fig. 2) was repeated five times.

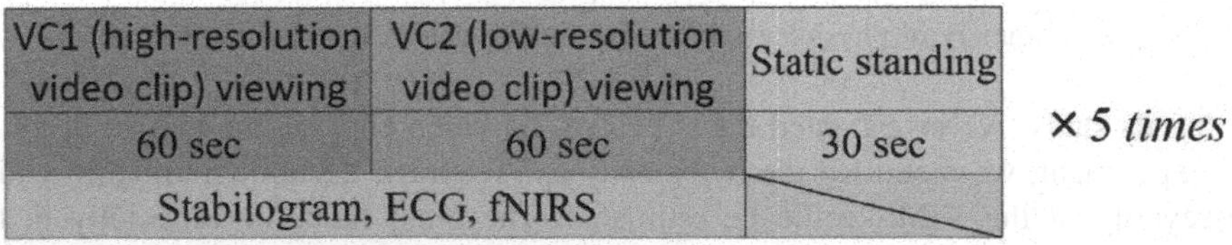

VC1 (high-resolution video clip) viewing	VC2 (low-resolution video clip) viewing	Static standing	
60 sec	60 sec	30 sec	× 5 *times*
Stabilogram, ECG, fNIRS			

Fig. 2. Experimental protocol in Experiment 1

For NIRS, the FOIRE-3000 (Shimadzu, Kyoto) was used. Channels were arranged as follows: 1–12 ch on the frontal lobe, 13–24 ch on the left temporal lobe, 25–36 ch on the right temporal lobe, and 37–48 ch on the occipital lobe (Fig. 3). The probe caps to fix the channels were set to the bilateral preauricular points with plane α covering the nasion (root of the nose) and plane β parallel to plane α. The distance between planes α and β was 3 cm, and plane β was positioned vertically upward of plane α. The occipital lobe was fixed in order to set the center of the probe cap to the inion in the occipital region (external occipital protuberance).

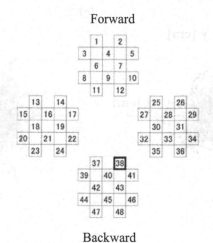

Fig. 3. Arrangement of channels in NIRS measurement

2.2 Experiment 2

Measurements were taken from 10 healthy males and females seated in a dark room. Following a test with the subjects' eyes closed (Cnt), stereoscopic video clips on an liquid crystal display (LCD), 55UF8500-JB (LG Electronics, Seoul), were played back in visual pursuit for 70 s and then in the peripheral vision for 70 s in succession. This protocol was repeated five times, and the changes in the CBF at 12 locations each in the frontal lobe, left/right temporal lobe, and occipital lobe were measured and recorded at 55 Hz (Fig. 3) using a FOIRE-3000 (Shimadzu Corp, Kyoto). This study focused on the dorsal stream among the recorded time series data on channel 38, which were then classified as the resting period, visual pursuit, and peripheral vision. Low-pass filters with different cutoff frequencies (0.1, 0.2, 0.3, 0.5, 1, 1.5, and 2 [Hz]) were applied. For each result, the translation error (see Appendix) was calculated using the Wayland algorithm [27].

Through the experiment, since the regularity of the changes in CBF were indicated, the first set of results from each of the subjects were compared for transitional errors during the resting period, visual pursuit, and peripheral vision. The nonlinearity of the results was also analyzed using the Fourier Shuffle Surrogate Data method [28].

3   Results

3.1   Experiment 1

Sway values such as the area of sway, total locus length, total locus length per unit area, and sparse density [29, 30] were estimated from the stabilograms (Figs. 4, 5).

By using the Wilcoxon signed-rank test, we compared the sway values while viewing the VCs for a trial as follows. The statistical significance was herein set to be 0.05.

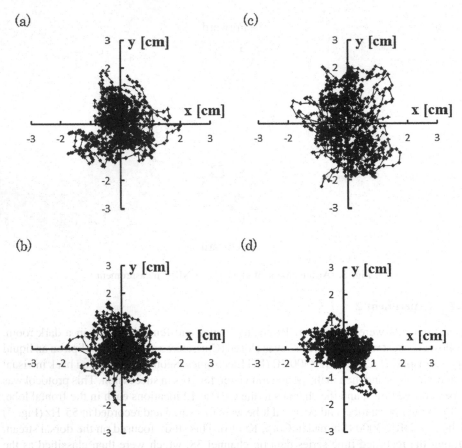

Fig. 4. Typical stabilograms while viewing VC1; for the first trial (a), for the second trial (b), for the third trial (c), and for the fourth trial (d).

There was no statistical significance in the difference between the sway values while viewing the VCs during the trials except for the third one (Fig. 6c). In the third trial, the total locus length per unit area while viewing VC1 tended to be different from that while viewing VC2 ($p < 0.1$).

The oxygenated hemoglobin concentration in the cerebrum blood flow recorded while viewing VC2 was compared to that while viewing VC1. Significant changes were observed in the frontal lobe, temporal lobe, and upper occipital lobe (Fig. 7).

For the total locus length, area of sway, and sparse density, the sway values for the n-th trial ($n = 3, 4, 5$) were significantly greater than those for the first trial while viewing VC1 ($p < 0.05$). In addition, all sway values for the n-th trial ($n = 3, 4, 5$) were significantly greater than those for the first trial while viewing VC2, as shown in Fig. 6 ($p < 0.05$).

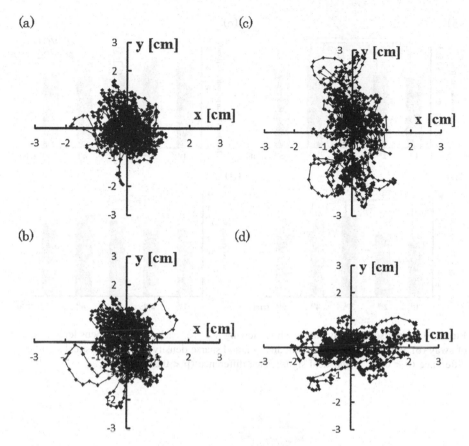

Fig. 5. Typical stabilograms while viewing VC2; for the first trial (a), for the second trial (b), for the third trial (c), and for the fourth trial (d).

3.2   Experiment 2

With eyes closed (Cnt), nonlinearities were observed in the raw data of the CBF (38 ch) and their low-pass filtered signals at cutoff frequencies below 0.5 Hz (Fig. 8). It was also observed that the translation error peaked at a cutoff frequency of

Nonlinearities were observed while tracking the stereoscopic sphere for raw data and their low-pass filtered signals at cutoff frequencies of 0.1, 0.3, 0.5, and 1 Hz (Fig. 8b). However, statistically significant differences were not observed at 0.2 Hz. As was the case when the eyes were closed, there was also a tendency for the translation error to peak at a cutoff frequency of approximately 0.5 Hz.

Nonlinearities were observed during peripheral viewing for the raw data and cutoff frequencies of 0.2, 0.3, and 0.5 Hz (Fig. 8c). Furthermore, since statistically significant tendencies were observed at 0.1 and 1 Hz, they were considered as possessing nonlinearities. Again, the translation error peaked at cutoff frequencies of 0.3–0.5 Hz.

(a)

(c)

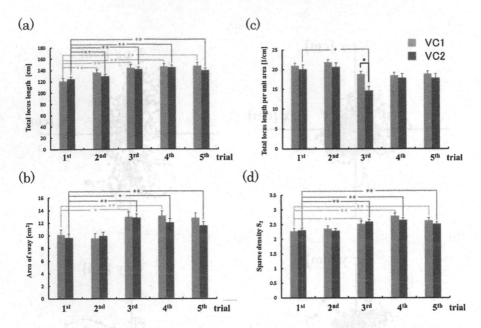

(b)

(d)

Fig. 6. Comparison of sway values while viewing VCs for each trial; total locus length (a), area of sway (b), total locus length per unit area (c), and sparse density S_2 (d); *statistical significance difference ($p < 0.1$), **statistical significance difference ($p < 0.05$)

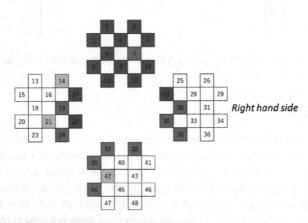

Fig. 7. Changes in oxygenated hemoglobin concentration in the cerebrum blood flow recorded while viewing the VC2 compared to that while viewing the VC1; ■ significant increase ($p < 0.01$), ■ significant increase ($p < 0.05$), ■ significant increase ($p < 0.1$) approximately 0.5 Hz

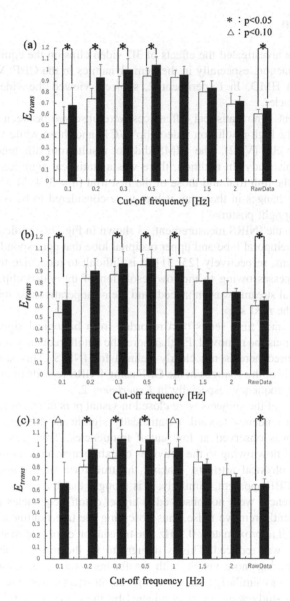

Fig. 8. Results of FS surrogate data analysis of CBF (a) with eyes closed as control (*Cnt*), (b) visual pursuit, and (c) peripheral vision. □ translation error estimated from time series data, and ■ translation error estimated from surrogate data

4 Discussion

In this study, we investigated the effects of 3D video clips on the equilibrium function and the brain function, especially in the hemodynamics in the CBF. Video clips were projected on an HMD. In Experiment 2, subjects viewed the video clips through polarizing spectacles.

In Experiment 1, no statistical differences were observed between the sway values while viewing the high-resolution video clip (VC1) and those while viewing the low-resolution video clip (VC2). The VIMS did not result from differences between the resolutions in this study. In addition, there was a statistical significance between the sway values of the n-th trial and those of the first trial (n = 3, 4, 5) while viewing any video clip. The changes in the sway values were considered to be owing to acclimatization in the upright posture.

According to the fNIRS measurement, as shown in Fig. 7, significant changes were observed in the temporal lobe and upper occipital lobe that corresponded to the ventral and dorsal streams, respectively [25, 31]. It is difficult to recognize the visual objects and motion processes owing to the low resolution of the video clip. Activity in the ventral and dorsal streams was enhanced, and their cooperativeness might be expected to be found in the next step.

Meanwhile, since time series data recorded from biological signals are prone to noise, the noise must be removed. Furthermore, the cutoff frequency appropriate for the low-pass filter used here is not clearly defined for fNIRS. This study performed a nonlinear analysis of the changes in the CBF using fNIRS records in order to determine a suitable cutoff frequency, especially in *Experiment 2*.

With the eyes of the subjects were closed in visual pursuit and peripheral vision, in each instance, a tendency toward a statistically significant difference in the mathematical model was observed at low cutoff frequencies. This was attributed to the changes in blood flow owing to the activities of extraocular muscles among others and the removal of physical artifacts, making the true form of the nonlinearity of the changes in the CBF apparent. Similarly, it is thought that the reason why statistically significant differences were not observed at higher cutoff frequencies is because of the failure to sufficiently remove noise, thus obscuring the true nonlinearity.

With a peak at approximately 0.5 Hz, the translation error was minimized when the cutoff frequency was reduced. This is thought to be the result of the actual control mechanism becoming more visible with the further removal of noise. However, the translation error was similarly reduced at high cutoff frequencies. The changes in CBF measured in this study were not only affected by the dorsal stream but also included various effects such as changes in blood flow owing to muscular activities and physical artifacts. Hence, it is thought that the periodicities of larger noises were affected and the probabilities of the changes were reduced as a result.

The translation errors were compared according to the cutoff frequencies f_0. At $f_0 = 0.2$ Hz, translation errors estimated in the visual pursuit and in the peripheral vision were significantly greater than those observed while the eyes were closed (*Cnt*). Hence, the visual effect is thought to lie in the 0.1–0.3-Hz band.

In order to evaluate the differences between the raw data and surrogate data, a t-value was herein calculated at f0 = 0.2 Hz. The values were estimated as 6.77, 1.09, and 3.52 for the Cnt, the visual pursuit, and the peripheral vision, respectively. For the visual pursuit and peripheral vision, the t-value was reduced compared to the Cnt. Thus, it was difficult to observe the nonlinearity in the CBF while viewing stereoscopic video clips. Compared to that for the peripheral vision, the t-value was reduced for the visual pursuit. This is thought to be the effect of increased activity in the dorsal stream that governs subjects' spatial awareness with respect to the object being viewed. This manifested itself more strongly when viewing stereoscopic video clips [31]. For this reason, it is thought that a low-pass filter with a cutoff frequency of approximately 0.2 Hz is suitable for observing the nonlinearity and changes in the CBF during the viewing of stereoscopic video clips.

The number of elderly people with dementia in Japan is estimated to reach approximately 7 million people by 2025, which means that 1 of 5 of those aged 65 and above will have dementia. Dementia is a disease that is close to home and can affect anyone. Based on the comprehensive strategy to accelerate dementia measures set by the Health, Labor and Welfare Ministry of Japan (called the New Orange Plan) that is aimed toward friendly community planning for the elderly with dementia, community planning that enables people to live a life in the manner they choose by prevention and the early diagnosis of/response to dementia is being studied.

One question remains: compared with the impact of viewing 3D videos with peripheral vision on the balance system, the amount of sway during viewing is small. Presently, we have not directly captured the instability in the balance system during the peripheral viewing of 3D videos. Therefore, it would be meaningful to improve the measurement precision of the impact on the balance system through numerical models. Considering research ethics, as it would lessen the burden on the subjects, this would not be limited to the design evaluation analysis of ultrahigh-definition images and VR, but could also contribute to hygiene and biomedical engineering.

In this study, by continuing the research challenges described above, we verified the illusion of self-motion (vection) induced by 3D video viewing. As an application, we determined new research topics. Is vection induced by 3D video viewing caused selectively by peripheral vision? Does uncoordinated movement of central and peripheral vision cause vection, inducing visually induced motion sickness? We plan to elucidate these questions. By working on new research topics, we may be able to propose a guideline for the safe viewing of 3D videos.

We developed games for people with mild cognitive impairments (MCIs). Their medical evaluations are now conducting, using electroencephalograms (EEG) [32] and near-infrared imaging (fNIRS). The basic experiments will be also stated in detail for the virtual space and the video games in the next paper.

5 Conclusion

We focused on the visual consciousness and examined whether the hemodynamics in the CBF depend on the consciousness (visual pursuit/peripheral vision). Despite the consciousness, the CBF contains body artifacts owing to the cardiovascular system and extraocular muscles in accordance with a nonlinear analysis of the CBF filtered at cutoff frequencies >0.5 Hz. In other words, noise at high frequency (>0.5 Hz) exhibits regularity. On the other hand, noise at low frequency (<0.5 Hz) can be removed by low-pass filters, as shown in Experiment 2. The most suitable cutoff frequency for viewing the effects from the dorsal stream was determined to be between 0.1 and 0.3 Hz in an FS surrogate data analysis of the CBF.

Acknowledgements. This work was supported in part by TAKEUCHI Scholarship Foundation, the Japan Society for the Promotion of Science, Grant-in-Aid for Research Activity Start-up Number 15H06711, Grant-in-Aid for Young Scientists (B) Number 16K16105, and that for Scientific Research (C) Number 17K00715.

Appendix

The Wayland algorithm assumes that the difference vectors $v(t) = x(t + \tau \, \Delta t) - x(t)$ in the embedding space [33] characterize the nonlinear variations of the trajectories and estimate the translation error in an m-dimensional embedding space ($m = 1, 2,..., 10$). Here, $1/\Delta t$ is 55 Hz. A linear correlation between adjacent vectors $x(t)$ and $x(t + \tau \, \Delta t)$ is eliminated by resampling the time series with respect to each embedding delay τ.

  (i)   A series of delay coordinate vectors $\{\mathbf{x}(t)\}$ is embedded in each space.
 (ii) M onset periods t_0 are randomly selected.
(iii)   The values of

$$E_{\text{trans}}(t_0) = \frac{1}{K+1} \sum_{i=0}^{K} \frac{|\mathbf{v}(t_i) - \bar{\mathbf{v}}|}{|\bar{\mathbf{v}}|} \tag{1}$$

are standardized by the average of the difference vectors at $K + 1$ points $\{\mathbf{x}(t_i)\}_{i=0}^{K}$.

$$\bar{\mathbf{v}} = \frac{1}{K+1} \sum_{i=0}^{K} \mathbf{v}(t_i) \tag{2}$$

is obtained at every onset period, where the K points nearest $\mathbf{x}(t_0)$ are selected as $\{\mathbf{x}(t_i)\}_{i=0}^{K}$.
 (iv)   The median of the M values of Eq. (1) is extracted.
  (v) Q medians are obtained by repeating the above steps. The translation error E_{trans} is estimated by the expectation value of these Q medians.

In this study, we set the conditions of coefficients M, K, and Q to 51, 3, and 10, respectively [27].

References

1. Toates, F.M.: Vergence eye movements. Doc. Ophthalmol. **37**, 153–214 (1974)
2. Cruz-Neira, C., Sanding, D. J., DeFanti, T.A.: Virtual reality: the design and implementation of the CAVE. In: Linehan, T. E. (ed.) SIGGRAPH 1993 Proceedings of the 20th Annual Conference on Computer Graphics and Interactive Techniques, pp. 135–142 (1993)
3. Hoffman, D.M., Girshick, A.R., Akeley, K., Banks, M.S.: Vergence-accommodation conflicts hinder visual performance and cause visual fatigue. J. Vis. **8**(3), 33.1–33.30 (2018). https://doi.org/10.1167/8.3.33
4. Shibata, T., Kim, J., Hoffman, D.M., Banks, M.S.: The zone of comfort: predicting visual discomfort with stereo displays. J Vis. **11**(8), 1–29 (2011)
5. International Standard Organization: IWA3:2005 image safety-reducing determinism in a time series. Phys. Rev. Lett. **70**, 530–582 (1993)
6. Brizzee, K.R.: Mechanics of vomiting: a mini review. Can. J. Physiol. Pharmacol. **68**, 221–229 (1990)
7. Takada, H., Miyao, M., Fateh, S. (eds.): Stereopsis and hygiene. Springer, Singapore (2018)
8. Patterson, R.: Human factors of stereo displays: an update. J. SID **17**(12), 987–996 (2009)
9. Nagata, S.: Distribution of vergence fusional stereoscopic limits (VFSL) of disparity in a stereoscopic display. TVRSJ **7**, 239–246 (2002). (in Japanese)
10. Nagata, S.: The binocular fusion of human vision on stereoscopic displays: field of view and environments. Ergonomics **39**(11), 1273–1284 (1996)
11. Chiarelli, A.M., Zappasodi, F., Di Pompeo, F., Merla, A.: Simultaneous functional near-infrared spectroscopy and electroencephalography for monitoring of human brain activity and oxygenation. Neurophotonics **4**(4), 041411 (2017). https://doi.org/10.1117/1.NPh.4.4.041411
12. Fukuda, M., Mikuni, M.: A study of near-infrared spectroscopy in depression. J Clin. Exp. Med. **219**, 1057–1062 (2006)
13. Zardecki, A.: Multiple scattering corrections to the Beer–Lambert law. In: Proceedings of SPIE, pp. 103–110 (1983)
14. Wray, S., Cope, M., Delpy, D.T., Wyatt, J.S., Reynolds, E.O.: Characterization of the near infrared absorption spectra of cytochrome AA 3 and hemoglobin for the non-invasive monitoring of cerebral oxygenation. Biochem Biophys Acta **933**, 184–192 (1988)
15. Kato, T., Kamei, A., Takashima, S., Ozaki, T.: Human visual cortical function during photic stimulation monitoring by means of near-infrared spectroscopy. J. Cereb. Blood Flow Metab. **13**, 516–520 (1993)
16. Hoshi, Y., Tamura, M.: Detection of dynamic changes in cerebral oxygenation coupled to neural function during mental work in man. Neurosci. Lett. **150**, 5–8 (1993)
17. Elwell, C.E., Cooper, C.E., Cope, M., Delpy, D.T.: Performance comparison of several published tissue near-infrared spectroscopy algorithms. Anal. Biochem. **227**, 54–68 (1995)
18. Takada, M., Fukui, Y., Matsuura, Y., Sato, M., Takada, H.: Peripheral viewing during exposure to a 2D/3D video clip: effects on the human body. Environ. Health Prev. Med. **20**, 79–89 (2015)
19. Phillips, A.A., Chan, F.H.N., Zheng, M.M.Z., Krassioukov, A.V., Ainslie, P.N.: Neurovascular coupling in humans: physiology, methodological advances and clinical implications. J. Cereb. Blood Flow Metabol. **36**, 647–664 (2016)
20. Donders, F.C.: Die bewegungen des gehirns und die vera: Nderungen der gefa¨ssfu¨llung der pia mater. Schmid's Fahrb. **69**, 16–20 (1851)
21. Mosso, A.: Sulla circolazione del cervello dell'uomo. Atti R Accad Lincei **5**, 237–358 (1880)

22. Roy, C.S., Sherrington, C.S.: On the regulation of the blood-supply of the brain. J. Physiol. **11**, 85–158 (1890)
23. Attwell, D., Iadecola, C.: The neural basis of functional brain imaging signals. Trends in Neurosci. **25**, 621–625 (2002)
24. Lauritzen, M.: Reading vascular changes in brain imaging: is dendritic calcium the key? Nat. Rev. **6**, 77–85 (2005)
25. Uludag, K., Dubowitz, D.J., Yoder, E.J., Restom, K., Liu, T.T., Buxton, R.B.: Coupling of cerebral blood flow and oxygen consumption during physiological activation and deactivation measured with fMRI. Neuro Im. **23**, 148–155 (2004)
26. Silva, R.: 720p vs. 1080p: a comparison. Lifewire.com (2018). Accessed 31 Jan 2019
27. Wayland, R., Bromley, D., Pickett, D., Passamante, A.: Recognizing determinism in a time series. Phys. Rev. Lett. **70**, 580–582 (1993)
28. Theiler, J., Eubank, S., Longtin, A., Galdrikian, B., Farmer, J.D.: Testing for nonlinearity in time series: the method of surrogate data. Phys. D **58**, 77–94 (1992)
29. Takada, H., Kitaoka, Y., Ichikawa, M., Miyao, M.: Physical meaning of geometrical index for stabilometry. Equilib. Res. **62**(3), 168–180 (2003)
30. Japan Society for Equilibrium Research: Standard of stabilometry. Equilib. Res. **42**, 367–369 (1983)
31. Ungerleider, L.G., Mishkin, M.: Two cortical visual systems. In: Ingle, D.J., Goodale, M.A., Mansfield, R.J.W. (eds.) Analysis of Visual Behavior. MIT Press, Cambridge (1982)
32. Rogers, M.A.M., Langa, K.M.: Untreated poor vision: a contributing factor to late-life dementia. Am. J. Epidemiol. **171**(6), 728–735 (2010)
33. Takens, F.: Detecting strange attractors in turbulence. In: Rand, David, Young, Lai-Sang (eds.) Dynamical Systems and Turbulence, Warwick 1980. LNM, vol. 898, pp. 366–381. Springer, Heidelberg (1981). https://doi.org/10.1007/BFb0091924

Author Index

Abbas, James II-250
Abdallah, Wajih II-3
Abel, Troy D. I-3
Abramson, Jennifer II-116
Aceves Gutiérrez, Luis Carlos I-191
Adiani, Deeksha II-13
Adjouadi, Malek II-282
Agatsuma, Shotaro II-363
Al Thani, Dena II-32
Alcañiz, Mariano I-646
Alef, Yael I-465
Al-khazraji, Sedeeq I-258
Allen, Anna II-116
Almeida, Leonelo Dell Anhol I-284
Alnahari, Mona I-201
Aloba, Aishat II-385
Alonso Jr., Miguel II-403
Alqahtani, Yahya II-23
Al-Thani, Dena I-268
Anand, Kruthika II-32
Andrade, Rossana II-209
André, Elisabeth I-601
Anthony, Lisa II-385
Aqle, Aboubakr I-268
Arshad, Kamran II-419

Bajireanu, Roman I-628
Banire, Bilikis I-268, II-32
Barakat, Basel II-419
Baranauskas, Maria Cecília Calani I-39
Barbosa, Simone Diniz Junqueira I-445
Barreto, Armando II-282
Barros, Rodolfo M. II-49
Barros, Vanessa T. O. II-49
Barroso, Isabel II-506
Barroso, João II-160, II-312, II-455, II-506
Becker, Manuela I-389
Becker, Valdecir I-377, I-526
Benner, Alexandra I-389
Bica, Paulo I-628
Bishop, Grayson II-193
Böhlen, Marc I-13
Bolivar, Santiago I-408
Bonacin, Rodrigo I-39

Bondin, Luca II-87
Borg, Katrin I-389
Brandão, Anarosa I-481
Brukamp, Kirsten I-57
Bühler, Christian II-98

Camargo, Murilo C. II-49
Camba, Jorge D. I-646
Camilleri, Vanessa II-64
Cañavate, Francisco J. F. I-159
Cardoso, Pedro J. S. I-420, I-628
Carlsen, Jonas Ege I-365
Carrasquillo, Armando I-408
Carvalho, Tathia C. P. II-49
Cavas-Martínez, Francisco I-159
Chakraborty, Joyram I-201, II-23
Chalki, Panagiota I-433, II-575
Chan, Ya-Hui I-312
Chang, Ting-Ya II-431
Chen, Chung-Jen I-244
Chen, Jing I-133
Chen, Weiqin I-342
Cheng, Kuang-Ting II-445
Chowdhury, Abhik II-224
Connor, Olcay II-32
Contero, Manuel I-646

da Silva Filho, Sandro G. I-526
da Silva, José Valderlei I-39
Darin, Ticianne II-209
Das, Swagata II-556
de Brandão Damasceno, André Luiz I-445
De Silva, Madhuka I-211
de Souza, Helder Bruno A. M. I-377, I-526
de Vasconcelos, Edvaldo I-377, I-545
De-Juan-Ripoll, Carla I-646
del Rio Guerra, Marta Sylvia I-191
Desrochers, Breanna II-77
Dias, Kapila I-211
Dieker, Lisa I-555
Dingli, Alexiei II-64, II-87
Dirks, Susanne I-28
Dong, Hua I-113
Dong, Yuzhu II-385

Dos Reis, Julio Cesar   I-39
dos Santos Ribeiro, Dalai   I-445
dos Santos, Andressa Cristina   I-39
dos Santos, Lillian   I-545

Edvinsen, Nikolai   I-365
Eicher, Cornelia   I-57
Eid, Mohamad   II-150

Fakhri, Bijan   II-224
Feng, Chia-Hui   I-244
Feng, Jinjuan Heidi   II-23
Fernández-Pacheco, Daniel G.   I-159
Ferreira Silva, Felipe Eduardo   I-229
Figueredo de Santana, Vagner   I-229
Filipe, Vitor   II-455
Flutura, Simon   I-601
Fremstad, Karl   I-365
Fujita, Kosuke   II-468

Gandy, Maribeth   I-301
Georgi, Leon   II-477
Gialanella, John   I-69
Giannoumis, George A.   II-511
Gjøsæter, Terje   I-342, II-523
Goethe, Ole   I-91
Greuèl, Marius   I-57

Haddod, Foaad   II-64, II-87
Hassan, Mehedi   II-234
Hastall, Matthias R.   II-98
Heitplatz, Vanessa N.   II-98
Herdeiro, Cláudia   I-420
Hirskyj-Douglas, Ilyena   I-91
Huber, Tobias   I-601
Huenerfauth, Matt   I-258, I-507
Hughes, Charles E.   I-555
Hüls, Jan   I-389
Hung, Yu-Hsiu   I-244
Hynes, Michael   I-555

Ingraham, Kathleen   I-555

Jain, Eakta   II-385
Jewel, Jacob   I-569
Jordan, J. Bern   I-353
Juhlin, David   II-116

Kajimoto, Hiroyuki   II-363
Kannekanti, Abhishek   I-258

Kaplan, Gabe   II-250
Keates, Simeon   I-100, II-419
Kegel, Karl   II-477
Khanal, Salik Ram   II-160, II-455
Khowaja, Kamran   I-268, II-32
Kiemel, Diana   I-57
Kinoshita, Fumiya   II-468
Kiselev, Jörn   I-57
Kishishita, Yusuke   II-556
Kobayashi, Makoto   I-494
Koch, Marina   I-389
Korn, Annabelle   I-389
Korres, Georgios   II-150
Korzetz, Mandy   II-477
Kost, Annika   I-389
Kühn, Romina   II-477
Kurita, Yuichi   II-556, II-587

Lam, Roberto   I-420, I-628
Law, Effie L.-C.   I-91
Leite, Patricia da Silva   I-284
Lelevé, Arnaud   II-334
Levy, Dalit   I-465
Levy, Laura   I-301
Li, Fang   I-113
Liberato, Margarida   II-312
Lima, Nelson   I-481
Lin, Chia-Tzu   I-244
Lin, Ming-Chyuan   I-133
Lin, Shu-Ping   I-312
Loi, Daria   II-491
Luc, Annie   II-385
Lueg, Marie-Christin   I-389

MacKenzie, I. Scott   II-234
Magee, John   II-77, II-234
Maier, André   I-57
Maike, Vanessa Regina Margareth
       Lima   I-39
Makki, Mustapha   II-32
Mancini, Drew   II-116
Mansoor, Bilal   II-32
Martín-Gutiérrez, Jorge   I-191
Martins, Paulo   II-312
Mata, Omar   II-300
Matsuura, Shu   I-494
McDaniel, Troy   II-224, II-250, II-300
McGuire, Michael   II-23
Méndez Mendoza, Yusseli Lizeth   I-39
Mesquita, Lana   II-262, II-353

Mikropoulos, Tassos Anastasios I-433, II-575
Minissi, Maria Eleonora II-133
Mitchell, Kimberly I-69
Miyanaga, Kazuya II-468
Miyao, Masaru I-578, I-669
Molina, Arturo II-300
Monteiro, Maria João II-506
Moreau, Richard II-334
Morelli, Tony I-569, II-323
Morris, Chris II-116
Motus, Daniel I-601

Nagamune, Kouki I-590
Nascimento, Marcos I-481
Neto, Amaro I-545
Nie, Guangtao II-123
Nieto, José I-159
Noleto, Jaqueline D. I-526
Nouaille, Laurence II-334
Novales, Cyril II-334
Nyaga, Casam II-373

O'Brien, Amanda II-116
O'Sullivan, Eric II-323
O-larnnithipong, Nonnarit II-282
Oleimeulen, Ursula I-57
Oliveira, Francisco I-481, II-353
Oliveira, Thiago I-481
Omokawa, Reika I-494
Ortega, Francisco R. I-408, II-282
Osthoff, Dominique I-389

Pallavicini, Federica II-133
Panchanathan, Sethuraman II-224, II-250
Paredes, Hugo II-160, II-312
Park, Wanjoo II-150
Parras-Burgos, Dolores I-159
Patricia McKenna, H. I-146
Paupini, Cristina II-511
Pelka, Bastian I-389
Pepe, Alessandro II-133
Pereira, Rui Penha I-420
Perez, Daniel I-408
Pettersen, Frida Margrethe Borge I-365
Pham, Minh Tu II-334
Ponce, Pedro II-300

Qaraqe, Marwa II-32
Qui, Guo-Peng I-133

Radianti, Jaziar I-342, II-523
Ramos, Célia M. Q. II-538
Ramos, Renato I-481
Rangelova, Stanislava I-601
Ratchatanantakit, Neeranut II-282
Reis, Arsénio II-312, II-506
Ren, Xiangshi I-91
Retore, Ana Paula I-284
Ribeiro, Paula I-545
Ripke, Taylor II-323
Rishe, Naphtali D. I-408
Rizvi, Syed Asad R. II-77
Rocha Façanha, Agebson I-617
Rodrigues, João M. F. I-628, II-538
Rodrigues, Liliana II-353
Rodrigues, Nuno I-420
Rodrigues, Vitor II-506
Rosenberger, Carina I-389

Saga, Satoshi II-363
Salehzadeh Niksirat, Kavous I-91
Sampaio, Jaime II-455
Sánchez, Jaime I-617, II-209, II-262
Sandnes, Frode Eika I-365
Santana, Matheus II-49
Sarkar, Nilanjan II-13, II-123
Satterfield, Debra I-177
Sattler, Helene I-389
Schlegel, Thomas II-477
Schlosser, Ralf II-116
Schmaltz, Peter II-116
Schmidt, Michael II-13
Schumann, Franz-Wilhelm II-477
Seita, Matthew I-507
Sénac, Thibault II-334
Shafriri, Yuval I-465
Shah, Utsav I-507
Shane, Howard II-116
Sharma, Prabin II-160
Sharma, Shashank II-224
Silva, Lidiane I-481
Siqueira da Silva, Isabel Cristina I-326
Soares, Maikon II-353
Soares, Salviano II-506
Soler-Dominguez, Jose L. I-646
Soni, Bhavica II-224
Spittel, Susanne I-57
Sugiura, Akihiro I-657
Sun, Huatong I-91

Sun, Qiming   II-172
Swanson, Amy R.   II-13, II-123

Tadayon, Ramin   II-250, II-556
Tahir, Samra   II-150
Takada, Hiroki   I-578, I-657, I-669
Takada, Masumi   I-578, I-669
Takahashi, Shin   II-363
Taliaferro, Lindsay A.   I-555
Tanaka, Kunihiko   I-657
Tang, Tiffany Y.   II-182
Tangnimitchok, Sudarat   II-282
Thakar, Ashka   II-193
Tomita, Hirobumi   II-363
Toscano, Rafael M.   I-377, I-526
Touyama, Hideaki   II-468
Tredway, Tom   I-177
Tseng, Kevin C.   II-431, II-445
Tsiara, Angeliki   I-433, II-575
Tsuzuki, Yujiro   I-590
Tunold, Siv   I-342
Tuson, Ella   II-77
Twanabasu, Amrit   II-160

Ullal, Akshith   II-123
Upadhaya, Mala Deep   II-160

Val, Thierry   II-3
Van den Bossche, Adrien   II-3
Vanderheiden, Gregg C.   I-353
Vega Ramirez, Antonio   II-556, II-587

Veiga, Ricardo J. M.   I-628
Vella, Frédéric   II-3
Viana, Windson   I-617
Vieyres, Pierre   II-334
Vigouroux, Nadine   II-3
Vinbæk, Ellen Opsahl   I-365

Wade, Joshua   II-13
Wang, Ruiyun   II-363
Wario, Ruth   II-373
Warren, Zachary E.   II-123
Warren, Zachary   II-13
Wassell, Ian   II-419
Weerasinghe, Thushani   I-211
Weitauf, Amy S.   II-123
Weitlauf, Amy   II-13
Wendt, Oliver   II-193
Westers, Nicholas J.   I-555
Williams, Adam S.   I-408
Winoto, Pinata   II-172, II-182
Woelfel, Wesley   I-177
Woodward, Julia   II-385

Xu, Jiasheng   II-182

Yamamoto, Masataka   II-556
Yamamoto, Syota   I-669
Yu, Christina   II-116

Zhang, Rong   II-385
Zhou, Xue Hua   I-133

Printed in the United States
By Bookmasters

Printed in the United States
By Bookmasters